COLLEGE

O9-ABE-829

F222.1507 C8869 c.2
CCraigie, Peter C.
TThe Book of Deuteronomy

DEMCO

Peter C. Craigie was educated in Edinburgh. He has studied at the University of
Edinburgh, the University of Durham, and the
University of Aberdeen, and holds the doctor-
ate from McMaster University in Hamilton,
Ontario. He is associate professor of religious
studies at the University of Calgary, Alberta.

THE NEW INTERNATIONAL COMMENTARY ON THE OLD TESTAMENT

R. K. HARRISON, *General Editor*

The Book of
DEUTERONOMY

by
PETER C. CRAIGIE

Associate Professor of Religious Studies
The University of Calgary

WILLIAM B. EERDMANS PUBLISHING COMPANY

Copyright ©1976 by William B. Eerdmans Publishing Company
255 Jefferson Ave. S.E., Grand Rapids, Mich. 49502
All rights reserved
Printed in the United States of America

Library of Congress Cataloging in Publication Data
Bible. O.T. Deuteronomy. English. Craigie. 1976.
   The Book of Deuteronomy.

   (The New international commentary on the Old Testament)
   Bibliography: p. 69.
   Includes indexes.
     1. Bible. O.T. Deuteronomy — Commentaries.
I. Craigie, Peter C. II. Title. III. Series.
BS1273.C7   222'.15'07   75-45372
ISBN 0-8028-2355-6

R
2.2.2.,1507
B58
C.1.

Baker & Taylor

6.91

1 Feb 77

55542

TO MY FATHER, IN GRATITUDE

AUTHOR'S PREFACE

Deuteronomy is a book about a community being prepared for a new life. Hardship and the wilderness lie behind; the promised land lies ahead. But in the present moment, there is a call for a new commitment to God and a fresh understanding of the nature of the community of God's people. Though the scene is set more than three thousand years in the past, Deuteronomy is still a book of considerable contemporary relevance. Then, as now, the surrounding world was experiencing a time of change, of political tension and military engagement. But in the midst of world events, a relatively small community was being urged by Moses, the "man of God," to commit itself wholeheartedly to the Lord, before engaging in the struggle for the promised land. The kingdom of God's chosen people was coming of age, unnoticed by the great powers of the time, and struggling against what were, by human standards, impossible circumstances. The book provides a paradigm for the kingdom of God in the modern world; it is a time for renewing commitment within the New Covenant and turning to the future with a view to possessing the promise of God.

The book of Deuteronomy, however, is not only a book of contemporary relevance. It has been, and continues to be, one of the most important and debated works in modern biblical scholarship. The varieties of opinion over Deuteronomy are enormous and they are likely to increase in the coming years. The traditional methods of Old Testament scholarship are being refined and modified, though as yet they are leading to no consensus regarding Deuteronomy. And new methods are being employed which will contribute increasingly to the diversity of opinion. The "New Criticism" (*Werkinterpretation*) is gradually being introduced to the Old Testament scholarly world, with its refreshing stress on the study of literature as a finished product, rather than emphasizing the antecedents to the extant form. It is too early to estimate the results of this approach. "Structural Analysis," too, though different in nature, places emphasis on the

7

text as a finished product. And the "New Stylistics" (*Neuen Stilistik*) is also beginning to make its emphasis felt in Old Testament studies. Along with this relatively new diversity in method, there is a growing body of secondary literature relating to every aspect of Old Testament studies; in biblical research, as in other fields, there is a "knowledge explosion" taking place, with the result that it is virtually impossible to encompass all the relevant secondary material on a given subject.

Against this background, I think it is wise to make a few comments concerning the nature of this commentary. It is written with one basic presupposition: that Deuteronomy is a part of the Word of God and not simply the product of human imagination. I have tried to articulate the implications of this perspective, as they relate to Deuteronomy, in Appendix I. In the Introduction, I have not attempted to give a history of previous scholarly work on Deuteronomy; this is done very competently in Sigrid Loersch's book, *Das Deuteronomium und seine Deutungen* (1967). I have deliberately singled out what I consider to be the most significant secondary literature and have dealt with it briefly in arguing my own case. However, as an aid to students of Deuteronomy, I have included in the text and footnotes, both in the Introduction and in the Commentary, many references to secondary literature, in which are expressed opinions very different from my own. Lest the commentary become burdensomely long, I have not always argued in detail with such writers. My debt to other authors will be evident immediately from the many references to their works throughout the commentary. This debt is to all those from whom I have learned, whether or not I have agreed with their conclusions.

One area of research that is making an increasingly large contribution to Old Testament studies is the study of Ugaritic (Canaanite) texts. I have attempted to include as much of the relevant material from Ugaritic studies as possible; it appears, for the most part, in the footnotes to the text and commentary. The index to Ugaritic texts at the end of the volume should be of assistance to those who wish to pursue this topic in more detail.

The translation is neither absolutely literal nor particularly literary. I have attempted, however, to indicate something of the character of the Hebrew. Often, for example, the Hebrew writer uses a series of conjunctions (*and*) where a series of commas would be more appropriate in English. On points such as this, I have adhered to the Hebrew text. Where the translation of a Hebrew idiom has been rendered in an appropriate English idiom, I have noted the idiom of the original in a footnote.

I have tried to keep in mind the readership for whom this series of commentaries is designed, which is defined by the editor as "pas-

8

tor, scholar, and student alike." My own first attempt at serious biblical study began while I was serving as an officer in the Royal Air Force. I was advised by a friend to read St. Luke's Gospel with the help of Geldenhuys' commentary, published in the New International Commentary on the New Testament, the companion series to that in which the present volume appears. At that time I had no University training and knew no Greek, but the work of Geldenhuys was invaluable. He could not apply Luke to my situation, but he could help me understand the meaning of the text, and from there I could grasp the implications of the text for myself. I have tried to keep that memory in mind while writing, though I cannot hope to have had the success of Geldenhuys. Because of this very personal past association with the series, I am greatly indebted to the William B. Eerdmans Publishing Company for the privilege of participating in the same venture.

There are many to whom I would express my thanks in the completion of this work, but I must limit myself to a few. Mrs. Grace Gordon and Mrs. Jeanette Fyfe have provided invaluable assistance in the preparation of the manuscript. I am grateful to the editor, Professor R. K. Harrison, not only for issuing the invitation to contribute to the series, but also for his advice and encouragement during the time in which the book was being written. I owe a great debt to my colleague, Professor Eugene Combs. He has not read this work and might not agree with much of it, but for the intellectual stimulus and the insight which his own words and work have provided, I cannot hope to repay him. My wife, Betty, has been patient and understanding throughout, and to her I owe the greatest debt of all.

P. C. C.

CONTENTS

11

PRINCIPAL ABBREVIATIONS

Akk.	Akkadian
ANET	J. B. Pritchard, ed., *Ancient Near Eastern Texts*
ANET(S)	J. B. Pritchard, ed., *Supplement* to *ANET*
Arab.	Arabic
Assyr.	Assyrian
AV	Authorized Version (Bible)
BA	*Biblical Archaeologist*
BASOR	*Bulletin of the American Schools of Oriental Research*
BDB	Brown, Driver, Briggs, *Hebrew and English Lexicon of the Old Testament*
*BH*³	R. Kittel, ed., *Biblia Hebraica* (3rd ed.)
BHH	Reicke and Rost, eds., *Biblisch-historisches Handwörterbuch*
BJRL	*Bulletin of the John Rylands Library*
BZ	*Biblische Zeitschrift*
BZAW	Beihefte zur *ZAW* (below)
CBQ	*Catholic Biblical Quarterly*
CTA	A. Herdner, ed., *Corpus des tablettes en cunéiformes alphabétiques*
DJD	*Discoveries in the Judaean Desert of Jordan*
E.T.	English translation
Gk.	Greek
GKC	*Gesenius' Hebrew Grammar* (ed. E. Kautzsch, trans. A. E. Cowley)
HUCA	*Hebrew Union College Annual*
IDB	G. A. Buttrick, ed., *Interpreter's Dictionary of the Bible*
IOT	R. K. Harrison, *Introduction to the Old Testament*
JBL	*Journal of Biblical Literature*
JNES	*Journal of Near Eastern Studies*
JSS	*Journal of Semitic Studies*
KAI	Donner and Röllig, eds., *Kanaanäische und Aramäische Inschriften*

13

KB	Koehler and Baumgartner, *Lexicon in Veteris Testamenti Libros*
LXX	Septuagint
MT	Massoretic Text
NBC(R)	*New Bible Commentary (Revised* 1970)
NBD	J. D. Douglas, ed., *New Bible Dictionary*
NICNT	New International Commentary on the New Testament
OTS	*Oudtestamentische Studiën*
PEQ	*Palestine Exploration Quarterly*
PRU	*Le palais royal d'Ugarit,* ed. C. Schaeffer
RB	*Revue biblique*
RS	Ras Shamra
RSP	L. R. Fisher, ed., *Ras Shamra Parallels*
RSV	Revised Standard Version (Bible)
Sam.	Samaritan text of Deuteronomy
SJT	*Scottish Journal of Theology*
SVT	Supplements to *VT*
TB	*Tyndale Bulletin*
TDOT	Botterweck and Ringgren, eds., *Theological Dictionary of the Old Testament* (E.T. 1974ff.)
ThZ	*Theologische Zeitschrift*
UF	*Ugarit-Forschungen*
Ugar.	Ugaritic
UT	C. H. Gordon, *Ugaritic Textbook* (1965)
VT	*Vetus Testamentum*
VTE	D. J. Wiseman, ed., *The Vassal-Treaties of Esarhaddon, Iraq* 20 (1958)
ZAW	*Zeitschrift für die alttestamentliche Wissenschaft*

The Book of
DEUTERONOMY

INTRODUCTION

I. TITLE

The fifth book of Moses traditionally has been entitled *Deuteronomy;* interpreted literally, the title would mean "second law." The use of this title arose because of the Greek (LXX) translation of Deut. 17:18; the translators apparently misunderstood the Hebrew ("a copy/ repetition of this law") and took it to mean "second law," implying thereby a body of legislation different from that contained in the previous books of Moses (which would have been, by implication, the "first law"). In a sense, the title (interpreted literally) is misleading, for the fifth book of Moses does not contain a second and distinct law. It does, however, repeat much of the legislation contained in the preceding books, though the context and form of that repetition is peculiar to Deuteronomy.

In the Hebrew Bible, the book is given its proper title, *'ēlleh hadde*ḇārîm ("these are the words"); this title, in accord with ancient custom, consists of the first words of the first line of the text of the book. It is a better title in that it describes more accurately the content of the book. The major part of the book consists of the words Moses addressed to Israel immediately prior to the entry into the promised land. It is an important title for the proper understanding of the book. Deuteronomy is not primarily a corpus of law, nor even an historical record; it purports rather to be a record of *words* addressed by Moses to the Israelites. The style is hortatory, that of an orator addressing his congregation with words designed to move them to obedience and commitment to the Lord of the covenant. Thus although Deuteronomy, in its present form, is a piece of literature, it is important to bear in mind the book's self-description as a report of words which were spoken.

The title in the Hebrew Bible also indicates the form and structure of the book of Deuteronomy. The plan of the book is based on the form of Hebrew covenant documents, which in turn find their

17

THE BOOK OF DEUTERONOMY

formal antecedents in the pattern employed for the expression of political treaties in the ancient Near East. (This topic is covered in more detail in section III below, "Unity of Composition.") The Near Eastern political treaties often began in a manner similar to Deuteronomy: "These are the words of. . . ."[1] Deuteronomy, as a finished work, is thus a literary record of a spoken address (or series of addresses) which has been given the form of a covenant document.

II. BACKGROUND

The events described in Deuteronomy occur right at the end of the Mosaic period and immediately prior to the entry of the Israelites into the promised land. The historical background to the book is described within the opening portions of the address of Moses (principally in chs. 1–4); the events of the past are employed within the address to emphasize to the people the importance of the present moment. The present envisaged in the book of Deuteronomy was a particularly critical time; past history had been leading, within the plan and promise of God, to a future goal. But that future goal was contingent upon the obedience and commitment of the Israelites to their God. Hence the book of Deuteronomy has to be understood in the context of the past history of the Israelites and in the perspective of their future history. The most significant event in the immediate background to the book was the Exodus from Egypt, which was followed in turn by the formation of the covenant at Sinai (Horeb).

The Exodus marked the liberation of the Hebrews from a long period of servitude in Egypt.[2] The end of servitude and the beginnings of liberation were in effect the birth of Israel as a nation whose king was God (Exod. 15:18); yet the Israelites were a nation without a land and without a constitution. The constitution was formed at Sinai in the covenant sealed between the Lord and his people in which Moses acted as mediator. The covenant was in part a renewal of the older

1. See *ANET*, pp. 202a, 203b; *ANET(S)*, p. 93a. Cf. M. G. Kline, *The Structure of Biblical Authority* (1972), p. 135.
2. The history of Israel from the Exodus to the conquest will not be recounted in detail here; one or two points will simply be emphasized which are of particular significance for Deuteronomy. For studies of the historical period, see the following: J. Bright, *A History of Israel* (²1972), pp. 97-127; D. M. Beegle, *Moses, The Servant of Yahweh* (1972); K. A. Kitchen, *Ancient Orient and OT* (1966), pp. 57-75. There are differences in the approaches represented by these works, but all are positive to some extent in their assessment of the period of Moses. Other scholars, by reason of their historical and literary method, consider it virtually impossible to reconstruct historically this early period. See particularly M. Noth, *The History of Israel* (E.T. 1960), pp. 42-50. For the point of view from which this commentary is written, see the remarks in the Preface, together with Appendix I, following the sections of the Introduction.

18

covenants made with the patriarchs; like the earlier covenants, the Sinai Covenant continued to hold forth the promise of God for the future, the promise that the Israelites would become God's special nation. In the covenant, the people were required to be obedient to God, the Lord of the covenant, who had liberated them from the Egyptian bondage. In summary, the covenant was the constitution of a theocracy. God was king and had claimed his people for himself out of Egypt; the people, who owed everything to God, were required to submit to him in a covenant which was based on love. Israel now had a constitution, but still it did not have a land to call its own.

Following the events at Sinai, the Israelites undertook further travels through the wilderness regions south of Palestine, and then eventually they began to move northward, travelling to the east of the Dead Sea and the great rift valley. Here they began to encounter a number of relatively small states,[3] situated in the mountainous country rising to the east of the rift valley and limited on their eastern side by the boundary of the desert. Some of these small states were deliberately avoided, but as the Israelites moved further north toward the lands on the east side of the Jordan, they began to fight the first preliminary battles of the conquest that lay before them. The promised land on which their eyes were fixed, however, lay to the west of the river Jordan; the events described in Deuteronomy took place immediately before the crossing of the Jordan and the beginning of the conquest in the fuller sense.

The movements of the Israelites during these years were critical for their continued existence as a potential nation; but on the larger canvas of history, they must have appeared to contemporary neighbors to have been relatively insignificant. There is no detailed extrabiblical evidence to shed further light on the movements of the Israelites,[4] but it is possible to reconstruct some of the details of the history of the contemporary world within which the Israelites lived.[5] For those living in Palestine, the great powers of the time were Egypt to the south and the Hittite empire to the north; neither of these two

3. On the archeological evidence relating to the settlement in Transjordan during the 13th century B.C., see N. Glueck, *The Other Side of the Jordan* (1940); see also G. E. Wright and D. N. Freedman, eds., *The Biblical Archaeologist Reader* (1961), pp. 1-21.
4. Historical evidence and archeological data make possible the preliminary reconstruction of the background and environment of the Israelites, but they do not provide any detailed information concerning the movements of the Israelites as a people. The one exception is the brief reference to Israel, among other peoples and nations, in the Egyptian stele of Merneptah (dated c.1230-1220 B.C.); see *ANET*, pp. 276-78; the text probably refers to the presence of the Israelites in southwest Palestine, soon after the events described in Deuteronomy.
5. For more detailed treatments, see B. Mazar, ed., *The World History of the Jewish People* III, *Judges* (1971), pp. 1-93; A. Gardiner, *Egypt of the Pharaohs* (1961), pp. 247-280; G. Roux, *Ancient Iraq* (1966), pp. 227-239.

powers, however, was at a particularly strong point in its history. Egypt, during the thirteenth century B.C., was governed by the Nineteenth Dynasty (Sethos I, c.1309-1290; Ramses II, c.1290-1224). Early in the century, Egypt began trying to reassert its control over Palestine and Syria, but this led inevitably to conflict with the Hittites. Early in Ramses' reign, the two powers met in battle in the vicinity of Qadesh in Syria;[6] though Egypt claimed victory, the result was in effect a stalemate, and fighting continued in a desultory fashion for several years before a treaty between the two powers was sealed. Thus, during the latter half of the thirteenth century, the Hittite power was gradually on the decline. The peace with Egypt enabled the Hittites to attempt to stave off threats from the west (various groups coming from the Aegean area) and the east (Assyria), but eventually their empire came to an end at the close of the thirteenth century B.C.[7] For Egypt, the latter half of the thirteenth century B.C. was relatively peaceful, but following the death of Ramses II, the country was again becoming threatened by external forces which seriously undermined its peace and power.

The geographical region of Palestine (or Canaan) was under the political control of Egypt during the latter half of the thirteenth century B.C. It was not a state, but rather a large collection of relatively small city-states which owed their allegiance to Egypt. Though these city-states shared a common culture and, to a large extent, a common religion, they were politically and militarily weak. The decline in Egyptian control and strength in Palestine contributed to a growing situation of social and political chaos. It was into this situation that the Israelites were to enter immediately following the events described in Deuteronomy.

III. UNITY OF COMPOSITION

The traditional view concerning the Mosaic authorship of Deuteronomy had as a corollary the understanding that the book was a unified literary whole. In recent scholarship, however, it is commonly held that the unity of the book marks a late stage in its development and that it may be possible to discern the component parts that underlie the formal unity.[8] In general terms, there are two reasons for this kind of approach to a study of the unity of the work. (1) If Deuteronomy, as a finished work, is believed to be essentially a

6. See A. Gardiner, *The Kadesh Inscription of Ramesses II* (1960); R. O. Faulkner, "The Battle of Kadesh," *Mitteilungen des Deutschen Archäologischen Instituts* (Cairo) 16 (1958), pp. 93-111.
7. For a fuller treatment, see O. R. Gurney, *The Hittites* (²1954), pp. 26-39.
8. By "recent scholarship," I mean post-Reformation, but with the emphasis on the last hundred years. The beginnings of the trend described here, however, seem to start

product of the seventh century B.C., then it is natural to attempt to discern older material which might have been incorporated in the work during the seventh century. (2) There are, in the view of some scholars, internal clues which might provide a means of discerning different strands in the composition of the book.[9] The first reason is clearly the primary one in significance, for if an argument is made for the antiquity of the book, then the second reason (internal evidence) appears in a somewhat different perspective. The analysis of the internal textual material has been undertaken in recent years by means of form-criticism, with the current emphasis turning toward redaction-criticism.[10] This last method, redaction-criticism, is in principle more positive, but it presupposes to a large extent the work of the earlier analysis and reflects the view that Deuteronomy is not a product of the period it describes.

There have continued to be a number of scholars who, for a variety of reasons, have argued for the essential unity of Deuteronomy as a whole.[11] They have been a minority, and the

---

with Spinoza, following some clues in the work of Ibn Ezra: see *Tractatus Theologico-Politicus* VIII, "The Authorship of the Pentateuch"; see also T. Hobbes, *Leviathan* part III, ch. 33.
9. The type of internal evidence employed might consist of data such as the following: (a) the supposed duplication of headings or introductions (e.g., 1:1; 4:44f.; 6:1; 12:1); (b) the alternation in the use of number (2nd person singular/plural) in verbs and pronouns; (c) various types of literary analysis (e.g., form-critical studies of particular passages within the book). For a useful survey of the debate on the structure and unity of the book, and the variety of interpretations that have been offered, see E. W. Nicholson, *Deuteronomy and Tradition* (1967), pp. 18-36. Nicholson's position is a good example of the kinds of positions that have been advocated. The following is his tentative suggestion concerning the development of the book: (a) original book: singular passages in chs. 5–26, plus part of ch. 28; (b) ch. 28 was expanded after 586 B.C. and ch. 30 was added to it; (c) the work was incorporated in the Deuteronomistic history, and given a framework (chs. 1–3, 4, parts of 31 and 34; after Noth); also, passages in the plural were added, and probably chs. 27 and 29 were added; (d) there was further editorial expansion, with additions to ch. 31, and the addition of chs. 32 and 33. These additions may have been made when Deuteronomy was united with Genesis-Numbers to form the Pentateuch.
10. Form-critical studies in Deuteronomy were pioneered by G. von Rad; see, e.g., his *Studies in Deuteronomy* (1951). A slightly different analysis is undertaken by N. Lohfink, who employs the so-called New Stylistics in his study of chs. 5–11: *Das Hauptgebot* (1963). Lohfink's book is a very penetrating study, but the nature of the literary method is such that the conclusions must be more tentative than Lohfink suggests; cf. H. Huffmon, *JBL* 83 (1964), pp. 197f. A work on redaction-criticism, which also contains a brief survey of earlier literary studies, is that of G. Seitz, *Redaktionsgeschichtliche Studien zum Deuteronomium* (1971). For other literary studies dealing with particular sections of Deuteronomy, see J. G. Plöger, *Literarkritische, formgeschichtliche und stilkritische Untersuchungen zum Deuteronomium* (1967); R. P. Merendino, *Das deuteronomische Gesetz* (1969).
11. For a useful summary, see E. W. Nicholson, *Deuteronomy and Tradition,* p. 37, n. 1. Among more recent representatives of this point of view, see the following: G. T. Manley, *The Book of the Law* (1957); M. H. Segal, "The Composition of the Pentateuch — a Fresh Examination," in C. Rabin, ed., *Scripta Hierosolymitana* 8 (1961),

differences they have maintained against a growing consensus have been based, to a large extent, on a very positive assessment of the early (Mosaic) period of Israelite religion. Given a positive assessment of the early period of Israel's history, the radical doubt[12] of the authenticity of Deuteronomy in its early setting is to a large extent removed.

In the last two decades, however, there has been an important new direction in OT research which is of great significance for the study of Deuteronomy. A number of scholars have argued convincingly that there is a relationship in form between the Hebrew covenant and the ancient Near Eastern vassal treaty.[13] The thesis was applied initially to texts describing the formation of the covenant at Sinai and also to various passages describing the renewal of the covenant (e.g., Josh. 24). Subsequently, the insights of this new thesis were applied to Deuteronomy, initially with reference to particular passages within the book (e.g., chs. 4, 28), but then on a larger scale which encompassed virtually the whole book. Among the first to apply this approach to all of Deuteronomy were M. G. Kline and K. A. Kitchen;[14] others are also pursuing this line of investigation, though with results radically different from those of Kline (see M. Weinfeld, *Deuteronomy and the Deuteronomic School* [1972], pp. 59-157). The implications of this approach for questions relating to date and authorship will be examined in section IV of the Introduction; for the moment attention will be focused on the form of Deuteronomy and its relation to the pattern of the Near Eastern vassal treaty.

In its classical form, the Near Eastern vassal treaty has the following component parts:

---

pp. 68-114; *idem, The Pentateuch* (1967). For a quite different approach, employing the method of "new criticism," see M. Weiss, *The Bible and Modern Literary Theory* (Hebrew) (1962); for Weiss, the biblical text must be studied as it is, with a perception of its wholeness and an emphasis on its intrinsic properties, which alone can explain the text.

12. By way of comment, it may be that current biblical scholarship (as one part of Western thought) has as its working principle *radical doubt,* which probably finds its roots in the epistemology of Descartes.

13. Particularly G. E. Mendenhall, "Ancient Oriental and Biblical Law," *BA* 172 (1954), pp. 26-46; *idem,* "Covenant Forms in Israelite Tradition," *BA* 17/3 (1954), pp. 50-76; K. Baltzer, *The Covenant Formulary* (E.T. 1970); D. J. McCarthy, *Treaty and Covenant.* There has been an enormous amount of work undertaken in this field in recent years; for a very valuable survey of current opinions, see D. J. McCarthy, *OT Covenant.*

14. See M. G. Kline, *Treaty of the Great King* (1963); *idem, The Structure of Biblical Authority;* K. A. Kitchen, *Ancient Orient and OT,* pp. 90-102; *idem,* "Ancient Orient, 'Deuteronomism' and the OT," in J. B. Payne, ed., *New Perspectives on the OT* (1970), pp. 1-24; see also J. A. Thompson, *The Ancient Near Eastern Treaties and the OT* (1964), p. 22.

22

UNITY OF COMPOSITION

1. *Preamble* ("These are the words . . .").
2. *Historical Prologue* (Baltzer: "antecedent history," i.e., events leading to and forming the basis of the treaty).
3. *General Stipulations* (Baltzer: statement of substance concerning the future relationship, which (1) is intimately related to the antecedent history, and (2) summarizes the purpose of the specific stipulations).
4. *Specific Stipulations.*
5. *Divine Witnesses:* various deities are called to witness the treaty.
6. *Blessings and Curses:* relating respectively to the maintenance or breach of the covenant.

There are in addition a number of other sections in certain texts which deal with the deposition of the treaty, its public reading, ceremonies of oath, and various formal procedures. (The debate over whether or not there were certain basic differences between the treaties of the second millennium and the first millennium is noted in section IV below.)

The vassal treaty was employed within the Near East when a great power (the suzerain king) imposed certain conditions of vassaldom on a smaller state (the vassal), which would normally have been conquered by the more powerful state in battle. The treaty explained the reasons for imposition and the nature of the conditions imposed on the smaller state, and made certain provisions relating to the maintenance of the treaty. The same basic type of treaty seems to have been employed throughout the Near East, and there is evidence of its use, in simpler form, in Mesopotamia as early as the third millennium.[15] In Egypt, there is some evidence to suggest that the treaty form was employed not only in relation to external vassal states, but also in relation to foreign (labor) groups within Egypt; for more details, see Appendix II following the Introduction.

The Hebrews adapted the treaty form for their own use in order to express the nature of their relationship to God. For many years they were in effect vassals to Egypt, but that old bondage was brought to an end in the Exodus from Egypt. Being liberated from bondage to an earthly power, they then submitted themselves in the Sinai Covenant to become vassals of God, the one who had liberated them from Egypt. The nature of this new submission, expressed in the covenant, finds its dramatic expression through the utilization and adaptation of the treaty form. While other small states might serve Egypt or the Hittite Empire as vassals, the Israelites owed their allegiance only to their suzerain God. This treaty form, in which their

15. See D. J. McCarthy, *Treaty and Covenant,* p. 12, for a chronological list of Near Eastern treaty texts.

23

covenant was set, finds striking expression in the book of Deuteronomy as a whole; in broad outline, the treaty form of the book may be described as follows:

1. *Preamble* (1:1-5); "These are the words which Moses addressed to all Israel. . . ."
2. *Historical Prologue* (1:6–4:49).
3. *General Stipulations* (chs. 5–11).
4. *Specific Stipulations* (chs. 12–26).
5. *Blessings and Curses* (chs. 27–28).
6. *Witnesses* (see 30:19; 31:19; 32:1-43).

The last two points can be expressed more broadly to encompass the whole work: (5) chs. 27-30, curses and blessings, with exhortation; (6) provisions for the continuity of covenant and a successor for Moses.[16]

This overall structure of the book of Deuteronomy suggests that it can be regarded essentially as a unity. The relation of chs. 33–34 to the rest of the book is doubtful, but they may also be integral to the whole (see sections IV and V below). The book is thus a literary account of the renewal of the covenant with God on the plains of Moab. The literary (treaty) pattern may be more than merely a literary device; it is probable that it reflects also the ceremony during which the covenant was renewed and a successor to Moses was appointed. The apparently unified composition of the book has certain implications for questions relating to date and authorship; while the treaty pattern underlying the structure of Deuteronomy does not automatically solve those questions, it does reduce to some extent the number of answers that are viable.[17]

IV. DATE AND AUTHORSHIP

The book of Deuteronomy, the fifth book of Moses, was traditionally regarded in both Christianity and Judaism as the work of Moses and

---

16. See J. A. Thompson, *The Ancient Near Eastern Treaties and the OT,* p. 22. The more detailed aspects of the treaty/covenant form are examined in section V, "Occasion."

17. It should be noted that the overall unity of the work does not preclude the possibility of a number of editorial revisions and notes over the course of the book's history. When one considers the history of a work such as this, the need for such notes becomes apparent. If Deuteronomy was indeed the work found in the temple during Josiah's reign, then the fact that the work survived at all is quite remarkable. Again, after the vicissitudes of the Exile, it may be that the time and perspective separating the people from the contents of the law were such that the text required explanation and clarification (Neh. 8:8). For possible examples of such minor additions, see: 2:10-12, 20-23; 3:9-11 and 13b-17; see further the commentary. Cf. Harrison, *IOT,* pp. 637-640.

was therefore dated in the Mosaic era. Since the Enlightenment, however, scientific biblical scholarship has advocated a large variety of hypotheses regarding the date and authorship of the work. The book has been ascribed to Moses,[18] Samuel, priests, prophets, and wisemen; it has been dated in various periods from the time of Moses to the time of the Exile, a time span of some seven centuries. H. H. Rowley, writing in 1951, said of the study of Deuteronomy: "It is here that the greatest fluidity in the whole field of Old Testament study is to be found today, though it cannot be said that any agreed pattern is emerging from the welter of challenge to the older views."[19] More than twenty years later, the same fluidity still exists, but it may be possible to discern a pattern emerging from the varieties of opinion; the pattern, however, does not remove all the difficulties attending the date and authorship of Deuteronomy.

The pattern that seems to be emerging in studies of Deuteronomy is to be found in the increasing recognition being given to the relationship between the overall structure of the book and the form of the ancient Near Eastern vassal treaty.[20] This recognition, however, leads to two basic alternatives with reference to the dating of Deuteronomy. The first possibility is that the treaty structure of the book indicates a date in the Mosaic period or very shortly thereafter; the second is that Deuteronomy is a seventh-century B.C. composition.

M. G. Kline and others (see n. 14) have argued that the treaty-covenant structure of Deuteronomy indicates that it must be dated in the Mosaic age. The thrust of this argument rests on several bases, but two may be singled out as being of particular importance. (1) Deuteronomy reflects the pattern of the suzerainty treaties in its total structure; (2) in particular, the whole work reflects "the classic legal form of the suzerainty treaties of the Mosaic age."[21] The second point is important, for it points to a distinction Kline makes in his analysis of the history of the form of the suzerainty treaties in the Near East. This point will be returned to below, but first we shall examine the second alternative.

18. For further details, see Harrison, *IOT*, pp. 637-653; E. W. Nicholson, *Deuteronomy and Tradition*, pp. 37f. For recent works on the Mosaic authorship of Deuteronomy and the Pentateuch, see W. Möller, *Grundriss für alttestamentliche Einleitung* (1958); B. Mariani, *Introductio in libros sacros Veteris Testamenti* (1958).
19. H. H. Rowley, ed., *The OT and Modern Study* (repr. 1956), p. xxvii.
20. It would not, of course, be universally agreed that this was the major pattern emerging from the variety of current opinions in scholarly writings. But M. Weinfeld has a pertinent remark, which is of interest in relation to the continuing analytic literary studies of Deuteronomy: "Though the book of Deuteronomy quite probably consists of different editorial strands, no established criterion exists by which we can determine either the extent of each strand of its composition or its ideological teaching." *Deuteronomy and the Deuteronomic School* (1972), p. 7.
21. Kline, *The Structure of Biblical Authority*, p. 132.

The argument of Frankena and Weinfeld is to the effect that the treaty structure of Deuteronomy indicates a date for the work in the seventh century B.C.[22] Weinfeld, whose work is more recent and more detailed, takes the position that the form and phraseology of Deuteronomy have their closest affinities in substance with the seventh-century Assyrian state treaties of Esarhaddon. He admits that the major sections of the Hittite treaties are present in Deuteronomy, but stresses rather a different point. The Hittite treaties have very short and generalized curse formulas, but Deuteronomy contains a long and elaborate series of curses after the fashion of the Aramean and Syrian treaties. The latter point is then worked out in detail by a close analysis of similarities in language between the curse sections in Deuteronomy and the treaties. It is clear that there are fairly basic differences between these two types of argument which are presented within the framework of similar data, and the short summaries given here cannot pretend to do justice to the strengths and weaknesses of either position. Two points, however, seem to be of particular significance to the debate and will be submitted to further examination. The first point has to do with the structure of the Near Eastern treaties which form the basis for comparison with Deuteronomy. The question may be put as follows: Is there a clear distinction in form between the treaty pattern of the second millennium and that of the first millennium? Those who advocate an early date for Deuteronomy claim that there is such a distinction; the treaty form of the second millennium had as the second section of the pattern an historical prologue. In the first-millennium treaties, it is argued, the historical prologue was no longer a standard section of the treaty.[23] Weinfeld admits that the historical prologue is found in Deuteronomy, and that it was not (normally) present in the first-millennium treaties; however, he does not consider this fact to be a strong argument against his view. He presents a number of arguments, including the observation that several of the first-millennium treaties are mutilated at the beginning just where the historical prologue ought to be.[24] But then Weinfeld presents a second argument as

22. R. Frankena, "The Vassal Treaties of Esarhaddon and the Dating of Deuteronomy," OTS 14 (1965), pp. 122-154; Weinfeld, Deuteronomy and the Deuteronomic School, pp. 59-157.
23. See Kline, The Structure of Biblical Authority, p. 9. The primary work of Mendenhall had made this distinction: BA 17/3, pp. 56f. Note that the presence of the historical prologue is not the only difference between the treaties of the second and first millennia; K. A. Kitchen notes four important areas of difference: Ancient Orient and OT, pp. 95f. It is also interesting to note the remarks of K. Baltzer in the preface (1971) to the English translation of his work: "It remains, however, a striking and historically unexplained fact that the Old Testament resembles most closely the highly developed formulary of the Hittite treaty." The Covenant Formulary, p. xii.
24. Deuteronomy and the Deuteronomic School, p. 67. It should be noted also that a

an alternative to the first; he suggests that the arrogance of Assyrian kings may have led them to omit the historical prologue, because they did not feel the need to provide any justification for their actions which were promulgated in the treaties. In other words, there are two quite different lines of argument to explain the absence of the historical prologue.

Of the two alternatives, the former seems to me to be the more acceptable position. The reason for this preference, however, lies not simply in the clear presence of the historical prologue in the second-millennium treaties, but also in a number of other features which distinguish the earlier treaties from those of the first millennium. Kitchen has presented four significant differences.[25] (1) In the early treaties, the divine witnesses almost always are placed between the stipulations and curses; they do not occur in this position in the extant first-millennium treaties. (2) The matter of the historical prologue—see above. (3) The blessings in the second-millennium treaty are a regular balance to the curses; the curses in the later texts do not have corresponding blessings. (4) There is a more consistent order to the elements of the early treaties than appears in the first-millennium treaties.

Having expressed this general agreement, however, it must be added that the Near Eastern textual parallels do not necessarily provide absolutely firm evidence for dating Deuteronomy either in the early period or the later period. There are two reasons for this uncertainty. First, the treaty texts that form the external data are the product of archeological discovery, but it is the nature of such discovery that there cannot be absolute certainty that the evidence is truly representative of a given culture or period. The evidence which was survived could give a distorted or unbalanced picture of what was actually the case. Second, the use of the treaty form in the Hebrew tradition must necessarily have involved adaptation. At the most obvious level, there was the adaptation of a political document for a specifically religious purpose. But there may have been further adaptation, which, in the absence of evidence, has not come to attention in modern research. These points are mentioned to stress the need for caution. The second-millennium treaties give reasonable grounds for dating Deuteronomy in the Mosaic era, but they do not prove or verify that conclusion; there must be further evidence to add weight to the earlier dating.

Within the perspective of this commentary, a part of that further evidence is the overall understanding of the history of Israelite

---

recently published fragment of an Assyrian treaty may contain a part of an historical prologue; see A. F. Campbell, *Biblica* 50 (1969), pp. 534f.
25. *Ancient Orient and OT,* pp. 95f.

religion;[26] if there are not conclusive reasons why Deuteronomy should *not* be placed in the earlier period, which it purports to describe, then the external evidence may add some further support to the preliminary view. There is, however, a further line of argument which is important both for the date of Deuteronomy and for an understanding of its theology. This line of argument may be opened by posing a question: If indeed the Hebrew covenant is set in the form of the vassal treaties, what was it that made the treaty form so suitable for adaptation to this new purpose? It is probable that the answer to this question lies in the nature of the covenant itself.[27] The covenant does not simply function to bind the people of Israel to their God, but it also marks the liberation of the people from subservience to a worldly power, namely, Egypt. In this context the significance of the treaty pattern emerges, for the form that symbolizes worldly vassaldom is transposed to another context, that of Israel's relationship to God. Like the other small nations that surrounded her, Israel was to be a vassal state, but not to Egypt or the Hittites; she owed her allegiance to God alone.[28]

Both the form of the book and the religious significance of that form make it not unreasonable to assume that the book comes from the time of Moses or shortly thereafter; the nature of the evidence, however, is not such that the date can be either proved or disproved. Given a general dating in the early period, then it must be asked whether more precise comments can be made. In dealing with this question, it is important to note that the formal background, the treaty form, may provide some clue. The authority of the vassal treaties lay in part in their written form; by being written down (inscribed on a tablet), the words of the treaty, which governed the suzerain-vassal relationship, gained authority and permanence.[29] It is probable, therefore, that Deuteronomy, as a covenant renewal document, was written down soon after the renewal ceremony.[30]

The scribe who wrote or recorded the final form of the book is not known. In terms of the major substance of the book, the source (or

26. For a valuable summary statement, see K. A. Kitchen, "The OT in Its Context, 6," *TSF Bulletin* 64 (1972), pp. 2-10. See further section IX of the Introduction, in which a number of specific problems are examined in detail.
27. The point made here is elaborated in more detail in section VIII, "Theology."
28. If Deuteronomy was indeed the book discovered in the temple during the reign of Josiah (2 K. 22:8-13), then the subsequent significance of the treaty form becomes evident. Judah's new independence from servitude to the Assyrian Empire could be given more definite and significant form in renewing the treaty-covenant commitment to God.
29. See *ANET*, p. 205b; cf. W. Beyerlin, *Origins and History of the Oldest Sinaitic Traditions* (E.T. ²1965), pp. 145-47.
30. For further discussion, see section V, "Occasion."

verbal author) is described regularly as Moses himself.[31] There are several references to writing within the book, but the references are often ambiguous; it is not always clear whether they refer to the book of Deuteronomy, or the earlier Book of the Covenant (Exod. 24:7), which may have been the original record of the Sinai Covenant and would therefore have formed the basis for the renewal of the covenant.[32]

The manner in which the original book was written is equally uncertain. The injunction to write "all the words of this law" on plastered stones after the crossing of the Jordan could refer to Deuteronomy, but it could also refer to the Book of the Covenant or to the legal section of Deuteronomy (see 27:1-8 and commentary). It is more likely that at some point following the death of Moses (34:1-12), the whole work was written down, perhaps on stone or tablets, but more likely on a leather scroll. The latter possibility is illustrated from Egypt by the so-called "Annals of Thutmose III" (c.1490-1436 B.C.).[33] The Annals, which were carved on the walls of the great temple at Karnak, are only one of several accounts of the pharaoh's campaigns in Syria and Palestine; shorter accounts are contained on a red granite stele found at Armant and on a granite stele from Jebel Barkal. A memorial stele, which once stood in the temple at Karnak, praises the pharaoh's victories in the form of a victory hymn. The point of interest, however, is that there is a reference in the Annals to a more detailed account of the campaigns which was contained on a leather roll and lodged in the same temple. The roll has unfortunately not survived, but apparently it contained the detailed reports of each day of the campaign from which the Annals were compiled. The leather roll seems to have served as a portable, but fairly durable substance on which records could be made during the travels through Syria and Palestine. It is possible that a similar mode of recording was employed by the Hebrews (who had resided in Egypt for so long). The writing of the law on plastered stones had a more temporary and ceremonial function.

---

31. It is important to stress that "authorship" of a book such as Deuteronomy has to do with the *substance* (viz., the "words that Moses spoke") and not primarily with the mechanical process of writing or recording. The relationship between the substance and the written form is, in the nature of the evidence, outside the scope or ability of literary-critical investigation.
32. E.g., 17:18; 28:58, 61; 29:20f., 27; 30:10; these passages could refer either to the Book of the Covenant or (on the analogy of the Hittite treaties) to Deuteronomy per se. 31:24 may refer to the legal section of Deuteronomy. 27:3-8 refers to writing at a future date, namely, at the ceremony to be held in the vicinity of Shechem. 31:19 refers to the writing of Moses' Song of Witness.
33. For the text of the Annals, see *ANET*, pp. 234-38.

V. OCCASION

There are two levels on which the occasion of Deuteronomy can be discussed. The primary level is that which is reflected internally in the book, namely, the renewal of the Sinai Covenant on the plains of Moab. The second level is related to the further renewal of the covenant immediately after the initial stages of the conquest (Josh. 8:30-35).

The renewal of the covenant on the plains of Moab is essentially the subject matter of the book of Deuteronomy; the emphasis, however, is not on the details of the renewal ceremony, but on the words that Moses addressed to the people gathered together for the occasion. There are two principal perspectives within which the renewal ceremony is to be understood. The first relates to the matter of the succession in human leadership in the covenant community; the time of Moses' death was drawing near and Joshua was to take up the responsibilities of leadership. The second perspective is that of the military conquest which lay in the immediate future of all the people assembled on the plains of Moab; after years of preparation and disciplining, they were now poised on the eve of events which would bring to fruition those ancient promises of God given first to the patriarchs.

The approaching death of Moses provided the initial basis for the renewal of the covenant. Moses' role in the first forging of the covenant at Sinai had been so significant that, for many of the people, Moses and the covenant must have seemed inseparable. But the time of Moses' death was approaching; this was not simply a result of old age, but was precipitated in part by the course of events. The time had come to cross the Jordan, but Moses had been forbidden by God to set foot in the promised land. The conquest had to continue and Moses had to withdraw from his people; but it should be noted that in the fullest sense, it was not a change in leadership that was contemplated. The true leader of the covenant people was God himself; Moses' role was that of mediator and effective leader from the human point of view. The matter of succession was related to the human leader, the representative and spokesman of God before the covenant community; and for all the importance of Moses in the Israelite tradition, the time had come when he had to step aside. The description of the termination of Moses' leadership of his people contains elements both of sadness and of acceptance. The sadness appears in Moses' prayer (3:23-28), when he recalled how he had pleaded with God to be allowed to enter the land, but was only to be permitted to see it from a distance. The acceptance and surrender appear in the concise but moving description of the death of Moses (34:1-8); though he did not set foot in the land, nevertheless his last moments were spent once again in communion with God on a mountain.

During the renewal ceremony, Moses thus addressed his people as one who would be with them no longer; and the force of the exhortation to obedience throughout the book is to be understood against this background. But Moses also passed on the office he had held to Joshua and encouraged the people to grant him their allegiance. The succession of human leadership was neither a power struggle nor a democratic process; it was a matter of divine appointment. On the occasion on which Moses had pleaded with God for permission to enter the promised land, he had been told to charge Joshua with the responsibility of leading the Israelites. Thus, at a certain point in the ceremony, Moses summoned Joshua and appointed him to his new role (31:7-8).

In addition to the change in leadership, the second perspective for the occasion described in Deuteronomy is to be found in the conquest to be undertaken in the immediate future. The covenant at Sinai had been sealed *after* the great victory of God against Egypt in the Exodus (Exod. 15:1-18); the covenant was to be renewed *before* the entry into the promised land. In the Exodus the people had discovered, perhaps for the first time, that their God was a "man in battle";[34] that is, they had learned that God participated in the events of human history to bring about the fulfilment of his promises to his people. But now that they knew the character of their God, they renewed their covenant allegiance to him before entering into battle; the outcome of future battles lay not in their military prowess, but in the power of God and the wholeheartedness of their commitment to God. The renewal of the covenant by the Israelites was thus an acknowledgement that they were about to set forth on an impossible task, but that with God all things would be possible. Obedience, however, to the God of the covenant would be essential and it is to this end that Moses, who anticipates his death, encourages his people to wholehearted commitment.

Some of the details of the ceremonial occasion emerge from the text of Deuteronomy, but they are not always clear, for the primary purpose of the book is to be found in the record of the words of Moses. All the people ("All Israel," 1:1) were gathered together on the plains of Moab to be addressed by Moses, and as the address continued, some particular events and actions appear. (1) The people

---

34.   See Exod. 15:3. For an examination of the theological difficulties relating to the understanding of God as a warrior, see P. D. Miller, "God the Warrior: A Problem in Biblical Interpretation and Apologetics," *Interpretation* 19 (1965), pp. 39-46; P. C. Craigie, "Yahweh Is a Man of War," *SJT* 22 (1969), pp. 183-88; R. Tomes, "Exodus 14: The Mighty Acts of God," *SJT* 22 (1969), pp. 455-478.

formally declared their allegiance by affirming that the Lord was their God (26:16-17). (2) Instructions were given for the next renewal of the covenant (ch. 27), based on the fact that "this day you have become the people of the Lord your God" (27:9-11). (3) Blessings and curses were announced to the people (ch. 28), which made clear to them the results that would follow obedience or disobedience to the law set down by the God of the covenant. (4) Joshua was appointed as Moses' successor, both in public ceremony (31:7-8; 34:9) and privately in the tent of meeting (31:14-23). (5) Instructions were given regarding the deposition of the text of the covenant in the ark (31:9, 26). (6) General instructions were given for the normative covenant renewal procedure in the more distant future (31:10-13). (7) Moses wrote down the "Song of Witness" (32:1-43) and taught it to the people (31:22, 28); the singing of the song may have marked the formal conclusion of the renewal ceremony.

In summary, these features indicate the occasion reflected within the book, but it may be that the book in its final form is to be related to a later occasion, a further renewal of the covenant within the promised land, which was conducted under the direction of Joshua (Josh. 8:30-35). This further perspective is already noted within Deuteronomy (see 11:29-30 and 27:1-13); the covenant was to be renewed in the vicinity of Shechem, to the north of which was located Mount Ebal, with Mount Gerizim to the south. The choice of Shechem as the site for the renewal of the covenant within the promised land may well have been determined by the ancient memory of Jacob's association with the place; Jacob had erected an altar there and called it "El-Elohe-Israel" ("God, the God of Israel"; Gen. 33:18-20). The renewal of the covenant at Shechem was a mark of the first successes that had been experienced in the possession of the land; it was fitting, therefore, to recall the ceremony, conducted by Moses, that had immediately preceded those successes. Joshua, in the ceremony at Shechem, did not omit any of the words Moses had commanded (Josh. 8:35). It is possible that the text of Deuteronomy, substantially in its present form, is to be associated with the covenant renewal ceremony at Shechem.

VI. CANONICITY

Although the detailed history of the formation of the OT canon is difficult to reconstruct, there has never been serious doubt as to the place of Deuteronomy (the fifth book of Moses) within the canon.[35] It

---

35. For a discussion of the problems relating to the history of the canon, see Harrison, *IOT*, pp. 260-288.

was from an early date recognized as a fundamental part of the canonical writings, and was not the subject of debate (as was the case, for example, with Esther and the Song of Solomon). Furthermore, in the history of Christian thought, Deuteronomy has played an important role in the understanding of the canon; the Second Helvetic Confession of 1566, for example, adduced passages in Deuteronomy (4:2; 12:32) as commandments of God having reference to the canonical writings of both Testaments.[36]

The many quotations from Deuteronomy in the New Testament and in the Qumran writings (see Appendix III, below) indicate that before the beginnings of the Christian era, the Torah (which included Deuteronomy) was widely accepted as an authoritative and canonical work. In the NT, quotations from and references to Deuteronomy occur in the Gospels and Acts, in the Epistles, and, in a more veiled manner, in the concluding verses of the Revelation.[37] Judging by the materials discovered in the vicinity of the Dead Sea, Deuteronomy was one of the most popular books among the sectarians who lived in the vicinity of Qumran.[38]

Deuteronomy, moreover, has a particular place in the developing history of the canon. The emergence of the idea of canon is closely related to the concept of covenant,[39] and in the OT, Deuteronomy is a covenant document par excellence.[40] It was in the nature of the covenant that it be set down in writing, thus becoming authoritative, so that a written covenant and the concept of canon no doubt grew together from a very early period in Israel's history. That is to say, even though the OT in its *complete* canonical form was a relatively late product (postexilic), many of the component parts of the complete canon may well have had canonical status at a much earlier date.

Recently, a new hypothesis has been advanced in regard to the nature and historicity of the canonicity of the OT. M. G. Kline has expanded his studies of the relationship between the Near Eastern treaties and the Hebrew covenant in order to bring further light to bear on the matter of canon.[41] He notes the importance of a written

---

36. See E. G. Kraeling, *The OT since the Reformation* (1955), p. 35.
37. See Matt. 4:1-11 (Luke 4:1-13); Mark 7:9-12; 10:17-19; Acts 3:23f.; Rom. 10:6-9; Gal. 2:10, 13; Heb. 10:28; Rev. 22:18f.
38. F. M. Cross, *The Ancient Library of Qumran* (1958), p. 43.
39. See O. Loretz, *The Truth of the Bible* (E.T. 1968), pp. 96-101. See also R. E. Clements, *God's Chosen People* (1968), pp. 89-105: "Thus the idea of a canon derives from the fact of the covenant, and the need to provide in written form a declaration of what this covenant entailed" (p. 100). Clements stresses the importance of Deuteronomy in relation to the developing principle of canonicity in the late 7th century B.C.
40. The expression "book of the covenant" in 2 K. 23:2 may well refer to Deuteronomy.
41. *The Structure of Biblical Authority*, pp. 27-110.

33

form for the political treaties and also for various other types of Near Eastern texts; the presence of document clauses and curses, designed to prevent the texts from being unlawfully changed, enables Kline to describe the Near Eastern texts as "canonical documents." The adaptation of the treaty form in the Hebrew tradition included adoption by the Hebrews of the canonical principle. Hence, Kline concludes: "The beginnings of canonical Scripture thus coincided with the formal founding of Israel as the kingdom of God. In the treaty documents given by Yahweh at the very origins of the nation Israel, the people of God already possessed the ground stratum of the old Testament canon."[42]

VII. THE HEBREW TEXT

The Hebrew text[43] of Deuteronomy has been preserved in remarkably good condition, in contrast to the text of other OT books (e.g., the books of Samuel or Job). Even though the principal textual evidence is as late as the tenth century A.D.,[44] there are very few places in which it is difficult to grasp the meaning of the Hebrew. The major difficulties arise in the two poetic chapters (32 and 33), and there the difficulties are part of the larger problem of understanding ancient Hebrew poetry, rather than being specifically textual problems. At a number of points the evidence of the Versions indicates a Hebrew text slightly different from that which we now have; for the most part, however, these variations are not of great significance.[45]

Toward the end of the nineteenth century, a great manuscript discovery was thought to have been made, which would have been particularly relevant to the study of Deuteronomy. Moses Wilhelm Shapira, a Jerusalem dealer in antiquities and manuscripts, offered for sale an apparently ancient manuscript, which was said to have been discovered in a cave in the region of the Dead Sea. The Hebrew script used in the manuscript was very similar to that already known from the Moabite Stone. The manuscript contained quite extensive sections from Deuteronomy, and on the basis of a comparison with

42. *Ibid.,* p. 38.
43. The text on which the translation is based in this commentary is that of *Biblia Hebraica*[3] (ed. R. Kittel; Deut. ed. J. Hempel).
44. For a full discussion of the OT text, see Harrison, *IOT,* pp. 211-243. On the transmission of the Hebrew text of Deuteronomy, see section IX.6 of the Introduction.
45. The majority of the variations concern such matters as the presence of the conjunction, and the person or number of pronominal suffixes. The points at which there seem to be more substantial variations are discussed in the commentary. The evidence of the LXX, *on minor points,* may not be of great value, for its stylistic elegance is such that it may not truly represent the Hebrew at all points; see Buis and Leclercq, *Le Deutéronome* (1963), p. 28.

the Moabite Stone, it was thought that they might be as old as the ninth century B.C. The manuscript, however, was declared a forgery, largely through the influence of the French scholar Clermont-Ganneau. Soon after this declaration, the unfortunate Shapira (who was blamed with complicity) committed suicide.[46]

In recent years, the question of the authenticity of the manuscript has been reopened. There are several scholars who now think that it may indeed have been an ancient text.[47] Although it may not have been as ancient as Shapira thought, the manuscript may at least have been contemporary with the recently discovered Dead Sea Scrolls, though written in a more archaic script. Unfortunately the manuscript seems to have been lost, but there are a number of translations and transcriptions still in existence. In view of the continuing debate over the authenticity of the Shapira manuscript, its evidence has not been employed in this commentary. If, however, the debate is resolved in the future, then this surviving evidence may have to be taken into account in subsequent studies of Deuteronomy.

Although the evidence of the Shapira manuscript is still under suspicion, new evidence for the Hebrew text of Deuteronomy was provided by the discovery of the Dead Sea Scrolls in the vicinity of Qumran in 1947 and the years following. For the most part, the evidence of the Scrolls shows the remarkable accuracy with which the ancient Hebrew text had been transcribed from an early date. The majority of the variations between the MT and the Dead Sea texts are minor in nature; the main differences are to be found in orthography. In one case (Deut. 32:43), the Qumran text is longer than the MT and has certain similarities to the longer text preserved in the LXX at this point. This variation and other significant differences are discussed in the body of the commentary.

The Qumran evidence for Deuteronomy consists of several different kinds of manuscripts. There are many fragments comprising remnants of scrolls which at one time contained the whole or part of Deuteronomy. The wide distribution of these fragments indicates that Deuteronomy must have been a popular book among the inhabitants of the Qumran region. In addition to these fragments, sections of Deuteronomy are quoted in other types of religious texts. The text 4QTestimonia, for example, brings together several biblical prophecies; among these are three quotations from Deuteronomy. Portions of Deuteronomy are also preserved in three *phylacteries* and one *mezuzah;* these are discussed more fully in the commentary on Deut. 6:6-9 and 11:18-21 (see also Exod. 13:1-10).

46. For a discussion see J. Allegro, *The Shapira Affair* (1965).
47. See L. Deuel, *Testaments of Time. The Search for Lost Manuscripts and Records* (1970), pp. 402-421.

A concordance of the principal Qumran evidence for the text of Deuteronomy is provided below (see Appendix III), as an aid to those who may wish to study the texts in detail. It is evident immediately that the evidence is quite extensive. The list, however, may be a little misleading, for in many cases the texts from Qumran are extremely fragmentary and may preserve only one or two words of any given verse. Thus there can be no question of the Qumran text replacing the much later texts upon which we have depended up to the present. In one or two cases, the evidence is valuable in clarifying a reading that was formerly doubtful. For the most part, the value of the Scrolls is indirect, namely, in increasing our confidence in the general trustworthiness of the texts upon which we have had to depend prior to the discoveries made in the region of the Dead Sea.

VIII. THEOLOGY

It is not possible to summarize all the details of the theology of Deuteronomy in an adequate way; the full riches of the theological thought of the book will emerge from a careful reading of the text. Therefore, this section on the theology of Deuteronomy will simply highlight some of the more important theological features in order to provide a general background to the book as a whole. The nature of Biblical Theology as a discipline is currently the subject of considerable debate;[48] the debate will not be resumed here, but it may be helpful to indicate in a preliminary fashion the method to be used for examining the theology of Deuteronomy. The basic principle for interpreting the theology of Deuteronomy rests upon its character as a covenant document. It is the covenant, then, that provides the framework within which the details of theology are to be expressed.[49] In the paragraphs that follow there will first be an examination of the general theological nature of the Israelite covenant, as it is expressed in Deuteronomy. Second, the details will be examined further by taking up consecutively the main sections of Deuteronomy; that is, those sections of Deuteronomy which find a parallel in the Near Eastern political treaties will form an interpretative framework for examining the theology of the book. The interpretation, once again, will be general; an attempt will be made to grasp the broader issues, without summarizing the content of the book. Inevitably, there will be

48. For a valuable discussion, see G. Hasel, *OT Theology: Basic Issues in the Current Debate* (1972).
49. It may be argued that the covenant provides a basic principle for interpreting not only Deuteronomy, but the whole biblical tradition; see F. C. Fensham, "The Covenant As Giving Expression to the Relationship Between the Old and the New Testament," *TB* 22 (1971), pp. 82-94.

some topics that do not receive full examination in this approach; for that reason, a special select bibliography has been added at the end of the section to give some indication of alternative approaches to the study of the theology of Deuteronomy.

The primary feature of the covenant lies in its nature as a bond between God and man, or more specifically, between the Lord and his chosen people. The source of the covenant bond lies in God alone; it represents an act of God's loving kindness, initiated by him in love. The recipients of this offer of relationship were God's chosen people, the Israelites; to ask "Why this choice" is to pose an impossible question, for though the acts and words of God may be revealed to man, the reason for his ways lies deeper in mystery. The question can be given only partial answers; it was because God loved his people (7:8) and, in a larger sense, it was because this was a part of the will of God for man. But in principle, the nature of God's covenant relationship to man is beyond the probing of philosophical questions; man must be content with that which is revealed and leave the secret things to God (29:29). The essence of the covenant, it must be stressed, lies in the relationship between God and man, and though God is the first and free mover in establishing that relationship, nevertheless a relationship requires response from man. The operative principle within the relationship is that of love; God moved first toward his people in love and they must respond to him in love. The law of the covenant expresses the love of God and indicates the means by which a man must live to reflect love for God.

The covenant at Sinai was not a once-and-for-all event that had only historical significance. It inaugurated a continuing relationship (which had already been anticipated in the earlier covenants) between God and his people; because it was a continuing relationship, the covenant was to be renewed regularly, but in each renewal the event at Sinai was recalled. The renewal of the covenant was undertaken, not because God changed, but because each generation had to recommit itself regularly in love and obedience to the Lord of the covenant. In the address of Moses, the most powerful exhortation is used to move the people to new and wholehearted commitment to God. The tendency to view the covenant as a legal contract automatically binding man to God had to be countered; the nature of the covenant, as an expression of a living relationship, demanded of man not a legalistic acquiescence, but a loving commitment to God.

The treaty structure of the covenant was a reminder to the people of their liberty in this world and of their total commitment to God. They had been in bondage, vassals to the worldly power in Egypt, but God's intervention in history at the Exodus had freed the Israelites from that human vassaldom; in the encounter with God at Horeb, they had submitted to a new vassaldom under God. In the old servitude, Israel had served a worldly master and had no freedom to worship God (Exod. 8:1); in the new covenant, Israel had freedom to worship God and was servant to no worldly state. The domination of Egypt had been exchanged for the Kingship of God (Exod. 15:18), who had broken the fetters of the old bondage. It is this relationship between God and man which will now be explored more fully by taking up the treaty-covenant sections of the book (for an outline of the sections, see "Unity of Composition" above).

1. Preamble: The Prophetic Word

The preamble in the Hittite suzerainty treaties normally opened by identifying the words contained in the treaty as those of the Hittite king. Deuteronomy opens in a similar, but distinctive manner: "These are the words that Moses addressed to all Israel . . ." (1:1). The formal similarities are clear, but the difference in substance is noteworthy; the book does not open by identifying the words contained in it as those of God, the true King of Israel. The human words are those of Moses. This difference does not mean that Moses was in effect king of Israel; it points rather to his role as the spokesman or prophet of God.

Having noticed this difference from the treaty form, however, it must be stressed immediately that the substance of the words of Moses finds its source in God. The relationship between the words Moses speaks and their source and authority in God may be expressed in several ways. In the first words ascribed to Moses in the book, he quotes words of God addressed to the people at Horeb (1:6), but on other occasions he speaks his own words (1:9). The general principle involved is expressed in 5:22-31; at Horeb, the people had been afraid to listen to the voice of God and requested Moses to listen on their behalf and then speak to them the words of God. Part of Moses' role at Horeb had thus been to act as God's spokesman; on the plains of Moab, he elaborates the meaning of those words once again in the ceremony of renewal.

Moses was thus the first of a distinguished line of prophets in Israel.[50] As a prophet, he entered into close communion with God and received God's word for man. It was as the first prophet, too, that he communicated to Israel certain basic guidelines which determined the nature and function of prophecy for subsequent generations (13:1-5; 18:15-22). And, in the last verses of the book, when Moses had died, it was said that there had not been a prophet like him since then; what distinguished Moses was that he was a man "whom the Lord knew face to face" (34:10).

---

50. Abraham is also called a prophet (Gen. 20:7), though in relation to Israel as a nation (after the Exodus), it is Moses who is the first and normative prophet.

In his role as prophet, Moses not only presented the words of God, but expounded them with emphasis in his preaching. He had responsibility under God for the Israelites, and from his long experience as their leader, he knew of all their weaknesses and failings. Thus, in his preaching, he employs the various devices of rhetoric in his presentation of the substance of the covenant, in order to bring the people to wholehearted commitment to their God. The prophetic role, in other words, was not simply to announce the word of God, but to persuade men of its living force, to call them to love and obedience, and also to warn them of the consequences of falling away from the intimacy of the covenant relationship. Moses was not simply the "microphone" of God, but was a man with responsibility; he was responsible under God for the faithful presentation of the divine words and he was responsible for the people whom God had committed to his charge.

From the Christian perspective, there is a further aspect to the prophetic role of Moses in Deuteronomy. In Deut. 18:15-22, there is a description of the nature of prophecy, but the passage is in itself prophetic in foreshadowing another Prophet who was to come, namely, Jesus.[51] As Moses was the first prophet in the covenant community founded at Sinai, so too Jesus had a prophetic role in the inauguration of the New Covenant. During the early ministry of John the Baptist, John was asked if he was "the prophet" (see John 1:21-25),[52] and he answered negatively; he was only a forerunner. Jesus was that coming Prophet, but he was more than a prophet. Thus, in the old covenant, the opening words were those of Moses, representing the true King of Israel; in the new covenant, the kingdom was inaugurated by the incarnate King himself, who could speak his own words.

2. Historical Prologue: The Theology of History

History plays a particular role in the covenant; in the covenant prologue, the recounting of history indicates those events antecedent to the founding of the covenant, which were of fundamental importance. History, however, in the biblical tradition, does not have the same connotations as do modern conceptions of history.[53] History is not an unbroken continuum of causes and effects, which is an en-

51. On the question of Jesus as prophet, see particularly H. E. W. Turner, *Jesus, Master and Lord* (1964), pp. 145-155.
52. Cf. C. K. Barrett, *The Gospel according to John* (1965), p. 144, for further details on the hope and beliefs regarding the coming prophet.
53. See G. P. Grant, *Philosophy in the Mass Age* (1959), pp. 42f. Grant describes the emergence of the modern conception from its Judeo-Christian origin; the modern idea is termed "history as progress" in contrast to the Christian idea of history as the "divinely ordained process of salvation" (p. 49).

closed system, free from the intervention of a transcendent God. Rather, history reflects the will of God, in word and in deed, within the creation of God. To be particular, the historical prologue of the covenant is a description of the enacted will and word of God within the sphere of history; it provides the basis upon which the covenant between God and his people is compacted. Thus the central element of this history is the Exodus, but it cannot be called historical in the modern scientific sense. This does not mean that "it didn't happen"; but it means that the essence of the Exodus was an act of God, which by its very nature is transhistorical in relation to a modern concept of history.

History, then, in ancient Israel, was not a scientific discipline; nor was it a search for the past provoked by antiquarian interests, or even a philosophical quest for self-understanding in the context of past events. History revealed what God had done for his people; it intimated his will. The role of history in Deuteronomy is related to this central point. First, history was utilized to evoke memory; second, history served to produce vision and anticipation. That is to say, history embraces both the past and the future, but is only critical for the present; memory of God's past course of action and anticipation of his future course of action provide the framework for the present commitment to God in the renewal of the covenant. History is thus one dimension of a continuing relationship between God and his people. The past portrays the faithfulness of God within the relationship and holds the promise for the continuation of the relationship. Conversely, the past may remind the people of their unfaithfulness, or the unfaithfulness of their predecessors, and it may therefore impress upon them more urgently the need for present commitment in order that the future of the relationship might be secured.

This sense of history creates an air of immediacy and contingency which permeates the whole book of Deuteronomy; it is by no means confined to the historical prologue. The immediacy is created by awareness that centuries of complex events have been leading, within the plan of God, to the present moment. From Abraham and the patriarchs (1:8), from Egypt and the great liberation, from Horeb and the giving of the Law, from the testing travels which had brought Israel to the plains of Moab, from all these events came an awareness that the present was a moment of crucial importance for the covenant relationship. The contingency is stressed by the tension between the promise of God for the future and the weight of responsibility which therefore rested upon the Israelites to be faithful and obedient in their covenant commitment to God. In the renewal of the covenant, "now" is the significant moment which Moses stresses in his address; he brings his people to the moment at which he can declare: "Today you have become the people of God" (27:9).

3. General Stipulations: the Basic Principle of the Relationship

The general stipulations in the political treaty contain directives which relate to the future relationships between the parties of the treaty.[54] In Deuteronomy the basic principle underlying the relationship between God and his people is stated and then worked out in some detail in the address of Moses. The basic principle is *love;* it was in love that the covenant was initiated by God in the first place, and by love the people were to maintain their close relationship to God. The stipulation is stated first in the Ten Commandments (5:6-21), which present the dimensions and nature of the relationship, namely, love for God and love for fellow man. Second, the principle is stated in its more general and imperative form—man must love God with the totality of his being (6:5). In the remaining portions of the general stipulations, love is a recurring theme, both God's love for man and the love man must have for God.[55]

The imagery employed to illustrate the principle of love is important, for it indicates which of the many facets of love underlies the covenant relationship. The imagery is that of a father's love for his son; similar imagery is employed in the political treaties.[56] God's fatherly love has two characteristics. It may be expressed in his compassionate care for his people (see 1:31) or it may be expressed in his disciplining them (see 8:5); but the two aspects of God, compassionate and stern, are both aspects of fatherly love. From the human perspective, the father-son imagery clarifies the reason why love can be stipulated; just as in the commandments the young could be instructed to honor their parents (5:16), so too in the covenant relationship, the people of God could be commanded to love him (6:5). The command to love, however, does not reduce the covenant to a legalistic relationship. Love must be a response toward God from man's heart; the command to love does not reduce the element of response, but recognizes that it is in the nature of man to forget[57] and to be faithless.

54. Baltzer notes the following features in the third section of the treaties: (1) it is closely related to the historical prologue ("antecedent history"), which contains the facts constituting the basis of the treaty relationship; (2) it contains in summary form the purpose of the following specific stipulations; (3) it consists primarily of general imperatives requiring loyalty on the part of the treaty signatory: see *The Covenant Formulary,* pp. 12f.
55. On God's love for his people, see 7:8f. and 12f.; 10:15. On man's love for God, see 7:9; 10:12; 11:1, 13, 22. On love for the alien resident in Israel, see 10:19.
56. For further details, see the commentary on 6:5. On the implications for the NT, see G. E. Mendenhall, *The Tenth Generation. The Origin of the Biblical Tradition* (1973), p. 14, n. 62.
57. Man's ability to "forget" appears several times in chs. 5–11 as a striking contrast to the injunction to love; see 6:12; 8:11, 14, 19; 9:7 (see also 4:9, 23). God, in contrast, does not forget his covenant (4:31).

The nature of the nascent state of Israel was thus to be based on the love of God and love for God. Love, the basic principle, finds its expression in the Decalog, the constitution of the state whose king was God. In other words, love was not simply a principle or abstract ethical concept; it was given clear expression in the commandments, which showed the way in which a man's love for God and for his fellow man must be given expression. And the commandments were vital to the continued welfare and existence of the Israelites. To break the commandments was to disrupt the relationship of love; when there was no love, there could be no covenant.

The renewing of the covenant thus consisted in a new commitment in love to the God of the covenant. From a human perspective, the whole procedure may seem extraordinary; Israel, a potential/nation in Palestine, was basing its existence on love of an invisible, yet personal God. The political treaties called for "love" of the suzerain king, a real physical person, who executed the human power to ensure that "love." Israel's nationhood was based on no human ruler, no democratically elected government, but on the living God, the knowledge of whom was so real that philosophical questions as to his existence would have seemed ridiculous. Just as God is presupposed in all the religious thought expressed in the OT, so too is he presupposed in the political structure.

4. Specific Stipulations: The Dimensions of Covenant Life in Detail

The details contained in the specific legislation are in many ways the most distant and foreign element in Deuteronomy to the modern reader. The matters touched on in this exposition of the law of the covenant are numerous and varied; some appear to be of the greatest importance while others appear to be relatively insignificant. There are laws relating to the sanctuary, to idolatry, to the major religious festivals, to sexual crimes, to the conduct of war, to foodstuffs, to slaves and the year of release, to prophecy and priesthood, to birds' nests, to financial matters, and to kidnapping, to name only a few. There appears to be a mixture of ceremonial, religious, civil, and criminal law. No area of human living is outside the perspective of the law and the covenant.

In the modern world, a distinction may often be made between the religious and the secular, or the sacred and the profane. To Israel, such a distinction would be artificial, not because there was no distinction made in the spheres of life within which the law was operative, but because all of life was under the dominion of God, the Lord of the covenant. Hence the broad scope of the specific stipulations is significant; the stipulations do not cover every possible contingency that could arise in human living, but they indicate by their breadth and diversity that no area of life is irrelevant or unimportant to the member of the covenant community. The laws embrace communal and individual responsibility, and implicit in the laws is the relationship between the two; the community remains healthy in its relationship to God only as long as its members are faithful. But the individual's responsibility was vital, not only for his own well-being, but because each of his actions was a part of the life of the whole community. "No man is an island": he was part of the community, and though he was responsible for his own sin and could be punished for it, the whole community was endangered by the sins of its members. If a crime were committed and the criminal were not brought to justice, then the community was responsible to deal with the wickedness that had been done and to seek God's forgiveness (21:1-9).

The significance of the specific stipulations emerges once again in the *relationship* between God and his people. The people declared that the Lord was their God (26:18). God's declaration involved the promise that he would set his people above all other nations; they were to be a holy people (26:19). The people's declaration was not simply a statement of fact, but a submission of obedience to the law of God. The obedience was necessary, for their declaration would be null and void if their lives did not testify to the reality of the declaration. To declare that the Lord was their God, but to live as others lived, would be more than hypocrisy; in the eyes of the world, it would blemish the knowledge of God for whom Israel had made their declaration. Hence, the detailed nature of the specific stipulations sets out the totality of the manner of life which would be fitting for a people who claimed a relationship to the Lord of the covenant. And running through the specific stipulations are warnings concerning the dangers of foreign religious practices; the warnings illustrate the ways in which allegiance to God might be disrupted and in which the true covenant relationship with God could be brought into danger. In summary, the object of the specific stipulations is the maintenance of a true and living *relationship* with the Lord of the covenant.

5. Blessings and Curses: Reward and Punishment

The chapters containing the blessings and curses (chs. 27–28) provide a somber tone to the book of Deuteronomy. The emphasis is placed on the curses rather than on the blessings, in terms of the length of treatment given to each topic. The curses function as a solemn warning to those who renewed their allegiance to the God of the covenant; it was no light matter to enter into a relationship with the Lord. The perspective within which the blessings and the curses are set is that of the community as a whole; obedience to the Lord of the covenant would result in blessing, long life, and the possession of the promised land, while disobedience would lead to disaster. Thus, when Israel renewed its covenant with God, the bright prospect of a future with God was contrasted with the bleak despair of a future without God; by emphasizing the curses, Moses brought home to his people the awesome responsibility of the commitment they were making.

There are two themes running through both the blessings and the cursings which are significant for a proper understanding of the nature of God as it is expressed in Deuteronomy; God is the Lord of history *and* of the world of nature.[58] He controls other nations *and* the course of nature, whether it be health, the fruitfulness of the land, or any other part of the created order. In other words, God has total control of all the factors that might affect the future well-being of Israel. If his people were obedient, he had the power to grant blessing: he controlled the affairs of nations and could therefore give Israel peace; and he could give them health, long life, and bountiful crops as the Lord of his created world. But if Israel were disobedient, there was no sphere of life in which Israel could escape God; the strength of their army or the richness of the land would be of no avail when the living relationship with God was broken.

The tragic element is introduced by the knowledge the reader has of the subsequent history of Israel. The blessing of God is at first realized, but then a decline sets in so that the curses dominate that history, until at last the history of the nation is terminated with the curse of exile from the promised land (28:36). In the light of Israel's history, the emphasis given to the curses loses something of its character and function as a *warning,* and comes to be seen rather as a prophetic anticipation of the course of Israel's history. But the sad story is not written to enable us to pass judgment on the men of ancient Israel. It serves rather as a paradigm of the nature of man. Granted the highest possible privilege, an intimate relationship with God, man nevertheless goes his own way, forgetful of that high calling, until he brings upon himself the curse of God. The curse of God is not something inflicted with vindictive pleasure; rather, it appears to be the inevitable outcome of life that is lived regardless of God, by rejecting a relationship with God whose essence is love.

The darkness of the picture given by the emphasis on the curses in Deuteronomy is illuminated by words Paul wrote to the Galatians. He quotes Deut. 27:26; everyone who does not abide by everything written in the book of the law comes under the curse. The paradigm of ancient Israel finds emphatic expression, for "it is evident that no man is justified before God by the law" (Gal. 3:10f.). Where, then, is hope to be found? How can man be redeemed from

58. Cf. G. E. Mendenhall, *The Tenth Generation,* p. 29.

the curse of the law? Paul provides the answer by quoting Deuteronomy once again and applying the passage to Christ: "Christ redeemed us from the curse of the law, having become a curse for us, for it is written: Cursed be every one who hangs on a tree" (Gal. 3:13; cf. Deut. 21:23). Through the death and resurrection of Jesus Christ, the blessing of God may be set before man once again.

Select Bibliography on the Theology of Deuteronomy

V. J. Almiñana Lloret, "El pecado en el Deuteronomio," *Estudios Bíblicos* 29 (1970), pp. 267-285.

E. P. Blair, "An Appeal to Remembrance: The Memory Motif in Deuteronomy," *Interpretation* 15 (1961), pp. 41-47.

W. Brueggemann, "The Kerygma of the Deuteronomic Historian," *Interpretation* 22 (1968), pp. 387-402.

D. Daube, "The Culture of Deuteronomy," *Orita* (Ibadan Journal of Religious Studies) 3 (1969), pp. 27-52.

F. Dumermuth, "Zur deuteronomistischen Kulttheologie und ihren Voraussetzungen," *ZAW* 70 (1958), pp. 59-98.

J. G. Gammie, "The Theology of Retribution in the Book of Deuteronomy," *CBQ* 32 (1970), pp. 1-12.

N. K. Gottwald, " 'Holy War' in Deuteronomy: Analysis and Critique," *The Review and Expositor* 61 (1964), pp. 296-310.

S. Herrmann, "Die konstruktive Restauration. Das Deuteronomium als Mitte biblischer Theologie," in H. W. Wolff, ed., *Probleme biblischer Theologie. Gerhard von Rad zum 70. Geburtstag* (1971), pp. 155-170.

J. Malfroy, "Sagesse et loi dans le Deutéronome," *VT* 15 (1965), pp. 49-65.

D. J. McCarthy, "Notes on the Love of God in Deuteronomy and the Father-Son Relationship Between Israel and Yahweh," *CBQ* 27 (1965), pp. 144-47.

R. A. F. McKenzie, "The Messianism of Deuteronomy," *CBQ* 19 (1957), pp. 299-305.

P. D. Miller, "The Gift of God: The Deuteronomic Theology of the Land," *Interpretation* 23 (1969), pp. 451-465.

J. M. Myers, "The Requisites for Response: On the Theology of Deuteronomy," *Interpretation* 15 (1961), pp. 14-31.

J. J. Owens, "Law and Love in Deuteronomy," *The Review and Expositor* 61 (1964), pp. 278-283.

M. Roberge, "Théologie de l'alliance sinaitique dans le Deutéronome," *Revue de l'Université d'Ottawa* 34 (1964), pp. 101-119.

L. E. Toombs, "Love and Justice in Dt. A Third Approach to Law," *Interpretation* 19 (1965), pp. 399-411.

M. Weinfeld, "The Origin of Humanism in Deuteronomy," *JBL* 80 (1961), pp. 241-47.

J. N. M. Wijngaards, *The Dramatization of Salvific History in the Deuteronomic Schools* (Leiden, 1969).

IX. PROBLEMS IN THE INTERPRETATION OF DEUTERONOMY

1. Introduction to the Problems

In the preceding sections of the Introduction, it has been argued that Deuteronomy is essentially Mosaic, and a similar perspective is taken throughout the commentary which follows. Although in a technical sense the author (or actual writer) is not known, the main substance of Deuteronomy is referred to internally as the "words" of Moses; even though the process and implications of the reduction of words to writing are not fully known, the interpretation of those words in this commentary has taken seriously the ascription of them to Moses. But it will already be evident to the reader of the foregoing sections of the Introduction that the conservative perspective taken throughout this commentary is by no means typical of the majority of views concerning Deuteronomy, held by modern OT scholars.

That there are so many differences of opinion over Deuteronomy indicates that there are fundamental problems pertaining to the interpretation of the book. To some extent, this variety of opinion arises from the theological and philosophical perspectives of different scholars; see Appendix I. But in addition, the variety of opinion may be based in part on the interpretation of the evidence contained within Deuteronomy, and also in the OT as a whole, which provides the broader framework within which Deuteronomy must be interpreted.

Hence, in this section of the Introduction, some attempt will be made to look at those problems of interpretation which have given rise to such diversity of opinion. From the vast number of such problems, those which are deemed to be most significant have been selected. If the problems are not solved to the satisfaction of those who hold interpretations of Deuteronomy different from that which is presented in this work, it is at least to be hoped that the following points will clarify somewhat the perspective from which this commentary has been written.

The following topics and problems will be examined respectively: Deuteronomy and Josiah's Reformation; "northern" and "southern" aspects of Deuteronomy; the background of the laws in the book; the religion of Israel at the time of Moses; the transmission of the text of Deuteronomy.

2. Deuteronomy and Josiah's Reformation

From an early period in the history of the interpretation of Deuteronomy, the book has been linked with the reformation of Josiah in the seventh century B.C. Jerome, and certain other church fathers, suggested that the lawbook discovered in the temple during

Josiah's reign was the book of Deuteronomy.[59] It was not until the beginning of the nineteenth century, however, that a more radical view was advocated, namely, that Deuteronomy was essentially the *product* of the reign of Josiah, not merely an already ancient book which was discovered at that time.[60] This hypothesis has continued to play a significant role in studies of Deuteronomy, although it is now modified considerably from the form in which it was initially expressed. Let us examine Josiah's reformation and the nature of the book that was discovered at that time.

The principal historical sources for Josiah's reformation are contained in 2 K. 22–23 and 2 Chr. 34–35. Because these two sources provide different emphases in their account of the reign of Josiah, each must be summarized briefly before the significance of both is examined for the relationship between the reformation and the book of Deuteronomy.

According to 2 K. 22–23, in the eighteenth year of Josiah's reign, word was sent to the king that a "book of the law" had been discovered in the temple. When the content of the book was read out to the king, he was greatly distressed. After confirming the authenticity of the book, Josiah summoned representatives of the people, together with prophets and priests; the newly discovered book was then read aloud to the assembled audience. Thus the discovery of the book of the law led directly to a ceremony of the renewal of the covenant. Then, according to the narrative, certain reform measures were undertaken throughout the kingdom and beyond it, directed against the symbols and practice of foreign religion, and against impurities in the worship of the true Israelite religion. Finally, the feast of the Passover was celebrated.

The narrative in 2 Chr. 34–35 gives additional information and it also provides different emphases from those contained in 2 Kings. In the eighth year of Josiah's reign, the young king began to "seek the God of David his father." In the twelfth year of his reign, Josiah began reform measures, cleansing Jerusalem of things pertaining to foreign religion. Then, in the eighteenth regnal year, the book of the law was

---

59. The point is made in Jerome's *Commentary on Ezekiel* (at 1:1). Jerome, however, cannot be called an "unwitting" predecessor of De Wette (see n. 60), for he seems to have accepted the already traditional view of Mosaic authorship, while at the same time being open to the view that Ezra, at a later date, may have made editorial revisions. See *Liber adversus Helvidium de perpetua virginitate B. Maria* (A.D. 383). *The Fathers of the Church* 53 (1965), pp. 19f.

60. W. M. L. De Wette, *Dissertatio Critica* . . . (1805). De Wette's view was radical only in contrast to the orthodoxy of his generation. One hundred thirty-five years earlier, for example, Spinoza, in his *Tractatus Theologico-Politicus*, had argued that the "book of the law" referred to in Neh. 8:8 was the book of Deuteronomy, which was "written, set forth, and explained by Ezra"; see *The Chief Works of Benedict de Spinoza* I (1951), p. 130.

discovered; the sequence of the following events is similar to that in 2 Kings. A covenant renewal ceremony was held, and Josiah continued his reform measures (2 Chr. 34:33); finally, the Passover was celebrated.

When these two accounts are compared, it becomes evident that the writer or editor of the account in 2 Kings has provided a summary statement of Josiah's reform, concentrating on the eighteenth regnal year. His account must therefore be supplemented by that of the Chronicler for a more complete picture. The complete picture is significant; the reforming trend of Josiah's reign is evident as early as his eighth regnal year, and by the twelfth year actual reforms were already being undertaken. The reforms which began in the twelfth year of Josiah's reign may in fact be implied in 2 K. 22, for there it is clear that renovations were being undertaken in the temple when the book of the law was discovered. When both sources for the reign of Josiah are taken into account, it is clear that the reform measures were already underway *before* the discovery of the book of the law. In both sources, however, there is no doubt that the discovery of the book of the law led to great anxiety on the part of the king, and that it resulted *directly* in a covenant renewal ceremony being held.

On the basis of these two sources, it seems reasonable to confirm the view that the book of the law discovered in the temple during Josiah's reign was none other than Deuteronomy. The reasons for this confirmation, however, do not include all those which are traditionally given.[61] The two principal reasons for identifying Deuteronomy as the book of the law are the following, taken together. (a) The reading of the book caused the king great consternation, even though reform measures were already being undertaken. There is a strong possibility that it was the "curse" section of Deuteronomy (27–28) which caused such consternation; this interpretation may find some confirmation in the words of Huldah (2 K. 22:19; 2 Chr. 34:24). (b) The immediate response to the discovery of the book, on the part of the king, was to hold a ceremony of the renewal of the covenant. This action would be entirely consistent with the nature and purpose of Deuteronomy as a covenant document.[62]

61. That is, the identification of Deuteronomy as the book of the law is not based on a comparison of the actual reform measures undertaken by Josiah and the law contained in Deuteronomy, for the reform measures (in part at least) antedate the discovery of the lawbook. It is possible that a distinction might be made between reforms initiated in the twelfth year, and additional reforms initiated in the eighteenth year, the latter arising from the distinctive legislation of Deuteronomy; the nature of the sources, however, makes such a distinction difficult. 2 K. 23:24 would provide a starting point for such distinctions.

62. The celebration of the Passover would also be consistent with the identification of the lawbook with Deuteronomy, though it is less precise in contributing to that identification in the first instance.

The following preliminary conclusion may be drawn from the evidence: that the reformation of Josiah provides a reasonably certain *terminus ad quem* for the date of Deuteronomy. In the argument presented so far, however, it is not clear whether the book of the law which was discovered was the whole book of Deuteronomy, or an earlier form of the present Deuteronomy (*Urdeuteronomium*). It is here that item (b) in the preceding paragraph takes on particular importance. The discovery of the book of the law prompted immediately a covenant renewal ceremony; it is therefore probable that the book that was discovered was not, for example, simply the legal section of Deuteronomy (12–26), but was in fact the majority (if not the whole) of Deuteronomy in its present form, all of which *together* constituted a covenant document.[63]

ADDITIONAL NOTE:
The Central Sanctuary and Josiah's Reformation

The centralization of worship in the Jerusalem temple was a significant aspect of Josiah's reformation; it should be stressed, however, that centralization of worship was the result of the reformation, rather than its theoretical purpose. *High-places* were destroyed and idolatrous priests were deposed, because they represented either foreign religion or a syncretistic form of the Israelite religion (2 K. 23:5, 8; 2 Chr. 34:3). It is difficult to argue that the centralization aspect of the reform presupposes, or is in any way dependent on Deuteronomy, for the following reasons. (a) The theoretical question of centralization is not of primary concern in Deuteronomy; see the commentary on ch. 12. (b) There is no explicit reference in Deuteronomy to either *high-places,* a temple, or to Jerusalem. (c) The only sanctuary mentioned in Deuteronomy is in the vicinity of Shechem, at Mount Ebal and Mount Gerizim (Deut. 11:29-30; 27:11-14). The treaty structure of the book is such that ch. 27 is an integral part of Deuteronomy, viz., a document clause,[64] and attempts to make this passage a later insertion are therefore suspect.[65] Hence, while in principle Josiah's reformation is not in conflict with Deuteronomy, it is difficult to provide an explanation for the reference to Mount Ebal and Mount Gerizim, if Deuteronomy is believed to be a seventh-century composition, designed in part to promote centralization of worship in Jerusalem.

63. Note that Josiah's book of the law is also called the "book of the covenant" (2 K. 23:2; 2 Chr. 34:20); this is a technical term for a covenant document. The thrust of the argument lies in the fact that a covenant document would require all the principal sections; hence to keep some parts of Deuteronomy and omit other parts would undermine the essential structure of the book. See further section III of the Introduction, "Unity of Composition."
64. See G. J. Wenham, "Deuteronomy and the Central Sanctuary," *TB* 22 (1971), p. 117.
65. For a fuller discussion of this issue, see section 3 (c) below.

3. "Northern" and "Southern" Aspects of Deuteronomy

If it is accepted that Josiah's reformation provides a reasonably certain *terminus ad quem* for the date of Deuteronomy, then two further possibilities arise which must be subjected to critical assessment. The first possibility is that there are aspects of Deuteronomy which suggest a provenance of the book in the northern state of Israel (or perhaps among the northern tribes). The second possibility is that there are aspects of Deuteronomy suggesting a provenance of the book in the southern state of Judah. In each case, the evidence consists both of features internal to the book, and of correspondences between Deuteronomy and certain external aspects of the history and religion of Israel.

(a) First, then, let us examine the evidence which might suggest a northern provenance of Deuteronomy. The following points must be taken into consideration. (i) The reference to a sanctuary in the vicinity of Shechem (viz., Mounts Ebal and Gerizim) implies some kind of affinity with the north; see 11:29-30 and 27:1-26. (ii) The strong similarities, in certain features, between Deuteronomy and Hosea suggest some affinity with the northern kingdom.[66] (iii) To this evidence can be added the parallels between Deuteronomy and the northern prophetic movement, in such matters as the latter's concern for the ancient ideology of war. (iv) The law of kingship (17:14-20) might be taken to reflect northern ideology. This type of evidence, however, is notoriously ambiguous, for while it does reflect the northern theory and (to some extent) practice of kingship, the legislation could equally well have been promulgated in the southern state as a reform measure. (v) Deuteronomy's so-called "name theology" might also be of a northern character, though this too is a very ambiguous type of evidence.[67] In summary, there is evidence to suggest some kind of relationship between Deuteronomy and the northern state of Israel (or the northern tribes), though the evidence by itself does not demand a northern *provenance* of the book.

(b) There is also evidence that might suggest a southern prove-

66. See, e.g., the early evidence adduced by S. R. Driver, *Deuteronomy*, pp. xxviif. See also G. T. Manley, *The Book of the Law*, pp. 143-49; M. Weinfeld, *Deuteronomy and the Deuteronomic School*, pp. 366-370.
67. See E. W. Nicholson, *Deuteronomy and Tradition*, pp. 71f., who argues that the absence of the ark from the northern kingdom, following the disruption of the united monarchy, led to the creation of the "name theology." It is a plausible thesis and could account for the popularity of Deuteronomy in the north. There are difficulties with the thesis, however: (a) as Nicholson admits, the ideology of war in Deuteronomy implies the ark, which was central to that ideology; (b) the ark is mentioned in Deuteronomy, though infrequently (10:1-5; 31:9, 25f.) and hence these references have to be described as secondary; (c) the possible military and conquest overtones of the "name theology" (see G. J. Wenham, *TB* 22 [1971], pp. 113f.) tend to reinforce its association with the ark.

nance of the book. (i) The discovery of Deuteronomy during Josiah's reign would support such a suggestion; see section 2 (above). (ii) It might be argued that the centralization of worship during Josiah's reign, and its supposed dependence on Deuteronomy, supports links with the southern state, but see the ADDITIONAL NOTE on this topic in section 2. (iii) The strong similarities between Deuteronomy and certain aspects of the Prophecy of Jeremiah suggest some kind of relationship between these two writings,[68] and hence the presence of Deuteronomy in the southern state. (iv) The production of the "Deuteronomistic History" suggests a knowledge of Deuteronomy in the southern state and during the Judean Exile.[69]

(c) How are these "northern" and "southern" aspects of Deuteronomy to be interpreted? It is clear that hypotheses which focus exclusively on either the "northern" or the "southern" evidence will be subject to strong criticism. If this type of data is to be used in the formulation of an argument concerning the date and provenance of Deuteronomy, then clearly *both* categories of evidence must somehow be included.

Let us begin with a critical assessment of E. W. Nicholson's *Deuteronomy and Tradition;* Nicholson has been chosen, as representative of a variety of modern hypotheses, because he presents a cogent and clearly argued case and attempts to incorporate both categories of evidence into this hypothesis. His view, in summary form, is as follows. The origin of Deuteronomy is to be found in the prophetic circles of northern Israel. After the fall of the northern kingdom (721 B.C.), the northern circle responsible for Deuteronomy fled to Judah. There they formulated their old (northern) traditions into a program of reform, which they intended the Judean authorities to carry out, for they had come to believe that the future of Israel lay in the south. Given their intentions, they attempted consciously to integrate their own traditions with those of the south, specifically with the reforming attempt of Hezekiah to achieve centralization of worship in Jerusalem. Thus the actual composition of Deuteronomy very probably took place during the reign of Manasseh (N.B. "Deuteronomy" here does not mean the whole book in its present form; see n. 9, above, for Nicholson's view of the process of compilation). The strength of Nicholson's hypothesis lies in that it gives serious consideration to the northern aspects of Deuteronomy, while at the same time providing a plausible account of the arrival and presence of the book in the southern kingdom.

68. See S. R. Driver, *Deuteronomy,* pp. xcii-xciv; cf. Weinfeld, *Deuteronomy and the Deuteronomic School,* pp. 27-32, 359f.
69. "Deuteronomistic History" normally refers to Deuteronomy–Kings; however, since Deuteronomy is currently the text under discussion, the expression is used here to refer to Joshua–2 Kings, for practical purposes.

The principal weakness of the hypothesis, in my view, is that it fails to give serious attention to the most significant evidence for the northern associations of Deuteronomy, namely, the references to a sanctuary in the vicinity of Shechem (see section (a), (i) above).[70] Nicholson's position with reference to Deut. 27 may be summarized as follows. (i) Deut. 27 is widely recognized as a secondary insertion because it interrupts the flow of the narrative.[71] To this it may be responded that it is possible to regard Deut. 11:29-30 and 27:1-26 as being thoroughly integrated in the narrative structure, from a literary perspective; see the introduction to the commentary on 11:26-32. (ii) The secondary nature of Deut. 27 is further said to be demonstrated by its being cast in the third person, and not the customary second person, form of address.[72] But it may be argued in response that there are particular reasons for this form of address; see the introductory remarks in the commentary on Deut. 27:1-8. (iii) Because the ceremonies legislated in Deut. 27 are recorded as having been fulfilled in Josh. 8:30-35, Deut. 27 may come from the Deuteronomist, who constructed it on the basis of older materials.[73] But, as G. J. Wenham has noted,[74] its insertion cannot easily be ascribed to the deuteronomistic historian, whose principal message was that all sanctuaries other than Jerusalem were sinful. (iv) In his discussion of the relationship between Deuteronomy and the treaty-covenant pattern, Nicholson does not make use of Deut. 27, on the basis that he has already shown it to be secondary material.[75] But in this omission, he removes a vital part of the treaty structure, and of the nature and purpose of the covenant renewal festival.[76] In summary, there are not good grounds for omitting as secondary Deut. 27 (and 11:29-30); but, if these passages are retained as primary material, then they tend to undermine some of the principal features of Nicholson's argument. To be more specific, it would be difficult to understand why the northern circle responsible for Deuteronomy should maintain the traditions concerning the sanctuary in the vicinity of Shechem, if they were consciously attempting to integrate their northern traditions with the southern tradition of centralization of worship; in a sense, that would undermine their purpose quite radically. Furthermore,

70. One key issue will be critically examined in this paragraph, though it is evident that this is not the only point of contention the present writer has with Nicholson's interpretation. This is stressed, lest the argument that follows be taken to have more weight than it deserves.
71. *Deuteronomy and Tradition*, pp. 19, 21, 34.
72. *Ibid.*, p. 34.
73. *Ibid.*
74. *TB* 22 (1971), p. 118.
75. *Deuteronomy and Tradition*, p. 45.
76. See M. G. Kline, *The Structure of Biblical Authority*, pp. 144f.; G. J. Wenham, *op. cit.*, p. 117.

Deut. 27 (and 11:29-30) speak of the future renewal of the covenant; as we have seen (section 2, above), the discovery of the lawbook in Josiah's reign prompted directly a covenant renewal ceremony, suggesting not only that Deut. 27 was a part of the lawbook, but also that the lawbook was not primarily concerned with centralization (which had been undertaken in Hezekiah's time without any remarkable discoveries), but rather was concerned with covenant renewal.

Given this rejection of Nicholson's interpretation of the "northern" and "southern" aspects of Deuteronomy, let us now attempt to interpret the data in terms of the dating of Deuteronomy at the end of the Mosaic period. The argument that follows is necessarily a hypothetical reconstruction, given the nature (and relative absence) of the evidence.

Deuteronomy has been interpreted as essentially Mosaic (see the earlier sections of the Introduction); its final form, including the account of Moses' death, is linked provisionally with Joshua's renewal of the covenant in the vicinity of Shechem (Josh. 8:30-35), which in turn marks the fulfilment of the inner objectives of Deuteronomy (11:29-30 and ch. 27). Deuteronomy is thus a covenant document. It may perhaps have been used again in the covenant renewal at Shechem which was undertaken at the end of Joshua's life (Josh. 24), and the account of the latter renewal ceremony may have been preserved along with Deuteronomy (Josh. 24:26). Since it was a covenant document, it may be supposed that the text of Deuteronomy was kept in the ark (see Deut. 31:9 and commentary). If so, then it would eventually have been taken to Jerusalem along with the ark, after a dangerous history during the time of the settlement and conquest.

With the disruption of the united monarchy after Solomon's time, one of two possibilities may have occurred. (i) Deuteronomy may have remained in Jerusalem, but a copy was also taken to the northern kingdom. (ii) Deuteronomy was taken from the ark in Jerusalem to the northern kingdom. It seems clear, at least, that Deuteronomy still exerted some influence at the end of the united monarchy; Rehoboam's fruitless journey to Shechem to be made king of all Israel (1 K. 12:1-20) indicates that Shechem still played an important role in the institution of a new national leader or monarch.[77] And, following the disruption, Jeroboam's building program at Shechem, and his use of Shechem as the capital city in the north for a short time, imply that the Shechem traditions of Deuteronomy were influential in the north. The evidence of the continuing importance of Deuteronomy in the north, as has been noted above, may be seen in the prophetic traditions in general, and in Hosea in particular.

77. See further G. J. Wenham, *ibid.*, pp. 106f.

Whether Deuteronomy played a significant role in the early history of Judah is uncertain, but the reformation of Josiah indicates its return to importance. It is possible that the Davidic dynasty, with its particular ideology, caused the temporary eclipse of Deuteronomy. Alternatively, Deuteronomy may indeed have been taken from Jerusalem after the disruption, then brought back again by northern refugees after the fall of Samaria, lodged in the Jerusalem temple, and eventually rediscovered a hundred years later in the time of Josiah. The rediscovery of Deuteronomy in the seventh century seems to have led to significant results: (i) it led to the ceremony of the renewal of the covenant during the reign of Josiah; (ii) it appears to have exerted influence upon Jeremiah and his circle; (iii) it started a tradition of history writing in Israel (the so-called "Deuteronomistic School"), which was to culminate in the compiling of a large-scale history of Israel, interpreted (in part, at least) from the distinctive covenant perspective of the book of Deuteronomy.

4. The Background of the Laws in Deuteronomy

It was argued in section IV of the Introduction ("Date and Authorship") that the treaty form indicated a very early date for the book in essentially its present form. And, in the immediately preceding paragraphs, an argument has been presented to the effect that the early dating of Deuteronomy makes possible the development of an hypothesis which is flexible enough to encompass both the "northern" and "southern" aspects of Deuteronomy. It must now be asked whether the legal content of Deuteronomy is compatible with an early dating and indeed whether it contributes to the argument for the early dating of Deuteronomy.

First, however, it will be recalled from the observations in section 3 above, that many modern writers who argue for a seventh-century date of the principal composition of the book allow that much of the content is very much older, some of it going back to the pre-monarchic period; this older material, it is argued, has been worked into the present composition. Thus the general antiquity of much of Deuteronomy is not the point at issue; rather, it must be asked whether the material is compatible with the Mosaic Age, and that is a more difficult question. Again, however, it is stressed that what is being attempted here is not the *proof* of the Mosaic origin of the law; it is the more modest task of inquiring after the compatibility of the law of Deuteronomy with the Mosaic Age. The treatment of material in the following paragraphs is necessarily selective; a fuller understanding of the view presented here will be gained from reading the commentary on chs. 12–26.

(a) The first point to be noted is that a large amount of the law in

Deuteronomy has precise parallels in other Ancient Near Eastern legal collections. These parallels are referred to in the footnotes to the commentary, but one example will be given here by way of illustration. Many parallels in social legislation exist between Deuteronomy and the Law Code of Hammurabi.[78] There are several ways of interpreting such parallels. It could be that both Deuteronomy and Hammurabi's Code reflect, quite independently of each other, the existence of an ancient and widespread common core of Semitic legal tradition. But, equally, the nature of the crimes in question is such that one might expect to find legislation on them in most societies, ancient and modern; the parallels between Deuteronomy and Hammurabi's Code, in other words, may be largely coincidental. There may have been similar legislation in ancient Egypt, though the nature of the evidence makes such a claim uncertain.[79] But in summary, laws of this kind in Deuteronomy, with parallels in other Near Eastern law codes, cannot be said to be anachronistic in the Mosaic period.[80]

(b) There are many laws in Deuteronomy that seem to presuppose a knowledge of conditions in Palestine. For example, the legislation in 12:1-3 (cf. 7:5) presupposes a knowledge of Canaanite religious practice. The detailed food and dietary laws in Deut. 14 also appear to presuppose a considerable knowledge of local conditions in Palestine. To material of this kind can be added those laws whose meaning may be clarified on the basis of the Ugaritic (Canaanite) texts, such as the legislation contained in 21:1-10 and 23:17-18.[81] It might be argued that legislation of this kind must be a product of the Hebrew experience of living within the land, and that such legislation could not have been anticipated prior to the settlement.

In addressing these difficulties, it is important to bear in mind the following points. (i) It is a fundamental part of the Hebrew patriarchal traditions that prior to the residence of the Hebrews in Egypt, their ancestors had experience of both Palestine and Mesopotamia.

78. The following table provides examples only:

Deuteronomy	(subject)	Code of Hammurabi
19:21	lex talionis	196, 197, 200
22:22	adultery	129
22:23-27	rape	130
24:7	manstealing	14

79. There are no precise parallels to Mesopotamian (and Hittite) law codes in the Egyptian sources; for a discussion of law in ancient Egypt, see A. Théoridès, "The Concept of Law in Ancient Egypt," in J. R. Harris, ed., The Legacy of Egypt (²1971), pp. 291-321.
80. Hammurabi's Law Code was first promulgated c.1726 B.C. It should be added, however, that the fact that certain laws are not anachronistic in the Mosaic period does not establish that they are early. Taken independently of their context, laws of this kind cannot be dated precisely.
81. See the Index to Ugaritic Texts for further examples.

As will be shown in section 5(a), below, the patriarchal traditions form an important subtheme running throughout Deuteronomy. It is thus not unreasonable to suppose that the living patriarchal tradition, which was maintained during the Hebrew residence in Egypt, included information about Palestine. (ii) There were apparently Canaanites resident in the delta region of northern Egypt when the Hebrews were in Egypt; the place name *Baal-Zephon* in Exod. 14:2 probably indicates the presence of a sanctuary to Baal in the delta region, for which there is also archeological evidence.[82] (iii) Aspects of Canaanite religion were present in Egypt, sometimes in syncretistic form, from at least the end of the Eighteenth Dynasty; the god Baal was even represented by his own priesthood and the goddess Anat was also popular.[83] (iv) During the Eighteenth Dynasty, the Amarna Letters indicate a good knowledge of Syria-Palestine in Egypt; in the Nineteenth Dynasty, under Sethos I, Egyptian control of Palestine was maintained, and thus a man of Moses' upbringing and circumstances might certainly be expected to have some familiarity with conditions in Palestine.[84]

On the basis of the preceding four points, it is clear that one should not think of Moses and the early Hebrews as if they lived in some kind of cultural and historical vacuum. Both internal biblical evidence, and also external evidence, indicate a variety of possible sources from which the Hebrews in Egypt might have gained information about Palestine and the religion of the Canaanites. However, the four points listed above by no means prove the Mosaic, or even early, nature of many of the laws in Deuteronomy; but they do reduce the strength of the argument to the effect that the laws *necessarily* reflect a period when the Hebrews were already settled in the land.

(c) Certain laws in Deuteronomy have a theoretical character about them, indicating a background of limited experience, but lofty aspirations. A good example of this kind of legislation can be seen in the laws of war, particularly those contained in Deut. 20 (see the commentary for fuller details). The general religious perspective (20:1-4) and the grounds for exemption from military service (20:5-9) point to a thoroughgoing conviction that victory in war was dependent principally on the strength of God, not on the numerical size of the army. The perspective is similar to that of the Song of the Sea (Exod. 15:1-18), in which victory over Egypt is attributed solely to

---

82. See J. Gray, "Canaanite Mythology and Hebrew Tradition," *Transactions of the Glasgow University Oriental Society* 14 (1953), pp. 47-57. For further discussion and bibliography, see F. E. Eakin, *The Religion and Culture of Israel* (1971), pp. 65f.
83. See *ANET*, pp. 249f. Cf. R. Stadelmann, *Syrisch-Palästinensische Gottheiten in Ägypten* (1967).
84. On this topic, see particularly K. A. Kitchen's remarks in *NBD*, pp. 343f. Kitchen describes Dynasty XIX as the "most cosmopolitan in Egyptian history."

God. There is certainly no suggestion in Deut. 20 either of a standing army, or of a more subdued attitude toward victory which might have developed later as a result of experience.

In conjunction with this religious understanding of warfare expressed in Deut. 20:1-9, there is a thoroughly realistic theory of war expressed in 20:10-18. A brief digression may help to illustrate this point. One of the most influential philosophers of war in modern times was Carl von Clausewitz (1780-1831). Clausewitz defined war as an act of violence undertaken in order to compel an enemy to fulfil the will of an aggressor.[85] In the expansion of his definition, however, he made an important and necessary distinction in his analysis of war; he distinguished between the theoretical or abstract conception of war on the one hand, and real wars on the other. From the theoretical point of view, war must end in victory for the aggressor, for otherwise it would be pointless to initiate war in the first place. To obtain victory, no effort was to be spared, and von Clausewitz insisted that it would be absurd to introduce a principle of moderation in the philosophy of war. The reality of war, however, very often differed from the theory of war, in that certain factors might arise (such as chance, or the morale of troops) which could not be completely accounted for on a theoretical basis. From a military perspective, Clausewitz argued, there were three principal objectives in war: (i) the military power of the enemy must be destroyed, so that the enemy could no longer undertake war; (ii) the enemy's country had to be conquered, for from that country a new military force could emerge; (iii) war would be terminated fully only when the enemy's will to fight had been subdued.

When the laws of war in Deut. 20 are compared with this recent theory of war, some significant points emerge. Deut. 20:10-15 (the treatment of enemy cities not in the promised land) and 20:16-18 (the treatment of enemy cities in the promised land) both provide for the use of force and killing, the latter passage being particularly harsh in legislating indiscriminate killing. The degree of severity in each of these two sections follows a certain logic; the treatment of cities not in the promised land would serve as a warning, whereas the treatment of those within the promised land would be terminal. In the latter passage, 20:16-18, all three of von Clausewitz's military objectives would be achieved in a single stroke; the military power of the enemy would be destroyed, the country (or city-state) would be conquered so that no new enemy could emerge, and the will of the enemy would be mortally subdued. A further dictum of von Clausewitz would also have been fulfilled, namely, that no principle of moderation would have been introduced into the theory of war.

85. C. von Clausewitz, *On War* (1968; 1st German ed. 1832), pp. 101-103.

The above comments seem to indicate clearly enough that Deut. 20:10-18 contains a theory (or "philosophy") of war; the practice of war very often did not match the theory.[86] That Deut. 20 contains a theoretical statement of war does not mean that it was written by someone uninformed about war; in fact, the very opposite is likely to be true, and (as will be seen from the footnotes to the commentary on Deut. 20) there are many parallels between Deut. 20 and the theory and practice of war in various Near Eastern countries. What is highly significant, however, is the perspective presupposed by this particular theory of war: (a) the wars would be aggressive wars of conquest, not defensive wars for the preservation of a state; (b) the wars would be waged by a nonprofessional army. In summary, the laws of war in Deut. 20 are expressed in language reminiscent of the ideology of war contained in the Song of the Sea, but they are at the same time thoroughly pragmatic from a *theoretical* point of view. When these points are taken in conjunction with the general predominance of the topic of war in Deuteronomy (see section 5(b) below), and with the prospect of war which is anticipated in the covenant renewal ceremony on the plains of Moab (see section V of the Introduction, "Occasion"), then Deuteronomy's laws of war may be seen to fit most naturally at the end of the Mosaic period.

(d) Finally, some comments must be made on those aspects of the law in Deuteronomy which are so thoroughly integrated with the essence of covenant renewal, that the substance of the law and the treaty- or covenant-framework within which the law is set are brought together into an intimate relationship with each other. Two examples will be given concisely.

First, it may be noted that one of the dominant themes occurring in Deuteronomy is the criticism of foreign religion. This theme occurs throughout the book, not only in the legal section.[87] Taken alone, this theme need not be indicative of a specific date, for throughout the history of Israelite religion, foreign religions posed a threat and were the subject of criticism.[88] What is significant in Deuteronomy, however, is the relationship between this theme and the covenant; a fundamental aspect of the covenant (and also of the

86. Compare, e.g., the narrative in 1 Sam. 15 with Deut. 20.
87. The theme has different aspects; e.g., criticism of, and legislation against, foreign gods; legislation against "abominations"; legislation against particular religious practices. To give only one example of the pervasiveness of one aspect of the theme, see the following passages relating to foreign gods: 6:14; 7:4; 8:19; 11:16, 28; 13:2, 6, 13; 17:3; cf. 28:14, 36, 64; 29:26.
88. However, G. T. Manley makes the significant point that the legislation in Deuteronomy is not directed to *reform* (e.g., cleansing the temple from foreign religious objects, as in Josiah's time), but presents, as it were, an absolute choice between Yahweh, on the one hand, and foreign gods, on the other: *The Book of the Law,* pp. 100f.

treaty, on which the covenant form was based) is the demand for loyalty on the part of the people for their God. The criticism of foreign religion, and the prohibition of foreign religious practices among the Israelites, are the covenant counterparts of the treaty demands for the undivided allegiance of vassals to their suzerain. In other words, this theme, so dominant throughout Deuteronomy, ties the substance of the book very closely to its form, that of a covenant document in the form of a vassal treaty.

A second example of a different kind will illustrate a further dimension of the subject. Throughout Deuteronomy, there are frequent references to *resident aliens*. [89] The concern for resident aliens finds more compassionate expression in Deuteronomy than anywhere else in the Pentateuch; not only are the legal rights of aliens protected, but the Hebrews are enjoined to *love* their resident aliens (10:19). The significance of this emphasis in Deuteronomy is to be found partly in the nature of the covenant and partly in the experience of the Hebrews in Egypt. In the past, the Hebrews had been resident aliens in Egypt (10:19; 23:7); and prior to the Exodus from Egypt, their status had been, in effect, that of vassals of the Egyptian pharaoh (see further the hypothesis in Appendix II). The Exodus from Egypt had liberated the Hebrews from their former vassaldom and resident alien status; the Sinai Covenant had introduced them to a new relationship, that of being vassals to God alone and to no earthly power. But, as they had learned from their experience of bondage in Egypt, God loved resident aliens (cf. 10:18), and thus their covenant with God had built into it the expression of concern for aliens, arising out of past experience. The concern for resident aliens is thus not a concern which arose at a late date, once the promised land had been settled; rather it is a concern integral to the whole experience of Exodus and Covenant. Thus, again, the frequent references to resident aliens throughout the book of Deuteronomy tie the substance of the book very closely to its form, that of a covenant document.

5. The Religion of Israel in the Time of Moses

The problem of the nature of Israelite religion in the time of Moses is being examined for a particular reason. If Israelite religion, in the Mosaic Age, is believed to be of a relatively primitive and undeveloped form, then it would be impossible to locate Deuteronomy in the Mosaic Age, given the developed and relatively sophisticated religious thought of the book. To put the problem another way, the dating of Deuteronomy will depend to a considerable extent on the view that is taken of the development of Israelite religion. This is a

89.   See the following passages: 1:16; 5:14; 10:18f.; 14:21, 29; 16:11, 14; 23:7; 24:17, 19-21; 26:11-13; 27:19; 28:43; 29:11; 31:12.

serious and important issue, even though it is usually more implicit than explicit in modern writing on Deuteronomy; the assignment of a late date to the book, and consequently the interpretation of its contents in the light of that date, tends to be tied to a view of Israelite religion which perceives the true flowering of Israelite religious thought during the monarchy, and during and after the Exile.

Before a way of dealing with this problem is suggested, it is important to clarify the full dimensions of the difficulty. The root of the problem lies in the nature of the sources from which earliest Israelite religion is to be reconstructed. It is generally maintained in contemporary OT scholarship that the relevant sources for earliest Israelite religion, in their present form, are to be dated considerably later than the period they describe, and consequently it is difficult to distinguish within those sources between that which is characteristic of earliest Israelite religion and that which is characteristic of later theological reflection on the early period. For example, even if the so-called "J" source (or Yahwist source) of the Pentateuch is dated relatively early, around the tenth century B.C., there is still an extensive chronological gap between this early major source and the period in which earliest Israelite religion developed. Although an early source such as "J," according to the hypothesis, is very likely to be dependent upon still earlier traditions, it is possible that its present form may be more indicative of later theological reflection than it is of the real nature of earliest Israelite religion. In the opinion of many modern scholars, the same principle would be applicable to Deuteronomy.

At this point, scholarly arguments (my own included) tend to become enmeshed in a net of circularity. On the one hand, the view one holds of the history and development of the religion of Israel will depend to a large extent upon one's interpretation of the sources. But, conversely, the interpretation of any particular source will be governed to some extent by one's view of the history and development of Israelite religion. The now dated work of Julius Wellhausen, in the nineteenth century, will illustrate the problem. On the one hand, Wellhausen was largely responsible for the refinement of literary or documentary analysis as a tool for interpreting the Pentateuchal sources. But, on the other hand, he applied to those sources a developmental or evolutionary theory of religion, the background to which was to be found partly in the philosophical thought of Hegel.[90] The combination of a literary method for the interpretation of the

90.   It may be, however, that Wellhausen's debt to Hegel has been overstated, and that his work should be seen as the culmination of a tradition which has its roots in the work of Herder and other representatives of German Romanticism. See R. J. Thompson, *Moses and the Law in a Century of Criticism Since Graf* (1970), pp. 35-49.

sources, and a particular theory of religion, led Wellhausen to the view that the Mosaic period was, at best, *germinal* in the history of Israelite religious thought.[91]

But let us return to the problem at issue. Inasmuch as contemporary OT scholarship sees in the major sources of the Pentateuch the difficulties described above, is there any other way of attempting to describe the religion of Israel at the time of Moses, which in turn will enable us to form an assessment of whether or not the religious content of Deuteronomy would be anachronistic or unsuitable in the Mosaic Age? We cannot go outside the OT, for archeology, at this point, provides at best indirect evidence. In the following paragraphs an alternative, but limited, route will be suggested.

There are contained in the Pentateuch, and in the books of Joshua and Judges, a number of poetic passages inserted into the prose narrative; these can be examined somewhat independently of the source problems associated with the prose narrative. These poetic passages appear to be very ancient *in their present form,*[92] and thus they may provide evidence of a particular kind for the study of earliest Israelite religion. Rather than examine all this early poetry for the light it may shed on early Israelite religion,[93] one passage will be examined in detail. The passage chosen is the "Song of the Sea" (Exod. 15:1-18); it has been chosen because there are good grounds for arguing that in oral form, if not in written form, this song is approximately contemporary with the events described within Deuteronomy.[94] In the following paragraphs, a summary statement of

91. In fact, Wellhausen described the time of Moses and the Exodus as the "properly creative period in Israel's history." *Prolegomena to the History of Ancient Israel* (E.T. 1885; repr. 1957), p. 432. And yet Moses, in Wellhausen's view, created only a sense of tribal unity, and "gave no new idea of god to his people" (*ibid.*, p. 440). At best, the early period can only be described as germinal in Wellhausen's treatment, with the real flowering of Israelite religious thought taking place several centuries later.

92. Since the nature of the poetry depends upon *form,* poetry is to be expected to be left relatively free from revision, when the passage of time necessitated the linguistic revision of prose passages. There are two principal reasons for the recent growth in knowledge of early Hebrew poetry. First, the increasing number of literary and epigraphic discoveries by archeologists in the Syro-Palestinian area has provided a fuller knowledge of northwest Semitic languages and poetry. Second, the application of controlled linguistic methods to both "archeological" and biblical literary data has established a relatively precise chronological framework for early northwest Semitic poetry.

93. For a preliminary study in this direction, see P. C. Craigie, "The Conquest and Early Hebrew Poetry," *TB* 20 (1969), pp. 76-94.

94. Pioneering work was done on the Song of the Sea in the study of F. M. Cross and D. N. Freedman, "The Song of Miriam," *JNES* 14 (1955), pp. 237-250, following an important study by W. F. Albright, "The Oracles of Balaam," *JBL* 63 (1944), pp. 207-233. Albright, in *Yahweh and the Gods of Canaan* (1968), p. 10, dated the song in

aspects of early Israelite religious thought will be presented, as they appear in the Song of the Sea; brief comments will indicate parallels in Deuteronomy.

(a) First, there are several points in the Song of the Sea at which it is possible to detect aspects of religious thought and tradition predating the event at the Reed Sea. The principal example of this is to be found in the indirect references to the religion of the patriarchs. The patriarchal tradition is implied in the epithet "my father's God" (Exod. 15:2); the linking of this epithet with the name *Yahweh* implies the continuation which was believed to exist between Yahweh, whose mighty works had been experienced at the Reed Sea, and the God of the fathers. The continuity between the song and the patriarchal tradition may also be implied in Exod. 15:13; the reference there to the "holy encampment" and the pastoral character of the language call to mind the nature of the patriarchal God as that of "Shepherd" (Gen. 49:24f.; cf. "God of your fathers" in the same context).

There are two implications arising from the continuity of the song with the patriarchal tradition. First, the general sense conveyed by the song is one of covenant. As the song purports to date from a period earlier than the Sinai covenant, it is not surprising that there is no clear reference to Sinai.[95] The sense of covenant in the song, then, is presumably a continuation of the patriarchal covenant tradition. In the ancient tradition concerning the covenant with Abraham, one of the divine covenant promises was that Abraham's progeny would possess a land (Gen. 12:1-3; 15:7). If this tradition has indeed preserved accurately an aspect of the old patriarchal covenant, it may be that Exod. 15:17 contains a reflection of that tradition. In that verse, the time is anticipated when the Israelites would settle in the land, "the mountain of Yahweh's inheritance." On this evidence, it would seem that prior to the event at the Reed Sea, the people who celebrated that event in the song had a tradition of covenant; that it was a living tradition is confirmed in that the event celebrated in song was

---

the early 13th century B.C. F. M. Cross, in *Canaanite Myth and Hebrew Epic* (1973), p. 123, suggests a date in the 10th century, or earlier, for its reduction to written form. See also S. Segert, "Versbau und Sprachbau in der althebräischen Poesie," *Mitteilungen des Instituts für Orientforschung* 15 (1969), pp. 312-321. The early dating of the song has not gone unchallenged; see particularly S. Mowinckel, " 'Psalm Criticism between 1930 and 1935'; Ugarit and Psalm Exegesis," *VT* 5 (1955), pp. 13-33. However, the recent study of D. A. Robertson, *Linguistic Evidence in Dating Early Hebrew Poetry* (diss., Yale University, 1966; repr. in the SBL Dissertation Series), seems to have established the antiquity of the Song of the Sea beyond reasonable doubt; Robertson argues for a twelfth-century date. The argument to be presented above assumes the existence of the song in oral form from a date very close to the event it celebrates.
95. In early Hebrew poetry *after* the Sinai experience, a reference to Sinai became a standard feature, often part of the Prologue; Deut. 33:2; Judg. 5:4f.; Ps. 68:7f. Cf. Hab. 3:3f.

undertaken by God on behalf of the people, and also by the description of the people as "your people, Yahweh" (Exod. 15:16).

The second implication arising from the continuity with the patriarchal tradition and from the covenantal atmosphere of the Song of the Sea is that prior to the event at the Reed Sea, there was a commitment to one God only. There is no way of determining, however, on the limited basis of this one passage, whether the earlier belief was monotheistic or monolatrous in nature. It is not implied, however, that the earlier tradition of the Hebrews was polytheistic;[96] the nature of the covenant tradition, as being an agreement between two parties, argues in favor of a prior commitment to one God.

In the light of this evidence, it is urged that the truly *germinal* period[97] in the Israelite religious tradition is to be found in the religion of the patriarchs. The pattern was already set within which subsequent religious thought was to develop. The tradition of covenant and the commitment to one God were to play a determinative role in the later development of Israelite religious thought. It was within this framework, which had so limited a sphere of reference in the time of the patriarchs, that the creative movements in Israelite religion were to find full expression at the time of the Exodus.

In Deuteronomy, similar recollections of the ancient patriarchal tradition appear; they form, in effect, one of the subthemes running throughout the book (Deut. 1:8; 6:10; 9:5, 27; 29:13; 30:20; 34:4). The references to the patriarchal tradition in Deuteronomy include both the *land* which was promised (e.g., 6:10) and also the covenant *word* of promise (e.g., 9:5). The patriarchal traditions function in a similar way in both the Song of the Sea and Deuteronomy; they stress the continuity between past and present, and also the present reality of a God who had been working out his purposes for his people since ancient times.

(b) What is more significant in the Song of the Sea is the evidence it provides of a truly creative period in Israelite religious thought. While an historical Exodus cannot be reconstructed in detail from this short passage alone, nevertheless the dramatic event celebrated in song had a significant part to play in the development of Israelite religion.

Perhaps the most important new feature in the Song of the Sea is the conception of Yahweh as a warrior and the related ideology of

96. The only possible evidence for such an argument is Exod. 15:11, but in that verse the significance is that the incomparability of Yahweh is expressed in the context of his divine assembly. Cf. C. J. Labuschagne, *The Incomparability of Yahweh in the OT* (1966), pp. 80-82.
97. The expressions "germinal period," and "creative period" in a later paragraph, are used as descriptive terms; theologically, they refer to stages in the history of revelation.

Holy War.[98] Neither of these features was novel in principle in the context of Near Eastern religions, nor is it possible to say that there was no similar religious thought incipient in the patriarchal traditions. The element that introduced novelty was the "international" plane on which the Israelites interpreted their experience at the Reed Sea. The victory that was celebrated was over the pharaoh and his Egyptian armies; the enemies of the future were the Canaanite states. The actual event at the Reed Sea may have had little significance in world affairs at that time; what is important, however, is not the magnitude of the event in an objective sense, but the magnitude of the Israelite interpretation of the event. The event at the Reed Sea was determinative in the maturing and growth of Israelite religious thought. The interpretation of Yahweh's victory at the international level was the beginning of an Israelite self-consciousness in terms of nation status. The self-consciousness outpaced the reality, but (as is indicated in Deuteronomy) adherence to that self-consciousness was significantly determinative in bringing about the reality. Thus the Song of the Sea marks the inception of the idea of the Lord as the Warrior, and of an ideology of war on an international level, which was dominant in early Israelite religious thought.

Closely related to the conception of God as Warrior is the expression of the kingship of Yahweh (particularly in Exod. 15:18); this too would seem to be new religious thought finding its first clear expression in the Song of the Sea. Once again, the linking of kingship with God is not necessarily new in principle; the novelty arises from the setting and broader horizons of the conception. The richness in the expression of royal divinity in the song has two contributing factors. First, the mythological motifs of Canaanite poetry, which have been adapted in the song,[99] have served to give the kingship theme a cosmological character; the adaptation of these motifs is such that Yahweh's kingship is expressed in terms of the *creation*[100] and sustenance of his people (Exod. 15:16-17). Second, the kingship of Yahweh finds its fullest expression in the nature of God the Warrior.

---

98. The explicit reference to the Lord as "Warrior" or "Man in battle" is in Exod. 15:3. The epithet is particularly suitable in a victory song. Because God is a warrior, he can be described as the "refuge and protection" of his people—Exod. 15:2; on the translation of this verse, see P. C. Craigie, *VT* 22 (1972), pp. 145f. It is because the Lord is a warrior that power and majesty are evident in the defeat of the Egyptian enemy (Exod. 15:6-7). The incomparability of the Lord in the divine assembly (Exod. 15:11) is based on his victorious achievement as a warrior. The future purposes of God for his people (Exod. 15:14-17) would be achieved by further military victories.
99. For a detailed account of the adaptation of Canaanite motifs, see P. C. Craigie, "The Poetry of Ugarit and Israel," *TB* 22 (1971), pp. 19-26.
100. The comment is based on the translation of the last line of Exod. 15:16: "... the people whom you have created...." See F. M. Cross and D. N. Freedman, *art. cit.*, p. 249.

As a victorious Warrior, God rules over his people, and his conquering power is exerted against their enemies.

In summary, these two themes—God as Warrior and God as King—are central in the Song of the Sea. The same two themes have an important part to play in Deuteronomy. First, let us examine God as King in Deuteronomy. The only explicit reference to God as King is to be found in Deut. 33:5 (see the commentary for fuller discussion), in a passage which has thoroughly military associations. But what is much more significant is the treaty-form of the whole book of Deuteronomy; the treaty-form stresses that the covenant was made, and renewed, between God *as King,* on the one hand, and his *vassal* people, on the other hand. In other words, the whole book of Deuteronomy presupposes the kingship of God; furthermore, it presupposes the Exodus upon which that kingship was initially based, for the Exodus was the key element in the historical antecedents to the covenant making.

While God is not explicitly identified as a "Warrior" or "Man in battle" in Deuteronomy, nevertheless the ideology of war, and the association of God with war, occur at many points throughout the book. In Deut. 1:30, God is identified as the one who fought for Israel, just as he had done in the Exodus from Egypt. In Deut. 7, the subject of war becomes a central theme in the address of Moses, and again there is a reference to God's victorious achievement in the Exodus (7:18). Or, to take another example, both the introduction and the conclusion of the Blessing of Moses (Deut. 33:2-5 and 33:26-29) breathe an atmosphere of war and of reliance upon God for victory. In summary, both the kingship of God and the association of God with war are key themes in the book of Deuteronomy, just as they are in the Song of the Sea.

(c) Let us now summarize the implications of this limited comparison and then draw some preliminary conclusions. The Song of the Sea is a celebration of the Exodus, particularly of the event at the Reed Sea; this event is important in Deuteronomy as one of the principal antecedents to the covenant. In both the song and Deuteronomy, there is a reflection of the patriarchal traditions, pointing to an age in the distant past. The key conceptions of God in the Song of the Sea, God as Warrior and as King, are fundamental also in Deuteronomy. And the anticipation of future victories in the song (Exod. 15:14-16) is partly realized and partly still anticipated in Deuteronomy.

It would be hazardous to draw too firm conclusions from these limited results, principally because the Song of the Sea is a very limited basis for comparison. But this much can be said: in certain key features, the book of Deuteronomy is in essential harmony with the Song of the Sea, a passage that can with reasonable certainty be dated to the Mosaic Age in oral form, and to a date soon after that in written form. This evidence (together with that referred to in n. 93) is an additional part of the reason why I do not feel the need for radical doubt concerning the authenticity of Deuteronomy.

6. *The Transmission of the Text of Deuteronomy*

In the preceding section, it was noted that there were certain poetic passages in the OT which could be given a thoroughly early date in their present form. The criteria by which such passages were dated included critical analyses of their syntax, and their morphological, lexicographical, and orthographical features. Why, it might be asked, if it is possible to date poetry by this means, cannot similar criteria be applied to Deuteronomy, if it is indeed a genuinely old (essentially Mosaic) book?

Before attempting to deal with this question, let us begin with a few observations on the nature of the text of Deuteronomy. First, it is necessary to note that in its present form, the Hebrew text of Deuteronomy is an orthographic "palimpsest."[101] To give the most obvious example, the pointing (or vocalization) of the Hebrew text reflects a relatively late development in Hebrew writing;[102] the original text (whether an early or late date is proposed) would have contained only alphabetic Hebrew characters. Furthermore, the present "alphabetic" (or consonantal) text, without pointing, is that of the classical period of Hebrew writing; it represents the system developed by approximately the sixth century B.C.[103] If, as it has been argued above, the original writing of Deuteronomy occurred at the end of the Mosaic Age, then that original text would have been purely consonantal, without the use of internal or final *matres lectionis;* furthermore, it would have been characterized by certain differences of syntax and morphology.

It must be admitted, however, that the unpointed text of Deuteronomy, as it now stands, is essentially that of the period of the classical Hebrew writing system (reflecting the exilic and postexilic periods). Unlike the passages that have been identified as early Hebrew poetry, Deuteronomy (with the exception of chs. 32 and 33) does

101. Viz., it reflects various "layers" of orthographic practice in the history of Hebrew writing.
102. The Massoretic vocalization of the Hebrew text is to be dated, approximately, in the 7th century A.D.
103. See F. M. Cross and D. N. Freedman, *Early Hebrew Orthography. A Study of the Epigraphic Evidence*. American Oriental Series 36 (1952). For suggested modifications to the system of Cross and Freedman, see J. C. L. Gibson, "On the Linguistic Analysis of Hebrew Writing," *Archivum Linguisticum* 17 (1969), pp. 131-160; G. Garbini, "Studi aramaici," *Annali dell' Istituto Orientale di Napoli* N.S. 19 (1969), pp. 1-15.

not contain traces of an earlier form. This fact, however, does not militate against an early date, for two principal reasons. First, exactly because Deuteronomy was a part of a *living* tradition, one would expect it to be revised and updated from time to time, in respect to syntax, morphology, and orthography; an analogy can be seen in the frequent new editions of the English Bible, which are produced for essentially the same reasons (compare the printing customs and grammar reflected in the seventeenth-century Authorized Version with those of the New English Bible in the present century). Second, there are reasons why poetry, as distinct from prose, tends to retain aspects of older forms, even after revision; poetry, unlike prose, depends on such features as particular syntax and morphological forms to maintain its function *qua* poetry. Prose is not so limited, and hence it must be subjected to thorough revision if it is to retain its directly communicative function. In summary, the present text of Deuteronomy does not militate against the argument for an early date, whereas the archaic features preserved in Deut. 32 and 33, insofar as those chapters are thoroughly integrated in the prose narrative, may give cautious support to the argument for an early date.[104]

X. ANALYSIS OF CONTENTS

The analysis presented here is intended to serve as a practical guide to the contents of Deuteronomy; it also serves to divide the text into relatively concise sections for the purposes of the commentary. For the unity and formal structure of the book, the reader should refer to section III (above). In the section containing specific legislation, the material has been treated chapter by chapter for the sake of convenience; as can be seen from the table prepared by G. Seitz (*Redaktionsgeschichtliche Studien zum Deuteronomium*, pp. 92f.), there is a wide variety of opinion regarding the inner structure of chs. 12-26.

I. Introduction to Deuteronomy (1:1-5)
II. The Address of Moses: Historical Prologue (1:6–4:43)
   A. The Experience of God in History (1:6–3:29)
      1. Recollections of Horeb (1:6-18)
      2. Recollections of Kadesh-barnea (1:19-46)
      3. Recollections of Mount Seir (2:1-8)
      4. Recollections of Moab and Ammon (2:9-25)
      5. The conquest of Heshbon (2:26-37)
      6. The conquest of Bashan (3:1-11)

---

104. See further the select bibliographies and introductory remarks in the commentary on Deut. 32 ("Song of Moses") and Deut. 33 ("Blessing of Moses").

XI. SELECT BIBLIOGRAPHY

In the select bibliography, the more important recent works have been noted, together with some of the old works in English which are still valuable. In view of the enormous quantity of secondary literature which has appeared in recent years, this bibliography is clearly selective; however, as a guide to further study, a number of books have been marked with an **asterisk** to indicate that they contain additional extensive bibliographies. In addition, special bibliographies have been provided at certain points in the commentary to aid the investigation of particularly important passages.

A. Commentaries and Books

Allis, O. T., *The Five Books of Moses* (1949).
Bächli, O., *Israel und die Völker. Eine Studie zum Deuteronomium* (1962).
Baltzer, K., *The Covenant Formulary in OT, Jewish and Early Christian Writings* (E.T. 1970).

THE BOOK OF DEUTERONOMY

Beegle, D. M., *Moses, the Servant of Yahweh* (1972).
Blair, E. P., *The Book of Deuteronomy. The Book of Joshua.* Layman's Bible Commentary V (1964).
Brinker, R., *The Influence of Sanctuaries in Early Israel* (1946).
Buis, P., *Le Deutéronome.* Verbum Salutis: Ancien Testament IV (1969).
Buis, P., and J. Leclercq, *Le Deutéronome* (1963).
Cazelles, H., translator, *Le Deutéronome.* La Sainte Bible (1966).
Claburn, A. W. E., *Deuteronomy and Collective Behavior* (diss., Princeton, 1968).
Clements, R. E., *God's Chosen People. A Theological Interpretation of the Book of Deuteronomy* (1968).
Cunliffe-Jones, H., *Deuteronomy.* Torch Bible Commentaries (1964).
Driver, S. R., *A Critical and Exegetical Commentary on Deuteronomy.* International Critical Commentary (1895).
Gottwald, N. K., "The Book of Deuteronomy," in C. M. Laymon, ed., *The Interpreter's One-Volume Commentary on the Bible* (1971).
Harrison, R. K., *Introduction to the OT* (1969).
Harrison, R. K., and G. T. Manley, "Deuteronomy," in D. Guthrie and J. A. Motyer, eds., *The New Bible Commentary (Revised)* (1970).
Hertz, J. H., ed., *The Pentateuch and the Haftorahs, V: Deuteronomy* (1936).
Horst, F., *Das Privilegrecht Jahves: Rechtsgeschichtliche Untersuchungen zum Deuteronomium* (1930).
Jocz, J., *The Covenant. A Theology of Human Destiny* (1968).
Keil, C. F., and F. Delitzsch, *The Pentateuch* (n.d.).
Kitchen, K. A., *Ancient Orient and OT* (1966).
Kline, M. G., *Treaty of the Great King. The Covenant Structure of Deuteronomy: Studies and Commentary* (1963).
Idem, The Structure of Biblical Authority (1972).
Loersch, S., *Das Deuteronomium und seine Deutungen.* Stuttgarter Bibel-Studien 22 (1967).
*Lohfink, N., *Das Hauptgebot. Eine Untersuchung literarischer Einleitungsfragen zu Dtn. 5-11* (1963).
Idem, Höre, Israel! Auslegung von Texten aus dem Buch Deuteronomium (1965).
Maarsingh, B., *Onderzoek naar de Ethiek van de Wetten in Deuteronomium* (1961).
Manley, G. T., *The Book of the Law* (1957).
McCarthy, D. J., *Treaty and Covenant* (1963).
Idem, OT Covenant. A Survey of Current Opinions (1972).
Mendenhall, G. E., *Law and Covenant in Israel and the Ancient Near East* (1955).
Merendino, R. P., *Das deuteronomische Gesetz. Eine literarkritische, gattungs- und überlieferungsgeschichtliche Untersuchung* (1969).
*Nicholson, E. W., *Deuteronomy and Tradition* (1967).
Phillips, A., *Ancient Israel's Criminal Law: A New Approach to the Decalogue* (1970).
*Plöger, J. G., *Literarkritische, formgeschichtliche und stilkritische Untersuchungen zum Deuteronomium* (1967).

70

Rad, G. von, *Deuteronomy: A Commentary* (E.T. 1966).
Idem, Studies in Deuteronomy (E.T. 1953).
Rennes, J., *Le Deutéronome* (1967).
Segal, M. H., *The Pentateuch: Its Composition and Authorship and Other Biblical Studies* (1967).
*Seitz, G., *Redaktionsgeschichtliche Studien zum Deuteronomium* (1971).
Smith, G. A., *The Book of Deuteronomy* (1918).
Steinmann, J., *Deutéronome* (1961).
Thompson, J. A., *The Ancient Near Eastern Treaties and the OT* (1964).
Watts, J. D. W., "Deuteronomy," in C. J. Allen, ed., *The Broadman Bible Commentary* II (1970).
*Weinfeld, M., *Deuteronomy and the Deuteronomic School* (1972).
Welch, A. C., *The Code of Deuteronomy. A New Theory of Its Origin* (1924).
Idem, Deuteronomy. The Framework to the Code (1932).
Wijngaards, J., *The Formulas of the Deuteronomic Creed* (1963).
Idem, Deuteronomium (1971).
Wright, G. E., "Deuteronomy," in *The Interpreter's Bible* II (1953).

B. Articles

Alt, A., "Die Heimat des Deuteronomiums," *Kleine Schriften* II (1953), pp. 250-275.
Blenkinsopp, J., "Are There Traces of the Gibeonite Covenant in Deuteronomy?" *CBQ* 28 (1966), pp. 207-219.
Braulik, G., "Die Ausdrücke für Gesetz im Buch Deuteronomium," *Biblica* 51 (1970), pp. 39-66.
Clements, R. E., "Deuteronomy and the Jerusalem Cult Tradition," *VT* 15 (1965), pp. 300-315.
Cross, L. B., "Commentaries on Deuteronomy," *Theology* 64 (1961), pp. 184-88.
Eissfeldt, O., "Deuteronomium und Hexateuch," *Kleine Schriften* IV (1968), pp. 238-258.
Frankena, R., "The Vassal Treaties of Esarhaddon and the Dating of Deuteronomy," *Kaf-Hē: 1940-1965 Jubilee Volume.* OTS 14 (1965), pp. 122-154.
Fretheim, T. E., "The Ark in Deuteronomy," *CBQ* 30 (1968), pp. 1-14.
Hertz, J. H., "Deuteronomy: Antiquity and Mosaic Authorship," *Journal of Transactions of the Victoria Institute* 72 (1940), pp. 86-103.
L'Hour, J., "Formes littéraires, structure et unité de Deutéronome," *Biblica* 45 (1964), pp. 551-55.
Keller, C. A., "Von Stand und Aufgabe der Moseforschung," *ThZ* 13 (1957), pp. 430-441.
Kitchen, K. A., "Ancient Orient, 'Deuteronomism' and the OT," in J. B. Payne, ed., *New Perspectives on the OT* (1970), pp. 1-24.
Idem, "The OT in Its Context, 2. From Egypt to the Jordan," *TSF Bulletin* 60 (1971), pp. 3-11.
Idem, "The OT in Its Context, 6," *TSF Bulletin* 64 (1972), pp. 2-10.
Lindars, B., "Torah in Deuteronomy," in P. R. Ackroyd and B. Lindars, eds., *Words and Meanings* (1968), pp. 117-136.

Lohfink, N., "Der Bundesschluss im Land Moab," *BZ* N.F. 6 (1962), pp. 32-56.
Idem, "Die Bundesurkunde des Königs Josias," *Biblica* 44 (1963), pp. 261-288; 461-498.
de Tillesse, G. Minette, "Sections 'tu' et sections 'vous' dans le Deutéronome," *VT* 12 (1962), pp. 29-87.
Weinfeld, M., "Deuteronomy—The Present State of Inquiry," *JBL* 86 (1967), pp. 249-262.
Idem, "Traces of Assyrian Treaty Formulae in Deuteronomy," *Biblica* 46 (1965), pp. 417-427.
Wenham, G. J., "Deuteronomy and the Central Sanctuary," *TB* 22 (1971), pp. 103-118.
Williams, D., "Deuteronomy in Modern Study," *The Review and Expositor* 61 (1964), pp. 265-273.

APPENDIX I

A PERSPECTIVE FOR THE STUDY OF DEUTERONOMY

The book of Deuteronomy is one of the most comprehensive accounts in the OT of the covenant between God and his people. It is a book that is vital for understanding the complexities of biblical theology, for the majority of that theology is concerned with the covenant relationship between God and man. In quite a different context, however, Deuteronomy has also been of crucial significance, namely, in the scientific (or higher-critical) study of the OT, particularly as it has been conducted during the last two centuries. Since the presentation of de Wette's hypothesis, near the beginning of the nineteenth century, Deuteronomy has become a cornerstone in much of the scientific study of the history, literature, and religion of Israel. De Wette's thesis has undergone a number of modifications and changes, but nevertheless it is still of considerable relevance to many current views on Deuteronomy.[1] De Wette linked Deuteronomy with the reform of King Josiah in the seventh century B.C. At this point, he was not breaking new ground, for the link had already been noted by a number of the Church Fathers; the novelty of the thesis was that Deuteronomy (in part, at least) was a product of Josiah's reign, not simply an ancient work whose rediscovery had prompted reform. In more recent studies, Deuteronomy is viewed not simply as a product of the seventh century; rather it is thought to be a compilation of very much older traditions, which have, nevertheless, been reworked in the period of the reform.[2]

There has been a tradition in biblical scholarship, however, which has continued to maintain the older position, namely, that

1. See M. Weinfeld, "Deuteronomy — The Present State of Inquiry," *JBL* 86 (1967), pp. 249-262.
2. These comments are generalizations, (1) because the wide variety of modern hypotheses are more complex than the brief summary given here, and (2) because there are numerous hypotheses not included in these general statements. See further section IX of the Introduction.

Deuteronomy, as a part of the Pentateuch, is substantially the work of Moses. In the context of contemporary scholarship, this point of view would have to be described as a minority opinion, being represented principally by the works of conservative Christian and Jewish scholars. The tradition of Christian conservative scholarship has debated the new directions introduced in the nineteenth century, sometimes on the ground of method per se and sometimes in relation to the conclusions presented; the basis for this conservative reaction was to be found in a particular theological understanding of the nature of inspiration and revelation.

It should be noted that the new directions that appeared in nineteenth-century scholarship tended to outpace the changes of opinion within the churches, so that it was not until the early part of the twentieth century that the more radical views of those scholars who followed in the path of de Wette came to be accepted with equanimity, in certain sections of the Christian Church. It is worth illustrating this point briefly, for it helps to clarify one of the theological difficulties that has accompanied the study of Deuteronomy. Friedrich Delitzsch described the shock he experienced as a student when he was taught that Deuteronomy was not written by Moses.[3] On further questioning, Delitzsch's teacher admitted that although Deuteronomy might be a falsification, such a view should not be admitted publicly. The ecclesiastical authorities at that time could have tried a scholar on a charge of heresy for making such an admission. The effect on Delitzsch was to indicate to him the hypocrisy of the situation and, perhaps in reaction, his writings on the OT were extremely negative. The OT, he believed, was fraudulent and immoral, unworthy of being considered a part of divine revelation.

An example of a different kind brings out another dimension of the situation. William Robertson Smith, the most distinguished Scottish biblical scholar of the nineteenth century, was brought before the high courts of his church on the issue of whether a late date for Deuteronomy (Smith proposed dating the book in the seventh century) was consistent with the inspiration of the book. The church considered that it was not and Smith had to vacate his Chair in the Church College. Robertson Smith's response to the charges laid against him, however, is illuminating.[4] He continued to affirm the inspiration of Scripture:

3. See E. G. Kraeling, *The OT since the Reformation* (1955), p. 150. The details come from the preface to Delitzsch's two-volume work, *Die grosse Täuschung* (1920/21). Friedrich should not be confused with his father, who had the same initial.
4. The quotation is from Smith's *Answer to the Form of Libel* (1878), p. 21, which is quoted by R. J. Thompson, *Moses and the Law in a Century of Criticism since Graf* (1970), p. 65. For a valuable study of Smith's work in relation to the present context, see W. M. Bailey, *Theology and Criticism in William Robertson Smith* (diss. , Yale, 1970).

... because the Bible is the only record of the redeeming love of God; because in the Bible alone I find God drawing nigh to man in Jesus Christ and declaring his will for our salvation. And the record I know to be true by the witness of his Spirit in my heart. . . .

It is somewhat ironical that the date and authority of Deuteronomy were not the real problems in either of these two incidents; they were simply an outward manifestation of a much larger problem. The larger problem, in general terms, related to the doctrines of inspiration and revelation. In particular, it was the nature of the relationship between these doctrines, on the one hand, and the scientific study of the Bible, on the other, that constituted the principal difficulty. For Delitzsch, there was a great gap between that which was believed about the Bible, as inspired, and the results of a scientific study of the Bible; what seemed to him to be a hypocritical situation produced in him a negative response. The irony of Smith's situation, on the other hand, was that he agreed with his church that the Bible was the inspired word of God. His view of inspiration, however, was such that it was able to accommodate the findings of his scientific studies of the Bible;[5] the more traditional view of his church could not accommodate those findings.

Before pursuing the implications of these two illustrations further, it is worth turning briefly to the contemporary situation, for the mood has changed quite radically in many ways. Biblical scholarship is undertaken in freedom, for the most part, from any oversight by ecclesiastical authorities. The scientific approach to the Bible has become so prevalent that it is the scholarly world, rather than a body in the church, which tends to pass judgment (though not in the form of a trial!). Today, it is the scholar who maintains the Mosaic authorship of Deuteronomy who is likely to be severely criticized in the pages of the academic journals. For example, reference may be made to G. T. Manley's *The Book of the Law: Studies in the Date of Deuteronomy;* L. B. Cross, in a short review of commentaries and books on Deuteronomy, had the following words for Manley's work:[6]

> This book is a *tour de force* in favour of the Mosaic dating of Deuteronomy. Its author claims to have made an independent study of the evidence, but there are few signs of this. His main concern is to refute the conclusions of source criticism. Internal and external evidence which conflicts with his views is ignored, and his representation of the views of some present-day writers is a travesty of them. It is tragic to find the expressions of a scholarly mind so limited by theological prejudice.

5. See, e.g., Smith's preface to the 1st edition of *The OT in the Jewish Church* (1881).
6. L. B. Cross, "Commentaries on Deuteronomy," *Theology* 64 (1961), pp. 184-88 (*p. 186).

The tone of Cross's review is unfortunate, for Manley's work (whether right or wrong) is presented humbly as a modest attack on an old problem. Implicit in Cross's final comment, however, is the assumption of what might be called the new orthodoxy in biblical scholarship. That assumption is that the Bible must be studied scientifically, objectively, and free from theological prejudice.[7] This methodology does not normally intend to deny that the Bible is the word of God, but stresses only that the primary method of approach must be scientific. There has thus been a reversal since W. Robertson Smith's trial. At that time, one of the charges laid against Smith was that his work was dictated by "rationalistic assumptions"; Manley's work, in contrast, had been dictated by "theological prejudice."

The problem indicated in this contrast is not simply a hangover from the nineteenth century. It is a problem which antedated the nineteenth century and which still poses radical difficulties in the twentieth century: the problem lies in defining the relationship between theology and scientific (or higher-critical) method in biblical study.[8] How are theology and scientific method to be related? On the one hand, the Bible is a body of revelation; it is the inspired word of God. That this is so is maintained as an act of faith and conviction by the Christian, or (to use Smith's words), "the record I know to be true by the witness of his Spirit in my heart." On the other hand, the divine revelation took historical form in a book, and the contents of that book had historical settings as word and deed. It is the historical setting that opens the Bible to scientific examination in terms of its history, language, and literature.

For a number of reasons, there must inevitably be a tension between the scientific and theological approaches to the Bible. The nature of the Bible as revelation is such that it is, *ipso facto,* beyond reason in terms of the truth it imparts. The mercy and faithfulness of a loving, personal God cannot be independently established by reason. But because the revelation takes the form of historical words and

7. Although the growth of the discipline of scientific biblical study occurred most notably during the 19th century, the real roots of the method per se are probably to be found in Spinoza. "I determined to examine the Bible afresh in a careful, impartial, and unfettered spirit, making no assumptions concerning it, and attributing to it no doctrines, which I do not find clearly therein set down" (from Spinoza's preface to his *Tractatus Theologico-Politicus;* R. H. M. Elwes, *The Chief Works of Benedict de Spinoza* I [1951], p. 8). Spinoza's thoroughly scientific method, however, is rooted in a critique of revealed religion. See particularly L. Strauss, *Spinoza's Critique of Religion* (1965).
8. For an example of the problem before the 19th century, see the correspondence between Spinoza and William van Blyenbergh, which anticipates in many ways the current dilemma, in J. Wild, ed., *Spinoza Selections* (1958), pp. 417-439. On the contemporary problem, see H. J. Kraus, *Die Biblische Theologie. Ihre Geschichte und Problematik* (1970), p. 370. See also J. Barr, *The Bible in the Modern World* (1973), p. 5.

deeds, reason (in the form of scientific study) is just as inevitably brought to bear. The tension lies in seeking to determine how far the scientific method can go in its examination of historical deeds and words that are affirmed to be revelatory.

In practice, it is not easy to maintain a balance between the theological and scientific approaches to the biblical text. It seems wise, therefore, to indicate the basic point of departure that has been taken in the writing of this commentary: the approach to the text might be described as theological-historical, or theological-scientific.[9] Thus, it is not assumed at the outset that the biblical text, and Deuteronomy in particular, is a purely human work, the product of man's imagination.[10] The assumption (or belief) that the source of the work is God, though its mediation is human, means that scientific method is employed with certain limitations. These comments do not mean that this work is ahistorical or ascientific, but the role that historical and scientific method are granted is, relatively, a subsidiary one. Insofar as scientific and historical criticism are an aid to understanding, they are valuable, but they are not considered to be the *sine qua non* for interpreting the OT.[11] Because of the distance in time

9. Cf. G. E. Ladd, *The NT and Criticism* (1967), p. 40; G. Hasel, *OT Theology: Basic Issues in the Current Debate* (1972), pp. 81-95. By theological-historical, I mean a concept of history that makes allowance for the intervention of a transcendent God. This is a (theological) assumption; the concept thus differs from an alternative point of view, according to which history is seen as an unbroken continuum of causes and effects, which involves the further assumption that there can be no transcendental intervention in historical process. It should also be stressed that I do not necessarily consider the texture of history in biblical times to be the same as that of modern times. That is, the biblical revelation may reflect the particular intervention of God in history, rather than the normative relationship of God to history. Therefore, the biblical text does not necessarily reflect normal events which are interpreted in a particular way by the biblical writers; the events themselves may be abnormal or extraordinary.

10. If it is correct to trace the origins of biblical science to the work of Spinoza, then it is significant to note the role given to *imagination* in Spinoza's assessment of the biblical writers. With the rise of biblical science in the 19th century, a quite different view of imagination was maintained from that of Spinoza, but nevertheless a basic premise underlying that science was that the biblical text was the product of human imagination (e.g., the *interpretation* of ordinary events as the acts of God). The link between Spinoza and 19th-century scholarship is probably to be found in J. G. Herder. Herder has a more positive assessment of human imagination than does Spinoza; however, his study of OT poetry, *Vom Geist der Ebräischen Poesie* (1782/83), has as its working principle the view that the Bible is essentially the product of human imagination. See L. Strauss, *Spinoza's Critique of Religion*, pp. 263f. See also H.-J. Kraus, *Geschichte der historisch-kritischen Erforschung des AT* (²1969), pp. 335f.

11. There is thus basic disagreement with ch. 7 of Spinoza's *Tractatus Theologico-Politicus*, "Of the Interpretation of Scripture." A modern emphasis on the role of history (and sociology) may be seen in the work of G. E. Mendenhall, *The Tenth Generation* (1973), particularly pp. 1-19. For Mendenhall, the biblical message lies, in the last resort, in a sociological, anthropological, and historical analysis of Israel's history in its Near Eastern context.

separating us from the era of ancient Israel, scientific and historical criticism may help us bridge a gap of understanding. But it is always important to remember that there are those in our modern world who have, without the aid of scientific scholarship, grasped the meaning of the Bible in a manner that may evade scholars.[12]

Both in the pages of the Introduction and in the Commentary, Deuteronomy has been interpreted as essentially "Mosaic." This is not entirely a theological judgment, but is partly an historical judgment. By the latter remark, I mean that my understanding of Near Eastern history as a whole, and of Israelite history in particular, is such that I do not find radical problems in setting Deuteronomy in the context of the close of the Mosaic period.[13] There are two provisions, however, that should be added to this general position. First, I do not think that one can *prove* the historicity or "Mosaicness" of Deuteronomy by scientific method; I shall not attempt to do so and I do not believe that the value of Deuteronomy is contingent upon historical verification. Second, I do not assume that those many works which adopt a viewpoint very different from the one presented here are therefore "wrong" or without value. Skepticism of method does not necessarily involve skepticism of belief.[14] The one unchanging fact (of faith) underlying this work is that Deuteronomy is a part of the word of God. In contrast, we are dealing very largely with matters of hypothesis in attempting to answer questions of date and history.[15]

It would require more than one volume to deal in detail with the varieties of opinion about Deuteronomy, and such treatment would have appeal only to specialist interests. However, within certain limits, I have tried to note in the footnotes and in the occasional bibliographies the variety of opinions on various difficult topics. These references, often without comment, are intended to serve as a guide to those who wish to pursue the intricacies of particular topics at greater length.

12. To illustrate the point, reference may be made to a news item in the Hamilton (Ontario, Canada) *Spectator,* April 2, 1973, p. 1. The article describes the release of a Canadian missionary, Lloyd Oppel, from a prisoner-of-war camp in Indochina. Oppel's comments to the press are illuminating: " 'I'd like to say that the main reason I'm home is because of God,' he said. He then quoted from Deuteronomy, which he said he had been studying the night before his capture: 'Be strong and of good courage, fear not, nor be afraid of them: For the Lord thy God, He it is that goeth with thee; He will not fail thee, nor forsake thee' (31:6)."
13. Here I am in essential agreement with the position stated concisely by Kitchen in his article, "The OT in Its Context, 6," *TSF Bulletin* 64 (1972), pp. 2-10. A number of problems relating to the conservative interpretation of Deuteronomy are examined in section IX of the Introduction.
14. See, e.g., Robertson Smith (n. 4, as above).
15. On the relationship between such matters and inspiration, see, e.g., B. M. Metzger, "Literary Forgeries and Canonical Pseudepigrapha," *JBL* 91 (1972), pp. 3-24; W. Harrington, *Irish Theological Quarterly* 29 (1962), pp. 23f. (quoted by Metzger, p. 22).

APPENDIX II

A PROPOSED EGYPTIAN BACKGROUND
FOR THE TREATY FORM OF THE HEBREW COVENANT

In the foregoing pages of the Introduction, it has been noted that the structure of Deuteronomy seems to be based on the pattern of the Near Eastern vassal treaties of the second millennium. This hypothesis, however, raises a number of questions; two of the most obvious questions may be posed: (1) Why did the Hebrews adapt the form of the vassal treaty to express their covenant with God? (2) Why is it that the *Hittite* treaties provide the closest formal similarity to the Hebrew covenant? This appendix is presented in an attempt to answer questions of this type. It must be stressed, however, that the substance of the following paragraphs is a hypothesis and that in light of the currently available evidence, it may not be possible to move beyond the hypothetical stage.

The starting point for the hypothesis is an obvious one. The Sinai covenant, and the renewal of that covenant in Deuteronomy, was made *after* the Exodus from Egypt. Therefore, one might expect to find the clues for the adaptation and use of the treaty form in Egypt.[1] I will begin by presenting the data on which the hypothesis is dependent.

A. Egyptian Data

The Hebrew word for "covenant" is *bryt*. A cognate word, *brt/bryt*, occurs several times in Egyptian texts from the Nineteenth Dynasty and later; it is a Semitic loanword.[2] The use of the word in Egyptian

---

1. Egyptian evidence has previously been utilized with a slightly different purpose, namely, to explain the use of *diathēkē* in the LXX to translate Heb. *bᵉrît;* see J. Swetnam, *"Diathēkē* in the Septuagint Account of Sinai: A Suggestion," *Biblica* 47 (1966), pp. 438-444. I do not think, however, that Swetnam's suggestion regarding the early period of Israel's history (pp. 442f.) is altogether convincing, though his comments regarding the LXX translation are valuable.

2. M. Burchardt, *Die altkanaanäischen Fremdworte und Eigennamen im Aegyptischen* II (1910), p. 20; W. F. Albright, *The Vocalization of the Egyptian Syllabic Orthography* (1934), p. 40.

79

indicates an interesting and perhaps significant semantic range, as the following examples show.

(1) In the Nauri Decree of Seti I,[3] the word *brt* is used three times; in one case, it is accompanied by the "strong arm" determinative. The meaning of the word has occasioned some difficulty. The immediate context in which it appears is a prohibition against removing personnel from the royal foundation at Abydos by various methods, in order to put them to work at some other task. The meaning seems to be related to "contract" and could perhaps be rendered "contractual labor,"[4] though the nature of the contract is not known.

(2) In an historical text of Ramses III, the word is used twice in the description of an Egyptian campaign against the Meshwesh (Libyans). It is used in this context with a different determinative ("man with hand to mouth") and has been translated "covenant."[5] In the first instance, the word is put into the mouths of the Meshwesh: "Let us make a covenant (*brt*). . . ."The second occurrence of the word is found in the Egyptian description of the defeated Meshwesh: "They all make a covenant (*brt*)." From the context, it seems reasonably certain that the term *brt* denotes some kind of vassal treaty.

(3) In quite a different kind of text, Papyrus Anastasi II, the word occurs again in a slightly different form (*bryt*).[6] The passage contrasts the difficult life of the stable-master with the better life of a scribe; one of several misfortunes that befall the stable-master is the loss of his maid-servant into *bryt*, namely, some kind of contractual labor (perhaps forced labor). The meaning of the word *bryt* in this context is very close to that of *brt* in the Nauri Decree.

Summarizing the evidence up to this point, the word *brt*/*bryt* is used in Egyptian with two senses, sometimes distinguished by a determinative: (a) "contract, contractual labor"; (b) "covenant, treaty."

B. Semitic Cognates to Egyptian BRT

On the basis of the Semitic cognate words, the primary meaning of the loanword *brt* in Egyptian is probably "contract, contractual labor."

3. See F. L. Griffith, "The Abydos Decree of Seti I at Nauri," *Journal of Egyptian Archaeology* 13 (1927), pp. 193-208; see lines 32, 43, and 46.
4. Griffith translates tentatively "corvée," though he suggests "agreement" in a footnote (*ibid.*, p. 200). Likewise, W. F. Edgerton renders the word as "corvée"; see "The Nauri Decree of Seti I," *JNES* 6 (1947), p. 221. Sir Alan Gardiner ("Some Reflections on the Nauri Decree," *Journal of Egyptian Archaeology* 38 [1952], p. 28), while admitting the sense "contract," notes that the meaning cannot be exactly "corvée," since that is the meaning of the word *bḥw* which follows immediately.
5. W. F. Edgerton and J. A. Wilson, *Historical Records of Ramses III. The Texts in Medinet Habu* (1936), plates 80-83, lines 38 and 52.
6. R. A. Caminos, *Late Egyptian Miscellanies* (1954), p. 51. Caminos suggests the

However, the attempt to specify the Semitic antecedents to *brt* is difficult,[7] as it is for the Hebrew word *bryt*. There seem to be two viable alternatives: (a) The Egyptian word is related to Akkadian *birtu* (Assyr. *biritu*) "link, clasp, fetter." If this is the source, then it may be that the Akkadian word had already acquired the sense "contract, covenant," as in the expression *TAR be-ri-ti*, which is used in a document from *Qatna* in Syria to be dated approximately in the fifteenth century B.C.[8] (b) Alternatively, the Egyptian word may be related to the Akkadian preposition *birit*, "between." This word is used in a contractual document from Mari, which has been studied by M. Noth.[9] The preposition may have already assumed a nominal sense in Semitic ("mediation, contract"?) prior to its assimilation into the Egyptian language.

It may not matter which of the two alternatives is accepted. What is important is that in both contexts, Qatna and Mari, the potential Semitic antecedent cognates occur in contexts dealing with contracts or agreements. In neither instance is there clear reference to a vassal treaty. From this evidence, it may be argued that the meaning "covenant, treaty" for *brt* in Egyptian is a secondary development from the primary sense ("contract, contractual labor"). If the argument is correct, the reason for the two senses of the word *brt* in Egyptian may lie in the nature of contractual agreements. As a working hypothesis, it is suggested that the nature of Egyptian contracts with "foreigners" (viz., vassal treaties) was essentially the same as that of certain types of Egyptian contracts with labor groups (perhaps non-Egyptian labor groups) employed within the state.

There is one further point to be made before turning to the Hebrew material. The *form* of Egyptian vassal treaties during the Nineteenth Dynasty is not known. However, there is clear evidence that the form of the Egyptian parity treaty was essentially the same as that of the Hittites.[10] It is likely, therefore, that Egyptian vassal treaties were also similar in form to those of the Hittites, during the

---

translation "hired gang" (p. 53). On the different forms of the word, see A. Gardiner, *op. cit.*, pp. 28f.

7. The difficulty arises over cognate *antecedents,* not simply over cognates. Thus Burchardt and Gardiner (nn. 2 and 4) both cite Heb. *bryt* as a cognate. It is not likely, however, that the Egyptian word was borrowed from the Hebrew.

8. See W. F. Albright, "The Hebrew Expression for Making a Covenant in Pre-Israelite Documents," *BASOR* 121 (1951), pp. 21-23. Note, however, that Albright's interpretation of *be-ri-ti* has been questioned; see J. A. Soggin, "Akkadisch TAR *BERĪTI* und Hebraisch כרת ברית," *VT* 18 (1968), pp. 210-15. If Soggin's suggestion is accepted, then the Qatna evidence can be subsumed under alternative (b) below.

9. M. Noth, "OT Covenant-Making in the Light of a Text from Mari," *The Laws in the Pentateuch and Other Studies* (E.T. 1966), pp. 108-117.

10. See *ANET*, pp. 199-203, for the Egyptian and Hittite forms of the parity treaty between Ramses II and Hattusilis.

Egyptian New Kingdom. This is not totally an argument based on probability; it is in the nature of treaties, parity and vassal, to have a common and "internationally" accepted form. The significance of this tentative observation will be taken up in the next section.

C. The Hebrew Covenant

The Hebrew term for "covenant" (*bryt/bᵉrît*) has a number of different nuances and has been the subject of several detailed studies.[11] In the present context, it is important to note that both before and after the sojourn in Egypt, the Hebrews were bound to their God in a covenant relationship; there appears to be a difference, however, between the form of the older patriarchal covenant and that made at Sinai. The Sinai covenant, and the various renewals of that covenant, are given the form of the political treaties in their written state. In other words, after the Exodus the form of the older covenants is given a new expression by means of the treaty pattern; it may be assumed that the new form has particular significance for the religion of early Israel.

Prior to the Exodus from Egypt, the Hebrews were employed by the Egyptians for heavy labor; taskmasters were appointed to control that labor and to make sure that the Hebrews did not rebel against their Egyptian masters (Exod. 1:8-14). It is at this point that the hypothesis comes in. I am suggesting that the nature of the relationship between Egypt and the Hebrews may have been described in Egyptian by the word *brt*. That is, the Hebrews were under some kind of contract to the Egyptian pharaoh (which amounted to a requirement for slave labor). It has already been suggested (section B, above) that *brt*, which is used in Egyptian to signify a vassal treaty, may also have described a contract or internal treaty with (foreign) labor groups within Egypt; both types of *brt* may have employed the form of a political vassal treaty such as that known from the Hittite texts. Thus the Hebrews in Egypt, according to the hypothesis, may have been bound to their Egyptian overlords by a "covenant, treaty" (*brt*). It may be significant that in the Hebrew account of the bondage in Egypt, the Egyptians are described as being afraid of the Hebrews; the Hebrews had become so numerous that they were a potential threat to the security of Egypt (Exod. 1:10). In this sense, the Hebrews within Egypt presented an internal threat similar to the kind of external threat that might be posed by a state beyond the Egyptian border. Egypt imposed upon a threatening power, whether internal or external, a vassal-type treaty.

If it is correct that the Hebrews in Egypt were bound to their

---

11. For bibliography and a detailed study, see *TDOT* II, *s.v. bᵉrîth* (Weinfeld), pp. 253-279.

overlords by some type of covenant (*brt*) in which the treaty form was used, then the form given to the Sinai Covenant becomes all the more significant. In the Exodus, the Hebrews were liberated from the Egyptian *brt* by their God. At Sinai, they entered a new covenant, though one that was given a similar structure to the older one they had known in Egypt. Since their suzerain God had delivered them from the power of Egypt, it was to God alone that the Hebrews could submit in allegiance to the new covenant. It is for this reason that the Exodus and the Sinai Covenant mark the birth of the new nation of Israel, rather than the settlement in the promised land. In the Exodus, the power of the suzerain was broken; the pharaoh, the god-king of Egypt,[12] was defeated and therefore lost his right to be Israel's suzerain lord; the Lord had conquered the pharaoh and therefore ruled as King over Israel (Exod. 15:18). As their deliverer, God had claimed the right to call for his people's obedient commitment to him in the covenant.

In conclusion, it should be repeated that the argument presented in this appendix is an hypothesis. However, the hypothesis does provide answers to the two questions posed in the opening paragraph. (1) Why did the Hebrews adapt the form of the vassal treaty to express their covenant with God? Because prior to the Sinai Covenant, they had been bound to Egyptian overlords by a similar kind of treaty. By employing the same form, the freedom from worldly authority and the submission to the Lord are given particular emphasis. (2) Why is it that the Hittite treaties provide the closest formal similarity to the Hebrew covenant? The answer to this question is to be found in part in the fortuitous nature of archeological discovery. It is the Hittite treaties that are known, but according to the hypothesis, the Hebrew covenant would be similar to the no longer extant Egyptian vassal treaties.[13] Finally, it should be noted that the early uses of *brt* that are known in Egyptian texts come from the period of the pharaoh who is thought to have been in power at the time of the Exodus.[14]

---

12. The pharaoh was believed to be a divine-king in Egypt; thus his defeat in the Exodus (Exod. 15:4-10) by the Lord of the Hebrews was in effect a denial of any real divine power lying in his hands.
13. See also A. Alt, *Kleine Schriften* III, p. 104.
14. Either Seti (Sethos) I or Ramses (Ramesses) II. The early uses of *brt* in Egyptian occur in texts dating from the period of Seti I (Dynasty XIX) and Ramses III (Dynasty XX).

APPENDIX III

CONCORDANCE OF PRINCIPAL QUMRAN MANUSCRIPTS
RELATING TO DEUTERONOMY

Text in Deuteronomy	Location of text (and bibliography)	Number of text: comments
1:7-9	*DJD* III, p. 60	2Q10.1
1:9-13	*DJD* I, p. 58	1Q5.1
1:22	*DJD* I, p. 54	1Q4.1
4:47-49	*DJD* I, p. 54	1Q4.2
5:1-14	*DJD* III, pp. 149-157	8Q3.20-25 (phylactery)
5:1-22	*DJD* I, pp. 73f.	1Q13.1-18
5:1–6:1	*Scrolls from the Wilderness of the Dead Sea* (British Museum, 1965), pp. 31f.	4QDeut.
5:23-27	*DJD* I, p. 74	1Q13.19 (phylactery)
5:28-29	*DJD* V, pp. 57-60 Cf. J. M. Allegro, *JBL* 75 (1956), pp. 182-87	4QTestimonia (quotation)
5:29	*DJD* V, p. 3	4Q158.6 (paraphrase)
5:30-31	*DJD* V, p. 3	4Q158.7-8 (paraphrase)
6:1-3	*DJD* III, pp. 149-157	8Q3.12-16 (phylactery)
6:4-9	*DJD* II, pp. 83f. Cf. R. deVaux, *RB* 60 (1953), pp. 268-275	Mur. Phyl. (phylactery)
6:4-9	*DJD* III, pp. 149-157	8Q3.4-6, 8 (phylactery)
7:15-24	*DJD* III, p. 174	5Q1.1.i
8:5-10	*Scrolls from the Wilderness of the Dead Sea*, p. 31	4QDeut.
8:5–9:2	*DJD* III, p. 171	5Q1.1.ii
8:8-9	*DJD* I, p. 58	1Q5.2
8:18-19	*DJD* I, p. 54	1Q4.3-4

9:10	*DJD* I, p. 58	1Q5.3
9:27-28	*DJD* I, p. 54	1Q4.5
10:1-3	*DJD* II, p. 79	Mur. Deut.
10:8-12	*DJD* III, pp. 61f.	2Q12.1
10:12-17	*DJD* III, pp. 149-157	8Q3.17-19, 21 (phylactery)
10:12-11:21	*DJD* III, pp. 158-161	8Q4.1 (mezuzah)
10:13(?)	*DJD* III, pp. 149-157	8Q3.26-27 (phylactery)
10:17-18	*DJD* I, p. 74	1Q13.20 (phylactery)
10:19	*DJD* III, pp. 149-157	8Q3.21 (phylactery)
10:20-22	*DJD* III, pp. 149-157	8Q3.12, 15-16 (phylactery)
10:21-11:1	⎰ *DJD* I, p. 74	1Q13.21-22 (phylactery)
	⎱ *DJD* III, pp. 149-157	8Q3.26-29 (phylactery)
11:2	*DJD* III, pp. 149-157	8Q3.26-27
11:2-3	*DJD* II, p. 79	Mur. Deut.
11:3(?)	*DJD* III, pp. 149-157	8Q3.26-27
11:6-12	*DJD* III, pp. 149-157	8Q3.27-29
11:8-11	*DJD* I, p. 74	1Q13.23-25 (phylactery)
11:12	*DJD* I, p. 75	1Q13.26-27 (phylactery)
11:13-21	⎰ *DJD* II, pp. 83f.	Mur. Phyl. (phylactery)
	⎱ *DJD* III, pp. 149-157	8Q3.4, 7-11 (phylactery)
	Cf. R. deVaux, *RB* 60 (1953), pp. 268-275	
11:27-30	*DJD* I, p. 55	1Q4.6
11:30-33	*DJD* I, p. 58	1Q5.4
12:25-26	*DJD* II, p. 79	Mur. Deut.
13:1-4	*DJD* I, p. 55	1Q4.7-8
13:4-6	*DJD* I, p. 55	1Q4.9
13:13-14	*DJD* I, p. 55	1Q4.10
14:21	*DJD* I, p. 55	1Q4.11
14:24-25	*DJD* I, p. 56	1Q4.12
15:14-15	*DJD* I, p. 58	1Q5.5
16:4	*DJD* I, p. 56	1Q4.13
16:6-7	*DJD* I, p. 56	1Q4.14
17:12-15	*DJD* III, pp. 60f.	2Q11.1
17:16	*DJD* I, p. 58	1Q5.6
18:18-19	*DJD* V, pp. 57-60	4QTestimonia (quotation)
	Cf. J. M. Allegro, *JBL* 75 (1956), pp. 182-87	
18:18-20, 22	*DJD* V, p. 3	4Q158.6
21:8-9	*DJD* I, p. 58	1Q5.7
24:10-16	*DJD* I, p. 58	1Q5.8
25:13-18	*DJD* I, p. 59	1Q5.9
26:19(?)	*DJD* III, pp. 106f.	6Q3.1
28:44-48	*DJD* I, p. 59	1Q5.10
29:9-11	*DJD* I, p. 59	1Q5.11

29:12-20	*DJD* I, p. 59	1Q5.12-13
29:20(?)	*DJD* I, p. 61	1Q5.28
30:19–31:6	*DJD* I, p. 59	1Q5.13
31:7-10	*DJD* I, p. 60	1Q5.14
21:12-13	*DJD* I, p. 60	1Q5.15
32:8	See P. W. Skehan, *BASOR* 136 (Dec. 1954), pp. 12-15	
32:17-21	*DJD* I, p. 60	1Q5.16
32:20-21(?)	*DJD* III, p. 171	5Q1.2-3
32:21-22	*DJD* I, p. 60	1Q5.17
32:22-29	*DJD* I, p. 60	1Q5.18-19
32:37-43	See P. W. Skehan, *BASOR* 136 (Dec. 1954), pp. 12-15; *idem,* SVT 4 (1957), p. 120; *idem, JBL* 78 (1959), pp. 21f.	
33:1-2(?)	*DJD* III, p. 171	5Q4-5
33:8-11	{ *DJD* V, p. 56	4QFlorilegium (quotation)
	{ *DJD* V, pp. 57-60	4QTestimonia (quotation)
	Cf. J. M. Allegro, *JBL* 75 (1956), pp. 182-87	
33:12(?)	*DJD* V, p. 56	4QFlorilegium (quotation)
33:12-17	*DJD* I, p. 61	1Q5.20
33:18-19	*DJD* I, p. 61	1Q5.21
33:19-21	*DJD* V, p. 56	4QFlorilegium (quotation)
33:21-23	*DJD* I, p. 61	1Q5.22
33:24	*DJD* I, p. 61	1Q5.23

TEXT AND
COMMENTARY

I. INTRODUCTION TO DEUTERONOMY (1:1-5)

1 *These are the words that Moses addressed to all Israel in Transjordan, in the wilderness, in the Arabah opposite Suph, between Paran on the one hand and Tophel and Laban and Hazeroth and Dizahab on the other.*

2 *It takes eleven days from Horeb to Kadesh-barnea by the Mount Seir Road.*

3 *And in the fortieth year, in the eleventh month, on the first of the month, Moses addressed to the Israelites all that the Lord had commanded him concerning them.*

4 *It was after his defeat of Sihon, king of the Amorites, who lived in Heshbon, and Og, king of Bashan, who lived in Ashtaroth and in Edrei.*

5 *In Transjordan, in the land of Moab, Moses undertook to expound this law, saying:*

These verses form a preamble to the entire book[1] and serve a function similar to that of the preamble in the Near Eastern treaties (see Introduction). The great covenant, which was made at Sinai between the Lord and his people, is to be renewed prior to the transference of the leadership from Moses to Joshua and the Israelites' entry into the promised land. In this renewal of the covenant, the persons involved, the place, and the time are all specified explicitly.

1 The principal content of Deuteronomy is defined first. The book does not contain simply an historical account of the renewal of the covenant, but contains the *words* of Moses. The words are addressed to *all Israel,* a common expression in Deuteronomy, which is used in both the first and last verses of the book and at many points

---

1. It has been suggested that these verses (or at least 1:1-3) are not an introduction to Deut., but a conclusion to Num.; see the discussion in Buis and Leclercq, *Le Deutéronome* (1963), p. 31. They do form a link with the foregoing narrative, but are best understood as the preamble to Deuteronomy.

THE BOOK OF DEUTERONOMY

between.[2] The expression is often said to be typical of the style of Deuteronomy, but this may be misleading. The principal theme running throughout is the covenant, and the unity of Israel is of the essence of the covenant; hence, the words *all Israel* are primarily an emphasis of that unity, rather than an indication of style. It is interesting that the book does not call for unity, but assumes unity to be existing already.[3]

Having indicated the persons involved, the verse then specifies the place in which the events took place. Many of the place names that follow have caused considerable difficulty and the exact location of all the places mentioned is not known. The general region is called *Transjordan,* viz., the region around the river Jordan.[4] The word *Arabah* has a wide sphere of reference, denoting the great rift valley that extends from the Sea of Tiberias in the north to the Gulf of Aqaba in the south. In this context, it is specified as that part of the Arabah in the region of *Suph,* but unfortunately the location of Suph is uncertain. It is probably to be located in Moab in the vicinity of the Arnon River.[5] The names that follow are all uncertain; the context suggests that they are all in the region of Moab, but one or two seem to be further afield. There is a region known as *Paran* in the Sinai Peninsula, which was traversed by the Israelites after the Exodus (Num. 10:12; 12:16) and has been identified with modern Feiran; but whether it is the same Paran referred to here is uncertain. *Tophel* is mentioned only here in the Bible. A location in Edom at the site Tafileh has been suggested tentatively,[6] but a more likely solution is that Tophel was further north in Moab.[7] *Laban,* too, is unknown, though it may be in the plains of Moab.[8] As for *Hazeroth,* there was a place of that name on the Israelites' desert itinerary (Num. 11:35; 12:16; 33:17), but again it is uncertain whether it is the same place as

2. The words occur at least fourteen times in various contexts: 1:1; 5:1; 11:6; 13:12; 18:6; 21:21; 27:9; 29:1; 31:1, 7, 11 (twice); 32:45; 34:12.
3. Cf. R. E. Clements, *God's Chosen People* (1968), p. 31.
4. The translation "beyond the Jordan" (RSV) is possible philologically and was known to the older commentators. As early as the 12th century A.D., it had been taken by Ibn Ezra to imply the east bank of the Jordan from the point of view of one standing on the west bank; this view was known and shared by Spinoza (*Tractatus Theologico-Politicus* VIII, "Of the Authorship of the Pentateuch") and has been assumed by many commentators since that time. It seems best in this context to take the general sense *Transjordan:* see B. Gemser, "Be'eber Hajjarden: in Jordan's Borderland," *VT* 2 (1952), pp. 349-355; and G. T. Manley, *The Book of the Law* (1957), p. 49.
5. See E. G. Kraeling, "Two Place Names in Hellenistic Palestine," *JNES* 7 (1948), p. 201. Suph (lit. "Reed") is linked by Kraeling to the site with the Greek name Papyron, mentioned in Josephus *Antiquities* xiv.33.
6. D. Baly, *Geographical Companion to the Bible* (1963), pp. 42f., fig. 10.
7. Cf. H. Cazelles, "Tophel (Deut. 1:1)," *VT* 9 (1959), pp. 412-15.
8. The identification with Libnah (Num. 33:20) is possible, though if correct, its significance would be uncertain.

90

that mentioned here. *Dizahab* ("place of gold") is also mentioned only here in the Bible and its location is uncertain.[9]

2 The difficulties associated with the place names in 1:1 continue into this verse; the immediate sense is clear, but the significance of the verse in its context is uncertain. *Horeb* is the general term for the locality within which Mount Sinai was located[10] and it is the word normally employed in Deuteronomy for Sinai, with the exception of the specific statement in 33:2. Kadesh-barnea[11] was eleven days' journey from Horeb by the Mount Seir Road,[12] a fact that has been confirmed by travellers in more recent times.[13] It may be that the verse relates to the place names in 1:1, some of which may have been in the Sinai Peninsula. Alternatively, it has been suggested that the verse should follow 1:19, where a direct reference is made to the journey from Horeb to Kadesh-barnea.[14]

3 Now the date of the address of Moses and the renewal of the covenant is added: the beginning of the eleventh month of the fortieth year of wilderness wandering since the Exodus. It is the only exact date given in the book and presumably it was the only date that was necessary, since it specifies the starting point of all the words and events contained in the book. This specific method of dating is known from both biblical and Near Eastern sources.[15] On this date, Moses addressed the Israelites; 1:3 then adds more information to that already provided in 1:1. The substance of the message Moses delivered to the Israelites was *all that the Lord had commanded him concerning them.* Moses is thus a man under orders; the demand for obedience is a prominent theme throughout Deuteronomy, and in declaring that demand, Moses was himself living his message.

4 The details contained in this verse illuminate further the date already noted in 1:3; some victories had already been experienced and the address of Moses anticipates further victories in the future. The victories over Sihon and Og are recalled in greater detail

---

9.   Y. Aharoni, *The Land of the Bible,* p. 180 (map 13), suggests identifying the place with Dhahab.
10.   See M. H. Segal in *Scripta Hierosolymitana* 8 (1961), p. 90.
11.   The possible locations are (a) 'Ain Qudeis or (b) 'Ain Qudeirat; see K. A. Kitchen, *NBD,* p. 687.
12.   For details of this road, see Y. Aharoni, *The Land of the Bible,* p. 40, map 3, and p. 52; Y. Aharoni and M. Avi-Yonah, *The Macmillan Bible Atlas,* map 10.
13.   See S. R. Driver, *Deuteronomy* (1895), pp. 5f.
14.   See M. H. Segal, *The Pentateuch: Its Composition and Authorship and Other Biblical Studies* (1967), p. 95.
15.   For Egyptian examples, see the Annals of Thutmose III (*ANET,* pp. 234-38); the Stele of Amenhotep II (*ANET,* pp. 245-47); the Campaigns of Ramses II (*ANET,* pp. 255f.). It is unnecessary to suppose that 1:3 is an addition from the so-called P-source, which is said to employ this type of dating procedure; see G. von Rad, *Deuteronomy: A Commentary* (E.T. 1966), p. 36. The substance of Deut. requires only one date.

in 2:26-37 (Sihon) and 3:1-22 (Og); see the commentary on these passages.[16]

5 The final verse of the preamble recalls the first verse[17] and introduces directly the opening words of Moses' address. Once again, some further information concerning the address of Moses is added to the statements of 1:1 and 1:3; *Moses undertook to expound this law*.[18] The word *expound* (*bēʾēr*) has the sense of making something absolutely clear or plain; the same verb is used in 27:8 to indicate the clarity or legibility with which the words of the law were to be inscribed in stone. *This law*, which Moses was to expound, is probably to be understood as *all that the Lord had commanded* (1:3); it was this that formed the basis of the covenant relationship between the Lord and his people. It is important to stress that the content of Deuteronomy is an *exposition* of the law; the book does not simply contain a repetition of the earlier legal material known in Exodus and Numbers, to which a few new laws have been added. It is true that there is a common core of law with the earlier books, but here the law is to be explained and applied by Moses to the particular situation of the Israelites. They were about to enter the promised land, and the law of the covenant could not lie as a dead letter. It had to be expounded and emphasized to all the Israelites, for the success of the events lying ahead of them depended on this critical point. Success in possessing the promised land lay not in military prowess and strength, but in an unbroken covenant relationship with the Lord, who alone could bring further victories like those over Sihon and Og (1:4).

16. *Ashtaroth* is not mentioned in 3:1-22; on the location of Ashtaroth, probably in Bashan, see W. F. Albright, "The Land of Damascus Between 1850 and 1750 B.C.," *BASOR* 83 (1941), p. 33.
17. The framework of the preamble has chiastic form:

A	(1:1)	These are the words that Moses addressed to all Israel
B		In Transjordan, in the wilderness . . .
B	(1:5)	In Transjordan, in the land of Moab,
A		Moses undertook to expound the law.

The significance of the structure is uncertain, but there are other points in Deut. where a similar structure appears; see the commentary at 7:10.
18. The word *law* (*tôrāh*) can be used with either a broad or a specific sense; for a detailed study of the word in Deut., see B. Lindars, "Torah in Deuteronomy," in P. R. Ackroyd and B. Lindars, eds., *Words and Meanings* (1968), pp. 117-136.

II. THE ADDRESS OF MOSES: HISTORICAL PROLOGUE (1:6–4:43)

A. THE EXPERIENCE OF GOD IN HISTORY[1] (1:6–3:29)

1. RECOLLECTIONS OF HOREB (1:6-18)

6 *The Lord our God addressed us in Horeb, saying: you have remained long enough on this mountain.*

7 *Get ready and begin your journey and go to the hill country of the Amorites and to all their neighbors in the Arabah, in the hill country, and in the Shephelah, and the Negeb, and by the coast of the sea; that is, the land of the Canaanites and the Lebanon as far as the great river, the river Euphrates.*

8 *Look! I have set the land before you. Go and take possession of the land which I promised by oath to your fathers, to Abraham, to Isaac and to Jacob, to give to them and to their posterity after them.*

9 *And at that time I spoke to you, saying: Alone, I cannot take responsibility for you.*

10 *The Lord your God has made you grow in number, so that today you are as numerous as the stars in the sky.*

11 *May the Lord God of your fathers add to your number a thousand times as many as you are now and may he bless you just as he said to you!*

12 *Alone, how can I take responsibility for your burden, and for your load, and for your disputes?*

13 *Provide for yourselves wise, discerning, and experienced men among your tribes and I will appoint them as your leaders.*

14 *And you answered me and said: The thing that you have told us to do is right.*

---

1. For specialized studies of this section, see N. Lohfink, "Darstellungskunst und Theologie in Dtn. 1:6–3:29," *Biblica* 41 (1960), pp. 105-134; J. G. Plöger, *Literarkritische, formgeschichtliche und stilkritische Untersuchungen zum Deuteronomium* (1967), pp. 1-59.

15 *So I took the leaders of your tribes, wise and experienced men, and I appointed them leaders over you; commanders of thousands, and commanders of hundreds, and commanders of fifties, and commanders of tens, and officers among your tribes.*

16 *And at that time, I commanded your judges, saying: Adjudicate between your brethren and judge righteously between a man and his brother and his resident alien.*

17 *You shall not show favoritism in judgment; you shall adjudicate exactly alike for the small and for the great. You shall not be afraid of man, because the judgment belongs to God; and the case that is too hard for you, you shall bring to me and I will adjudicate it.*

18 *And at that time, I commanded you all the things which you should do.*

The historical prologue, though it repeats material from the other books of the Pentateuch in shorter and sometimes different form, serves a particular purpose in its present context. The Near Eastern treaty, in its historical prologue, described the events underlying the treaty. In Deuteronomy, likewise, the historical basis for the covenant begins with the covenant promise made to Abraham and then it continues to the initial stage in the realization of that promise at Sinai/Horeb.[2] The importance of history has two focal points: (a) there is the covenant tradition of promise, from Abraham to Moses; (b) there is the experience of God in history working out in deed the content of the promise. Thus, for the renewal of the covenant described in Deuteronomy, the prologue recalls not only the covenant's history, but also the ability of the Lord of the covenant to fulfil his promise. What God had done in the past, he could continue to do in the future. There is thus a presentation of a faithful God, whose demand was for a faithful people. In Deuteronomy, the historical prologue does not have the concise form of the treaty prologue, but it is developed in the address of Moses for an instructional purpose. Hence, a further theme in the prologue is that though God was faithful, the Israelites tended constantly toward unfaithfulness. Though the success in the past was cause for hope in the events that lay beyond the Jordan, the failures of the past provided a warning. The recital of history thus gave strength and warning to the people; the address of Moses solemnly prepares the people for the call to commitment and obedience that would be laid upon them. The address begins with recollections of Horeb/Sinai:

6 *The Lord our God addressed us in Horeb.* As soon as

2. Note, however, that the themes are not presented in strictly chronological fashion; the covenant with the patriarchs is a theme interwoven into the narrative, which begins with Sinai/Horeb. See Buis and Leclercq, *Le Deutéronome,* p. 35.

Moses begins his address, he quotes the words of the Lord; the quotation extends from vv. 6b-8. The syntax of the Hebrew sentence places the emphasis on *the Lord our God,*[3] thus providing a suitable introduction to the essence of Moses' discourse. The words emphasize the covenant character of the God of Israel, for it is only on the basis of the covenant that Moses can say, identifying himself with his people, that the Lord is *our God.* But the covenant privilege carries with it heavy responsibilities, and the words of the Lord required action from the Israelites. *You have remained long enough on this mountain.* The events of Horeb were completed and it was time to move. The formation of the covenant at Horeb had made the Israelites potentially a nation; there could be no rest until that potential was a reality. Hence at Horeb, and again at Mount Seir,[4] and now in the plains of Moab, where Moses addressed the people, the call comes constantly to move on, until the promised land is the possessed land.

7   The call was to go toward the promised land; and the dimensions of it, as described in this verse, are enormous. Virtually all of Palestine and Syria are included by these terms, an area larger than Israel ever possessed in fact, even during the reigns of David and Solomon. The terms employed indicate the principal geographic divisions of the land.[5] The land included the *hill country of the Amorites* (viz., the central mountainous regions of Judah and Mount Ephraim), the *Arabah* (see 1:1), and the *Shephelah,* a range of low hills situated between the Judean mountains and *the coast of the sea* (viz., the plain in western Palestine bordering the Mediterranean). The *Negeb* is the dry land in southern Palestine, extending from north of Beersheba to the Judean mountains. All these areas can be placed under the general term, *the land of the Canaanites.*[6] To the north of the land of the Canaanites lay *the Lebanon,* and even further to the northeast were the upper reaches of the *river Euphrates.*

This large vision of the land is a reflection of the patriarchal

3.   Here, the subject is placed first in the sentence, whereas normally in Hebrew it follows the verb. The words *Lord our God,* and variations such as *Lord your God,* occur frequently in Deut.; see G. A. Smith, *The Book of Deuteronomy* (1918), p. 6. While the words may be an indication of the style of Deut., they are primarily a further indication of content (cf. "all Israel" and the comment at 1:1). The centrality of the covenant in Deut., together with its nature as being principally an address of Moses, make these forms of divine reference particularly suitable.
4.   See Deut. 2:3, where the same Hebrew idiom is used (with a different verb).
5.   On the geographical terms, see Y. Aharoni, *The Land of the Bible,* pp. 37f. On some of the implications of this description of the promised land, see Gordon, *UT,* p. 459 (19.1899).
6.   See the discussion in J. C. L. Gibson, "Observations on Some Important Ethnic Terms in the Pentateuch," *JNES* 20 (1961), pp. 217-238.

covenant; the promise made to Abraham was that the Lord would give to his descendants the land from "the river of Egypt to the great river, the river Euphrates" (Gen. 15:18).

8 *Look![7] I have set[8] the land before you.* The charge the Lord gives to his people is one that requires vision, but now it must be vision that prompts action: *Go and take possession of the land.* In 1:7, the land was described according to its geographical divisions. Here it is described as a part of the plan and promise of the Lord: *the land which I promised[9] by oath to your fathers.* The vision required of the people of the Lord is one that sees more than the mundane, physical regions of the land; it is the significance of the land in the promise, soon to be realized, that provides the strength necessary for commitment and obedience.

9 Moses, having begun by citing the words of the Lord, now resumes his address and recalls how, prior to leaving Horeb,[10] it had been necessary to undertake some organization of the Israelites. *Alone, I cannot take responsibility for you* (lit. "I cannot bear/carry you"). The responsibility, which was both a privilege and a burden, was to be distributed among others.

10 The reason for the need to delegate responsibility was directly related to the Lord's fulfilment of his promise; thus, these verses on the practical organization of the Israelites are directly related to the earlier quotation of the words of the Lord and the reference there to the promise made to the patriarchs. *The Lord . . . has made you grow in number*—hence, it became an increasingly difficult task for Moses, by himself, to undertake all the aspects of the leadership of his people, both judicial and military. The growth, so that now the Israelites had become *as numerous as the stars in the sky,* was in part a fulfilment of the promise of the Lord: "Look toward heaven and number the stars, if you are able to number them. Then he (the Lord) said to him (Abram): so shall your descendants be" (Gen. 15:5; see also Gen. 22:17).

7. MT has *r'h* (singular); and later imperatives in this verse are plural, so that one might expect a plural form for the first imperative. A Qumran fragment gives grounds for reading *r'w,* the plural (see *DJD* III, p. 61); this reading is strengthened by the renderings of Sam., LXX, and Syriac.
8. Heb. *nāṭattî* ("set"; the verb has also the sense "give" and is used, in the context of the covenant promise, of that which would be "given" to the descendants of the patriarchs [1:9]).
9. MT *nishba' yhwh* ("the Lord promised"); the reading suggested by Sam. and LXX (*nishba'tî*), "I promised," is more likely since the verse is a part of the address of the Lord to Moses and the people.
10. The expression used is *at that time,* occurring here and in vv. 16 and 18. It is an expression used commonly in the historical section of Deut.; see S. R. Driver, *Deuteronomy,* p. 15; S. E. Loewenstamm, "The Formula *b'ṭ hhw'* in Deuteronomy," *Tarbiz* 38 (1968/69), pp. 99-104.

11 *The Lord God of your fathers.* Earlier in the discourse, the divine titles have indicated primarily *relationship* (the Lord our God, 1:6; the Lord your God, 1:10). Now the emphasis lies in the *continuity of relationship,* stressing once again the theme of the covenant with the patriarchs. The Lord was "their God" and he is "your God," Moses is saying, and his request was that the promise made to the fathers, already fulfilled in the sons, might be fulfilled still further in the sons' sons. Moses' request for further increase and further blessing makes it clear that his need to delegate responsibility, stated already (1:9) and to be repeated more emphatically (1:12), was in no sense a complaint.

12 The statement of 1:9 is repeated here more emphatically by indicating the nature of Moses' responsibility for the Israelites' *burden, load,* and *disputes.*[11]

13 Moses therefore requests the people: *provide for yourselves*[12]. . . *men*—the people would select men and then Moses would formally appoint them, or commission them, to their new tasks. The men chosen, however, were to have certain essential qualifications. They were to be *wise, discerning,* and *experienced;*[13] that is, they were to have the benefit of acquired knowledge (wisdom), and the ability of discernment, together with the knowledge that can come only with experience. Their task was a difficult one, and the required qualifications were high.

14 The people readily agreed with Moses' plan. Perhaps Moses reminded the people of their agreement, since the newly appointed men were those to whom the people would now owe their immediate obedience. All might agree on the need to obey God, and his representative Moses, but such obedience was distant and the immediate demand for obedience would come from the officers lower down in the organizational structure. Yet, in the conquest lying beyond the plains of Moab, obedience would not be a lofty theological concept, but an immediate demand made by the officers immediately over the people.

15 With the agreement of the people, Moses proceeded to appoint *leaders.*[14] The first group, *commanders (śārîm),* had primar-

11. *Burden (ṭōrah)* is uncommon in the OT; see its use in Isa. 1:14. *Your load* is derived from the verb used in the first part of the sentence (*nś', "*to carry, bear"). *Disputes (rîḇ)* implies legal cases, as will become evident in the following verses; see also the commentary on Deut. 17:8.
12. The grammatical construction is the so-called *dativus commodi;* GKC § 119 s.
13. *Experienced (yᵉduʿîm),* from *yāḏaʿ, "*to know"; see the discussion in J. A. Emerton, "A Consideration of Some Alleged Meanings of *yd'* in Hebrew," *JSS* 15 (1970), pp. 145-180, esp. pp. 175f.
14. The "leaders" (lit. "heads") could have both judicial and military responsibilities; for a detailed study, see J. R. Bartlett, "The Use of the Word *r'sh* as a Title in the OT," *VT* 19 (1969), pp. 1-10.

ily a military function, for beyond Horeb, and indeed beyond Moab, the people were to launch into a battle for the land promised to them. The divisions (*thousands, hundreds, fifties, tens*) refer to units of different sizes rather than to specific numbers.[15] Although there was not yet a "standing army" in Israel, such as was to be formed during the monarchy, the Israelites as a whole were, in effect, the army of the Lord. The word *officers (shōṭᵉrîm)* probably indicates a more administrative than purely military function; it might be equivalent approximately to the modern term "quartermaster."[16]

16 Moses also appointed *judges (shōpᵉṭîm)*; this term, too, may have both judicial and military implications (as in the book of "Judges"), though here the reference is specifically to those appointees who would assume a judicial office. They were to *judge righteously;* that is, there was a "righteous law/judgment" (Deut. 16:18) which was to be applied by them. It applied not only to the full Israelites (i.e., *between a man and his brother),* but also to the *resident alien (gēr).* The resident alien was a foreigner who resided with the Israelites under their protection, and though he was not equal in all respects to the Israelites, under the law he was treated as they were. The Israelites knew from bitter experience the status of an alien in a foreign land (see Deut. 10:19); their own resident aliens were not to be treated as they were in the land of Egypt, but they were to have the same status in law as a freeman.

17 Likewise, in the administration of justice, no distinction was to be made between *the small* and *the great,* that is, the poor and the rich, the unimportant and the important. Nor were the judges to be afraid of man, if untoward pressure was brought to bear on them, for the measure by which they adjudicated was that of God. The principle that *judgment belongs to God* was enormously important,[17] for it removed the basis and the authority of the law from the human realm and placed it firmly on an absolute principle of divine authority. But there would still be cases *too hard* for the judges; the principle of law may be clear, but the application of the principle to situations where evidence was unclear or contradictory could be very difficult. Such cases were to be referred to Moses for his adjudication.

18 The section closes with a summary statement referring to all the legislation given at Horeb; the function of the historical prologue is such that only selected recollections were described, insofar as they fitted into the purpose of Moses' address.

15. See the general discussion in R. deVaux, *Ancient Israel: Its Life and Institutions* (²1965), pp. 216f.
16. The meaning of the root, by analogy with its Semitic cognates, is "write"; Assyr. *šaṭâru,* Arab. *saṭara.* In Exod. 5:6-19, the role of the *shōṭᵉrîm* (RSV "foremen") was to keep tally of the building supplies.
17. For an examination of the implications of the principle, in the area of legal theory, see J. Ellul, *The Theological Foundation of Law* (1969), pp. 37-45.

2. RECOLLECTIONS OF KADESH-BARNEA (1:19-46)

19 *And we set out from Horeb and we travelled through all that great and terrible wilderness which you saw, en route for the hill country of the Amorites, just as the Lord our God commanded us: and we came to Kadesh-barnea.*

20 *And I said to you: You have come to the hill country of the Amorites which the Lord our God is about to give us.*

21 *Look: the Lord has set the land before you. Go up! Take possession, just as the Lord God of your fathers said to you. Do not be afraid and do not be dismayed.*

22 *Then all of you approached me and said: Let us send men ahead of us and they will explore the land for us and they will bring us word about the route by which we must go up, and about the cities to which we shall come.*

23 *And the plan was agreeable to me and I took twelve men of you, one man per tribe.*

24 *And they prepared and went up to the hill country and they came to the Eshcol Valley, and they explored it on foot.*

25 *And they took in their hands some of the fruit of the land and they brought it down to us, and they brought us back news and they said: The land is good which the Lord our God is about to give us.*

26 *But you did not consent to go up and you rebelled against the command of the Lord your God.*

27 *And you murmured in your tents and you said: Because the Lord hated us, he brought us out of the land of Egypt to hand us over into the power of the Amorites, to exterminate us.*

28 *Where are we going to go? Our brothers have intimidated us, saying: People are bigger and taller than us! Cities are huge and fortified up to the sky! And we even saw sons of Anakim there!*

29 *But I said to you: Do not stand in awe of them and do not be afraid of them.*

30 *The Lord your God is the one going before you; he will fight for you, just as he did for you in Egypt before your very eyes—*

31 *and in the wilderness, where you saw how the Lord your God carried you as a man carries his son—and in every road which you travelled until you came to this place.*

32 *Yet in spite of this, you did not trust in the Lord your God,*

33 *the one who walked ahead of you in the road to seek out a place for you to pitch camp—in the fire by night, to show you in which road you should travel, and in the cloud by day.*

34 *And the Lord heard the sound of your words and he was angry; and he made an oath, saying:*

35 *Not one of these men—this evil generation!—shall see the good land which I promised by oath to give to your fathers.*

36 *Except for Caleb, son of Jephunneh—he shall see it! And to him and to his sons shall I give the land through which he travelled, because he has followed the Lord wholeheartedly.*

37 *Even with me, the Lord was angry on your account, saying: Even you shall not go in there!*

38 But Joshua son of Nun, he who is standing before you, he shall go
in there. Encourage him, for he shall cause Israel to inherit it.

39 And your little ones, whom you said would become captives, and
your children, who today do not distinguish between good and
evil, they will go in there and I shall give it to them and they will
possess it.

40 But as for you, prepare yourselves and set out for the wilderness
by the Reed Sea Road.

41 Then you answered and said to me: We have sinned against the
Lord. We shall go up and we shall fight, just as the Lord our God
commanded us. And every man bound on his weapons of war and
thought it easy to go up to the hill country.

42 And the Lord said to me: Say to them: You will not go up and you
will not fight—for I am not among you—lest you be struck down
before your enemies.

43 So I spoke to you, but you did not listen; and you rebelled against
the command of the Lord, and you acted presumptuously, and
you did go up to the hill country.

44 And the Amorites living in that hill country came out to confront
you and they pursued you as bees do, and they slew you from Seir
as far as Hormah.

45 Then you returned and wept before the Lord, but the Lord did not
listen to your voice and did not pay attention to you.

46 So you remained in Kadesh many days, the days you remained
there.

19 This verse serves as a link between the previous recollections concerning Horeb and the new focus of interest, Kadesh-
barnea; the latter place acted as the first base camp from which an
attack was to be launched on the promised land. The journey took the
Israelites through a *great and terrible wilderness*, namely, an almost
waterless limestone plateau. It was a journey of more than one
hundred miles, and over those dusty and dry miles the prospect of the
promised land must have become very inviting. The journey was
undertaken *just as the Lord commanded us*, a reference perhaps to
the words of the Lord in 1:7.

20-21 Moses then addressed the people again on their arrival
at Kadesh-barnea, and he described the region in which they had
arrived as the land *which the Lord our God is about to give us*.[1]
Kadesh was not literally the land, but on the border of the land. The
call to vision of 1:8 was then reiterated; in 1:8, the call had been a part

1. *About to give* is expressed in Hebrew by the participle of the immediate future; on
its use here and frequently elsewhere in Deut. (1:25; 2:29; 3:20; etc.), see P. Joüon,
Grammaire de l'Hébreu Biblique (1947), p. 339; W. F. Stinespring, "The Participle of
the Immediate Future and Other Matters Pertaining to Correct Translation in the OT,"
in H. T. Frank and W. L. Reed, eds., *Translating and Understanding the OT.*
Festschrift H. G. May (1970), pp. 64-70.

ל ה ל אֶת

of the words of the Lord which Moses addressed to the people. Here, Moses was encouraging the people by repeating the Lord's word to them. They were to *take possession* of the land in obedience to the command of *the Lord God of your fathers,* a further reference to the continuity of their God and the God of the patriarchs. The verb used (*yārash*) has the sense both of "possessing" and "dispossessing"; the land to which they were going was already inhabited, and in order to possess it, the Israelites must first dispossess the former inhabitants. The "dispossessing" of the Canaanites was going to require strength and courage; hence the words of Moses close with a call for courage: *Do not be afraid and do not be dismayed.*[2]

22   The words of Moses in the two previous verses have stressed the great vision of the land lying before them which God would give to them. The people, perhaps lacking the vision of Moses, wanted to take practical measures first. They requested that spies be sent ahead to *explore the land;* the spies would then be able to advise on the best line of attack and give the people some idea of the kind of opposition to expect and the size of the cities.

23   Moses approved the plan and appointed twelve men, *one man per tribe.* In the parallel account (Num. 13:1f.), the command to send men was made by the Lord to Moses; the extra information added here indicates, perhaps, that though the plan was initiated by the people, Moses first consulted with the Lord and received divine approval and injunction.

24   The spies entered enemy territory, came to the Eshcol Valley, and *explored it on foot.*[3] Eshcol was a valley or wadi in the region of Hebron; the exact location of the ancient site is not known.[4]

2.   There is a difficulty introduced in the Hebrew at this point which is not evident in the English translation. The Hebrew alternates between the 2nd person singular and the 2nd plural in the forms of verbs and pronouns (both appear in English as "you, your," etc.). The previous verses were in the plural, this is in the singular, and the alternation continues in the succeeding verses. There have been a number of attempts to explain this anomaly, none of which has been entirely satisfactory, and the matter remains something of a mystery. G. Minette de Tillesse (*VT* 12 [1962], pp. 29-87) suggests that the plural passages are later additions which introduce the concept of conditional rewards and punishments; see also H. Cazelles, "Passages in the Singular Within Discourses in the Plural of Deut. 1-4," *CBQ* 29 (1967), pp. 207-219. In contrast, N. Lohfink, *Das Hauptgebot* (1963), pp. 239-260, discussing the problem as it appears in the later chapters of the book, is doubtful whether the interchange in number indicates a composite narrative. He suggests the singular material is parenetic in character, the plural principally historical, and the abrupt changes were used to stimulate the listeners' attention. None of the proposed solutions is entirely convincing, and for the moment the problem remains unsolved.
3.   The verb *rāgal* (here Piel) is a denominative formation from the noun "foot." The object of the verb in MT is "it"; however, the Qumran evidence suggests that the object was "the land" (*h'rṣ;* see *DJD* I, p. 54), a reading that has support from the Vulgate, Syriac, and Coptic versions.
4.   D. Baly, *Geographical Companion to the Bible,* p. 171.

LINCOLN CHRISTIAN COLLEGE

The general region is known, however; there are vineyards even today in the vicinity of Hebron that are famous for the quality of their grapes.[5] The land that the spies explored was a striking contrast to the great and terrible wilderness through which the Israelites had recently passed.

25 As Moses continues his recollection, he is selective in his choice of topics. In this verse he recollects how the spies returned, bringing not only news, but also samples of the fruit of the land; it was a good land that they were about to possess.

26-28 In contrast, the people's vision had been not on the goodness of the land, but on the difficulty they would experience in possessing it. Hence they were rebellious and unwilling to go up and possess the land. As they saw the land, its conquest was full of difficulty—as Moses saw it, it was the promised land that the Lord was about to give them as he had promised. The "facts" were the same for both, but Moses, the man of vision and faith, could minimize the difficulties because of his strong conviction in the Lord's promise; the people, with little vision, could not lift their sight above the formidableness of their opponents.

The people's rebellion completely perverted their understanding of the nature of their God. They said *the Lord hated us,* and yet the essence of the covenant was the *love* of God. They said their God had only brought them out of Egypt to deliver them *into the power*[6] *of the Amorites:* the truth of the Exodus was that the Lord had brought them out of Egypt and would deliver the Amorites into their hands. They said that God would *exterminate* them; the purpose of God was to give them life.

The information that the spies had brought back had thoroughly terrified the Israelites (note in 1:21 the admonition not to be afraid). Their enemies were bigger than they were, as enemies usually are when a man is afraid (the contrast with David and Goliath is noteworthy!). Their enemies' cities were *fortified*[7] *up to the sky,* and to cap it all, there were even *Anakim*[8] in the land.

29 Moses recollects how again he encouraged the people, urging them not to fear (see 1:21). The remembrance of former en-

5. G. T. Manley, *NBD,* p. 391.
6. *Into the power* (lit. "into the hand of"). The idiom is common, not only in Deut., but also in other Near Eastern historical texts; see the examples in B. Albrektson, *History and the Gods* (1967), p. 39.
7. Contrast the statement here with 28:52. The Israelites would be in fortified cities, trusting in their strong walls—but without God, the walls would be useless. Here, if the Lord is in the midst of his people, the walls of the enemy are equally useless.
8. The Anakim were traditionally giants; see the comments in G. A. Smith, *The Book of Deuteronomy,* pp. 19f. Though the word probably came to be used as a general term for "giants" (LXX renders *giganton*), in more ancient times it probably referred to a particular tribe or ethnic group. In the Egyptian Execration Texts, reference is made to a "ruler of Iy-'anaq" (*ANET,* p. 328).

couragements and former failures continues the procedure in Moses' address of employing the past both to encourage and to warn the people about the future.

30-31   The reason why the Israelites need not have feared is now provided; their God went ahead of them, and with such a precursor, the murmurings of the people (vv. 27-28) were futile. If the enemies they encountered were strong, they were to remember that the Lord *will fight for you*. It was a lesson that the Israelites should have learned already at the Exodus, for in the great hymn celebrating that event, they had extolled the Lord as a "Man of War" (Exod. 15:4).[9] This is the event referred to in v. 30b: *just as he did for you*[10] *in Egypt before your very eyes*. Their God would help them not only in war, but also in the dangers of their journeys. In the terrors of the wilderness (see 1:19), the Israelites had already experienced *how the Lord your God carried you just as a man carries his son*.[11] The father/son imagery is one of several ways in which the theme of the *love* of God is developed in Deuteronomy (see Introduction). Although the theme of love reflects to some extent the treaty terminology, in this context it seems to be a more general use of language to elaborate on the protective care of a fatherly God.[12]

32   In spite of having already experienced both the strength and protection of God, still the people did not trust him. This short verse emphasizes once again the need of the reflection on history in the address of Moses. To experience God in their history was not sufficient for the people; they had to be constantly reminded of that experience in order to overcome their anxieties which tended to blot out the memory.

33   The address of Moses reverts again to the theme introduced in v. 30.[13] God would go ahead of the people *to seek out a place for you to pitch camp*.[14] The words *to seek out* (Heb. *tûr*) introduce an

9.   On some of the theological difficulties of this verse and the associated ideas, see P. D. Miller, *Interpretation* 19 (1965), pp. 39-46; P. C. Craigie, *SJT* 22 (1969), pp. 183-88; R. Tomes, *SJT* 22 (1969), pp. 455-478.

10.   On the syntax of *'et* (plus pronominal suffix) in this verse, see R. J. Williams, *Hebrew Syntax* (1967), p. 61 (no. 341); the particle is used to express *advantage*.

11.   The syntax of vv. 30-31 is somewhat abrupt; the introduction to v. 31 (*and in the wilderness* . . .) appears to return to the theme, introduced in v. 30, of the Lord *going before you*. The second abrupt transition in v. 31 (*—and in every road* . . .) also returns to the theme introduced in v. 30.

12.   See also Deut. 8:5; 32:5; cf. D. J. McCarthy, *CBQ* 27 (1965), pp. 144-47. See also Paul's use of the theme in his address in the synagogue at Antioch in Pisidia (Acts 13:18).

13.   The same rather abrupt syntax is evident here as in v. 31. The verse begins with the theme of God walking ahead; it comments briefly on the theme (*to seek out a place*), then returns to the theme: "(he who walked ahead of you) in the fire by night. . . ."

14.   The LXX (*hodēgōn*) suggests the Heb. root *nhh*, "to guide," which is possible if metathesis is assumed to have taken place. The translation would then read: "to seek out a place for you, *to guide you* in the fire by night. . . ."

ironic element. With God "seeking out/exploring" the land ahead of them, there was no ground for rebellion and fear, but the people could not lift their sight above the fears induced by the reports of their own men who *explored* the land ahead of them.

34-35 Although the words of rebellion had been whispered in the secrecy of the tents (v. 27), the Lord knew of the Israelites' rebellion and was angry: *he made an oath.* The verb used (Niph. of *shāba‘*) is the same as that employed for the covenant promise to the patriarchs and to the Israelites. The promise was contingent on obedience in the context of the covenant, and hence the rebellion of the people against the first oath of God (which held out the promise of the land) induced another oath with a less pleasant prospect. The oath made here, however, applied to one rebellious generation; the promise of the first oath passed from generation to generation and was still the promise Moses held out to the people on the plains of Moab. The substance of the oath was that *this evil generation*[15] would not see the promised land. This element of Moses' recollection acts as a further warning to the people whom he addressed. Rebellion and disobedience could mean that they too would not see the promised land. But there is more than warning in this verse; it was just because there was a new generation gathered at Moab, with new hope among them, that the renewal of the covenant was necessary before launching the attack on the promised land.

36 There was to be one exception to the oath; Caleb and his family would be granted the privilege of seeing the promised land. Caleb and his sons would be given the land *through which he travelled.* The verb *travelled (dārak)* might have a future point of reference (i.e., be equivalent to a future perfect tense in English), or it may be indicative of action completed in the past. Caleb was one of the spies sent out from Kadesh (Num. 13:6), and in spite of the dangers in the land he had explored, he had advocated immediate attack (Num. 13:30). Thus the promise contained in this verse seems to signify that when the land was possessed, Caleb would be apportioned the good fruit-growing land through which he had travelled as a spy. In Josh. 15:13, Caleb was given land in the vicinity of Hebron, in the same vicinity, that is, as the valley of Eshcol which he had explored on foot. The general reason given here for Caleb's special promise is *because*[16] *he has followed the Lord wholeheartedly.* The Hebrew idiom, rendered literally, would be: "he completely filled (himself) after the Lord"; although English does not have an exactly equivalent idiom,

---

15. The LXX omits this phrase; it is probable that it is a later addition to the MT, since its position in the Heb. sentence is rather awkward.

16. "Because," *ya‘an,* is used with an oracular function; i.e., it introduces words spoken either by God himself, or by a representative of God. See D. E. Gowan, "The Use of *ya‘an* in Biblical Hebrew," *VT* 21 (1971), pp. 168-185.

the literal translation gives some sense of the total obedience and dedication of Caleb.

37 The Hebrew word order places the emphasis on Moses in this verse, so that his statement approaches indignation: *Even with me,* he says, speaking of himself; *"Even you,"* quoting the Lord's words addressed to him. The reason for Moses' exclusion from the promised land, in this context,[17] seems to be directly related to his responsibility for the Israelites (i.e., *on your account*) before the Lord. Although Moses was personally without blame for the failures of the Israelites at Kadesh-barnea, his identification with the people as their leader meant that he also accepted with them the result of their failure.

38 Because Moses would not go into the land with the new generation of the people, a new leader would have to be appointed, namely, Joshua. It is not clear, in the context of the address, whether this verse means that Joshua was singled out for leadership as early as Kadesh-barnea,[18] or whether Moses' recollection of his own debarment from the land prompts an aside, referring to the present; Joshua, *he who is standing before you* (now), was going to take Moses' place (see Deut. 31:1-29).

39 Along with Caleb, those children who were beneath the age of discernment *(who today do not distinguish between good and evil)* would be permitted to enter the promised land; their age freed them from any responsibility for the cowardly position adopted by the adults. It seems, too, that the adults had used the children *(whom you said would become captives)* as an excuse in their rebellion against the command of the Lord. Their concern for the children was valid, but it was misplaced since it implied that the Lord ("who carried you just as a man carries his son," v. 31) was not able to protect his own people, young and old alike.

40 Moses' address now returns to those who had been debarred from the promised land because of disobedience. They were to *set out for the wilderness by the Reed Sea*[19]*Road.* The Reed Sea Road ran to the east of Kadesh-barnea, extending from Elath in the south to the southern region of the Dead Sea (by Zoar) in the north.[20]

17. That is, the reference here is not to the incident described in Num. 20:10-12, in which Moses presumptuously struck the rock with his rod. That incident took place some time after the events described in the region of Kadesh. See the discussion of the problem in S. R. Driver, *Deuteronomy,* pp. 26f.
18. In Num. 27:15-18, the appointment of Joshua is described as taking place several years after the events at Kadesh-barnea.
19. Heb. *yam šup* is Reed (*sûp*) Sea, not the Red Sea, as often translated; it was located at some point between the northern limit of the Red Sea and the Mediterranean coastline of northern Egypt. See W. Stinespring, "Some Remarks on the New English Bible," in J. Reumann, ed., *Understanding the Sacred Text* (1972), pp. 92-94.
20. See Y. Aharoni, *The Land of the Bible,* p. 53 and map 14 (p. 186).

41 Too late, the people finally responded to the earlier command to go in and possess the land: *We shall go up and we shall fight.*
. . . But they were inspired by a false confidence, and the momentary confidence that elicited their words was primarily a result of their final realization of the enormity of their rebellion against the Lord. The statement, made in shame, had still no real appreciation of what it was that their God was demanding of them: they had *thought it easy to go up to the hill country.* There was a fine balance in the nature of the covenant that they constantly failed to grasp. First, they could not really trust in the Lord, who would fight for them and protect them. Then, when they rose to shallow confidence in the Lord, they forgot the seriousness of their task.

42 The Israelites could only have success when the Lord was with them—then they needed fear nothing. But disobedience meant that the Lord could withdraw his presence. So the Lord told Moses to forbid the people to fight; if they did fight, disaster would meet them, for the Lord said: *I am not among you.* To a young aspiring nation, whose future lay in the hands of their covenant God, there could hardly have been a more awful proclamation.

43 But the perversity of the people continued. Moses warned them, but they failed to heed the warning; they rebelled against this command just as they had rebelled against the first command. *You acted presumptuously*—the verb (*zûd*) suggests an action undertaken with insolence, which was just the attitude taken by the Israelites toward their God.

44 The result of their insolent and presumptuous action was inevitable. When the Israelites met the Amorites, they were defeated and put to flight, because the Lord was not in their midst. Going out to meet the enemy, "every man bound on his weapons of war" (1:41); but without the presence of their God, they were as naked men on the battlefield. The Amorites pursued them *as bees do,*[21] a suggestive simile describing the headlong flight of the Israelites from the battle. The simile is reversed in Deut. 7:20 (see commentary). The Israelites were pursued by the Amorites as far as *Hormah,* a town to the northeast of Kadesh-barnea.[22]

45-46 Like spoiled children, whose insolence had achieved nothing for them, the Israelites returned to Kadesh and *wept before the Lord,* to no avail. In the recollections of Kadesh-barnea, it would have been very easy for those listening to Moses' address (and for the

---

21. See the similar use of language in Ps. 118:12; Isa. 7:18 (and see E. J. Young, *The Book of Isaiah* I [1965], pp. 296f.).
22. Y. Aharoni, *The Land of the Bible,* map 13 (p. 180). It is possible, however, to take the term as a general description rather than a specific site; see W. M. F. Petrie, *Palestine and Israel* (1934), p. 66. The word means something like "devoted to destruction."

modern reader!) to be astonished and critical at the sheer perversity of the Israelites; in a sense, such a reaction is called for in Moses' address. But the words of Moses held out warning, for the events at Kadesh-barnea typified man's natural tendency to perversity. It was easy looking back to see the errors and failures, but at that time and in those circumstances it was not so easy. And it was just because the Israelites, gathered in the plains of Moab, would soon be faced with similar temptations to rebellion that now—before crossing the Jordan—it was important to warn them of the dangers lying ahead.

3. RECOLLECTIONS OF MOUNT SEIR (2:1-8)

1 *Then we turned and we set out for the wilderness by the Reed Sea Road, just as the Lord had said to me; and we went around Mount Seir many days.*

2 *And the Lord spoke to me saying:*

3 *You have spent long enough going around this mountain. Turn yourselves toward the north,*

4 *and command the people, saying: You are about to pass through the territory of your brethren, the sons of Esau, they who dwell in Seir. And they will be afraid of you, so you will take great care.*

5 *Do not engage them in war, for I shall not give you a portion of their land, even so much as a stepping place for the sole of the foot, because I have given Mount Seir to Esau for a possession.*

6 *You shall purchase food from them with silver, so that you may eat, and you shall even buy water from them with silver, so that you may drink.*

7 *For the Lord your God has blessed you in all the work of your hands. He knew of your travelling through this great wilderness. These forty years, the Lord your God was with you. You have not lacked a thing.*

8 *So we passed on, away from our brethren, the sons of Esau who dwell in Seir, away from the Arabah Road, away from Elath and from Ezion-geber. And we turned and we passed onto the Wilderness of Moab Road.*

1 After spending a long time in the oasis at Kadesh-barnea, the Israelites set out once again at the command of the Lord through Moses:*just as the Lord had said to me.* They set out in a southeasterly direction toward the Gulf of Aqaba, and spent many days travelling in the vicinity of Mount Seir, the mountain range of Edom, south of the Dead Sea and extending down the eastern flank of the Arabah.

2-3 The Lord addressed Moses again. The people had spent long enough in the vicinity of Mount Seir and now the command came:*Turn yourselves toward the north.* The departure from Kadesh, a place associated with failure, had been in a southeasterly direction, *away* from the promised land. Now, at last, the command had come to turn again northward, in the direction of the promised land. But there were particular instructions about the route and the procedure the people should follow.

4 The exact route the Israelites took is uncertain, but it may have been around the southern border of Edom (i.e., the land occupied by the sons of Esau) and then up the eastern border following the caravan route alongside the desert.[1] The territory of Edom, or Mount Seir, is described as belonging to *your brethren, the sons of Esau*. The settling of this land by Esau, brother of Jacob, is described in Gen. 36:1-8, and here in Deuteronomy the descendants of Esau were still looked on with relative equanimity. At a later date, Edom was thought of with more enmity.[2] However, because of the tension, evoked by fear,[3] between the descendants of Esau and the Israelites, the people were to act cautiously.

5 *Do not engage them in war*—since the territory was not a part of the area designated as the promised land, there was to be no fighting; war was to be undertaken only with the object of dispossessing former inhabitants in order that the Israelites might possess the land promised to them by the Lord. *Because I have given Mount Seir to Esau for a possession*[4]—the Israelite understanding of the nature of their God extended beyond the boundaries of their own covenant society. The Lord had promised to give his own people a land; but other peoples, too, had been granted possessions by God. This verse is one of several clues in Deuteronomy to the concept of the nature of God and the realm of his power over peoples and nations other than Israel.

6 Following the words of the Lord (vv. 3-5), the narrative now returns to the words of Moses. The people were given instructions to purchase food and water during their passage through Mount Seir,[5] in this way seeking to avoid unnecessary tension with the descendants of Esau. On the route they followed, the purchase of

1. There are useful comments on the geographical aspects in G. A. Smith, *The Book of Deuteronomy*, pp. 30f.
2. Jer. 49:7-22; Obad. 8-21.
3. The fear had been anticipated in the Exodus "Song of the Sea": "now are the chiefs of Edom dismayed" (Exod. 15:15).
4. There may be a parallel to the events described here in the Ugaritic Keret Legend. See C. F. A. Schaeffer, *Cuneiform Texts from Ras Shamra-Ugarit* (1939), p. 75. King *Pbl* sends a messenger to King Keret: "Beset not '*udm* the Great, even '*udm* abundant in water. '*udm* is the gift of El, even the present of the Father of Men." Translation from J. Gray, *The KRT Text in the Literature of Ras Shamra* (²1964), p. 14. The general parallel is interesting: "'*udm* is the gift of El," but whether the sense here is similar to that in Deut., namely that Mount Seir (Edom) was God's gift to the sons of Esau, is uncertain. See the discussion in Gray, *ibid.*, p. 53.
5. Note that while this incident is described in Num. 20:19, the overall account in Deut. is once again a shortened and selective account, the choice of materials and emphases being determined by the purpose of the historical prologue in Deuteronomy.

water might have been a practical necessity, for water was scarce in eastern Edom and closely guarded by those living near the springs and wells.

7 They could afford to deal equitably with the inhabitants of Mount Seir because *the Lord your God has blessed you in all the work of your hands.* [6] With the failures at Kadesh now in the past, and with the people moving again toward the promised land, Moses was able to give some comfort to his people: *He knew of your travelling through this great wilderness.* For forty years God had been with his people and provided for their needs, despite their failures at Kadesh.

8 In the short account in Deuteronomy, the details of the journey through the region of Mount Seir are not specified. The account is concluded with some rather vague words describing the departure of the Israelites away from their brethren, *away from the Arabah Road,* [7] *away from Elath and from Ezion-geber,* located at the northern limit of the Gulf of Aqaba. [8]

The second part of v. 8 marks the conclusion of the recollections of Mount Seir and leads into the next section, the recollections of Moab and Ammon. *The Wilderness of Moab Road* followed the eastern border of Moab, lying between the habitable land and the desert.

4. RECOLLECTIONS OF MOAB AND AMMON (2:9-25)

9 *And the Lord said to me: Do not treat Moab as an enemy and do not engage with them in battle, for I shall not give you any of their land as a possession, because I gave Ar as a possession to the sons of Lot.*

10 *Formerly the Emim lived there, a people that were great and numerous and tall like the Anakim.*

11 *They too are considered to be Rephaim like the Anakim, but the Moabites called them Emim.*

12 *And formerly the Horites lived in Seir, but the sons of Esau dispossessed them and exterminated them from before them and settled down in place of them, just as Israel has done to the land of its possession, which the Lord gave to them.*

13 *Now, get up and cross over the brook Zered. So we crossed over the brook Zered.*

14 *And the time that we travelled from Kadesh-barnea until we crossed over the brook Zered was thirty-eight years, until the whole generation, namely the men of war, were finished from the*

---

6.   MT has singular "hand"; there is good evidence, however, for reading the plural "hands" (several Heb. mss., Sam., LXX, Syriac, Vulgate).

7.   Y. Aharoni, *The Land of the Bible,* map 14 (p. 186).

8.   Elath and Ezion-geber may be two places very close to each other. It is more likely that there are here two names for the same site; see N. Glueck, "The Topography and History of Ezion Geber and Elath," *BASOR* 72 (1938), pp. 2-13.

midst of the encampment, just as the Lord had sworn by oath to them.

15 *And indeed the hand of the Lord was against them to cast them in confusion from the midst of the encampment, until they were finished.*

16 *And so when all the men of war were completely deceased from the midst of the people,*

17 *then the Lord spoke to me saying:*

18 *Today, you are about to cross the border of Moab, that is Ar.*

19 *And you shall approach to opposite the sons of Ammon. Do not treat them as an enemy and do not engage them in battle, because I shall not give to you as a possession any of the land of the sons of Ammon, for I gave it as a possession to the sons of Lot.*

20 *That too was considered to be the land of the Rephaim. Formerly the Rephaim lived there, but the Ammonites called them Zamzummim,*

21 *a people that were great and numerous and tall like the Anakim, and the Lord exterminated them from before them and they dispossessed them and settled down in place of them,*

22 *just as he did for the sons of Esau, who are living in Seir, before whom he annihilated the Horites and they dispossessed them and they settled down in place of them until this very day.*

23 *And as for the Avvim, living in the villages as far as Gaza, the Caphtorim, coming from Caphtor, annihilated them and they settled down in place of them.*

24 *Get up! Begin your journey and cross over the Arnon Valley. Look! I have delivered into your power the Amorite Sihon, king of Heshbon, together with this land. Begin to take possession and engage with him in battle.*

25 *This very day, I shall begin to put the dread of you and the fear of you upon the peoples that are under all the heavens, who have heard report of you, and they tremble and are weak because of you.*

9 The Moabites were to be treated with a similar respect to that shown to the descendants of Esau. Moab, a land lying to the east of the Dead Sea, was named after the incestuous son of Lot (Gen. 19:37). Because the land had been allocated to the descendants of Lot *as a possession*, the Israelites were not to provoke fighting, for the land was not a part of their "promised land." *Ar* appears here to be a synonym for Moab (see also v. 18), though it may in certain contexts refer to one of the principal cities in Moab (see Num. 21:28).

10-12 These three verses comprise one of several explanatory notes which apparently have been inserted into the original text of the address of Moses.[1] The verses provide brief comments of his-

1. See M. H. Segal, *The Pentateuch*, p. 95. At what point in time the explanatory note was added is uncertain; see the comments in the introductory section on "Date and Authorship."

torical interest regarding the background to the events that are being recounted in the address. In v. 9, Moses had been recounting the Lord's words to him, and that section finishes in v. 13a after this explanatory note.

The *Emim* (apparently a Moabite rather than a Hebrew word)[2] were the predecessors of those descendants of Lot who inhabited Moab at the time of Israel's passage. On the *Anakim,* see the commentary at 1:28. The *Rephaim* were also inhabitants of Palestine in more ancient times (see Gen. 15:20), though they had almost died out by the time of the Israelites (see Deut. 3:11). Whether the terms *Emim* and *Rephaim* are ethnic terms, or whether they are simply descriptive in function, is uncertain; they may mean simply the "terrible ones" and the "defunct ones" respectively. In later passages in the OT the *Rephaim* appear to be shades or ghosts, a sense already known in the Canaanite (Ugaritic) literature from a date slightly earlier than the time of Moses.[3]

The *Horites* were the Hurrians, a non-Semitic people who appear in groups at various places in Syria and Palestine (and in Mesopotamia);[4] those living in the region of Seir had been displaced by the descendants of Esau. The displacement of the Horites was analogous to the Israelites' possessing of their own land: *just as Israel has done to the land of its possession.* This latter clause is one of the indications that the verses (10-12) were added at some point after the address on the plains of Moab.

13 *Now, get up and cross over the brook Zered*—these may be the words of Moses, or they may conclude the words of the Lord to Moses which were begun in v. 9. The brook Zered ran through one of the wadis extending from the southeast of the Dead Sea, though its exact location is uncertain. It seems to have constituted the southern boundary of Moab. In contrast to the disobedience and failure associated with Kadesh-barnea, the address of Moses indicates how at Zered there was a new spirit among the people. The command to cross over was followed by obedience: *so we crossed over the brook Zered.*

14 The crossing of the Zered marked an important point in

2. The evidence of the Moabite Stone suggests that Hebrew and Moabite were closely related languages which differed only in a dialectal sense. On the presence of foreign words in Hebrew, here and at 2:20; 3:9, see E. Ullendorff, "The Knowledge of Languages in the OT," *BJRL* 44 (1962), pp. 455-465.
3. For later biblical passages, see *NBD,* p. 1084. The Rephaim are still puzzling and have been the subject of much study: see J. Gray, "The Rephaim," *PEQ* 81 (1949), pp. 127-139; *idem,* "DTN and RPUM in Ancient Ugarit," *PEQ* 84 (1952), pp. 39-41; A. Jirku, "Rapa'u, der Fürst der Rapa'uma—Rephaim," *ZAW* 77 (1965), pp. 82f.; A. Caquot, "Les rephaim ougaritiques," *Syria* 37 (1960), pp. 75-93.
4. See H. W. F. Saggs, *The Greatness That Was Babylon* (1968), pp. 91f.; G. Roux, *Ancient Iraq* (1966), pp. 210-13; I. J. Gelb, *Hurrians and Subarians* (1944).

the history of the wilderness wanderings. Thirty-eight years had elapsed since the departure of the Israelites from Kadesh-barnea,[5] and during that time the rebellious generation, who had been debarred from the promised land by the oath of the Lord (see 1:35), had all died. The language with which they are described is slightly sarcastic; they are called *the men of war,* which is just what they should have been, had they not failed to obey the command of the Lord. The crossing of the Zered here seems to mark a new beginning. Just as the crossing of the Reed Sea had marked a new beginning of freedom from Egyptian bondage, so the crossing of the Zered marked freedom from the oath of the Lord against the "men of war." And beyond the plain of Moab, where Moses addressed the people, the crossing of the Jordan would mark the beginning of a new era in the freedom of the promised land. The death of the "men of war," employed in Moses' address as a warning, is used in the same manner by Paul in his use of history for instruction.[6]

15 This verse elaborates a little further on the unhappy end of the rebellious Israelites. They did not die a natural death from old age, but their end was hastened by the direct action of the Lord. The event is mentioned in the Epistle of Jude (v. 5) as one of the most serious warnings that could be presented; it is followed (Jude 7) by a reference to Sodom and Gomorrah. They are said, among other crimes, to have "rejected authority" (Jude 8), a warning to obedience which the recipients of the Epistle were to heed. The mention of the event of the "men of war" in the NT stresses the nature of history, both there and in Moses' address, as having a didactic function.

16-18 With the final decease of the "men of war," the Lord once again addressed Moses: *you are about to cross the border of Moab.* The translation of this verse poses a number of difficulties,[7] particularly because of the concise nature of the historical account in the address of Moses. If it is correct to interpret v. 13 as the crossing *into* Moab, it seems that v. 18 refers to the preparation for the crossing *out of* Moab and on into the territory of the Ammonites (or Amorites; see below).

19 The Ammonites were to be treated in the same manner as

5. Perhaps the first departure from Kadesh and the unsuccessful campaign against the Amorites mark the beginning of the time span. In this case, many of the thirty-eight years would have been spent in the vicinity of Kadesh-barnea (see 1:46); cf. G. T. Manley, *The Book of the Law,* p. 53.
6. 1 Cor. 10:5-6.
7. See the discussion in A. R. Hulst, *OT Translation Problems* (1960), *ad loc.* The problems arise because: (a) $g^e b\hat{u}l$ can mean "territory" or "boundary"; (b) the verb *'āḇar* can be "travel through" or "cross over"; (c) Ar may be a synonym for Moab, or the name of a town in Moab. Normally any one of these difficulties could be solved by reference to the immediate context. However, with the three problems coming together in an extremely concise piece of writing, the translation is slightly doubtful.

the Moabites, for according to the Hebrew tradition (Gen. 19:38), the Ammonites were the descendants of the second incestuous son of Lot. They occupied land north of Moab, situated between the river Arnon in the south and the Jabbok in the north. The people were to approach *to opposite the sons of Ammon*—that is, when they came to the Arnon, the northern border of Moab, they would be just opposite the territory of the Ammonites.[8]

20-23   These verses constitute a second explanatory note (see vv. 10-12 above). *Zamzummim* is apparently another term foreign to Hebrew, used by the Ammonites to describe their precursors in the land.[9] Whereas vv. 20-22 illustrate the event recounted in Moses' narrative, the comment on the *Avvim* (v. 23; see also Josh. 13:3-4) seems to be added simply as a further example of one people dispossessing another. The Avvim, according to the note, were the ancient village dwellers of southwestern Palestine (*as far as Gaza,* the city considered to be the southern limit of Palestine). They were dispossessed by the *Caphtorim,* apparently an early name for the Philistines, who came to Palestine from *Caphtor* (possibly Crete).[10]

24   Now the address of Moses (citing the words of the Lord) is taken up from where it was left off at the end of v. 19. The command was given to cross the Arnon and move on and attack Sihon, a king ruling an Amorite kingdom from his capital at Heshbon. Sihon's kingdom at the time extended north from the Arnon and between the Dead Sea and the Jordan on the west and the kingdom of the Ammonites on the east. The Israelites could advance with confidence in the word of the Lord to them: *I have delivered into your power*[11] *the Amorite Sihon. . . .* The previous rebellious generation had said in their perversity that the Lord was going to give them into the power of the Amorites (1:27), but to the new and obedient generation, the Amorites were to be delivered into the Israelites' power. At last the Israelites were to begin to taste the promise of the land, for not only would the Lord deliver the Amorites to Israel, but their land also was to be given over.

25   With the promise of the Lord beginning to take effect, *the dread of you and the fear of you* (i.e., of the Israelites) would begin to

---

8.   Josh. 13:25 (in RSV) suggests that in spite of the injunction in Deut. 2:19, some of the Ammonite territory was occupied by the Israelites. For a discussion of this difficulty, see B. Obed, "A Note on Josh. 13:25," *VT* 21 (1971), pp. 239-241.

9.   It is possible that they are the same as the *Zûzîm* (Gen. 14:5).

10.   For discussion of the problem of the identity and origin of the Caphtorim (and the Philistines), see T. C. Mitchell, *NBD,* p. 199; J. Prignaud, "Caftorim et Keretim," *RB* 71 (1964), pp. 215-229; Buis and Leclercq, *Le Deutéronome,* p. 47; W. F. Albright, *Cambridge Ancient History* (rev. ed.) fascicle 51 (1966), pp. 24-33; A. Malamat (ch. 2) and B. Mazar (ch. 8) in *The World History of the Jewish People* III (1971).

11.   *Into your power* (lit. "hand")—the same idiom is used in one of the Mari Letters (see *ANET*, p. 623).

take hold of the Canaanites. *Who have heard report of you*—these words may refer to the Exodus from Egypt, where the event was celebrated as a victory which would strike terror into the hearts of the Canaanite chiefs (Exod. 15:14-16). The Moabite "Oracles of Balaam" indicate that the news of the Exodus had become well known (see Num. 23:22 and 24:8). The crossing of the brook Zered had marked the end of a "rebellious generation"; the crossing of the Arnon marked the beginning of Israel's possessing of the land east of the Jordan.

5. THE CONQUEST OF HESHBON (2:26-37)[1]

26 *Then I sent messengers from the wilderness of Kedemoth to Sihon, king of Heshbon, with words of peace, saying:*

27 *Let me pass through your land. I shall travel only along the highway; I shall not turn aside to the right hand or to the left.*

28 *You will sell me food for silver so that I may eat, and you will give me water for silver so that I may drink. Only let me pass through on foot,*

29 *just as the sons of Esau, who live in Seir, did to me, and the Moabites, who live in Ar, until I cross the Jordan into the land which the Lord our God is about to give us.*

30 *But Sihon, king of Heshbon, was not willing to let us pass through, for the Lord your God had made his spirit stubborn and had made his heart obstinate, in order to deliver him into your power, as at this very day.*

31 *And the Lord said to me: Look! I have begun to give you Sihon and his land. Begin to dispossess in order to possess his land.*

32 *Then Sihon, both he and all his people, came out to battle at Jahaz.*

33 *And the Lord our God delivered him to us and we attacked him and his sons and all his people.*

34 *And we captured all his cities at that time, and we completely destroyed every city, men and women and children. We did not leave anything remaining.*

35 *We took only the cattle as spoil for ourselves, and the booty of the cities which we captured.*

36 *From Aroer, which is on the side of the valley of Arnon, and the city that is in the valley, and as far as Gilead, there was not a town that was too high for us. The Lord our God delivered everything to us.*

1. For specialized literary studies of this section, see W. A. Sumner, "Israel's Encounters with Edom, Moab, Ammon, Sihon and Og according to the Deuteronomist," *VT* 18 (1968), pp. 216-228; J. van Seters, "The Conquest of Sihon's Kingdom: A Literary Examination," *JBL* 91 (1972), pp. 182-197. For both literary and geographical comments, see J. R. Bartlett, "Sihon and Og, Kings of the Amorites," *VT* 20 (1970), pp. 257-277.

37 *Only you did not approach the land of the Ammonites, both banks of the Jabbok Valley, and the cities of the hill country, according to all that the Lord our God had commanded.*

After a peaceful transit through the previous lands, Israel came to the point of conflict; Sihon's land was to be possessed (2:24) and would become a part of the promised land. The way in which the recollection is phrased is such that the emphasis falls on the plan of the Lord to give the Israelites the land. They were not to provoke battle and take aggressive military action; in the plan and promise of the Lord, the means of victory would become plain.

26   The campaign thus began on a peaceful note: messengers of peace were sent ahead of the main body to speak with *Sihon, king of Heshbon.* Sihon, an Amorite king, had his capital city at Heshbon, situated about 15 miles east from the point at which the Jordan runs into the Dead Sea. Here, however, Heshbon probably refers to the whole Amorite kingdom ruled by Sihon. The kingdom extended approximately from the Arnon in the south to the Jabbok in the north, with the Jordan and the Dead Sea forming the western boundary. Some of this territory had been captured by Sihon from the Moabites, an event that has been celebrated in an ancient fragment of victory poetry, the "Song of Heshbon" (Num. 21:27-30). At any event, Sihon's kingdom presented a formidable obstacle to the Israelites. The main body of the people remained in *the wilderness of Kedemoth* while the ambassadors took the message of peace to Sihon. Kedemoth was probably a few miles inside Sihon's territory, north of the Arnon and quite near to the eastern border of the Amorite state.[2]

27-29   The message of the ambassadors to Sihon. The message is phrased in the first person singular, as a personal communique from Moses (representing his people) to Sihon. *I shall travel only along the highway.*[3] Although a large number of people passing through his land would pose a threat for Sihon, the message makes clear the peaceful intent of the Israelites. By keeping to the highway and purchasing food and water, the Israelites would not have ravaged the land or destroyed the crops; they would, in fact, have brought some material prosperity to the Amorites. The good intention lying behind the message is stressed in two ways (v. 29). First, the Israelites had already passed through Seir and Moab peacefully; their transit had not been without incident, as is clear in the account in Numbers, but there had not been war. The reference to Seir and Moab strengthens Moses' statement that he simply wanted to pass through

2.   Y. Aharoni, *The Land of the Bible,* map 14 (p. 186).
3.   Heb. *badderek badderek*—"in the highway, in the highway." See GKC § 123 e.

the Amorite territory. Second, Moses makes it clear that the Amorite territory was not his main objective: *until I cross the Jordan into the land which the Lord our God is about to give us.* As events turned out, the Amorite territory became a part of Israelite land, but the substance of the covenant promise lay beyond the Jordan.[4]

30 Sihon, however, *was not willing to let us pass through.* Whether his unwillingness stemmed from fear, or whether it was confidence in his own military strength, is uncertain. It may well have been confidence, for he had already experienced military successes against the Moabites. The *spirit (rûaḥ)* and *heart (lēḇāḇ),* in this context, probably refer respectively to the "will" and "mind" of Sihon. It should be noted that the words here express an understanding of Sihon's action in retrospect. In the account in Numbers (21:23), Sihon's actions are attributed to unfriendliness. But beyond the event, it was possible to look back and see the event in the context of the plan of God. Thus the statements about Sihon *(the Lord your God had made his spirit stubborn . . .)* do not reflect a view of determinism, but reflect rather a part of the Hebrew theology of history.[5] Man is free and responsible in action, but the actions of all men are set within the sphere of history, and God was the Lord of history.[6]

31 *Look!*—see also 1:8, 21, and the commentary at that point. *Begin to dispossess in order to possess his land*—the translation is somewhat doubtful because of the peculiar idiom used in the Hebrew.[7] A simpler rendering would be: "begin to possess his land."[8]

32 Sihon came out to engage the Israelites in battle at *Jahaz;*[9] though the ancient site is not known with certainty, it appears to have been a few miles to the north of Kedemoth, and is probably to be related to the modern Khirbet el-Medeiyneh.[10]

33-36 The battle at Jahaz. Verse 33 indicates in a different way the Hebrew understanding of God in history, of which warfare was a part. *The Lord our God delivered him to us*—that is, victory was assured from the start, for the Lord was with his people, participating within the realm of human history. But victory was not miraculous or

---

4. See Keil and Delitzsch, *The Pentateuch,* p. 295.
5. See Buis and Leclercq, *Le Deutéronome,* p. 48.
6. See G. T. Manley and R. K. Harrison, *NBC(R),* pp. 209f.: "The OT steadily refuses to see any inconsistency between human freedom and divine sovereignty." "Because the ancient Hebrews ascribed all causality to God, it was both natural and proper for them to see the response of Sihon in the light of the larger activity of God."
7. See GKC § 69f. The sentence reads: *hāḥēl rāsh lareshet*—"begin, possess to possess." Note that *yārash* has the sense of "possess" and "dispossess."
8. S. R. Driver, *Deuteronomy,* p. 44, considers that the function of *lareshet* is simply to strengthen *rāsh.* Alternatively, following the clue of the LXX, *rāsh* can be deleted, giving in effect the same translation with slightly less force.
9. Jahaz is referred to in line 19 of the inscription on the Moabite Stone: *ANET,* p. 320.
10. Y. Aharoni, *The Land of the Bible,* p. 379.

an act of God alone: *we attacked him and his sons*[11] *and all his people.*
The people of God did not sit back and observe the acts of God; they
entered the battle and experienced the presence of God in their active
obedience and commitment. The cities and their inhabitants were
completely destroyed (or "devoted to destruction"). This practice of
complete destruction (*ḥerem*) was also used by other nations in Palestine;[12] for fuller details, see the commentary on Deut. 20:10-18, in
which the laws of warfare are stated. The battle and the accompanying destruction extended far beyond the battlefield at Jahaz. The city
of *Aroer*, on the northern bank of the Arnon, marked the southern
limit of the victory, and also marked the southern limit of Sihon's
kingdom. *And the city that is in the valley*—this unnamed city may
either have been a suburb of Aroer, further into the valley and close to
the water's edge, or else it may have been further up the valley and
thus it would have indicated the southeastern limit of Sihon's kingdom and of the Israelites' victory.[13] *And as far as Gilead*—these
words define the northern limit of the victory, Gilead[14] being to the
north of Sihon's territory. In all the region that the Israelites conquered, *there was not a town that was too high for us.* At this point the
didactic nature of Moses' address becomes very clear. When the
people had been rebellious at Kadesh-barnea, they had claimed that
the cities they would have to attack were fortified up to the sky (Deut.
1:28); in their fear, they had refused to obey the Lord. In the conquest
of Sihon's kingdom, the people were obedient and their God was with
them; under those circumstances, there was no obstacle too great for
them. Whereas the events at Kadesh-barnea had served as a severe
warning in Moses' address, the victory over Sihon is employed as a
source of strength and encouragement: *The Lord our God delivered
everything to us.*

37   The theme of obedience is reiterated in this concluding
verse. The Israelites did not, in the elation of victory, exceed their
orders and grasp more territory for themselves than had been permitted by the Lord. The territory described in this verse is that of the
Ammonites; the Israelites had already been commanded not to attack
it (Deut. 2:19).

6. THE CONQUEST OF BASHAN (3:1-11)

1 *Then we turned and we went up the Bashan Road; and Og, king of
Bashan, he and all his people, came out for battle at Edrei.*

11.   The consonantal text has the singular, "his son"; the suggested reading (Qere),
supported by the majority of the versions, is the plural "his sons."
12.   See the Moabite Inscription, line 17: *ANET*, p. 320.
13.   See the geographical comment in G. A. Smith, *The Book of Deuteronomy*, p. 44.
14.   For a fuller discussion of Gilead, see M. Ottosson, *Gilead. Tradition and History*
(1969).

2 *And the Lord said to me: Do not fear him, for I have delivered him into your power, along with all his people and his land. And you will do to him just as you did to Sihon, king of the Amorites, who was living in Heshbon.*

3 *And the Lord our God delivered into our power even Og, the king of Bashan, along with all his people, and we smote him until not a single survivor was left to him.*

4 *And we captured all his cities at that time; there was not a town which we did not take from them: sixty cities, all the region of Argob, the kingdom of Og in Bashan.*

5 *All these were cities fortified by high walls, gates, and bars, besides a very large number of unprotected cities.*

6 *And we completely destroyed them, just as we did to Sihon, king of Heshbon, destroying every city, men, women, and children.*

7 *But we took as booty for ourselves all the cattle and the spoil of the cities.*

8 *And at that time we took the land from the power of the two kings of the Amorites who were in Transjordan, from the Arnon Valley up to Mount Hermon—*

9 *the Sidonians call Hermon Sirion, but the Amorites call it Senir—*

10 *all the cities of the plateau, and all Gilead, and all Bashan to Salecah, and Edrei, the cities of the kingdom of Og in Bashan.*

11 *For only Og, the king of Bashan, remained from the last of the Rephaim. Indeed his couch was an iron couch: is it not in Rabbah of the Ammonites? It is nine cubits long and four cubits wide according to the common cubit.*

1   The account of the victory over Sihon's kingdom is followed by a description of the next military success of the Israelites, this time over *Og, king of Bashan.* Bashan was the northernmost district of Transjordan, and its southern border, normally marked by the Yarmuk, was probably farther south in the region of Gilead during the reign of Og. Bashan was a rich and fertile land, whose prosperity was referred to scathingly at a later date by the prophet Amos (4:1).

The conquest of Bashan took the Israelites off their route slightly, in that the land lay considerably to the north of the point at which they would cross the Jordan for the conquest of western Palestine. From a military point of view, the conquest of Bashan was wise, for it meant that the right flank of the Israelites would be protected when they prepared to cross the Jordan for the main assault.[1] The battle took place in the vicinity of Edrei, a city located on one of the tributaries of the Yarmuk, and apparently one of the royal residences of Og (Deut. 1:4).

2   The word of the Lord came to Moses again, urging courage because Og, his people and his land, would be delivered into the

---

1.   G. A. Smith (*The Book of Deuteronomy*, p. 46) notes that Pompey attempted the same tactic and that, at a later date, the first Muslim invaders used a similar tactic successfully.

power of the Israelites. This time the word of encouragement was able to draw upon the experience of the Israelites. They had seen already, in the conquest of Heshbon, that the Lord's promise was good and one on which they could depend.

In the concise nature of this recollection, the entire battle is virtually reduced to this one verse. *The Lord our God delivered into our power even Og.* The theology is important; there is no doubt that the people were involved in the reality of the battle, but in the recollection of military success, that success was seen as the Lord's doing. Hence in this verse, God's action is referred to first; he delivered Og into the Israelites' power. Man's action is stated second: *and we smote him until not a single survivor was left to him.* The same total destruction, or *herem,* was applied to the kingdom of Bashan as it had been to the kingdom of Heshbon (see Deut. 2:34).

4   The Israelite victory was a total success: *there was not a town which we did not take from them: sixty cities*—the number seems very large, but it should be remembered that the term "city" does not imply quite the same magnitude as the English word.[2] There were, in fact, many settlements in northern Transjordan (Bashan), largely because of the fertility of the soil and because of Mount Hauran. This mountain, rising in the east of Bashan to a height of more than 5,000 feet, attracted rainfall and extended the usable land further to the east of the Jordan than was the case in southern Transjordan.[3] *The region of Argob*[4]—although the exact details are uncertain, Argob was apparently a fertile region within the larger kingdom; further details are provided at 3:14 (below).

5   Some of the cities were heavily fortified with *high walls* (see also 2:36 and commentary), *gates, and bars.* In addition, there were *unprotected cities*—literally, perhaps, "cities of the country people," or agricultural settlements which were too small, or too poor, to be defended properly.

6   This verse is a summary statement of what was done, but it links up with v. 2. In v. 2, the Lord had said to Moses: *you will do to him just as you did to Sihon.* The faithfulness of the word of the Lord is emphasized in this summary statement after the brief description of the battle: *and we completely destroyed them, just as we did to Sihon* . . . (see also 2:34).

2.   S. R. Driver, *Deuteronomy,* p. 49, cites Wetzstein's comment concerning the region: "the E. and S. slopes of the Jebel Hauran contain some three hundred deserted cities and villages." In recent years, there has been little archeological activity in this area.
3.   Y. Aharoni, *The Land of the Bible,* pp. 34f.
4.   H. Cazelles, *Le Deutéronome* (La Sainte Bible, 1966), translates "the *confederation* of Argob"; this is possible, since the Heb. (*hebel*) may designate either territory or a "band" of men. The verbal root has the sense "bind, pledge." Following Cazelles' rendering, the "confederation" would be in apposition to "sixty cities," viz., those places which made up the confederation.

7 As in the defeat of Sihon (2:35), the cattle and the spoil were kept by the Israelites as booty.

8 This verse is a summary statement of the two conquests, of Heshbon and Bashan respectively; the summary and repetitive statements have to be seen in the context of the address of Moses, where the emphasis and repetition serve to hammer home to the listeners the truth of God's faithfulness. The summary statement indicates the total extent of the conquest east of the Jordan, which extended from the Arnon in the south (the southern border of Sihon's kingdom) to *Mount Hermon* in the north; the whole territory was that of the *two kings of the Amorites who were in Transjordan* (see the commentary on Deut. 1:1). Mount Hermon was a part of the Anti-Lebanon mountain range, its highest point reaching to an altitude of over 9000 feet. As a natural physical barrier, it formed the northern limit of the kingdom of Bashan.

9-11 These verses probably form another of the explanatory notes inserted into the text of the address.[5] Hermon, a natural physical barrier, and therefore often a border between ancient states, was given various names by the kingdoms that surrounded it. The Sidonian name, *Sirion*, is now also known from the Ugaritic texts, coming from a region of Syria to the north of Sidon.[6] The Amorite name, *Senir*, is known in extrabiblical sources from an historical account of Shalmaneser.[7] *All Bashan to Salecah*—the words seem to indicate the eastern limit of Bashan. Salecah is probably to be identified with Ṣalḥad, referred to in a later Nabatean inscription,[8] and lying on the southern heights of Mount Hauran.

Og's kingdom is described as an Amorite kingdom, but he himself was one of the last of the Rephaim (see 2:11). *His couch was an iron couch*—the word *couch ('ereś)* may be rendered better by "sarcophagus"[9] so that the reference would be specifically to the *deceased* Og. *Rabbah* is the modern Amman in Jordan. The *common cubit* (lit. "cubit of a man") appears to have been originally the distance from the elbow to the tip of the middle finger,[10] a distance of approximately 18 inches. Thus the approximate dimensions of Og's sarcophagus or couch would have been 13½ x 6 feet (4.1 x 1.8 m.).

---

5.   M. H. Segal, *The Pentateuch,* p. 95. It is possible that v. 10 should be excluded from the note and linked directly with v. 8.
6.   For the Ugaritic reference, see *CTA* 4.VI.19, 21 (= *UT* 51.VI.19, 21). Cf. Gordon, *UT,* p. 495. For a possible reference in Egyptian Execration Texts, see A. Alt, *Kleine Schriften* III (1959), p. 67.
7.   Cf. I. M. Price, *The Monuments and the OT* ([6]1909), p. 154.
8.   See G. A. Cooke, *A Text-book of North-Semitic Inscriptions* (1903), p. 253.
9.   See *ibid.,* p. 187.
10.   See C. M. Laymon, ed., *The Interpreter's One-Volume Commentary on the Bible* (1971), p. 1283.

7. ALLOCATION OF LAND EAST OF THE JORDAN (3:12-22)

12 *And at that time we possessed this land. I gave to the Reubenites and to the Gadites from Aroer, which is on the bank of the Arnon Valley, and half the hill country of Gilead, together with its cities.*

13 *And I gave the remainder of Gilead, and all Bashan, the kingdom of Og, to the half-tribe Manasseh: and all that land of Bashan is called a land of Rephaim.*

14 *Jair, the Manassite, took the whole region of Argob as far as the boundary of the Geshurites and the Maacathites, and he named them (that is, Bashan) after his own name, Havvoth-jair, as they are to this day.*

15 *And I gave Gilead to Machir.*

16 *And I gave to the Reubenites and to the Gadites a part of Gilead and as far as the Arnon Valley, the middle of the valley as a boundary; and as far as Jabbok, the valley that is a boundary of the Ammonites;*

17 *and the Arabah, and the Jordan as a boundary from Chinnereth and as far as the sea of the Arabah, the salt sea beneath the mountain slopes of Pisgah to the east.*

18 *And at that time I commanded you, saying: The Lord your God has given to you this land to take possession of it. You shall cross over equipped for war before your brethren, the Israelites, all you heroic men!*

19 *Only your women and your children and your cattle—I know that you have many cattle — they will reside in your cities which I gave to you,*

20 *until the Lord grants rest to your brethren as to you, and they too take possession of the land which the Lord your God is about to give them beyond the Jordan. Then each man of you shall return to his possession, which I gave to you.*

21 *Then at that time I commanded Joshua, saying: Your eyes have indeed seen all that the Lord your God has done to these two kings. Just so will the Lord do to all the kingdoms to which you are about to cross over.*

22 *You shall not be afraid of them, because the Lord your God—he is the one fighting for you.*

With the completion of the conquest east of the Jordan, the newly captured land was divided among some of the tribes. In these verses, there is first a description of the division of the land between the tribes (vv. 12-17)[1] and then a reminder to those tribes that, although they

1. These verses contain a number of difficulties, partly grammatical and partly geographical. Segal (*Pentateuch*, p. 95) suggests vv. 13b-17 are added as an explanation of the initial statement; this is uncertain. It seems reasonable to argue that vv. 12-13 state the general allocation of the land and that vv. 14-17 specify it in more detail, either as an addition for clarity, or as an integral part of the address.

had already come into possession of their land, nevertheless their responsibilities had not ceased until the conquest was complete.

12 The general statement in this verse gives in broad outline the territory allocated to the tribes of Reuben and Gad. It extended *from Aroer, which is on the bank*[2] *of the Arnon Valley*—that is, the southern limit of the territory of the two tribes—*and half the hill country of Gilead,* namely, the northern portion of their territory. This block of land allocated to the two tribes was approximately (perhaps exactly) the territory that had formerly been Sihon's kingdom (see Deut. 2:36).

13 The half-tribe Manasseh were given *the remainder of Gilead, and all Bashan.* Both these territories were probably part of Og's kingdom of Bashan. Bashan, as a *geographical* region, extends to the north of the Yarmuk, though under Og, the *kingdom* Bashan included both northern Gilead and the geographical region of Bashan. On the *Rephaim,* see the commentary at 2:11.

14-15 The details of the allocation of territory to the half-tribe Manasseh are now given. *Jair, the Manassite,* received the northern sector of what had formerly been Og's kingdom. This territory consisted of the fertile *region of Argob* (see the commentary at 3:4), the limits of Argob being determined in the north and west by the *boundary of the Geshurites and the Maacathites.*[3] Maacah was a small state to the south of Mount Hermon, probably bridging both banks of the upper reaches of the Jordan; Geshur was another small state, further south than Maacah, situated on the eastern shore of the sea of Chinnereth (later called the sea of Galilee). Jair *named them (that is, Bashan)*[4] *after his own name, Havvoth-jair.*[5] Jair renamed the collection of villages in the territory allocated to him after himself, for he had been the one who was responsible for capturing them from the enemy (Num. 32:41). *And I gave Gilead to Machir*—that is, the northern sector of the geographical region known as Gilead was given to Machir, the southern section going to Reuben and Gad (v. 12). The term *Machir* refers to the descendants of Machir, the son of Manasseh, and came to be used as virtually synonymous with Manasseh.

2. MT *'al naḥal;* the translation above assumes *'al śᵉpaṯ naḥal,* for which there is good evidence from Heb. mss. and the versions.
3. See B. Mazar, "Geshur and Maacah," *JBL* 80 (1961), pp. 16-28. Y. Aharoni, *The Land of the Bible,* map 15 (p. 196). Mazar notes references to Geshur in the Amarna Letters (viz., *ga-ri*) and possible references to Maacah in Egyptian texts.
4. Heb. ("the Bashan") is syntactically anomalous, and seems to be added to clarify "them," apparently the villages of Bashan, for which there is no direct grammatical antecedent.
5. Heb. *hawwāh* probably means "tent villages" (*BDB,* p. 295). Alternatively, it may mean the "house" or even "realm" of Jair, if the Heb. word is taken to be cognate with Ugar. *ḥwt,* "house, dynasty, realm"; see *UT,* p. 395, no. 850. It should be noted, however, that the Ugaritic word is used in a monarchical context.

The allocation of this territory to Machir was because the descendants of Machir had been the ones directly responsible for capturing it from the Amorites (Num. 32:39).

16 The Reubenites' and Gadites' territory is now described in more detail, though it should be noted that the translation of this verse has certain grammatical difficulties.[6] *A part of Gilead*[7]—the southern section of Gilead is intended, as distinct from that portion of it assigned to the half-tribe Manasseh. *And as far as the Arnon Valley, the middle of the valley as*[8] *a boundary*—the valley marked the southern limit of the allocated territory, the river itself being the exact and natural boundary line. *And as far as Jabbok, the valley that is a boundary of the Ammonites*—the Jabbok would have formed the boundary between Gad and the half-tribe Manasseh, but it is possible that the reference here is not to the main valley of Jabbok leading into the Jordan. The note that it was a *boundary of the Ammonites* may specify it as one of the upper tributaries of the Jabbok, specifically the tributary that turned south and then slightly west, forming a kind of semicircle around southeastern Gilead. If this is the case, then the details given here specify the northern border, setting off the territory of Reuben from that of the Gadites, who were located between Reuben (to the south) and the half-tribe Manasseh (to the north).

17 This verse, concluding the short passage describing the allocation of land east of the Jordan, contains details of the western border of all the tribes whose territory has just been defined; it sets off their land from that of their brethren who would be settling west of the river. *The Arabah* defines this western border in its broadest sense, *the Jordan* being one part of the border in the Arabah. The Jordan acted as a boundary from *Chinnereth,* the northern limit, with Geshur on its eastern shore, and as far south as *the sea of the Arabah, the salt sea,* which is now called the Dead Sea. *Pisgah* may be a particular mountain range to the east of the Dead Sea, or perhaps it should be taken as a general term meaning "a ridge crowning a hill or mountain."[9] See further the commentary on Deut. 34:1.

18 When the land had been allocated, Moses had special orders for the tribes who were to settle east of the Jordan. Their land

6. For a general discussion, see A. R. Hulst, *OT Translation Problems,* p. 13.
7. Reading the *min-* as partitive *min;* see GKC § 119 w (n. 2).
8. Heb. has the conjunction "and" /w/; the translation assumes a reading "as" /k/, the consonants /w/ and /k/ being easily confused in early Heb. script, since both were characterized by a strong vertical stroke. Alternatively, the /w/ could be rendered (somewhat artificially) by "also"; see S. R. Driver, *Deuteronomy,* p. 57. The same reading is assumed in the translation "as a boundary" in v. 17, below.
9. See G. T. Manley, *NBD,* p. 1000. See also D. Baly, *Geographical Companion to the Bible,* pp. 53f.; Baly suggests "the Pisgah" has a sense similar to the modern Arab. *neqb,* meaning the high precipitous slope which marks the edge of a plateau. A number of scholars, however, have identified Pisgah with the mountain range or massif of

had not been acquired solely through their own merits: *the Lord your God has given you this land to take possession of it*. The Lord had *given* the land through his victorious presence among all the Israelite tribes, but the other tribes had yet to possess their lands. For this reason, the eastern settlers were reminded of their responsibility to all Israel: *you shall cross over equipped for war*. . . . The reminder was necessary, for it would have been easy for the eastern tribes to lose interest in the remaining conquest, when they were already in possession of their land. Thus Moses' words are a further emphasis on the unity of all Israel. In later times, after the initial stages of the conquest, the eastern tribes sometimes failed their western brethren and came in for severe criticism.[10]

19 Because the tribes addressed by Moses already possessed their land, they could leave the women and children behind. The now deceased rebellious generation had used their children as an excuse for their disobedience (see Deut. 1:39 and commentary); the new generation had obeyed the Lord and their obedience meant that now they could leave their families in the security of their newly acquired towns. *Your cattle—I know that you have many cattle*—the many cattle were the spoil from the initial campaigns (Deut. 2:35 and 3:7). There were many of them because the land east of the Jordan, and particularly Bashan, was ideal cattle country. The emphasis here is on the new wealth of the inheritance of the eastern tribes, for cattle were a far more significant sign of prosperity in the ancient Near East than a healthy bank balance would be in the modern age.

20 They (Reuben, Gad, and the half-tribe Manasseh) were to continue fighting and were not to return to their new homes and their families, until such time as their fellow tribes had also come into possession of their land, *which the Lord your God is about to give them beyond the Jordan*.[11]

21-22 Moses then recalled his command given at that time to Joshua. Although these two verses form a unit by themselves, they follow from what has gone before. The first recollection of history was coming to a close, with the eastern conquest complete and the land having been allocated. One of the more important points in the recollection of history had been Moses' exclusion from the land of promise (Deut. 1:37), so that having reminded the eastern tribes of their

---

which Nebo was the summit; see J. Gray, *Joshua, Judges and Ruth*. Century Bible (1967), p. 125; K. Elliger, *BHH*, col. 1475; Buis and Leclercq, *Le Deutéronome*, p. 53. The modern name is Ras el-Siyaghah.

10. See, e.g., Judg. 5:15-17, where they are criticized for failing to help their brethren in Deborah's war against a Canaanite confederation.

11. On *beʻeber hayyardēn*, see the commentary on Deut. 1:1. The use of the phrase here is one of three occasions where it is used of Palestine west of the Jordan (see also v. 25 and 11:30), rather than Transjordan in general.

responsibilities in the west, he then turned his attention to Joshua, who would take his place and lead the Israelites into the land of promise. *Your eyes have indeed seen all that the Lord your*[12] *God has done to these two kings*—Moses employs here the now familiar technique of eliciting courage for the future on the basis of the experience of the past. Joshua had a formidable task before him, but he was called upon to undertake it in the sure knowledge of a God who had already shown himself faithful. As the Lord had done in the past, *just so will the Lord do to all the kingdoms to which you are about to cross over.*

The words to Joshua are completed by a charge not to fear man, the visible and tangible enemy, for the Lord, though invisible and intangible, *he is the one fighting for you.*

8. MOSES' REQUEST AND ITS REFUSAL (3:23-29)

23 *And at that time, I sought the favor of the Lord, saying:*
24 *Lord God, you have begun to show your servant your greatness and your powerful hand. What god is there in heaven or on the earth, who does deeds and mighty acts like yours?*
25 *Please let me cross over so that I may see the good land which is beyond the Jordan, that good hill country and the Lebanon.*
26 *But the Lord became furious with me because of you and he did not listen to me. And the Lord said to me: That is enough! Do not continually speak to me on this matter.*
27 *Go up to the summit of Pisgah and raise your eyes toward the west and the north and the south and the east; and look with your eyes, for you will not cross over this Jordan.*
28 *But charge Joshua, and strengthen him and assure him, for he will pass over before this people and he will cause them to inherit the land which you will see.*
29 *So we remained in the valley opposite Beth-peor.*

In the short prayer of Moses, there is a new insight concerning the nature of his relationship with the Lord. In the recollections up to this point, the Lord spoke to Moses on several occasions, but Moses' role was that of representative between the Israelites and the Lord. Now Moses recalls how he approached God in prayer on a personal matter. The prayer of Moses comes first (vv. 24-25) and is then followed by the response of the Lord to his request (vv. 26-28). The response of the Lord introduces Joshua again (see also vv. 21-22), thus returning to one of the most important themes in the book, the succession of the leadership from Moses to Joshua.

23-25 The prayer of Moses. *I sought the favor of the Lord*—

12. MT; LXX suggests the reading "our God."

the verb used (Hithp. of *ḥānan*) is a strong one, implying a solemn request for the Lord to be compassionate (see Ps. 30:7-8 [E.T.]for a similar use). *Lord God*—the Hebrew is *'aḏōnāy yhwh*. This name or title for God is used only twice in Deuteronomy and on both occasions it appears in a prayer of Moses (here and at 9:26).[1] It is indicative of the deeply personal tone of the request Moses brings to the Lord. *You have begun to show your servant your greatness and your powerful hand*—Moses refers to himself as *your servant*, conscious of his position before the Lord, yet knowing the boldness of his request in the light of the Lord's earlier prohibition against his entering the promised land (Deut. 1:37). The words show the deep pathos and tragedy of Moses' position. He had begun to see the marvellous works of the Lord, from the Exodus to the conquest of the lands east of the Jordan. But now, just when the climax was drawing near, he would be unable to see the Lord's fulfilment of the ancient promise. It was a promise to which he had devoted his whole life, and the thought that he would not see its fulfilment was too much for him to accept without question.

What god is there in heaven or on the earth, who does deeds and mighty acts like yours?—these words are prompted by the memory of the past (*you have begun to show . . .*) and are elicited primarily by the greatest wonder of them all, the Exodus from Egypt. In the celebration of the Exodus, Moses had sung: "Who is like you, O Lord, among the gods? Who is like you, majestic in holiness, terrible in glorious deeds, doing wonders?" (Exod. 15:11). The words of both these passages do not imply that Moses acknowledged the existence of other gods. Rather they are a rhetorical question, expressed in the form of praise, to which no answer can be given other than that there is no other living god like the Lord.[2] The Exodus from Egypt had been a dramatic event in the history of Israel's theology. It had shown dramatically that God was not limited to the circle of the Hebrews, but was God par excellence in the world, moving in the events of history toward the fulfilment of the covenant promise to his people.

Please let me pass over so that I may see the good land. The prayer began with a recollection of God's activity in the past, which was followed by words praising the incomparable character of the Lord. Now Moses voices his request to be permitted to pass over the Jordan. The words of the request are related directly to the earlier part of the prayer; Moses wished to cross over so that he could *see the*

---

1. While the title is not used only in prayer, it is common in that context; it appears in the prayer of Abraham, in the context of the covenant of the Lord (Gen. 15:2 and 8). Joshua uses it in a prayer of desperation during the early period of the conquest (Josh. 7:7-9).

2. See C. J. Labuschagne, *The Incomparability of Yahweh in the OT* (1966), pp. 22-24.

good land. He desired the completion of the vision that had grown toward fulfilment over more than forty years. Though he would have been too old to savor for long the experience of the land, just to set foot on it would have been sufficient reward for the years of struggle and anticipation.

26 The request, however, was not to be granted: *the Lord became furious with me because of you.* The reason for the denial of the request is the same as that given in 1:37; Moses would not see the land because, though individually blameless, he had to accept the responsibility for the acts of the rebellious generation in Kadesh-barnea. The tone of the refusal seems very strong (*became furious*), and yet in a sense it is indicative of the intimacy of the relationship. It was a relationship of love, but the status of Moses was always that of servant (or vassal) before the Lord, his suzerain God. *He did not listen to me*—that is, the Lord did not accede to the request of Moses. *That is enough! Do not continually speak to me on this matter.*[3] The very persistence of Moses in prayer, which aroused the anger of the Lord, was nevertheless one of his greatest gifts; it was his dogged faith and persistence that had finally brought the Israelites to the plains of Moab. So the request made by Moses was probably not in itself illegitimate. But there is a sense in which the great vision of Moses had slightly lost its focus. The vision of the promise had become a consuming passion to set foot in the land, but the vision had slipped from the Lord of the promise to the promise itself. It was the Lord himself who was to remain the true promise and vision of Moses.

27 Though the request to cross the river had been denied, Moses would be granted the privilege of looking at the land from the summit of Pisgah: see the commentary at 3:17 and see also 34:1.

28 With all possibility of Moses crossing the Jordan removed, the words of the Lord then turned to Joshua. Moses was charged to *strengthen him and assure him,* a task for which Moses himself would require great strength and graciousness, for it was not easy to pass on the office of command to a younger and less experienced man. The whole book of Deuteronomy is evidence that Moses was obedient to this command of the Lord. The renewal of the covenant on the plains of Moab was a time when the people renewed their allegiance to their God, not only under the direction of Moses (as at Sinai/Horeb), but also under Joshua, who during the ceremony would assume his new role of leadership.

29 The people *remained in the valley opposite Beth-peor* (see also 1:5); they remained there following the allocation of tribal land

---

3. The Heb. implies that Moses had been extremely persistent in his request: lit. "do not continue to speak to me again on this matter."

described earlier in the chapter. Though the exact location is uncertain, Beth-peor was situated east of the Jordan, probably opposite Jericho; it may have been in one of the wadis leading into the mountainous area identified as Pisgah.[4]

B. THE CALL FOR OBEDIENCE TO GOD'S LAW (4:1-40)[1]

1. THE LAW AS THE FOUNDATION OF THE NATION (4:1-8)

1 *And now, Israel, listen to the statutes and to the ordinances which I am about to teach you to do, so that you may live and go in and take possession of the land which the Lord God of your fathers is about to give to you.*

2 *You shall not add to the word which I am about to command you and you shall not detract from it, so that you may keep the commandments of the Lord your God, which I am about to command you.*

3 *Your eyes have seen what the Lord has done in Baal-peor. For every man who followed the Baal of Peor, the Lord your God annihilated him from your midst!*

4 *But you who kept close to the Lord your God, all of you are still living today.*

5 *Look, I have taught you statutes and ordinances, just as the Lord my God commanded me, so that you may act accordingly in the midst of the land into which you are about to enter in order to take possession of it.*

6 *And you will keep them and you will do them, because that will be your wisdom and your discernment in the eyes of the peoples who will hear of all these statutes, and they will say: Surely this great nation is a wise and discerning people!*

7 *For what great nation is there that has God as close to it as is the Lord our God, whenever we call on him?*

8 *And what great nation is there that has statutes and righteous ordinances like all this law which I am about to set before you today?*

In the first three chapters of Deuteronomy, the address of Moses contains an account of the experience of God in history, set within a

---

4. See O. Henke, "Zur Lage von Beth Peor," *Zeitschrift des deutschen Palästina-Vereins* 75 (1959), pp. 155-163.

1. Several scholars have noted that the principal elements of the treaty/covenant form occur in ch. 4: see D. J. McCarthy, *Treaty and Covenant*, pp. 131f.; M. G. Kline, *Treaty of the Great King*, p. 31. For a study dealing with the literary relationships between vv. 1-40 and certain historical sections of 1 Kings, see G. Braulik, "Spuren einer Neuarbeitung des deuteronomistischen Geschichtswerkes in I Kön. 8:52-53, 59-60," *Biblica* 52 (1971), pp. 20-33.

general chronological framework. In this fourth chapter the recollection of God in history continues, but it now assumes a subsidiary role. Deut. 4 is in essence a miniature sermon on the covenant and the law, in which historical recollection is employed in a more general didactic fashion. The "sermon" prepares the way for the presentation of the Decalog and the other laws which begins in ch. 5.

1 *And now, Israel, listen to the statutes and to the ordinances*[2]—the subject matter of this part of the address is the law (*statutes* and *ordinances*) which forms the basis of the covenant relationship. Although the actual pronouncement of the law does not begin until the following chapters, the nature and purpose of the law are expounded here, so that the obedience that is called for will not be blind obedience, but an obedience based on understanding. *Which I am about to teach you to do*—these words are important for a proper understanding of the law contained in Deuteronomy. The law here is not simply a written code; rather it is a presentation of law in the context of *education* ("to teach you") and *application* ("to do"). It is important to bear in mind the form of presentation of law in Deuteronomy, in the context of an address designed to educate, if comparison is to be made between this law and the other laws contained in the Pentateuch. Moses then states the purpose of his teaching of the law; it is *so that you may live and go in and take possession of the land*. The life of the Hebrews as a nation would depend on the law, not in a totally legalistic sense, but in that the law was the basis of the covenant, and in the covenant rested their close relationship to their God. (In contrast to *so that you may live,* see Moses' words in 4:22, "I am about to die.") For the immediate future, Moses was expounding the law, because only by obedience to the law would the Israelites take possession of the land after they had crossed the Jordan.

2 *You shall not add to the word*[3] *which I am about to command you and you shall not detract from it.* This "canonical formula" is similar in principle to other such injunctions known in ancient Near Eastern literature. A similar type of injunction was used for the

2. The words *statutes* and *ordinances* are used here, virtually synonymously, to describe all the law contained in Deut. 5–26. In certain passages, however, the words may have a more specific sense. For detailed studies of Hebrew legal terminology, see G. Braulik, "Die Ausdrücke für Gesetz im Buch Deuteronomium," *Biblica* 51 (1970), pp. 39-66; J. Morgenstern, "The Decalogue of the Holiness Code," *HUCA* 26 (1955), pp. 1-27; J. van der Ploeg, "Studies in Hebrew Law (I)," *CBQ* 12 (1950), pp. 248-259; cf. Z. W. Falk in *JSS* 5 (1960), pp. 350-54; *JSS* 12 (1967), pp. 241-44; *JSS* 14 (1969), pp. 39-44.
3. "Word" (*dābār*) has a wide semantic range; here it is synonymous with the whole law which was to be presented by Moses, or perhaps only with the Decalog; see the commentary at 4:13. Cf. O. Grether, *Name und Wort Gottes im AT.* BZAW 64 (1934), pp. 121-26.

guidance of scribes in ancient Egypt.[4] Of more direct relevance, however, is a warning contained in a vassal treaty of Esarhaddon against tampering with the text of the treaty.[5] In Deuteronomy, the injunction is analogous to that of the treaty. In the history of the Christian Church, this verse (see also Deut. 12:32) has often been taken, along with Rev. 22:18-19, as a commandment of God with reference to the canonical writings of both Testaments.[6] In its immediate context, however, the injunction relates to the *law* which Moses was about to present to the people (not to the book of Deuteronomy per se). It was the law, the gift of God at Horeb, that could not be supplemented or reduced.[7] This did not mean, however, that there could be no further revelation from God; the promise of a prophet like Moses (Deut. 18:15-18) pointed forward beyond the present situation.

3-4 The incident at Baal-peor. The incident is recited as a warning, designed to emphasize the encouragement to obey the law *so that you may live* (v. 1). The incident, which was not described in the earlier historical part of Moses' address, is given in Num. 25:1-5. Certain Israelites had indulged in sexual relationships with Moabite women; it is possible that this took place in the context of a religious ceremony in honor of the god Baal.[8] The behavior was quite contrary to the law of the Israelites and as a result the offenders were executed. The penalty was harsh, but implicit in the offense was a denial of a basic tenet of the Hebrew faith.[9] Those who had survived the incident and judgment at Baal-peor (presumably the same as, or close to, Beth-peor) were the ones *who kept close to the Lord,* and this was the life style that Moses encouraged in his address to the Israelites.

5-8 The call for Israel to become a distinctive people. The

---

4. See S. Morenz, *Egyptian Religion* (E.T. 1973), pp. 223f.; cited (in the German ed.) by G. von Rad, *Deuteronomy,* p. 48.
5. See M. G. Kline, *Treaty of the Great King,* p. 43. For earlier Near Eastern uses of similar language, see M. Fishbane, "Varia Deuteronomica," *ZAW* 84 (1972), pp. 349f.
6. Such a position was stated in the Second Helvetic Confession of 1566; see E. G. Kraeling, *The OT since the Reformation,* p. 35.
7. Note too that the reference is to the *essence* of the law, not the *letter* of the law. For example, the Decalog, as presented in Deut. 5, is worded differently at several points from its presentation in Exod. 20, but the essence of the law is quite clear and the same in both chapters. An example of how the law could be falsely adapted is shown clearly in the teaching of Jesus (Mark 7:9-13).
8. Baal, a principal Canaanite god, was responsible for fertility. In the cult of Baal, the performance of the sexual act seems to have been done as a type of imitative magic; just as the woman became pregnant through the sexual relationship, so too, it was hoped, the land would be made fertile by Baal in the coming agricultural season. The god mentioned here may have been a local manifestation of the Canaanite high-god Baal, or some other local deity, known as *the lord of (ba'al-) Peor.* There is no extrabiblical evidence for this particular manifestation of the god Baal.
9. That is, it was a contravention of the first commandment.

purpose underlying Moses' teaching of the law was directed toward the future life of the Israelites in the promised land: *so that you may act accordingly in the midst of the land.* Moses looked to the day when the Israelites would become a *great nation* (vv. 6, 7), but his ideal of a great nation was not that of Egypt or the other nations of the ancient Near East. It was not wealth or military power that provided the criteria of greatness; their greatness would lie in the wisdom and discernment that was the fruit of obedience to the law, so that their neighbors would say: *Surely this great nation is a wise and discerning people.* Thus the greatness would not even lie in the forms of government,[10] which were specified in the law of the covenant, for these too were similar in many ways to those of the nations of their time. Rather the distinctiveness would lie in the intimate relationship the covenant created between God and his people.

This distinctiveness in relationship is specified in v. 7: *for what great nation is there that has God*[11] *as close to it as is the Lord our God.* The covenant would establish a relationship with the Lord which would distinguish Israel from her neighbors. The relationship was a moral and spiritual one, for the Lord was close to the Israelites (*whenever we call on him*). In the context of the covenant relationship, the law itself was distinctive, for its source was the Lord and so its character was *righteous* (v. 8).

2. THE LAW AND THE NATURE OF GOD (4:9-24)

9 *Only guard yourself carefully and guard very carefully your desire, lest you forget the things your eyes have seen, and lest they slip from your mind all the days of your life; but you shall make them known to your children and your grandchildren.*

10 *The day that you stood before the Lord your God in Horeb, when the Lord said to me: Call together for me an assembly of the people and I shall cause them to hear my words, by which they shall learn to fear me all the days that they are alive upon the earth; then they will teach their children.*

11 *Then you approached and you stood beneath the mountain, and the mountain was burning with fire in the midst of the sky—there was darkness, cloud, and dense mist.*

10. Spinoza has so argued (*Tractatus Theologico-Politicus*, ch. 3, "Of the Vocation of the Hebrews"). "When therefore it is said in Scripture that the Lord is not so nigh any other nation as he is to the Hebrews, reference is only made to their government. . . ." Spinoza seeks to reduce the theological concern and leave only a kind of ethical and political system, but the essence of this passage is more religious and theological than Spinoza would allow.

11. Heb. *'elohim* (RSV "a god"); the Heb. could be "god" or "gods." However, the contrast here is not between the Lord and other gods, but between Israel, whose God is the Lord, and other nations; see C. J. Labuschagne, *The Incomparability of Yahweh*, p. 23.

12 *And the Lord your God spoke from the midst of the fire: you hear the sound of words, but you do not see a form—only the sound!*

13 *And he declared to you his covenant, which he commanded you to do, namely, the Ten Words, and he wrote them on two tablets of stone.*

14 *And at that time, the Lord commanded me to teach you statutes and ordinances, so that you may do them in the land into which you are about to cross over in order to take possession of it.*

15 *So guard your desires very closely—for you did not see any form on the day that the Lord spoke to you in Horeb from the midst of the fire —*

16 *lest you act corruptly and make for yourselves the image of a form, any statue in the shape of a male or a female;*

17 *the shape of any beast that is on the earth; the shape of any winged bird that flies in the sky;*

18 *the shape of any creeping thing on the ground; the shape of any fish that is in the waters beneath the earth.*

19 *And lest you raise your eyes heavenward and you see the sun and the moon and the stars, the whole host of heaven, and you are misled and you bow down to them and serve them, whom the Lord your God has assigned to all the peoples under the whole heaven.*

20 *But the Lord took you and brought you out from the iron furnace, from Egypt, to be a people of inheritance belonging to him, as at this day.*

21 *And the Lord became angry with me on account of your words and he swore that I would not cross the Jordan and I would not enter the good land which the Lord your God is about to give to you as an inheritance.*

22 *For I am about to die in this land. I am not going to cross the Jordan, but you are about to cross and you shall take possession of this good land.*

23 *Guard yourselves carefully, lest you forget the covenant of the Lord your God which he made with you, and you make for yourselves an image, in the shape of anything which the Lord your God has forbidden you.*

24 *For the Lord your God is a consuming fire! He is a jealous God!*

9 The passage begins with a warning, repeated again in v. 15 and v. 23: *only guard yourself carefully and guard very carefully your desire.*[1] The abstract nature of God in the Israelite religion, and the absence of any physical representation of him, imposed great difficulties for a people living in a world where all other men represented their gods in visual, physical form. To counter this difficulty would require great care and so Moses urged such care, *lest you forget the things your eyes have seen.* They had never literally seen their God, but they

---

1. The Heb. *nepesh*, sometimes rendered "soul" or used in a reflexive sense ("self"), is here rendered "desire"; see F. Hesse, *BHH* III, col.1755; *BDB*, p. 659.

had seen what God had done. That is, in the Exodus from Egypt, and in the travels that had brought them to the plains of Moab, they had seen God's work in the affairs of men. Their "seeing" was that of religious experience, not the literal seeing of a wooden or stone representation of their God. *And lest they slip from your mind*[2]—for a people who knew their God through experience, the memory of that experience became a vital part of their religious life. Religious life did not consist, however, only in remembering the experience of God in the past; memory, rather, functioned in order to produce the continuing obedience to the law of God, which in turn would lead to the continuing experience of the presence and activity of God. Thus the Israelites were not to forget their experience of God and, in addition, they had a responsibility to teach others about it: *but you shall make them known to your children and your grandchildren.* The theme of educating the children, which continues throughout Deuteronomy,[3] is important in the context of the covenant. The covenant promise of the land, made first to the patriarchs, moved forward by Moses, and still to be experienced by future generations, spanned time within the framework of the purpose of God. And yet the continuity of the covenant, in its fullness, was contingent upon the obedience of the people of God. Forgetfulness opened the door to failure, and so it was vital that the people of God not only remember their experience of God's mighty hand, but also that they pass on the memory, and thus the experience, to their children.

10   The verse, in English, begins rather abruptly and the style is still that of an address. The opening words continue from the admonition of the previous verse, so that the sense is: *(lest you forget) the day that you stood before the Lord your God in Horeb.* Horeb (Sinai), where the law was given, was one of the cardinal points of the faith which was to be remembered; the other high point was the Exodus from Egypt (see vv. 20, 34 below). At Horeb, the people had been called together to hear God's *words* (i.e., "commandments," see v. 13).

11-13   The details of the experience of God at Horeb/Sinai are recalled very vividly. As the people stood at the foot of the mountain, the mountain itself glowed with the light of a fire, its brightness contrasted sharply by the surrounding *darkness, cloud, and dense mist.* This theophany had a very profound religious effect, and the memory of it was such that it became a common feature (usually a part of the prologue) in many Hebrew hymns and poetic passages.[4] From

2.   The Heb. is lit. "and lest they turn aside from your heart." Heb. *lēḇāḇ* means "heart," but not the physical organ in this context; the sense is "mind" or "memory": see *NBD*, p. 509(b).
3.   Deut. 6:7, 20; 11:19; 31:13; 32:46.
4.   See Deut. 33:2; Judg. 5:5; Ps. 68:8; Hab. 3:3.

the fire came the voice of the Lord: *you hear the sound⁵ of words, but you do not see a form—only the sound!* The phrasing of this sentence is made very dramatic in the Hebrew by the use of active participles (rendered in English by the present tense). This experience the Hebrews were not to forget. If in their most profoundly moving encounter with their God there was no physical representation or form of him, but only his voice, any attempt to represent God in form would be totally inadequate and misleading. The voice of God communicated *the Ten Words,* that is, the Ten Commandments, which Moses was to set before the people once again (see Deut. 5). *He wrote them on two tablets of stone.* It has been pointed out that the *two* tablets contained two copies of the law⁶ (not several commandments on each, as often supposed). As in the suzerain/vassal treaties, each partner to the treaty had a copy of the agreement, so in the covenant, both the Israelites and the Lord had a copy of the covenant agreement.

14 Following the theophany at Horeb/Sinai, Moses was instructed *to teach you statutes and ordinances;* the object of this instruction was oriented toward the future contained in the covenant promise: *so that you may do them in the land.* The recollection of the teaching at the initial forging of the Sinai covenant anticipates the present task of Moses, once again teaching statutes and ordinances prior to the Israelites' entry into the promised land. Thus the address of Moses was itself an example, on a grand scale, of the injunction given in v. 9 to teach the children and grandchildren, for the people now standing before him were a post-Sinai generation.

15-19 A detailed warning against the dangers of idolatry. The principle is stated first⁷ and then it is followed by a detailed application. The principle is that when the Israelites had the profound experience of the presence of God on Mount Sinai, *you did not see any form.* The reality of God's presence could not be doubted, for they had heard his voice and sensed the awe of his presence in the fire; and yet the genuine danger of turning from a spiritual experience and resorting to physical representations was known already from the incident of the golden calf. Hence Moses presents the warning: they were to keep careful watch, *lest you act corruptly and make for yourselves the image of a form* (v. 16).

The first specific warning was against making *the image⁸ of a*

---

5. Lit. "voice (of words)."
6. See M. G. Kline, *Treaty of the Great King,* pp. 13-26; idem, *The Structure of Biblical Authority,* pp. 113-130.
7. The principle is that contained in the second commandment (5:8-10), and the verses following are an exegesis of the commandment.
8. Heb. *pesel* denotes basically an image cut from wood or stone.

form, any statue[9] *in the shape of a male or a female.* This was the greatest danger of all and for a very good reason. Since in the Israelite conception the Lord was a personal God, the most obvious way of attempting to represent him would have been in human likeness. And yet this would have been contrary to an essential part of Hebrew theology. Man was made in the image of God (Gen. 1:26-27) and yet man could not in any sense be said to be a complete representation of God, for God was transcendent (Gen. 1:1). To attempt to represent and limit God by human form in wood or stone would be to undermine the transcendence of God.[10] It should be stressed that the warning in this verse was not against the worshipping of other gods in the form of images, but against any attempt to represent the Lord in a physical manner. Thus the danger is equally one for the contemporary Christian. We may not be tempted to represent God in wood or stone, but like the Israelites we are constantly tempted to think that we can contain and limit God. The representation of God in wood or stone, even though it is acknowledged as only representative and not divine per se, is in effect a human attempt to contain and limit God. To contain or limit God, whether in material form or in theological proposition, is to fail to be aware of his transcendence and infinitude.

After the warning against images in human form, various other forms are also forbidden (vv. 17-19); the list reflects the temptation presented by other religions (principally Egyptian and Canaanite) to resort to various types of images. *The shape of any beast that is on the earth*—in one tradition of Egyptian religion, there were large numbers of "animal deities." The types of animal deities varied. In some cases a particular animal, or a whole species, was considered sacred, and in other cases a high deity of the Egyptian pantheon might be represented physically in a number of ways, of which the form of an animal would be one.[11] From the tombs of ancient Egypt, there have been recovered in large numbers mummified cats, dogs, crocodiles, bulls, and other beasts. Perhaps more significant, however, are the animal representations of important deities. The goddess Hathor was represented as a cow; Thoth could be manifested as a baboon or as an ibis; Min was normally represented in human form; other deities were represented in a cross between animal and human form. *The shape of*

---

9.   Heb. *semel* "statue"; *smlt* is used in a fourth-century B.C. Phoenician inscription to describe a statue of the female goddess 'Ashtart; see G. A. Cooke, *A Text-book of North-Semitic Inscriptions* (1903), p. 58.

10.   See P. C. Craigie, "Hebrew Thought about God and Nature and Its Contemporary Significance," *Canadian Journal of Theology* 16 (1970), pp. 3-11 (*p. 7).

11.   For fuller details of these aspects of Egyptian religion, see H. Frankfort, *Ancient Egyptian Religion* (1961), pp. 8-14; C. J. Bleeker, "The Religion of Ancient Egypt," *Historia Religionum* I (1969), pp. 51-73.

any winged bird that flies in the sky—several Egyptian deities were represented as birds, one of the most important being Horus, who was manifested as a falcon. These prohibitions against images in animal or bird form seem to reflect primarily the Israelite memory of their experience in Egypt.

The shape of any creeping thing on the ground—this further prohibition may be another example of the general prohibition against animal and bird images, though in Egypt "creeping things" play a less obvious role in this sphere. If Egypt still provides the background, however, it is possible that this prohibition is against the equivalent of the Egyptian scarab. The scarab, formally, was a representation of the "dung-beetle," but it could be used for a number of purposes. A common function of the scarab was to act as an amulet and as such it was considered to have certain magical qualities.[12] It was not strictly an image, but its supposed magical qualities could easily result in its being treated with special awe. Alternatively, however, the *creeping thing* may refer to a snake, which could symbolize the power of an Egyptian goddess.[13] Whatever the significance might be, it is to be noted that the *creeping thing*, in Hebrew thought, was a part of God's creation (Gen. 1:24) and as such it could in no sense be a proper representation of the Creator. *The shape of any fish that is in the waters beneath the earth*—the fish was not normally used as a representation of deity in the Near East,[14] but the reference here to *waters beneath the earth* may mean that images representing the mythological characters of the underworld in Egyptian or Canaanite thought were being forbidden. Alternatively the prohibition may again simply prevent any part of the order of creation (Gen. 1:20-23) from being used as an image of the Creator.

In v. 19, the warning and prohibition move from the animal world to the cosmic sphere. The warning here is not explicitly that of making an image, but rather of worshipping *the sun and the moon and the stars, the whole host of heaven*. The role of the heavenly host, in later Israelite religion, was to reflect the glory of God (Ps. 19:1), but the temptation for the Israelites was not to worship the Lord for the

12. See J. R. Harris, ed., *The Legacy of Egypt* (1971), p. 164. Scarabs might be produced to commemorate an event, but many had a magico-religious role. The "heart-scarabs" had a spell inscribed, designed to give protection in the judgment before the god Osiris; see A. Gardiner, *Egyptian Grammar* (³1957), p. 269.
13. See K. A. Kitchen, *NBD*, p. 1165. It is interesting to note that in the Proto-Sinaitic inscriptions, there are four references to a goddess known as the "Serpent Lady"; see W. F. Albright, *The Proto-Sinaitic Inscriptions and Their Decipherment* (1966), nos. 351, 353, 360, 361. The serpent-goddess *Ušḫr* is mentioned in one of the more recently discovered Ugaritic texts, RS 24.260. See *Ugaritica* 5 (1968), pp. 586-88; L. R. Fisher, "An Ugaritic Ritual and Genesis 1:1-5," *Ugaritica* 6 (1969), pp. 197-205.
14. Occasionally Atargatis, a fertility-goddess, is shown in fish-like form, but this was not the principal form of her representation.

136

glory of his creation, but to follow their Near Eastern neighbors in worshipping the sun, moon, and stars. In all the Near Eastern religions, the sun and the moon, and to a different extent the stars, were thought of as divine and worthy of praise,[15] and hence the temptation at this point was very dangerous. It should be noted that in the previous verses (17-18), the warning was against *making* an image, but in this verse (19), the warning is against a more subtle danger, that of taking something within the created universe (e.g., sun) and making it divine and the object of worship. The more sophisticated Egyptians and Canaanites no doubt understood that their physical images were not in themselves divine, but only representations of divinity. However, the sun (in Egypt, e.g.) was itself so awe-inspiring as to induce worship in its own right. In more sophisticated forms, the tendency to make the physical world divine and the object of worship is still present and constitutes a real danger to the Christian faith.[16] These false forms of worship, though assigned by God to other nations (v. 19), would be antithetic to the revelation of Israel's true religion.

20   The warning is summarized by a further reference to the Exodus from Egypt. *But the Lord took you and brought you out from the iron furnace,*[17] *from Egypt*—it was the Exodus that established a special relationship between the Israelites and their God (they became *a people of inheritance belonging to him*) and made any worship of images or natural phenomena false. Their faith had depended in the past on the experience and knowledge of God; to remain pure, the faithful had to avoid all tendencies toward images and continue to base their lives on the experience and knowledge of the living God.

21-22   Moses once again recalls that he was forbidden to enter the promised land: see Deut. 1:37 and 3:26. The words give emphasis for the need of great caution on behalf of the audience. There is a great poignancy in Moses' statement: *for I am about to die in this land.* The request for a change of decision had been denied (3:26), but the

---

15.   In Egypt, Thoth was originally a moon-god; Re was the principal sun-god (though Aten, the sun-disc, took preeminence during the reign of Akhenaten). In Mesopotamia, Sin was the moon-god, Shamash was the sun-god, and Ishtar represented the Venus star; see H. W. F. Saggs, *The Greatness That Was Babylon,* pp. 314-329. In Canaanite religion, Yaraḫ was moon-god, Shapash was sun-god, and Athtar represented the Venus star; see H. Gese *et al., Die Religionen Altsyriens, Altarabiens und der Mandäer* (1970), pp. 94-172; W. F. Albright, *Yahweh and the Gods of Canaan* (1968), pp. 122-26.
16.   See, e.g., Julian Huxley's essays "The Humanist Frame" and "The New Divinity" in J. Huxley, *Essays of a Humanist* (1966); Huxley, rejecting the "god hypothesis," substitutes as the object of man's worship the universe, seen as a "unitary and evolutionary process" (p. 113).
17.   The *iron furnace* suggests that the time in Egypt was a period of ordeal, testing, and purifying for the Hebrews; see also Isa. 48:10; Jer. 11:4.

137

longing could not be hidden; he would die in *this land* (v. 22a), not in *this good land* (v. 22b), beyond the river Jordan.

23 The warning and prohibitions of vv. 15-19 are here summarized succinctly; to make an image would be tantamount to forgetting the covenant, and to forget the covenant was to forget the relationship that provided the total *raison d'être* of the Israelites.

24 The Lord is described as a *consuming fire* and as a *jealous God*. The language is stern, but it is closely related to the theme of the love of God in Deuteronomy.[18] The covenant relationship was one of love, initiated in the covenant of God and demanding a response of love from the Israelites (see 6:5). To construct images would be to indicate that the first love of the Israelites had been forgotten, and to this the response of the Lord would be jealousy. Jealousy, however, does not represent a change in God, but is, as it were, the reverse of the coin of love; it was the people who were prone to change and forgetfulness, and from outside the relationship of love, God was indeed awesome like a *consuming fire*.

3. THE LAW AND JUDGMENT (4:25-31)

25 *When you bear children and grandchildren and you grow old in the land, and then you act perversely and make an image, the form of anything, and you do wrong in the eyes of the Lord your God, provoking him to anger:*

26 *I summon heaven and earth as witness against you today, that you shall certainly perish quickly from the land, toward which you are about to cross the Jordan in order to take possession of it; you will not live long in it, for you will certainly be annihilated.*

27 *And the Lord will scatter you among the peoples, and you will survive, few in number, among the nations to which the Lord will lead you.*

28 *And there you will serve gods, the fabrication of human hands, consisting of wood and stone, who do not see and do not hear and do not eat and do not smell.*

29 *And from there you will seek the Lord your God, and you will find him if you seek him with all your mind and all your desire, when you are in distress.*

30 *And all these things will happen to you in the days ahead; then you will return to the Lord your God and you will hear his voice.*

31 *For the Lord your God is a compassionate God; he will not fail you and he will not destroy you, and he will not forget the covenant of your fathers, which he swore to them by oath.*

25 *When you bear children and grandchildren and you grow old in the land*—as in the previous verses, the address continues to

18. See Buis and Leclercq, *Le Deutéronome*, p. 59.

anticipate the dangers and temptations the people would face when they had crossed the Jordan into the promised land. The future anticipated here is primarily the immediate future; that is, Moses is looking forward to a time when those standing before him would be thirty or forty years older and when they should be secure in the land. The temptation anticipated is that which has already been examined in the previous passage, namely, that the people *act perversely and make an image.*

26 *I summon heaven and earth as witness against you today.* *Today,* referring to the time of the address, indicates a present curse, implicit in the covenant, which would take effect in the future if the Israelites were not obedient to the terms of the covenant. The summoning of witnesses to the agreement was a regular part of the Near Eastern treaties; in those texts, however, which were essentially political documents between a suzerain king and a vassal state, gods were normally summoned as witnesses, the gods of the respective states being considered to have the power to enforce the threat against any breach of the treaty.[1] In some Near Eastern political treaties, "heaven and earth" might be included in the list of deities witnessing the treaty.[2] In the covenant, God was himself one partner of the agreement, so that *heaven and earth* were called to witness as a part of God's creation; the phrase is used frequently in the context of the covenant.[3]

Thus the making and renewing of the covenant were witnessed by *heaven and earth:* these "witnesses" were permanent things, unchanging in contrast to the fickleness of man. If the Israelites were, at some future date, unfaithful to the covenant and they were to make an image of their formless God, then that faithlessness would be known as certainly as the permanence of the heaven and the earth, and the people would suffer: *you will not live long in it, for you will certainly be annihilated.*[4]

27-30 The implications of a breach of the covenant are now given in more detail. *And the Lord will scatter you among the peoples*—although these words have a prophetic ring, when viewed against the subsequent history of Israel, their immediate reference is

---

1.   See J. A. Thompson, *The Ancient Near Eastern Treaties and the OT.*
2.   See, e.g., certain Akkadian political decrees recovered from Ras Shamra-Ugarit, on the coast of Syria: *PRU* 4, 17.365 and 17.338.
3.   See also Deut. 30:19; 31:28-30; 32:1; for a discussion of the expression in the covenant context, see M. Delcor, "Les attaches littéraires: l'origine et la signification de l'expression biblique 'prendre à témoin le ciel et la terre'," *VT* 16 (1966), pp. 8-25.
4.   The consonantal text of the Hebrew in the earlier part of the verse *(that you shall certainly perish)* is *ky 'bd t'bdwn;* there is some reflection of the fulfilment of this threat in the Moabite inscription of Mesha, where it is said of Israel that she *'bd 'bd 'lm.* See J. C. L. Gibson, *Textbook of Syrian Semitic Inscriptions* I (1971), p. 78.

still to a point in the near future and in the promised land. They were about to cross over into a land already occupied, not by a single state, but by many small states, some of whom might unite on particular occasions to face a common threat. The principal danger facing the Israelites, once they had crossed the Jordan, would be that of failing to maintain their unity as they began to settle in their new land.[5] The principal source of unity among the Israelite tribes, from a religious point of view, was their covenant with the Lord. Thus a breach of the covenant had as an automatic result the effect of undermining the unity of the tribes. When that unity was gone, the people, losing their distinctiveness, would quickly be scattered and lost among the Canaanites (that is, *the nations to which the Lord will lead you,* v. 27). They would survive, *few in number*—although they would not be completely wiped out, to survive *few in number* would be a tragic contrast to the promise of the covenant, according to which the Israelites were to become as numerous as the stars of heaven.[6]

If the Israelites were scattered among the Canaanites, they would have no option but to *serve gods, the fabrication of human hands.* This principle is at the core of the covenant promise and the necessity of the conquest. The religion of the Israelites was so closely bound by the nature of the covenant to the people as a whole that it was inconceivable to think of somehow maintaining a purely individual faith in the land. The whole of Canaanite society, even that which would nowadays be called secular, was permeated by the belief structure and world view of the Canaanites. Simply to live among the Canaanites would involve concessions on the part of individual Israelites. The covenant promise anticipated a state, a theocracy, but the fulfilment of that vision depended on the unity of the people, by which alone such a state could be brought into being.

There are two positive sides to the warning, however. First, if the people were so punished through disobedience, the consequences of their action would drive them back to their God. Though in human weakness it was easy to forget their experience of God, nevertheless the experience of serving gods, *who do not see and do not hear and do not eat and do not smell,* would by its very futility awaken again memories of their living God. The Israelites would be driven by circumstances to look again for God (v. 29). Second, even in the midst of the warning, there was an element of promise; though the people might be unfaithful, yet God would remain faithful. In other words, breach of the covenant, though deserving only punishment, was not

---

5.   A good example of this danger taking effect may be seen in Judg. 5, celebrating the victory of Deborah and Barak over a confederation of Canaanite states. Several tribes participated in the victorious war, several tribes were criticized for not participating, and other tribes (the southern group) are not mentioned at all.
6.   See Gen. 15:15 and Deut. 1:11.

totally irreparable: *you will find him if you seek him with all your mind and all your desire,*[7] *when you are in distress.*[8]

And all these things will happen to you in the days ahead[9]—the primary reference is still to the immediate future, and the book of Judges provides some insight into the type of disunity that appeared in the period following the initial part of the conquest. But as history unfolded, the danger contained in this warning was illustrated more dramatically in the fall of the two kingdoms and the subsequent dispersal of many of the Israelites from their promised land.

31 The section closes on a more positive note, emphasizing the nature of God as *compassionate.* His compassion lay in his continuing readiness to receive his people back to himself, despite the fact that a breach of the covenant dissolved, in a legal sense, the commitment of God to his people. The positive note contrasts sharply the different characters of the two "partners" in the covenant. The Israelites were prone to be forgetful of the covenant and their experience of God; forgetfulness led to acts of disobedience, such as idolatry, contrary to the stipulations of the covenant. In contrast, God *will not forget the covenant of your fathers, which he swore to them by oath.*

4. THE LAW AND THE GOD OF HISTORY (4:32-40)

32 *For inquire now about days gone by, which were before your time, from the day that God created man upon the earth, and from one extremity of the heaven to the other: Has there happened anything like this great deed or has anything been heard of like it?*

33 *Is there a people that has heard the voice of God speaking from the middle of the fire, as you indeed heard it? And you are still living!*

34 *Or has a god tried to go and take for himself a nation from the midst of a nation, by tests, by signs and by wonders, and by war, and with a strong hand, and with an outstretched arm, and by great and terrifying actions, according to all that the Lord your God has done for you, before your very eyes in Egypt?*

35 *You were shown this in order to know that the Lord, he is God: there is none other apart from him.*

36 *From heaven, he made you hear his voice in order to discipline you. And on the earth he made you see his great fire and you heard his words from the middle of the fire.*

7. See the commentary on 4:9 (n. 1).
8. The verse break is placed after *distress* (following Sam.), rather than after *nepesh,* as in *BH*[3] (see AV and RSV).
9. "In the days ahead" (or "in the latter days") comes to have an eschatological significance at a later date, though in this context the reference is simply to the future; for a study of the use of the phrase, see E. Lipiński, *"b'hryt hymym* dans les textes préexiliques," *VT* 20 (1970), pp. 445-450.

37 *And because he loved your fathers and chose their seed after them, and he brought you out from Egypt in his presence by his great strength;*

38 *in order to dispossess because of you nations greater and stronger than you, to cause you to enter, in order to give you their land to be an inheritance, as on this day:*

39 *so that today you know and you call to mind that the Lord, he is the God in the heaven above and on the earth beneath: there is no other.*

40 *So you shall keep his statutes and his commandments which I am about to command you today, which will be good for you and your children after you, and so that you may live long on the land which the Lord your God is about to give you permanently.*

In the earlier part of the address, heaven and earth were called on to witness the covenant between the Lord and Israel, and their permanence reflected the certainty of the distress that would follow upon a breach of the covenant. In these verses, witness is summoned to testify to the nature of God, and that witness is provided by history. The elaboration of the wonderful evidence of God's work in history further illuminates the compassionate and faithful nature of God (v. 31). From a literary point of view, these verses are among the most beautiful in Deuteronomy. They are prosaic in form, but poetic in their evocation of the marvelous acts of God. The occasion for the more elevated style is provided by the subject matter; not until the end of the passage does the focus shift from God and his acts back to man and his need of obedience (v. 40).

32 A rhetorical question opens the section: *Has there happened anything like this great deed[1] or has anything been heard of like it?* The question has no limits chronologically: *inquire now . . . from[2] the day that God created man upon the earth.* Neither has it geographical limits: *from one extremity of the heaven to the other.* The invitation is thus to explore into the whole panorama of human history, within the limits—but to the extremities—of time and space, to see whether anything similar to Israel's experience of God had been known before. The rhetorical question is "loaded," for the beginning of human history is described as *the day that God created man upon the earth,* specifying God's role not only as Creator, but also as the Lord of history.

33 The rhetorical questioning continues: Has any other

1. "This great deed" (singular) describes the whole act of God in history, consisting in (a) the making of the covenant at Horeb/Sinai; (b) the Exodus from Egypt; (c) the beginning of the possession of the promised land. All three themes are developed in the following verses.

2. On the uncommon *lᵉmin-,* indicating here *terminus a quo,* see S. R. Driver, *Deuteronomy,* p. 75.

people had an experience of God similar to that of the Israelites on Mount Sinai? The answer could only be "No." The astonishing part of that experience for the Israelites was not only that they had heard God's voice, but that they had survived so awesome an experience (*and you are still living*[3]).

34 A further rhetorical question follows, once again implying a negative response. The liberation of the Israelites and their Exodus from Egypt constituted an act of God unique in human knowledge and experience. Though it had not been done before, God took *for himself a nation from the midst of a nation,* a think no god had *tried*[4] to do. God's action and presence in human history had been clearly shown to the Israelites by the events accompanying the Exodus: *by tests, by signs . . . and by great and terrifying actions.*[5]

35 *You were shown this in order to know that the Lord, he is God.* The knowledge of God for the Israelites sprang from God's revelation of himself in word and in deed. Thus right from the beginning, the Bible presupposes the existence of the living God. The question "Does God exist?"—though a legitimate question per se—was nevertheless an irrelevant question in the light of a knowledge of God, of which the source was revelation and in which the conviction was provided by experience. Thus, for the Israelites, the two primary sources of the knowledge of God were Sinai and the Exodus, which together formed the framework of their belief. These two themes, both presupposing the activity of God in history, are a paradigm for the Christian faith. The incarnation, providing a new and intimate knowledge of the presence of God in human history, is the prerequisite for the death of Jesus and the resurrection of Christ. Thus for the Christian, while the Exodus and Sinai remain important, it is of the death and resurrection that it can be said, in the words of Moses' address: *you were shown this in order to know that the Lord, he is God. There is none other apart from him*—the faith of Israel was monotheistic; that is to say, it was a faith in which the existence of one God was affirmed and the reality of all other gods was denied. This did not mean, of course, that the Israelites were unaware that there were believed, by others, to be many gods, and the viewpoint of Deuteronomy toward other gods, *in the faith of other nations,* was remarkably tolerant (see v. 19). But a major thrust of the whole book

3. Heb. *wayyeḥî*; the translation above supposes a text *watteḥî*, following the evidence of the LXX.
4. Heb. *nissāh,* "tried," or perhaps even "dared"; see J. C. L. Gibson, *Textbook of Syrian Semitic Inscriptions* I, p. 40, who notes the use of the same word in the Lachish Ostraca iii.9.
5. It has been noted that several of the expressions used in the sequence have similarities to common Egyptian expressions: A. S. Yahuda, *The Language of the Pentateuch in Its Relation to Egyptian* (1933), pp. 66 and 81. The language thus not only elevates the Lord, but implicitly mocks the ineffectiveness of the Egyptian gods.

was to warn Israel against the dangers of serving other gods. The reason was that though there were many gods in the religions of Israel's neighbors, only the Lord was a true and living God. And the proof of the reality of the Lord their God lay not in any philosophical argument, but in the acts and words of God in history, principally in the Exodus and at Sinai.

36-39 The themes of the previous verses (Sinai, Exodus, and the promised land) are now treated with a slightly different emphasis. The voice of God, which was heard from the middle of the fire (v. 36), was *in order to discipline you.* The verb *discipline* (Piel of *yāsar*) is used in Deut. 8:5 of a man disciplining his son and it has a similar sense here. The covenant provided a father/son relationship between the Lord and Israel; at Sinai, they were *disciplined* in the sense that the manifestation of the glory of God made Israel aware of its position in relation to the Lord and thus inclined toward obedience. The acts of God, beginning with the promise made to the patriarchs (v. 37) and continuing through the Exodus to the beginning of the possession of the land (vv. 37-38), together culminated at one point and for one purpose in the present: *so that today you know . . .* (v. 39; see also v. 35).

40 The discourse on God's role in history concludes with a further charge to *keep his statutes and his commandments. Which I am about to command you today*—the address of Moses is still at a preliminary stage (see the outline in the Introduction), and following this fourth chapter the actual presentation of statutes and commandments begins. *Which will be good for you and for your children after you*—at first reading, the emphasis on law in Deuteronomy may seem severe, but the purpose of the law and of obedience to the law was a lofty one. The good life, for the Israelites, lay in obedience to the law of God rendered out of love. Obedience would make the people *live long* (lit. "prolong days") *on the land which the Lord your God is about to give you permanently* (lit. "all the days," indicating continuity: see also 5:29 [E.T.]; 6:24; 11:1; 14:23; 18:5; 19:9; 28:29, 33).

C. NOTE ON THE CITIES OF REFUGE (4:41-43)

41 *Then Moses set aside three cities in Transjordan, that is, in the east;*

42 *so that the manslayer might seek refuge there, he who kills his neighbor without forethought, when he did not previously hate him; and he shall seek refuge in one of those cities and live.*

43 *They are Bezer, in the wilderness on the plateau, for the Reubenites, and Ramoth in Gilead for the Gadites, and Golan in Bashan for the Manassites.*

These verses, which are not a part of the address of Moses, describe an action undertaken between the preliminary address (the Historical Prologue) and the subsequent address in which the Law is presented and expounded. They describe the allocation of three eastern cities of refuge, and the appointment of them at this point in the course of the narrative seems suitable. The historical prologue had described the experiences of the Israelites up to the present moment on the plains of Moab; that part of the address which follows has its specific focus on the future. Yet there was one bit of unfinished business relating to the past, the setting aside of cities of refuge for the two and a half tribes who had already been allocated land east of the Jordan. The reasons for such cities and the legislation concerning them are presented in detail in 19:1-13 (see commentary) and will not be pursued further at this point; the present remarks will be confined to some brief notes on matters of geography.

The exact location of *Bezer,* in the territory allocated to the Reubenites (see 3:12-17), is uncertain, though an identification with the modern Umm el-'Amad has been suggested.[1] *Ramoth in Gilead* was situated in the eastern part of the Gadites' territory, approximately between the Yarmuk and the Jabbok. An identification with the modern site Tell-Rāmîth seems fairly certain.[2] *Golan,* the northernmost city of refuge, was located in the Manassite territory of Bashan, but again, its exact location is uncertain; it is possible that it should be identified with Saḥm el-Jōlân,[3] but the fact that a whole territory was later named after it (Gaulanitis) makes the specific identification uncertain.

1. Y. Aharoni, *The Land of the Bible,* pp. 308, 375. Bezer is mentioned in line 27 of the Moabite inscription of Mesha, though the reference does not help in marking its location.
2. N. Glueck, "Ramoth-Gilead," *BASOR* 92 (1943), pp. 10-16; Y. Aharoni, *The Land of the Bible,* p. 383.
3. Aharoni, *ibid.,* p. 377.

III. THE ADDRESS OF MOSES: THE LAW (4:44–26:19)

A. INTRODUCTION TO THE DECLARATION OF THE LAW (4:44-49)

44 *And this is the law which Moses set before the Israelites.*
45 *These are the testimonies and the statutes and the judgments which Moses proclaimed to the Israelites when they came out of Egypt,*
46 *in Transjordan, in the valley opposite Beth-peor in the land of Sihon, king of the Amorites, who lived in Heshbon, whom Moses and the Israelites had defeated, when they came out of Egypt.*
47 *And they took possession of his land and the land of Og, king of Bashan, the two kings of the Amorites who were in Transjordan, in the east:*
48 *from Aroer, which is on the edge of the Arnon valley, and as far as Mount Sirion, that is Hermon,*
49 *and all the Arabah that is in Transjordan to the east, and as far as the sea of the Arabah, beneath the slopes of Pisgah.*

These verses are introductory to the second major section of Moses' address, the declaration of the law. *This is the law which Moses set before the Israelites* (v. 44) refers to all the law that is about to be presented in chs. 5–26. The law about to be presented is then clearly identified as the same law (*testimonies, statutes,* and *judgments*) that was proclaimed to the Israelites at Horeb/Sinai after the Exodus from Egypt (v. 45); it is not a new covenant in Deuteronomy, but the renewing of an old covenant. But while the law is the same as that given earlier, its form is slightly different in this context, since it is presented and expounded in Moses' address. The place and time are then specified (vv. 46-49) in a summary section gathering together briefly many of the themes already dealt with at length in chs. 1–3.

46 See 2:26-37 and 3:29.
47 See 3:1-11.

48-49   See 3:8-22. Note on Sirion: the reading *Sirion* here is based on the evidence of the Syriac, though the MT reads *śî'ōn*. In the original text, the reading was probably *śrn*, before the use of medial *mater lectionis*, introduced around the sixth century B.C. This was misread at an early date as *ś'n*, the /r/ and /'/ being easily confused in early Hebrew script; compare the respective forms in the Gezer calendar. With this wrong reading, when orthographic revisions were made, the /y/ was placed in the wrong position, *śy'n*, on the basis of the ancient misreading, the proper form being *śryn*. The basis for the initial misreading probably lies in that *śryn* was not a Hebrew word, but from a North Canaanite dialect, Sidonian (see 3:9).

B. THE BASIC COMMANDMENTS:
EXPOSITION AND EXHORTATION (5:1–11:32)

1. THE SUMMONS TO OBEY THE LAW (5:1-5)

1 *And Moses summoned all Israel and said to them: Hear, O Israel, the statutes and the judgments which I am about to proclaim in your hearing today; and you will learn them and you will take care to do them.*
2 *The Lord our God made a covenant with us in Horeb.*
3 *The Lord did not make this covenant with our fathers, but with us, each one of us, these present today, all of us who are living.*
4 *The Lord spoke with you face to face on the mountain, from the middle of the fire.*
5 *I was standing between the Lord and you at that time, to declare to you the word of the Lord—for you were afraid because of the fire and you did not come up into the mountain—saying:*

1   *All Israel* (see also 1:1) are called to hear Moses' proclamation of the law, which was binding on all of them as members of the covenant community. *Hear, O Israel*—see also 4:1; 6:3, 4; 9:1; 20:3; 27:9. The verb *hear* (*shāma'*) carries with it the sense "obey": hearing that leads to obedience is demanded of the people. The verb is used with the same sense in the context of the Near Eastern treaty.[1] The full implications of a proper hearing of the law (*statutes* and *judgments*) are stated at the end of the verse: *you will learn them and you will take care to do them.*

2   The statutes and judgments which the people were about to hear had been presented first in the covenant made at Horeb. For most of the people standing before Moses, the covenant at Horeb had been made with a previous generation, but their identification with

1.   In the Aramaic Sefiré document; see J. A. Thompson, *The Ancient Near Eastern Treaties and the OT*, p. 36.

that generation is emphasized by the title given to God, *the Lord our God*. Here, and in the verses that follow, there seems to be an emphasis on the living reality of the covenant relationship between the people and their God which transcends the boundaries of time.

3 Thus the words in this verse emphasize that the covenant was not simply an event of the past, or something of historical interest: *the Lord did not make this covenant with our fathers*. In a literal sense, the covenant was made with the fathers of most of those standing there on the plains of Moab. The essence of the covenant, however, was its present reality, so that Moses drives home very forcefully the direct identification of the principally new and young generation with those involved in the making of the Horeb covenant. It was made *with us, each one of us, these present today, all of us who are living*—the syntax of this part of the Hebrew sentence is at first sight rather awkward, but it functions effectively in a hortatory sense to drive home the direct relationship between the people present and the Lord of the covenant.

4 *The Lord spoke with you face to face*—the Hebrew idiom *face to face* is not to be taken in a literal sense. In 4:12, it is clear that the people heard God's voice, but they did not see any form of God. The idiom implies something like "person to person,"[2] or simply that the Lord spoke to the people "directly." The verse continues to press the reality of the event, the experience of God speaking *from the middle of the fire,* by identifying the present hearers with those present at the original covenant ceremony.

5 The role of Moses had been a mediatory one at Horeb, *standing between the Lord and you*. They had all heard the sound of God's voice, but it was on Moses that the responsibility lay *to declare . . . the word of the Lord*. The people had been terrified by the experience of the presence of the living God. Thus the essence of what Moses had declared at Horeb, and was about to repeat on the plains of Moab, was the *word* (or "commandment," see 4:13) *of the Lord*. Moses was not the creator of that word, only its mediator; its source was God alone. But in mediating the law, Moses applied it to the contemporary situation, and his repetition of the Decalog and laws in the verses and chapters that follow in Deuteronomy differs at a number of points from the initial presentation of the law in the book of Exodus. To give only one example, the wording of the sabbath commandment here in Deuteronomy is different from that of Exod. 20:8-11. The application of the Decalog in the address of Moses does not change the law per se, but elucidates its relevance and meaning to the ongoing life of the covenant community.

2. So Augustine, cited by Buis and Leclercq, *Le Deutéronome,* p. 36.

2. THE DECALOG (5:6-21)

6 *I am the Lord your God, who brought you out of the land of Egypt, out of the house of bondage.*

7 *You shall not have other gods besides me.*

8 *You shall not make for yourself an image or any form of that which is in heaven above, or of that which is in the earth beneath, or of that which is in the waters under the earth.*

9 *You shall not bow down to them and you shall not serve them, for I, the Lord your God, am a jealous God, punishing the iniquity of the fathers on the children, and on the third and fourth generation of those that hate me;*

10 *but acting with loving kindness toward thousands, toward those that love me and keep my commandments.*

11 *You shall not take the name of the Lord your God in vain, for the Lord will not leave unpunished him who takes his name in vain.*

12 *Take care to make holy the sabbath day, just as the Lord your God commanded you.*

13 *You shall labor six days and do all your work.*

14 *But the seventh day is the sabbath of the Lord your God. You shall not do any work, neither you, nor your son nor your daughter, nor your male servant nor your female servant, nor your ox nor your ass, nor any of your cattle, nor the resident alien who is within your gates: so that your male servant and your female servant may rest just like you.*

15 *And you shall remember that you were a servant in the land of Egypt and the Lord your God brought you out from there with a strong hand and with an outstretched arm; therefore the Lord your God commanded you to keep the sabbath day.*

16 *Honor your father and your mother as the Lord your God commanded you, so that you may live long and it may go well for you on the land which the Lord your God is about to give to you.*

17 *You shall not kill.*

18 *And you shall not commit adultery.*

19 *And you shall not steal.*

20 *And you shall not give vain witness against your neighbor.*

21 *And you shall not covet your neighbor's wife, and you shall not strongly desire your neighbor's house, his field, or his male servant or his female servant, his ox or his ass, or anything that belongs to your neighbor.*

The Decalog is at the heart of the message of Deuteronomy. It is the divinely given foundation of the covenant relationship, the standard set by the suzerain God as a basis for the continuing relationship with his vassal people. In one sense, the Decalog is the legal basis of the covenant relationship, but to stress its nature as law would be to fail to appreciate its true role. It was the legal aspect of the covenant relationship in a sense similar to the role a legal wedding contract plays in a marriage. A marriage may be legalized by a marriage license, but it is a true marriage only when the legal terms of the contract are representative of a love leading to and maintaining the marital relationship. Thus, too, the law was legally binding, but not in a restrictive sense; it was representative of God's love for men and it called in turn for a response of love (6:4-5). The Decalog was representative of God's love in that its injunctions, both negative and positive, led not to restriction of life, but to fullness of life. It demanded a response of love, not because obedience would somehow accumulate credit in the sight of God, but because the grace of God, experienced already in the liberation from Egypt and in the divine initiative in the covenant promise, elicited such a response from man in gratitude.

The principles embodied in the commandments are of abiding value, but the application of the principle changes, just as does the environment of the man who is within the covenant relationship. Thus the immediate significance of some of the commandments might differ from one environment to another. The meaning of the commandments to the Israelites in the newly formed theocracy may assume a different shape for modern man living under a form of technocracy. But the principles remain the same. Hence the commandments continue to be valid in the NT (e.g., Matt. 19:16-20) and are still considered to be of vital importance to the contemporary Christian. In the commentary that follows, an attempt will be made first of all to interpret the commandments in the context of the covenant community of early Israel. Then some comments will be ventured which seek to indicate the application of the principles of the Decalog to our contemporary situtation.

Special Select Bibliography

(Works marked with * contain useful additional bibliographies.) The Decalog, both here and in Exod. 20, has been the subject of many detailed studies. The following works are taken selectively from various types of modern approaches to the Decalog; for those who wish to go further back in the history of scholarship, the bibliographies contained in these works will be of great assistance. Group (a) contains more specifically works of biblical scholarship; group (b) contains works that examine the significance of the Decalog for modern man.

(a) J. J. Stamm and M. E. Andrew, *The Ten Commandments in Recent Research* (²1967); contains a useful summary and evaluation of scholarship prior to 1967. S. Goldman, *The Ten Commandments,* ed. M. Samuel (1956); a valuable Jewish study of the Decalog. W. Beyerlin, *Origins and History of the Oldest Sinaitic Traditions* (E.T. ²1965). H. Graf Reventlow, *Gebot und*

Predigt im Dekalog (1962). N. Lohfink, "Zur Dekalogfassung von Deut. 5," *BZ* N.F. 9 (1965), pp. 17-31. E. Hamel, *Les dix paroles. Perspectives bibliques* (1969). A. Phillips, *Ancient Israel's Criminal Law. A New Approach to the Decalogue* (1970).

(b) K. Hennig, *God's Basic Law. The Ten Commandments for the Man of Today* (1969). H. G. G. Herklots, *The Ten Commandments and Modern Man* (1958). G. A. F. Knight, *Law and Grace. Must a Christian Keep the Law of Moses?* (1962). R. S. Wallace, *The Ten Commandments. A Study of Ethical Freedom* (1965).

Additional studies are referred to in the footnotes of the pages following.

6 *I am the Lord your God*[1]—these opening words are a declaration at the head of the Decalog and form a context for what follows, rather than being simply a part of the first commandment. The words indicate the nature of the speaker of the commandments and give divine authority to the commandments themselves. *Who brought you out of the land of Egypt, out of the house of bondage*—it was because of what God had done for his people that he was in a position to lay upon them certain obligations. But the initiative of God in participating in the lives of his people came prior to the obligations contained in the Decalog, and this sequence provides an important principle for interpreting law and the requirement for obedience. The law was not an arbitrary prescription placed randomly on a group of people. God had delivered or redeemed (Exod. 15:13) his people from a situation of slavery; then, at Horeb, he enacted with them the covenant. Thus the Exodus is the "gospel" placed at the head of the law. In the language of treaty and covenant,[2] his people had formerly been vassals subject to the suzerain authority of the worldly power of the pharaoh; the liberation of the Exodus took them away from the subjection to the old suzerain authority, but introduced them to a new suzerain authority, God himself. The new authority, however, had acted in love for the people and the obligations imposed upon them in the covenant reflected no less the love of God. This, then, is the context in which the Decalog is to be understood; it was law for a people already redeemed, not designed per se to redeem the people. It was, nevertheless, at the heart of the covenant relationship, for the health and the continuity of the covenant depended on the relationship of the people to their God and to their fellow men, and it was to this end that the Decalog gave direction to the people.

7 *The first commandment:* the prohibition of gods other than the Lord. The first commandment clearly establishes the responsibility of the people of God in the covenant relationship, namely, the

---

1. Alternatively, the Hebrew may be rendered: "I, the Lord, am your God."
2. For fuller details at this point, see the discussion of treaty and covenant in the Introduction.

responsibility of absolute faithfulness. They had already experienced the faithfulness of God toward them (5:6) and a response of faithfulness was called for. The commandment is expressed negatively, but it is full of positive implications. Negatively, the Israelites were not to have *other gods*—they were not to commit themselves in any fashion to foreign gods,[3] either those remembered from Egypt or those to be encountered in Canaan. They were to be totally faithful to the God to whom they were bound in the covenant. *Besides me* (Heb. *'al-pānāy*)—the specific meaning of the words has aroused some debate,[4] but seen in the context of the covenant, the sense seems fairly clear. The words are completely exclusive, removing the possibility of a relationship to any other supposed-god. The implications are monotheistic, but in a sense it is misleading to introduce the theme of monotheism at this point. Monotheism is a modern term with philosophical implications, whereas the first commandment is concerned primarily with a direct relationship to the living God, whose reality had already been experienced.

The nature of the temptation presented by *other gods* introduces in a roundabout way the modern significance of the commandment. To take one example, when the Hebrews began to settle in the promised land they would have to assume an agricultural way of life; at first, it would be strange to them, after the years wandering in the desert and, before that, the years in servitude in Egypt. In Canaan they would find that agriculture and religion were closely related. Man depended on the harvest of his crops, and a good harvest was not a fortuitous thing, but a result of the bountifulness of the gods of fertility. For the Canaanite farmer, it may be conjectured, the role of the fertility-gods was at least as important as the necessary task of plowing the field and planting the seed; agriculture was a religious activity, as was all life. The Hebrews, however, would have to learn to become farmers, using the same farmers' tools, but dispensing with the gods of fertility. Their God was God not only in the realm of history, but also in the realm of nature. He would grant the harvest of the field. But the temptation to seek the more visual, palpable assurance that the fertility cult pretended to offer would be difficult to

---

3. S. Goldman, *The Ten Commandments,* p. 135, notes that the words *other gods* occur 64 times in the OT and are in effect a technical description for heathen gods.
4. That is, they have been taken in a henotheistic sense, to imply that the Lord was supreme and first among the gods, but was not necessarily the only God. This interpretation seems to be precluded by the solitary nature of the covenant God. An alternative approach is to render the words "before my face," that is, "in my sight"; the implication would then be that no other gods were to be placed in the shrine of Yahweh (cf. R. Knierim, "Das erste Gebot," *ZAW* 77 [1965], pp. 20-39). The interpretation seems possible at a secondary level, but the primary sense of the commandment in the covenant context is directed rather toward the sphere of relationships and commitments.

avoid. The Hebrews had known their God in the Exodus, had sensed his presence in the desert, but would they also be able to find his presence in the new life style they were about to adopt? Here, in a sense, lies not only the obligation, but also the challenge of the commandment. In the future, which would be a time of radical change, a step into the unknown, the Hebrews were to maintain their total commitment to the Lord. The experience ahead might be new, but their god had already proved his faithfulness. He was to be in the future, as he had been in the past, the total horizon of their lives and experience.

Thus the implications and obligations of the first commandment are far-reaching in their significance. The commandment calls for a style of life dominated by a relationship to God. The commandment was not merely "theology," nor was it concerned simply with the proper form of worship. It affected the whole life of the whole covenant community. Its implications remain the same today; the relationship to one God must dominate every sphere of life, whether the life of action, of thought, or of emotion. There can be no area of life in which a person or thing comes before the commitment to the one God. The *other gods* may take on forms more subtle than wooden images or stone idols; indeed anything that relegates the relationship with God to second place functions in effect as "another god."

8-10   *The second commandment:* the prohibition of images. The second commandment prohibits the making of images intended to represent in some physical way God himself. In other words, it is not images of other gods that are prohibited—that possibility has already been excluded in the first commandment, in which other gods are forbidden outright. Thus the second commandment guards against two possible dangers: (a) that while maintaining the faith and worship of the one Lord, the expression of that faith and worship might adapt itself to the forms (viz., imagery) of the Near Eastern religions; (b) that thereby the Israelite faith and worship might implicitly confine the greatness and transcendence of God.

You shall not make for yourself an image—the first and most immediate danger was that of attempting to render the Lord in human form. Since, on the one hand, God was conceived in personal terms and, on the other hand, man was made in the image of God (Gen. 1:27), the human form represented the most obvious means of attempting to give some visual expression to God. But any such representation would be totally inadequate, for God himself is greater than any attempt to represent him within the created order. *Or*[5] *any form*—after human form, the next danger guarded against was that of

5.   For the translation "or," see 4QDeut. 5:8, which has support from various Heb. mss. and the majority of the versions.

employing anything, animate or inanimate, from the created order in an attempt to represent the Creator. For a fuller discussion, see the commentary on 4:16-19. The only manner in which God could be represented was by means of language. Language, too, is a means of imagery, but it is necessary in order to articulate the knowledge and experience of God. By excluding all means other than language, God was kept free from all human attempts to impose limits on the conception of him. And even language, it may be noted, may become a form of imagery in an illegitimate sense. To construct, by theological propositions, a definition of the nature of God and then to claim adequacy for that definition, would be to construct an image as real as any wooden image. Theology is not thereby forbidden, but its limitations are to be recognized; it may clarify our understanding of the God of revelation, but it cannot confine or circumscribe God to definitions or propositions.

You shall not bow down to them and you shall not serve them—the danger of imagery is that the object, which was intended to function only in a representative fashion, may easily become confused with that which it was intended to represent. Hence the image may become the thing that is worshipped, and this would detract from that proper kind of worship which was a response of love (6:5). It is for this reason that there is a return to the theme already mentioned in 4:24: *I, the Lord your God, am a jealous God.* To worship an image of God was to succumb to the tendency to externalize and formalize the object of worship and as such it detracted from the true response of love. Anything that detracted from this essential relationship of the covenant, the commitment of love, led to the jealousy of God (see the commentary on 4:24). And such false forms of worshipping the Lord inevitably had consequences for future generations (*punishing the iniquity . . .*), for it meant that children and grandchildren would not be instructed properly concerning the covenant relationship which was essential to their life and well-being (see 4:10). Thus, in the covenant community, no man was an island; his acts had repercussions for others and the breach of this commandment could affect his posterity for more than one generation.

One of the effects of the proper observance of this commandment was to preserve the distinctiveness of the Israelite religion in the context of the religions of Israel's neighbors. It has been noted that the giving of this commandment was "perhaps the *unlikeliest* thing that ever happened."[6] The Near Eastern neighbors of Israel used a variety of images to represent their deities, but Israel alone (so far as is known) refused to employ imagery. Israel thus preserved not only

6. Quoted from O. Barfield, *Saving the Appearances. A Study in Idolatry* (n.d.), p. 109.

an external distinctiveness, but also a religious one, for though the Lord could be known immanently in the world of history or nature, he was not confined to those worlds, but was transcendent, as Creator of the world; and that transcendence was preserved in this commandment.

The second commandment contains not only warning but also promise: *acting with loving kindness[7] toward thousands, toward those that love me and keep my commandments.* The element of promise emphasizes again that the thrust of the commandment as a whole is the preservation of the relationship between God and man which is characterized by love. The attempt to limit God to some visual form, and the tendency to worship the attempted representation, meant that the essential love relationship became distorted. Conversely, the prohibition of images, eliminating any visual substitutes for God, meant that man was constantly cast back upon his knowledge of God gained from the experience of God's living reality, especially the experience of the Exodus (5:6), so that he responded in love to an invisible but no less real God.

11 *The third commandment:* the prohibition against the improper use of God's name. Whereas the second commandment guarded against imposing a limitation on God that would disrupt the relationship of love, the third commandment is concerned with a different kind of imposition, that of attempting to manipulate God for purely personal ends. The commandment has often been taken as a prohibition against blasphemy; blasphemy (in the simple sense), however, is too narrow a subject for the commandment in its original setting.[8] The commandment is concerned rather with the *name* of God, which God had revealed to his people.[9] That God had revealed his name (the *Lord* or *Yahweh*) gives some clue to the intimacy of the covenant relationship. However, the *name* of a person or god, in the Near East, was also considered to contain certain implicit power. Hence Balak, the Moabite king, attempted to employ Balaam for the purpose of magically cursing the Israelites in the name of the Lord.[10]

---

7. Heb. *hesed.* The word is difficult to translate with its full implications, but it describes essentially the love of God toward his people within the relationship of the covenant (Deut. 7:9, 12; see also 1 K. 8:23; Neh. 1:5; 9:32; Dan. 9:4). For a detailed study of the word, see N. Glueck, *HESED in the Bible* (1967).

8. A. Phillips, *Ancient Israel's Criminal Law,* p. 53, makes the observation that for the Israelite, "to curse Yahweh would have amounted to suicide. Self-interest made such legislation unnecessary." To illustrate this point in the context of Near Eastern society, there is an Egyptian stele in the British Museum (BM Stele 589) from Dynasty XIX, which was set up by a man who had been struck blind as a punishment for swearing falsely by the god Ptah. See T. E. Peet, *A Comparative Study of the Literatures of Egypt, Palestine and Mesopotamia* (1931), p. 89.

9. See Exod. 3:14 and 6:3.

10. Num. 22–24.

That incident is just one that indicates the variety of types of magic and cursing in the Near East.[11] Thus, at least one of the things prohibited by the third commandment is the use of God's name in magic, which was an explicit attempt to harness God's power for personal ends or for a "worthless purpose."[12] Not only did the commandment forbid the use of God's name in magic, but in positive terms it meant that the Israelite, by faith in the Lord, was free from any influence from the world of magic.[13]

The implications of the commandment, however, in both ancient and modern times, reach beyond the sphere of magic. Any attempt to manipulate God for personal ends comes under the prohibition. Thus, the name of God may be called on in prayer, and prayer is a right and proper form of communication in the covenant community. But prayer too may be misused and may result in an attempt to channel God's power toward some worthless purpose. And in more evident and overt terms, to link God's name to some purely selfish human purpose, whether it be the conduct of war or the undertaking of some human enterprise, may be to use God's name in vain. All such improper uses of God's name have suspended over them a warning, *for the Lord will not leave unpunished him who takes his name in vain.* In contrast, those bound to God in covenant, who know his name in the relationship of love, learn to live within the family of God.

12-15 *The fourth commandment:* the observance of the sabbath. The fourth commandment differs from the preceding three commandments in that it is set in positive form initially (vv. 12-13), though the negative implications are also stated (v. 14). The commandment imposes in effect a double obligation,[14] that of making holy the sabbath day (v. 12) and that of working for six days (v. 13). It is the first part, however, that is most significant and for which a reason is provided (v. 15). The positive formulation of the commandment has some small differences which distinguish it from the form of the commandment in Exod. 20:8-11, and which are further evidence of the hortatory style in which the commandment is presented in Deuteronomy. The Hebrew word used in v. 12 is *shāmôr*, "take care"; in Exod. 20:8, it is rather *zākôr*, "remember" or "remembering."[15] *Just as the Lord your God commanded you*—the words refer back to the first giving of the commandment at Horeb/Sinai.

11. See further the commentary on Deut. 18:9-14, in which the prohibition of magic is discussed.
12. Heb. *shāwe'* has the sense of "vanity" or "worthless purpose."
13. A. Phillips, *op. cit.,* p. 55.
14. See. E. Hamel, *Les dix paroles,* p. 67.
15. See J. D. W. Watts, "Infinitive Absolute as Imperative and the Interpretation of Ex. 20:8," *ZAW* 74 (1962), pp. 141-45. See also A. S. Yahuda, *The Language of the Pentateuch in Its Relation to Egyptian,* p. 11; he notes the use of the infinitive in

On the seventh day, the sabbath, work was forbidden to the master of the house, his children, his servants, his working beasts, and resident aliens. It has been suggested that there is no mention of wives in the otherwise comprehensive list in order to avoid any suggestion that the law also applied to domestic activities.[16]

The reason given for the fourth commandment here (v. 15) differs from that given in Exod. 20:11. Here the Exodus from Egypt is referred to as the antecedent of the sabbath. God had brought his people out of Egypt *with a strong hand and with an outstretched arm; therefore the Lord your God commanded you to keep the sabbath day*.[17] In Exodus, reference is made to the creative work of God undertaken in six days, after which God rested on the seventh day. The two reasons complement each other and both emphasize man's dependence on God. To rest on the sabbath day was to remember that man, as a part of God's created order, was totally dependent on the Creator; man's divinely appointed task to have dominion over the created order (Gen. 1:26) carried with it also the privilege of sharing in God's rest. The Exodus, too, was a type of *creation* and thus forms an analogy to the creation account in Genesis. The Exodus from Egypt marks in effect the creation of God's people as a nation,[18] and the memory of that event was also a reminder to the Israelites of their total dependence upon God. Whereas at one time the Israelites had been slaves in Egypt, with no appointed day of rest from their continual and monotonous labor, God's deliverance made them potentially a nation, and the sabbath was to function as a day of rest in which the deliverance from the former bondage could be remembered with thanksgiving.

The word sabbath is a noun related to the verb *shābat* meaning "cease, rest." Although cognate forms of this verb are found in other Semitic languages, there is no clear evidence of a *sabbath day* (or of time construed as a week)[19] apart from the Israelite tradition. Thus the fourth commandment once again established a point of distinction between the religion of Israel and that of her neighbors.

Egyptian with imperative force when it is used in official diction, citing, by way of evidence, the opening lines of the Merneptah Stela.

16. See A. Phillips, *op. cit.,* p. 69.

17. In one of the Qumran mss. (4QDeut. 5:15; see the concordance in the Introduction), the commandment is given the same reason as in Exod. 20:11.

18. The Heb. of Exod. 15:16(b), part of the song celebrating the Exodus, may be rendered: "till your people pass by, O Lord; till your people whom *you have created* (*qānîtā*) pass by."

19. See W. Rordorf, *BHH* III, p. 1633. The Flood (in the Gilgamesh Epic, tablet XI) lasted for a week, as did the subsidence of the flood waters, but this does not seem to have been a standard division in the reckoning of time in Mesopotamia. See also the account of the Flood in the Epic of Atrahasis: W. G. Lambert and A. R. Millard, *Atra-ḫasīs: The Babylonian Story of the Flood* (1969), pp. 96f. (iv.24-25).

The relationship expressed between the sabbath and the Exodus in this commandment is directly analogous to the relationship between the Lord's Day (Rev. 1:10; the first day of the week) and the resurrection of Jesus Christ in the Christian faith. The Exodus, marking the liberation and "creation" of a new people, was linked to the sabbath; the Exodus had been the redemption of Israel by their God from slavery (Exod. 15:13). Likewise, the resurrection of Jesus Christ marked liberation from an old life and entry into a new life, which was the gift of God in love.[20] Thus, for the Christian, the principle of the fourth commandment remains in force, though the day has been changed. The principle thus provides us with three themes to remember on the day of rest, all of which indicate our dependence upon God. We are creatures of our Creator God, and therefore dependent on him for our life. We are participators in that tradition which goes back in history to the Exodus, when God revealed to his people his activity in human history by liberating his chosen people. We are reborn through our identification with the risen Christ, who may work in us a new creation, recalling the first creation (Exod. 20:11) and the creation of the people of Israel (Deut. 5:15).

16 *The fifth commandment:* the honor of parents. In the second commandment, the parents of children were aware of a heavy responsibility; the danger of imagery could lead to a false relationship with the Lord of the Covenant, which in turn could affect even their great-grandchildren (5:9). Here, the reciprocal side of that responsibility is stated; children were charged: *honor your father and your mother.*[21] The second part of the verse clarifies the specific significance of the commandment—*so that you may live long and it may go well for you on the land.* The close parallel between these words and 4:40 indicates that the basic issue involved in the commandment was the continuity of the covenant. Parents were responsible to teach their children concerning the covenant, and by so doing, both children and parents would prosper in the land (4:9-10, 40) and see the fulfilment of the covenant promise of God. But to teach effectively, there must be a receptive audience. If children did not honor their parents and were rebellious and self-centered, they would not be able to learn about the covenant relationship with God which had been so central to the lives of their parents. And as a consequence of dishonoring their parents, they would not prosper in the promised land, for they would not know intimately the Lord of the covenant promise.

Although the primary significance of the commandment had to do with the continuity of the covenant, one of the fruits of children

20. Eph. 2:4-10.
21. The words following (*as the Lord your God commanded you*) do not occur in Exod. 20:12, and are a further example of the hortatory or sermonic style employed in Deuteronomy.

honoring their parents was to provide a solid family structure for the Israelites. Since the father/son relationship (1:31) was analogous to the God/Israel relationship, this fifth commandment indicates clearly how the covenant community depended on two levels of relationships. The first four commandments were concerned with the man/ God relationship; without a proper relationship to God, a proper relationship to fellow man was impossible. The last five commandments deal specifically with man/man relationships (within the covenant); the proper relationship to God was dependent on a proper man/man relationship. The fifth commandment, falling between these two poles and dealing specifically with the family situation, is in a sense the sphere of the most intimate relationship and is at the core of the covenant community.

The emphasis of the commandment on the continuity of the covenant community presupposes the faithfulness of the covenant God. God had made a promise in the covenant according to which he would bless his people with land and progeny. The fulfilment of the promise of the covenant God, however, would be experienced only as the parents taught their children and as the children honored their parents and learned from the faith of their fathers. Just as the covenant itself involved certain commitments from both parties to the covenant, God and his people, so too there were to be joint commitments within the human family.

17 *The sixth commandment:* the prohibition of murder. This commandment deals specifically with murder and not with all forms of taking life. Thus it does not eliminate the possibility of capital punishment, which was present in Israelite legislation (see Deut. 17:2-7 and 19:12 with commentary), nor does it prohibit war (see Deut. 20–21 for the legislation on war). The verb used in the commandment is *rātsah,* which is employed of killing persons, either in the sense of murder (premeditated killing) or of manslaughter (accidental killing). The commandment forbids the former; manslaughter, which involves accidental death and therefore requires a different type of legislation, is dealt with in Deut. 19:1-13. The prohibition of this commandment is thus against the act of murder by a member of the covenant community for personal and illegitimate reasons.

The reasons underlying the commandment are both social and religious. The commandment protected the individual within the covenant community from any danger at the hands of a fellow member of the community and thus enabled him to experience the blessing of God, which was *long life* (see 4:40) in the promised land. Since each individual Israelite was bound to the Lord in the covenant, his life lay in God's hands. God alone, who had made man in his own image, had the right to terminate life. Thus an act of murder involved the abrogation of divine power, the taking away of that which God had given and which God alone could give, namely life itself.

Premeditated killing involved certain processes of thought culminating in action, and both the process and the act contravened the commandment. However, since the commandment functioned initially as the legislation of a human society, the covenant people of God, it was the act that was prohibited legally and the act that could be punished. The process leading potentially to the act indicates the wider sphere of the commandment and is clarified in the teaching of Jesus on the law (Matt. 5:21-22). In both Testaments, the path toward obedience and fulfilment of the law is characterized as a path of love toward God and toward fellow man (Deut. 6:4-5; Rom. 13:9-10). Love for fellow man involves accepting him as a fellow creature of God; to murder is to ignore man's created nature, to ignore his worth in the sight of God and to eliminate him for purely personal reasons.

18 *The seventh commandment:* the prohibition of adultery. The seventh commandment deals specifically with *adultery* and not with the various other matters relating to sexual and conjugal behavior; these latter are dealt with in detail in the legislation in Deut. 22–25. The prohibition here is against sexual relationships between two persons, one or both of whom are married to another party or parties. The legislation probably considers "betrothed" girls as being the equivalent (in law) of married women (see Deut. 22:23-24).

The reason why adultery is singled out for attention in the Decalog is because adultery, more than other illicit sexual behavior, has to do with unfaithfulness in a relationship of commitment. Marriage was a binding commitment of faithfulness between two persons and it was in principle similar to the covenant relationship itself. The crime of adultery was the social equivalent to the religious crime of having *other gods* (5:5); both offenses involved unfaithfulness and both were therefore reprehensible to the God of the covenant, whose character it was to be totally faithful. It is this emphasis, that faithfulness (expressed in obedience) must permeate every sphere of life, both the religious and the secular, that gives a distinctive character to the Israelite law on adultery. Adultery of one partner in a marriage involved not only unfaithfulness to the other partner, but also unfaithfulness to God.[22]

Thus the primary emphasis of the law is a guarding against unfaithfulness in the marriage relationship. The theme of this law, in both its negative and positive aspects, becomes conversely one of the important analogies employed in the Bible for describing the covenant relationship between God and his people. It was employed to show, negatively, the constant tendency by the people of God toward

---

22. Adultery of a wife in Near Eastern law was primarily a secular offense against the husband: see, e.g., the Code of Hammurabi, law 129 (*ANET*, p. 171). See also W. Kornfeld, "L'adultère dans l'Orient Antique," *RB* 57 (1950), pp. 92-109.

"spiritual adultery" and, positively, the faithfulness and love of God for his people despite their unfaithfulness.[23]

19 *The eighth commandment:* the prohibition of theft. At first sight, the commandment seems to be a simple prohibition of theft, that is, the unlawful acquisition of the property or possessions of another person or group of persons. However, although simple theft was forbidden in Israelite law (see, e.g., Exod. 22:1-13), something more specific is specified by this commandment. The commandment, unlike the more general legislation on theft, is concerned specifically with relationships between persons within the covenant community, rather than with property. Thus the primary prohibition of the commandment is against manstealing, or something akin to kidnapping;[24] see Deut. 24:7 for a more elaborate description of the crime.

By manstealing is meant the taking of a person, presumably by force, and the "sale" of that person for personal profit or gain. The clearest example of the kind of crime envisaged by the commandment is provided in the account of the capture and sale of Joseph by his brothers to some travelling Midianite traders (Gen. 37:22-28). The brothers gained personal profit from the transaction, but the effect of the crime on Joseph was to cut him off completely from his family. If this is indeed the type of crime envisaged by the commandment, it can be seen, once again, to be a crime that would disrupt the basic covenant relationship between a man and his God. Though not so final as the crime of murder, it was similar in principle in that it involved a human act which removed a man from the covenant relationship. It was thus an act directly contrary to the love and will of God as expressed toward man in the covenant. It was an act in which one man assumed control of the life and fate of another man for his own personal gain, thereby assuming a right that properly belongs only to God.

The modern variations of the act prohibited in this commandment are numerous and constantly in the news. One exclusively contemporary crime is the hijacking of passenger airplanes. In general terms, such a crime involves a violation of the eighth commandment, for it is an act in which human lives are held in ransom for personal gain of some kind. The various types of kidnapping also fall under the condemnation of this command. The law assumes the inviolable freedom of man under God; the crime both transgresses that freedom and intervenes in a realm in which only God has a right to

---

23. See, e.g., Ezek. 16; Hos. 1–3.
24. See, *inter al.,* A. Alt, "Das Verbot des Diebstahls im Dekalog," *Kleine Schriften* I (1953), pp. 333-340; E. Hamel, *Les dix paroles,* pp. 82-87; A. Phillips, *Ancient Israel's Criminal Law,* pp. 130-32.

act. But it is not usually in these dramatic forms, but in more subtle forms, that the danger presents itself. Any act that involves the manipulation of another human being for personal gain is tantamount to the crime, and in a day when promotion and personal progress have been described as a "rat race," the temptation to manipulate other people may often confront us. In this sense, the eighth commandment forms a parallel to the third; the improper use of God's name amounted to an attempt to manipulate God for personal gain, just as manstealing was an attempt to manipulate one's fellow man for personal gain.

The foregoing comments do not mean that the commandment had nothing to do with simple theft; they point rather to the worst form of theft, manstealing, which disrupted the relationship between a man and the community of God. The prohibition of simple theft follows as a natural corollary in the wider implications of the commandments.

20 *The ninth commandment:* the prohibition of false witnesses. The wording of the commandment indicates that the primary prohibition has to do with the process of law. *Vain*[25] *witness*—the word *witness* (*'ēd*) refers to a statement given against a *neighbor* (a fellow member of the covenant community) in a legal case. Since the evidence given against the defendant in a case determined his future, it was vital that all evidence that was given be true evidence. (These matters are discussed more fully in the commentary on 19:15-21, where the detailed legislation is given.) The worst type of false witness would be that which led to the death sentence, but any false witness led to the possibility of a miscarriage of justice.[26]

The principle involved, once again, was that the breach of the commandment undermined a basic characteristic of the covenant, namely, *faithfulness*—of God to man, of man to God, and of man to fellow man. To bring false witness against a fellow member of the covenant community involved lying and various forms of deception; it would be motivated by self-interest. The result (if successful) would be the false punishment of a neighbor, and even if unsuccessful, it could cast doubt by implication on the character of that neighbor. In other words, even if false witness did not lead directly to a miscarriage of justice, its effects could be tantamount to slander and defamation of character. The focus of the commandment is thus again on the matter of personal human relationships, and it emphasizes the integrity and

25. The Heb. here is "vain" (*shāwe'*); in Exod. 20:16 it is *shāqer*, "false, deceptive," though the general meaning would appear to be the same. See Phillips, *ibid.*, p. 142.
26. The Code of Hammurabi begins with four laws specifying various types of false witness: (a) bringing an unproved charge of murder; (b) bringing an unproved charge of sorcery; (c) false witness in a capital case; (d) false witness in a civil case (*ANET*, p. 166).

honesty required within the community of God. Though the immediate context of the commandment was in the sphere of legal process, the implications applied to the activities of daily life. A God of faithfulness, who did not deal deceitfully with his people, required of his people the same transparency and honesty in personal relationships.

21 *The tenth commandment:* the prohibition of coveting. The last commandment has aroused a certain debate about its meaning,[27] for which there are a number of reasons. Unlike the previous nine commandments, the tenth is concerned primarily with motivation rather than with act. This emphasis produces difficulty because since the commandments, in their initial setting, were the laws of a community under God, they set down regulations for a way of life; disobedience of those regulations required legal action on the part of the community, in order that the relationship to the Lord of the community might be maintained. How then, it might be asked, could a breach of this commandment be known by the community to have taken place? Although it has been suggested that the verb "covet" (*ḥāmaḏ*) means desire leading to action (and thus the action would indicate the contravention of the law), that possibility does not seem to be the case in the wording of the law here. In the first clause, *ḥāmaḏ* is used, and then a synonym is used in the second main clause, "strongly desire" (Hithp. of *'āwāh*), which quite clearly expresses desire or longing.

It is likely that this tenth and final commandment should be interpreted simply as a probition of desire or coveting, without there being any suggestion of an act. As such it forms a suitable conclusion for the Decalog, and in particular it is an effective summary of the spirit of commandments 6-9. In all those commandments, the normal motivation involved, which would lead to the transgression, would be self-interest. A sane man does not kill for the love of killing, but in the hope of attaining personal benefit. The act of adultery involves interest in another person, but again that is closely related to self-interest. A similar thread of self-interest has been traced in the kinds of acts prohibited by the eighth and ninth commandments. Self-interest, or selfishness, may be a dangerous thing when it assumes a dominant role in a man's life. But in more specific terms, the nature of the covenant community required that there be two primary foci for a man's life—the God of the covenant and the fellow members of the

27. In addition to the general works already referred to, see the following: J. R. Coates, "Thou shalt not covet," *ZAW* 52 (1934), pp. 238f.; G. W. Buchanan, "The 'Spiritual' Commandment," *Journal of the American Academy of Religion* 36 (1968), pp. 126f.; C. H. Gordon, "A Note on the Tenth Commandment," *Journal of Bible and Religion* 31 (1963), pp. 208f.; *idem*, "The Ten Commandments," *Christianity Today* 8 (1964), pp. 624-28; W. L. Moran, "The Conclusion of the Decalogue," *CBQ* 29 (1967), pp. 543-554.

covenant community of God. Thus all the last five commandments prohibit a wrong attitude to neighbors; commandments 6-9 prohibit wrong acts toward them and commandment 10 is comprehensive in prohibiting *desire* leading to any such act. It is comprehensive also in delineating the areas in which covetous desire might—but must not—be evoked; there must be no coveting of persons, possessions, or property.

It is this dimension of the commandments that is taken up in the teaching of Jesus (Matt. 5:21-48). Not only the act, but also the desire is condemned, partly because the desire is what leads to the act, and partly because whether or not the desire leads to the act, it betrays the same wrong attitude toward a neighbor. By setting the commandments in this light, to include both desire and act, the life of total obedience seems suddenly remote, but thereby the true dimensions of the law are revealed. The member of the family of God is once again cast back on the grace of the Lawgiver (see the commentary on 5:6), but this in turn stresses the true spirit of the commandment: *you shall love the Lord your God . . .* (6:5). And then, from the relationship of love, the commandment remains, but in a different light. The neighbor's world is not one to be coveted, but the neighbor is to be loved as a fellow member of the family of God.

3. MOSES' MEDIATORY ROLE AT HOREB (5:22-33)

22 *The Lord proclaimed these words with a great voice to all your assembly on the mountain, from the middle of the fire, the cloud, and the dense mist; and he did not add to them. And he wrote them on two tablets of stone and he gave them to me.*

23 *And when you heard the voice from the midst of the darkness, and the mountain was burning with fire, then you approached me, all the chiefs of your tribes and your elders,*

24 *and you said: Behold, the Lord our God has revealed to us his glory and his greatness, and we have heard his voice from the midst of the fire. This very day we have seen God speak with man and he still lives!*

25 *But now, why should we die? For this great fire will surely consume us! If we continue to hear the voice of the Lord our God still further, then we shall die!*

26 *For who is there of all mankind that has heard the voice of the living God speaking from the middle of the fire, as we have, and he still lives?*

27 *You go near and hear all that the Lord our God says. Then you proclaim to us all that the Lord our God proclaims to you, and we shall listen and we shall act.*

28 *And the Lord heard the sound of your words, when you spoke to me, and the Lord said to me: I have heard the sound of the words of this people which they have spoken to you. They are right in all that they have said.*

29 *Would that they were continually of this mind, to fear me and to keep all my commandments, so that it might go well for them and for their children for ever.*
30 *Go, say to them: Return to your tents.*
31 *But as for you, stand here with me and let me speak to you about the whole commandment, and about the statutes and the judgments which you must teach them, so that they will do them in the land which I am about to give them to possess.*
32 *So you must take care to do just as the Lord your God has commanded you. You shall not turn aside to the right hand or to the left.*
33 *You must walk in all the way that the Lord your God has commanded you, so that you may live and prosper and you may prolong your life in the land which you will possess.*

22   This verse acts as a conclusion to the Ten Commandments (*these words*) and leads into the next section concerning Moses' role as a mediator of the covenant. The verse emphasizes in conclusion the divine origin of the commandments (*the Lord proclaimed these words*) and their comprehensive and complete nature (*he did not add to them*—see also 4:2). Their continuity and fixed nature is affirmed by God inscribing them *on two tablets of stone* (see 4:13) and delivering them to Moses. The event itself is described in very concise terms, but it is presented in more detail in 9:9–10:5. The emphasis in this verse on the awe-inspiring phenomena that accompanied the revelation of God (*the fire, the cloud, and the dense mist*) leads directly into the following section, in which the people, awed by their experience, bring a request to Moses.

23-27   The people request Moses to act on their behalf and to continue in the presence of God to hear the words God intends for them. The request arises directly out of the apprehension that God's presence evoked. They delegate their chiefs (see 1:15) and elders to approach Moses with their request (*you approached*[1] *me*). Their anxiety, specifically, arose from having heard God's voice and survived to tell of the experience (v. 24). The words give some insight into the people's concept of the reality and awesomeness of their God. Though he could not literally be seen, God could be known, but to *see* the phenomena surrounding his presence was exceptional rather than normal. It was the exceptional occurrence that terrified the people and reminded them of their *mortality.*[2] It is easy to have too small a view of God in the mind, but the experience of the presence of God may shatter the inadequacy of such a view and impress rather the awesomeness of *the living God* (v. 26). Therefore

---

1. Heb. *tiqreḇûn.* Alternatively the verb may be rendered as *"they* approached," assuming a 3rd masc. plur. imperfect with preformative /t/, as occasionally in Ugaritic.
2. *Mankind* (v. 26) is Heb. *baśar* (lit. "flesh"), which implies mortality and fragility (see Jer. 17:5).

they request Moses to go into God's presence and then afterward to communicate to them the words of God. They were not consciously trying to avoid their responsibilities and they committed themselves to hear and obey Moses in his role as mediator[3] between them and God: *we shall listen and we shall act* (v. 27).

28-31 The Lord responds to Moses and the people, having heard and approved their request (v. 28). *Would that they were continually*[4] *of this mind*—the attitude expressed in the people's request was a proper and a reverential one, but unfortunately it was not a typical attitude. On a previous occasion when God had overheard the people's words, as here, he was provoked to anger (1:34). The reverence shown now was in response to the phenomena accompanying God's revelation, and though it was not thereby any less genuine, it was nevertheless regrettable that the people could not show the same reverence in the more mundane affairs of daily life. It was not only that lack of reverence betrayed the wrong attitude to God, but also that such a lack was not good for the people themselves. If they always maintained an attitude of true reverence, then indeed it would *go well for them and for their children for ever* (v. 29).

The people were then sent to their tents while Moses continued in the intimacy of the presence of God: *but as for you, stand*[5] *here with me and let me speak to you. . . .* The whole commandment was delivered to Moses and he was charged to deliver it to the people in order that they might live obediently in the promised land.

32-33 The foregoing verses (22-31) have been in the now familiar form of recollection (see Deut. 1–4); Moses presented his recollection of the events immediately following the giving of the commandments at Horeb. Now his attention returns to the present, to the people assembled before him on the plains of Moab, and he emphasizes the significance of past events for the present and the future. The people are charged to *take care to do just as the Lord your God has commanded you.* But the people had not literally heard God pronounce all the statutes and judgments (see v. 31) and the temptation to disobedience could take the form of assuming that the law was, after all, only the word of Moses. The wrongness and impossibility of such an assumption has been emphasized by Moses in the previous verses; hence the words he has spoken and will be speaking are words

3. The mediatory role of Moses in the covenant parallels that of the third party often involved in the making of a treaty: Buis and Leclercq, *Le Deutéronome,* p. 73.
4. Heb. "all the days."
5. In some of the Gnostic sects contemporary with early Christianity, this theme was developed: Dositheus, a leader of one such sect, is referred to as the *standing one,* who thus claimed to have knowledge of the true commandments of God. See R. M. Grant, *Gnosticism and Early Christianity* (1966), p. 92. In contrast, Moses' mediatory role involved no arrogant claims for himself; he assumed the role in response to the people's request and with the permission of God.

from God and as such they require obedience. Moses' role as mediator meant that he communicated the revelation of God to the people, but the authority of that revelation lay in its source, God, not in the mediator. On v. 33, see 4:26 and 40 with commentary. The focus in the address of Moses remains on the land beyond the Jordan, the land in which he would not set foot, yet one that the people would soon possess for themselves.

4. THE PRINCIPAL COMMANDMENT: TO LOVE GOD (6:1-9)

1 *And this is the commandment, the statutes and the ordinances, which the Lord your God commanded me to teach you, so that you may act accordingly in the land into which you are about to cross over to possess;*

2 *so that all the days of your life you may fear the Lord your God by keeping all his statutes and commandments, which today I am about to command you and your son and your grandson; and so that you might prolong your life.*

3 *So you shall hear, O Israel, and you shall take care to act accordingly, so that it may go well for you and so that you might increase greatly, just as the Lord God of your fathers said to you (a land flowing with milk and honey).*

4 *Hear, O Israel. The Lord our God is one Lord.*

5 *And you shall love the Lord your God with all your heart and with all your soul and with all your strength.*

6 *And these commandments, which I am about to command you today, shall be upon your heart.*

7 *And you shall repeat them to your children, and you shall talk about them when you are sitting in your house and when you are walking in the road, and when you are lying down and rising up.*

8 *And you shall bind them as a sign upon your hand, and they shall be as frontlets on your forehead.*

9 *And you shall write them on the doorposts of your house and on your gates.*

1-3 These three verses are introductory to the next great portion of Moses' address, the "first and great commandment" to love God. *This is the commandment, the statutes and the ordinances*—the singular (*commandment*) may refer to the same principle underlying all the law (though see 5:31), in which case *statutes* and *ordinances* are in apposition, describing the general laws based on the first principle. *Which the Lord your God commanded me*[1] *to teach you*—the words may refer back to 5:22-33, where Moses' mediatory role is described. He remained in the presence of the Lord to receive his word, and then went out to teach it to the people in order

---

1. "Me" is provided for the sense in English, but is not present in the Hebrew.

that the people might *act accordingly* (Heb. "to do": see also v. 3) in the promised land. The object of Moses' teaching of the law was life-long *fear* (or reverence) of *the Lord your²* God; the evidence of this reverence would be seen in the obedience of the Israelites to God's law, and its fruit would be long life (see also 5:33). Therefore, the people are commanded to *hear* (or "obey": see 5:1) in order that they might find the full prosperity of life promised by *the Lord God of your fathers* (v. 3). A *land flowing with milk and honey³*—the phrase occurs a number of times in Deuteronomy (11:9; 26:9, 15; 27:3; 31:20) and describes the richness of the land which the Israelites were soon to possess.

Verses 4-9,⁴ known in the Jewish tradition as the *Shemaʿ*,⁵ contain what have been called "the fundamental truth of Israel's religion" and "the fundamental duty founded upon it."⁶ The fundamental truth has to do with the nature of God as one (v. 4); the fundamental duty is the response of love which God requires of man (v. 5). Both themes are taken up in the teaching of Jesus (Mark 12:29-30; see also Matt. 22:37 and Luke 10:27). The relationship of the two themes to the law and their importance to the Israelite are examined in vv. 6-9.

4 *Hear, O Israel*—see also 5:1,⁷ where the same phrase opens the chapter containing the Decalog, just as here the words introduce a major and important part of Moses' address. *The Lord our God is one Lord.* The Hebrew at this point can be rendered in a number of different ways,⁸ and it is possible that "one" is intended as a name or title of God: C. H. Gordon has suggested the rendering, "Yahweh is our God, Yahweh is 'One.' "⁹

---

2. The Heb. reverts in this verse to the 2nd person singular, after using the plural in v. 1.
3. The phrase seems to be out of place in its present position. RSV resolves the difficulty by adding a preposition ("*in* a land"), though there is no textual evidence to support this. The best solution may be to transpose the phrase to the end of v. 1, which may have been its original position and where it complements the sense.
4. For exegetical studies of this passage, see W. Rupprecht in H. Breit and C. Westermann, eds., *Die alttestamentlichen Texte*. Calwer Predigthilfen 3 (1964), pp. 145-153; N. Lohfink, *Höre, Israel! Auslegung von Texten aus dem Buch Deuteronomium* (1965), pp. 54-71.
5. For the significance of the *Shemaʿ* in rabbinic thought, see S. Schechter, *Aspects of Rabbinic Theology* (1965 printing), pp. 65-79.
6. S. R. Driver, *Deuteronomy*, p. 89.
7. On the use of these words in Deut. (esp. chs. 5-11), see N. Lohfink, *Das Hauptgebot*, p. 66.
8. The Heb. may also be rendered: "the Lord our God, the Lord is one" (compare with Mark 12:29); "the Lord is our God: the Lord is one." See further the notes above. On the use of the *litera majuscula* at the end of the first and last words of v. 4, see Keil and Delitzsch, *The Pentateuch*, p. 322; S. R. Driver, *Deuteronomy*, p. 90; GKC § 5 n.
9. "His Name is 'One'," *JNES* 29 (1970), pp. 198f. M. Dahood suggests rendering the

These words, which have been called the fundamental monotheistic dogma of the OT,[10] have both practical and theological implications. The Israelites had already discovered the practical implications when they celebrated the Exodus in song: "Who is like you, O Lord, among the gods?" (Exod. 15:11), a rhetorical question inviting a negative response—there were no gods like the Lord! In the Exodus, the Israelites had discovered the uniqueness of their God and that the Egyptian "gods" could do nothing to stop the Lord's people leaving Egypt. It was because they had experienced the living presence of their God in history that the Israelites could call the Lord *our God*. Thus the oneness and reality of the Lord were practical knowledge to the people.

But there were also theological implications and the context of this verse indicates its source as a direct revelation from God (v. 1). The word expresses not only the *uniqueness* but also the *unity* of God. As one God (or the "Unique"), when he spoke there was no other to contradict; when he promised, there was no other to revoke that promise; when he warned, there was no other to provide refuge from that warning.[11] He was not merely first among the gods, as Baal in the Canaanite pantheon, Amon-Re in Egypt, or Marduk in Babylon; he was the one and only God and as such he was omnipotent. It was this all-powerful Unique God who imposed on Israel the charge to love him, thereby revealing another aspect of his character.

5   *You shall love the Lord your God*—this command, based on the statement of the previous verse, is central to the whole book of Deuteronomy. E. W. Nicholson, commenting on the sermon-like style of the book, has noted that "it is in a very real sense true to say that the entire book is a commentary on the command which stands at its beginning: 'You shall love the Lord your God . . . .'"[12] The command to love is central because the whole book is concerned with the renewing of the covenant with God, and although the renewal demanded obedience, that obedience would be possible only when it

whole verse: "Obey, Israel, Yahweh. Yahweh our God is the Unique." See *RSP* I (1972), p. 361.

10. W. Rupprecht, in Breit and Westermann, *op. cit.,* p. 149 ("Grunddogma").

11. There is a striking contrast here to Mesopotamian religious thought, where the multiplicity of gods could produce a great tension in man's life. Though man might perform his religious duties diligently, he could not be guaranteed security, for if there was strife among the gods, that could radically affect his life. This type of tension and unease is shown, for example, in the Flood account of Gilgamesh XI, where the flood seems to be a result of Enlil's whim; it was only through the goodness of Ea (Enki) that Utnapishtim was forewarned and escaped. The polytheistic belief structure included deities both benevolent and malevolent toward man; though one god might promise much, a more powerful god might threaten disaster. As a consequence, this tension in man led to a strongly pessimistic element in that religion.

12. *Deuteronomy and Tradition,* p. 46.

was a response of love to the God who had brought the people out of Egypt and was leading them into the promised land. The language of love is reminiscent both of treaty language[13] in the Near East and also of the analogy of the father/son relationship[14] which has already been employed in Deuteronomy. The language of loving God, however, is not drawn directly from the treaty terminology;[15] rather it is one of the features of the Hebrew relationship to God which made possible the use of the treaty terminology in the first place, and also the use of the father/son analogy.

The injunction to love was based on the precedent of God's love, which had been shown to the Israelites principally in the Exodus, and, in a larger context, in their election and calling from the time of Abraham. The people were called upon to love God with their whole beings—*with all your heart and with all your soul and with all your strength.*[16] The all-encompassing love for God was to find its expression in a willing and joyful obedience of the commandments of God; this theme is developed in the next four verses.

6-9 The commandments, which provided the framework within which the Israelites could express their love of God, were to be *upon your heart*—that is, the people were to think on them and meditate about them, so that obedience would not be a matter of formal legalism, but a response based upon understanding. By reflecting on the commandments, they were reflecting on God's words (6:1); and by understanding the path of life set down by the commandments, they would at the same time be discovering the way in which God's love for them was given expression. Having understood the commandments for themselves, the people were then responsible for their children: *you shall repeat*[17] *them to your children* (a theme already familiar; see Deut. 4:9). The commandments were to be the subject of conversation both inside and outside the home, from the beginning of the day to the end of the day. In summary, the commandments were to permeate every sphere of the life of man.[18]

---

13. For details see W. L. Moran, "The Ancient Near Eastern Background of the Love of God in Deuteronomy," *CBQ* 25 1963), pp. 77-87; M. Weinfeld, *Deuteronomy and the Deuteronomic School* (1972), pp. 333f.; N. Lohfink, *Höre, Israel!* p. 63.
14. D. J. McCarthy, *CBQ* 27 (1965), pp. 144-47. See also J. W. McKay, "Man's Love for God in Deuteronomy," *VT* 22 (1972), pp. 426-435.
15. See R. E. Clements, *God's Chosen People*, p. 83.
16. The words have been translated in the traditional manner, but on the meaning of *heart* and *soul*, see the commentary on 4:29. On the rendering of these words in the LXX and the NT, see Keil and Delitzsch, *The Pentateuch*, p. 324.
17. Heb. *shinnantām*, "repeat"; the meaning of the verb has been clarified by Ugaritic. See G. R. Driver, *Canaanite Myths and Legends* (1956), p. 151; M. Dahood, *Ugaritic-Hebrew Philology* (1965), p. 74.
18. Verses 7-9 have many similarities to Prov. 6:20-22; see the study of P. D. Miller, "Apotropaic Imagery in Proverbs 6:20-22," *JNES* 29 (1970), pp. 129f.

The injunctions given in vv. 8 and 9 continue to emphasize the important role the commandments were to play in man's life. It is uncertain whether the verses were intended to be taken literally in their initial context, or whether they had a metaphorical sense. In either case, they came to be taken literally during the course of Jewish history. *They shall be as frontlets*[19] *on your forehead.*[20] The frontlet, or phylactery, came into use as a small container enclosing a parchment on which a number of biblical verses were written.[21] A number of examples of such frontlets have been found among the discoveries made in the region of the Dead Sea.[22] *And you shall write them on the doorposts of your house and on your gates.*[23] This injunction, too, has been interpreted literally: the word translated *doorposts (m^ezûzot)* has become a proper noun, *mezuzah.* The mezuzah was a small box containing a parchment; a mezuzah discovered in one of the Qumran caves contained the text of Deut. 10:12–11:21.[24] Whether taken literally or metaphorically, the signs described in vv. 8-9 indicate that the individual (v. 8), his home, and his community (v. 9) were to be distinguished in their character by obedience to the commandments as a response of love for God.

5. INSTRUCTIONS CONCERNING THE PROMISED LAND (6:10-25)

10 *And it shall be that the Lord your God will bring you in to the land which he promised to your fathers — to Abraham, to Isaac, and to Jacob — to give to you: great and good cities which you did not build;*
11 *and houses filled with every good thing which you did not fill; and hewn cisterns which you did not hew; vineyards and olive trees which you did not plant. Then you shall eat and you shall be satisfied.*

19.   The Heb. (*tōṭāpōt*) is sometimes rendered "phylactery" after the Gk. translation of the Heb. word. The etymology and ancient significance of the word are uncertain, but see the careful study of E. A. Speiser, in *Jewish Quarterly Review* 48 (1957), pp. 208-217.
20.   The Heb. is literally "between your eyes"; for the translation "forehead," see S. R. Driver, *Deuteronomy*, p. 93, and on the basis of the Ugaritic evidence, Gordon, *UT*, p. 96, n. 1; G. R. Driver, *Canaanite Myths and Legends*, p. 83. See also Deut. 11:18.
21.   The texts seem to vary slightly; the standard texts included were Exod. 13:1-10 and 11-16; Deut. 6:4-9; 11:13-21; sometimes the Decalog was also included.
22.   For examples, see *DJD* II (1961), pp. 83f.; *DJD* III (1962), pp. 149-157.
23.   M. Dahood's implication (in *RSP* I, p. 158) that the words here translated "house" and "gates" are synonymous (based on the parallel use of the words in Ugaritic in Ps. 122:1-2) seems unlikely. The words specify rather the smaller and larger communities; the sign was to be on the doorpost of the *house* (representing the family) and the *gates* (representing the community: the village or the town).
24.   See *DJD* III (1962), pp. 158-161.

12 *Take care lest you forget the Lord, who brought you out from the land of Egypt, from the house of slavery.*

13 *You shall fear the Lord your God and you shall serve him and you shall swear in his name.*

14 *You shall not go after other gods, from the gods of the peoples who will be round about you,*

15 *lest the Lord your God's anger be kindled against you and he exterminate you from the face of the earth, for the Lord your God is a jealous God in your midst.*

16 *You shall not put the Lord your God to the test as you put him to the test at Massah.*

17 *You shall diligently keep the commandments of the Lord your God, together with his testimonies and his statutes which he commanded you.*

18 *And you shall do what is right and good in the eyes of the Lord, so that it may go well for you and you may enter and take possession of the good land, which the Lord promised to your fathers,*

19 *by ejecting all your enemies before you, just as the Lord has said.*

20 *When, in time to come, your son shall ask you, saying: What is the meaning of the testimonies and the statutes and the judgments which the Lord our God commanded you?*

21 *then shall you say to your son: We were slaves of pharaoh in Egypt. Then the Lord brought us out from Egypt with a strong hand.*

22 *And the Lord provided great and calamitous signs and wonders against Egypt, against pharaoh, and against all his household before our very eyes.*

23 *Then he brought us out from there, so that he might bring us in to give to us the land which he promised to our fathers.*

24 *And the Lord commanded us to do all these statutes, to fear the Lord our God, for our own good always, to keep us alive at this very day.*

25 *And we shall have righteousness, if we are careful to do this whole code of law in the presence of the Lord our God, just as he commanded us.*

10-11 Anticipation of the promised land. In the days ahead, the Lord was going to lead his people into the land that had been anticipated since the promise given to Abraham. There is here an explicit identification of that ancient promise to the patriarchs with the generation now present before Moses on the plains of Moab: *the land which he promised to your fathers . . . to give to you.* That the ancient promise was so close to being fulfilled gave cause not only for joy, but also for solemnity in view of the responsibility that the promise imposed. Moses expresses the joy by describing the bounty of the land God was going to give: the clauses beginning with *great and good cities* (or perhaps "towns") are all descriptive of the *land* (v. 10a) and indicate its "ready-made" character. The lines have a poetic quality about them which seems to serve a particular function. The poetic quality can be set out as follows:

Great and good cities,	*Which you[1] did not build;*	(3+3)
And houses filled with every		
good thing,	*Which you did not fill;*	(3+3)
And hewn cisterns,	*Which you did not hew;*	(2+3)
Vineyards and olive trees,	*Which you did not plant;*	(2+3)
Then you shall eat	*And you shall be satisfied.*	(1+1)

Following this passage, in which the pleasantness of the land is portrayed, there is a dramatic change of emphasis.

12 *Take care lest you forget the Lord*—this would be the danger facing the people when they settled in the land. The preaching style here has effectively expressed the danger Moses was concerned about. The meditation on the pleasantness of the land (vv. 10-11) evokes pleasure and anticipation, and then the relaxing tone of the poetic lines is sharply interrupted by the imperative — *Take care*. In the land, its very richness and goodness could lull the people into an attitude of forgetfulness which would be disastrous. In the good land, they were to remember their past and the *Lord, who brought you out from the land of Egypt* (v. 12).

13 *You shall fear[2] the Lord your God[3] and you shall serve him.* You shall serve (*ta'ᵃbod̠*) is in contrast to the house of *slavery* (*ᵃbād̠îm*); both words are derived from the same root and contrast vividly the old and the new masters of Israel. The pharaoh (who was considered a god in the Egyptian religion) had for a long time been the suzerain lord of the Israelites in a literal, worldly sense; in the Exodus, the Lord had broken the old ties binding his people to Egypt and had thus won the right to call them his vassals. Since the basis of nationhood in their new land was established on the power of their God, the Israelites were not to forget their liberation, but rather they were to continue to serve their Lord. *And you shall swear in his name* — the context suggests that the reference of these words is to the oath of allegiance to God as the Lord of the covenant; because he had liberated his people from Egypt, they committed themselves solemnly to him in obedience and love. The words come to be synonymous with the true worshipper of the Lord (see Ps. 63:11, E.T.).[4]

---

1. Though rhyme is not a regular feature of Hebrew poetic style, the ending of each line in -*tā* creates an effect similar to rhyme by means of repetition. The numbers in brackets indicate the stress count per line.
2. The *fear* or reverence of the Lord has already been emphasized in Deut. 4:10; 5:29; 6:2; it continues to be an important theme in the following chapters.
3. This grammatical object, and the two other objects in this verse, are all placed before their respective verbs in the Heb. for reasons of emphasis.
4. On the significance of v. 13 (as a whole) for Jesus, see Matt. 4:10; Luke 4:8. On the relationship between the latter part of the verse and Matt. 5:34, see R. V. G. Tasker,

14-15 On *other gods,* see the first commandment (5:7) and commentary. Although the thought of following *other gods* might have seemed a remote possibility to the people as they were assembled in Moses' presence, it could become a very real possibility the moment they forgot (v. 12) the Lord, their Deliverer. To follow other gods would automatically arouse God's anger, since it would be an act of unfaithfulness. It would be tantamount to going back into Egypt, for to follow another god was to confess a god or suzerain other than the Lord and to reject thereby the grace of God already shown to them during the course of their history. A *jealous god* — see the commentary on 4:24.

16 For the incident at Massah, see Exod. 17:1-7 (see also Deut. 9:22).[5] At *Massah* (the place of *testing*), the Israelites had *put the Lord . . . to the test;* they had behaved rebelliously against the Lord and Moses in a situation calling for faith and trust. Many similar situations would arise during the course of the settlement in the promised land, and so Moses employs the incident from the past as a reminder and warning relevant to the future.

17-19 Rather than testing God, the people were to be diligent in their obedience of his commandments. Only by obedience would the people prosper in the land: the land was essentially good (vv. 10-11), but the people would experience its goodness (v. 18) only when they were obedient to the Lord who had promised the land. The preaching style is evident in these verses. Many themes are repeated which have already been mentioned earlier in Deuteronomy (compare vv. 17-18 with 1:35; 4:1, 5; 5:29; 6:1; etc.): the repetition seeks to drive home the requirement of obedience on which the success of events still lying in the future depended.

20-25[6] A son's question and a father's answer. The son asks: *What is the meaning[7] of the testimonies . . . ?* The nature of the question implies a good family relationship, the kind envisaged by the positive implications of the fifth commandment (see 5:16 and commentary). The positive nature of the question is shown by the identification of the questioner with the God of the covenant, even though he was not present at the initial making of the covenant; thus he is asking about the commandments *which the Lord *our God commanded *you.* It is a question from a youth growing to maturity in the covenant

---

The Gospel According to St. Matthew. Tyndale NT Commentaries (1961), pp. 66f. On the subsequent debates relating to these verses, see E. G. Kraeling, *The OT since the Reformation,* p. 27, who discusses the differences between Calvin and the Anabaptists on this point.

5. See Matt. 4:7 (Luke 4:12) for Jesus' use of this verse in refuting Satan during the temptation in the wilderness.
6. For a discussion of the view that vv. 21-25 were an ancient "creed," see the commentary on 26:5-9.
7. The Heb. is simply "what" (*māh*). - "

community, already instructed in obedience, but wishing to know and understand the meaning and significance of the commandments that shaped the course of his daily life.

The answer that the father was to give to his son's question contains a condensation of the principal elements of the faith of the Israelites; in order to present that condensation clearly, it is given in outline form below:

INTRODUCTION
1. *The previous situation:* vassals of the Egyptian pharaoh (v. 21).
THE REVELATION OF GOD IN HISTORY
2. *The experience of God:* the deliverance of the Exodus (v. 21).
3. *The judgment of God:* God's dealings with Egypt (v. 22).
4. *The purpose of God:* to grant his people the promised land (v. 23).
THE REVELATION OF THE WORD OF GOD
5. *The word of God:* the giving of the law (v. 24).
6. *The conditions given:* obedience and reverence (v. 24).

These points contain the essence of the covenant theology: God revealed himself both by act and by word. Both the acts and the words of God revealed his concern and his purpose for his people. Both the acts and the words imposed a responsibility on God's people, to revere and obey God in order that they might continue to experience his presence in history and continue to hear his words. The result of this reverence and obedience is stated in v. 25: *we shall have righteousness.* . . . Righteousness in this context describes a true and personal relationship[8] with the covenant God (see also Gen. 15:6), which not only would be a spiritual reality, but would be seen in the lives of the people of God. Thus the answer to the son's question finally focuses on the proper relationship of a man to God, and the fruit of that relationship in daily life.

6. ISRAEL'S POLICY OF WAR (7:1-26)

1 *When the Lord your God brings you into the land, which you are about to enter in order to take possession of it, and he clears away before you many nations: the Hittites, and the Girgashites, and the Amorites, and the Canaanites, and the Perizzites, and the Hivites, and the Jebusites, seven nations more numerous and powerful than you are;*

2 *when the Lord your God sets them before you and you attack them, you must destroy them completely. You shall not make a treaty with them and you shall not grant them favor.*

3 *And you shall not undertake a marriage alliance with them: you shall not give your daughter to his son, nor shall you take his daughter for your son.*

8.   See Buis and Leclercq, *Le Deutéronome,* p. 79.

4 *For he would turn your son aside from following after the Lord and they would serve other gods. Then the Lord's anger would be aroused against you and he would annihilate you quickly.*

5 *But you shall deal with them as follows: you shall break down their altars, and you shall smash their sacred pillars, and you shall chop down their asherim, and you shall burn their idols in the fire.*

6 *For you are a holy people to the Lord your God and the Lord your God has chosen you to be for himself, a people prized more highly than all the peoples who are on the face of the earth.*

7 *It was not because you were more numerous than other peoples that the Lord cared for you and chose you, for you were the smallest of all the peoples.*

8 *It was because of the Lord's love for you and his keeping of the oath which he swore to your fathers, that the Lord brought you out with a strong hand and he ransomed you from the house of slavery, from the power of pharaoh, king of Egypt.*

9 *So you shall know that the Lord your God, he is the God, the faithful God maintaining the covenant and loving kindness with those that love him and those that keep his commandments, for a thousand generations;*

10 *but recompensing the one that openly hates him, by destroying him: he does not delay — he destroys the one who openly hates him.*

11 *So you shall keep the commandment, and the statutes and the judgments, which I am about to command you today, by doing them.*

12 *And it shall be that, as a result of your hearing these judgments and keeping and doing them, the Lord your God shall keep with you the covenant and the loving kindness which he promised to your fathers.*

13 *And he will love you and bless you and make you numerous; and he will bless the fruit of your womb and the fruit of your ground, your grain and your new wine and your fresh oil, the offspring of your cattle, and the young ones of your flock, in the land which he swore to your fathers to give to you.*

14 *You shall be blessed more than all the peoples. There shall not be a sterile male or barren female among you or among your cattle.*

15 *And the Lord will turn aside from you all sickness, and he will not inflict upon you all the terrible diseases of Egypt, which you knew, but he will impose them on all those that hate you.*

16 *And you shall devour all the peoples whom the Lord your God is about to deliver to you; your eye shall not look upon them with compassion and you shall not serve their gods, for that would be a snare to you.*

17 *But you may say in your heart: These nations are more numerous than I am! How can I dispossess them?*

18 *You shall not be afraid of them. You shall remember diligently what the Lord your God did to pharaoh and to all Egypt:*

19 *the great trials which your eyes beheld, and the signs and the*

wonders, and the powerful hand and the outstretched arm by which the Lord your God brought you out — thus shall the Lord your God do to all the peoples of whom you are afraid.

20 *And also the Lord your God shall send the hornet among them, until those who are left and those hiding from you are destroyed.*

21 *You must not tremble because of them, for the Lord your God is in your midst, a great and fearful God.*

22 *And the Lord your God will clear away these nations before you little by little. You may not put an end to them quickly, lest the wild beasts become too numerous for you.*

23 *And the Lord your God will deliver them to you, and he will disturb them with great unrest until their annihilation.*

24 *And he will deliver their kings into your power and you shall cause their names to perish from under the heavens; no man shall take a stand against you until you have annihilated them.*

25 *You shall burn the images of their gods in the fire; you shall not covet the silver or gold upon them and take it for yourself, in case you are ensnared by it, for it is an abominable thing to the Lord your God.*

26 *And you shall not bring an abominable thing into your house, or you will be fit for destruction just as it is. You shall thoroughly detest it and utterly abominate it, for it is fit for destruction.*

1-5   The policy — the destruction of the Canaanites. (For a discussion of the theological aspects of the problem of war, see the Introduction.) In summary, when the Israelites conquered their new land, they were to destroy the old inhabitants, refusing to enter into any kind of treaty with them, either political or marital. Any kind of treaty would be a compromise and would lead to disaster; therefore the Israelites were to destroy systematically the physical religious "furniture" of their enemies, indicating thereby their complete lack of recognition for the gods of their enemies.

The inhabitants of Palestine, whom the Israelites would meet and fight, are listed more comprehensively here than normally;[1] these *seven nations* would be relatively small states by modern standards, controlling areas of land usually centered around one or more fortified cities. The exact implications of all the terms are uncertain, due in part to the antiquity of the references and the obscurity of some of the terms. The *Hittites,* properly speaking, came from Anatolia, though from an early date there were Hittite migrants settling in Palestine (e.g., Ephron, who resided in the vicinity of Hebron: Gen. 23). Very little is known of the *Girgashites:* they are referred to elsewhere (Gen. 10:16; 1 Chr. 1:14; Josh. 3:10; 24:11) and the name is attested in the

---

1. See S. R. Driver, *Deuteronomy,* p. 97, for a detailed note of similar passages; see also G. T. Manley, *The Book of the Law,* pp. 62f.

Ugaritic texts.[2] They may have been a tribal people living in the north of Palestine. *The Amorites, and the Canaanites* — these two terms have a wide sphere of reference,[3] though in this context they refer to specific (though unidentified) groups settled in Palestine. The Amorites were probably located in the Judean hill country and the Canaanites further west, toward the coast land (see Josh. 5:1; 11:3). The *Perizzites*, like the Amorites, appear to have been a group living in the central hill country (Josh. 11:3).[4] The *Hivites*, perhaps "tent-villagers," were located in the north of Palestine in the vicinity of the Lebanon mountains (Judg. 3:3), though they may have been distributed more extensively. The *Jebusites* were a group of people controlling the region of Jerusalem and the territory surrounding the city, and they were to prove to be among the most stalwart in their resistance to the Israelite settlers. These seven nations made up the enemy Israel was to face, and together they were *more numerous and powerful than you are* (v. 1). The strength and numbers of the enemy, however, were not to cause the Israelites alarm, for God would set the enemy before his people and they were then to *destroy them completely* (v. 2). The God of the covenant would grant to his people the strength for victory.

You shall not make a treaty with them (v. 2) — the word translated *treaty* here is *bᵉrîṯ*, the same word employed for "covenant." The word gives a clue to the reason for the harsh policy of war to be employed by the Israelites. The Israelites were bound primarily by their *bᵉrîṯ* (covenant, treaty) with the Lord, and though this was a religious bond, it was also a political bond, for it set aside Israel as a distinctive nation among other nations. To make a treaty with other nations would indicate a lack of faithfulness on the part of the Israelites to their suzerain God.[5] Likewise, the Israelites were forbidden to *undertake a marriage alliance with them;* although there may be a prohibition of mixed marriages between Israelites and non-Israelites implicit here,[6] the specific prohibition probably has in mind the forg-

2. See F. Gröndahl, *Die Personennamen der Texte aus Ugarit* (1967), p. 332; Gordon, *UT*, p. 381.
3. See the full discussion in J. C. L. Gibson, "Observations on Some Important Ethnic Terms in the Pentateuch," *JNES* 20 (1961), pp. 217-238.
4. Unless the term is taken in a nonethnic sense as "villagers" or even "warriors"; see Judg. 5:7, 11 and P. C. Craigie, "Some Further Notes on the Song of Deborah," *VT* 22 (1972), p. 350.
5. The Near Eastern treaties may also stipulate the nature of a vassal's relationships with other nations: see *ANET*, p. 204b.
6. Hebrew law does not prohibit mixed marriages outright, and certain regulations are laid down for a Hebrew desiring to marry a foreign woman taken as a prisoner in war; see Deut. 21:10-14. Moses himself was married to a non-Hebrew (Exod. 2:21), as were other Hebrew leaders; there was always a danger inherent in such marriages, however, as is evident in Ahab's marriage to Jezebel (1 K. 16:31-34).

ing of political treaties by means of marriage. This course of action, as with the making of a treaty (v. 2), would be an indication of compromise and could lead to a disruption of the covenant faithfulness to the one God: *he would turn your son aside from following after the Lord and they would serve other gods.*[7] Thus both prohibitions (vv. 2-3) have in mind the preservation of the covenant relationship with the Lord by forbidding any relationship that would bring that first and most important relationship into danger. The covenant relationship was to be guarded further by positive action, namely the total destruction of the various types of religious equipment employed in Canaanite religion (v. 5): *altars, sacred pillars, asherim,* and *idols* (for a fuller discussion, see the commentary on 12:3 and 16:21-22). The destructive action would remove any consequent temptation for the Israelites to follow the religious practices of the nations they were to displace from the land.

6-11   The reason for Israel's policy of war lay in her election and holiness, two important religious themes which are related directly to the covenant. The Israelites were a *holy people* because of their relationship to God, which *separated* them, or *cut* them *off* (apparently the original sense of the root *qdš*, "holy"), from other peoples and practices. Their holy character does not indicate inherent merit, but rather divine choice; God had chosen Israel to be *a people prized more highly than all the peoples who are on the face of the earth.* The Heb. *sᵉgullāh,* translated *prized . . . highly,* describes the special relationship between the Lord and his people; the cognate Akkadian word (*sikiltu*) is used in a treaty seal from Alalaḫ to describe the king as a "treasured possession" of his god.[8] Thus Israel's character as a holy people gave them no ground for pride, but imposed on them the responsibility of their calling.

The negative and positive dimensions of Israel's election are expressed in vv. 7-8. Negatively, they were not chosen on the basis of their numerical strength;[9] they were numerically a very small people in the context of other Near Eastern peoples and nations. Positively, they were chosen because the Lord loved them; the reason for God's special love, though it contained within it a purpose, remains essen-

---

7.   There are some ambiguities in the Heb. of v. 4. The subject *he* probably denotes the foreign father-in-law referred to in v. 3 (*his* son, *his* daughter); it is in effect generic for the enemy. *The Lord*—MT has "me," which is possible and would be a case of Moses relapsing into the use of God's words to him. In either case, the meaning is *the Lord. They* would refer to sons and daughters entering into mixed marriages.
8.   See J. A. Thompson, *The Ancient Near Eastern Treaties and the OT,* p. 35. See also the discussion and references in M. Weinfeld, *Deuteronomy and the Deuteronomic School,* p. 226, n. 2. See further Deut. 14:2 and 26:18.
9.   Though numerical strength was one of the blessings inherent in the covenant promise from the time of Abraham; Gen. 15:5 and 17:2.

tially a mystery. On the basis of that love, God had called Abraham and his descendants and had made the covenant promise to them. And on the basis of the covenant promise, he had charted his people's course through the events of history, liberating them from the bondage of Egypt (v. 8), and bringing them to the present moment on the plains of Moab, on the eve of the fulfilment of the ancient promise to the fathers. Thus God's love and choice of his people could not be known clearly in a philosophical or theological sense; it was known rather through the experience of God maintaining his *covenant and loving kindness* (v. 9) with his faithful people *for a thousand generations* (a phrase which has its beginning in the past, but which has relevance still for the future). His faithful people were known by two characteristics: they were *those that love him and those that keep his commandments.* The close relationship between the love of God and obedience to his commandments has already been described in 6:4-9. In contrast, *the one that openly hates him*[10] (and as a consequence disobeys God's commandments) invites God's speedy retaliation and judgment. These words probably apply both to renegade Israelites and (in the context of the chapter as a whole) to those of the surrounding nations whom Israel was to encounter in war. On the basis of this divine love and choice, the Israelites are therefore persuaded to be obedient to the whole law (*the commandment, and the statutes and the judgments,* v. 11) which Moses was about to set before them.

12-16 The prosperity, health, and success of the Israelites would be contingent upon obedience; only as they heard and were careful to obey God's word would they continue to experience God's faithfulness and loving kindness. It is this note of contingency that adds such solemnity to Moses' discourse, for although God's faithfulness and ability were beyond question, the course of the future would be dependent very largely on the people responding to their covenant obligations. This did not mean that obedience merited divine blessing, but rather that obedience maintained the proper covenant relationship with God; and his people could experience the blessing of God only when the covenant relationship, which involved reciprocal responsibilities, was properly maintained. Contingent upon this obedience would be their prosperity and fruitfulness in the land (vv. 13-14), their good health (v. 15), and their military success in the conquest (v. 16).

Their prosperity and fruitfulness in the land, which would be a further example of God's love and blessing for his people (see also v. 8), would extend to all spheres of their lives. They would have many

10. MT has plural here: "those that hate him"; the singular translation is based on one Heb. ms., and is supported by the repetition in the singular of the same word in the latter part of the verse.

children (*the fruit of your womb*) and thus would experience the fulfilment of the promise to Abraham (Gen. 15:5). The ground would be fruitful and produce *grain, new wine*, and *fresh oil;* these three terms, denoting the substances in their simple or unmanufactured states, encompass the three principal food products of Palestine.[11] Their animals too would produce calves (*offspring*[12] *of your cattle*) and lambs, so that the increase in the population would be matched by an increase in the food supply. Furthermore, the people would be blessed with good health. *He will not inflict upon you all the terrible diseases of Egypt* — this reference to Egypt is particularly apt for Moses' audience, for they and their parents would still have been able to remember the particular afflictions associated with that land. In ancient Egypt, such diseases as elephantiasis, various types of boils, and afflictions of the eyes and bowels were particularly common and unpleasant.[13] The Israelites would no longer be plagued with such sickness, but God would inflict it upon their enemies.

The reference to military success (v. 16) brings back the focus to the theme of the chapter as a whole. All the blessings described earlier could come to pass only after the Israelites had expelled the previous occupants of the land and possessed it for themselves. Here, however, it is not an injunction to fight but a promise of military success that is given: *you shall devour* (lit. "eat") *all the peoples*, and the reason for the success would be God's part in the action — *peoples whom the Lord your God is about to deliver to you*. The Israelite military action was to be without *compassion*, so that the people would not be tempted to *serve their gods;* such an action *would be a snare to you*, in that it would involve a breach of the first commandment.

17-26   This last paragraph of the chapter deals explicitly once again with the war in which the Israelites were about to engage. There was a danger that they might let their minds reflect on the strength of their enemy (v. 17), rather than upon the strength of their God. In a previous military action, this wrong mental attitude had led to defeat (see 1:27-28). Hence Moses encourages the people to think positively and not to fear; the remedy for fear was memory — *you shall remember diligently what the Lord your God did to pharaoh and to all Egypt* (v. 18). The people would see a repetition of the marvellous events associated with the liberation from Egypt if they trusted in the strength of their God. Just as when the people had not trusted in God,

11. See S. R. Driver, *Deuteronomy*, p. 103.
12. On the Heb. *sheger*, see Gordon, *UT*, p. 488 (19.2384).
13. For a general description of sickness and medicine in ancient Egypt, see F. Marti-Ibanez, ed., *A Pictorial History of Medicine* (1965), pp. 33-51 (and bibliography, pp. 283f.); see also G. A. Smith, *The Book of Deuteronomy*, p. 114.

they had been chased as if by *bees* (1:44) from the battlefield, so by trusting in God they would see the reverse happen: *God shall send the hornet*[14] *among them . . .*, indicating, perhaps metaphorically, that there could be no hiding place from the victorious pursuit of God's people. The Israelites were not to *tremble because of them* (v. 21); when they remembered that their God, *a great and fearful God,* was in their midst, they would regain their proper focus as warriors of the Lord. When in times past the Israelites had celebrated God's victory at the sea, they had sung of the fear of their enemies: "the people have heard, they tremble; pangs have seized on the inhabitants of Philistia" (Exod. 15:14). That was their proper perspective prior to engaging in battle.

In v. 22, there is expressed an awareness of the gradual nature of the military task lying ahead of the people: *the Lord your God will clear away these*[15] *nations before you little by little.* The initial conquest would be sudden, but the process of settlement and complete conquest would be more gradual, while the Israelites grew sufficiently in number (i.e., while the promise of v. 13 was being fulfilled) to enable them to populate the land.[16] The gradual changeover would thus avoid the danger of the land returning to a primitive state of natural anarchy: *lest the wild beasts*[17] *become too numerous for you.* But during the gradual course of the conquest and settlement, God's hand would be at work, and even those not immediately conquered would become anxious as they anticipated their own defeat: *he will disturb them with great unrest until their annihilation* (v. 23).

In the concluding verses, the complete destruction both of the people of Canaan (v. 24) and of their religion (v. 25) is anticipated. The kings of the enemy states would be defeated and their temporal power and authority would be lost in the forgetfulness of human history. Their religion, pretending reality, would have its symbolic forms burned in fire. Even the precious metals (silver and gold) employed for decorating the idols, though they were valuable in themselves, were to be discarded as an *abominable thing*[18] (vv. 25, 26). The

14. The Heb. is *tsir'āh;* see G. Cansdale, *NBD,* p. 538. The translation of the word has caused some debate; L. Köhler suggested translating "panic" (*ZAW* 44 [1926], p. 291) and later suggested "depression, discouragement" (KB, p. 817).
15. Heb. *hā'ēl;* the translation assumes *hā'ēleh* (for which Kennicot cites ms. evidence), the *mater lectionis* perhaps having been accidentally omitted during the course of the grammatical revision of the text at some date subsequent to its initial written form.
16. Thus the verse anticipates the contrast between the book of Joshua and the statements at the beginning of Judges.
17. Lit. "beast of the field" (collective), field having the sense of countryside. The reference is not to domestic animals.
18. It has been suggested that the noun *tô'ēḇāh,* "abominable thing" (and the denominative verb) may be borrowed from Egyptian *w'b;* see A. S. Yahuda, *The Lan-*

association with false religions made the metals totally unsuitable for use within the Israelite community, which might again be tempted to misuse the materials to make a representation of God as had been done in the past (see Exod. 32).

7. THE WILDERNESS AND THE PROMISED LAND (8:1-20)

1 *You shall take care to do all the law which I am about to command you today, so that you may live and grow in number and enter and take possession of the land, which the Lord promised by oath to your fathers.*

2 *And you shall remember all the way that the Lord your God led you in the wilderness for these forty years, in order to discipline you and to test you, to know what was in your heart, whether or not you would keep his commandments.*

3 *And he disciplined you and made you hungry; then he fed you manna, which you did not know and your fathers did not know, in order to make you realize that man does not live by bread alone, but man lives by every utterance of the mouth of the Lord.*

4 *For these forty years, your coat did not wear out on you and your foot did not become swollen.*

5 *So you know with your mind that just as a man disciplines his son, so the Lord your God is disciplining you;*

6 *and you shall keep the commandments of the Lord your God, by walking in his ways and by fearing him.*

7 *For the Lord your God is about to bring you into a good land, a land with brooks of water, springs and deep waters flowing forth in the valley and in the hill country;*

8 *a land of wheat and barley and vines and fig trees and pomegranates; a land of olives, oil, and honey:*

9 *a land in which you may eat bread, not in scarcity; a land whose stones are iron and from whose hills you may mine copper.*

10 *Then you shall eat and be satisfied, and you shall bless the Lord your God because of the good land which he has given to you.*

11 *Be very careful lest you forget the Lord your God, by not keeping his commandments and his judgments and his statutes which I am about to command you today;*

12 *lest you should eat and be satisfied and build beautiful houses and live in them;*

13 *and your herd and your flock grow numerous, and silver and gold accumulate for you, and everything that you have;*

14 *then you may become proud and forget the Lord your God, the*

---

guage of the Pentateuch in Its Relation to Egyptian, pp. 75, 95. The cognate word is also used, e.g., in a Phoenician inscription on an Egyptian-style sarcophagus from Sidon: "an abomination (t'bt) of Ashtart." See G. A. Cooke, A Text-book of North-Semitic Inscriptions, p. 29.

one who brought you out of the land of Egypt, out of the house of slavery;

15 *the one who led you in the great and terrible wilderness —the fiery serpent and scorpion and thirsty ground that was waterless! —the one who brought forth water for you from the flint-hard rock;*

16 *the one who fed you manna in the wilderness, which your fathers had not known, in order to discipline you and in order to test you, to do good for you in the end.*

17 *But you may say to yourself: My power and the strength of my hand have made this wealth for me!*

18 *So you may forget the Lord your God, that he is the one giving you power to make wealth, in order to establish his covenant, which he promised by oath to your fathers, as on this very day.*

19 *And it shall be that if indeed you forget the Lord your God and you follow other gods and serve them and bow down to them, I bear witness against you today that you shall certainly perish.*

20 *Like the nations which the Lord makes to perish before you, so also you shall perish, because you would not listen to the voice of the Lord your God.*

1   The chapter is introduced in familiar terms (see also 4:1); the people are urged to obey the commandment which is to be declared to them, in order that they might prosper in the land promised by God to their forefathers. In the portion of the address that follows, there are two double-themes which are employed to emphasize the call to obedience: (a) "remember/forget"; (b) "wilderness/promised land." In the structure of the chapter, the two double-themes are closely interwoven,[1] and lead eventually to a solemn warning in vv. 17-20, which indicates the basic danger threatening the covenant faith. The general structure of the chapter, after the introductory verse, can be expressed as follows:

2-6:   *remember* the *wilderness* and God's presence there:
7-10:   God will bring his people into the *promised land:*
11-16:   beware of *forgetting* God in the *promised land:*
          beware of *forgetting* God who was present in the *wilderness:*
17-20:   beware of presumption: *remember* God, the source of strength:
          do not *forget* God and follow other gods:
          forgetfulness leads to disaster:

The two double-themes emphasize the sense of history, the immediacy and contingency of the present moment and of all future present

---

1. N. Lohfink, *Höre, Israel!* p. 76, traces a chiastic structure in the chapter as a whole; the analysis is valuable, but it may be too precise in that it involves a breakdown that does not fit well with the natural punctuation of vv. 11-16 (17). See also Lohfink, *Das Hauptgebot,* pp. 189-199.

moments (see Introduction VIII, "Theology"). The act of *remembering* prompts obedience to the covenant law, for it brings to the forefront of the mind the reality and faithfulness of God; forgetfulness is tantamount to disobedience, for the self and human concerns have pushed into the background of the mind the reality and claims of God.

2-6   Remember the wilderness and God's presence there. The desolation of the wilderness is in stark contrast to the richness of the promised land. God had led his people through the wilderness, however, for a particular purpose; the forty years were to be a time of testing and disciplining, *to know what was in your heart,*[2] *whether or not you would keep his commandments* (v. 2). The wilderness tested and disciplined the people in various ways. On the one hand, the desolation of the wilderness removed the natural props and supports which man by nature depends on; it cast the people back on God, who alone could provide the strength to survive the wilderness. On the other hand, the severity of the wilderness period undermined the shallow bases of confidence of those who were not truly rooted and grounded in God. The wilderness makes or breaks a man; it provides strength of will and character. The strength provided by the wilderness, however, was not the strength of self-sufficiency, but the strength that comes from a knowledge of the living God.

When the people were hungry, God fed them manna; the provision of manna was not simply a miracle, but it was designed to teach the Israelites a fundamental principle of their existence as the covenant people of God. The basic source of life was God and the words of God to his people; *every utterance of the mouth of the Lord* (v. 3) was more basic to Israelite existence than was food. This principle did not mean that the Israelites were to expect at all times the miraculous provision of food, as in the instance when God provided manna. Normal circumstances would involve the normal acquisition of food supplies. But if the command of God directed the people to do something or go somewhere, the command should be obeyed; shortage of food or water, lack of strength, or any other excuse would be insufficient, for the command of God contained within it the provision of God. The principle contained in v. 3 was employed by Jesus in his own period of testing in the wilderness. He was directed by the Spirit into the wilderness, and after forty days and nights was tempted to perform a miracle by turning stones into bread.[3] The miracle would have been similar, in principle, to that which was performed by God in the desert for the Israelites. But Jesus

---

2. *Heart* — the word has been translated elsewhere as "mind." The reference is to the basic attitudes of the people toward God and his commandments.
3. Matt. 4:1-4; note that in response to all three temptations, Jesus quoted Deuteronomy. See also Luke 4:1-4.

did not perform the miracle, for he knew that he would be sustained by God; following the temptation, "angels came and ministered to him" (Matt. 4:11). The complete dependence on the word of God and God's ability to provide is always a hard lesson for man to learn, whether in ancient times or modern. Man knows that he must work in order to provide the essentials for physical existence, but in that very labor, he may easily forget that, in the last resort, it is God who makes provision for man's life. Thus, when the divine command comes, or when a period of testing is entered, man's self-sufficiency is undermined, for his own ability to provide for his needs is removed and he must learn again that his existence, physical and spiritual, can only be grounded in God.

The reference to manna in v. 3 is emphasized further in v. 4; *your coat did not wear out on you and your foot did not become swollen.* [4] God provided not only food for the journey, but also clothing and physical strength. These lessons in the desert had taught the Israelites the nature of God's dealings with them: *just as a man disciplines his son, so the Lord your God is disciplining you* (v. 5). [5] The disciplinary action of God may involve admonition, correction, and severity, but it is prompted by the love of God for his people. The wilderness period was thus the time of adolescence in Israel's history, when the people learned to understand by experience the way in which God wished them to walk. Adolescence and education in the ways of God may involve trials and hardship, but there was a prospect, beyond the growing pains, of the good land that was promised by God; if the people were obedient to God and feared him (v. 6), then they would move from adolescence to maturity, the time anticipated in the following verses.

7-10 God will bring his people into the promised land. The description of the land contained in these verses is expressed in glowing terms; it has been suggested, quite plausibly, that the description may be modelled on, or even quoted from, a hymn-like poem extolling the beauties of the land. [6] There is first a description of the bountiful water supply of the land (*brooks of water, springs and deep waters*), which stands in contrast to the dryness of the desert mentioned in the previous verses (see also v. 15). The land was also rich in crops, fruit, oil, and honey, so that it was a land *in which you may eat*

4. See also Neh. 9:21. *Swollen*—Heb. *bātsēqāh;* the word is used only here and in the repetition of the line in Neh. 9:21. LXX (in Deut. 8:4) renders *etylōthēsan,* indicating the sense of getting hard skin or callosity.
5. See also 4:36 and 6:5 (together with the references there in n. 14).
6. G. von Rad, *Deuteronomy,* p. 72. M. Weinfeld, *Deuteronomy and the Deuteronomic School,* pp. 71f., notes that the historical prologue of the political treaties often contains a land grant, which may be followed by a description of the land containing details similar to those described in the present context.

bread, not in scarcity. The land contained in addition mineral deposits; *iron* could be found there and *copper* could be mined in the hills (v. 9). It becomes clear from the final reference that the conception of the promised land that underlies the description of these verses is a very large one. Copper and iron could be mined for the most part in the vicinity of the Arabah, particularly from the Dead Sea to the Gulf of Aqaba; there may also have been deposits of iron ore in Transjordan.[7] Thus it is clear that the land described in these verses is not just Palestine to the west of the Jordan; there is a larger conception of the promised land, which should perhaps be related to the description contained in Deut. 1:7-8. When God had brought his people into the good land promised to them, then they would *eat and be satisfied.* In their new prosperity and satisfaction, they were always to remember the source of their blessed estate: *you shall bless the Lord your God because of the good land which he has given to you* (v. 10). The possibility of forgetting God in the land, and not blessing him, is the theme of the following section.

11-16   The danger of forgetting God. The essential nature of forgetfulness is described in v. 11; failure to keep God's *commandments and his judgments and his statutes* indicates that God has been forgotten. That is, forgetfulness is not simply a state of mind, or something akin to absentmindedness. Facts may still be remembered, in a literal sense, but they have ceased to be part of a living memory of the reality of God, who no longer seems to be a living and real presence. The reality of the living God is not bounded by time; but finite man, pressed continually by the pressures of the present moment, is constantly tempted to limit his horizons to that which is immediately known and experienced. When the immediate experience is one of security and tranquillity, then the living memory of the reality of God fades and easily ceases to be the governing principle of daily life. The danger was a constant one, so the people were warned by Moses: *Be very careful lest you forget the Lord your God* (v. 11).

The anticipation of the good land promised by God had been a source of strength to the Israelites during their time of testing in the wilderness; following the conquest, however, the good land itself could become a source of testing for the Israelites (vv. 12-14a). They would have sufficient food and good homes; they would have numerous livestock and would acquire wealth in silver and gold. These benefits were all part of the blessing God had prepared for his people; but the blessing of God, which is good in itself, brings with it further temptation. Having received good things from God, the temptation lay in the possibility of coming to think that those good things were

7.   See J. Gray, *Archaeology and the OT World* (1962), p. 14; F. V. Winnett, "Mining," *IDB* III, pp. 384f.; D. Baly, *Geographical Companion to the Bible,* p. 57.

actually acquired through human ability. As the Israelites came to rejoice in the prosperity of their newly acquired land, it would be easy to remember how hard they had fought for it, how much they deserved it after so many trials — but at the same time to forget that the land was the gift of God, that any military success they might have had was only because of God's presence in the midst of the people. Prosperity, in other words, could very easily lead to pride; to be proud was to think that the prosperity had been achieved as a result of their own human achievement, and to think in this way was to *forget the Lord your God* (v. 14a).

There follows a series of descriptions of God (vv. 14b-16), in each of which there is mention of some gracious act of God on behalf of his people. Each description is presented as something that might easily be forgotten in the future prosperity, but in the address of Moses, each one serves as a further reminder of the gracious acts of God on behalf of his people. (a) *The one who brought you out of the land of Egypt, out of the house of slavery* (v. 14b). The Exodus event had been the liberation of Israel from human servitude and had made possible submission to God in the covenant formed at Sinai. Israel was not a free nation, though the newly found prosperity in the promised land might lead to the delusion of freedom. The freedom from Egypt was significant only in that it formed the basis for a new allegiance, the allegiance given to God in the covenant. The belief in self-sufficient freedom and independence would be a dangerous thing in the new state of Israel. There could be freedom from Egypt, freedom from worldly domination, but only insofar as Israel was absolutely committed to God in a covenant relationship which totally permeated every aspect of its life.

(b) *The one who led you in the great and terrible wilderness* (v. 15a). Having brought his people out of Egypt, God continued with them. He was first their Liberator (a) and then their Leader (b). The liberation from Egypt did not lead immediately to the promised land; first, the Israelites entered a period that was as testing physically as was their former life in Egypt.[8] Thus the first lesson to learn was trust in God, before the experience of prosperity; hardship in Egypt was followed by hardship in the desert, but in the desert, the people knew the guidance of God. (c) *The one who brought forth water for you from*

---

8. The terrifying nature of the wilderness is emphasized by the reference to the *fiery serpent, scorpion,* and *thirsty ground*. The significance of *fiery* in relation to a snake is uncertain; if the term *śārāp* does mean "fiery" or "burning," then the reference may be to the burning inflammation that results from snakebite (see G. A. Smith, *The Book of Deuteronomy,* p. 122). Alternatively, the meaning may be *venomous serpent,* "fiery" referring to the nature of the venom; cf. H. Cazelles, *Le Deutéronome,* p. 54; D. J. Wiseman, "Flying Serpents?" *TB* 23 (1972), pp. 108-110.

the flint-hard rock (v. 15b) — as their Leader through the dry wilderness, God provided water for his people.[9] (d) *The one who fed you manna in the wilderness* (v. 16a) — see also v. 3 (above).

In each of these four descriptions of God, there is contained a reminder to the people of God's disciplining and testing of his people; the purpose of it all was in order that God could *do good for you in the end* (v. 16). The danger of which Moses warns the people is that when they come to experience the good for which God was preparing them, then they might forget the actions of God that had led to that good and they would thereby forfeit the good estate God had granted to them.

17-20 The danger of presumption. The final verses of the chapter stress once again the initiative of God in the covenant and the promise it contained. For the member of the covenant community, it would be gross presumption to speak of the accomplishments of *my power* or the *strength of my hand* (v. 17). Yet precisely because the purpose of God was achieved through cooperation with man, there was inevitably a temptation for man to boast of his achievements. God grants power and ability to his people for a special purpose: it is *in order to establish his covenant, which he promised by oath to your fathers* (v. 18). *As on this very day* — the reference is to the present time during which the covenant was being renewed on the plains of Moab. The words, however, indicate all three temporal dimensions of the covenant. The immediate context refers to the *future* establishing of the covenant in the promised land. The initiation of the covenant in the *past* is also in mind: (the covenant) *which he promised by oath to your fathers*. But both past and future are related to the *present* renewal of the covenant in Moab.

The chapter ends with a further note of warning; forgetting God may lead to the worst kind of disaster. When God is no longer in the forefront of the mind, Moses warns, it would become easy to *follow other gods and serve them and bow down to them* (v. 19), and to do this would be to break the first commandment. The result would inevitably be death, for the Israelites would be behaving as the Canaanites behaved and, like the Canaanites, they would die or be ejected from the promised land (v. 20). It has been suggested that vv. 19-20 were not originally part of the sermon, on the grounds that the warning against strange gods does not really fit in with its theme.[10] The significance of the last two verses, however, should be set in the context of the book as a whole. A basic theme of Deuteronomy is the demand for covenant allegiance, and always this is contrasted with

9. See Num. 20:11; Exod. 17:1-6; Ps. 78:15-20; 114:8.
10. See G. von Rad, *Deuteronomy*, p. 73. Note that there is similar material to that contained in the last two verses in 4:25-26; 6:14-15.

the danger of unfaithfulness to the covenant God and following other gods. Thus, the last two verses of the chapter serve to tie the particular themes of the chapter more closely to the overall themes of the book.

8. THE STUBBORNNESS OF ISRAEL (9:1-29)

1 *Hear, O Israel. Today you are going to cross the Jordan, to go in and dispossess nations that are greater and more powerful than yourself, cities that are large and fortified to the skies;*
2 *a people large and tall, sons of the Anakim, whom you know about and of whom you have heard it said: Who can hold his ground before the sons of Anak?*
3 *But today you know of the Lord your God, that it is he who crosses over ahead of you as a devouring fire; it is he who will destroy them and it is he who will humble them before you; and you shall dispossess them and destroy them speedily, just as the Lord said to you.*
4 *When the Lord your God drives them out before you, do not say to yourself: Because of my righteousness, the Lord brought me in to take possession of this land. For it is on account of the wickedness of these nations that the Lord is going to dispossess them before you.*
5 *It is not because of your righteousness or the uprightness of your heart that you are going to go in to possess their land, but it is because of the wickedness of these nations that the Lord your God is going to dispossess them before you, and so that he might establish the word which the Lord promised by oath to your fathers, to Abraham, to Isaac, and to Jacob.*
6 *And you should know that it is not because of your righteousness that the Lord your God is going to give you this good land to possess, for you are a stubborn people.*
7 *Remember! Do not forget that you provoked the Lord your God to anger in the wilderness; from the very day that you departed from the land of Egypt up to your coming to this place, you were rebellious against the Lord.*
8 *You provoked the Lord to anger even in Horeb, and the Lord became so angry with you that he almost destroyed you.*
9 *When I ascended the mountain to receive the stone tablets, the tablets of the covenant which the Lord made with you, I remained on the mountain forty days and forty nights; I ate no bread and I drank no water.*
10 *And the Lord gave me the two stone tablets, written by the finger of God, and on them were all the words which the Lord spoke with you on the mountain, from the midst of the fire, on the day of the assembly.*
11 *And at the end of forty days and forty nights, the Lord gave to me the two stone tablets, the tablets of the covenant.*

190

12 *And the Lord said to me: Get up! Go down quickly from here, for your people, whom you brought out of Egypt, have acted perversely; they have quickly turned aside from the path that I commanded for them. They have made a molten image for themselves.*

13 *Then the Lord said to me: I have seen this people and they are indeed a stubborn people.*

14 *Leave me alone and I will destroy them and I will wipe out their name from under heaven, and I will make you to be a nation more powerful and numerous than they.*

15 *So I turned and came down from the mountain and the mountain was burning with fire; and the two tablets of the covenant were in my two hands.*

16 *And I looked, and lo, you had sinned against the Lord your God; you had made a molten calf for yourselves; you had quickly turned aside from the way that the Lord had ordained for you.*

17 *And I seized the two tablets and flung them from my two hands, and I shattered them before your very eyes.*

18 *Then I prostrated myself before the Lord as beforehand, forty days and forty nights; I ate no bread and I drank no water, because of all your sin which you committed by doing what was wrong in the eyes of the Lord, by provoking him to anger.*

19 *For I was afraid on account of the anger and wrath which the Lord bore against you, intending to destroy you; but the Lord listened to me on that occasion also.*

20 *And the Lord was very angry with Aaron, intending to destroy him, but I interceded on Aaron's behalf also at that time.*

21 *And I took your sinful thing, the calf which you had made, and I burned it in the fire; and I crushed it, grinding it thoroughly until it was fine as dust, and I threw its dust into the brook running down from the mountain.*

22 *And at Taberah, and at Massah, and at Kibroth-hatta'avah, you were provoking the Lord to anger.*

23 *And when the Lord sent you forth from Kadesh-barnea, saying: Go up and possess the land which I have given to you – then you rebelled against the word of the Lord your God and you did not believe him and you did not listen to his voice.*

24 *You have been rebellious against the Lord from the day that I knew you.*

25 *Then I prostrated myself before the Lord forty days and forty nights, for the Lord intended to destroy you.*

26 *And I prayed to the Lord and I said: Lord God, do not destroy your people and your inheritance, whom you redeemed in your greatness, whom you brought out from Egypt with a mighty hand.*

27 *Remember your servants, Abraham, Isaac, and Jacob; look neither at the stubbornness of this people, nor at their wickedness, nor at their sin;*

28 *lest the land, out of which you brought us, say: Because the Lord was unable to bring them into the land which he promised them,*

191

THE BOOK OF DEUTERONOMY

and because he hates them, he has led them out into the wilder-
ness to kill them.
29 *But they are your people and your inheritance, whom you brought*
out by your great strength and by your outstretched arm.

In the previous chapter, the address centered on the contrast
between memory and forgetfulness; a living memory of God aided in
the maintenance of a living relationship with God, but forgetfulness
undermined the continuity of love which was the basis of the covenant relationship. In this chapter there is a shift in emphasis, and now
the stubbornness of Israel becomes the focal point of attention. Stubbornness can be a good quality, but it is not an unyielding, stubborn
faithfulness to the covenant that is described in this portion of the
address. Israel is described rather as being stubborn in its perversity,
stubborn in its continual provocation of God. Thus the theme serves
once again as an element of warning in Moses' address; the people
and their predecessors had been stubborn in the past, but they must
learn to yield to the graciousness of God. The scene is set first by an
anticipation of the conquest of the promised land (vv. 1-3). Then
Moses reminds the people in advance that the land will come to them
from God's graciousness and judgment, not through any righteousness of their own (vv. 4-6). In the following verses (7-21), the perverse
stubbornness of the people becomes the central topic and it is illustrated by reference to past events, particularly the events associated
with Horeb/Sinai; that the illustrations could easily be multiplied,
however, is made clear by the brief summary statement in vv. 22-24.
Finally the chapter concludes with Moses' prayer on behalf of the
people committed to his charge (vv. 25-29).

1-3 These opening verses set the scene by bringing together
many themes that have already been mentioned earlier in
Deuteronomy.[1] The people were poised on the verge[2] of the conquest. Beyond the river were more powerful nations, heavily fortified
cities, and the gigantic Anakim. But the people knew that their
strength and hope of victory lay in God's strength and in his word of
promise. The contrast is between the weakness of Israel and the
strength of the Canaanites, but the latter are eclipsed by the power of
God. In v. 3, the power of God is described in three ways:
It is he who crosses ahead of you as a devouring fire;
It is he who will destroy them;
It is he who will humble them before you.

1. On v. 1, see 1:28; 2:18; 4:38; 5:1; 6:4; 7:1. On v. 2, see 1:28 and 7:15. On v. 3, see
4:24; 7:21-24.
2. *Today you are going to cross the Jordan* (9:1) — the *today* probably means the
immediate future rather than the same day; i.e., "today, you are ready to cross the
Jordan."

There is thus a strong emphasis on the role of God in giving military victory to his people in the coming conquest, but nevertheless the people are not simply bystanders or observers. After the threefold emphasis of God's role, it can then be said: *you shall dispossess them and destroy them speedily.* The people participate in the work of God, but the verses that follow immediately contain a warning that the people should not be mistaken in understanding the nature of their participation.

4-6 In contrast to the threefold emphasis of God's role, the people are now warned three times that the gift of the land would not be *because of*[3] (Israel's) *righteousness.* (a) When God expelled the Canaanites before them, the Israelites were to beware of saying to themselves[4] that their righteousness was God's reason; the reason for God dispossessing the Canaanites was to be found partly in his judgment of them: *it is on account of the wickedness of these nations* (v. 4). God was not only the God of Israel, but the God of all nations in his sovereignty; hence the expelling of the Canaanites from Palestine was not to be understood as an arbitrary divine act, but as an act of judgment by a just God. (b) *It is not because of your righteousness or the uprightness of your heart* — the second emphasis seems at first to be similar to the preceding one. God was going to dispossess the Canaanites because of their wickedness (v. 5). There is an important addition, however; God's act of dispossession was not only one of judgment, but it was in order to *establish the word which the Lord promised by oath to your fathers, to Abraham, to Isaac, and to Jacob.* That is, the action of God was a part of the fulfilment of the ancient promise made to the patriarchs. The first two emphases are closely related; the covenant promise to Abraham contained not only the gift of the land, but also the understanding that the gift would follow the divine judgment coming upon the inhabitants of the land (Gen. 15:16). Thus the gift of the land was first an act of judgment by God (v. 4), and second an act arising out of God's faithfulness to the covenant promise made long ago. (c) The third reason why the gift of the land should not be regarded as a reward for righteousness is the most compelling of all for the audience listening to the address: *you are a stubborn people.* If, in fact, the gift of the land was to be contingent upon the righteousness of the people, it was a gift that would never be received. The third emphasis thus highlights the graciousness of God in the gift of the land. But v. 6 also introduces a matter of delicate balance which is expounded further in the remain-

---

3.   On the relatively rare nuance "because of" for the preposition /b/, see T. L. Fenton, "Ugaritica-Biblica," *UF* 1 (1969), p. 64, n. 4.
4.   *Do not say to yourself*—a literal rendering of the Hebrew would be: "do not say *in your heart.*"

der of the chapter. The gift of the land could not be a reward for righteousness; it was a gift of God's graciousness. On the other hand, the continuing possession of the land by the Israelites would certainly be contingent upon obedience. Disobedience to the covenant could lead to forfeiting the land, and the Israelites would join the Canaanites as ex-residents.

7-14 An illustration of the stubbornness of the people. *Remember! Do not forget* (v. 7) — the emphatic call to remember is reminiscent of the theme of ch. 8, but it is prompted by the topic of vv. 4-6. If the people were ever foolish enough to claim that the gift of the land was a result of their righteousness, then they would be suffering from a severe case of religious amnesia. They are called, therefore, to remember the long history of their stubbornness and provocation of God, which had extended from the time of the Exodus from Egypt up till the present moment on the plains of Moab (v. 7b).

Though there were many events that could have been drawn on to illustrate Israel's history of provocation, the events associated with Horeb are chosen and are presented in the form of historical recollection, similar to the various themes in Deut. 1:6–3:29. The choice of Horeb was no doubt dictated by its central significance; if there was a time above all others when the people should have been faithful, it was during the events associated with the formation of the covenant in Horeb (*you provoked the Lord to anger even in Horeb*, v. 8). But the people's behavior at Horeb was such that God almost destroyed them; clearly, there could be no ground to argue that the gift of the land would be reward for righteous behavior!

The recollection of the events at Horeb[5] is also significant in that the renewal ceremony in Moab was a renewal of that first great forming of the covenant. The relevance of the historical recollection is thus all the more apparent, for if the people had been guilty of provoking God even in the midst of the awe-inspiring events associated with Horeb, then the danger was no less present on the plains of Moab. At the first forming of the covenant, Moses had ascended the mountain, fasted for forty days and forty nights, and had received from God the two stone tablets, *written by the finger of God,* containing the covenant words of God (vv. 9-10). The nature of Moses' fast emphasizes his complete dependence upon God; he neither ate nor drank day or night.[6] But the contrast is drawn sharply in v. 12; while Moses was in communion with God, the people had already *turned aside from the path* God had commanded for them. They had acted

5. The principal parallel passage is Exod. 32:7-20. See also Deut. 5:22-33. For a more detailed tabulation of the parallel passages, see S. R. Driver, *Deuteronomy,* pp. 112-14.
6. By way of contrast, the fast advocated during the month of Ramadān in Islam consists in abstinence from food and drink during the hours of daylight only: see *Quran* 2:180-84 (A. J. Arberry, *The Koran Interpreted,* pp. 24f.).

perversely by making a molten image for themselves (v. 12b). Moses was therefore commanded to go down from the mountain to the people for whom he was responsible.

The theme of stubbornness returns in v. 13: *I have seen this people and they are indeed a stubborn people.* The previous reference to the stubbornness of the people (v. 6) had been on the lips of Moses; this time, it is spoken by God himself and it has awesome implications. God threatens to destroy the people and obliterate all memory of them from the world of men. According to the principle of human or self-righteousness (vv. 4-6), there was no reason why God should not have so acted with justice; but, as we shall see, the divine *Leave me alone* (v. 14a) was taken by Moses, not as a direct prohibition, but as an invitation to intercession. That he could interpret the words in this way was made possible only through the closeness of his communion with God during the preceding forty days and forty nights. Before interceding, however, Moses recalls how first he went down from the mountain to deal with the immediate problem.

15-21 Moses came down from the mountain, which was still *burning with fire,* holding in his hands the two tablets of the covenant which God had given to him (see 4:11-14 and commentary). Coming directly from the glory of God's presence, Moses was faced immediately with the awfulness of the people's sin: *you had made a molten calf for yourselves* (v. 16). The construction of the calf may have been a lapse into idolatry, or it may have been an attempt to make a physical representation of the Lord, or even to make an object symbolizing the footstool of God.[7] In any case, the construction of the molten calf constituted a breach of the first or second commandment (see 5:7-10). The nature of the crime explains the violence of Moses' reaction which is described in v. 17: *and I seized the two tablets and flung them from my two hands, and I shattered them before your very eyes.* Moses' act was not simply a spontaneous reaction of anger, in which he shattered the tablets because they just happened to be in his hands. Rather the evil act of the Israelites had violated the covenant God had just granted to them. Thus Moses' act of smashing the covenant tablets symbolized in a very forceful way the potential meaning of the Israelites' act in constructing the calf. At the very time that God had given the people the tablets of the covenant through Moses, the people broke the conditions of the covenant and potentially rendered it null and void. Once again, Israel could never claim

7. Cf. Buis and Leclercq, *Le Deutéronome,* p. 89. On the potential Egyptian background to the bull or calf-cult, see K. A. Kitchen, *NBD,* pp. 179f. The Heb. word for "calf" is *'ēgel;* the cognate Ugar. word, *'gl,* is used several times in association with deities. The word is used in simile to describe Anat's yearning for Baal (*CTA* 6.II.7, 28). The god Mot is described as the "calf of El": *CTA* 3.III.41, but following the reading of Gordon, *UT,* p. 255.

that the gift of the land would be because of their righteousness; they were so stubborn and perverse that they had broken the covenant on the same day that Moses had returned to them from the mountain with the tablets of the covenant.

Having shattered the tablets, symbolizing thereby that the covenant was already potentially broken, Moses immediately began to intercede. First, he prayed for the people (v. 18), for their behavior had been such as to invite destruction by a just God (v. 19). This first act of intercession is recalled in detail in vv. 25-29, but here Moses recalls how the Lord heard his intercession on that occasion (v. 19b). Second, Moses interceded on behalf of Aaron, on whom the immediate responsibility for the Israelites' sin rested (v. 20); Aaron had thus incurred the wrath of God and his life was in danger.[8] Then Moses systematically destroyed the objectionable calf (v. 21). *I burned it in the fire* — the heat would reduce the gold to a lump, at the same time removing the symbolic shape. *I crushed it, grinding it thoroughly until it was fine as dust* — the lump of gold was reduced to a fine powder. Note that the actions of Moses indicate that for him, the object had no sacred associations whatsoever; in the eyes of those who made the calf, however, the acts of "profaning" the image emphasized that it was indeed nothing more than precious metal. *I threw its dust into the brook running down from the mountain* — the final symbolic act disposed of the gold dust beyond retrieval. The people, by their acts, had brought on the smashing of the tablets of the covenant. Then the golden calf, which they had constructed, had also been destroyed, until at last they were left with nothing — except Moses to intercede on their behalf.

22-24 Further examples of the people's stubbornness and sin. The recollection of the people's provocation of God at Horeb was one of several examples Moses could have drawn upon to emphasize to the people that the gift of the land could never be a direct reward for righteousness. It was the most important example in that the events occurred at the time of the making of the covenant in Horeb. At Taberah, the people had complained of their misfortunes and had been saved from the burning anger of God only by the intercession of Moses (Num. 11:1-3). At Massah, they had been finding fault with everything and in presumption had put God to the test; Moses had called on God for guidance (Exod. 17:1-7). At Kibroth-hatta'avah (lit. "graves of desire/lust"), the people had again incurred God's anger and several had perished as a result (Num. 11:31-35). At Kadesh-barnea, the people had been disobedient to the command of God.[9] All

---

8. On Aaron's role in the affair of the calf, see Exod. 32:1-6 and 21-26. The intercession on behalf of Aaron is not mentioned elsewhere.
9. See Deut. 1:19-40 and commentary. The last example was particularly relevant in that people on the plains of Moab faced a divine command similar to that given at Kadesh-barnea.

these examples[10] are employed by Moses to establish the point of this portion of his address; *You have been rebellious against the Lord from the day that I knew you* (v. 24; see also v. 7). The history of Israel's stubborn rebellion against God thus emphasized all the more the graciousness of God. But for God's grace in the past, they would not even be standing in the plains of Moab, renewing their covenant with God.

25-29   The intercession of Moses.[11] Verse 25 refers back to v. 18. Moses' prayer opens with the words *Lord God* ('ǎḏōnāy yhwh); in Deuteronomy, this title for God is used only in the introduction to prayer and may indicate the relationship between Moses and God on which the petition was based, namely the recognition of God's Lordship and sovereign power.[12] Moses first stated his request in this intercessory prayer: *do not destroy your people and your inheritance* (v. 26). His purpose in intercession was to turn aside the divine wrath and judgment which the people had incurred by their evil behavior. But even in stating simply his request, Moses has begun already to argue his case: it was not his own people he was praying for, but God's people (*your people/inheritance*). They are the people whom God *redeemed* by liberating them in the Exodus from the bondage of Egypt. Thus the first basis on which Moses requested forgiveness was God's former gracious act of liberation; though the people deserved judgment, there had been a divine purpose in the Exodus, and Moses' request was that that purpose not be frustrated through the people's unfaithfulness. The second basis for the request goes even further back than the Exodus: *Remember your servants, Abraham, Isaac, and Jacob* (v. 27). It is interesting to compare Moses' use of history and memory in his prayer and in his address to the people. To the people, Moses recalls that history which shows their unfaithfulness, and on this basis he calls them to obedience and faithfulness. In prayer to God, Moses recalls the long history of God's covenant faithfulness and seeks God's forgiveness for the people on the basis of God's nature, not the people's worthiness. If merit were the criterion, the covenant would already be void; therefore Moses beseeches God in prayer — *Look neither at the stubbornness of this people, nor at their wickedness, nor at their sin* (v. 27b). The third basis of Moses' request was related to the vindication of the honor of the Lord in the eyes of Egypt; if the people had perished in the wilderness, the Egyptians could have interpreted that event as reflecting God's inability to fulfil his promise, and his hate for his people (v. 28). The prayer concludes by repeating, for the sake of emphasis, the theme of v. 26:

10.   Keil and Delitzsch, noting that the examples are not given in chronological order, have suggested that the sequence moves from the smaller to the more serious forms of guilt: *The Pentateuch*, pp. 338f.
11.   See also Exod. 32:11-13. Cf. S. R. Driver, *Deuteronomy*, p. 116.
12.   See also 3:24.

they are your people . . . whom you brought out . . . by your outstretched arm.

The prayer of Moses expresses his understanding and knowledge of God: the justice of God is balanced by the mercy of God, and it was to God's mercy that Moses appealed. But the prayer expresses boldness, for it involved the attempt, in humility, to turn aside the wrath of a righteous God. Thus the recollection of the prayer in Moses' address served to bring a sobering influence on his audience; in the past, there had been moments when the whole future of the people of Israel had been in the balance. In the present, therefore, the people were to remember the past mercies of God and to commit themselves wholeheartedly in allegiance to their Lord.

9. THE TABLES OF THE LAW AND THE ARK (10:1-10)

1 *At that time, the Lord said to me: Hew out for yourself two stone tablets like the original ones and come up to me on the mountain; you shall also make for yourself a wooden ark.*

2 *And I shall write upon the tablets the words that were on the original tablets which you smashed; then you shall place them in the ark.*

3 *So I made an ark of acacia wood and I hewed out two stone tablets like the original ones, and I ascended the mountain with the two tablets in my hand.*

4 *And he wrote upon the tablets the same substance as the original writing, namely, the ten words which the Lord spoke to you on the mountain from the midst of the fire on the day of the assembly; then the Lord gave them to me.*

5 *And I turned and came down from the mountain and I placed the tablets in the ark which I had made, and there they were, just as the Lord commanded me.*

6 *And the Israelites travelled from Be'eroth Bene-ja'akan to Moserah. There, Aaron died; he was buried there too, and his son Eleazar served as priest in his place.*

7 *From there, they set out for Gudgodah, then from Gudgodah to Jotbathah, a land with streams of water.*

8 *At that time, the Lord set aside the tribe of Levi to carry the ark of the covenant of the Lord, to stand before the Lord to minister to him, and to bless in his name, to this very day.*

9 *Therefore, Levi did not have a portion or inheritance along with his brethren; the Lord — he was his inheritance, according to what the Lord your God had told him.*

10 *And I stood on the mountain, as in the former days, for forty days and forty nights, and the Lord heard me on that occasion also; the Lord did not wish to destroy you.*

The opening section of ch. 10 is closely related to the substance of ch. 9; it provides a conclusion to the example of Horeb employed in the immediately preceding section of Moses' address. First, there is a description of the second giving of the Decalog and the depositing of the tables of the law in the ark (vv. 1-5). There then follows a short passage (vv. 6-9) which has the appearance of an editorial addition, providing brief further comments on the travels of the Israelites, the death of Aaron, and the role of the Levites. The concluding verse refers back to 9:25.

1-5 The tablets of the law and the ark. *At that time* (v. 1) — the time indicated is the time of Moses' intercessory prayer on behalf of the people (9:25-29), and it is significant for the interpretation of the verses immediately following. The following verses indicate that the request in Moses' prayer was granted, for after the prayer (*at that time*) he was instructed to undertake certain preparations which indicated, by their nature, that God would not destroy his people and that the covenant was not irreparably broken.

The substance of the historical recollection at this point is based substantially on Exod. 34:1-4, though the sermonic style of the text in Deuteronomy is such that particular parts are emphasized and other items are added (the ark) which do not appear in Exodus.[1] Moses was commanded to prepare two stone tablets,[2] similar to those which had been broken (9:17), on which the basic law of the covenant was to be written once again. He was also to make the wooden ark which was to be the receptacle for the covenant tablets. It should be noted that Moses prepared the stone tablets, but it was God who would write upon them the divine words (v. 2). The ark, constructed from acacia wood,[3] contained the tablets of the covenant and was thus similar in function to the religious shrines in which copies of the Near Eastern political treaties were deposited.[4]

Moses ascended the mountain with the prepared tablets and God wrote upon them *the same substance as the original writing,*[5] *namely, the ten words . . .* (v. 4). The "ten words" are the Ten Commandments: see 4:13 and commentary. *Then the Lord gave them to me* (v. 4b) — more is involved than simply that another copy of the law was provided because the first two tablets unfortunately got broken. The shattering of the first tablets symbolized the breaking of

1. On the relationship between vv. 1-5 and the narratives in Exodus, cf. Driver, *Deuteronomy*, pp. 117f.; Keil and Delitzsch, *The Pentateuch*, p. 340.
2. See also 4:13 and commentary, and 5:22.
3. *Acacia* — or shittim. According to Num. 33:49, the Israelites had pitched camp in the vicinity of Abel-shittim, the "meadow/grove of acacia trees." On the nature of the wood, see G. A. Smith, *The Book of Deuteronomy*, pp. 132f. Acacia was also one of the basic types of wood used for carpentry in Egypt; J. R. Harris, ed., *The Legacy of Egypt*[2], p. 94.
4. Cf. A. Phillips, *Ancient Israel's Criminal Law*, p. 6.
5. On the translation here, see A. R. Hulst, *OT Translation Problems*, p. 14; the similarity lies in the substance, not the form, of the writing.

the covenant relationship because of Israel's sin in making the calf. The second writing of the law and the gift of the tablets is indicative of the graciousness of God and the response of God to the intercession of Moses. Moses then returned down the mountain and placed the two newly inscribed tablets in the ark, as he had been commanded (v. 5). This recollection of the renewal of the relationship in Horeb emphasized to the Israelites, who were engaged in a further renewing of the covenant in Moab, that the graciousness of God was to be seen in their very survival to that present moment as the covenant family of God.

6-9 These verses serve to bring together various themes that have appeared in the foregoing section of the address and to provide them with a natural conclusion. Verses 6-7, or even all four verses, may be an addition to the text.[6] The four place names mentioned are to be associated with the places named in Num. 33:31-33,[7] though the location of the ancient sites is no longer known with any certainty.[8]

Aaron died and was buried at Moserah (v. 6). The verse refers back to 9:20 and more generally to Aaron's responsibility in the incident of the golden calf (9:16-21). God had been angry with Aaron and ready to destroy him (9:20) because of the calf incident; Moses, however, had prayed for him, and the brief reference to Aaron here (in 10:6) indicates that that prayer had been answered. Aaron had not died in Horeb as a result of his sin, but had lived longer and died at Moserah, which was presumably in the vicinity of Mount Hor (see Num. 20:27-28). Thus 10:6 is parallel in function to 10:1-5, in that both passages indicate that Moses' intercession, described in ch. 9, was answered by the Lord.

The responsibilities of the tribe of Levi are described in vv. 8-9; for further details on the Levites, see 18:1-8 and commentary.

6. Verses 5 and 10 both have verbs in the 1st person singular, indicating the address of Moses. Verses 6-7 seem to be an extract from a travel itinerary similar to that in Num. 33. On the difficulty here, see G. T. Manley, *The Book of the Law*, p. 157; H. M. Segal, *The Pentateuch*, p. 95. Keil and Delitzsch (*The Pentateuch*, p. 341) think that Moses quoted from an account of the journeys and that "he lets the history itself speak." See also S. R. Driver, *Deuteronomy*, pp. 118-121, for a critical assessment of attempts to harmonize the verses with Num. 33. Verses 8-9 may refer back to 10:1 (see *at that time*, in both places) and may therefore be integral to the address.
7. Be'eroth Bene-ja'akan is the full form of Bene-ja'akan (Num. 33:31). Moserah ("chastisement") is given a plural form, Moseroth, in Num. 33:31. Gudgodah is to be identified with Hor-haggidgad (probably "cave of Gidgad/Gudgod") in Num. 33:2. Jotbathah is the same in both passages. The differences in the form of the place names indicate that there is not a direct relationship between the texts in Deut. and Numbers.
8. The specific geographical locations of Be'eroth Bene-ja'akan and Moserah are not known with any certainty; the former, however, may be related to the family or tribe of Akan (Gen. 36:27). Gudgodah may be identified tentatively with the vicinity of Wadi Hadahid (Manley, *NBD*, p. 495). Jotbathah may be identified tentatively with Bīr Tabā in the southern Arabah; D. Baly, *Geographical Companion to the Bible*, p. 174.

Here, three principal responsibilities of the Levites are set forth: (a) *to carry the ark of the covenant of the Lord* (v. 8). The earlier reference to the ark (10:1-5) likely prompted the mention of the ark here and the responsibility for it with which the Levites were charged. Responsibility for the ark meant responsibility for the tablets of the covenant contained within the ark; the Levites were to carry the ark, and the covenant tablets within it, during the travels of the Israelites. (b) *to stand before the Lord to minister to him* — the Levites were also to be responsible for the conduct of worship, the offering of sacrifices, and other matters related to the sanctuary, in which the ark was kept. (c) *to bless in his name* — the name of the Lord was also connected with the sanctuary and the ark (12:5 and commentary). *To this very day* (v. 8b) — the words indicate that the duties assigned to the tribe of Levi at an earlier date still applied in the present. On v. 9, see 18:1-5 and commentary; the Levites, who were not to have a share in the promised land similar to that which was to be assigned to their fellow tribes, would nevertheless have a noble inheritance, namely, the Lord himself. They would live by participating in that which was given directly to the Lord. Though they would not have the physical security derived from their own personal property, they had the high honor of directly serving the Lord on behalf of their fellow Israelites.

10 The concluding verse of the section emphasizes the principal theme, namely, that Moses' prayer had been answered, the people had not been destroyed, and the covenant relationship between God and his people was still intact, only through the grace of God.

10. GOD'S REQUIREMENT OF ISRAEL (10:11–11:25)

11 *And the Lord said to me: Get up! go and journey in front of the people, so that they may enter and possess the land which I promised by oath to their fathers to give to them.*

12 *And now, O Israel, what is it that the Lord your God requires of you, but to fear the Lord your God, to walk in all his ways, and to love him, and to serve the Lord your God with all your heart and with all your soul;*

13 *to keep the commandments of the Lord and his statutes, which I am about to command you today, for your own good.*

14 *Lo, the heaven, and the heaven of heavens, the earth and all that is in it, belong to the Lord your God.*

15 *Only the Lord was drawn to your fathers to love them, and he chose their posterity after them, namely you, above all the peoples, as at this very day.*

16 *Circumcise, therefore, the foreskins of your heart and do not become stubborn again;*

17 *for the Lord your God is God of Gods and Lord of Lords, the great, mighty, and fearful God who is impartial and does not take a bribe.*

18 *He is the one enacting justice for the orphan and widow and loving the resident alien, providing him with bread and clothing.*

19 *So you shall love the resident alien, for you were resident aliens in the land of Egypt.*

20 *You shall fear the Lord your God and you shall serve him, and you shall keep close to him and you shall swear in his name.*

21 *He is your praise and he is your God, who did for you these great and fearful things, which you have seen with your own eyes.*

22 *Your fathers went down into Egypt with seventy persons, but now the Lord your God has made you like the stars of heaven in number.*

1 *And you shall love the Lord your God and you shall keep his injunction and his statutes and his judgments and his commandments always.*

2 *And today you shall know the discipline of the Lord your God — but not your children, who have not known and have not seen it — his greatness, his mighty hand and his outstretched arm,*

3 *and his signs and his deeds which he performed in the midst of Egypt, against pharaoh, king of Egypt, and against all his land;*

4 *and what he did to the Egyptian army, to its horses and its chariots; how he caused the waters of the Reed Sea to flow over them when they pursued you, and the Lord destroyed them, to this very day;*

5 *and what he did for you in the wilderness until you came to this place;*

6 *and what he did to Dathan and Abiram, the sons of Eliab, son of Reuben; how the earth opened its mouth and swallowed them, together with their families and their tents and every living person who followed in their footsteps, in the midst of Israel.*

7 *For your eyes have seen every great act of the Lord which he has done.*

8 *So you shall keep every commandment which I am about to command you today, in order that you may be strong and enter and possess the land, to which you are about to cross over in order to take possession of it;*

9 *and in order that you might prolong your life on the land which the Lord promised by oath to your fathers, to give to them and to their posterity, a land flowing with milk and honey.*

10 *For the land, into which you are about to enter to take possession of it, is not like the land of Egypt from whence you came, in which you used to sow your seed and water it with your foot, like a vegetable garden.*

11 *But the land, to which you are about to cross over in order to take possession of it, is a land of hills and valleys; it drinks water of the rain of heaven;*

12 *a land for which the Lord your God cares; the eyes of the Lord your God are continually upon it, from the beginning of the year to the end of the year.*

13 *And if you will indeed hear my commandments, which I am about*

to command you today, to love the Lord your God and to serve him with all your heart and with all your soul,

14 *then I will provide rain on your land in its season, the early rain and the spring rain, and you shall gather in your grain and your new wine and your fresh oil.*

15 *And I will provide grass in your field for your cattle, and you shall eat and be satisfied.*

16 *Take care for yourselves in case your heart is deceived and you turn aside and serve other gods and bow down in worship to them,*

17 *and the Lord's anger be kindled against you and he seal off the heavens so that there is no rain, and the ground does not bring forth its produce, and you perish quickly from the good land which the Lord is going to give to you.*

18 *And you shall set these words of mine in your heart and in your soul, and you shall bind them onto your hand for a sign, and they shall be between your eyes as frontlets.*

19 *And you shall teach them to your children, speaking about them when you are sitting in your house and when you are walking in the way, and when you lie down and when you rise up.*

20 *And you shall write them upon the doorposts of your house and on your gates,*

21 *so that your days and the days of your children may be numerous in the land which the Lord promised by oath to your fathers to give to them, as many as the days of heaven over the earth.*

22 *If only you will be careful to keep all of this law code, which I am about to command you, by doing it, by loving the Lord your God, by walking in all his ways and by clinging closely to him,*

23 *then the Lord will dispossess all these nations before you and you shall dispossess nations greater and more powerful than yourselves.*

24 *Every place on which the sole of your foot shall tread shall be yours; your border shall be from the wilderness and the Lebanon, from the river, the river Euphrates, and to the Mediterranean Sea.*

25 *No man shall be able to stand against you; the Lord your God has put fear of you and awe of you on all the land into which you shall march, just as he said to you.*

10:11   This verse serves as a transition from the substance of the previous passage to the new emphasis of Moses' address. The Horeb covenant was almost disrupted, but through the grace of God and the intercessory prayer of Moses, disaster was averted. The emphasis of the address now centers on God's present requirement of his people, but first Moses recalls briefly how the Lord had commanded them to begin their journeys once again. His prayer had been answered and the people had been spared; there was not only mercy but a full restoration of the covenant relationship. When God said: *Get up! Go . . .,* the command indicated that God would be with his people; he had not forgotten the covenant with the patriarchs and *the* *land which I promised by oath to their fathers to give to them.* Because it was through God's grace that the people were present on the plains of Moab, their responsibility to fulfil the requirements of God was all the more pressing.

12-13 God's requirements of his people are stated first of all in summary form and then serve as the basic texts for the portion of the sermon that follows.

(a) *Fear the Lord your God* (see also 10:20).

(b) *Walk in all his ways* (see also 11:22).

(c) *Love him* (see also 11:1, 13, 22; compare 10:15, 18, 19).

(d) *Serve the Lord your God* (see also 10:20 and 11:13).

(e) *Keep the commandments of the Lord* (see also 11:1, 8, 13, and 22). These basic texts are woven into the fabric of the sermon that follows and are illustrated and emphasized in a number of ways. Essentially, however, the various requirements have a common theme which can be stated in various ways. In broad terms, the common theme is *allegiance* to the God of the covenant; the particular requirements indicate the dimensions of the common theme of allegiance and are reminiscent of the language of the Near Eastern political treaties.[1] Expressed differently, the requirements may be seen as a positive sermon on the negatively stated first commandment: "You shall not have other gods besides me." The requirements stated in 10:12-13 indicate the positive nature of the total commitment to the One God. Still another way of looking at this portion of the address is to see it as a sermon on the "Great Commandment" (6:5) to love God; of the five requirements listed in the present context, love for God is the central one. The meaning of the various requirements is elaborated in the verses that follow; it is significant that the first theme taken up is *love*, not the requirement of love, but rather God's love for his people.

14-15 These verses present a contrast which is reminiscent of Ps. 8:3-4; God was creator and possessor of the cosmos in its entirety, but nevertheless he was *drawn to your fathers to love them*. The distinction between *heaven* and *heaven of heavens* (v. 14a) is uncertain.[2] *Heaven*, alone, may refer literally to the sky above (see the metaphorical use in 1:28), whereas *heaven of heavens* may imply something more cosmic,[3] similar to the modern connotations of the

---

1. See M. Weinfeld, *Deuteronomy and the Deuteronomic School,* pp. 83f.
2. The verse has a poetic character which might suggest that it would be artificial to make too firm a distinction between the meaning of the parts. Thus *heaven* / / *heaven-of-heavens* are further parallel to *earth* / / *all-that-is-in-it.* The phrase *heaven of heavens* may have a superlative sense, "the highest of heavens," perhaps even the "totality of heaven." See also the comments of M. Dahood, *Psalms, III.* Anchor Bible XVII A (1970), p. 142. The character of both v. 14 and v. 17 indicates that the words may have been quoted from some ancient hymn of praise.
3. See the similar use of language in 1 K. 8:27; if the sense is *sky* / / *heaven,* then the transcendence of God is given firm emphasis, for God is contained neither within the

term. The verse stresses the absolute sovereignty of God over all the created universe, both heaven and earth. Against the background of God's universal sovereignty, the election of his people in love is expressed: *he chose their posterity after them, namely you* (v. 15). Once again, the speaker brings the past to bear on the present; God's love for the patriarchs and his promise to them was beginning to find its full expression in the people gathered on the plains of Moab (*as at this very day*). The events of the past and the present moment were grounded essentially in God's love, and it was on the basis of God's prior love that Moses advocated love as a requirement for the people (v. 12).

16-17   On the theme of Israel's stubbornness, see also 9:1-29. *Circumcise, therefore, the foreskins*[4] *of your heart* — the metaphor is used in a slightly different way in 30:6. The metaphor of circumcision in this context seems to be prompted by the reference to the patriarchs in v. 15; the election of the patriarchs and God's covenant with them was marked by the sign of circumcision.[5] In the renewal of the covenant, however, it was not the outward sign of the covenant that was important, but the inward attitude of those who were renew-their allegiance to the God of the covenant. The metaphor thus aptly employs an act symbolizing the covenant relationship, but applies it to the present moment in a spiritual sense. God's requirement was that his people *love him* (10:12), but to do this, they required a particular attitude of heart or mind, which — like circumcision — involved decision and action symbolizing allegiance. Thus to circumcise the heart is to take an attitude to God which is the opposite of being *stubborn* (or stiff-necked).

The basis for this proper attitude toward God is stated in another hymnlike passage in v. 17. The description of God given here begins by emphasizing God's transcendent greatness and ends by indicating the character of God in relation to man. *God of Gods and Lord of Lords* — the Hebrew employs a superlative construction[6] so that the sense is: "the supreme God and the absolute Lord." God is God in the fullest and most complete sense and is absolute Lord or Sovereign.[7] But this dimension of the nature of God is beyond the

---

physical world limited by the sky, nor even within the cosmic heaven which is reflected in the mythology of the ancient Near East. As the completely transcendent God, his sovereignty extends over the earth and what is conceived as heaven.
4.   The plural reading here follows the Qumran evidence: see *DJD* III, pp. 158-161.
5.   See Gen. 17:9-12. Note that the metaphorical use of circumcision appears also in Jer. 4:4, though it is unlikely that there is a direct relationship between that passage and Deuteronomy. It is one of several metaphors employed by Jeremiah to emphasize his message.
6.   See GKC § 133 i (see also n. 2, p. 431).
7.   "Lord of Lords"/"Absolute Lord" implies the kingship of God; this verse may indeed be the background to "Lord of Lords and King of Kings" in Rev. 17:14. The

comprehension of man — he can only worship God in awe. The transcendent and almighty God, however, also revealed himself to man: *the great, mighty, and fearful God.* The language employed here to describe God directly implies the God of the Exodus,[8] the one who had participated in human events specifically on behalf of his chosen people. *Who is impartial* — rendered literally, the Hebrew idiom is "... who does not lift up faces."[9] The emphasis of the verse is now directly upon the relationship of God to man; God shows no partiality to man on the basis of his social or economic standing in the community.[10] What God requires of man is a proper attitude of heart (10:16). The impartiality of God also indicates judgment and justice, as do the last words of v. 17: *... and does not take a bribe.* The meaning of the words emerges once again in contrast to God's requirements of his people (10:12-13). God *does* require love; but those, for example, who outwardly obeyed the commandments, but did not love God, were in effect offering God a bribe. They were saying: "Look, I'm doing this and that correctly, so taking these things into account, perhaps the rest could be overlooked?" God required of man a wholehearted commitment in love, from which all other proper behavior stemmed; God saw what was in the heart and could not be persuaded or bribed into reducing his requirements of man.

18-19   The impartiality of God and the impossibility of bribing him are now illustrated with a particular example, to which an injunction is added. The more detailed legislation concerning orphans, widows, and aliens will be found in Deut. 24:17-22; in the present context, the topic is presented principally to illustrate the character of God and the implications of that character for the life of man. *He is the one enacting justice for the orphan and widow*[11] — that is to say, God had particular concern that those in the community whose social and economic status was not secure should receive just and proper treatment. *(He is the one) loving the resident alien, providing him with bread and clothing* — on the *resident alien,* see also 1:16 and commentary. Earlier, it was stated that God loved the patriarchs (10:15), whose posterity were gathered on the plains of Moab; now the impartiality of God is shown in his love for the resident alien, a person within the community who did not share full civil and religious rights with the Israelites. God provided food and clothing for the alien, just

---

Kingship of God in this context, however, has cosmic and universal implications, rather than the more specific implications contained in Exod. 15:18.
8.   *Mighty (gibbôr)* — see also Exod. 15:3(a), following the Sam. reading, for the expression: "the Lord is a warrior/mighty man." On *great* and *fearful,* see 10:21 (below).
9.   See also the similar idiom, describing the behavior of human judges, in Deut. 1:17.
10.   See also the use of this theme in the NT by Peter (Acts 10:34) and Paul (Gal. 2:6).
11.   Similar language is used of Danel in the Canaanite Aqhat Legend: see *CTA* 17.V.7-8. Cf. *RSP* I, 47f; II, 262f.

as he had done for his own people (see 8:3-4). There were two reasons, therefore, why the Israelites should love the resident aliens dwelling in their midst. First, the love of God extended not only to themselves, but also to the aliens; whom God loved, therefore, they should also love. Second, they were to remember that they too had been aliens in Egypt and there, in the latter years, they had not been treated with love and respect. Having experienced God's love and care during their own time as aliens, they were to express similar love and care to the aliens resident in their midst.

20 Note the similarity to 10:12-13; the theme of this part of the address is repeated here for emphasis. *You shall keep close to him* — the language indicates a very close and intimate relationship. The same verb *(dābaq)* is employed to describe the relationship between a man and his wife.[12] For further comments, see Deut. 6:13, which is similar, but slightly shorter, than 10:20.

21 *He is your praise and he is your God.* The basis for these two affirmations is gratitude and religious experience. The people had personally experienced the acts of God on their behalf from the Exodus to the present moment, and in gratitude they were to praise God,[13] and to recognize that he had an absolute claim to be their God. The worship of God was a vital part of the general requirements stated in 10:12-13, for in worship man gave an inward response and outward expression of his relationship of love to God.

22 See also 1:10 and 26:5, with commentary.[14] A part of the covenant promise to the patriarchs had already been fulfilled by the growth in Israel's numbers (see Gen. 15:5-6); the faithfulness and ability of God were therefore beyond question. But a part of the ancient promise still remained to be fulfilled, namely, the gift of the land (Gen. 17:8); the people were to know God's requirements of them in order that they might live to experience the fulfilment of all of God's promise to them.

In ch. 11, this portion of the address continues in the same manner; the requirements of God are reaffirmed and then applied and illustrated by a variety of particular themes:

(a) *Requirement:* love God and keep his commandments (11:1).
(b) *Illustration:* the lessons of history (11:2-7).[15]

---

12. Gen. 2:24. See also Job 19:20, where the verb describes "clinging" of human bones to skin.
13. G. A. Smith has noted that the sense of the words *He is your praise* may either be that God is the object of Israel's praise (see also Ps. 109:1) or that God's deeds for his people were the basis on which others praised Israel: *The Book of Deuteronomy*, pp. 142f.
14. On the number *seventy*, see also Gen. 46:27 and Exod. 1:5.
15. On the importance of these verses for an understanding of the Israelite conception of revelation, see L. Köhler, *Theologie des AT* (1936), p. 84.

(c) *Requirement:* Keep the commandments (11:8).
(d) *Illustration:* the good land compared with Egypt (11:9-12).
(e) *Requirement:* Keep the commandments, love and serve God (11:13).
(f) *Illustration:* the fertility of the good land (11:14-17).
(g) *Summary:* concluding the exposition on the basic commandments (11:18-25).

In each case, the statement of requirements refers back to 10:12-13, stressing different aspects of that summary statement; the two principal features are love and obedience.

11:1 (a) *Requirement.* In addition to 10:12, see also 6:5. *You shall keep his injunction* — the word *injunction* is used only here in Deuteronomy,[16] though the verb to which the noun is related is common throughout the book.

2-7 (b) *Illustration:* the lessons of history. Three things are singled out for mention in this concise passage: the Exodus, in some detail (vv. 2b-4); God's presence in the wilderness, stated in general terms (v. 5); the affair of Dathan and Abiram (v. 6). These items from history are presented as *the discipline of . . . God* (v. 2); discipline is not simply a negative term here, for the examples presented are both positive (Exodus) and negative (Dathan and Abiram) in relation to Israel. The discipline of God is thus the education of God, whereby he taught his people both by gracious acts on their behalf and by acts of judgment.[17] *And today you shall know the discipline* (v. 2) — the substance of that discipline had already been experienced by the people (11:7). In the address of Moses, however, the common experience of the past was turned into knowledge in the present; the sense is: "Today you shall know the meaning/relevance of that discipline." The people would understand that the divine education which they had been given, from the time they had left Egypt up to the present, was preparing them for the events still lying ahead of them. *But not your children, who have not known and have not seen it* (v. 2) — the syntax of this section is awkward,[18] but not altogether unusual given the rhetorical character of the address as a whole. The words are an interjection addressed to the younger people in the audience who had not actually experienced or seen the events about to be described and therefore would not know them with the same directness and intimacy as their parents.

The Exodus (vv. 2b-4) is described in familiar language. *His greatness, his mighty hand and his outstretched arm, and his signs*

16. S. R. Driver, *Deuteronomy*, p. 127.
17. For uses of the verb "discipline" (*yāsar*) in Deut., to which the noun (*mûsar*) employed here is related, see 4:36; 8:5; 21:18; 22:18.
18. See GKC § 117 1.

and his deeds . . .: see also 4:34. With vv. 3b-4, compare the Song of the Sea (Exod. 15:1-6). *To its horses and its chariots* (v. 4) — the pronominal suffix refers either to the army (*its*) or to the Egyptian pharaoh ("his").[19] The events associated with the great liberation of the Exodus are all attributed directly to God and not to the military strength or expertise of the Israelites. A part of God's purpose in the Exodus was still of direct relevance to those gathered on the plains of Moab; God not only brought his people out of the land of Egypt, but intended to bring them into the promised land (11:9-17; see also Exod. 15:17).

What he did for you in the wilderness (v. 5) — see also 8:2-15. The Exodus, the first of the lessons from history, had been a totally positive part of Israel's education in the ways of God. The wilderness period, mentioned here only in general terms, had broadened that education; Israel had experienced not only the provision and help of God, but also the chastisement and rebuke of God. The third example (v. 6) completes the balance by presenting a lesson from history stressing the failure of some Israelites and the judgment of God. For a full account of the rebellion in which Dathan and Abiram were involved, see Num. 16. The contrast between the Exodus and the rebellion is striking and relevant to the address of Moses. The Exodus had been the beginning of new life for Israel; the rebellion had led to the death of many and almost to the destruction of all the Israelites (Num. 16:45). The lessons of the past, therefore, stressed both the grace of God and the judgment of God, and the people were to remember these acts of the Lord (*your eyes have seen every great act of the Lord,* v. 7).

8 (c) *Requirement:* The people are urged once again to keep the commandments of God, but now the focus shifts from the lessons of history to the anticipation of the future. The people are to obey the law soon to be declared to them, not only because of their knowledge of God drawn from past experiences, but also because without such obedience, they would not find the strength necessary to take possession of the promised land.

9-12 (d) *Illustration:* the good land compared with Egypt. The promised land was *a land flowing with milk and honey.* In the rebellion of Dathan and Abiram, they had claimed that Moses had brought them *out of* the land flowing with milk and honey (Egypt!) but had not brought them *into* such a land (Num. 16:12-14). Perhaps to counter the reminiscences of that rebellion, Moses compares and contrasts Egypt with the promised land — *it is not like the land of*

---

19.   The word *rekeb* means "chariot," not "rider"; cavalry was not employed in Egypt until a later date: W. F. Albright, *Archaeology and the Religion of Israel* (²1946), p. 213, n. 25. The Aramaic cognate word is distinguished from riders in an Aramaic inscription: *lrkb (w)lprš* (*KAI* 202.B2).

Egypt from whence you came (v. 10). In Egypt, the land could be made
to produce a crop from the planted seed only when it was irrigated by
artificial means. *You used to sow your seed and water it with your
foot, like a vegetable garden* — the reference to watering the land by
foot probably reflects the practice of marking the ground with foot-
dug channels, through which irrigating water would flow.[20] In the
promised land, a vegetable garden might be watered artificially
(11:10b), but in contrast, virtually the whole Egyptian agricultural
system depended on irrigation. The land the Israelites were about to
possess was watered directly by *the rain of heaven* (v. 11). In the
promised land, therefore, they would be dependent not on human
techniques, but on the provision of God. The direct provision of God,
however, increased the responsibility for obedience which was incumbent upon the Israelites, as the third illustration makes clear
(11:14-17).

13 (e) *Requirement.* The requirement (obedience, love, and
service) is stated on this occasion in the form of a condition; if the
condition was upheld, then the people would receive provision and
prosperity from God in the future.

14-17 (f) *Illustration:* the fertility of the good land. Whereas
the previous illustration had contrasted the past with the future
(11:9-12), the focus is now entirely on the future and the good land
promised to Israel by God. *I will provide* (v. 14; see also v. 15) —
either Moses reverts temporarily to words spoken by God to him, or
else the text should read: "he will provide."[21] *The early rain and the
spring rain* — the two terms indicate the beginning and the end of the
rainy season in Palestine, extending approximately from October to
April. God promised to provide rain, in its season, which was necessary for the sustenance of men and beasts, provided that his people
lived in accord with his requirements of them. *Take care for yourselves in case your heart is deceived* (v. 16) — an alternative translation would be, "take care lest you become so open-minded that.
. . ."[22] The reference to the danger of turning to foreign religions,
though common in Deuteronomy, is introduced here for a particular
reason. The Canaanites believed that the gift of the rains lay in the

---

20. P. Montet, *Egypt and the Bible* (1968), pp. 83f. The words are not likely a
reference to the *shaduf,* which was operated by hand. The water-wheel (*saqqieh*),
which could be operated by foot or by the use of cattle, was probably not introduced in
Egypt until a later period.
21. Such a reading, which was already implied by Sam., some versions of LXX, and
the Vulgate, is now given additional weight by the quotation of the passage in a
mezuzah text from Qumran: *wntn (DJD* III, p. 161).
22. See T. J. Meek, "OT Notes," *JBL* 67 (1948), pp. 233-39 (*pp. 235f.); Meek
suggests the verb *pātāh,* "to be open," noting that this rendering has the support of the
LXX.

power of the god Baal/Hadad. The Israelites were to be careful to recognize the Lord as the giver of rain; if they failed to do so and worshipped other gods, they would learn the truth the hard way. God would *seal off the heavens so that there is no rain* (v. 17), and the result would be that Israel would not survive in the land which was God's gift to them.

18-25 (g) *Summary:* a conclusion to the exposition on the basic commandments. The substance of these verses is essentially repetition of material that has come earlier in the address of Moses, but the repetition serves once again a rhetorical purpose. It is a final exposition of the essential features of the basic commandments of the covenant, presented once more before the actual recitation and exposition of the law (in chs. 12–26). The main emphasis is still on the requirement of God for his people (law, obedience, and love), upon which the future blessing of God in the conquest and the possession of the promised land would be contingent. The main parallel passages are listed below and should be consulted for a fuller commentary:[23]

> Verse 18: see 6:8.
> Verse 19: see 6:7 and 4:9-10.
> Verse 20: see 6:9.
> Verse 21: see 4:40 and 6:2.
> Verse 22: see 6:17.
> Verse 23: see 4:38 and 9:1.
> Verse 24: see 1:7-8.
> Verse 25: see 2:25 and 7:23-24.

11. A BLESSING AND A CURSE (11:26-32)

26 *Listen! Today I am going to set before you a blessing and a curse:*

27 *the blessing for those of you who listen to the commandments of the Lord your God which I am going to command you today;*

28 *and the curse if you do not listen to the commandments of the Lord your God and you turn aside from the way which I am going to command you today, in order to go after other gods whom you have not known.*

29 *And it shall be that when the Lord your God brings you into the land, which you are about to enter in order to take possession of it, then you shall set the blessing on Mount Gerizim and the curse on Mount Ebal.*

30 *Surely they are beyond the Jordan, beyond the western road, in the land of the Canaanites who inhabit the Arabah, in the vicinity of Gilgal, beside the oaks of Moreh.*

---

23. It should be stressed that these verses are not exact repetitions of the earlier verses listed; they contain a repetition for emphasis of the substance or message of the earlier passages.

31 *For you are about to cross over the Jordan, to go in, to take possession of the land which the Lord your God is going to give to you; and you shall take possession of it and you shall inhabit it.*
32 *And you shall take care to do all the statutes and the judgments which I am about to set before you today.*

The context of this passage is important. It serves as a conclusion to the preceding part of the address in that it places the audience in a position of decision which will soon have to be made. *Today I am going to set before you a blessing and a curse* — the alternatives will be set before the people as the basis upon which the decision has to be made. The blessing and the curse, however, are contingent upon obedience to the law, which was about to be presented to the people in its detailed specifications. Thus the passage serves not only as a conclusion to the preceding part of the address, but also as an introduction to what follows, which sets the subsequent chapters within their immediate and proper perspective.

The framework within which the detailed presentation of the law is set can be seen in the following outline:

(a) The blessing and curse in the *present* renewal of the covenant (11:26-28).
(b) The blessing and curse in the *future* renewal of the covenant (11:29-32).
(c) The specific legislation (12:1–26:19).
(d) The blessing and curse in the *future* renewal of the covenant (27:1-26).
(e) The blessing and curse in the *present* renewal of the covenant (28:1–29:1).

Thus it can be seen that the specific legislation is set in a chiastic framework, stressing the importance of the blessing and curse contingent upon obedience to the legislation both in the present and in the future.

26-28 For fuller details, see ch. 28 and commentary and also the Introduction, section VIII/5. The nature of the commandments emerges in a striking manner in v. 28: *if you do not listen to the commandments . . . and you turn aside from the way. . . .* Again it becomes clear that the commandments were not simply a body of legislation which was to be obeyed for its own sake. The commandments reflected a way of life, the good way of life which God determined for his people; therefore, to disobey (or *not listen to*) the commandments was to *turn aside from the way* that alone could lead to happiness and prosperity in relationship with God, and to take a false trail that could lead only to separation from God and disaster. Thus, in the exposition of the details of the law that follows, Moses' role was not that of a great legalist or jurist, but was that of a man deeply concerned that the people who were under his charge should enter into the fullness of life that was potential in the covenant relationship with God.

29-32 For a fuller account of the future renewal of the covenant mentioned briefly here, see 27:1-26 and commentary.[1] The location of the two mountains is specified in v. 30. *Beyond the western road*[2] — while the reference of the words is not absolutely certain, they may indicate the road that lay to the west of the Jordan, linking Jericho in the south with Bethshan in the north. *In the vicinity of Gilgal* — since there are several different Gilgals mentioned in the OT,[3] the particular location is uncertain, but it may have been located near Shechem, toward the Jordan. *The oaks*[4] *of Moreh* — see also Gen. 12:6 for Abram's association with this vicinity.

C. THE SPECIFIC LEGISLATION (12:1–26:15)

1. REGULATIONS RELATING TO THE SANCTUARY (12:1-31)

1 *These are the statutes and the judgments which you are to be careful to do in the land which the Lord God of your fathers has given you to possess, all the days that you live on the land.*

2 *You shall completely destroy all the places where the nations, whom you are about to dispossess, serve their gods, on the high mountains, and on the hills, and under every luxuriant tree.*

3 *And you shall tear down their altars, and you shall shatter their pillars, and you shall burn their asherim in the fire, and you shall hew down the images of their gods, and you shall destroy their name from that place.*

4 *You shall not do thus toward the Lord your God.*

5 *But you shall resort only to the place that the Lord your God shall choose from all your tribes, to set his name there for his habitation, and you shall go there.*

6 *And you shall bring there your burnt offerings, and your sacrifices, and your tithes, and the contribution of your produce, and your vow offerings, and your free-will offerings, and the firstlings of your herd and your flock.*

7 *And there you shall eat before the Lord your God, and both you*

---

1. For a study of 11:26-32 in relation to Deut. 27 and Josh. 8:30-35, see O. Eissfeldt, "Gilgal and Shechem," in J. I. Durham and J. R. Porter, eds., *Proclamation and Presence* (1970), pp. 90-101. However, Eissfeldt's argument that some of the passages relate to Gilgal and some relate to Shechem seems, from the perspective of the present writer, to be based on a rather artificial analysis of the texts. On the authenticity and antiquity of 11:26-32 and ch. 27, see the Introduction, section IX. 3 (c).

2. Rendered literally, the Hebrew is: "beyond the road of the going in of the sun."

3. See K. A. Kitchen, "Gilgal," *NBD*, pp. 469f.

4. *'ēlônê* (plur.) — probably a singular should be read (as in Gen. 12:6), for which the majority of the versions offer good support.

213

and your families, whom the Lord your God has blessed, shall rejoice in all that you undertake.

8 *You shall not do according to all that we are doing here today, each man doing whatever is right in his own eyes;*

9 *because up to now you have not come to the rest and to the inheritance, which the Lord your God is going to give to you.*

10 *But you shall cross the Jordan, and you shall dwell in the land which the Lord your God is going to give you for an inheritance; and he will give you rest from all your surrounding enemies and you shall dwell in safety.*

11 *Then the place, which the Lord your God shall choose to cause his name to dwell there – to that place you shall bring all that which I am commanding you: your burnt offerings, and your sacrifices, and your tithes, and the contribution of your produce, and all the choicest of your vow offerings which you vow to the Lord.*

12 *And you shall rejoice before the Lord your God, you, and your sons, and your daughters, and your male servants, and your female servants, and the Levite who is in your settlements, for he does not have a portion or inheritance along with you.*

13 *You must take great care that you do not offer your burnt offerings in every place that you see,*

14 *but only in the place that the Lord chooses in one of your tribes; there you shall offer your burnt offerings and there you shall do all that I am commanding you.*

15 *However, in all your settlements you may slaughter and eat flesh as freely as you wish, according to the blessing of the Lord your God which he grants to you. The unclean and the clean may eat it — the gazelle, for example, or the hart.*

16 *However, you shall not eat the blood: you shall pour it out upon the earth like water.*

17 *In your settlements, you may not eat the tithe of your grain, or of your new wine, or of your fresh oil, or of the firstlings of your herd or your flock, or any of your vow offerings which you vow, or of your free-will offerings, or of the contribution of your produce;*

18 *but you shall eat it only before the Lord your God in the place which the Lord your God shall choose, you, and your son, and your daughter, and your male servant, and your female servant, and the Levite who is in your settlements. And you shall rejoice before the Lord your God in all that you undertake.*

19 *You must take great care that you do not neglect the Levite all your days upon your land.*

20 *When the Lord your God enlarges your border, just as he said to, and you say: "Let me eat flesh," for you desire to eat flesh —you may eat flesh as freely as you wish.*

21 *If the place, where the Lord your God chooses to place his name, is distant from you, then you may slaughter some of your herd or of your flock, which the Lord has given to you, just as I have commanded you, and you may eat in your settlements as freely as you wish.*

22 *Indeed, just as men eat the gazelle or the hart, so too you may eat it; the unclean and the clean alike may eat it.*
23 *However, be certain not to eat the blood, for the blood is the life force and you shall not eat the life force along with the flesh.*
24 *You shall not eat it; you shall pour it out upon the earth like water.*
25 *You shall not eat it in order that it may go well for you, and for your sons after you, because you are doing the right thing in the eyes of the Lord.*
26 *However, you shall take your holy things, which you shall have, and your vow offerings, and you shall go to the place that the Lord shall choose.*
27 *And you shall offer your burnt offerings, the flesh and the blood, upon the altar of the Lord your God; and the blood of your sacrifices shall be poured out upon the altar of the Lord your God, but you shall eat the flesh.*
28 *Take care and hear all these words which I am commanding you, in order that it may go well for you, and for your sons after you, for ever, because you do what is good and right in the eyes of the Lord your God.*
29 *When the Lord your God cuts off before you the nations, whom you are going to dispossess, then you shall dispossess them and you shall dwell in their land.*
30 *You must take great care that you are not thrust out after them, after they have been destroyed before you, and that you do not resort to their gods, saying: How do these nations worship their gods, that I too may do the same?*
31 *You shall not do thus to the Lord your God, because they do for their gods every abomination of the Lord, which he hates — because they even burn their sons and their daughters in the fire to their gods.*

1   This verse serves as an introduction to the next major portion of Deuteronomy, the portion containing the specific legislation (12:1–26:15).[1] The wording here is similar to the wording in the introductory sections of previous portions of the book (cf. 4:44-45; 5:1; 6:1-2). The *statutes* and *judgments* which follow in the subsequent chapters are designed with the future residence of the Israelites in the promised land in mind; the promised land, though not yet

1.   For detailed studies of the section, see R. P. Merendino, *Das deuteronomische Gesetz* (1969); F. Horst, "Das Privilegrecht Jahwes," *Gottes Recht: gesammelte Studien zum Recht im AT* (1961); C. A. Simpson, "A Study of Deut. 12-18," *Anglican Theological Review* 34 (1952), pp. 247-251. For studies dealing particularly with ch. 12 and the problem of the sanctuary, see G. J. Wenham, "Deuteronomy and the Central Sanctuary," *TB* 22 (1971), pp. 103-118; A. Rofé, "The strata of the law about the centralization of worship in Deuteronomy," *SVT* 22 (1972); V. Maag, "Erwägungen zur deuteronomistischen Kultcentralization," *VT* 6 (1956), pp. 10-18; and the article by the editor in H. Graf Reventlow, ed., *Gottes Wort und Gottes Land* (1965). Other articles and studies are referred to in the following notes.

possessed, was already a certain possession (*the Lord God of your fathers has given*[2]. . .).

This twelfth chapter is at the heart of much of the current debate in the study of Deuteronomy, but this debate will not be taken up in detail here. The commentary will attempt to focus on the significance of the verses in their ancient context, but will deal in a little more detail with those sections of the text relevant to the larger debate.

2-4 The injunction to destroy foreign sanctuaries. The foreign sanctuaries, which were to be destroyed, were located in places believed by the Canaanites to have particular religious significance. Some shrines were located on *high mountains* and *hills;* the mountain or hill was sometimes thought to be the home of a god,[3] and by ascending the mountain, the worshipper was in some symbolic sense closer to the deity.[4] There were also shrines located *under every luxuriant tree;* certain trees were considered to be sacred and symbolized fertility, a dominant theme in Canaanite religion.[5] It was not primarily the location of the foreign shrines that was abhorrent to Israelite faith, but the nature of the worship conducted there; that worship was characterized by *altars, pillars* (standing stones, symbolizing the deity in some manner),[6] *asherim* (a tree or wooden pole, symbolizing the fertility-goddess),[7] and *images of their gods.* These objects were to be systematically destroyed so that the places associated with them would be divested of any semblance of sanctity. The physical act of destruction was thus also a symbolic act of rejection, the rejection of the deities and of the efficacy of the religious system of the Israelites' predecessors on the land. The act of destruction not only removed any subsequent temptation for the Israelites to lapse into foreign forms of religion, but also obliterated *their name* (i.e., of foreign gods) *from that place.* There was only one name on which the Israelites could call; this is the theme of the next section.

5-7 *The place that the Lord your God shall choose from all*

---

2. The form of the verb(*nāṯan*) indicates a completed action, implying the certainty of God's promise.

3. There was a shrine to the god Baal, for example, on the mountain located northeast of the ancient city of Ugarit. See H. Gese *et al., Die Religionen Altsyriens, Altarabiens und der Mandäer,* p. 123; E. Jacob, *Ras Shamra et l'AT* (1960), p. 100.

4. The symbolic significance of a mountain or hill was also known to the Hebrews, though with a slightly different significance (e.g., Sinai and Zion). See also G. T. Manley, *NBD,* pp. 525f. It should be noted that the technical term *bāmôṯ* ("high places") is not used in this context, but is used in the context of Josiah's reform (e.g., 2 K. 23:5).

5. See the discussion in M. H. Farbridge, *Studies in Biblical and Semitic Symbolism* (1923; repr. 1970), pp. 27-49.

6. See notes and bibliography in A. R. Millard, *NBD,* p. 999; L. Delekat, *BHH* II, col. 1169.

7. See V. Maag, *BHH* I, cols. 136f.

your tribes. The place referred to here is in sharp antithesis to *the places* (v. 2) where the Canaanites worshipped. This part of Moses' address on the law is concerned with this antithesis, rather than with the theoretical question of whether there could be more than one sanctuary in the promised land. Negatively, the Israelites were to avoid all places associated with Canaanite worship; positively, they were to resort only to the place divinely chosen. The place would be identified as that in which God would *set his name*[8] *. . . for his habitation*[9] — that is, the place would be identified by the tabernacle and the ark within it. The tabernacle, and the ark containing the tablets of the law, was the place of meeting between God and his people (Exod. 33:7-11); God's name (the Lord, or *Yahweh*), which had been revealed to Moses (Exod. 3:14-15), made possible that meeting with him. Thus, though there was only one tabernacle, it would be moved from place to place; there would be many places over the course of time, but only one place at a time.[10] This legislation, however, does not either prohibit or permit other sanctuaries — that question is not directly relevant in the immediate context.[11]

To this divinely appointed place, the people were to bring their sacrifices and offerings and there they would partake of them in God's presence (vv. 6-7). The burnt offering and sacrifice were the normal types of animal sacrifices; the former was burned in its totality, thus symbolically all going to the Lord, while the latter was divided, the fat being burned as the Lord's portion, and the remaining parts going to the priests and to the offerer. In addition to the animal sacrifices, the Israelites were also to bring the various other types of their offerings to God's sanctuary,[12] and *there you shall eat before the Lord your God.* These sacrifices and offerings would arise out of the bounty that would accrue to the Israelites in the promised land; thus the very possibility of bringing sacrifices and offerings would exist only in the

---

8. For the background to the sense of this Hebrew phrase, see G. J. Wenham, *TB* 22 (1971), pp. 113f. Wenham suggests that there may be military overtones of the conquest in the phraseology here. This suggestion would also be strengthened by the association of the *place* with the ark, which accompanied the Hebrews in battle (see Num. 10:35-36).
9. Heb. *lᵉshiknô*, assuming a noun form (only here) of *shēken*. It is possible to vocalize the consonants as Piel inf. absol.; the present text could then perhaps be seen as a conflated version (see M. Weinfeld, *Deuteronomy and the Deuteronomic School,* p. 325, n. 4).
10. Cf. K. A. Kitchen, *TSF Bulletin* 64 (1972), pp. 9-10n.
11. M. H. Segal, however, argues that the law (here and at Exod. 20:24) permits a plurality of sanctuaries, provided that they were properly consecrated. Thus *the place* denotes a single class of sanctuaries, not a single place (other singulars of class are noted in 12:18 and 16:14). See Segal, *The Pentateuch,* pp. 87f.
12. For a detailed discussion of sacrifices and offerings, see R. J. Thompson, *NBD,* pp. 1113-22. On tithes, see Deut. 14:22-29. On vows, see 23:21-23. On firstlings, see 15:19-23.

fulfilment of God's promise, and the bringing of them would acknowledge and commemorate in an open manner the goodness of God as provider. The future anticipated in this law relating to the sanctuary is one of rejoicing in all things, because of God's blessing (v. 7); but this joyous vision of the future is yet contingent upon obedience and avoidance of the dangers noted in vv. 2-4.

8-12 *You shall not do . . . in his own eyes* (v. 8). The years preceding, and those which would follow immediately upon the events in Moab, were not to be typical of the Israelites' religious life in the future. Since the Exodus from Egypt, the people had no permanent resting place, and their itinerant life style meant that of necessity their forms of worship had to be adapted to the immediate situation. The stress given to this point is important, for memory played a significant role in the faith of Israel. When in the future the people remembered the wilderness years and God's presence and aid, they should also remember that the desert did not provide the paradigm for the settled life in the promised land. The legislation given in Moses' address provided the foundation for that anticipated future life, and would be applicable when the people received from God the promised *rest* and *inheritance* (see v. 9). Hence v.10 is a further word of encouragement to persevere in faithfulness to God in the events lying ahead. Following that perseverance, they would settle in the land and assume what would become a normative religious life; then they would bring their sacrifices and offerings to God's sanctuary (v. 11) and would rejoice in God's presence (v. 12). On the Levites, see the detailed legislation in 18:1-8.

13-14 These verses return to the theme of vv. 2-4, though with a slight change in emphasis. There the destruction of foreign sanctuaries had been commanded and the people were instructed to worship the Lord properly, not in the manner of the Canaanites (v. 4). There was also a danger, warned against in these verses, that the people might be tempted to offer their legitimate burnt offerings to the Lord in illegitimate places; the words *every place that you see* refer by implication to Canaanite religious sanctuaries (see v. 2), though they could also refer to any place not sanctified by the Lord's choice. Hence v. 14 repeats emphatically the note of v. 5, that the sacrifices could be offered only in the place chosen by God.

15-19 The following verses make some distinctions that would be necessary when the Israelites were settled in the land, but which were unnecessary during the years in the desert. During the journeys of the Israelites, their "settlement" and the sanctuary were in the same location; when they populated their new land, there would be many different settlements, but the sanctuary of God (the tabernacle, and later the temple) would be in a particular place (see the notes above on vv. 5-7). In this new situation, it would be quite legitimate to slaughter and to eat meat freely;[13] the slaughtering and eating would take place in any settlement, and it would not be necessary to be ritually clean to participate. Likewise, meat could be eaten in such circumstances as would not be permissible for sacrifices (the meat of the *gazelle* or *hart*). The only limitation on this general eating of meat was that the *blood* was not to be eaten, but to be poured out. Thus, although the eating described here is totally secular (i.e., in no way associated with a sacrificial meal or offering), nevertheless the blood was to be poured ritually upon the ground. The blood was treated with respect, regardless of whether the slaughter was carried out in a secular or ritual setting, because the blood symbolized *life,* that which God imparted to all living creatures. The freedom of eating meat, however, did not extend to those products and foodstuffs which were set aside specifically for God (v. 17); they could be eaten legitimately only in God's sanctuary (v. 19), as had already been stressed earlier in the chapter (vv. 6,11).

20-28   The permission of the previous verses is expanded somewhat here and repeated, the repetition emphasizing the importance of distinguishing what could be eaten only at the sanctuary and what could be eaten anywhere. The expansion foresees growth in the land area controlled by the Israelites, and consequently the majority of the Israelites would live further away from the sanctuary. It is repeated that in such a situation, meat could still be slaughtered and eaten locally. Verse 21 makes it clear that mutton and beef were included in the provision; in v. 15, the gazelle and hart had been mentioned. The latter could never be used sacrificially, but the former could be; thus the provision makes clear that beef and mutton, though employed sacrificially, could quite legitimately be eaten secularly in the local settlements. The importance of obedience is stressed in vv. 25, 28; by observing the law, the people and their posterity would prosper in the land.

29-31   In these closing verses, the attention is turned once again to the theme that has already formed a framework for the chapter as a whole, namely, the dangers of foreign religion (see also vv. 2-4, 13-14). The time envisaged in the warning is described in v. 29; the danger would come after the Israelites had taken possession of the promised land and driven out the former residents. The danger was that the Israelites too would be driven out of the land by acting in the same manner as the former inhabitants (v. 30). These words not only function as a warning to the Israelites, but they also present the religious justification for the expulsion and extermination of the Canaanites. They were not to be dealt with harshly simply at the Lord's whim, nor out of sheer political necessity, but because their

13. *As freely as you wish* — the Heb. is lit. "in every desire of your self (soul)."

life style, as reflected in their religion, had become repugnant to God, the creator of all men; *they do for their gods every abomination of the Lord, which he hates* (v. 31). The Israelites were not immune from God's wrath on account of the covenant relationship; if they behaved in the same manner as the Canaanites, they would also be liable to be driven from the land, unworthy to continue there as its residents.

The example given of the heinous nature of foreign religion is the practice of child sacrifice:[14] *they even burn their sons and their daughters in the fire to their gods.* Israelite law described child sacrifice as a capital offense (Lev. 18:21; 20:2-5), for it was tantamount to murder in spite of the supposedly religious reason for it. In spite of the horrible nature of the offense, there are cases of child sacrifice related during the later apostate periods of Israelite history. Both Ahaz (2 Chr. 28:3) and Manasseh (2 K. 21:6) were guilty of child sacrifice. Just as here in Deuteronomy, the crime is described as one that could lead to expulsion from the land (see v. 30), as in fact it happened with the northern kingdom (2 K. 17:17-18). To assume the right to sacrifice a child was to assume a prerogative that was God's alone, the prerogative over human life. In the fullness of time, God exercised that prerogative in the offering of his only Son as a complete sacrifice for the sins of men.

2. THE DANGERS OF IDOLATRY (13:1-19 [Eng. 12:32–13:18])

1 *You shall take care to do every word that I am commanding you; you shall not add to it and you shall not detract from it.*

2 *If there arises a prophet in your midst, or a dreamer of dreams, and he gives you a sign or a wonder;*

3 *and the sign or wonder of which he spoke to you comes to pass, so that he says: Let us follow after other gods (whom you do not know) and let us serve them;*

4 *you shall not listen to the words of that prophet or to that dreamer of dreams, because the Lord your God is testing you, to know whether you love the Lord your God with all your heart and with all your soul.*

5 *You shall follow after the Lord your God, and you shall fear him, and you shall keep his commandments, and you shall listen to his voice, and you shall serve him and you shall keep close to him.*

6 *But that prophet or that dreamer of dreams shall be put to death, because he has declared apostasy against the Lord your God —*

---

14. For studies dealing with child sacrifice in Syrian and Canaanite religion, see H. Gese *et al., Die Religionen Altsyriens, Altarabiens und der Mandäer,* pp. 175f.; O. Eissfeldt, "Adrammelek und Demarus," *Kleine Schriften* III (1966), pp. 335-39. The cult is associated with various deities in the Near East, but principally with the god Molech in the OT records: see J. A. Thompson, *NBD,* p. 836 for discussion and references.

the one who brought you out from the land of Egypt and who redeemed you from the house of slavery — to thrust you out of the way in which the Lord your God commanded you to walk; so you shall purge out the evil from your midst.

7 *If your brother, the son of your mother, or your son, or your daughter, or your beloved wife, or your closest friend allures you secretly by saying: Let us follow and let us serve other gods (whom neither you nor your fathers knew,*

8 *gods of the peoples who are around you, whether those near to you or those far from you, from one end of the land to the other end of the land);*

9 *you shall not yield to him, and you shall not listen to him and your eye shall not look on him with compassion, and you shall not spare him, and you shall not cover up for him.*

10 *But you shall certainly kill him; initially, your hand shall be against him to put him to death and afterward the hand of all the people.*

11 *And you shall stone him with stones so that he dies, for he sought to thrust you aside from the Lord your God, the one who brought you out of the land of Egypt, out of the house of slavery.*

12 *And all Israel shall hear and shall fear, and they shall not again do anything like this evil thing in your midst.*

13 *If you hear it said that in one of your cities, which the Lord your God is going to give to you to live there,*

14 *certain wicked men came out from your midst, and thrust aside the inhabitants of their city, saying: Let us go and let us serve other gods (whom you have not known):*

15 *then you shall make inquiries and investigate and question thoroughly, and if indeed the matter is true and certain, that this abominable thing was done in your midst,*

16 *you shall indeed smite the inhabitants of that city with the sword, exterminating it, and all those in it, and its cattle with the sword.*

17 *And you shall gather all its spoil to the midst of its town square, and you shall burn the city and all its spoil with fire, a whole-offering to the Lord your God, and it shall be a perpetual mound; it shall not be built again.*

18 *And nothing from what is to be exterminated shall cling to your hand, so that the Lord may turn away from the heat of his anger, and grant you compassion, and be compassionate to you, and make you grow in number, just as he promised by oath to your fathers;*

19 *provided that you listen to the voice of the Lord your God, keeping all his commandments which I am commanding you today, doing what is right in the eyes of the Lord your God.*

In the instructions relating to the sanctuary contained in ch. 12, one of the recurrent themes was the danger of resorting to Canaanite methods and places of worship (12:2-4, 13-14, 29-31). In ch. 13, the dangers presented by idolatry and foreign religion become the central

221

focus of attention. The chapter falls into three sections, each of which has a common subject, namely, the explicit temptation to renounce covenant allegiance: *Let us follow after other gods* (13:3, 7, 14).[1] The three sections specify the principal persons or groups within society that might be the source of the temptation.

(a) *Religious leaders* (vv. 2-6): the temptation might come from prophets or dreamers.
(b) *The immediate family* (vv. 7-12): various close relatives might be the source of temptation.
(c) *Urban revolutionaries* (vv. 13-19): the temptation might come from a group of men intent upon undermining the allegiance of a whole city.

In each of these sections, a number of points are emphasized in the address, dealing with the source and nature of the temptation, the legal penalty to be accorded to the criminals, and the positive action to be taken in order to maintain true allegiance to the Lord of the covenant. The legal penalties noted in this chapter may seem at first sight to be excessively harsh, but the reason for the severity lies in the nature of the crime. The continued existence of the covenant community depended literally upon allegiance to the Lord of the covenant. Thus the crime is considered not simply in light of the actions of the perpetrator, but in light of the effect of the crime on the welfare of the whole people of Israel. Of all potential crimes in ancient Israel, the one described in this chapter was the most dangerous in terms of its broader ramifications: to attempt deliberately to undermine allegiance to God was the worst form of subversive activity, in that it eroded the constitutional basis of the potential nation, Israel. In its implications, the crime would be equivalent to treason or espionage in time of war.

1 See also 11:32. *You shall not add to it and you shall not detract from it* — see also 4:2 and commentary. These words are the second canonical sanction[2] contained in Deuteronomy; they emphasize the solemnity of the law preceding and following. Neither the law nor the warning could be changed or adapted; hence there could be no excuse for a breach of the law or a lapse into the religious practices associated with the Canaanites.

2-6 (a) *Religious leaders.* The first source of temptation might be a *prophet* or a *dreamer of dreams.* Both prophecy and

1. The verse numbers in this chapter and throughout the commentary follow the Hebrew text. Some English translations (e.g., RSV) number v. 2 (Hebrew) as v. 1.
2. See the discussion in M. G. Kline, *The Structure of Biblical Authority*, pp. 27-44; Kline's argument for an early development of the concept of canonicity is based in part on the similarity of these sanctions to sanctions and inscriptional curses in the Near Eastern treaties.

dreams were legitimate means of reception of revelation in Israel;[3] thus what is envisaged is a man whose role or office carried particular religious authority in the community, but one who might abuse his position for his own evil ends. Such a person might perform or be instrumental in *a sign or a wonder* (v. 2). The coming to pass of a predicted sign or wonder (v. 3) would normally be one indication of the validity of the prophet (see 18:22 and commentary). In this particular case, however, the words of the prophet or dreamer after the fulfilment of the sign or wonder would immediately make it clear that he was a false prophet or dreamer: *Let us follow after other gods . . . and let us serve them.* No true prophet of God could speak such words, which would be in direct contradiction to the first commandment (5:7) and to the great commandment to love God wholeheartedly (6:5). *Whom you do not know* — the words are a rhetorical device employed by the speaker to emphasize the absurdity of the words of a false prophet (see also 13:7b-8 and 14). *Know* implies experience rather than intellectual knowledge; the Israelites *knew* God from their experience of his presence with them and word to them, but they had no such knowledge of any other supposed gods.

The Israelites were forbidden outright to *listen to the words of that prophet or to that dreamer of dreams* (v. 4); whatever claims to validity he might appear to have on the basis of his performance of a sign or a wonder, they were not to *listen* to him (i.e., "obey" him). *Because the Lord your God is testing you* (v. 4) — the words emphasize God's sovereignty and permission.[4] The temptation would test the true disposition of the hearts of the Israelites, and while the temptation was genuinely dangerous, the overcoming of that temptation would strengthen the people in their love of God and obedience to his commandments. The sovereignty of God is also seen in another manner: the performance of a sign or wonder did not mean that the gods advocated by a false prophet or dreamer had any real power, but only that the true God would permit certain things to happen in order to test and thereby strengthen his people. Moses then stresses once again God's basic requirements of his people: with v. 5, compare 10:12-13 and commentary.

The penalty for the false *prophet* or false *dreamer of dreams* (v. 6) was capital punishment because of the seriousness of the crime. The serious nature of the crime is shown by means of a striking contrast: *he has declared apostasy against the Lord your God —the one who brought you out from the land of Egypt. . . .* The false prophet was calling for faithlessness from a people redeemed by a God of faithfulness. He was calling for ingratitude from a people who should

---

3. More detailed legislation on prophecy is contained in 18:15-22. On the relation between prophecy and the gift of a vision in a dream, see Num. 12:6.
4. The principle implicit in the words is thus similar to Job 1–2.

know only gratitude to the God who brought them *from the house of slavery*. Just as the Exodus formed the preamble to the first commandment (5:6), so here it forms part of the warning against breaking that first commandment. *To thrust you out of the way* . . . — the intent of the false prophet, had it been achieved, would have automatically brought on the curse of God, as Moses had already warned the people (see 11:28). *So you shall purge out the evil from your midst* — the object of the severe penalty was not only the punishment of the evildoer, but also the preservation of the community.

7-12 (b) *The immediate family*. The temptation might also come from members of the immediate family or from an intimate friend. *Your brother, the son of your mother* — a blood-brother. *Your beloved wife* — the Hebrew idiom is "wife of your bosom." *Your closest friend* — the Hebrew idiom is "your friend who is like your self/soul." The temptation from the false prophet or dreamer would be made openly, based on a sign or wonder. In this second section, however, the temptation would be made *secretly* and would be based upon the intimacy of relationship or friendship. An unscrupulous person was in a position to wield strong influence on a close relation or friend in a way that an outsider could not; the temptation might seem less obvious when presented within the intimacy of a close relationship and (from another perspective) the tempter might feel safer and less liable to prosecution and punishment. The nature of the temptation, however, was essentially the same: *Let us follow and let us serve other gods* (v. 7). *Whom neither you nor your fathers knew* — see also 13:3 above; the parenthetic remark is expanded this time to include explicitly any foreign gods belonging to peoples from any part of the promised land (v. 8).

The treatment prescribed for the person with whom the temptation originated is essentially the same as that for the false prophet or dreamer, but it is stated in a fuller form, not only for reasons of emphasis, but also to remove any excuses that might arise on the basis of the intimacy of the relationship between the tempter and the tempted. *You shall not yield to him* (v. 9) — though the temptation to do so might be very strong, given the psychological pressure that could be brought to bear on the basis of an intimate relationship. *You shall not listen to him* — see also 13:4. *Your eye shall not look on him with compassion* — the tempter was to be treated with the same severity as the previous inhabitants of the land (see also 7:16), without regard to the closeness of relationship. *You shall not cover up for him* — not only were the people to resist the temptation, but they were also to bring the tempter to justice. To give in to the temptation would be sinful, but to fail to deal with the source of evil would also be wrong. Throughout these emphatic remarks, not only the evil of the temptation becomes clear, but also the terrible predicament that the tempter put on those to whom he was closest and dearest emerges into focus. The tempter's purpose was, in effect, to undermine the unity and allegiance of all Israel; but even if he failed to do this, he put enormous pressures on his immediate family and friends. In resisting the temptation, the family were then in the position of having to put to one side their natural love for the offender and deal with him under the law.

The penalty, as before, was capital punishment: *you shall certainly kill him* (v. 10). The person who reported the crime would cast the first stone against the accused person; then the rest of the community would join him in stoning the offender to death. The procedure of execution is significant: by casting the first stone (*initially, your hand shall be against him*), the person reporting the crime took responsibility for the execution, by symbolizing in this manner that his evidence, which brought about the execution, was true evidence. However, he did not have to carry the responsibility alone, for after he cast the first stone, the rest of the community shared in the act of execution. In the event of false testimony leading to an execution, the responsibility would revert to the accuser who had given the false testimony and thrown the first stone. With v. 11b, compare v. 6; the objective of the crime incurring capital punishment was the same in both instances — to undermine the status of the whole community of Israel; thus it was appropriate that the community as a representative whole should participate in the execution.

However terrible the nature of the crime, participating in the execution (particularly if the offender was a relative or friend) would have been a fearsome and awful experience. Nevertheless, it would serve in a preventive role, to remind the people of the consequences of breaking the first commandment — not so much the consequences for the particular offender, but the potential consequences for all Israel. Thus the nature of punishment was designed in part to prevent the people from doing in the future *anything like this evil thing in your midst* (v. 12).

13-19 (c) *Urban revolutionaries.* In this third section, a slightly different situation is envisaged; here, the crime of idolatry has already been committed on a large scale and measures are given concerning the means of dealing with such large-scale apostasy. *If you hear it said that in one of your cities*[5]. . . (v. 13) — the sense may be either that the apostasy in a particular city becomes generally known throughout the land, or that a report is brought to the central tribunal (see 17:8-13) concerning the state of affairs in a city. *Which*

---

5. *In one of your cities* — the words refer to the place where the crime was committed, not the place where the report was heard; on the translation, see G. A. Smith, *The Book of Deuteronomy*, p. 181.

the Lord your God is going to give to you . . . (v. 13b) — the statement that the city which becomes apostate is a part of the gift of God emphasizes all the more the heinous nature of the crime.

Certain wicked men (v. 14) — the Hebrew is "men, the sons of $b^e l\hat{i}ya'al$." By NT times, the noun was used as a proper name (*Belial*) virtually synonymous with Satan (2 Cor. 6:5), though in its older use it was probably a general noun, the etymology of which is uncertain.[6] The meaning, however, is quite clear: these men are wicked in that they are described as being successful in their attempt to turn a city from the true faith. The words by which the apostasy would be achieved are the same in substance as in the first two sections: *Let us go and let us serve other gods* (v. 14; see also vv. 3 and 7). The evil-doers are "urban revolutionaries" in that the action they advocated would be contrary to the constitution of the state and of the city (viz., the covenant with God) and (if successful) would have led to a total change in the nature of ancient Israel, which would have been disastrous in its effects.

The nature of the crime and the severity of the penalty were such that a very careful investigation would have to be carried out to establish *if indeed the matter is true and certain* (v. 15).[7] If the proof was beyond question that the crime (*abominable thing*) had been committed, then all the inhabitants of the city were to be executed. The penalty prescribed for the crime was essentially the same as the method of dealing with Canaanite cities,[8] and the nature of the crime was such that its result was to make an Israelite city Canaanite, even though those who had instigated the crime in the first place were Israelites (*men . . . from your midst:* v. 14). The inhabitants and cattle were to be executed; the spoil was to be gathered in the *town square*[9] and burned with the city, which would never again be rebuilt. The purpose of the harsh action was to turn aside God's anger and seek his compassion (v. 18). As in the previous two sections, the crime threatened the existence of all Israel and the continuation of God's ancient covenant promise to the patriarchs (v. 18b); only radical and prompt action could be a remedy for the situation. The Israelites were not only to deal with the crime, but were also to maintain the positive requirements of God; with v. 19, compare 4:2 and 6:18.

6. For a detailed study, including references to the Qumran literature, see H. W. Huppenbauer, *ThZ* 15 (1959), pp. 81-89. See also M. Dahood, *Psalms, I.* Anchor Bible XVI (1966), p. 105.
7. *nākôn* — for the sense "certain, trustworthy, sure," see G. Rinaldi, *"kwn," Bibbia e Oriente* 10 (1968), p. 206.
8. See 2:33-36 and commentary; the treatment prescribed for apostate Israelites in 13:16-18 is harsher than that actually accorded to Sihon's cities, when the cattle and spoil were spared.
9. Lit. the "broad place," where commercial and legal activities were undertaken.

ADDITIONAL NOTE on Deuteronomy 13

For further studies of the chapter, see J. L'Hour, "Une législation criminelle dans le Deutéronome," *Biblica* 44 (1963), pp. 1-15; M. Weinfeld, *Deuteronomy and the Deuteronomic School,* pp. 91-100. Weinfeld draws a number of valuable parallels between Deut. 13 and Hittite, Aramean, and neo-Assyrian political treaties; he notes that in the treaties, warnings concerning conspiracy and seditious agitation were the principal subject matter. Because the closest parallels are between Deut. 13 and the vassal treaties of Esarhaddon, Weinfeld concludes: "The present style of the laws and their affinities with political documents from the seventh century prove their connection with Josianic times" (p. 100). While there is no doubt the evidence adds weight to Weinfeld's case for a late date for Deuteronomy, I think "prove" is too strong a word given the general parallel with the substance of other treaties including the Hittite texts. The date of Deuteronomy, and its relation to the treaty texts, is discussed more fully in the Introduction, section IV.

3. LEGISLATION RELATING TO VARIOUS RELIGIOUS PRACTICES (14:1-29)

1 *You are sons of the Lord your God. You shall not lacerate yourselves and you shall not make a bald spot on your head for the dead;*

2 *because you are a holy people to the Lord your God, and the Lord has chosen you to belong to him, a people prized more highly than all the people who are upon the face of the earth.*

3 *You shall not eat any abominable thing.*

4 *These are the animals which you may eat: ox, sheep, and goat;*

5 *hart, and gazelle, and roebuck, and wild goat, and mountain goat, and antelope, and mountain sheep;*

6 *and every animal that divides the hoof, that splits the cleft into two parts, and those among the animals that chew the cud — those you may eat.*

7 *Nevertheless, of those chewing the cud and having the cleft hoof, you shall not eat the following: the camel, the hare, and the rock badger — because they chew the cud but do not divide the hoof; they shall be unclean to you —*

8 *and the swine, because it divides the hoof, but does not chew cud; it is unclean to you. You shall not eat their meat and you shall not touch their carcasses.*

9 *Of all that is in the water, you may eat the following: anything that has fins and scales you may eat;*

10 *but anything that does not have fins and scales, you may not eat. It is unclean to you.*

11 *You may eat every clean bird.*

12 *And the following are the ones you may not eat: the eagle, and the bearded vulture, and the osprey;*

13 *and the glede, and the vulture, and the kite, according to their kinds;*

14 *and every raven, according to its kind;*

15 *and the eagle-owl, and the short-eared owl, and the long-eared owl, and the hawk, according to their kind;*

16 *and the tawny owl, and the barn owl, and the little owl;*

17 *and the Scops owl, and the Egyptian vulture, and the fisher owl;*

18 *and the stork, and the heron, according to their kind; and the hoopoe, and the bat;*

19 *and every flying insect; it shall be unclean to you. These must not be eaten.*

20 *Every clean flying thing, you may eat.*

21 *You shall not eat any carcass. You may give it to the resident alien who is in your towns and he may eat it, or sell it to a foreigner; for you are to be a holy people to the Lord your God. You shall not boil a kid in its mother's milk.*

22 *You must tithe all the produce of your seed, which comes forth in the field year by year.*

23 *And you shall eat before the Lord your God, in the place where he shall choose to establish his name, the tithe of your grain, and of your new wine, and of your fresh oil, and the firstlings of your herd and of your flock, so that you may learn to fear the Lord your God always.*

24 *And if the distance is too far for you, so that you are not able to carry it, because the place, which the Lord your God shall choose to place his name there, is far away from home –for the Lord your God will bless you —*

25 *then you may exchange it for silver. And you shall bind the silver in your hand and you shall go to the place which the Lord your God shall choose;*

26 *and you shall exchange the silver for whatever you desire; cattle, or sheep, or wine, or strong drink, or anything that you want. Then you shall eat there before the Lord your God, and you shall rejoice, you and your family.*

27 *And you shall not forget the Levite who is in your towns, for he does not have a portion or inheritance along with you.*

28 *At the end of three years, you shall bring all the tithe of your produce in that year and you shall deposit it in your towns.*

29 *And the Levite, because he has no portion or inheritance along with you, shall come, and also the resident alien, and the orphan and the widow, who are in your towns, and they shall eat and be filled; so that the Lord your God may bless you in every work of your hand which you do.*

The contents of this chapter, which Driver has aptly entitled the "Holiness of the Laity,"[1] seem at first sight to be a diverse collection

1. S. R. Driver, *Deuteronomy*, p. 155.

of prohibitions and injunctions. The substance of the chapter may be presented in outline form as follows:

(a) prohibition of certain mourning rites (vv.1-2);
(b) clean and unclean animals (3-8);
(c) clean and unclean fish (9-10);
(d) clean and unclean birds (11-20);
(e) dead creatures (21a);
(f) cooking a kid (21b);
(g) tithes (22-27);
(h) the tithe of the third year (28-29).

However, with the exception of section (a), the common theme tying together the remaining sections of the chapter is food or that which may or may not be eaten; the verb "eat" (*'ākal*) occurs throughout these sections (vv. 3, 4, 6, 7, 8, 9, 10, 11, 12, 19, 20, 21, 23, 26, 29). The legislation covers both general dietary prescriptions (b-f) and specific matters relating to the eating of tithes (g-h).

1-2   (a) *Prohibition of certain mourning rites.* The principle underlying this short portion of legislation is stated in the opening words: *you are sons of the Lord your God.* Earlier in Deuteronomy, the conception of a father/son relationship between God and Israel had been used to illustrate God's provision and care for his people (1:31) and the reason underlying his disciplining of them (8:5). In this context, the emphasis is on the responsibility that rested upon the Israelites because of their intimate relation to God as "sons." The legislation in the previous chapter (13) concerning idolatry had been intended to cut off the possibility of a relationship with any other god. In this section, the prohibition stated in v. 1 indicated clearly that their behavior as sons of God would be distinct from that of those who worshipped other gods. The practices prohibited are those which characterized certain facets of foreign religion.

You shall not lacerate yourselves and you shall not make a bald spot on your head for the dead — the two practices prohibited here were associated with mourning customs of foreign religions[2] and may have been associated with a cult of the dead. Some information about these practices in Syria and Palestine has been provided by the texts recovered by archeologists from Ras Shamra/Ugarit, which the following brief notes describe: (i) In the mythological texts relating to Baal, there is a description of the mourning of El following the death of Baal.[3] Among a variety of mourning rites, El is described as lacerating himself. (ii) In the "Legend of Aqht," there is a reference to professional mourning women who also lacerate themselves to let

2. For a statement of sources (prior to the discovery of the Ugaritic texts), see Driver, *Deuteronomy*, p. 156.
3. The text is in Ugaritic; *CTA* 5.VI.14-18 (=*UT* 67).

blood flow.[4] (iii) In an Akkadian text recovered from Ras Shamra (the "Just Sufferer"), a man who is sick, but not yet dead, is treated as if he were already in the grave; "my brothers bathe in their blood like ones possessed."[5] It is clear from these texts that the laceration of the body with the consequent flow of blood was a part of the mourning customs employed in religions outside Israel. In addition to mourning, however, laceration may have been part of a seasonal rite within the Canaanite fertility cult;[6] in this context, the rite may have been a type of imitative magic, designed to revitalize the god Baal on whom the fertility of the land was believed to depend.[7] The Israelites are thus forbidden to participate in such actions; though the actions could in themselves appear to be innocent enough, they were associated with practices and beliefs that were reprehensible to the covenant faith and therefore were to be avoided. The Israelites were not to worship a god other than the Lord (14:1-2); they were *sons of the Lord*. The reason for the prohibition is stressed again in 14:2; the same words are also employed earlier in the address (see 7:6 and commentary) to express the holiness and election of God's people.

3-8 (b) *Clean and unclean animals.* Regarding this section and the two that follow (c-d), there has been debate over the principle underlying the regulations on permitted and prohibited foods. There are those who adopt the position that the underlying principle has to do with hygiene.[8] Thus, an American doctor conducted a series of experiments to determine the levels of toxicity in the meats of the animals, aquatic creatures, and birds mentioned in Deut. 14;[9] he discovered that the various types of prohibited meats contained a higher percentage of toxic substances than those which were permitted. Others have maintained that the principle underlying the legislation has to do with the association of some creatures with other religions; the animals that the Israelites were prohibited from eating were those revered and held sacred by various foreign religions.[10] The text does not make absolutely clear which position is correct, and

---

4. *CTA* 19.IV.173, 184 (=*UT* 1 Aqht). The translation of this text and that mentioned in n. 3 is difficult; for a detailed study and a discussion of laceration in mourning rites, see T. L. Fenton, *UF* 1 (1969), pp. 69f.
5. RS 25.460, line 11. See J. Nougayrol, "Textes suméro-accadiens des archives et bibliothèques privées d'Ugarit," *Ugaritica* 5 (1968), pp. 265-273. See also J. Gray, "The Book of Job in the Context of Near Eastern Literature," *ZAW* 82 (1970), p. 263.
6. See John Gray, *The Legacy of Canaan.* SVT 5 (²1965), p. 252 (n.).
7. See also 1 K. 18:28, where the prophets of Baal (in the "contest" with Elijah) lacerate themselves.
8. See, e.g., G. T. Manley and R. K. Harrison, *NBC(R),* pp. 219f.
9. D. I. Macht, "An Experimental Pharmacological Appreciation of Leviticus 11 and Deuteronomy 14," *Bulletin of the History of Medicine* 27 (1953), pp. 444-450.
10. See M. Noth, *The Laws in the Pentateuch and Other Studies* (E.T. 1966), p. 56. Cf. G. von Rad, *Deuteronomy,* p. 102.

it is possible that both positions have some merit, as the following comments will attempt to clarify.

You shall not eat any abominable thing (v. 3) — these words state a part of the principle pertaining to vv. 4-21. The word *tô'ēbāh* ("abominable thing") is used also in 7:25 and 12:31. In both those passages, the word indicates an association with foreign religions. In 7:25, for example, silver and gold were to be discarded because of their association with the images of foreign gods; simply as substances, however, silver and gold were not unclean or evil. Thus, on the basis of v. 3, it seems clear that at least part of the reason for the prohibition against eating certain types of meat was the association existing between those animals (birds, etc.) and foreign religions.

There follows a list of animals which could be eaten (vv. 4-5) and which could not be eaten (vv. 7-8); the list should be understood as representative, rather than comprehensive. Verses 6-7a explain the basis for the distinction: animals that chewed and had a fully cleft hoof were permitted, while an animal that did not fulfil one or both of these requirements was prohibited. The implications of this rationale for distinction might suggest a hygienic, rather than a religious reason for the prohibition of certain types of meats. In v. 8, the complexity of the issue can be seen clearly. The swine was prohibited *because it divides the hoof, but does not chew cud;* for that reason it was *unclean.* It is uncertain whether the terms *clean/unclean* as they are used in this chapter have a ritual or religious basis, or whether they have hygienic implications. It may be noted that in Egypt, the pig was considered to be unclean for "mythological" reasons; Horus became blind when looking at a black pig (actually Seth in the form of a pig), and therefore pig was taboo for Horus and all those faithful to him.[11] There is no evidence of this type of thinking in Deuteronomy. On the other hand, the sacred associations of the pig/boar with certain Canaanite-Syrian cults may have made the pig particularly reprehensible to the Hebrews, assuming that they knew of such associations.[12] This association with foreign religion, which would make the pig *unclean,* could have been at least part of the reason underlying the prohibition; a particular understanding of hygiene may have been a further basis for the prohibition.

It should be noted that the identification of many of the animals listed in this section, and of the birds in vv. 11-20, is uncertain.[13] Even

11. P. Montet, *Egypt and the Bible,* p. 102. For an English translation of the text, see *ANET,* p. 10; it may be significant that at the end of the text the pig is described as an "abomination" (see Deut. 14:3).
12. M. Noth, *The Laws in the Pentateuch and Other Studies,* pp. 57f. In certain Hittite rituals, a small pig was killed in order to protect the sacrificers from evil curses; *ANET,* p. 351.
13. See particularly G. Cansdale, *All the Animals of the Bible Lands* (1970); *idem,*

though several Ugaritic words, cognate to the Hebrew terms, are now known, the problems are by no means solved.[14]

9-10 (c) *Clean and unclean fish or aquatic creatures.* The normal kinds of fish, possessing fins and scales, were clean and could be eaten. Those without fins and/or scales, such as the catfish in the Sea of Chinnereth (Galilee), and eels, rays, and lampreys[15] in the Mediterranean coastal waters, were unclean and therefore not to be eaten.

11-20 (d) *Clean and unclean birds and flying insects.* In this section, a general category of clean birds (v. 11) and flying things (v. 20) is mentioned, and only the prohibited types are specified in some detail. *Birds* that could be eaten would include such types as quail, partridge, and doves; *flying things* that could be eaten would have included a certain type of locust.[16] The long list of birds whose meat was forbidden seems to consist mainly of birds of prey and scavenging birds, if the terms have been translated correctly; thus the basis of the prohibition may have been primarily hygienic. The meat of bats and certain types of flying insects was also prohibited.

21a (e) *Dead creatures.* Eating the meat of an animal that has died a natural death is prohibited. While it is possible that the meat was prohibited because of the likelihood of contamination, which would occur quickly in a hot climate, it is more likely prohibited because the animal had not been killed in the proper fashion and the blood drained out (see 12:16). For this reason, the animal could be eaten by a resident alien or sold to a foreigner, neither of which would have been possible if the meat was already bad. The Israelites were not to eat such meat, which would be ritually unclean, because they were a *holy people to the Lord* (see also 14:2).

21b (f) *Cooking a kid in its mother's milk.* This prohibition no doubt reflects a practice common in Canaanite religion, which was not to be permitted in the religion of the Israelites.[17] It is possible that one of the Ugaritic texts, which appears to contain a reference to "cooking a kid in milk," may provide a background to the specific rite prohibited in Deuteronomy;[18] if this external parallel could be sub-

"Birds of the Bible," *NBD*, pp. 154-57; F. S. Bodenheimer, *Animal and Man in Bible Lands* (1960); G. A. Smith, *The Book of Deuteronomy,* pp. 186-191.
14. See, e.g., *RSP* I, items III.33, III.37, III.83.
15. See F. S. Bodenheimer, *IDB* II, pp. 272f.
16. Lev. 11:21; see the comments of S. R. Driver, *Deuteronomy,* p. 163.
17. The suggestion goes back at least to Maimonides (*Guide to the Perplexed* iii.48), cited by H. L. Ginsberg, "Notes on 'The Birth of the Gracious and Beautiful Gods,' " *Journal of the Royal Asiatic Society* (Jan. 1935), p. 72 (Postscript); see also U. Cassuto, *The Goddess Anath,* pp. 50f.
18. The text is *CTA* 23.14 (=*UT* 52.14). For a discussion and further bibliography, see Anton Schoors, *RSP* I, pp. 29-32. Schoors is very confident of the parallel: "the biblical prohibition is certainly directed against the practice described in this text" (p. 31).

stantiated,[19] then the prohibited rite would be one that had close associations with the fertility cult.

22-27   (g) *Tithes. You must tithe* — the Hebrew construction is emphatic. The verb employed (Piel of *'āśar*) means to "tithe" or "take a tenth of." The tithe specified in these verses is only that of the agricultural produce which the land would provide,[20] namely *grain, new wine,* and *fresh oil* (v. 23; see also 7:13). The tithe would be taken to *the place where he shall choose to establish his name* (see 12:5 and commentary) and there it would be eaten in God's presence. By returning a tithe to God regularly, the people would *learn to fear the Lord* (v. 23) and know that their prosperity did not depend on irrigation or advanced agricultural techniques, but on the beneficence and provision of their God.[21]

In vv. 24-26, a provision is made which anticipates difficulties arising because of the size of the promised land that would soon belong to the Israelites.[22] If certain Israelites lived too far from the sanctuary for it to be practical for them to carry their tithe there, then they could exchange the tithe locally for money (*silver*) and subsequently convert the money back into substance at the sanctuary. With the money, they could purchase *cattle, sheep, wine, strong drink,*[23] *or anything that you want* (v. 26). The emphasis given to the tithe in these verses, in contrast to the more precise legislation contained in Num. 18:21-32 and Lev. 27:30-33, rests principally on the joyful meal of fellowship eaten by the whole family in the presence of God (v. 26) and the provision made for the Levites (v. 27: see also 12:12).

28-29   (h) *The tithe of the third year.* The time specified in v. 28 would seem to be year three and year six of the seven-year sabbatical cycle. On every third year in the cycle, the tithe was not taken to the sanctuary, but was to be set aside especially for certain

19.   There are two main reasons for doubting the Ugaritic parallel to the biblical prohibition. (a) The reading of the Ugaritic text is uncertain. See the reservations of A. Herdner, *CTA*, p. 98 (n. 9). Virolleaud, who has been followed with great confidence by subsequent writers, noted cautiously that his restitution of the text at the critical point was "simplement conjecturale"; "La naissance des dieux gracieux et beaux," *Syria* 14 (1933), p. 140. See also *CTA*, fig. 67 and pl. XXXII; J. M. Sasson, *RSP* I, p. 403; Gordon, *UT*, p. 379. (b) The Ugaritic text, even if the reading *ṭbḫ.gd* is accepted, does not specify that the kid is boiled in *its mother's milk,* and it does not, therefore, provide precise illumination of the prohibition in Deuteronomy.
20.   Hence the reference to the *firstlings* in v. 23 should not be understood as a part of the tithe; the *firstlings* are mentioned here presumably because they too would be eaten at the same place (see 15:20).
21.   See also 11:10-15 and commentary.
22.   See also 12:20-21 and 19:8-10 for similar anticipatory provisions.
23.   The Heb. (*shēkār*) indicates some kind of alcoholic beverage, or as Jerome described it, *omne quod inebriare potest* (G. A. Smith, *The Book of Deuteronomy,* p. 195).

less privileged classes of people. *You shall deposit it in your towns* — the tithe would be brought by each Israelite to his town (in or near which he lived) and there either stored for subsequent distribution when need arose, or else distributed immediately to the needy persons. The persons who were entitled to participate in the third year tithe were the Levites (who also shared in the annual tithe, v. 27), the resident alien, the orphan, and the widow; all these groups, for a variety of reasons, might be dependent on the community as a whole for their welfare.[24] The type of community envisaged and anticipated in the promised land was one in which the majority of men and families would be self-sufficient in terms of producing their sustenance and living from the land. There would inevitably be members of the community, however, who were not self-sufficient. The system of tithes described in these two verses enabled both groups to learn and understand their continual dependence upon God. The people with produce and income gave a portion back to God, who had made provision in the first place; year by year, they learned to know and remember that the source of their sustenance was God, and every third year they remembered particularly that not all others were blessed as they were. Those without regular means of subsistence, such as aliens, widows, and orphans, were thrown onto God, the Lord of the community, for provision. In receiving it from the tithe, which properly belonged to God, their needs were met. Thus the health of the community would be maintained and the people would continue to experience the blessing of God which led to prosperity (v. 29b).

4. THE YEAR OF RELEASE AND THE LAW REGARDING FIRSTLINGS (15:1-23)

1 *At the end of seven years, you shall enact a release.*
2 *And this is the nature of the release: every creditor shall release what he has lent to his neighbor; he shall not exact it from his neighbor or his brother, for the Lord's release is proclaimed.*
3 *You may exact it from the foreigner, but whatever is due to you from your brother, your hand shall release.*
4 *However, there shall not be any poor people among you, for the Lord will certainly bless you in the land which the Lord your God is about to give to you as an inheritance, for you to take possession of it —*
5 *provided that you listen carefully to the voice of the Lord your God, by taking care to do the whole of this code of law which I am commanding you today.*

24. These groups were also the subject of God's particular provision and justice; see 10:18 and commentary. On the topic as a whole, see esp. F. C. Fensham, "Widow, Orphan and the Poor in Ancient Near Eastern Legal and Wisdom Literature," *JNES* 21 (1962), pp. 129-139.

6 *For the Lord your God will bless you, just as he said to you; and you shall cause many nations to give pledges, but you shall not give a pledge, and you shall rule over many nations, but they shall not rule over you.*

7 *If there is a poor man among you, one of your brothers in one of your settlements in your land, which the Lord your God is going to give to you, you shall not harden your heart and you shall not be tightfisted with your brother, the poor man.*

8 *But you shall certainly be generous to him and you shall make him give a pledge sufficient for his need, whatever he needs for himself.*

9 *You must take great care lest there be a base thought in your mind, saying to yourself, "The seventh year, the year of release is near," and your eye is unfriendly toward your brother, the poor man, and you do not give to him; then he shall cry out to the Lord against you and it shall be held against you as a sin.*

10 *You shall certainly give to him and your attitude shall not be unfriendly when you give to him, because on account of this act, the Lord your God will bless you in all your work and in all your undertakings.*

11 *For the poor shall never cease from the midst of the land; therefore I am commanding you, saying: You shall certainly be generous to your brother, to your needy, and to your poor in your land.*

12 *If your brother is sold to you, whether a male or a female Hebrew, then he shall serve you six years and in the seventh year you shall send him away from you free.*

13 *And when you send him away from you free, you shall not send him away empty-handed.*

14 *You shall make rich provision for him from your flock, and from your threshing floor and from your wine-vat; just as the Lord your God has blessed you, you shall give to him.*

15 *And you shall remember that you were a slave in the land of Egypt and the Lord your God redeemed you; therefore, I am commanding you this word today.*

16 *And it shall be that if he says to you: "I will not go away from you," because he loves you and your household, because it is good for him to be with you;*

17 *then you shall take the awl and you shall pierce through his ear into the door, and he shall be your perpetual slave; and you shall do just the same to your slave-girl.*

18 *And it shall not seem hard to you when you send him away from you free, because, equivalent to the wages of a hired man, he has served you six years. And the Lord your God will bless you in all that you do.*

19 *You shall consecrate to the Lord your God every male firstling which is born in your herd and in your flock; you shall not do work with the firstling of your cattle and you shall not shear the firstling of your flock.*

20 *You and your household shall eat it year by year before the Lord your God in the place which the Lord shall choose.*

235

21 *But if there is a blemish in it, lameness or blindness or any serious blemish, you shall not sacrifice it to the Lord your God.*
22 *You shall eat it in your settlements, unclean and clean alike, as if it were a gazelle or a hart.*
23 *However, you shall not eat its blood; you shall pour it out on the ground like water.*

The substance of this chapter is an exposition of laws relating to the year of release and to firstlings,[1] but the occasion prompting this part of the exposition is the reference to various classes of needy persons in 14:27-29. Thus, especially in vv. 1-18, the details of the year of release are vague in comparison to other legislation on the subject,[2] and a humanitarian concern for the needy becomes the center of attention.[3]

1 *At the end of seven years* — see also 14:28: *At the end of three years.* After two three-year periods, each third year being the year of tithe for the needy, the cycle was completed by a seventh year of release. *Release* (*sheṭmiṭṭāh*) is a difficult term to define precisely in this context; the difficulty concerns whether the term means "suspension" or "termination" when it is applied to debts in the following verses.

2-6 The Year of Release. In v. 2, *the nature of*[4] *the release* is specified insofar as it relates to creditors and debtors. The difficulty referred to above is whether a debt was to be terminated permanently, or suspended for the year, meaning that repayment could not be demanded during the course of the seventh year.[5] The latter alternative seems more probable; in the seventh year, when the land was left fallow, many people would not have been in a position to repay a debt because of the temporary interruption of their normal source of income. Hence, to have insisted on the repayment of a debt during the year of release could have resulted in particular hardship for the debtor, such as entering into unpaid servitude (see vv. 12-18). A debt could still be exacted from a *foreigner* (v. 3; e.g., a foreign merchant who might live in an Israelite town), because he would not be subject to the provisions of the year of release and would therefore be in a

---

1. For studies relevant to the substance of this chapter, see F. N. Jaspers, "Preaching in the OT," *Expository Times* 80 (1968/69), pp. 356-361; M. Kessler, "The Law of Manumission in Jer. 34," *BZ* N.F. 15 (1971), pp. 105-108.
2. See Exod. 23:10-11; Lev. 25:1-7.
3. Cf. M. Weinfeld, *Deuteronomy and the Deuteronomic School*, pp. 282-84.
4. The idiom employed here is also used in the first line of the Siloam Tunnel inscription; see J. C. L. Gibson, *Textbook of Syrian Semitic Inscriptions* I, p. 23.
5. For a discussion of older views on the subject, see S. R. Driver, *Deuteronomy*, pp. 178-180. G. von Rad cautiously suggests that the logic of v. 9 implies a complete discharge of the debt (*Deuteronomy* p. 106), but it will be argued below that v. 9 has a different point of reference. The view adopted here follows essentially that of Keil and Delitzsch, *The Pentateuch*, pp. 369f.

position to repay the debt if it were demanded of him. The year of the release would be publicly proclaimed (v. 2), so that it would be known throughout the community that the stipulations of the release were in effect.

The statement in v. 4 that *there shall not be any poor people among you* is a conditional statement governed by the substance of v. 5 (*provided that*...). In fact, *the poor shall never cease from the midst of the land* (v. 11), which was a more realistic appraisal, but the significance of vv. 4-5 is that there *need not* be poor people in the land, *for the Lord will certainly bless you*. The fullness of that blessing, however, would be contingent on the completeness of Israel's obedience; thus vv. 4-5 are an encouragement and enticement to strive for the reduction of poverty, while at the same time they stress the abundance of the provision God would make in the promised land (vv. 4b, 6a). The anticipated prosperity of Israel is given a striking portrayal in v. 6b: the sense of the words is that Israel would become a major mercantile state, wealthy enough to lend to other nations and therefore ruling over them in a sense, but not needing to borrow from them and therefore not being subject to them.[6] The words point to the intimate relationship that would exist between internal and external affairs in the future state envisaged by Moses. The prosperity in external affairs described in v. 6b would be a result of the blessing of God, but God's blessing would be contingent upon the inner health of the nation, to which the requirements stated in this chapter are directed.

7-11 The requirement of generosity toward the poor. The attitude of the Israelites toward the poor in their community was to be one of warmth and generosity: *you shall not harden your heart and you shall not be tightfisted*[7]... (v. 7). The humanitarian spirit of the address comes clearly to the forefront in these verses, for the requirement of generosity extends beyond the letter of the law and points to a proper attitude which was to characterize the people's dealings with the poor. Note, however, that it is not charity, in the sense of almsgiving, that is advocated here; it is a charitable attitude to be expressed by lending the poor man *whatever he needs for himself,* while he pledged to repay the loan in due course (v. 8).

The dilemma of vv. 2-6 reappears in v. 9. A potential creditor might be unwilling[8] to make a loan to a poor man because of the proximity of the year of release. As in vv. 2-6, the sense still seems to be that the year of release would be a time when the loan could not be recalled. Thus, a poor man, borrowing before the year of release,

---

6.   See also G. A. Smith, *The Book of Deuteronomy,* p. 201, and his citation of Strabo from Josephus (*Ant.* vii.2).

7.   The Hebrew idiom (lit. "you shall not close your hand") is similar to the English.

8.   *Your eye is unfriendly* . ... (v. 9) — lit. "Your eye is evil. . . ."

would have a longer time to repay his debt, but the creditor would have a longer time to wait before he could recoup his expenditure; he might be less willing, therefore, to respond positively and generously to the poor man's request. The only way in which to avoid such a situation was to inculcate a generous attitude toward the poor, so that the creditor thought first of the predicament of the poor man, and was not concerned primarily with when he could get his money (or substance) back again. By acting generously, the people would experience God's blessing and would prosper (v. 10b).

12-18 Slavery and manumission.[9] Although slaves could be acquired in Israel by various means, such as capture in warfare (see 20:14), the substance of the foregoing verses makes it clear that a particular type of "slavery"[10] is described here. *If your brother is sold to you* (v. 12)—in the context of vv. 1-11, the reason for the sale would be default in the repayment of a debt, and a period of servitude would substitute for that repayment. *Then he shall serve you six years* — these are not the six years of the sabbatical cycle, but six years following the sale, with freedom being declared in the seventh year.[11] The principle, however, is the same as that underlying the sabbatical cycle, but the presence of the law in this chapter seems to be prompted by the theme of various types of needy persons (see above), rather than by the legislation relating to the year of release.

When a slave had completed his time of service, his former owner or guardian was to make ample provision for him, so that he would not begin his state of new freedom in destitution; once again, the humanitarian spirit of Deuteronomy is clear.[12] The basic requirement of the law was simply that the slave be set free in the seventh year (Exod. 21:2); Moses' exposition of the law draws out the principle of love, for God and for fellow man, which was so vital to the covenant community.[13] *And you shall remember that you were a*

9. For general studies of slavery and manumission, both in the OT and in the ancient Near East, see the following: I. Mendelsohn, "Slavery in the Ancient Near East," in E. F. Campbell and D. N. Freedman, eds., *The Biblical Archaeologist Reader* III (1970), pp. 127-143; *idem, Slavery in the Ancient Near East* (1949); K. A. Kitchen, "Slave, Slavery," *NBD,* pp. 1195-98.
10. The word "slavery" may not be appropriate, given the modern connotations and associations of the term. The "slaves" had certain rights and privileges both in Ugarit and Israel; see J. L. R. Wood, *Kingship at Ras Shamra-Ugarit, a Study of the Literary, Ritual and Administrative Documentation* (diss., McMaster University, 1972), pp. 89-96.
11. In the Law Code of Hammurabi (§117), the period of servitude was three years, with freedom being established in the fourth year; see *ANET,* p. 171.
12. ". . . It was not sufficient to give a man servant and maid-servant their liberty after six years of service . . . if they had nothing with which to set up a home of their own; but love to the poor was required to do more than this, namely, to make some provision for the continued prosperity of those who were set at liberty." Keil and Delitzsch, *The Pentateuch,* p. 372.
13. See the Introduction, section VIII/3.

slave . . . (v. 15)[14] — the call to remember was not simply in order to evoke pity or sympathy for the slave, which would lead to generosity. Rather, they were to remember that, when they had been slaves, God had loved them, freed them, and made ample provision for them; as sons of God (see 14:1), they should do no less to the manumitted slaves in the seventh year.

In certain circumstances, a slave might prefer to remain with a family after a required six years of servitude;[15] he would then be marked with a hole in his ear and would become a *perpetual slave* (*'eḇeḏ 'ôlām*, v. 17). This term, which occurs also in the Ugaritic literature,[16] implies somebody of value and importance, and does not seem to have any derogatory implications. The regulations and exhortation contained in vv. 12-17 applied equally to male and female slaves (v. 17b). Having had the free service of a slave for six years, there would be those who, for reasons of dependence or greed, would find it very difficult to release the slave. They were to free the slave willingly, however, for his six years of service were *equivalent to*[17] *the wages of a hired man* — that is, the slave had worked for no pay, and the wages that would have been paid to an employee for the same labor were to be considered as full repayment for the debt that had caused the slavery in the first instance. *And the Lord your God will bless you* . . . (18b) — see also vv. 4, 6, 10.

19-23   The law regarding firstlings; see also 12:6, 17; 14:23. The law is first stated briefly[18] and then becomes the subject of exposition, in accord with the general nature of the presentation of the

14.   Similar words are used in several contexts in Deut. to encourage the people to the proper behavior expected of them; see 10:19; 16:12; 24:18, 22, and also 5:15 (Decalog).
15.   In certain circumstances, the liberating of a slave could be an act of cruelty rather than of love. "Manumission was only an act of love when the person to be set free had some hope of success and of getting a living for himself; and where there was no such prospect, compelling him to accept of freedom might be equivalent to thrusting him away." Keil and Delitzsch, *The Pentateuch,* p. 373. For example, an old slave with no family, or perhaps a blind slave, or one who was particularly devoted, might prefer to remain in a household in which he was loved and well treated (v. 16b).
16.   See particularly *CTA* 14.II.55. The words *'bd. 'lm* occur six times altogether in the Keret Legend, in a stereotyped expression; see R. E. Whitaker, *A Concordance of the Ugaritic Literature* (1972), p. 474. The words have been translated "perpetual slave" (G. R. Driver, *Canaanite Myths and Legends,* p. 31) and "perpetual henchman"; see the discussion in John Gray, *The KRT Text in the Literature of Ras Shamra*[2], p. 52. For other occurrences of the phrase in biblical passages, see 1 Sam. 27:12 and Job 41:4 (E.T.).
17.   "Equivalent to" is a translation of Heb. *mishneh,* normally rendered "double, twice as much." Those who translate "double" may take the sense to be that a Hebrew slave served six years, "double" that which was required in the Code of Hammurabi § 117; cf. I. Mendelsohn, *Slavery in the Ancient Near East,* pp. 32f. The translation "equivalent to" seems preferable; it is based on the use of *mištannu* in texts from Alalaḫ. See D. J. Wiseman, *NBD,* p. 67; M. Tsevat, "Alalakhiana," *HUCA* 29 (1958), pp. 125f.
18.   For fuller details, see Exod. 13:11-15; 22:29-30; 34:19-20; Num. 18:15-18.

THE BOOK OF DEUTERONOMY

law in Deuteronomy. *Every male firstling* — the firstling was the first calf, lamb, etc., to be produced during the bearing-life of an animal; it was to be consecrated ("made holy") to the Lord. For that reason, a male firstling calf could not be put to work in plowing and a male firstling sheep could not be sheared for wool; that is, since the firstlings belonged to God, they could not be utilized in accord with the normal function of those animals on behalf of man. Rather, the firstlings would be sacrificed annually and the offerers would participate in the sacrificial meal (see 14:23). No animal that was imperfect could be sacrificed to God (17:1); the general principle is applied specifically to firstlings in v. 21. On vv. 22-23, see also 12:15-16 and commentary.

5. MAJOR FESTIVALS AND THE APPOINTMENT OF OFFICERS AND JUDGES (16:1-22)

The three major festivals or pilgrimages are dealt with first in this chapter: (a) Passover and Unleavened Bread (vv. 1-8); (b) Weeks, or "Pentecost" (vv. 9-12); (c) Booths (vv. 13-15); vv. 16-17 are a summary section relating to all three festivals and indicating the common theme linking the legislation in this section of Deuteronomy. The legislation concerning the officers of law (vv. 18-20) introduces further legislation relating to: the king (17:14-20); priests (18:1-8); prophets (18:9-22). Verses 21-22 contain a brief portion of legislation relating to the sanctuary of the Lord.

(a) Passover and Unleavened Bread (vv. 1-8)

1 *Observe the month of Abib and keep the Passover to the Lord your God, for the Lord your God brought you out from Egypt by night in the month of Abib.*
2 *And you shall sacrifice the passover-animal to the Lord your God, from the flock or from the herd, in the place that the Lord shall choose to establish his name there.*
3 *You shall not eat leavened bread in his presence. For seven days you shall eat unleavened bread in his presence, bread of affliction — for you went out of the land of Egypt in fearful haste — in order that you may remember the day of your exodus from the land of Egypt all the days of your life.*
4 *And in all your territory leaven shall not be seen in your possession for seven days; and of the flesh that you sacrifice in the evening on the first day, none shall remain overnight until the morning.*
5 *You may not sacrifice the passover-animal in any of your settlements, which the Lord your God is about to give to you,*
6 *but only in the place that the Lord your God shall choose to establish his name there. You shall sacrifice the passover-animal in the evening, when the sun goes down, the time of your exodus from Egypt.*

240

7 *And you shall cook and eat in the place that the Lord your God shall choose; then in the morning you shall turn and go to your tents.*
8 *For six days you shall eat unleavened bread, and on the seventh day there shall be an assembly to the Lord your God; you shall do no work.*

The detailed legislation regarding the Passover and Unleavened Bread is contained elsewhere in the Pentateuch;[1] here, in the address of Moses, only a summary statement is provided, in which certain themes are given particular emphasis in harmony with the address as a whole. Once again, both the past and the future provide an important part of the perspective. The exodus from Egypt is the period from Israel's past history which finds continuing commemoration in the festival (vv. 1, 3, 6). The future is anticipated by the reference to the place (*that the Lord shall choose,* v. 2) in the promised land in which the festival would be celebrated; the place is not specified geographically, but is identified as the place in which the sanctuary of the Lord would be located. The first celebration of the Passover within the promised land is described in Josh. 5:10-12.

1 *Observe the month of Abib.* Abib (which was later called Nisan) occurred in the spring (approximately March/April in the modern calendar). In the month of Abib, the Israelites were to *keep the Passover to the Lord;* the hortatory style of the legislation in Deuteronomy is such that the specific date is not mentioned, though elsewhere it is clear that the celebration was to be held on the fourteenth day of the month (Exod. 12:18) and the Unleavened Bread was observed for the next seven days (15th-21st Abib). *For the Lord your God brought you out from Egypt* — Passover was a celebration and commemoration of the event on which the covenant community of God was established. Because of the liberation from servitude which God had granted his people in the Exodus, the new commitment of the Israelites to God in the Sinai Covenant had become possible. Thus the Passover was a celebration of freedom, but at the same time it was a reminder that that freedom from Egypt and worldly domination had been exchanged almost immediately for a new commitment; the new commitment was made evident in that the celebration was made by the Israelites as the covenant people of God.

2 The word translated *passover-animal (pesah)* is the same word as that used in v. 1, where it was rendered *Passover;* the same term is employed to designate both the festival and the sacrificial animal which symbolizes the meaning of the festival. *From the flock*

---

1. See particularly Exod. 12; Lev. 23:5-8; Num. 28:16-25. For a fuller discussion of the subject, see R. de Vaux, *Ancient Israel. Its Life and Institutions,*[2] pp. 484-493; R. A. Stewart, *NBD,* pp. 936-38.

or from the herd—the words are somewhat ambiguous and are difficult to interpret. In Exod. 12:3-6, a lamb (either sheep or goat) is specified as the sacrificial animal, whereas the words here would seem to offer a greater choice. It has been suggested the words refer not specifically to the paschal lamb, offered on the first day, but to the animal sacrifices offered in the days of Unleavened Bread which immediately followed the day of Passover.[2] It is possible, however, that the passage of time between the first Passover (in Egypt) and the renewal of the covenant on the plains of Moab had led to a broadening of the original prescription. At the time of the renewal of the covenant on the plains of Moab, Reuben, Gad, and the half-tribe Manasseh had already taken possession of their land to the east of the Jordan; their newly possessed land was cattle country and already they were wealthy in cattle (see 3:19 and commentary). Thus the permission indicated in this verse may have in mind the state of affairs that existed at the preliminary stage of the conquest to the east of the Jordan. *In the place that the Lord shall choose to establish his name there* — see 12:5 and commentary, and in ch. 16, vv. 6, 7, 11, 15, and 16. The original Passover in Egypt had been performed by families in their homes; the blood sprinkled on the lintel and doorposts had provided protection from the destructive wrath of the Lord (see Exod. 12:21-27). The continuing celebration and commemoration of the Passover, however, was to be enacted in one place, where the sanctuary of the Lord was located; the change from the original event to the commemoration of that event may be significant. In Egypt, the Israelites had been a number of families under the suzerainty of a worldly power. After the Exodus and forming of the covenant at Sinai, Israel became a single nation, the family of God; thus the Passover became the act, symbolically speaking, of the one large family of God, celebrated in one place where the sanctuary or house of God was located.

3 Passover and Unleavened Bread are in effect the two constituent parts of a single major festival; in vv. 3 and 4, the second part of the festival becomes the center of attention. *You shall not eat leavened bread* — perhaps because the leavening process was considered to be impure and therefore unsuitable for the festal occasion.[3] *In his presence ('ālāyw)* — if the translation is correct (see also the following sentence, v. 3b),[4] the phrase refers to the sanctuary where the presence of the Lord would be experienced. *For seven days*

2. See, e.g., Keil and Delitzsch, *The Pentateuch,* p. 375.
3. See Exod. 12:15; 23:18; Lev. 2:11.
4. RSV renders "with it"; see also NEB. For the translation *in his presence,* see M. Dahood, *Biblica* 45 (1964), p. 283. If the translation "with it" is maintained, the antecedent (unexpressed) of "it" would be the sacrificial animals eaten during the days of Unleavened Bread; see Num. 28:19-24.

(15th-21st Abib) *you shall eat unleavened bread* — the unleavened bread perhaps symbolized the hurried nature of the flight from Egypt, for unlike leavened bread it could be made quickly.[5] But it may simply have been the case that unleavened bread was the staple diet of the Hebrews in Egypt, and thus its use in the festival would be a reminder of the old days of bondage; it has been suggested that the word *matstsôṯ* ("unleavened bread") may be related to the Egyptian word *ms.t/msw.t,* meaning "bread, cake,"[6] and could therefore have been the term employed to designate the Hebrews' food in Egypt.[7] *Bread of affliction* — *for you went out of the land of Egypt in fearful haste* — these words indicate that the unleavened bread might serve to symbolize both the affliction of the years in Egypt and the speedy departure[8] from that land. *The day of your exodus* — or "day of your going out." The whole festival, both Passover and Unleavened Bread, was to serve as a reminder of the manifold dimensions of the Exodus.

4 *And in all your territory* — although the context is concerned with the celebration of the festival at the sanctuary, the prohibition against leavened bread applied to the whole land. In this manner, the spirit of the festival affected the lives of all those in Israel, and not simply the males (see v. 16) who were present at the sanctuary. The prohibition of leaven and the complete consumption of the sacrificial meat during each night of the festival symbolized once again (see v. 3a, above) the theme of purity in the celebration. Leaven, as well as old meat (which would begin to decay in the heat of the day following its preparation), would have been a sign of impurity, and therefore they are forbidden during the festival.

5-6 In the foregoing verses, both Passover and Unleavened Bread have been mentioned; there now follow detailed specifications concerning the place and time of the sacrifice of the passover animal. The place of the sacrifice has already been noted in a positive sense (v. 2b), and now the point is made more certain by means of a prohibition: *You may not sacrifice the passover-animal in any of your settlements* (v. 5). That is, the sacrifice could not be offered randomly, wherever might have seemed appropriate or convenient, but only at the sanctuary of the Lord (see v. 2b and commentary). The animal was to be sacrificed *in the evening, when the sun goes down* (v. 6); the time of the act was to be the same as that of the first Passover (Exod. 12:6), to

5. Cf. Keil and Delitzsch, *The Pentateuch,* p. 375.
6. See A. S. Yahuda, *The Language of the Pentateuch in Its Relation to Egyptian,* pp. 95f.
7. Yahuda's suggestion must remain uncertain. R. O. Faulkner notes the word *mswk* meaning "a kind of bread" (*A Concise Dictionary of Middle Egyptian,* p. 117), but the term is not cognate to the Heb. word. The Egyptian word *msyt* ("supper, evening meal") might be relevant to the discussion.
8. *Fearful haste* — the word *hippāzôn* has connotations both of speed and anxiety.

commemorate more vividly the protection offered by the sacrificial animal during the night of the Lord's destruction (Exod. 12:29).

7 *And you shall cook⁹ and eat in the place that the Lord your God shall choose* — namely, in the vicinity of the sanctuary of the Lord. *Go to your tents* — the expression means, in effect, "go home." It should not be taken to mean "go home" in a literal sense, however; after the sacrifice of the passover-animal, and the night vigil which followed, then in the morning the people would return to their lodgings or tents, where they were staying for the duration of the festival. On the seventh day of Unleavened Bread, there was to be an assembly (NEB "closing ceremony") in which the days of the festival would be formally brought to an end. As on the first day of the festival (Num. 28:18), no work was to be done on the closing day (v. 8).

(b) Weeks, or "Pentecost" (vv. 9-12)

> 9 *You shall count seven weeks; you shall begin to count the seven weeks from the time you first put the sickle to the standing grain.*
> 10 *And you shall keep the Feast of Weeks to the Lord your God with a sufficient freewill offering of your hand, which you shall give according as the Lord your God shall bless you.*
> 11 *And you shall rejoice before the Lord your God, you, and your son, and your daughter, and your male servant, and your female servant, and the Levite who is in your settlements, and the resident alien, and the orphan, and the widow who are in your midst, in the place that the Lord your God shall choose to establish his name there.*
> 12 *And you shall remember that you were a slave in Egypt, and you shall take care to keep these statutes.*

The second of the annual major festivals is the Feast of Weeks, which is also called the "Feast of Harvest" (Exod. 23:16) and the "Day of Firstfruits" (Num. 28:26);¹⁰ the title "Pentecost" came into use at a later date, being based on the Greek (LXX) translation of the "fifty days" mentioned in Lev. 23:16. The Feast of Weeks was a celebration essentially of the gracious provision of God in the harvest; the feast would become an essential part of Israelite life in the future when agriculture became the basis of the society. In keeping with the rest of Moses' address on the law, these verses do not contain all the detailed prescriptions concerning the festival, but only emphasize certain points of importance within the context of the address as a whole.

9. The verb translated *cook* is the Piel of *bāshal;* the same verb is used in Exod. 12:9 in a context noting that the paschal offering was not to be boiled (the normal sense of *bāshal*), but roasted. In that passage, however, the sense "boil" is made clear by the addition of "in water," whereas in the present context, the more general sense of "cook" (in preparation for eating) is implied.
10. For more detailed legislation, see Exod. 23:16; 34:22; Lev. 23:15-21; Num. 28:26-31; see also R. de Vaux, *Ancient Israel*, pp. 493-95.

9   The dating of the feast is given in relative and imprecise terms in this context; seven weeks (hence the title of the feast, "Weeks") were counted from the beginning of the harvest of grain. In Lev. 23:15-16, the date is more explicitly defined as being fifty days (seven weeks, the fiftieth day being the day of the festival) after the offering of a sheaf at the beginning of Passover.

10   *A sufficient[11] freewill offering* — the offering was given freely in an amount determined by the offerer (see n. 11), and was not fixed as were the daily and sabbath offerings. The emphasis in the verse is on what the individual Israelites would offer, not on all the details of the festival; the future blessing of God in the land is anticipated once again.

Feast of Weeks — the word *ḥag* is traditionally rendered "feast" or "festival," but it has connotations not contained in these English words. It implies also the sense of "pilgrimage" (NEB renders "pilgrim-feast"),[12] for Weeks, and the other two festivals mentioned in this chapter, involved a journey to the place where the Lord's sanctuary was located (see v. 16). The pilgrimages served not only to bring the people to the central sanctuary at least three times a year, but also they were to be a regular reminder to the people of their nature as a community, the people of the Lord. The solidarity of the covenant community would thus be expressed and strengthened each year, even when the population of the country would be spread out over a large geographical area.

11   The festival was to be a time of rejoicing for all members of the community, for it celebrated the goodness of the Lord in the provision of food for another year at harvest time. For the terms employed in this verse, see also 12:7, 12, 18; 14:29.

12   In addition to celebrating God's provision in the harvest, the people were to remember, in the midst of their rejoicing, the time in the past when they had been in servitude in Egypt; the memory was not simply to be of the Exodus (see vv., 1, 3), but was to be the basis of generosity toward the various persons mentioned in v. 11 (servants, aliens, widows, and orphans; see also 15:15).

(c) Booths (vv. 13-15)

> 13 *You shall keep the Feast of Booths for seven days, when you gather the produce from your threshing floor and from your wine-vat.*

11. The word *missat* (translated *sufficient*) is a *hapax legomenon*. The sense of "sufficient/adequate" is determined by the clause at the end of the verse: *according as the Lord your God shall bless you*. The sufficiency of the offering a person made was determined not by its inherent value or its size, but by its relation to the provision of God in the harvest.

12. The Heb. *ḥag* is cognate to Arab. *ḥajj*. The Ḥajj is one of the five so-called Pillars of Islam, namely, the duty incumbent on every Muslim to undertake the pilgrimage to Mecca at least once during his lifetime (see, e.g., *Quran* 2:185-195).

14 *And you shall rejoice in your feast, you, and your son, and your daughter, and your male servant, and your female servant, and the Levite, and the resident alien, and the orphan, and the widow who are in your settlements.*

15 *For seven days you shall keep the feast to the Lord your God in the place that the Lord shall choose, for the Lord your God will bless you in all your produce and in all your undertaking, and you shall indeed be joyful.*

The *Feast of Booths* (or "Tabernacles" or "Huts") is also called the Feast of Ingathering (Exod. 23:16; 34:22).[13] Like the Feast of Weeks, the Feast of Booths is a harvest festival, but it occurs some months later, in the autumn, when all the produce has been gathered in.[14]

13 The festival was to last for seven days (with a closing ceremony on the eighth day: Lev. 23:36). In this context, the date is not specified precisely, the celebration being said to begin when all the fruit of the harvest was gathered in.[15]

14 See also v. 11; the festival was to be a time of rejoicing for all members of the covenant community.

15 The feast was to be celebrated at the sanctuary of the Lord (*in the place . . .*), as were the other two annual pilgrimage festivals. It would be a joyful celebration in thanksgiving for the good provision of God in the harvest of both crops and fruits.[16]

(d) Summary Section (vv. 16-17)

16 *Three times in the year, all your males shall appear before the Lord your God in the place that he shall choose: at the Feast of Unleavened Bread, and at the Feast of Weeks, and at the Feast of Booths; and they shall not appear before the Lord empty-handed.*

17 *A man shall give as he is able, according to the blessing of the Lord your God which he will have given you.*

With this summary section, compare Exod. 23:17; 34:23. *All your males* — these words seem to indicate the minimum requirement of the law, though it is clear from the preceding verses (particularly vv. 11, 14) that others could also attend the three annual festivals at the sanctuary of the Lord. *Shall appear before the Lord* — alternatively, the words could be rendered: "shall see the face of the Lord."[17] *They*

13. For detailed legislation, see Lev. 23:33-43; Num. 29:12-38; see also R. de Vaux, *Ancient Israel*, pp. 495-502.
14. Grapes, olives, dates, and figs were harvested in the summer months (June-September, on the modern calendar), some time after the barley harvest.
15. The date is specified more exactly in Lev. 23:34, the seven days beginning on the fifteenth day of the seventh month.
16. Every sabbatical year, the Feast of Booths would include additional elements, including the reading of the law; see 31:9-13 and commentary.
17. See the discussion in S. R. Driver, *Deuteronomy*, pp. 198f.

shall not appear before the Lord empty-handed — since the festival celebrated the provision of the Lord in the harvest, it was only fitting that each pilgrim bring with him an offering from the substance with which he had been blessed. On the principle of v. 17, see also v. 10 and commentary.

(e) The Appointment of Officers of the Law (vv. 18-20)

> 18 *You shall appoint judges and officers in all your settlements, which the Lord your God is about to give to you, according to your tribes; and they shall judge the people with righteous judgment.*
>
> 19 *You shall not pervert justice; you shall not show favoritism; and you shall not take a bribe, for the bribe blinds the eyes of wise men and undermines the words of righteous men.*
>
> 20 *You shall pursue justice, and justice alone, in order that you may live and take possession of the land which the Lord your God is going to give to you.*

With these verses, compare 1:13-18 and commentary. The legislation in these verses is of a general nature;[18] the manner of dealing with particularly difficult legal cases is described in 17:8-13.

18   *Judges and officers* — the judge's role was no doubt similar to that of the modern judge, while the "officer" probably represented the executive branch of the law and may have been analogous to the modern policeman. Each settlement would have its own legal authorities to deal with ordinary legal cases, only the more difficult cases being referred to a central tribunal (17:8).

19   The admonitions in this verse, although applying in principle to all men, are addressed particularly to the officers of the law. *You shall not pervert justice* — see also the more specific application of the prohibition in 24:17 (cf. Exod. 23:6). The man who was guilty of perverting justice would become subject to the curse of God (27:19), for such action is contradictory to the character and purpose of God. *You shall not show favoritism* — the idiom employed (lit. "you shall not recognize faces") is the same as that used in 1:7. *You shall not take a bribe* — see also Exod. 23:8. A bribe disrupted the true course of justice by appealing to the baser side of human nature. Justice would no longer be a "right"[19] of all men; what was called justice would become in effect a hypocritical system serving only those who were wealthy enough to manipulate it. Because "God does not take a bribe" (10:17), the action was wrong and fell under the curse of a righteous God (27:25).

18.   E.g., the actual procedure in making the appointments (v. 18) is not described; the emphasis in the verses is on the principle of justice.
19.   For a discussion of the principle in terms of human rights, see J. Ellul, *The Theological Foundation of Law*, pp. 79-81.

20 Both the people and the officers of the law were to *pursue justice, and justice alone,* rather than *pervert justice* (v. 19). The pursuit of *justice alone* provided a basis for the execution of the law that was not merely human, whereas perverting justice reduced the execution of the law to a human basis in which unjust criteria became operative. Justice, the principle underlying the law, was not man-made or conceived, but found its source and authority in God. Hence justice was the only sure and authoritative basis for law. The pursuit of justice and the execution of the law in justice could alone lead to prosperity, namely, life and the possession of the promised land (v. 20b).

(f) Legislation relating to the sanctuary (vv. 21-22)

> 21 *You shall not plant an asherah of any kind of wood beside the altar of the Lord your God, which you shall make.*
> 22 *And you shall not raise up a pillar for yourself, which the Lord your God hates.*

At first reading, these verses seem to be somewhat out of place in the context of chs. 16–17, but it is possible that the modern requirement of orderly presentation was not considered to be a prime requisite in a sermon on the law. As will become clearer in chs. 22–25, the discourse not only deals systematically with major topics, but also covers a variety of minor topics in a more cursory fashion.

The Israelites have already been commanded to destroy the *asherim* (plural of *asherah*) and pillars of the Canaanite cult centers (see 7:5 and the commentary on 12:3). Now they are explicitly forbidden to set up similar cult objects *beside the altar of the Lord* in the sanctuary. *An asherah of any kind of wood* — the Hebrew may be rendered literally: "an *asherah*, any tree. . . ."[20] *Which the Lord your God hates* (see also 12:30-31) — to set up an *asherah* or pillar would be indicative of syncretism with Canaanite religion and would therefore be repulsive to God.

6. LAWS RELATING TO SACRIFICE, COVENANT TRANSGRESSION, THE CENTRAL TRIBUNAL, AND KINGSHIP (17:1-20)

(a) Prohibition of Defective Animal Sacrifices (v. 1)

> 1 *You shall not sacrifice to the Lord your God an ox or a sheep in which there is a blemish, anything defective, for that is an abomination of the Lord your God.*

---

20. The translation "of any kind of wood" is based on the comments of M. H. Farbridge, *Studies in Biblical and Semitic Symbolism,* p. 33.

This law is related both to regulations concerning firstlings (15:19-23) and to the immediately preceding verses in the previous chapter (16:21-22). Just as the firstling was not to be defective (15:21), e.g., blind or lame, so too any other animal sacrificed to the Lord was to be free from blemishes. The principle was the same in both instances, that only the best and faultless could be offered to God. To offer less than the best would be, by implication, to mock God and to hold in low esteem the worship of God. As Malachi pointed out at a later time, to offer the defective and second best would be tantamount to despising God's name (Mal. 1:6-8). The act would undermine the very purpose of sacrifice, for it would widen further the rift between the worshipper and his God which the sacrifice was designed to bridge.

In relation to 16:21-22, the offering of a blemished sacrifice is similar in result to defiling God's sanctuary by the importation of things foreign to Israelite worship (the introduction of an *asherah* or pillar to God's sanctuary). It is possible that Canaanite religion did not have such a prescription,[1] and therefore that offering defective animals was a sign of further lapse into a syncretistic form of religion. Any type of syncretism with foreign religion would be *an abomination of the Lord your God.*

(b) The Transgression of the Covenant (vv. 2-7)

2 *If there is found in your midst, in one of your settlements which the Lord your God is about to give you, a man or a woman who does evil in the eyes of the Lord your God, by transgressing his covenant;*

3 *and he has gone and served other gods, and worshipped them, or the sun, or the moon, or the whole host of heaven, which I have not commanded,*

4 *and it is told to you or you hear of it: then you shall investigate diligently, and if indeed it is true, the matter is established, that this abomination has been done in Israel,*

5 *then you shall bring out to your gates that man and that woman who have done this evil thing, and you shall stone them —the man or the woman —with stones and they shall die.*

6 *On the testimony of two witnesses or of three witnesses, the one about to die shall be put to death; he shall not be put to death on the testimony of a single witness.*

7 *In the first instance, the hand of the witness shall be against him to*

1. The evidence is unclear. For example, several of the Proto-Sinaitic inscriptions refer to animal sacrifice, but do not specify fault-free animals. The texts, however, may be too brief to make the omission significant. For the texts, see W. F. Albright, *The Proto-Sinaitic Inscriptions and their Decipherment*, pp. 16-30. The Ugaritic Canaanite texts do not normally specify the condition of the animal to be sacrificed: see *CTA 32* (*=UT* 2); *CTA* 35 (*=UT* 3); *CTA* 36 (*=UT* 9); *CTA* 33 (*=UT* 5). However, *CTA* 34.1-2 (*=UT* 1.1-2) seems to indicate that sacrifices had to be *perfect* (*tm*), though the text is difficult; see *CTA*, p. 118, n.1.

put him to death, then afterward the hand of all the people; so shall you completely remove the evil from your midst.

2-3 The legislation contained in these verses, which is closely related to 4:15-24 and 13:1-18 in its subject matter, is dealing with the paramount crime in the Israelite community. That crime is *transgressing his covenant* (v. 2), which involves the worship of foreign deities and is therefore a breach of the first commandment, which called for total and undivided allegiance to the Lord. The crime undermined the very basis on which the covenant community existed and therefore it was to be dealt with very severely, for it threatened the security and life of all Israelites. Thus the crime, though religious in form, was political in significance. It is analogous to the modern crime of espionage or treason in time of war, for the net effect of both would be to weaken the security of the homeland. The crime involved certain acts, such as the worship and service of other gods (e.g., *sun, moon, the whole host of heaven:* see the commentary on 4:19).

4-5 When the crime is made known to the authorities, either by direct report (*it is told to you*) or[2] by rumor (*you hear of it*), then a careful investigation is to be undertaken to establish the facts of the matter. The word *abomination,* in this context, is equivalent to "crime," for the Lord was king of the theocratic state of Israel, and the act envisaged was one directly contrary to God's law, which in turn reflected his love and concern for his people. If the crime could be shown to have occurred, the criminal, either male or female,[3] was to be taken to the city gates[4] and executed by communal stoning.

6-7 There had to be at least two valid witnesses against the accused person in order for a case to be established and the death penalty to be put into effect. One witness was not sufficient in a case of this severity, for in the last resort, the evidence would consist merely in one man's word against that of another fellow Israelite. For the application of the principle of two or more witnesses in the NT, see Matt. 18:16, 2 Cor. 13:1, 1 Tim. 5:19. The way in which the execution was to be carried out emphasizes the burden of responsibility for truthful testimony that rested on the witness in a case involving

---

2. Alternatively, the Heb. may be rendered "and you hear. . . ."
3. In v. 5, the words *the man or the woman* are grammatically awkward. The Massoretic punctuation suggests taking the words with 5a, though the sense seems to be served better by taking them with 5b. However, there may be dittography here (see *that man and that woman* in 5a), in which case the words should be omitted, with LXX and Vulgate.
4. The word *sheʿārîm* may mean (a) *gates* or (b) *settlements,* "villages." The latter sense may be seen in vv. 2, 8. Here the meaning is *gates,* but whether the offender was to be taken outside the gates for execution (and therefore outside the area of residence), or was to be executed at the gates (viz., the place where the law courts assembled), is not altogether certain.

capital punishment. Although the execution was to be carried out communally, *in the first instance, the hand of the witness shall be against him* (v. 7). The witnesses, by casting the first stones, accepted the onus of the responsibility; in the event of further evidence establishing the innocence of the (now deceased) accused, and thereby the false testimony of the witnesses, they would then assume the responsibility for wrongful execution, in effect murder. On the other hand, having given true evidence, the witnesses cast the first stones, but shared the responsibility with the whole community. Thus, all together would *completely remove*[5] *the evil* (v. 7). The capital punishment of the offender removed that evil which had, by the nature of the crime, endangered the continuation of the covenant community of God.

(c) The Jurisdiction of the Central Tribunal (17:8-13)

> 8 *If there is a matter for judgment, which is too difficult for you, between one kind of death and another, between one kind of plea and another, between one kind of assault and another, matters of contention within your settlements; then you shall rise and go up to the place that the Lord your God shall choose,*
>
> 9 *and you shall go to the priests, the Levites, and to the judge who will be there in those days, and you shall inquire; and they shall declare to you the nature of the judgment.*
>
> 10 *Then you shall act according to the sentence of the law that they declare to you from that place which the Lord shall choose; and you shall take care to act according to all that they point out to you;*
>
> 11 *you shall act according to the sentence of the law that they point out to you and according to the judgment they announce to you. You shall not turn aside from the pronouncement they declare to you, to the right hand or to the left.*
>
> 12 *And the man who acts with presumption by not listening to the priest, the one standing there to minister to the Lord your God, or to the judge, then that man shall die and you shall completely remove the evil from Israel.*
>
> 13 *And all the people shall hear and fear and shall not behave presumptuously again.*

In 16:18-20, the local structure and principles of law were described. In these verses, there is described a central court of law whose particular function would be to deal with those legal cases which, for one reason or another, were too complex for the local courts. The complexity envisaged is specified in v. 8. *Between one kind of death and another* — although the general principle of the law was clear, it

---

5.   The verb employed (Piel of *bāʿar*) has the sense of "burning out, purging out by fire."

might not be clear in a particular case whether death had been caused deliberately or accidentally, and therefore whether the crime was homicide or manslaughter. The different types of *plea* perhaps involved cases in which, for example, it was difficult to distinguish whether the offense resulted from intention or negligence. *Assault* perhaps has primary reference to crimes involving bodily injury, where it was important to distinguish between cases of deliberate assault, accidental injury, or criminal negligence. Whatever the specific meaning of the phrases in v. 8, they are summarized as *matters of contention within your settlements.* The revealed law set down both the broad principles (the Decalog) and the specific applications (the casuistic law), but each offense was in practice unique and distinctive. In the course of time, a body of precedent judgments could make difficult cases easier to handle. But in all matters where a particular case proved to be too complicated for the local courts to give an adequate ruling, the case was to be referred to the central tribunal, located at the central shrine of Israel—*the place that the Lord your God shall choose* (v. 8).

At that central tribunal, the local judges were to inquire[6] about the case and they would receive a ruling either from the priests or from the judge. It is likely that referred cases were dealt with in the central tribunal by both priests and judges; the particular function of the priests would be to legislate on matters of ceremonial law, and that of the judge to legislate on matters of civil and criminal law. However, it should be remembered that in a theocracy, the distinction between religious and civil law is a somewhat artificial one and there may not have been a clear distinction drawn between the types of case ruled on by the priest and judge respectively.

The representatives of the local court were bound to act upon the ruling[7] of the central tribunal, whether or not they found it congenial. In this way, there was a central legal authority in Israel, with the power to resolve legal problems and conflicts. To refuse to carry out the rulings of the central tribunal carried a harsh penalty, death. But the purpose of the penalty, as in the previous section (17:7), was to *completely remove the evil from Israel* (v. 12). The legislation thus removed the possibility of a form of anarchy arising, in which each local region or authority manipulated the law to its own ends, overlooking the true principle of the law, which was *justice* (see 16:20). The harsh penalty was designed to enforce the ruling of the central

6. Verse 9: *and you shall inquire;* alternatively, following Sam. and LXX, it is possible to read a 3rd person masc. plur.: "and they shall inquire"; the reference would then be to the priests and the judge.
7. *The sentence of the law* ('*al-pî haddābār*) in v. 10, and *the sentence of the law* ('*al-pî hattôrāh*) in v. 11, seem to be synonymous. On *tôrāh* in Deut., see the commentary on 1:5; cf. the commentary on 17:18 below.

court and create reverence and respect in the people, thus deterring them from committing a crime.

(d) Laws Pertaining to Kingship (vv. 14-20)

14 *When you go into the land which the Lord your God is about to give to you, and you take possession of it and you dwell in it, then you will say: I will appoint a king over me, just like all the nations who are round about me.*

15 *You shall indeed appoint a king over you, whom the Lord your God shall choose. You shall appoint a king over you from among your brethren; you may not set over you a foreign man, who is not your brother.*

16 *Only he is not to increase for himself horses, and he is not to make the people return to Egypt in order to increase horses, for the Lord has said to you: You shall not return in this way again.*

17 *And he is not to increase for himself wives, or his heart may turn aside; and he is not to increase greatly for himself silver and gold.*

18 *And it shall be that when he sits upon the throne of his kingdom, he shall write for himself a copy of this law in a book, from the copy before the priests, the Levites.*

19 *And it shall be with him and he shall read in it all the days of his life, in order that he may learn to fear the Lord his God by keeping all the words of this law and these statutes, and by doing them,*

20 *so that his heart is not exalted above his brothers, and so that he does not turn aside from the commandment to the right hand or to the left, in order that he may prolong his days over his kingdom, he and his sons, in the midst of Israel.*

This section, containing laws relating to kingship, is the only one of its kind in the Pentateuch. It takes the form of permissive legislation, rather than positing a requirement. That is to say, it anticipates a time when, for practical and pragmatic reasons, kingship might become a necessity. But the legislation does not expound in detail the character of the kingly office; rather it specifies the attitudes and characteristics that would be required of a king in a state that was primarily a theocracy. As a theocratic state, Israel's only true king was the Lord,[8] and there was a sense in which it would seem presumptuous for a man to assume the title; the legislation given here makes certain that the king would remain aware both of his human status as a man among his brethren, and also of his status in relation to the kingship of God. But the law given here should not be looked to as a guide concerning the practical role of the king within the framework of the government.[9]

8.   The origin of the concept of the Lord as king may perhaps be found in the celebration of the Exodus (see Exod. 15:18; Deut. 33:5).
9.   M. H. Segal says of this section: "The height of impractical idealism is reached in the law relating to the king" (*The Pentateuch*, p. 79). Segal also notes that the law can

The law anticipates a time when, after having taken possession of the land, the Israelites would decide to have a king: *I will appoint a king over me, just like all the nations who are round about me* (v. 14). In the period between the Exodus and the monarchy, Israel (as a nonmonarchical state) was an exception in the Near Eastern world of that time.[10] If, therefore, a king were to be appointed, Israel's neighbors would provide the natural source for a model of kingship. Although the model would be viable in political matters, the Israelite kingship would be distinguished by the character of Israelite religion, as the following verses make clear.

The first specification is that the anticipated king would be divinely appointed (*whom the Lord your God shall choose*, v. 15); just as the sanctuary's location would be chosen by God (see ch. 12), so too would his royal representative be chosen. In theory, therefore, the office of the king would not be dependent on either popularity or military strength; it would be filled by a man approved by God. Further, the man so approved would be an Israelite, not a foreigner. At first sight, this legislation may seem a little peculiar, since it is hard to conceive of a situation in which a foreigner might be appointed to the office of king. There are a few points, both from Near Eastern history and from the OT, that cast light on this prohibition. It is possible that the Hebrews may have recalled, from the time of their sojourn in Egypt, the memories of great internal unrest and despair associated with the reign of the foreign Hyksos kings (Dynasties XV and XVI) in Egypt. But there are two incidents in the later biblical tradition that may be more significant. In the time of the judges, there are two rather enigmatic references to Shamgar (Judg. 3:31 and 5:6); Shamgar was apparently not a Hebrew (he was perhaps a Hurrian mercenary soldier[11]), though he acted on behalf of Israel. In some ways, he represents the danger of someone pro-Israelite, though foreign both ethnically and religiously (as is implied by his title *ben Anath,* Anath being a Canaanite goddess), who was in a position of strength in the Israelite community. A rather different illustration comes from the period immediately before the beginning of the monarchy with Saul. There was an abortive attempt at kingship by Abimelek; it has been argued that Abimelek may have been in part a foreigner (through his mother), and associated with the Canaanites at

hardly have been addressed specifically to Solomon. Though Solomon was censured for his weakness in old age toward his foreign wives (1 K. 11:2-4), his horses and wealth were not so criticized. For a general study of the laws relating to kingship, see A. Caquot, "Remarques sur la 'loi royale' du Deutéronome," *Semitica* 9 (1959), pp. 21-33; K. Galling, "Das Königsgesetz im Deuteronomium," *Theologische Literaturzeitung* 76 (1951), pp. 133-38.

10. See K. A. Kitchen, *TSF Bulletin* 64 (1972), p. 8.
11. For a fuller discussion, see P. C. Craigie, "A Reconsideration of Shamgar ben Anath," *JBL* 91 (1972), pp. 239f.

Shechem.[12] If this were the case, he would be disqualified from assuming the office of king. In any case, the prohibition against having a foreign king is designed to preserve the integrity of Israelite religion; none but a true Israelite could live within the legislation contained in vv. 18-20 (see below).

In vv. 16-17, there are three separate prohibitions relating to the activities and behavior of the king. The first has to do with horses. The king was not to accumulate a large number of horses. Horses represented wealth in the Near East, but their principal function was related to warfare, specifically chariot warfare and, to a lesser extent, cavalry troops.[13] In the early Israelite period, the conduct of war was largely undertaken with infantry. Strategically, infantry were weak when facing a chariot force, but in the Israelite conception, their military strength lay not in the number or type of their troops but in the strength and presence of their God in battle. They had already experienced God's aid against an enemy equipped with horse-drawn chariots (Exod. 15:1, 4). In the days ahead, there would be similar occasions. For example, in Deborah's war (Judg. 4–5), the Israelite forces were at a strong disadvantage in facing the chariot-equipped Canaanite forces, but once again victory was achieved through the intervention of God. In the early period, then, there seems to be a certain suspicion of the use of horses in military affairs, not because of any particular view about the animal itself, but because the horse represented the military tactics of Israel's enemies, against whom their principal strength was God himself.

In v. 16b, the prohibition is given more specific detail: *he is not to make people return to Egypt in order to increase horses.* The exact meaning of the words is somewhat uncertain. It may be that the legislation prohibits, in an anticipatory manner, the opening of diplomatic or trade relations with Egypt, one result of which would be trading in horses. Although Anatolia was the primary source of horses for trading purposes, the residents of Palestine would normally turn to Egypt as the main source of supply.[14] On the other hand, something other than diplomatic and commercial relations may be prohibited, as is implied by the words: *the Lord has said to you: You shall not return in this way again.* It is possible that what is in mind is trading men (i.e.,

12.   See D. Daube, " 'One from among your brethren shall you set king over you,' " *JBL* 90 (1971), pp. 480f. G. A. Smith (*The Book of Deuteronomy,* p. 225) notes, with reference to a later period, that it was this law that caused Agrippa I to burst into tears, because of his Edomite ancestry.
13.   For a very useful discussion of horses in the Ancient Near East, and of the Hebrew terms employed, see D. R. Ap-Thomas, "All the King's Horses," in J. I. Durham and J. R. Porter, eds., *Proclamation and Presence,* pp. 135-151. For the general history of horses, see G. Morgan, "The Heavenly Horses," *History Today* (Feb. 1973), pp. 77-83.
14.   Cf. Buis and Leclercq, *Le Deutéronome,* p. 133.

mercenary Israelite soldiers) in return for horses.[15] The net result of such action, for the men involved, would be separation from the freedom of the Israelite community and a return to the old bondage in Egypt. There could be few worse fates for an Israelite freeman.

Second, the king is forbidden to *increase for himself wives* (v. 17). The prohibition probably envisages an increase in foreign wives, which would incur a deviation from the true Israelite religion (*or his heart may turn aside;* see also 1 K. 11:1-4). The purpose in the acquisition of many wives would normally be political; a marriage to a foreign princess could add strength to a treaty with a neighboring state. But the danger in such a course of action has already been clarified in an earlier part of Moses' address (see 7:3-5 and commentary). And implicit in the procedure of a political marriage alliance is a deviation from the one and only true treaty of the Israelite state, namely, the treaty that finds its expression in the covenant with the Lord.

The third prohibition is directed against the accumulation by the king of personal wealth (*silver and gold,* v. 17). The accumulation of wealth would tend to give to the king excessive personal power, so that he would become separated from his brethren (cf. v. 15). But more specifically, the desire for the accumulation of wealth, which all too easily could become a consuming passion, would run contrary to the true character of the ideal king, as described in vv. 18-20.

The ideal king was to *write for himself a copy of this law in a book, from the copy*[16] *before the priests, the Levites.* The exact significance of these words is not easy to ascertain because of the ambivalence of the term *this law* in Deuteronomy.[17] It could be taken to refer to the legislation concerning the king (vv. 14-17). Or it could be taken to refer to Deuteronomy, either as a whole, or with specific reference to the legislative portion (chs. 12–26). However, it should be remembered that Deuteronomy as a whole describes the renewal of the Sinai Covenant, which had been recorded in writing at an earlier date. It may be, then, that *this law* refers to the original written document of the Sinai Covenant, perhaps the so-called Book of the Covenant (Exod. 24:7).[18]

15. See G. von Rad, *Deuteronomy,* p. 119; von Rad suggests that such action may have resulted in garrisons of Hebrew mercenaries in Egypt, such as that which existed at a later date in the island community at Elephantine in Upper Egypt. See also J. Gray, *The Legacy of Canaan*[2], p. 224.
16. The Heb. is literally "from before"; on the rendering "from the copy before," see *BDB,* p. 818. It may be, however, that the sense is simply "in the presence of the priests, the Levites."
17. See 1:5 and commentary.
18. The implications of the legislation are that even at this early date, there was a basic canon of God's revealed word for his community. See particularly the thesis proposed by M. G. Kline, *The Structure of Biblical Authority.*

This book was to be the king's *vade mecum*, his life-long companion and source of wisdom and strength. By reading and learning, he would express true reverence for his God, exemplified by his keeping of the law and statutes of God. True reverence for God would in turn keep the king mindful of his true relationship to his fellow Israelites (*so that his heart is not exalted above his brothers*, v. 20). He would avoid being cut off from his fellows by virtue of his position or wealth (cf. v. 17). Although the question whether or not kingship would be dynastic is not explicitly broached, the implications of v. 20 are conditionally dynastic. The true king would exercise his reign over the kingdom for a long time, as would his sons after him.

The role of the *book* in the life of the king is of importance for understanding the full dimensions of Israel's faith. In the early part of Moses' address, he recalled for his audience the events of past history; on the basis of the experience of God in history (one form of revelation), the Israelites drew strength for the future. But the revelation of the word of God, written down for successive generations, was also a source of strength. Both the acts of God and the words of God were recorded; but while the former gave evidence of the living reality of their God, it was the latter that provided in detail the guidance and wisdom for daily living, in the first place for the king.

7. LAWS RELATING TO THE LEVITES, FOREIGN PRACTICES, AND PROPHECY (18:1-22)

(a) The Levites (vv. 1-8)

1 *The priests, the Levites — the whole tribe of Levi — shall not have a portion and an inheritance with Israel; they shall eat offerings made by fire to the Lord, and his inheritance.*

2 *And he shall not have an inheritance in the midst of his brethren; the Lord is his inheritance, just as he said to him.*

3 *And this shall be the due of the priests from the people, from those offering a sacrifice, whether ox or sheep; they shall give to the priest the shoulder and the two cheeks and the stomach.*

4 *You shall give to him the firstfruits of your corn, your new wine and your oil, and the firstfruits of the wool of your flock;*

5 *for the Lord has chosen him from all your tribes to stand and serve in the name of the Lord, him and his sons continually.*

6 *And if the Levite should come from one of your settlements, from all Israel, where he resides — and he may come as freely as he wishes—to the place which the Lord shall choose,*

7 *then he may minister in the name of the Lord his God, like all his brother Levites, those standing there before the Lord.*

8 *They shall eat equal portions, besides what comes from his sale of the patrimony.*

The Levites, who have already been referred to several times in Deuteronomy,[1] are now the subject of some detailed legislation. It should be noted at the beginning that the Levites are the subject of several difficulties and uncertainties in OT studies; those difficulties cannot be fully resolved in the context of these verses, but an attempt will be made to clarify as far as possible this particular passage.[2]

1-2 *The priests, the Levites — the whole tribe of Levi*. The exact significance of the opening words is uncertain and is related to a larger problem, namely, the relationship between priests and Levites and the question as to whether all Levites were priests. From one point of view, the words may be taken to imply that all Levites were priests (though they might have had various and diverse functions). Alternatively, the sense may be that some Levites were priests and some were not;[3] if such was the case, then a distinction would have to be made in the following verses between legislation specifically relating to priests (vv. 3-5) and legislation referring more generally to all Levites (vv. 6-8).[4] Taking the latter point of view as a provisional hypothesis, vv. 1-2 will be interpreted as referring to *all* Levites, vv. 3-5 as referring to Levitical priests, and vv. 6-8 as referring to Levites who would not normally function as priests.

None of the Levites would share *a portion and an inheritance with Israel* (v. 1) — that is to say, the Levites as a tribe would not have a portion of the promised land assigned to them as tribal land or territory.[5] *They shall eat offerings made by fire to the Lord, and his*[6] *inheritance*. If the word *'ishsheh* means "offerings by fire," then the sense is that the Levites would participate in portions of such offerings (cf. v. 3 below). However, it is possible that the word should simply be translated "gifts, offerings," without any implications of sacrifice.[7] This possibility seems quite likely in the context of the most general part of the legislation; the Levites would be supported

1. See 10:8-9; 12:12, 18, 19; 14:27, 29; 16:11, 14; 17:9, 18.
2. For general discussions and further bibliography, see D. A. Hubbard, "Priests and Levites," *NBD*, pp. 1028-34; K. Koch, "Leviten," *BHH* II, cols. 1077-79.
3. G. E. Wright suggests that the sense of the words is: "the priests, the Levites, *and* all the tribe of Levi"; see "The Levites in Deuteronomy," *VT* 4 (1954), pp. 325-330. For a contrary opinion, see J. A. Emerton, "Priests and Levites in Deuteronomy," *VT* 12 (1962), pp. 129-138. An absolutely literal rendering of the Hebrew ("the priests, the Levites, the whole tribe of Levi") seems to leave open either possibility and the decision must be determined largely in the light of the view taken of the Levite problem as a whole.
4. Cf. D. A. Hubbard, *loc. cit.*, p. 1029(b).
5. However, there were to be certain cities set aside for them and there would be pasture land marked off for their use in the vicinity of these cities: Num. 35:1-8.
6. The grammatical antecedent of *his* is uncertain; (a) it could be the Lord, viz., the Levites would partake in other foodstuffs dedicated to the Lord; or (b) it could mean the Levites' own inheritance. See A. R. Hulst, *OT Translation Problems*, p. 15.
7. See J. Gray, *The Legacy of Canaan*[2], p. 198. Gray notes the use of Ugar. *'ušn* in the Keret Legend, where it seems to mean "gift," with no hint of sacrifice. See also J.

by the generosity of the people, who have already been urged not to forget or neglect them.[8]

3-5 The provisions to be allocated to the Levitical priests are now stated: they include food (portions of meat from sacrificial animals, corn, wine, and oil) and material from which clothing could be made (wool). These substances were given to the priests, but in a sense they were due payments for services rendered. Having no tribal territory, the priests were dedicated specifically to the service of the Lord and deserved to share in the bounty of the promised land (see v. 5).

6-8 These verses contain permissive legislation which envisages certain contingencies arising in the future. Certain Levites, residing in various Israelite settlements (see Num. 35:1-8), might wish to come to the main sanctuary (the tabernacle, with the ark, in *the place which the Lord shall choose*); they were to be permitted to do so *(he may come as freely as he wishes* — on the grammatical construction, see 12:15 and commentary) and there they would minister *in the name of the Lord* (v. 7). Since they would be performing the same duty as those normally serving in the sanctuary, *they shall eat equal portions.* The words that follow *(... besides what comes from his sale of the patrimony)* are obscure in the Hebrew and of uncertain meaning,[9] though they would seem to designate some source of income which was not to be affected by the Levite transferring his residence from one place to the main sanctuary.

(b) Prohibition of Foreign Religious Practices (vv. 9-14)

9 *When you have come into the land which the Lord your God is about to give to you, you shall not learn to behave according to the abominable practices of those nations.*

10 *There shall not be found among you one who causes his son or his daughter to be burned in the fire, one who practices divination, one who practices soothsaying, or one who interprets omens, or one who practices sorcery,*

11 *or one who casts magic spells, or one who inquires of a ghost or familiar spirit, or a necromancer.*

12 *For all who do these things are an abomination to the Lord, and the Lord your God is about to drive them out before you because of these abominations.*

13 *You shall be perfect before the Lord your God.*

14 *For these nations, which you are about to dispossess, listen to*

Gray, *The KRT Text in the Literature of Ras Shamra*[2], p. 53; Gordon, *UT,* p. 354 (no. 117).

8.   Deut. 12:18-19.

9.   See the discussion in Hulst, *OT Translation Problems,* p. 15; G. R. Driver, *Syria* 33 (1956), p. 77. Compare the rendering of H. Cazelles, *Le Deutéronome,* p. 83; Cazelles paraphrases, but suggests a reasonable sense for the passage.

soothsayers and diviners, but as for you —the Lord your God has not so granted.

The context of these verses is particularly significant for their interpretation. The beginning of the chapter dealt with the Levites (vv. 1-8), who ministered to the Lord in various ways on behalf of the people; the last section (vv. 15-22) deals with prophecy, the deliverance of God's word to his people. These two legitimate types of religious office are contrasted by this middle section, which contains prohibitive legislation against illegitimate types of religious functionaries and practices. The period envisaged, as is consistently the case in Deuteronomy, is the time when the Israelites would possess their promised land (v. 9); at that time, they must take great care not to copy their forerunners in the land in the matter of various religious offices and practices.

10-11 There follows a comprehensive list of the types of religious and magic functionaries who were to be forbidden in Israel. The exact significance of all the terms employed is now uncertain,[10] but the emphasis of the list is to be found in its character as a blanket prohibition of all types of divination, magic, and consultation with the spirit world, such as would be typical of the religion of the Canaanites.[11] *One who causes his son or his daughter to be burned in the fire* (see 12:31 and commentary) — the context indicates that the reference is not simply to child sacrifice, but to the offering of a child with the particular purpose of determining or discerning the course of events.[12] That is, the sacrifice would have a magical intention. *One who practices divination,*[13] *one who practices soothsaying, or one who interprets omens* — various methods of divining (i.e., employing supernatural means to discover the course of future events) are prohibited.[14] Magic was also to be forbidden; as distinct from divination,

10. For useful philological comments, see S. R. Driver, *Deuteronomy*, pp. 223-26; G. A. Smith, *The Book of Deuteronomy*, pp. 231f.
11. The Ugaritic texts from Ras Shamra provide a few clues relating to these topics in ancient Canaan. There may be an allusion to divining by birds in *CTA* 19.I.32-36 (=*UT*, 1Aqht, 32-36). Recent finds of liver models indicate the practice of divination by hepatoscopy; see M. Dietrich and O. Loretz, "Beschriftete Lungen- und Lebermodelle aus Ugarit," *Ugaritica* 6 (1969), pp. 165-69. Some texts contain magical incantations. The recently discovered text RS 24.244 contains magical incantations against snakes; see *Ugaritica* 5 (1968), pp. 564-572, and M. C. Astour, "Two Ugaritic Serpent Charms," *JNES* 27 (1968), pp. 13-36.
12. This seems to have been the motivation behind the Moabite king's sacrifice of his son: see 2 K. 3:26-27.
13. The root used for "divine" (*qsm*) is not always used negatively in the OT; here it is *foreign* forms of divination that come in for strong condemnation. See the discussion in J. Pedersen, *Israel: Its Life and Culture* (³1953, repr. 1963), pp. 124f.; H. H. Rowley, "Ritual and the Hebrew Prophets," *Myth, Ritual and Kingship* (1958), p. 247.
14. Cf. A. Guillaume, *Prophecy and Divination among the Hebrews and Other Semites* (1938).

magic was intended to influence events or persons by the use of supernatural methods. The methods to be forbidden were *sorcery* and the use of *magic spells* (v. 11), though the distinction between the two methods is not clear in this context. Finally, various types of consultation with the world of spirits (again with the purpose of knowing, and perhaps determining, the future) are to be forbidden. *One who inquires of a ghost* — the reference is to the kind of person who would conjure up and consult any ghost (see Saul's consultation with the witch at Endor, 1 Sam. 28:8-14). *Familiar spirit* — some practitioners consulted only known or particular spirits. Necromancy is also a form of prediction, by means of communicating with the dead.

12-14   These foreign offices and practices, which were an *abomination to the Lord,* were to be forbidden in Israel precisely because they were a part of the reason for God's judgment of the Canaanites, which would be seen in their ejection from the land. If the Israelites adopted similar practices, they too would become liable to ejection from the land. To maintain their possession of the promised land, the Israelites were to be *perfect before the Lord* (v. 13). In these verses, the essence of the covenant tradition appears once again. The covenant promise of the Lord held forth the gift of the land, but the continuing possession of the land would be dependent upon the Israelites' faithfulness to their covenant obligations, namely, that obedience which would make them perfect (or blameless).[15]

(c) The Prophet (vv. 15-22)

> 15 *The Lord your God shall raise up for you a prophet like me, from your midst, from your brothers; you shall listen to him —*
> 16 *just as you requested the Lord your God at Horeb, on the day of assembly, saying: I cannot continue to listen to the voice of the Lord my God, nor can I look at the great fire again, so that I will not die.*
> 17 *And the Lord said to me: They are right in what they have said.*
> 18 *I will raise up a prophet for them, from the midst of their brethren, just like you; and I will put my word in his mouth and he shall tell them all that I command him.*
> 19 *And it shall be that the man who does not listen to my word, which he shall speak in my name, I myself will hold him responsible.*
> 20 *But the prophet who acts presumptuously by speaking a word in my name, which I did not command him to speak, or who speaks in the name of other gods — then that prophet shall die.*
> 21 *And if you say to yourself: How shall we distinguish the word that the Lord has not spoken?*
> 22 *when the prophet speaks in the name of the Lord, and the word is not true or does not come to pass, that is a word that the Lord has*

---

15.   See Gen. 17:1. In the covenant with Abram, the promises (vv. 2-8) are preceded by the injunction: "walk before me, and be perfect."

not spoken. The prophet has spoken it in presumption. You shall not dread him.

Having forbidden certain illegitimate methods of attempted communication with the supernatural world (vv. 9-14), the sermon on the law now turns to prophecy, the true and legitimate means by which God's word would be delivered to his people.[16] The legislation that follows has two levels of significance.[17] Its immediate significance lies in the provision for the continuation of prophecy after the decease of the prophet Moses. But in addition, the passage is in itself prophetic, as the New Testament interpretation makes clear.

15 *A prophet like me, from your midst, from your brothers —* the primary sense in which the coming prophets[18] would resemble Moses would be in their function, which was to declare the word of God. The prophets would be fellow Israelites (not foreigners, as in vv. 9-14), who would speak the word of God and who would therefore be heard and obeyed (*you shall listen to him*).

16-19 The institution of this continued line of prophets was marked by the events at Horeb, when the people, afraid to listen directly to the voice of God, requested Moses to act as a mediator on their behalf (see 5:23-27 and commentary). The divinely appointed prophet, speaking directly God's word (v. 18), thus provided the Israelites with a way of knowing and understanding the course of human events that was totally at variance with the manner of their neighbors.[19] And because the word of the prophet was spoken with divine authority, to ignore that word would lead to divine judgment: *I myself will hold him responsible* (v. 19).

20-22 Given the serious nature of failure to obey the prophetic word, the legislation now turns to the matter of distinguishing between true and false prophecy. In addition, the criminal nature of false prophecy is stressed by the imposition of capital punishment for the offender. But in order to know whether to obey the prophetic word, and in order to condemn the false prophet, criteria had to be established by which a distinction between true and false prophets could be made. In some cases, at least, the distinction could be made easily; when a prophet in Israel spoke *in the name of other gods,* he was not only a false prophet, but he was also guilty of breaking the

16. See also 13:1-5 and commentary.
17. Cf. C. F. Keil and F. Delitzsch, *The Pentateuch,* pp. 394-97.
18. The singular (*a prophet*) is a collective form indicating a succession of prophets: see also the collective use of *king* (17:14). Cf. G. A. Smith, *The Book of Deuteronomy,* p. 233.
19. "It is now possible to sweep aside, as with a wave of the hand, the motley arsenal of mantic and occult practices, all the attempts to attain a share of the divine powers of divine knowledge. A quite different possibility has been disclosed to Israel, namely the Word of its prophet." G. von Rad, *Deuteronomy,* p. 123.

first commandment, and therefore was deserving of the death penalty. The more difficult case to distinguish would be that in which a prophet actually spoke his own words, but claimed to be speaking the words of God, and therefore — among other crimes — was guilty of gross presumption (v. 20). The criteria for distinguishing the true words of God are expressed very succinctly in two clauses. (a) *The word is not true* — the Hebrew rendered literally is "the word is not." The implication seems to be that the word has no substance, or that what the prophet says simply "is not so." That is, the word supposedly spoken by God through the prophet was not in accord with the word of God already revealed and it was therefore automatically suspect. (b) . . . *Or does not come to pass* — this clause describes prophetic words of a judgmental or predictive nature. The truth of the words would lie in their fulfilment.

It would probably be wrong to take these criteria as rules to be applied rigidly every time a prophet opened his mouth. When a prophet announced God's coming judgment and called for repentance, it would clearly be pointless to wait first to see if the judgment actually came to pass, and then to repent (too late!). Rather the criteria represent the means by which a prophet gained his reputation as a true prophet and spokesman of the Lord. Over the course of a prophet's ministry, in matters important and less significant, the character of a prophet as a true spokesman of God would begin to emerge clearly. And equally, false prophets would be discredited and then dealt with under the law.

Over the course of time, the verses concerning the prophet came to be recognized within later Judaism as having a future and prophetic point of reference.[20] In Peter's "Second Sermon," he quotes these verses from Deuteronomy[21] and finds their prophetic fulfilment in Jesus (Acts 3:22-23).[22] The parallel between Jesus and Moses, expressed here prophetically, is striking. The prophet Moses, in his role as leader of the people and spokesman for God, was

20.   See H. M. Teeple, *The Mosaic Eschatological Prophet. SBL Monograph* 10 (1957). The Essenes, as represented by the Qumran texts, expected the coming of an eschatological prophet; see 1QS 9:1 and 4QTestimonia. See also J. M. Allegro, "Further Messianic References in the Qumran Literature," *JBL* 75 (1956), pp. 174-187; F. M. Cross, *The Ancient Library of Qumran* (1961), pp. 218f. Likewise, there were debates among the Samaritans as to the specific identity of the "prophet" referred to in 18:15; see R. M. Grant, *Gnosticism and Early Christianity* (1966), p. 91. The Pharisees, too, seem to have had an expectation of a coming prophet: John 1:25.
21.   On the relationship between the quotation in Acts and the MT text, LXX text, and 4QTestimonia, see J. de Waard, *A Comparative Study of the OT Text in the Dead Sea Scrolls and in the NT* (1965), pp. 21-24 and 78-79; *idem, Biblica* 52 (1971), pp. 537-540; cf. J. A. Fitzmyer, "4QTestimonia and the NT," *Theological Studies* 18 (1957), p. 537.
22.   On Peter's method of OT exegesis, in the quotation of Deut., see R. N. Longenecker, "Can We Reproduce the Exegesis of the NT?" *TB* 21 (1970), pp. 3-38 (*22).

instrumental in founding the first kingdom, the kingdom of Israel. Though he was followed by many genuine prophets in the history of that kingdom, none of them was comparable to him in the significance of his work under God's direction. Likewise, Jesus also marked the coming of a new kingdom; it was not a political kingdom of this world, as was that of Moses, but the "kingdom of God." The prophet Moses mediated the covenant which was to be the constitution of the kingdom of Israel, whose true king was God. The prophet Jeremiah signalled the end of this age and pointed forward to a new covenant (Jer. 31:31-34) and a new kind of kingdom. These prophetic pointers in the past found their fulfilment in Jesus.

8. CITIES OF REFUGE AND LEGAL PROCEDURE (19:1-21)

(a) The Law Regarding the Cities of Refuge (vv. 1-13)

1 When the Lord your God cuts off the nations, whose land the Lord your God is about to give to you, and you dispossess them and live in their cities and in their houses,

2 you shall set aside for yourself three cities in the midst of your land, which the Lord your God is going to give to you to possess.

3 You shall fix the distance of the roads and divide into three the territory of your land, which the Lord your God will cause you to inherit, so that every manslayer might seek refuge there.

4 And this is the procedure for the manslayer who flees there to save his life. The one who kills his neighbor without intent and who did not hate him beforehand —

5 the one, for example, who goes with his neighbor into the forest to cut wood, and his hand swings the axe to cut down the tree, but the axe-head slips off the wooden haft and hits his neighbor, so that he dies — that man may flee to one of these cities and save his life;

6 lest the avenger of blood, while he is consumed with rage, pursue the manslayer and catch up with him, because the road is long, and take his life, even though he did not deserve the death penalty, because he did not hate him beforehand.

7 Therefore, I am commanding you: you shall set aside for yourself three cities.

8 And if the Lord your God extends your territory, as he promised by oath to your fathers, and gives to you the whole land which he promised to give to your fathers —

9 but you must be careful to keep the whole of this commandment which I am commanding you today, by loving the Lord your God and by walking in his ways always — then you may provide for yourself three more cities in addition to these three,

10 so that innocent blood will not be shed in the midst of your land, which the Lord your God is about to give to you as an inheritance, for you would be responsible for bloodshed.

11 *But if there should be a man who hates his neighbor, and he waits in ambush for him, and he rises up against him and takes his life, so that he dies, and then he flees to one of these cities,*
12 *then the elders of his city shall send and take him from there, and deliver him into the power of the avenger of blood, and he shall die.*
13 *Your eye shall not pity him and you shall purge out from Israel the guilt of innocent blood; then it will go well for you.*

The "cities of refuge"[1] have already been referred to briefly in 4:41-43; in that passage, three cities were mentioned by name and set aside to serve as cities of refuge for those tribes residing to the east of the Jordan valley. In these verses, no cities are mentioned by name, for the Israelites had not yet crossed the Jordan and taken possession of the land promised to them by God (v. 1). The verses describe both the procedure for appointing the cities and their function in relation to Israelite criminal law. The institution of cities of refuge seems to be an expansion of the simpler law contained in Exod. 21:12-14, where the altar (presumably that in the sanctuary of the Lord) offered protection to the manslayer, but not to the murderer. As the Israelites took possession of the land, however, the sanctuary and its altar would be located a considerable distance away from the majority of the population. The cities of refuge, strategically located throughout Israelite territory, would supplement this particular function of the sanctuary and its altar.[2]

2 *You shall set aside for yourself three cities* — bringing the total to six, including those to the east of the Jordan. *In the midst of your land* — the cities would be allocated on a geographical or regional basis, but not specifically in relation to tribal territory. The purpose of the distribution would be to provide places of refuge within easy access of all areas of Israel's future land; to have allocated one city per tribe might have defeated the purpose of the cities, by making the law in relation to manslaughter and murder a matter of tribal justice and revenge.[3]

3 *You shall fix the distance of the roads* — the meaning of this clause is difficult[4] but seems to be related to the relative location of the cities throughout the land.[5] The implication of the words is that the

1. The title "cities of refuge" is not used explicitly in Deut., but occurs in Num. 35:6, 11 (the cities of refuge being identified with Levitical cities).
2. For the detailed legislation on the cities of refuge, see Num. 35:9-34. For further studies of the subject, see N. M. Nicolsky, "Das Asylrecht in Israel," *ZAW* 48 (1930), pp. 146-175; M. Greenberg, "The Biblical Concept of Asylum," *JBL* 78 (1959), pp. 125-132.
3. Cf. J. Gray, *Joshua, Judges and Ruth.* Century Bible, pp. 25f.
4. For the rendering given here, see A. R. Hulst, *OT Translation Problems,* p. 15.
5. The translation in the RSV ("you shall prepare the roads"), if it is preferred, would

three cities were to be evenly distributed throughout the land, so that no fugitive should be at a particular disadvantage under the law because of the location of his residence in relation to the cities of refuge. *And divide into three the territory of your land* — see the comments on v. 2 (above).

4-7 *And this is the procedure* . . .⁶— in the verses that follow, the function of the cities of refuge in relation to the crime of manslaughter is described. The manslayer is defined as one who kills another man accidentally, *without intent* (i.e., without premeditation) and without there having been feelings of hate for the *neighbor* before his decease. A basic and simple example is provided in v. 5;⁷ two men go into the forest to cut wood and one is killed as a result of an accident due to a fault in his friend's axe. The man responsible for an accidental death of this kind could find shelter in the nearest of the three cities of refuge.

The avenger of blood *(go'ēl haddām)* (v. 6) — the exact meaning of this expression has been the subject of considerable debate. Traditionally, it has been taken to refer to the nearest male kinsman of the deceased, upon whom rested the responsibility for avenging the blood of the dead man.⁸ More recently, however, the expression has been interpreted as referring to a representative of the elders of the city in which the death took place; he was therefore an official (the "protector of blood"), not a close relative of the deceased.⁹

The meaning of the expression possibly lies somewhere between these two alternatives. The avenger of blood may well be the nearest male kinsman of the deceased; his responsibility, however, was not simply to kill the person responsible for the death (whether manslayer or murderer), but to bring him before the established courts of law in his home town, who would determine the case in the proper manner. If the death was manslaughter, the manslayer would be sent to the city of refuge;¹⁰ the city of refuge was not simply a place

---

mean that roads were to be made that would ensure easy access to the cities of refuge; cf. Driver, *Deuteronomy*, p. 231. NEB paraphrases, but gives the sense of the translation provided above: "and determine where each city shall lie."
6. For the idiom employed here, see 15:2 (". . . the nature of the release") and G. A. Cooke, *A Text-book of North-Semitic Inscriptions*, p. 17, with reference to the Siloam inscription.
7. The clear distinction between murder and manslaughter is made in a whole series of examples provided in Num. 35:16-24.
8. See Driver, *Deuteronomy*, p. 232.
9. For a clear presentation of this point of view, see A. Phillips, *Ancient Israel's Criminal Law*, pp. 102-105. Although it is quite possible, the difficulty with this view is that it involves a good deal of speculation, especially concerning the legal process in the city of the deceased, for which there is no firm evidence; it should be added, of course, that in the nature of the evidence, all views involve a degree of speculation.
10. See Lev. 35:24-25. The avenger of blood probably operated on the principle that the fugitive was guilty of murder, unless it was proved to be otherwise; hence he would

of safety, but a place in which the manslayer made atonement for the deed of which he was guilty.[11] If the death was determined to be murder, then the culprit would be executed.

The problem envisaged in v. 6 is that the avenger of blood might be *consumed with rage*[12] and kill the fleeing man; while such action seems to have been allowed for on a permissive basis,[13] there was a danger of injustice being done if the fugitive was in fact a manslayer (and therefore not deserving captial punishment) rather than a murderer (v. 6b). For these reasons, cities of refuge were to be set aside (v. 7).

8-10 Provision is made for the addition of three further cities of refuge (bringing the total to nine), in the event that an even larger portion of territory should be occupied by the Israelites than that envisaged in vv. 1-7. Such provision was necessary in that a part of the principle underlying the appointment of cities of refuge was ease of accessibility (see the commentary on v. 3 above), and if there was a major increase in land-holdings, the first three cities that were set aside would be a long distance from the residents of the new territory. *And if the Lord your God extends your territory* — whereas vv. 1-7 seem to envisage the land lying to the west of Jordan, these words indicate that much larger conception of the promised land already mentioned in 1:7 and 11:23-24. Since all this territory (from the borders of Egypt to the Euphrates) was never fully possessed by the Israelites,[14] the provisions mentioned in these verses do not seem to have been put into effect at any point during Israel's history. The condition (v. 9a) on which the acquisition of this larger territory would be contingent is very similar to that stated in 11:22; the words are another reminder of the sermonic style of the presentation of the law

---

immediately set out in pursuit. The procedure to be followed if the fugitive was a murderer, and reached the city of refuge before being apprehended by the avenger of blood, is described in vv. 11-13 (below).

11. Lev. 35:25-28; he was to stay there until the death of the high priest, after which he was at liberty to return to his residence. The death of the high priest served as an expiation for the man's bloodguilt; see M. Greenberg, *loc. cit.*, p. 130. The view of M. Weinfeld (*Deuteronomy and the Deuteronomic School*, p. 237), that in Deut. the city of refuge was only a place of protection, and not a place of punishment, seems to be unnecessary. The nature of the presentation of law in Deut., in the context of a hortatory address, is such that it is not the detailed prescriptions of the law that find expression (these are given elsewhere), but the spirit of the law within the purpose of the address. The sermonic nature of this particular section of Deut. emerges clearly in v. 9.

12. Following the interpretation of Phillips, these words would indicate excessive eagerness on the part of the official, rather than intense rage: *Ancient Israel's Criminal Law*, p. 105.

13. See Num. 35:26-27.

14. Much of it came under Israelite control during the period of the united monarchy, but it was not fully integrated as a part of Israel.

in Deuteronomy. This additional provision for further cities of refuge had the same purpose in mind as in vv. 1-7, namely, the avoidance of innocent bloodshed, with its attendant responsibility, in Israel (v. 10).

11-13 These verses indicate the method of dealing with the abuse of the cities of refuge. The crime described in v. 11 is murder, not manslaughter, for to lie in ambush for someone involves premeditation. The murderer might still flee to the cities of refuge, but the protection they offered did not cover the crime of which he was guilty. *The elders of his city* (v. 12) — namely, the city in which the criminal lived and presumably in which the crime had been committed. These elders, who were the guardians of the law in the city, demanded the extradition of the criminal. They would then *deliver him into the power* (lit. "hand") *of the avenger of blood* — if the interpretation suggested in the commentary on v. 6 is correct, then the sense is that the *avenger of blood* would act as prosecutor and present his evidence against the accused before the court of law (the elders) in his own town. On securing a conviction, the avenger of blood would then be responsible for the execution, together with other members of the community (see, e.g., 13:9). *Your eye shall not pity him* — see also 7:16. The reason for the stern action was to remove the stain from the land which resulted from the shedding of innocent blood; since the Lord was believed to dwell in the land with his people, it was not to be defiled (see Num. 35:34).

(g) Displacing a boundary marker (v. 14)

> 14 *You shall not displace your neighbor's boundary marker, which predecessors fixed, in your inheritance which you inherit in the land which the Lord your God is about to give to you to possess.*

On the nature of the boundary marker and the implications of displacing it, see the commentary on 27:17; in that passage, the displacement of a boundary marker comes under the curse of God.

The situation envisaged in the legislation would involve the exertion of undue pressure by a rich landowner on a poorer neighbor, perhaps in an attempt to acquire his land.[15] *Which predecessors* (perhaps "ancestors") *fixed* — the boundaries would be fixed once the land had been possessed and allocated among the Israelites, and the legislation has in mind a time further in the future, when attempts might be made to alter those boundaries. Inheritance, in this context, may refer to particular territories within the land, rather than the land as a whole.

---

15. This sense is clearer in Prov. 23:10: "Do not displace an ancient boundary marker, and do not enter the fields of orphans." See also the sixth chapter of the

(c) The Law Regarding Witnesses (vv. 15-21)

15 *A single witness may not testify against a man regarding any iniquity or any sin that he commits; a case must be established on the testimony of two witnesses or on the testimony of three witnesses.*

16 *If a malicious witness testifies against a man, charging him with defection,*

17 *then the two men who are parties to the dispute shall stand before the Lord, before the priests and judges who are in office in those days.*

18 *And the judges shall investigate diligently, and if indeed the witness is a false witness and has charged his brother falsely,*

19 *then you shall do to him what he intended to do to his brother and you shall purge out the evil from your midst.*

20 *And the rest shall hear of it and be afraid; and they shall not do again anything like this evil deed in your midst.*

21 *You shall not show compassion; a life for a life, an eye for an eye, a tooth for a tooth, a hand for a hand, a foot for a foot.*

The law regarding witnesses in criminal cases, which has already been stated concisely in relation to a particular crime (see 17:6), is now the subject of further elaboration; the basic statement (v. 15) is the same in substance as 17:6, though now it is not limited to the death penalty, which was incurred by the transgression of the covenant.[16]

Malicious (or "violent") *witness* (v. 16) — in spite of the requirement for more than one witness (v. 15), cases would inevitably arise in particular circumstances when there was only one witness.[17] The single witness could not ignore that a crime had been committed simply because there was not a second witness to confirm his story.[18] On the other hand, a case in which there was only one witness would be particularly difficult to determine and it would probably be referred

---

Instructions of Amenemope, *ANET*, p. 422.

16.   See also Num. 35:30. The law elaborated in these verses should probably be understood as an expansion of the apodictic prohibition of the ninth commandment (see 5:20). For a study of the place given to this law in the NT (and a comparison with later Greek and Roman law regarding testimony), see H. van Vliet, *No Single Testimony. A Study of the Adoption of the Law of Deut. 19:15 par. into the NT* (1958).

17.   Thus v. 15 states the general requirement of the law; vv. 16-21 attempt to provide a means of dealing with cases where circumstances might not allow the normal requirement to be met, and more particularly they attempt to cover any "loophole" that might arise in the exceptional (rather than normal) process of law, when only one witness was available. In legal process, the absence of witnesses or the existence of a single witness did not mean that no crime had been committed, but it made it exceptionally difficult to secure a conviction.

18.   In a genuine case, the single witness might not know at the time he brought the criminal charge that he was the only witness.

to the central tribunal (see 17:8-13). *Charging him with defection* (*sārāh*) — the word means literally "turning aside" (from the prescriptions of the law) and could perhaps be translated by "crime."[19] Thus the situation envisaged is one in which a false witness brought a criminal charge against his fellow Israelite; at the time when the charge was brought, it might have been imagined by the authorities that further witnesses would be forthcoming. In the absence of further witnesses, the legal problem was that of determining which of the two parties in the dispute was telling the truth.

The procedure to be followed was to send the two parties in the dispute to the central tribunal, located at the sanctuary of the Lord; there they would stand before the Lord (v. 17), a symbolic manner of referring to the sanctuary (see 17:8), and their case would be heard by the priests and judges who were currently holding office in the central tribunal. The judges would make a diligent investigation of the case (v. 18) and pass judgment on the basis of their findings. If it turned out that the witness bringing the charge was giving false testimony, then his punishment would be determined on the basis of the intention of the crime; the *lex talionis* would become operative (v. 19). On v. 20, see 13:12 and commentary; with v. 21a, compare v. 13a.[20] The *lex talionis* (law of retaliation) is stated more fully in Exod. 21:23-25 and Lev. 24:17-20.[21] With the exception of the first phrase relating to murder (*a life for a life*), it is uncertain how literally the remaining phrases should be interpreted; the force of the collocation of phrases may lie in asserting the principle of proportionate compensation.[22]

9. THE CONDUCT OF WAR (20:1-20)

War has already been the topic of an earlier portion of Moses' address (see 7:1-26); in this chapter, detailed instruction is given concerning the conduct of war. Further legislation on war and matters relating to military affairs occurs in 21:10-14; 23:9-14; 24:5; 25:17-19.[1] This legislation, like that on kingship (17:14-20), has a somewhat idealistic and

19. A. Phillips, *Ancient Israel's Criminal Law,* p. 143.
20. See also 7:16 and 18:9; M. Weinfeld (*Deuteronomy and the Deuteronomic School,* p. 2) has noted that the phrase is used whenever there was a danger that the punisher would be lenient or even unwilling to perform the punishment.
21. Contrast the different spirit in the quotation of the *lex talionis* in the teaching of Jesus, though the context there has to do with personal behavior and attitudes and not with the courts of law. For an example of *lex talionis* in Babylonian Law, see the Law Code of Hammurabi, § 197 ("bone for bone"; cf. Lev. 24:20); *ANET,* p. 175. On the possible development of this law from earlier Mesopotamian law codes, see A. S. Diamond, "An Eye for an Eye," *Iraq* 19 (1957), pp. 151-55.
22. See R. de Vaux, *Ancient Israel,* pp. 149f.

1. For particular studies of war in the OT, see G. von Rad, *Der Heilige Krieg im alten Israel* (⁴1965); F. M. Cross, "The Divine Warrior in Israel's Early Cult," in A.

unrealistic character,[2] which may reflect the antiquity of the passage and the relatively early stage in the conquest (namely, the conquest of land east of the Jordan) in which it is set. After an introductory section (vv. 1-4), there are laws relating to exemption from military service (vv. 5-9; cf. 24:5), the manner of dealing with enemy cities (vv. 10-18), and trees in the vicinity of enemy cities (vv. 19-20).

(a) General Introduction (vv. 1-4)

> 1 *When you go out to war against your enemies, and you see horses and chariots and a people more numerous than you are, you shall not be afraid of them, for the Lord your God, the one who brought you up from the land of Egypt, is with you.*
> 2 *And it shall be that when you draw near to war, then the priest shall come forward and shall address the people,*
> 3 *and shall say to them: Hear, O Israel. Today you are drawing near to war against your enemies. Let not your heart be timid! Do not fear, and do not be alarmed, and do not tremble because of them,*
> 4 *for the Lord your God is the one going with you, to fight for you against your enemies, to give you victory.*

1   When the Israelites engaged in battle, the greater numbers and superior military equipment (*horses and chariots* — the Israelite army would consist of infantrymen) of their enemies need cause them no anxiety. Israelite strength lay not in numbers, not in the superiority of their weapons, but in their God.[3] The strength of their God was not simply a matter of faith, but a matter of experience; in the Exodus from Egypt, God (*the one who brought you up from the land of Egypt*) had proved his strength and prowess in war against the strongest enemy that Israel had known.[4]

2-4   Immediately before the battle commenced, the priest[5]

Altmann, ed., *Biblical Motifs* (1966), pp. 11-29; F. Stolz, *Jahwes und Israels Kriege* (1972), *pp. 17-28. For the Near Eastern background to war in Israel, see A. Glock, *Warfare in Mari and Early Israel* (diss., University of Michigan, 1968); M. Weippert, "*Heiliger Krieg* in Israel und Assyrien," *ZAW* 84 (1972), pp. 460-495. For an examination of the subject of war in relation to the NT and Christian thought, see K. Hammer, *Christen, Krieg und Frieden* (1972), *pp. 9-33; R. H. Bainton, *Christian Attitudes Toward War and Peace* (1960). See also the articles cited in n. 34 of the Introduction.
2.   See M. H. Segal, *The Pentateuch*, p. 80. See further the discussion of the laws of war in the Introduction, section IX.4(c).
3.   A similar conception may appear in Judg. 5:8; see P. C. Craigie, *VT* 22 (1972), p. 351 (n. 4).
4.   In the song celebrating that victory (Exod. 15:1-18), the Lord is referred to as a "Man in Battle," but an Israelite "army" is not mentioned at all.
5.   Only one of the functions of the priest in relation to war is mentioned in this context. In addition, priests would be responsible for the offering of sacrifices before going into battle, and some priests would be present in the battle, attending the ark which accompanied the army of the Lord. The role of the priest in addressing the army could be assumed by the king in other Near Eastern countries; concerning Assyria, see

would *address the people*[6] (v. 2). His message, in substance, has already been summarized in v. 1; the people were to have no anxiety about the outcome of the battle, because their God would be present with them in the thick of the battle, and would grant to them the victory (vv. 3-4). In the context of Israelite faith, fear and trembling were to be the prerogative of enemies[7] — Israel's prerogative was victory!

In the NT the language of warfare is used frequently, though in a figurative sense; the war to be fought is not a "worldly war" (2 Cor. 10:3-4; see also Eph. 6:12), but is against a more subtle enemy. But just as the Israelite knew of the victorious strength of his God from the experience of the Exodus, so too the Christian is on the victorious side, for Jesus Christ, through his death and resurrection, "disarmed the principalities and powers" (Col. 2:15). As victory was the prerogative of Israel, so it is also for the Christian.[8]

(b) Exemptions from Military Service (vv. 5-9)

> 5 Then the officers shall address the people: What man is there that has built a new house and has not started to live in it? Let him go and let him return to his house, lest he die in the war and another man start to live in it.
>
> 6 And what man is there who has planted a vineyard and has not put it to use? Let him go and let him return to his house, lest he die in the war and another man put it to use.
>
> 7 And what man is there who has pledged to marry a woman, but has not taken her? Let him go and let him return to his house, lest he die in the war and another man take her.
>
> 8 Then the officers shall continue to address the people and they shall say: What man is there that is afraid and softhearted? Let him go and let him return to his house, so that he does not make the heart of his brethren melt like his own heart.

R. Labat, *Le caractère religieux de la royauté assyro-babylonienne* (1939), pp. 254f. Various priests, however, did accompany the armies of Mesopotamian states; for a fuller discussion of the subject see T. Fish, "War and Religion in Ancient Mesopotamia," *BJRL* 23 (1939), pp. 387-402; A. Haldar, *Associations of Cult Prophets among the Ancient Semites* (1945).

6.   The word *people* (*'am*), used here of Israel and in v. 1 of the enemy, may also have the sense "army," both in the OT and in certain Qumran texts; see P. C. Craigie, *TB* 20 (1969), pp. 89f.

7.   Compare v. 3, the priest's words of encouragement to Israel, with the joyful confidence of the Israelites after the Exodus from Egypt, Exod. 15:14-16a: "The peoples have heard — they trembled! Agony seized the inhabitants of Philistia! Even the chiefs of Edom were dismayed! Trembling seized hold of the leaders of Moab! All the inhabitants of Canaan were utterly panic-stricken! You caused terror and dread to fall upon them!"

8.   For further uses of the language of warfare in the NT, see 2 Tim. 2:3-4; 1 Pet. 2:11; Eph. 6:10-20. A very modern, readable, and provocative approach to the subject of war in the Bible is provided by V. Eller, *King Jesus' Manual of Arms for the Armless. War and Peace from Genesis to Revelation* (1973).

9 *And when the officers have finished addressing the people, then*
they shall appoint military captains at the head of the people.

The various exemptions from military service[9] stated here follow
from the logic of vv. 1-4; Israel's success in war would not be based on
military power superior to that of the enemy, but it would depend on
the presence and power of God in the midst of the army. Hence
exemptions from military service could be granted on the basis of
morale or for compassionate reasons; the object of the officers of the
people was not to get the *largest* possible army, but the *best* possible
army. The best possible army was the one wholly committed to God[10]
and absolutely confident in his strength and ability for the battle lying
ahead of the army.

5   After the people (army) had been addressed by the priest,
then the *officers*[11] would step forward to address them. First, they
announced three categories of exemption from military service on
compassionate grounds (vv. 5-7); as the military representatives of
the tribes, the officers would be in a position to know which men
qualified for these exemptions. The first category qualifying for
exemption consisted of those who had just built a house but had *not*
started to live in it;[12] they were to be permitted to live in the house for
a period before being required to undertake military service.[13]

6   The second group to be granted exemption were those who
had planted a vineyard, but had not yet put it to use. The procedure is
clarified in Lev. 19:23-25 (with reference to fruit in general). For the
first three years, no fruit would be taken from a tree; in the fourth
year, the fruit was dedicated to the Lord. In the fifth year, the orchard
could be put to common use and the fruit eaten. Thus those who were
still engaged in this lengthy and important process of preparing a

9.   For further studies, see S. B. Gurewicz,, "The Deuteronomic Provisions for
Exemption from Military Service," *Australian Biblical Review* 6 (1958), pp. 111-121
(with comments on relevant Near Eastern material); L. Landman, "Law and Con-
science: the Jewish View," *Judaism* 18 (1969), pp. 17-29. Landman notes that the
exemptions from military service stated in Deut. 20 were interpreted by the Mishnah to
apply to conscientious objectors, especially in an "optional" or aggressive war. See
also M. H. Segal, *The Pentateuch,* p. 80 and Mishnah *Sotah* viii.7.
10.   On the complete commitment of the people to God in war, see Judg. 5:2, and P. C.
Craigie, *VT* 18 (1968), pp. 397-99.
11.   See also 1:15b. Officers, representing the various tribes, had primarily an administrative function within the military. Combat officers are referred to in v. 9 (below).
12.   Most English translations render the verb here (*ḥānak*) by "dedicate." There is
no clear evidence, however, for the practice of dedicating a new house in ancient Israel.
The proper sense of the verb seems to be: "to initiate; to begin to use." See S. C. Reif,
"Dedicated to *ḥnk,*" *VT* 22 (1972), pp. 495-501; cf. J. Parkhurst, *An Hebrew and*
English Lexicon (1811), p. 225.
13.   A similar conception appears in line 50 of the Sumerian poem, "Gilgamesh and
the Land of the Living"; see *ANET,* p. 48. Gilgamesh's fifty volunteers are single men
who do not have a "house."

vineyard for use were to be exempted from military service. Although vines were grown in Palestine and would form an important part of Israel's future agricultural activity, it should be noted that the vine had been cultivated in the Delta area of Egypt from an early date,[14] and some of the Israelites may have been familiar already with the process of cultivating vines.

7 Finally, a man who was pledged to marry a woman was to be exempt from military service; here, the compassionate basis for exemption is most clearly evident. See also the similar exemption in 24:5, where a newly married man is granted one year's exemption from military service.

The basis of these exemptions becomes clearer against the background of the function of war in ancient Israel. The purpose of war in the early stages of Israel's history was to take possession of the land promised to the people by God; in the later period of history, war was fought for defensive purposes, to defend the land from external aggressors. The possession of the promised land, in other words, was at the heart of Israel's wars, and the importance of the land, in the plan of God, was that Israel was to live and work and prosper in it. The building of homes and orchards, the marrying of a wife, and other such things were of the essence of life in the promised land, and if these things ceased, then the wars would become pointless. Thus, in these exemptions from military service, it is clear that the important aspects of normal life in the land take precedence over the requirements of the army, but this somewhat idealistic approach (in modern terms) was possible only because of the profound conviction that military strength and victory lay, in the last resort, not in the army, but in God.

8 *Then the officers shall continue* — see also v. 5a; the repetition of the introductory clause does not necessarily indicate a later accretion to the text,[15] but marks rather a different category of exemption in this verse from those contained in vv. 5-7. The priest had already admonished the people not to be fearful in battle (vv. 3-4); nevertheless, there would inevitably be those who would be *afraid and softhearted*. These people were not to be bullied into battle, scorned for their fear, or court-martialled; they were to be sent home along with the others who qualified for exemption. The reason is clear, for fear in an army is like an infectious plague, which can quickly cripple the ranks with its debilitating effect. The strength of the army, it is true, lay in God's presence; but to experience God's

14. See P. Montet, *Eternal Egypt* (1968), pp. 112f.; for an artistic representation of the cultivation and harvesting of grapes in Egypt, see K. Michalowski, *Art of Ancient Egypt* (n.d.), pl. 19 (p. 53).
15. See, e.g., G. von Rad, *Deuteronomy*, p. 132.

presence in battle, the people were to be wholly committed to him, and fear undermined the wholeness of commitment.

9 Only after the address of the officers could the more detailed process of military organization take place. It is apparent in this verse that there is no conception of a permanent standing army, with regular officers and soldiers. After those granted exemption had departed, it would be clear who was available for military service; from those remaining, *military captains*[16] would be appointed, who would be responsible for their men in the approaching conflict.

(c) Enemy cities (vv. 10-18)

> 10 *When you approach a city to fight against it, you shall offer terms of peace to it.*
> 11 *And it shall be that if it requests terms of peace from you and it opens up to you, then all the people who are found in it shall become forced-laborers for you, and they shall serve you.*
> 12 *But if it does not seek terms of peace with you, but makes war with you, then you shall besiege it.*
> 13 *Then the Lord your God shall deliver it into your power and you shall put all its males to death by the sword;*
> 14 *only the women, and the children, and the animals, and everything that is in the city, all its spoil, you may take as booty for yourself; and you shall take pleasure in the spoil of your enemies, which the Lord your God will have given to you.*
> 15 *Thus shall you act toward all the cities that are a long way from you, which are not among the cities of these nations close at hand.*
> 16 *Only you shall not allow anything that breathes to live from the cities of these peoples, which the Lord your God is about to give to you as an inheritance,*
> 17 *but you shall certainly destroy them: the Hittites and the Amorites, the Canaanites and the Perizzites, the Hivites and the Jebusites, just as the Lord your God has commanded you;*
> 18 *in order that they may not teach you to act according to all their abominations, which they do for their gods, so that you would sin against the Lord your God.*

Two situations are envisaged in these verses, namely, the conquest of distant cities, on the periphery of or beyond the promised land (vv. 10-15), and the conquest of the cities belonging to those peoples whose land Israel was soon to possess as her own (vv. 16-18).

10-15 Cities in the first category were to be offered initially *terms of peace (shālôm);* the verse indicates that the Israelites were

---

16. Lit. "captains of hosts"; the expression probably covers all military officers responsible for combat duties. A more precise ranking of officers according to the number of men for which they were responsible is given in 1:15.

to offer to the inhabitants of such cities the terms of a vassal treaty.[17] If the city accepted the terms, it would open its gates to the Israelites, both as a symbol of surrender and to grant the Israelites access to the city; the inhabitants would become vassals and would serve Israel (v. 11). If the offer was rejected, the Israelites were to besiege the city, and when they were victorious (God's victory is taken for granted, see v. 13a), they would execute all the males; everything else was to be spared. The Israelites would *take pleasure in* (lit. "eat, consume") the spoil acquired in the victory God would grant them.[18] This relatively humane approach to military conquest was only to apply to the cities at some distance from the land, which it was Israel's first duty to acquire.

16-18 The treatment of those cities which the Israelites would encounter immediately after they crossed the Jordan was to be sterner; no living thing was to be allowed to survive. *You shall certainly destroy them* (v. 17) — the law of *herem* was to come into effect (see also 2:34 and 7:1-2). There are two reasons for this total destruction, only one of which is stated in this context. The unstated reason is that the Israelites were instruments of God's judgment; the conquest was not only the means by which God granted his people the promised land, but was also the means by which he executed his judgment on the Canaanites for their sinfulness (see 9:4). The second reason, which is stated, appears in v. 18; if the Canaanites survived, their unholy religion could turn Israel aside from serving the Lord.

To the six nations listed in v. 17, a seventh may be added, the *Girgashites,* following the evidence of the LXX and Samaritan versions; on these seven nations, see 7:2 and the commentary.

(d) Trees in the vicinity of enemy cities (vv. 19-20)

> 19 *When you besiege a city for many days, making war against it in order to capture it, you shall not ruin its trees by wielding an axe against them, because you may eat of them, but you shall not cut them down. For are the trees of the field human, that they should be besieged by you?*
>
> 20 *Only the trees that you know are not food-bearing trees may you ruin and cut down; then you may build siege-works against the city which is making war with you, until it falls.*

The practice of cutting down trees and laying waste the land was employed by the Egyptians and other military powers in the Near East.[19] In contrast to the total havoc wreaked by the great military

17. With *shālôm* in this verse, compare the use of *salīmum* in the Mari texts; see A. Glock, *Warfare in Mari and Early Israel,* pp. 62 (n. 79) and 215f.
18. For similar practices following victory, according to the texts from Mari, see J. M. Sasson, *The Military Establishments at Mari* (1969), pp. 47-49.
19. See the description of the destruction of trees in the accounts of the military

powers of that time, Israel was to discriminate in the use of its destructive power and to be guided by good sense and utilitarian requirements. Fruit trees were not to be cut down; not only would they provide food for the besieging army, but after the victory they would become a part of Israel's new possessions. *For are the trees of the field human . . .?*[20] — though trees might belong to the enemy, they were not an enemy, and they were not to be treated with vindictive wrath as if they were persons. Even non-fruit-bearing trees should not be cut down at random, but only in order to fulfil particular requirements, such as building siege-works. The exact significance of *siege-works (mātsôr)* is not certain, but it is known that battering-rams, siege-towers, and ladders were employed in Near Eastern warfare;[21] all these would have required wood in their construction. *Until it falls* — once again, eventual victory for the army of the Lord is taken as a certain outcome of the siege.

10. LAWS RELATING TO MURDER, WAR, AND FAMILY AFFAIRS (21:1-23)

(a) Murder by a Person Unknown (vv. 1-9)

> 1 *When a murdered man is found lying in the countryside in the land which the Lord your God is about to give to you to possess, and it is not known who struck him,*
>
> 2 *your elders and your judges shall go out, and they shall measure the distance to the cities that are in the vicinity of the murdered man.*
>
> 3 *And the elders of that city which is nearest to the murdered man shall take a heifer of the herd, which has not been used and which has not pulled in the yoke.*
>
> 4 *Then the elders of that city shall take the heifer down into a valley with a perpetually running stream, which has not been plowed and has not been planted, and there in the valley they shall break the neck of the heifer.*
>
> 5 *And the priests, the sons of Levi, shall come forward, for the Lord your God has chosen them to minister to him and to bless in the*

campaigns of Thutmose III, *ANET,* pp. 239f. See also F. Stolz, *Jahwes und Israels Kriege,* p. 27 (n. 54).

20. *Human* — lit. "man." The interrogative, *he-,* is read following the evidence of certain versions (LXX, Syriac), so that the line is understood to be a rhetorical question.

21. On battering-rams and siege-towers, see J. M. Sasson, *The Military Establishments at Mari,* pp. 33f. An Egyptian scene depicting the attack of Ramses III on the city of Tunip provides valuable illumination on these verses; see H. H. Nelson and U. Hölscher, *Medinet Habu Reports* (1931), p. 32 (fig. 19). The picture shows the Egyptian forces using ladders to gain access to the besieged city; in the background, Egyptians are cutting down trees.

*name of the Lord, and every dispute and every case of assault
shall be settled by their word.*

6 *And all the elders of that city nearest to the murdered man shall
wash their hands over the broken-necked heifer in the valley;*

7 *and they shall make response and say: Our hands have not shed
this blood and our eyes did not see it happen.*

8 *Forgive your people, Israel, whom you have ransomed, O Lord,
and do not set the guilt of innocent blood in the midst of your
people, Israel, but let the bloodguilt be forgiven them.*

9 *And so you shall purge out the guilt of innocent blood from your
midst, when you do the right thing in the eyes of the Lord.*

In the earlier legislation, distinctions have been made between manslaughter and murder, together with the manner of dealing with such
crimes (17:8; 19:4-13). In this passage it is envisaged that a crime has
taken place (presumably murder, though it could have been manslaughter), but the authorities do not know who was responsible for
the crime. Because of the religious implications of murder, incurring
guilt for the whole land, the matter could not simply be left (to use
modern language) as an open file at the police headquarters. Some
action had to be taken immediately, though the action described in
these verses does not preclude the continuing investigation into the
cause of the death by the officers of the law. Both the crime and the
procedure involved have parallels in Near Eastern literature and legal
texts,[1] though at a number of points the Israelite practice is quite
distinctive.

1   The *murdered man* (lit. "the one pierced") is found *lying in
the countryside;*[2] the body is presumably found by accident, perhaps
by a farmer or a passer-by. The qualifying clause that follows (*in the
land which . . .*), though typical of Deuteronomy, nevertheless indi-

1.   Though parallels occur in a variety of Near Eastern texts, the most immediately
relevant are those from the Ugaritic texts. (a) *CTA* 19.III.148–IV.168 (=*UT* 1 Aqht,
148-168); in the Aqhat Legend, there is a description of Danel locating the place in
which his son was murdered; there he curses the unknown murderer and also the cities
closest to the scene of the crime. For further discussion of this passage, see T. H.
Gaster, *Thespis* (1966), pp. 364f.; T. L. Fenton, "Ugaritica-Biblica," *UF* 1 (1969), p.
68; J. Gray, *The Legacy of Canaan*², pp. 122, 241. Another Ugaritic text may provide
some illumination on the biblical text, namely *PRU* 4.62 (=RS 17.146), which indicates
the procedure to be followed if a merchant is killed while he is away from home. (b) For
laws relating to a similar crime, see the Code of Hammurabi, § 24, *ANET*, p. 167. (c) For
parallels in Hittite law, see H. A. Hoffner, "Some Contributions of Hittitology to OT
Study," *TB* 20 (1969), pp. 39f. (d) A similar procedure for a different (but unsolved)
crime is known also in the Nuzu texts; C. H. Gordon, "Biblical Customs and the Nuzu
Tablets," in D. N. Freedman and E. F. Campbell, eds., *The Biblical Archaeologist
Reader* II (1964), p. 31.
2.   The Heb. *śādeh* (*countryside*) may refer to open country as distinct from cultivated
ground; see H. A. Hoffner, *loc. cit.*, p. 39. On the use of the verb *nāpal*, with the sense
"lying," compare Ugar. *npl.l'arṣ*, "lying on the ground"; *CTA* 5.VI.8 (=*UT* 67.VI.8).

cates the serious nature of the discovery, for the land in which the corpse is discovered is the land in which the Lord dwells (Num. 35:34).

2 Since the person responsible for the crime would be unknown, a particular legal procedure was to be followed. The elders and judges referred to in this verse are the representatives of a central legal authority, rather than a local authority (as in v. 3). These men were to *measure the distance to the cities*,[3] in order to determine which city was closest to the dead man; the closest city would undertake responsibility for the procedure that follows.

3-4 The elders of the city that was to accept responsibility for the crime were to take a heifer. The heifer was specified as one that had not been employed for farm work;[4] it could therefore be considered sacred for its use in the symbolic act. The heifer was to be taken to a place outside the city; the place (like the heifer) had to meet certain specifications. It was to be a valley, or ravine, with a perpetually running stream; the stream, in other words, would be fed by a spring, unlike those streams in wadis, which flowed only after a heavy fall of rain.[5] Furthermore, the valley was not to have been plowed, nor were crops to have been planted in it; as with the heifer, the land in the valley was not to have been subjected to human use. Then the neck of the heifer was to be broken in the valley; it should be noted that this was not a sacrifice in the normal sense, for the text does not state explicitly that blood would be shed. The animal was simply to be killed by breaking its neck.

5 The Levitical priests also had a role to play in the ceremony;[6] their presence seems to be primarily as representative of the central tribunal. In a criminal (capital) case, where there was a person charged with an offense, the priests would have been involved in the passing of judgment (17:8-9). Even though the guilty party was not known in the present situation, their presence was required here also. It may be too that the priests had an explicit part to play in the ceremony; see the comments on v. 7 (below).

6 The elders of the city that accepted responsibility for the dead man washed their hands over the broken-necked heifer. The symbolism of the various actions now becomes clear:[7] the crime deserved to be punished, as the broken neck of the heifer indicated,

---

3. Measurement was also made according to Hittite law, though a maximum distance within which responsibility could be allocated was also specified; H. A. Hoffner, *loc. cit.*, p. 39.

4. In the NEB, the heifer is described as one "that has never been mated or worn a yoke." On this translation, see G. R. Driver, "Three Notes," *VT* 2 (1952), pp. 356f.

5. See G. A. Smith, *The Historical Geography of the Holy Land* (repr. 1966), pp. 70f.

6. For the language employed in this verse, see 10:8 and 18:5.

7. Cf. M. H. Farbridge, *Studies in Biblical and Semitic Symbolism*, p. 275.

but the hand-washing of the elders showed that, although they accepted responsibility for what had happened, they were nevertheless free from the guilt attached to the crime. The symbolic action is reinforced by the spoken words of the subsequent verses.

7 *And they shall make response* — the verb employed is the same as that in the ninth commandment (*'ānāh*), so that the sense could be: "and they shall testify" (RSV). However, the simple meaning of the verb ("answer, respond") may be intended; it may have been the role of the priests (v. 5) to pronounce the words, which would have then been repeated, or responded to, by the elders of the city.[8] First, the elders declare lack of direct guilt in the crime; they had not committed the crime (*our hands have not shed this blood*) nor did they see it happen. The last clause in v. 7 probably indicates more than that they were not eyewitnesses; it may indicate that they had not seen and did not know anything which might lead to the conviction of the guilty party. In speaking these words, the elders spoke not only for themselves, but also for the city of which they were the representatives.

8 After declaring innocence of the act and of knowledge of the act, the elders then prayed for forgiveness, indicating that in spite of innocence, the community must still shoulder responsibility for the crime. The forgiveness is sought for the whole people (*Israel* is mentioned twice in the prayer for forgiveness), not simply for the city nearest the crime. A basis for forgiveness is offered in the prayer; it is not the merit of Israel, but the fact that God had ransomed (see also 7:8) his people from the bondage of Egypt. The act of ransom had been an act of grace, and on the basis of such glorious precedent, the elders sought another act of grace in receiving the forgiveness of God. But further, if all the land were punished on account of an act of murder by a person unknown, then the great work of God, initiated in the Exodus, could be brought to an untimely end. Thus the prayer for forgiveness has in mind not only the well-being of the people, but also the purpose of God.

Verse 9 summarizes the section; in the case of murder by an unknown hand, the procedure described would *purge out*[9] *the guilt of innocent blood from your midst*.

(b) Marrying a Female Prisoner of War (vv. 10-14)

> 10 *When you go out to war against your enemies, and the Lord your God delivers them into your power, and you take them captive,*
> 11 *and you see among the captives a woman of beautiful appear-*

8. Cf. Buis and Leclercq, *Le Deutéronome*, p. 147, who note this possibility, but reject it.
9. This verb is used frequently in Deut.; see also 13:6; 19:13.

ance, and you desire her, then you may take her for yourself as a wife;

12 *but you shall bring her into your house, and she shall shave her head and cut her nails.*

13 *Then she shall discard the garment of her captivity, and she shall live in your house and weep for her father and her mother for a full month. Then after that, you may go in to her and be her husband, and she shall be your wife.*

14 *And if it happens that you have no pleasure in her, then you shall let her go where she wants; but you shall not sell her for money, you shall not treat her as merchandise, because you have humiliated her.*

10   The legislation on war now continues, beginning with the same words as the previous section on war (20:1). A situation is imagined in which war is undertaken against *enemies,*[10] victory is granted by God, and some of the enemy are taken captive;[11] the last clause of v. 10 makes it clear that the war envisaged would be one against a distant enemy, a circumstance in which it was permissible to take captives (see 20:13-15 and commentary).

11   If a man sees a beautiful woman among those taken captive and desires her, he is free to *take her*[12]. . . *as a wife.*[13] The marriage, however, was not to be consummated immediately.

12-13   First, the captive woman was to be taken back to the man's home. There she was to shave her head, cut her nails, and *discard the garment of her captivity* (presumably the clothing she was wearing at the time of her capture, rather than some kind of prisoner-of-war uniform). These actions may have a double significance. They indicate her transference from a foreign community into the family of Israel;[14] they may also indicate her mourning. For a full month, she was to weep for her father and mother; although the mourning could indicate the death of the woman's parents in war, it may simply point to her removal by force from the parental home. Only after the expiry

10.   Perhaps the singular ("enemy") should be read, following the evidence of some mss.; such a reading would be better in view of the singular pronominal suffixes in the sentence that follows.

11.   On the use of *shebî* and *shibyāh* in vv. 10-11 (both meaning "captivity, captive"), see U. Cassuto, *The Goddess Anath,* p. 45.

12.   The translation assumes a fem. sing. suffix on the verb, following a variant Heb. reading and the evidence of Sam. and LXX.

13.   Cf. 7:3; in the commentary on that verse, however, it was argued that the particular prohibition was against the forging of treaties by means of marriage. Furthermore, the context of 7:3 indicates a war against the nearer nations, not the more distant enemies (20:13-15), for whom different regulations applied.

14.   Farbridge suggests that the acts were intended to "disguise" the woman, in order to show that she had been translated from one religion to another; *Studies in Biblical and Semitic Symbolism,* p. 238.

of this month was the man to be permitted to consummate the marriage.

14 A contingency clause is added at the end of the basic statement of the law. If, after the consummation of the marriage, it was not successful (from the husband's point of view), because of some kind of incompatibility, then the husband could divorce[15] the woman. The woman, however, was to have certain rights; she was free to go *where she wants* (lit. "according to her desire"). The man was not free to sell her as a slave for money, or to *treat her as merchandise;*[16] that is, she could not be given in exchange for some other person or goods. The rights given to the woman seem to be designed as some sort of compensation for the losses incurred by the marriage and subsequent divorce.

(c) Law relating to wives and first-born sons (vv. 15-17)

> 15 *If a man has two wives, the one loved and the other hated, and both the loved and the hated have borne him sons, but the first-born son belongs to the hated wife;*
> 16 *then on the day that he assigns to his sons as an inheritance that which he possesses, he may not treat the son of the loved wife as the first-born, in preference to the son of the hated wife, the real first-born son.*
> 17 *But he shall recognize the first-born, the son of the hated wife, by giving him a double share of all that he has, for he is the first issue of his procreative power; the right of the first-born belongs to him.*

Although monogamy was the normal form of marriage, polygamy was permitted in Hebrew law, though the latter tended to be subject to a variety of problems, as these verses and many others make clear.[17] It may be significant that this section occurs in a context containing several references to war (20:1-20; 21:10-14). In time of war, there would be a shortage of men through death in battle, and polygamy was one way of dealing with what could become an acute social problem.[18] Note, too, that polygamy was apparently a very ancient practice in the Near East (Gen. 4:19).

15 The situation imagined in this passage is similar to that already known from earlier times in the life of Jacob (Gen. 29:30).

---

15. The Piel of the verb *shālaḥ* (here translated "let go") may have the technical sense of "divorce"; see 22:19, 29.

16. The precise meaning of the verb (Hithp. of *'āmar*), translated by "treat as merchandise," is uncertain; it is used in the OT only here and in 24:7. For the translation given here, see A. R. Hulst, *OT Translation Problems,* p. 16; M. David, *"Hit'āmēr* (Deut. 21:14; 24:7)," *VT* 1 (1951), pp. 219-221. See also the use of *tgr* in the Targum.

17. For further discussion, see R. de Vaux, *Ancient Israel,* pp. 24-26.

18. A similar situation existed in earliest Islam; see, e.g., *Quran* 4:3 and the discussion in W. Montgomery Watt, *Muhammad, Prophet and Statesman* (1964), pp. 151-55.

Thus it is clear that the law here is not intended to initiate certain rights for the first-born, but it is designed to safeguard rights already belonging to them. The language of the verse conceives a situation of the most extreme type, one wife being loved and the other hated, in order to anticipate thereby all potential situations, many of which might be expected to be less acute.

16 *The day that he assigns to his sons . . .* — since the father would be alive, the action is equivalent to making a will, in which would be designated the portions of property that would accrue to the sons following the death of the father. In this situation, the father is forbidden to follow his natural inclination, which would be to show preference to the eldest son of his beloved wife, even though the son of the hated wife was the first-born (to him) and as such had particular legal rights.

17 The law safeguarded the rights of the first-born son, despite the father's feelings for his mother, to receive a *double share*,[19] for regardless of the father's feelings, he was *the first issue* (lit. "the first") *of his procreative power.*[20]

(d) A Rebellious Son (vv. 18-21)

> 18 *If a man has a rebellious and refractory son, who will not listen to the voice of his father or the voice of his mother, and they admonish him, but he does not listen to them,*
> 19 *then his father and his mother shall take hold of him and take him to the elders of his city, at the gates of his place of residence.*
> 20 *And they shall say to the elders of his city: This son of ours is rebellious and refractory. He will not listen to our voice. He is a glutton and a drunkard.*
> 21 *Then all the men of his city shall stone him with stones and he shall die. And you shall purge out the evil from your midst, and all Israel shall hear and shall fear.*

The legislation contained in these verses provides details for the procedure to follow in particular cases involving parents and children; the general law covering this topic is the fifth commandment, prohibiting the dishonoring of parents by their offspring.[21] As has been suggested in the commentary on the fifth commandment, the kind of behavior that is envisaged in this legislation would be of a very serious nature; whatever the explicit form of that behavior, its implicit threat would be against the security and continuity of the cove-

---

19. The Heb. idiom is "mouth of two." A double portion for the first-born occurs also in Middle Assyrian Law; see *ANET*, p. 185 (B,1).
20. On the translation *procreative power* for Heb. *'ōnô*, see G. Fohrer, "Twofold Aspects of Hebrew Words," in P. R. Ackroyd and B. Lindars, eds., *Words and Meanings*, p. 99. The more general sense is "strength."
21. 5:16. For similar legislation, see Exod. 21:15, 17 (= Lev. 20:9).

nant community of God. As such, it was to be dealt with firmly and severely. The context of the behavior in the family unit, however, would have made it very difficult for parents to prosecute their own children, knowing that the result of such prosecution would be a sentence of death. Perhaps for this reason, the dishonoring of parents comes under the curse of God (see 27:16 and commentary), so that even without formal prosecution, those guilty of such a crime would experience the wrath of God.

18 First, an example of the situation is given. The son is guilty of wrongdoing on two counts: (a) he is *rebellious and refractory,* and though the nature of the rebellion is not specified, it clearly involves the dishonoring of his parents (and, by implication, the dishonoring of God); (b) even after warning and admonishment, in which the consequences of his behavior would be explained, the son still refuses to listen to his parents. In such a situation there would appear to be no hope that the son would amend his ways.

19 The responsibility would then fall upon the parents to prosecute their son and take him to the elders, who were responsible for law in the local community and who performed their legal function *at the gates.*[22]

20 Then the parents would state their case to the elders, identifying themselves as the ones responsible for the youth (*this son of ours*). They stated his crime (*he will not listen to our voice*) and indicated that his character was not befitting a member of the covenant community of God: *he is a glutton and a drunkard.* The latter words do not specify the crime, but indicate, by way of example, the kind of life that has resulted from disobedience to parental authority. The crime, in other words, is disobedience, but the result of the crime is the dissolution of a proper style of life.

21 The verses provide a very compact description of the legal process, so that not all the details are provided. When the parents had delivered their son and given their evidence, the case would be heard in the proper manner, and after due deliberation, judgment would be passed; at this point, further details are provided. *All the men of his city* would participate in the execution by stoning.[23] Here, the allocation of responsibility within the community is made clear. The parents had a responsibility to prosecute their son for the offense in question; they could not take the law into their hands, however. Judgment would then be carried out by the men of the city. The reason for the men carrying out the judgment lies in the nature of the crime; although it took place initially within the sphere of the family, the crime was

22. Cf. *CTA* 17.V.4-8; in the Aqhat Legend, Danel sat by the gates to execute judgment.
23. On death by stoning, see 13:9-10.

one affecting the whole community of God. Therefore it was to be punished by representatives of that larger community. *And you shall purge out the evil* — see also v. 9.

(e) A Hanged Man (vv. 22-23)

> 22 *And if there is a man who has committed a crime incurring the death penalty and he is put to death, and you hang him on a tree,*
> 23 *his body shall not remain overnight on the tree, but you shall be careful to bury it on that same day, for a hanged man is an object accursed of God; and you shall not pollute your land, which the Lord your God is about to give to you as an inheritance.*

22 The sequence in this verse indicates that hanging was not a method of execution, but something that was done after the death of a criminal, on the same day. When the man was dead, he would be hanged on a *tree* or a "wooden post"[24] of some kind; the gruesome sight would then serve as a warning to the population of the results of breaking those laws which were punishable by death. Although the practice of hanging bodies on trees was employed in military operations,[25] the context here indicates its use with those executed for breaking certain laws of the covenant community. The legislation, however, does not initiate the practice, which seems to be very ancient, but it only imposes certain limitations on the use of the practice.

23 The limitation imposed on the practice was that the body was to be removed from the tree or wooden post at sunset, and then it was to be buried. To have left the body hanging would have been to *pollute* the land, not only literally (through the decay of the body in a warm climate), but symbolically, for the land belonged to God and would be given to Israel by him.

An object accursed[26] *of God.* The body was not *accursed of God* (or lit. "curse of God") because it was hanging on a tree; it was hanging on a tree because it was accursed of God. And the body was not accursed of God simply because it was dead (for all men die), but it was accursed because of the reason for the death. To break the law of God and live as though he did not matter or exist, was in effect to curse him; and he who cursed God would be accursed of God. To break the law of God and incur thereby the penalty of death, was to

---

24. The word *'ēts* is used both for "tree" and "wood"; see the commentary on 16:21.
25. Thus the practice can be seen, e.g., in Josh. 8:29; 10:26-27; the reason for hanging in those texts, however, is not the same as that envisaged in the passage under discussion. For a similar practice among the Assyrians in time of war, see T. Fish, *BJRL* 23 (1939), p. 397.
26. Or perhaps the words should be rendered "repudiation of God"; see the discussion in A. Phillips, *Ancient Israel's Criminal Law*, pp. 25f.

die the worst possible kind of death, for the means of death was a formal and terminal separation from the community of God's people. Hence the use of this verse in Paul's Epistle to the Galatians is very forceful. Christ took upon himself the curse of the law, the penalty of death, thereby redeeming us from the curse of the law.[27] The manner of his death, crucifixion, symbolized dramatically the meaning of his death. His separation from the family of God made possible our admission to the family of God, because the curse of the broken law — which would have permanently barred admission — had been removed.

11. MISCELLANEOUS LAWS AND THE REGULATION OF SEXUAL BEHAVIOR (22:1–23:1 [Eng. 22:1-30])

(a) The Assistance to Be Given a Neighbor (vv. 1-4)

1 You shall not see your brother's ox or his sheep going astray, and then take no notice of them. You shall be careful to return them to your brother.

2 And if your brother does not live near you, or you do not know him, then you shall take it to your house, and it shall remain with you until your brother comes looking for it, and you will return it to him.

3 And you shall do the same with his ass, and you shall do the same with his garment, and you shall do the same with all your brother's lost property, which he loses and you find. You are not to take no notice of them.

4 You shall not see your brother's ass or his ox lying on the road, and then take no notice of them. You shall be careful to help him lift them up.

The law, in the address of Moses, not only contains prohibitions, but also requires positive action on the part of the Israelites in particular circumstances. Here, it is prescribed that an Israelite offer assistance to his fellow Israelite (brother[1]); such assistance would require personal effort and initiative. The law counters a natural human tendency not to get involved or not to go out of one's way to help another. Two categories of assistance are noted: (a) the restoration of lost property (vv. 1-3); (b) direct aid to a neighbor in a difficult circumstance (v. 4). The principle underlying the legislation is the same in both instances.[2]

27. Gal. 3:13. See also the discussion at Deut. 27:26.

1. It is not a blood-brother that is meant, but a brother within the covenant family of God. Hence (v. 2), it is quite possible not to know a brother.

2. For a shorter statement of the law, see Exod. 23:4-5. In the Law Code of Hammurabi, §§ 9-12 deal with lost property (ANET, p. 166), but they do not form a precise parallel to the verses in Deuteronomy. They envisage a situation in which theft of lost property has taken place, and the possibility of a "fence," or middle man, who has sold the lost property for personal gain.

1-3   A man may see his neighbor's ox or sheep going astray; the animals are noted simply by way of example, an ox or an ass being mentioned in Exod. 23:4. The lost animal was to be returned to its proper owner, unless the owner lived at a distance from the finder, or was unknown to him, in which case he was responsible to come and look for his property. The law was to apply to all lost property, not only the more valuable possessions such as domestic animals. The principle expressed by the popular expression, "finders-keepers," did not apply, but the procedure noted in v. 2 indicates that if property was found, the owner of which was unknown, and if a claim was not made for it, then presumably the lost property would remain in the keeping of the finder.

The expression *take no notice* is a translation of the Hebrew verb *hiṭ'allēm,* which means literally "to hide oneself." The verb gives a good indication of the spirit of the Hebrew law. Unlike Babylonian law (see n. 2), it is not concerned primarily with a criminal act such as the illegal appropriation of lost property; rather, it deals with shouldering responsibility as a member of the covenant community. A man was not to "hide himself" from responsibility, or to take no notice of the happenings around him that required some positive action on his part.

4   The second category specifies that direct help was to be given to a neighbor in a situation of crisis. If a beast of burden was lying on the road, a man was to help his neighbor get the animal back on its feet. The animal would be heavily laden with baggage, and therefore it would not be able to get up by itself and it would be too heavy for one man.[3] A difficult task would thus be made much easier with the assistance that was to be offered by a fellow Israelite.

(b) Transvestism (v. 5)

> 5 *A woman shall not wear man's things, and a man shall not put on a woman's garment, for anyone doing these things is an abomination to the Lord your God.*

This short verse does not refer simply to fashions or styles of dressing, as the warning contained in the final clause makes clear. It refers at first reading to the practice of transvestism, a deviant form of sexual behavior, though this definition must be qualified, as below. *Man's things* — the Hebrew does not refer specifically to male clothing, but to things pertaining to the male. The words would thus include not only clothing, but ornaments, weapons, etc., normally associated with men. In the second clause, women's clothing is specified explicitly.

---

3. For examples of the principle in action in more recent times, see G. A. Smith, *The Book of Deuteronomy,* p. 260.

While transvestism may appear to be a relatively harmless deviation, either or both of two aspects may underlie the present legislation. First, transvestism tends to be associated with certain forms of homosexuality; second, in the ancient world, it is probable that transvestite practices were associated with the cults of certain deities.[4] In either or both of these instances, the practice of transvestism would be *an abomination to the Lord your God.* In Lev. 18:22 and 20:13, homosexual behayior is described as an *abomination.* There is less evidence to establish the association of transvestism with foreign cults in the external sources,[5] though a collection of Assyrian Wisdom texts may provide indirect evidence.[6] If transvestism was indeed associated with foreign religious practices, it should be noted that things associated with foreign religions are described as an *abomination* in Deuteronomy (see 7:25 and 18:12).

(c) Birds in the Nest (vv. 6-7)

> 6 *If by chance you come across a bird's nest in the road, in any tree, or on the ground, containing young birds or eggs, and the mother bird is brooding over the young birds or over the eggs, you shall not take the mother bird with the young ones.*
> 7 *You shall take care to release the mother bird, but you may take the young ones for yourself, in order that it may go well for you and you may prolong your life.*

This legislation, which is peculiar to Deuteronomy, is stated quite concisely, so that the meaning is no longer clear to the modern reader, though it would have been in its original context. Among the varieties of interpretation that have been suggested, it is often stated that the legislation reflects some kind of humanitarian concern for the parental relationship in the animal world. It is not clear, however, how taking young birds, but releasing the mother, can be considered as a humanitarian act.

It is more likely that the law has to do with the conservation of food supplies. The Israelites were permitted to eat certain clean birds (14:11); the obvious reason for taking the young birds (v. 7) would be in order to provide food for the family. Since the birds in question would not be domesticated fowls, this source of food would be of a

---

4. On both these points, see C. Allen, *A Textbook of Psychosexual Disorders* (1962), pp. 243-46.
5. Driver (*Deuteronomy*, p. 250) provides some detailed evidence of sources, most of which, however, come from the Greco-Roman period in the Near East. Note the comment of C. Allen, *op. cit.,* p. 243: "Again, in some religions it has been the custom for priests to assume a quasi-female or even completely female garb, and . . . this usually occurred when the deity was a goddess rather than a god."
6. See W. G. Lambert, *Babylonian Wisdom Literature* (1960), pp. 226, 230. It is debatable, however, whether the passage in question refers to transvestism or homosexual practice.

casual or accidental nature (v. 6a). Given this context, the provisions of the law may become clearer. If a nest was found with a mother bird and eggs or young birds in it, the natural thing to do would be to take all of them, thereby acquiring more food. The effect of such action, however, would be bad; in commercial language, it would be exchanging a long-term profit for an immediate gain. To take and kill the mother would be to terminate a potential future supply of food. To take the mother and leave the others would not be possible, for they would not be able to survive without the mother. Thus by taking the young birds (or eggs), but letting the mother go, food was acquired without the source of food for the future being cut off. The legislation thus has something in common with modern conservation laws. The large-scale killing of any species can lead to a serious diminution in its numbers and to eventual extinction.

(d) A Safety Precaution in House Building (v. 8)

> 8 *When you build a new house, then you shall make a parapet for your roof, so that you do not bring bloodguilt on your house, if someone should fall from it.*

The roof of a house would be used for many purposes, such as sleeping (in summertime), a number of household chores, and entertaining.[7] Because of this regular use, a parapet was to be built round the outside of the roof area, to act as a retaining wall for safety purposes. Although the construction of such a parapet would involve additional expense and time, it was to be required by law.

If an accident occurred and someone fell from the roof, either killing or injuring himself, the householder could not be held responsible if his house had a parapet (and the accident would be less likely to happen in the first place!). Without a parapet, however, the householder could be held liable for manslaughter or damages, since failure to provide the required safety precaution amounted in law to criminal neglect. Apart from the legal implications of the verse, however, the legislation reflects a concern for the value and protection of human life. Safety precautions were to be taken in order to protect life, which was the gift of God; as in vv. 6-7, the law reflects what we sometimes consider to be a very modern concern.

(e) Prohibition of Certain Mixtures (vv. 9-11)

> 9 *You shall not sow your vineyard with two different kinds of seeds, lest you forfeit the full yield, both the seed which you sow and the produce of the vineyard.*

---

7. See also J. Gray, *Archaeology and the OT World*, p. 170. "To judge from modern Arab custom, the roof was the place of entertainment, and in view of possible conviviality it was a wise provision which prescribed a parapet on the roof."

10 *You shall not plow with an ox and an ass together.*
11 *You shall not wear mixed material, wool and linen woven together.*

The reason (or reasons) underlying this legislation are no longer clear to the modern reader. The legislation may reflect a theological concern, namely, in maintaining the distinctions of the created order.[8] The laws may combat certain practices employed in other countries, which may have had magical associations.[9] Or there may have been some pragmatic or utilitarian concern intended by the legislation. The three laws are grouped together because they all contain prohibitions against mixing, but each law may have a particular intent or different reason lying behind it.[10]

9 *Lest you forfeit* — lit. "lest you make sacred, set apart." The sense seems to be that a breach of the law would result in the whole yield of the vineyard being turned over to God's sanctuary, as if it were something captured from an enemy in war.[11] The law would prohibit customs such as planting vegetables in a vineyard between the rows of vines, or perhaps mixing vines and other fruit trees in the vineyard. It is possible that the Hebrew law reflects a certain antipathy toward Egyptian practice. There are a number of Egyptian paintings, from Eighteenth and Nineteenth Dynasty tombs, showing gardens and orchards in which various types of fruit-bearing trees are growing side by side.[12]

10 It should be noted that of the two animals mentioned here, the ox was "clean," but the ass was "unclean," in terms of the dietary laws prescribed earlier in Deuteronomy (14:1-8).

11 Again, although the precise reason for the prohibition is uncertain, it may have been related to some custom practiced in Egypt. The word *sha'aṭnēz*, which is not Hebrew, appears to be a word taken over from Egyptian;[13] this may indicate that the reason for the prohibition is to be found in Egypt. It may be noted that during the Eighteenth Dynasty, various complicated types of pattern weaves were being introduced in Egypt, perhaps from Syria,[14] and they may therefore have had reprehensible associations (no longer known) for the Israelites.

8. See, e.g., Keil and Delitzsch, *The Pentateuch*, p. 410.
9. See, e.g., Buis and Leclercq, *Le Deutéronome*, p. 151.
10. For similar legislation, see Lev. 19:19.
11. See Josh. 6:18-19, and G. A. Smith, *The Book of Deuteronomy*, p. 262.
12. See K. Michalowski, *Art of Ancient Egypt*. The plate on the front endpaper, from the tomb of Rekhmira in Thebes, shows a garden scene in which different types of fruit-bearing trees grow around the perimeter of a pond. Plate 20 (p. 53) portrays a more agricultural scene, with different types of fruit trees growing in a field side by side.
13. Suggested by W. F. Albright; see T. O. Lambdin, "Egyptian Loan Words in the OT," *Journal of the American Oriental Society* 73 (1953), pp. 145-155.
14. J. R. Harris, ed., *The Legacy of Egypt²*, p. 92.

(f) Tassels (12)

12 *You shall make tassels for yourself at the four corners of your cloak, with which you cover yourself.*

After the negative proscription concerning clothing material (v. 11) a positive prescription is now added. *Tassels* (lit. "twisted threads") are to be prepared and attached to the four corners of the cloak, *with which you cover yourself.*[15] The reason is not stated in this verse, but it is given in the fuller legislation on the topic in Num. 15:37-41. The tassels served to remind the people of all the commandments of the Lord, and thus, in remembering, they were to obey them and not go their own ways. By attaching the tassels to the garment that was used the most frequently (see n. 15), the people would be reminded of the law of God continually. If this law is placed after that contained in v. 11 for a specific reason, then perhaps it is that the *mixed material* in that verse might have reminded the people of other religious practices (from Egypt), contrary to the law of their God.

(g) Allegations Concerning the Virginity of a Newly Married Wife (vv. 13-21)

13 *If a man takes a wife and goes in to her, and then he hates her,*

14 *and he makes baseless charges against her and brings her a bad name, by saying: I took this woman and when I came near to her, I did not find in her the signs of virginity;*

15 *then the father of the young woman, together with her mother, shall take and bring out the young woman's tokens of virginity to the elders of the city at the gate,*

16 *and the father of the young woman shall say to the elders: I gave my daughter to this man for a wife, but he hated her.*

17 *And now he has made baseless charges, claiming: "I did not find signs of virginity in your daughter," but these are my daughter's tokens of virginity. Then they shall spread out the garment before the elders of the city.*

18 *And the elders of that city shall take the man and they shall chastise him,*

19 *and they shall fine him one hundred pieces of silver, and he shall pay the father of the young woman, because he has brought a bad name on an Israelite virgin. And she shall be his wife and he may not divorce her all his days.*

20 *But if this charge was true — tokens of virginity were not found for the young woman —*

21 *then they shall bring out the young woman to the door of her father's house, and the men of her city shall stone her with stones, and she shall die, for she has acted disgracefully in Israel, by*

---

15.   The cloak served both as a coat for daytime use and as a blanket for overnight covering.

committing fornication in her father's house. And you shall purge out the evil from your midst.

Two situations are in view in this legislation, both of which relate to the virginity of a new bride. In the first situation, a man and a woman are married; for some unspecified reason, the man comes to hate the woman. In an attempt to get rid of her, he charges her — falsely — with premarital intercourse with another man and with not being a virgin at the time of the wedding. Because the charge is false, and is discovered to be so, the man is punished and fined. The second situation, stated briefly, concerns the eventuality that the man's charges are true, and it states the penalty to apply to the woman.

13 Although the time sequence is not clearly specified, it is probable that the action stated in the last clause (*he hates her*) follows immediately upon the consummation of the marriage. Likewise, the reason for the hate is not made explicit, though it could have been related to some factor unknown before the wedding, such as lack of sexual compatibility.

14 The man then lays public charges against the woman; the charges have no foundation in fact, and therefore they bring the woman a bad name. The specific charge is that the man did not find the woman to be a virgin at the time of the consummation of the marriage.

15 When such charges were made, the legal responsibility for defending the young woman rested on her parents. They were responsible because they had given their daughter to the man in marriage, and by that act they had indicated that the girl was qualified for marriage (i.e., a virgin). The parents of the woman took their case to the elders of the city, to whom, it may be assumed, the man made his initial charge (v. 14); the role of the parents was to present a proper defense for their daughter against the charges that had been laid. The legal case was conducted at the *gate* of the city, the normal place for such transactions (see 21:19 and commentary). The parents took with them to the defense of their daughter her *tokens of virginity*.[16]

16-17 The father made spoken response to the charges, first identifying himself as the father who had given his daughter in marriage; then he repudiated the charges and provided his evidence, which was exhibited to the court. The evidence consisted of his daughter's tokens of virginity; a token would have been a sheet or garment marked with blood, coming from the marriage chamber of

---

16. The word *bᵉṯûlîm*, rendered here by "tokens of virginity," is the same word translated "signs of virginity" in v. 14. The husband's evidence would be the physical evidence known only to him and his wife (hence "signs"), whereas the evidence of the parents would be the bloodstained "token" of the wedding night. Cf. *TDOT* II, p. 342 (Tsevat).

the daughter on the wedding night. The blood would be evidence that, at the time of the consummation of the marriage, the young woman had been a virgin.

18-19 The full proceedings of the court are not described. However, when it was determined in this instance that the man was guilty of laying false charges, he was to be punished. There was a double punishment, corporal and financial. *They shall chastise him* — the Hebrew word (*yissēr*) implies corporal punishment, such as a flogging. Further, he was fined a hundred pieces of silver, presumably shekels, which were paid to the father as damages, in recompense for the injury to the family incurred by the baseless and slanderous charges. The last clause seems unfair to the woman in the circumstances (*he may not divorce her . . .*), but prevented the man from achieving in the end what he had set out to do in the first place.[17]

20-21 If the charges made by the husband were shown in the court case to be true, then the woman would be executed by stoning (cf. 13:9) outside the father's house.[18] The location of the execution pointed to the shame resting on the family. Although there is no suggestion that the father knew of his daughter's offense (and therefore he was not guilty of deliberate misrepresentation in giving his daughter to the man in marriage), nevertheless, as head of the household, he was in part responsible for his daughter's behavior. *By committing fornication in her father's house* — the sense is not that the act was done literally in the house (though it could have been), but that the woman was guilty of fornication while still resident in the family home, before her marriage. Her act was tantamount to making the family home a "house of ill-repute." The severe punishment appointed for the woman was not only for the sin of fornication, but for misrepresenting herself, both to the father and the bridegroom, as a virgin. Just as Israel's honor was at stake in the vindication of an innocent woman (v. 19), so too an evil act brought discredit and disgrace on all Israel (v. 21). To maintain the purity of the covenant community of God, the people were to *purge out the evil* (cf. 21:21) from their midst.

(h) Adultery and Rape (22:22–23:1 [Eng. 22:22-30])

> 22 *If a man is found lying with a woman, another man's wife, then the two of them shall die, the man lying with the woman and the woman too. And you shall purge out the evil from Israel.*

---

17. Note, too, that the prohibition of divorce in this instance protected the legal rights of inheritance belonging to the woman and her first-born child. The law stated in 21:15-17 (protecting the legal rights of a "hated wife") should be read alongside the law under discussion.
18. John Gray has noted that among the Bedouin, in more recent times, the father has the right of life and death of an offending daughter; *The Legacy of Canaan*[2], p. 241 (n.).

23 *If there should be a young woman, a virgin who is betrothed to a man, and a man finds her in the city and lies with her,*
24 *then you shall take the two of them out to the gate of that city, and you shall stone them with stones and they shall die — the young woman on the basis that she did not cry for help in the city, and the man on the basis that he humiliated his neighbor's wife. And you shall purge out the evil from your midst.*
25 *But if it is in the countryside that the man finds the betrothed young woman, and the man seizes her and lies with her, then only the man who lay with her shall die;*
26 *but you shall not do anything to the young woman; the young woman has not committed a capital crime, for as when a man rises against his neighbor and murders him, so it is in this case,*
27 *for he found her in the countryside; the betrothed young woman cried for help, but there was no one to rescue her.*
28 *If a man finds a young woman, a virgin who is not betrothed, and he takes hold of her and lies with her, and they are found,*
29 *then the man who lay with her shall give to the father of the young woman fifty pieces of silver, and she shall be his wife, because he humiliated her. He may not divorce her all his days.*
23:1 *A man shall not take his father's wife and he shall not uncover his father's skirt.*

After the legislation concerning the virginity of a newly married woman, there now follows a series of laws relating to various types of illicit sexual behavior. The general principle underlying the whole series is expressed in the seventh commandment, the prohibition of adultery (5:18), and it is with the matter of adultery that the series begins.

22 (i) Adultery;[19] for further details, see the commentary on 5:18. The crime of adultery was to be punished by death. Both parties were put to death, since the crime involved consent from both.

23-24 (ii) The seduction of a betrothed woman.[20] The betrothed (but not yet married) woman is treated under the law as if she were married. The reason for this is clear when it is remembered that the crime consists not only in the act, but also in the lack of faithfulness signified by the act. Both the married woman and the betrothed woman were committed to a particular relationship with a man; the crime involved breaking that relationship through an unfaithful act. Although rape could take place in the city, the case in question is not an example of rape, for if the woman had cried out for help, help

19. See also Lev. 18:20; 20:10; Code of Hammurabi, § 129 (*ANET*, p. 171); Middle Assyrian Law, A, 13-14 (*ANET*, p. 181).
20. See the Hittite Laws, § 197 (*ANET*, p. 196); see also Middle Assyrian Law, A, 12 (*ANET*, p. 181), describing a case of rape in the city in which there was no response to the cry for help.

would have come. Because there was no evidence that the woman had called for help, it could be assumed that she had consented to the advances of the man. Thus, as in the case of adultery, both parties were to be executed by stoning.

25-27 (iii) The rape of a betrothed woman in the countryside.[21] Several features distinguish this case from (ii) above. First, the crime takes place in the countryside; thus although the woman cries for help, there is no one available or nearby to come to her help. Second, it is clear that the man employs force. In case (ii), a man "finds" the woman, then "lies" with her; in this instance, the man "finds" her and "seizes" her (v. 25), then "lies" with her. Though both parties had consented in case (ii), the woman had not consented in this case and therefore she was not guilty of any crime. Only the man was to be executed for the crime of rape. (As in a murder case, the woman was an unwilling victim of an attack; she suffered as a result of that attack, but was in no sense culpable.)

28-29 (iv) The rape of a single woman.[22] The man uses force on the woman, who is a virgin and is not betrothed to a man; the two are discovered while the crime is being committed. In this case, the man must pay damages to the father, in the amount of fifty pieces (shekels) of silver, and he must marry the woman. The penalty is less severe than in the case of adultery with a married woman or a betrothed woman, since this crime does not involve a breach in a relationship in the sense that it does with adultery. By insisting that the man marry the woman, the law protected the woman and any child that might be born as a result of the union. The woman was protected further by the law in that the man was prohibited from divorcing her.

23:1 (v) Adultery with the father's wife.[23] The law probably specifies that a man may not have sexual relationships with his stepmother, rather than his real mother. For further discussion of the language and expression used in this verse, see the commentary on 27:20, where it is noted that this crime comes under the curse of God.

12. MISCELLANEOUS LAWS (23:2-26 [Eng. 23:1-25])

(a) Admission to the Assembly of the Lord (vv. 2-9)

> 2 *One whose testicles are crushed or whose male organ is cut off shall not enter the assembly of the Lord.*
> 3 *A bastard shall not enter the assembly of the Lord; even to the tenth generation, his descendants shall not enter the assembly of the Lord.*

21. See the Code of Hammurabi, § 130 (*ANET*, p. 171); the Laws of Eshnunna, § 26 (*ANET*, p. 162).
22. See Exod. 22:16-17; Middle Assyrian Law, § 55 (*ANET*, p. 185).
23. See Lev. 18:8; 20:11.

4 *An Ammonite or a Moabite shall not enter the assembly of the Lord; even to the tenth generation, their descendants shall not enter the assembly of the Lord for ever,*

5 *on the basis that they did not come out to meet you on the road with bread and water when you came out from Egypt; and that they hired against you Balaam son of Beor, from Pethor, Mesopotamia, to curse you.*

6 *But the Lord your God did not want to listen to Balaam, and on your behalf, the Lord your God converted the curse into a blessing, for the Lord your God loved you.*

7 *You shall not seek their peace or their friendship all your days, for ever.*

8 *You shall not abominate an Edomite, for he is your brother. You shall not abominate an Egyptian, for you were a resident alien in his land.*

9 *Children that are born to them of the third generation may enter the assembly of the Lord.*

The common theme running through the laws contained in this section[1] is the question of admission to the *assembly of the Lord* (vv. 2, 3, 4, 9). The *assembly* (*qāhāl*) of the Lord refers to the covenant people of God, particularly when they are gathered in his presence. Although the normal use of the noun (and the related verb) in Deuteronomy appears in a context dealing with Horeb/Sinai,[2] here the word has general reference to Israel as a worshipping community.[3] Thus to *enter the assembly of the Lord* would indicate a person who became a true Israelite and who therefore shared in the worship of the Lord. The expression is somewhat narrower in its intent than *Israel,* taken as a whole, for there would be resident aliens and others who, though a part of the community,[4] were nevertheless not full members of it. Various categories of people were either to be barred permanently from the community of the Lord, or to be admitted under certain specified conditions.

(i) A man who had been emasculated was not to be granted admission to the assembly of the Lord. This prohibition is probably not intended to bar from the community those whose state of emascu-

1. The style and contents of this section have given rise to a number of hypotheses about its composition and the dates reflected by the component parts. For particular studies, see K. Galling, "Das Gemeindegesetz in Deuteronomium 23," in *Festschrift Alfred Bertholet* (1950), pp. 176-191; S. Mowinckel, "Zu Deuteronomium 23:2-9," *Acta Orientalia* 1 (1923), pp. 81-104; G. von Rad, *Deuteronomy,* pp. 145f. The main difficulties will be examined in the commentary and notes that follow.
2. See 4:10; 5:22; 9:10; 10:4; 18:16.
3. The LXX translates *qāhāl* by *ekklēsia;* the same Greek word is used in the NT to designate a "congregation" or "church," not in the sense of a building, but a group of people who together worship God.
4. On the love and protection to be given resident aliens in the community, see 1:16; 10:18-19.

lation had been brought on by accident or illness.⁵ "The self-castrated, who carry on their bodies the sign of their recognition of another god, shall not enter the congregation."⁶

(ii) A bastard (*mamzēr*) was not to be granted admission to the assembly of the Lord (v. 3). The term *mamzēr* is used only twice in the OT and its specific sense is uncertain (see also Zech. 9:6). It may refer to children who were born as a result of incestuous relationships.⁷ It is possible, however, that something more specific is intended; the term *mamzēr* might refer to children born to cult-prostitutes (see vv. 18-19, below).⁸ In this case, the children would have been conceived and born in an environment directly related to the cult of a foreign religion, and therefore would be an abomination in the eyes of the Israelites and God. As such, they could not enter the assembly of the Lord.

(iii) Ammonites and Moabites are prohibited permanently from access to the assembly of the Lord (vv. 4-7). Their permanent exclusion is given emphasis in v. 4: *to the tenth generation . . . for ever.*⁹ The two principal subordinate clauses in v. 5 refer to the Ammonites and Moabites respectively,¹⁰ rather than to the two of them together. The Ammonites are criticized for not having freely offered hospitality (*bread and water*) to the Israelites; the Moabites are criticized for their attempt to use Balaam to bring down the curse of God on the Israelites (see Num. 22–24). What is not mentioned, but may be implied, is that in Hebrew tradition both the Moabites and the Ammonites were believed to be descendants of the incestuous relationships between Lot and his two daughters (Gen. 19:30-38). This point may suggest a link between the prohibition in these verses and that contained in v. 3. A further reason for the prohibition of the Moabites emerges from the Balaam incident.¹¹ The Moabites had

5.   Thus, in Isa. 56:3-5, the eunuch (*sārîs*) is by no means cut off from the blessing of God; if the castration was not self-imposed, it implied nothing concerning a man's religious commitment.
6.   A. C. Welch, *The Code of Deuteronomy* (1924), p. 200. See also H. W. F. Saggs, *The Greatness That Was Babylon*, p. 332; Saggs notes classes of temple personnel in Mesopotamia (*Kurgarru* and *Assinnu*), probably eunuchs, who seem to have participated, in female clothing, in cultic performances relating to Ishtar.
7.   Note that the provision that a man should be required to marry a single woman whom he had raped (22:29) prevented a child being born out of wedlock as a result of the rape.
8.   In support of this suggestion, the following etymology is suggested: *mamzēr* < *manzēr* (Hiph. participle of *nzr*, "dedicate, consecrate"). The *mamzēr* would thus be the child "dedicated" to a foreign god, by reason of its conception during some kind of temple fertility ritual.
9.   Keil and Delitzsch (*The Pentateuch*, p. 414) note that "ten" in vv. 3, 4 "is the number of complete exclusion."
10.   See also the discussion of Ammonites and Moabites in 2:9-25, and commentary.
11.   It is possible, though not implied elsewhere, that the Ammonites conspired with the Moabites in the Balaam incident, and hence both would have come under censure.

attempted to bring a curse on the people of God through the mediacy of Balaam; their attempt had been frustrated because of the Lord's love for his people, which had changed the curse into a blessing (v. 6). However, the Moabite attempt would have a "boomerang" effect, for in attempting to bring a curse on the people of God, they could only succeed in bringing God's curse upon themselves (see Gen. 12:3). As a people cursed by God, they could not be admitted to the assembly of the Lord.

The Israelites were also forbidden to negotiate political treaties with Ammon and Moab. The language employed in v. 7 (*peace, friendship*) reflects directly the terminology of Near Eastern political treaties.[12]

(iv) Edomites and Egyptians were not to be abominated, and could be granted access to the assembly of the Lord in the course of time (vv. 8-9). The verb *abominate* indicates an attitude directly opposite to the loving kindness (*ḥeseḏ*) to be expressed and experienced within the covenant community.[13] Neither Edomites nor Egyptians were to be abominated, but they were to be treated with some respect. The Edomite was a *brother* of the Israelite; according to Hebrew tradition, the Edomites were descendants of Edom/Esau.[14] The sojourn in Egypt, though in its latter days a time of hardship, had nevertheless been the period in which the growth toward Israel's nationhood had begun (26:5). Thus, for varying reasons, Edomites and Egyptians were to be treated differently from Ammonites and Moabites. If either Edomites or Egyptians took up residence in Israel, then the children of the third generation of immigrants could be granted admission to the assembly of the Lord. After the lapse of three generations, there would be no doubt that the Edomites and Egyptians resident in Israel were genuine in their desire to become full members of the worshipping family of God.

(b) Purity in the Military Camp (vv. 10-15)

> 10 *When you go out against your enemies and are in camp, then you must be on your guard against anything unclean.*
> 11 *If there is a man among you who is not clean because of what happens at night, then he shall go outside the camp; he shall not come into the midst of the camp,*

---

12. See W. L. Moran, "A Note on the Treaty Terminology of the Sefire Stelas," *JNES* 22 (1963), pp. 173-76; D. R. Hillers, "A Note on Some Treaty Terminology in the OT," *BASOR* 176 (1964), pp. 46f. On the use of *shālôm*, see also the commentary on 20:10.
13. Cf. N. Glueck, "Deuteronomy 23:8,9," in *Mordecai M. Kaplan Jubilee Volume* (1953), pp. 261f. However, Glueck's attempt to identify the *Edomites* with Judaized Idumeans and *Egyptians* with the Jews of Elephantine (in a later period in Israel's history) seems to be somewhat artificial and unnecessary.
14. See Gen. 36:1-19. See also Deut. 2:1-8.

12 *but toward the evening, he shall wash in water, and he may come in to the midst of the camp when the sun sets.*
13 *And you shall have a sign outside the camp, and you shall go to that place outside.*
14 *And you shall have a trowel among your implements, so that when you sit down outside, you may dig a hole with it; then you shall turn and you shall cover up your excrement.*
15 *For the Lord your God walks about in the midst of your camp, to deliver you and hand over your enemies before you; so your camp must be holy, so that he does not see something indecent in it and turn away from you.*

This further piece of military legislation relates to the standards of cleanliness to be maintained in the camp during a military campaign. The general principle is stated first (v. 10) and then is followed by two specific examples (vv. 11-12, 13-15), though no doubt the principle would extend beyond the two examples stated here. The legislation has to do with matters of hygiene, but hygiene was closely related to an important religious concern, namely, God's presence in the military camp (see v. 15). The Israelites were to be on their guard against anything *unclean (rā'); the adjective ra', depending on its context, may mean "bad, unpleasant, evil, unclean, etc." The context of v. 10 indicates the sense is *unclean,* both hygienically and ritually.

The first example relates to a man who is unclean *because of what happens at night* (v. 11). On the analogy of Lev. 15:16, these words are often interpreted as signifying the nocturnal, involuntary emission of semen; the Hebrew in this passage, however, is different and less specific than that of Lev. 15:16, and it is possible that something else is intended. The references may simply be to urinating in the camp at night, either involuntarily or else because a man was too lazy (or tired) to get up and go outside his camp. This interpretation seems to provide a more natural parallel to the legislation contained in vv. 13-15, and it would thus refer to a more typical and common occurrence in any military camp. A man who had behaved in this manner was to remain outside the camp the following day; toward evening he would wash himself, again for hygienic and ritual reasons, and he would be permitted to reenter the camp after sunset.

The second part of the legislation relates to the provision and maintenance of toilet facilities outside the camp. *You shall have a sign* . . .[15] — the sense is that the procedure described in v. 14 would take place in one locality, which would be indicated by a sign at the exit of the camp. *You shall have a trowel among your implements* — each man would not be required to have such a tool (*trowel,* "scraper"), but there should be one among the camping equipment, which would

15. Heb. *yād* (lit. "hand") may mean *sign;* see *BDB,* p. 390, and the NEB translation of this verse. A modern analogy may be seen in the use of signposts cut in the shape of a pointing hand.

be placed in the appropriate location when camp was pitched. In this way, human excrement would not be left lying on the surface of the ground, but would be covered up by means of the trowel in a hole dug for that purpose.[16] The hygienic reasons for such a procedure, especially in a warm climate, are obvious; the modern traveller, especially in the country areas of the Near East, is often aware of the absence of such a procedure.

The reason given for this legislation is to be found in the fact of God's presence in the military camp (v. 15).[17] *The Lord your God walks about in the midst of your camp* — although these words express what was a religious or spiritual reality to the Israelites, they may also allude to the presence of the ark in the camp, which visually symbolized God's presence.[18] Because of the presence of God, the camp was to be holy. There was to be nothing visible that was *indecent ('erwāh)* — the word indicates something that was "unseemly" or "unbecoming," without necessarily having any connotations of morality. Although the legislation made requirements of the people because of God's presence, conversely the purity in the camp would serve to remind the people of God's presence in their midst.

(c) Legislation Concerning Escaped Slaves (vv. 16-17)

> 16 *You shall not hand over a slave to his master, who has escaped from his master to you.*
> 17 *He shall remain with you, in your midst, in the place that he chooses in one of your settlements, wherever seems good to him. You shall not maltreat him.*

Legislation on *Hebrew* slaves is contained in 15:12-18, though in that passage there is no provision made for the way of dealing with an escaped Hebrew slave. In the present context, however, the legislation deals with a situation in which a slave escapes from his master in a foreign country and seeks refuge in Israelite territory; this meaning seems clear from the wording of v. 17.[19] In such a situation, the escaped slave was to be given sanctuary in Israel and was not to be returned to his master; he could live where he wished and would not be subject to maltreatment from the Israelites. This short portion of legislation is important for the indirect light it sheds on the political implications of the covenant or treaty between God and Israel. In both the parity and suzerainty treaties of the Near East, provisions were made for the extradition of various types of fugitives from one

---

16. Cf. Josephus *Wars* ii.147-49. Josephus describes a similar method of burying excrement which was employed among the Essenes.
17. See also 20:4.
18. Cf. G. J. Wenham, *TB* 22 (1971), p. 110.
19. Contra M. Weinfeld, *Deuteronomy and the Deuteronomic School*, p. 272, n. 5.

country and their return to their country of origin.[20] Israel, however, was not to have such extradition agreements, at least in relation to runaway slaves. To do so would be to imply a treaty with a foreign power, undermining thereby the total commitment required of Israel by the covenant with the Lord. The legislation thus not only provided sanctuary for runaway slaves (such as the Israelites had been themselves in their recent past), but also preserved the sanctity of the covenant relationship.

(d) Legislation Concerning Prostitution (vv. 18-19)

> 18 *There shall not be a cult-prostitute from among the daughters of Israel, and there shall not be a cult-prostitute from among the sons of Israel.*
> 19 *You shall not bring a prostitute's wage or the hire of a dog into the house of the Lord your God in payment for any vow, for the two things are an abomination of the Lord your God.*

There are two distinct laws here; they have presumably been placed together because of their common relationship to the matter of prostitution. First, young women and young men in Israel were not to become cult-prostitutes.[21] A *cult-prostitute* (Heb. *qādēsh/qᵉdēshāh:* lit. "holy one")[22] was a person belonging to a particular class of temple personnel in certain of the religions of Israel's neighbors.[23] They carried out their function in relation to the fertility rituals of certain deities. Both because of the association with foreign religion, and because of the nature of the act per se, cult-prostitution was forbidden in Israel as an *abomination of the Lord your God.*

The second part of the legislation prohibits the payment of a vow to God with "dirty money." When a vow was to be paid to God, it was not as though God required the money; the payment betokened

---

20. See *ANET*, pp. 200f., 203f.
21. As later history shows, the law was frequently broken; see 1 K. 14:24; 15:12; 22:46; 2 K. 23:7.
22. Though in Israelite eyes the cult-prostitute was anything but holy, he or she would be considered to be holy within the context of the foreign religion.
23. On this practice in Mesopotamia, see H. W. F. Saggs, *The Greatness That Was Babylon,* pp. 334f. See also W. G. Lambert, *Babylonian Wisdom Literature,* pp. 102f.: "Do not marry a prostitute, whose husbands are legion, a temple harlot who is dedicated to a god." It is interesting to note the derogatory tone of the quotation. The *qdšm* who are mentioned in a number of Ugaritic administrative texts may have been cult-prostitutes, though the contexts in which the word is used do not permit certain identification; see *CTA* 71.73; 73.1; 75.2; 77.3. For discussion, see W. von Soden, "Zur Stellung des 'Geweihten' (*qdš*) in Ugarit," *UF* 2 (1970), pp. 329f. Although von Soden is probably correct in his analysis of the Ugaritic term (in the light of current evidence), his doubt about the translation "cult-prostitute" for the Hebrew term is without good foundation. The context provided by v. 18 seems to make the rendition "cult-prostitute" in v. 17 fairly certain.

an attitude of gratitude for God's gracious provision, but money that had been acquired by sinful means could not be a part of God's gift, and therefore could not be used in paying a vow to him. *A prostitute's wage* — the term translated *prostitute* (*zônāh*) indicates a common prostitute, not specifically a cult-prostitute. *The hire of a dog* — the meaning of these words is doubtful, though they are commonly taken to refer to wages acquired from male prostitution.[24] Because the activities that provided the funds were an *abomination,* the money could not be brought to the house of God.

(e) Legislation Concerning Lending on Interest (vv. 20-21)

20 *You shall not lend on interest to your brother: interest on money, interest on food, interest on anything that is lent.*

21 *You may lend on interest to the foreigner, but you may not lend on interest to your brother, in order that the Lord your God may bless you in all that you undertake in the land which you are about to enter in order to take possession of it.*

In the modern world, bank loans, commercial loans, and so on, have become an integral part of daily life, so that it is easy for the modern reader of Deuteronomy to assume that legislation such as this relates to a similar practice. At the time reflected in the book of Deuteronomy, however, Israel's society was not based on a complex commercial and financial structure. Loans were normally made in an attempt to alleviate poverty, as is made clear by the parallel legislation to these verses.[25] Since loans would be made to a fellow Israelite (*brother,* v. 20) in a time of crisis, to *lend on interest*[26] would be an improper thing to do for two reasons. First, it would tend in the long run to aggravate the crisis that had produced the need for the loan in the first place. Second, it would betray an attitude unworthy of a member of the covenant community. The man wealthy enough to make a loan would be wealthy only because of the gracious provision of God; if, then, he lent something on interest (money, food) to a

24. Alternatively, *klb* may point to some other type of temple personnel, and not mean "dog." See J. Gray, *The KRT Text in the Literature of Ras Shamra*[2], p. 64. See further G. A. Cooke, *A Text-book of North-Semitic Inscriptions,* p. 68; D. W. Thomas, *VT* 10 (1960), p. 424.

25. Exod. 22:25; Lev. 25:35-36. For further studies of the subject, see S. Stein, "The Laws on Interest in the OT," *Journal of Theological Studies* N.S. 4 (1953), pp. 161-170; H. Gamoran, "The Biblical Law against Loans on Interest," *JNES* 30 (1971), pp. 127-134. In Syria, it may have been the practice among free men to make interest-free loans to one another. This seems to be implied in an Akkadian letter (RS 15.11) from Ugarit; see *ANET(S),* p. 629.

26. The noun *neshek,* which is normally used of interest on money (as distinct from food), is used in these verses in a broad sense, applying to all kinds of loans. See S. E. Loewenstamm, "*nšk* and *m/trbyt*," *JBL* 88 (1969), pp. 78-80.

fellow in crisis, he would be abusing God's provision. He should lend freely, without interest, reflecting thereby his own thankfulness to God, and receiving the continued blessing of God (v. 21b).

The Israelite was permitted, however, to lend on interest to a foreigner.[27] Since the foreigner was not a member of the covenant community, it was not considered necessary to treat him in the same way as a fellow Israelite.

(f) The Making of Vows (vv. 22-24)

> 22 *When you make a vow to the Lord your God, you shall not be tardy in making it good, for the Lord your God will certainly require it from you, and it would be a sin in you.*
> 23 *But if you refrain from making a vow, it will not be a sin in you.*
> 24 *Take care concerning what you say and do it; what you have vowed to the Lord your God is like a freewill offering that you promise in your own words.*

When a man made a vow to God, either to perform a certain act, or simply as an expression of his devotion,[28] then he was to be careful to carry out what he had vowed. Having once made a vow, a man was required not only to fulfil it, but to do so within a reasonably short period of time. Failure to fulfil the vow, or indefinite procrastination, would amount to a sin (v. 22b). It would be better not to make a vow at all than to make one and not fulfil it.

The people are thus urged to be very careful in their spoken words of commitment, which would be binding on them. When a man made a vow to God of his own free will, it would be pleasing to God, but only insofar as the spoken word found fulfilment in the concomiant act. The principle underlying the injunction is rooted in the nature of the covenant. God spoke his promise in words to his people; his spoken word was reliable and would be fulfilled — it was not a spoken bribe to secure the allegiance of the people. To make a vow to God, then fail to fulfil it, would be contrary to the whole spirit of the covenant.

(g) Eating in the Countryside (vv. 25-26)

> 25 *When you go into your neighbor's vineyard, then you may eat grapes freely, until you are satisfied, but you shall not put them into your container.*
> 26 *When you go in among your neighbor's standing grain, then you may pluck off the ears with your hand, but you shall not take a sickle to your neighbor's standing grain.*

27. See also 28:12: "You shall lend to many nations, but you shall not borrow." Cf. 15:6 and commentary.
28. Cf. E. E. Ellis, "Vow," *NBD*, p. 1313.

The situation envisaged in this legislation is that of a man travelling through the country from one place to another.[29] When he passes through a vineyard or through fields of standing grain, he may satisfy his hunger by picking grapes and eating them, or plucking off the ears of grain. This privilege was not to be denied to a man; the harvest was a part of God's gracious provision. Any privilege, however, may easily be exploited, and the legislation prohibits the removal of foodstuffs from the vineyard or field. In other words, property rights are recognized; the grapes or grain properly belonged to the farmer who grew them and tended them. He was to be generous in letting passers-by refresh themselves, but the harvesting of the crop and removal of it could be done only by him.[30]

13. MISCELLANEOUS LAWS (24:1-22)

(a) Legislation Concerning Marriage, Divorce, and Remarriage (vv. 1-4)

1 When a man takes a woman and becomes her husband, if she does not find favor in his eyes, because he finds something indecent in her, and he writes a bill of divorce for her and puts it in her hand and sends her away from his house,

2 and she departs from his house and goes and gets married to another man,

3 but the latter man hates her and writes a bill of divorce for her and puts it in her hand and sends her away from his house, or if the latter man who took her for his wife should die,

4 her former husband, who sent her away, may not remarry her, taking her to be his wife again, after she has been defiled, for that would be an abomination before the Lord. And you shall not bring about sin in the land which the Lord your God is going to give you as an inheritance.

In precise terms, there is only one piece of legislation in this passage,[1] that contained in v. 4a. The first three verses, which form the grammatical protasis, specify exactly the conditions that must apply for the execution of the legislation in v. 4 (the apodosis). Thus, strictly speaking, the legislation relates only to particular cases of remarriage; the protasis contains incidental information about marriage and di-

29. It is unlikely that the verses imply that whenever a man is hungry, he simply goes to the nearest vineyard or field for a meal, then returns home. The verses imply rather the generosity to be extended to travellers.
30. Note that in the NT incident, when the disciples pluck ears of grain, the legal dispute centers on the sabbath, not the plucking of grain. See Matt. 12:1; Mark 2:23; Luke 6:1.
1. For parallel material, see Jer. 3:1; cf. J. D. Martin, "The Forensic Background to Jeremiah III 1," *VT* 19 (1969), pp. 82-92.

vorce, but does not specifically legislate on those matters. The verses do not institute divorce, but treat it as a practice already known, which may be either a matter of custom or of other legislation no longer known.[2]

The procedure for divorce is contained in vv. 1, 3; the statement is so succinct that all the details are no longer clear. The woman does not *find favor* in the eyes of the man; the reason for this lack of favor is because there is *something indecent in her*. *Something indecent ('erwaṯ dāḇār)* may have been a technical legal expression; the precise meaning is no longer clear. The same expression is used in 23:14, where it suggests something impure, though the words do not seem to have normal connotations. In this context, the words may indicate some physical deficiency in the woman, though this meaning is uncertain.[3] A physical deficiency such as the inability to bear children may be implied.[4]

If the man decided to divorce the woman, he was to write out a bill of divorce and formally serve it on the woman. She was then sent away from the man's house, but possession of the bill of divorce gave her a certain protection under law from any further action by the man. In the situation envisaged by this particular piece of legislation, the divorced woman then remarries another man. The second marriage is terminated, either by a second divorce or by the death of the second husband. Now comes the specific legislation: under all these circumstances, the first man may not remarry his former wife. *After she has been defiled* — the language (*defiled*) suggests adultery (see Lev. 18:20). The sense is that the woman's remarriage after the first divorce is similar to adultery in that the woman cohabits with another man. However, if the woman were then to remarry her first husband, after divorcing the second, the analogy with adultery would become even more complete; the woman lives first with one man, then another, and finally returns to the first. Thus the intent of the legislation seems to be to apply certain restrictions on the already existing practice of divorce. If divorce became too easy, then it could be abused and it would become a "legal" form of committing adultery.

2. Hence, in Jesus' response to the Pharisees (Mark 10:4), he is not so much changing the law of Deut. 24:1-4, as bringing out its true meaning: cf. C. E. B. Cranfield, *The Gospel According to Saint Mark* (1959), p. 319. See also Matt. 5:31; 19:7; cf. U. Nembach, "Ehescheidung nach alttestamentlichem und jüdischem Recht," *ThZ* 26 (1970), pp. 161-171.
3. It is clear that the meaning cannot be "adultery," for adultery was punishable by death (22:22), though elsewhere in the Near East adultery could provide grounds for divorce under particular circumstances. See further J. J. Rabinowitz, "The 'Great Sin' in Ancient Egyptian Marriage Contracts," *JNES* 18 (1959), p. 73; W. L. Moran, "The Scandal of the 'Great Sin' at Ugarit," *JNES* 18 (1959), pp. 280f.; L. R. Fisher, *The Claremont Ras Shamra Tablets* (1972), pp. 14-19.
4. There may be a parallel in an Old Assyrian marriage contract; *ANET(S)*, p. 107.

THE BOOK OF DEUTERONOMY

The legislation thus restricts what may have been a loophole in the older custom. The purpose of the restriction is to keep free from sin the land which God would soon be giving to his people as an inheritance.

(b) A Further Exemption from Military Service (v. 5)

> 5 *If a man marries a new wife, he shall not go out with the army, nor shall any responsibility be assigned to him; he shall be free at home for one year and he shall make happy the wife whom he has married.*

For further grounds for exemption from military service, see 20:5-8. The present legislation, in its context, provides a positive balance to the negative substance of vv. 1-4, where certain abuses of the state of marriage are countered. Here, a positive prescription is set forth, which is intended to promote the health and growth of a new marital relationship. A man who is just married is exempted for one year from (a) military service[5] and (b) any responsibility.[6] The legislation thus guards against the untimely death of the husband, which would result in the woman becoming a widow almost immediately after her marriage, and also the absence of the husband from the home for a prolonged period of time immediately after the wedding. This safeguard was intended to promote the growth of the family relationship, which reflected, in miniature, the larger family of the covenant people of God. By remaining at home for one year, the man would *make happy*[7] his new wife.

(c) Legislation Concerning Millstones (v. 6)

> 6 *A man shall not take in pledge millstones or an upper millstone, for that would be taking a life in pledge.*

In an earlier passage (23:19), a man is forbidden to lend on interest to a fellow Israelite; he could make a loan to his fellow Israelite, however, in order to help him in distress, provided that he did not charge interest. The person receiving the loan would provide some collateral to the lender, signifying thereby his intention of repaying the loan (failing which, the collateral would be forfeited). This legislation

5. The customary exemption of a newly married man from military service was known elsewhere in Syria-Palestine. In *CTA* 14.II.100-102 (=*UT* Krt 100-102),ᵗthere is a description of the suspending of the practice, but in circumstances in which war was being undertaken to acquire a new wife for King Keret.
6. The Heb. is literally: "any thing shall not pass upon him" (following a variant reading noted by Kennicot). The reference would be to some kind of public service which (like military service) might be required of a man from time to time.
7. Alternatively, the text could be translated: "rejoice with his wife" (pointing the verb as Qal, after the suggestion in the Targums — Onqelos and Jonathan).

concerns collateral provided in pledge of repayment to the man making the loan. The lender is prohibited from taking in pledge the *millstones* or *upper millstone*.[8] In every Israelite family home, a small milling machine would be a basic and essential part of culinary equipment. Each morning, the housewife would use it to prepare flour in order to provide the family with its daily bread.[9] Thus, to take the millstones (or even just the upper stone, which would make the machine useless) would be to cause real hardship to the family, and would be contrary to the spirit of generosity which should characterize the lender.[10] *Taking a life in pledge* — the sense is "taking in pledge a means of livelihood."

(d) Legislation Concerning Kidnapping (v. 7)

> 7 *If a man is found stealing the life of one of his brothers from among the Israelites, and treating him as merchandise or selling him, then that thief shall die; and you shall purge out the evil from your midst.*

For a fuller discussion of the substance of this legislation, see the commentary on the eighth commandment (5:19). The crime is kidnapping, though not in the literal sense of abducting a child and returning it on receipt of a ransom payment. The theft would be followed by sale into slavery, either for a direct payment of money, or in exchange for merchandise.[11] *Stealing the life* — the crime is social murder, for though the victim does not literally die, by being sold into slavery he is effectively cut off from the covenant family of God. Hence the penalty for the crime is severe — death![12] To cut a man off from the covenant community was to cut him off from sharing in the blessing of God for his people in the promised land.

(e) Legislation Concerning Leprosy (vv. 8-9)

> 8 *Take care, in an outbreak of leprosy, to be very diligent in doing all that the Levitical priests instruct you; what I commanded them, you shall be careful to do.*
> 9 *Remember what the Lord your God did to Miriam, on the route of your exodus from Egypt.*

This short passage is interesting in that it refers to a large section of legislation, already in existence, without specifying at all the sub-

8.   On *reḳeb*, "upper millstone," see K. J. Cathcart, *VT* 19 (1969), p. 122.
9.   See Jer. 25:10; the "grinding of the millstones" was a sound typical of the life of an ordinary family.
10.   Cf. the commentary on 23:19.
11.   On the verb translated "treat as merchandise," see the commentary on 21:14 (n. 16).
12.   A similar penalty applies in the Law Code of Hammurabi § 14, *ANET*, p. 166.

stance of that legislation.[13] The exhortation at this point thus assumes that the legislation on leprosy is known to the audience, and Moses simply exhorts the people to be diligent in their observation of that legislation. *Leprosy (tsāra'at)* — the Hebrew term may not be so specific as the modern medical term,[14] but may indicate a variety of malignant and infectious skin diseases. The exhortation to obey the law concerning leprosy is illustrated and emphasized by a call to *remember* (v. 9) the case of Miriam's leprosy and the procedure of purification by which the people dealt with it (Num. 12:9-16).

(f) Further Legislation Relating to Pledges (vv. 10-13)

10 *When you make any kind of loan to your neighbor, you shall not enter his house to take his pledge.*

11 *You shall stand outside, and the man to whom you are lending shall bring the pledge to you outside.*

12 *And if he is a poor man, you shall not sleep in his pledge.*

13 *You shall certainly return the pledge to him when the sun goes down, so that he may sleep in his garment and bless you. And it shall be counted as righteousness for you before the Lord your God.*

On pledges, see also v. 6 (above); v. 17b (below); Exod. 22:25-27. The legislation offers further protection to the poor who are required by force of circumstance to request a loan from a fellow Israelite. (a) The man making the loan may not enter the house of the recipient of the loan; he must wait outside, where the pledge will be brought to him (vv. 10-11). This requirement protects the privacy of the recipient's home and leaves to him the choice of the article to be given as collateral for the loan. It means that a man can borrow with honor, without having his personal possessions made open to the creditor for his selection of an item to be taken in pledge. (b) In the case of a very poor man, he would only have his *garment* to offer as pledge (vv. 12-13). The *garment* is a blanket-like piece of clothing, used as a cloak by day and as a bed-covering by night. *You shall not sleep in his pledge* — that is, where the creditor took a *garment* in pledge, he was not to put it to his own use at night, thereby depriving the borrower of his only protection against the chill night air.[15] The spirit of both parts

13. The legislation is contained in Lev. 13-14; cf. G. T. Manley, *The Book of the Law,* p. 94.
14. *Leprosy,* as a modern medical term, refers particularly to the mildly infectious disease caused by the organism called *mycobacterium leprae.* For a detailed study of leprosy in the Bible, see R. K. Harrison, *IDB* III, pp. 111-13.
15. For an example from a later period in history, see the Yavneh-Yam ostracon; J. C. L. Gibson, *Textbook of Syrian Semitic Inscriptions* I, p. 27. The text describes an appeal by a farmworker to the governor against a minor official, who had confiscated the farmworker's garment.

of this legislation breathes the humanity and charity that were to characterize the covenant community of God. There would inevitably be needy people among the Israelites (15:11), but their hardship would be alleviated by legislation such as this, which reflected in its terms the covenant love of God for his people.

(g) Legislation Against Oppressing the Poor (vv. 14-15)

> 14 *You shall not withhold the wage of the poor and needy, whether one of your brethren or one of your resident aliens, who are in your land and in your settlements.*
> 15 *You shall give him his wage on the same day, before the sun goes down, for he is a poor man and he sets his heart on it. Then he will not cry out to the Lord against you, so that it would be a sin in you.*

The theme linking these verses to the previous section is a concern for the welfare of the poor; in this instance, however, the poor man is working for another man in order to meet his need for sustenance. *You shall not withhold the wage* — alternatively, the Hebrew could be rendered, "You shall not oppress the hired laborer."[16] Poor men who worked as laborers were to be paid at the end of their day's work, whether they were Israelites or aliens resident in Israel. The legislation refers specifically to the hire of poor people, whose need was such that to be paid on a weekly (or longer) basis would cause real hardship. The money would be needed each day to feed a family each day; the legislation expresses once again humanitarian concern for those within Israel who would be less fortunate than their fellows.

Failure to behave in this manner would bring down sin on Israel as a community (v. 15b), for the poor and needy would cry to God for help in their distress. God does bring aid to the oppressed; but when that help should have been offered by the people of God in the first place, the people, by their failure, bring down the judgment of God on their own heads. The use of this legislation in the NT (Jas. 5:4) makes clear that it protects not only the poor, but also the rich; the rich men, fulfilling their obligations to their poor laborers, maintain the integrity of the community. But failure to deal honestly in transactions of this sort brings severe condemnation (Jas. 5:1-6).

(h) Individual Responsibility within the Family (v. 16)

> 16 *Fathers shall not be put to death on account of sons, and sons shall not be put to death on account of fathers; each man shall be put to death for his own sin.*

16. MT: *lo'-ta'ashoq śākîr;* the translation above reads *śekar* (cstr. of *śākār*), "hire, wages." This is a probable interpretation of the Qumran text, *śkr (DJD* I, p. 58). The verb *'āshaq,* which in general has the sense "oppress," means specifically the withholding of property rightly belonging to another.

In the preceding chapters, the death penalty has been noted several times as the judgment to be awarded following certain types of crimes. This short piece of legislation relates to the practice of capital punishment; the principle is that a man was responsible for his own *sin* (or "crime") and must pay the penalty.[17] If a father was condemned to death, the son was not to be executed with him or in his place, and vice versa. This piece of legislation must be held in balance with another principle, stated in 5:9. On the one hand, a man was treated as an individual in terms of his criminal responsibility under law. On the other hand, the nature of a father's criminal act (for example) was such that his children were inevitably affected; see the commentary on 5:9. The individual responsible for crime must accept the legal punishment under law, but the repercussions of the act spread beyond him to affect his family. This short piece of legislation makes clear a principle underlying all the law in Deuteronomy, namely, that the presence of law, and the requirement that it be obeyed, placed upon every man a responsibility for his actions, both within the covenant community and before God.

(i) The Resident Alien, the Orphan, and the Widow (vv. 17-22)

> 17 *You shall not pervert the justice due to a resident alien or an orphan, and you shall not take in pledge a widow's clothing;*
> 18 *but you shall remember that you were a slave in Egypt, and that the Lord your God redeemed you from there. Therefore, I am commanding you to do this law.*
> 19 *When you gather your harvest in your field, but you forget a sheaf in the field, you shall not return to fetch it; it belongs to the resident alien, to the orphan, and to the widow. So the Lord your God will bless you in all that you undertake.*
> 20 *When you beat your olive trees, you shall not strip them after you; it belongs to the resident alien, to the orphan, and to the widow.*
> 21 *When you gather grapes from your vineyard, you shall not glean after you; it belongs to the resident alien, to the orphan, and to the widow.*
> 22 *And you shall remember that you were a slave in the land of Egypt. Therefore I am commanding you to do this law.*

This is the fourth section of legislation relating to various classes of needy persons in this chapter; see also vv. 6, 10-13, and 14-15 (above). The classes referred to, aliens, widows, and orphans, have already been the subject of charitable legislation earlier in the presentation of the law (14:29).[18]

---

17. For a general parallel, see Middle Assyrian Law, A, § 2 (*ANET*, p. 180); a woman convicted of blasphemy was to bear the penalty of her crime, but her husband and children were not to be punished.
18. For parallel material, see Exod. 22:21-24; Lev. 19:9-10; 23:22.

17 *You shall not pervert the justice . . .*— see 16:19 and commentary. On clothing as a pledge, see vv. 12-13 (above).

18 This verse is essentially the same as v. 22 (below); see 15:15 and commentary.

19-22 Provision is to be made for feeding underprivileged people, such as aliens, orphans, and widows. (a) When the fields were harvested, any sheaf left in the fields by mistake was to become the proper possessions of aliens, orphans, and widows;[19] removing such a sheaf would not be considered theft. The generous farmer might even contrive to "forget" a few sheaves. (b) Olive trees would be beaten so that the olives fell to the ground and could then be collected. After the beating, the farmer was not then to check every branch and make sure it was stripped bare of fruit; any remaining fruit (*it belongs . . .*, v. 20b) was left for the aliens, orphans, and widows. (c) A similar procedure was to be employed when grapes were gathered from the vine. The spirit of this legislation expresses clearly the awareness that was to exist within the covenant community for all classes of people. Throughout Deuteronomy, there is a strong anticipation of the promised land, which was soon to be in the possession of the Israelites. The majority of Israelite families would be allotted a portion of the land and they would harvest the produce of the land, crops and fruit. But there would be some who would not be landowners and who could easily feel left out of the life of the community in that they did not share directly in the possession of the land promised and given by God. This legislation makes sure that resident aliens, orphans, and widows, though not owning land for themselves, might nevertheless share in the fruit of the land. The manner of their participation in the fruit of the land would be such that they could maintain their honor and self-respect. They would not have to beg or seek a "hand-out"; they would go into the fields and orchards after the harvest, and like the farmer, they would work for their own small harvest, as they searched and gleaned for the grain and fruit that had been left there. And the farmers, who had allowed some produce to remain, were not simply being charitable to those less fortunate than themselves; they were expressing their gratitude to God, who had brought them out of the slavery in Egypt and given to them a land of their own.

14. MISCELLANEOUS LAWS (25:1-19)

(a) Legal Disputes and Punishment (vv. 1-3)

> 1 *If there should be a dispute between men, and they take it to court, and the judges pass judgment between them, and they declare the one man righteous and declare the other man guilty,*

---

19. See also the account in Ruth 2.

2 *and if the guilty man deserves to be beaten, then the judge shall make him to lie down and be beaten in his presence with a number of lashes proportionate to his guilt.*
3 *He may beat him forty times; he shall not do more, lest, if he should go on beating him with many lashes beyond these, your brother would be humiliated in your eyes.*

In the early part of the discourse on the law, it was noted that when a man brought false charges concerning the virginity of his new wife, he was not only to pay damages, but was also to receive corporal punishment; see the commentary on 22:18. In this section of the discourse, the legislation is more general and relates to the proper procedure for the administration of corporal punishment. There is a legal dispute between two men; the nature of the dispute is not known, nor is there parallel legislation to clarify the situation. In order to settle the matter, the men take their dispute to court to receive a legal judgment. *The judges pass judgment . . .* — the Hebrew is simply "they judge." The guilty party is determined by the judges and they set the penalty to be administered in light of the gravity of the act. Two decisions have to be made: (i) whether the offense warrants corporal punishment, and if so, (ii) how many lashes should be given, the number increasing in proportion to the gravity of the offense. If the judge declared that corporal punishment was in order, then the flogging was to be carried out in his presence; in this way, the judge was able to see that the sentence was properly executed and that the offender was not treated too leniently or too harshly by the officer of the law entrusted with the task. The flogging would probably be done with a rod,[1] and the maximum number of lashes was set at forty.[2] The substance of this legislation makes it very clear that corporal punishment was subject to many safeguards designed to avoid its abuse. Corporal punishment could be inflicted only after proper trial, and then it was to be carried out, within the specified limit, under the supervision of the judge. In this way, care was taken to see that the punishment was appropriate to the crime, on the one hand, and that the criminal was not grossly maltreated on the other hand; the guilty party was still *your brother* (v. 3b; a fellow Israelite) and was not to be publicly humiliated.

(b) Legislation Relating to the Ox (v. 4)

4 *You shall not muzzle an ox when it is threshing grain.*

1. Cf. Exod. 21:20.
2. By way of contrast, the Law Code of Hammurabi specifies sixty lashes for insubordinate action: § 202 (*ANET,* p. 175). By NT times, thirty-nine lashes became a standard number, in order to be sure of keeping under the maximum permitted by law; 2 Cor. 11:24.

This brief passage of legislation, which has no exact parallels in the other legal material in the Pentateuch,[3] does not appear to have any particular relationship to its immediate context. It expresses concern for the animal, perhaps emanating from the general concern implicit in 5:14. One method of threshing in the Near East was by means of an animal (*ox*, though horses are also used in more modern times) trampling across the threshing floor, thereby separating the ears of grain from the stalk. Sometimes the ox would pull a threshing sledge, which would have the same effect. Presumably the prohibition against muzzling the ox was in order that it could eat from time to time; the animal should not be grudged sustenance when it was working on behalf of man.[4]

(c) Levirate Marriage (vv. 5-10)

> 5 *If brothers live together, and one of them dies and has no son, the dead man's wife shall not go outside to a strange man; her brother-in-law shall go in to her and take her to be his wife, and he shall act like a brother-in-law.*
> 6 *And it shall be that the first-born whom she bears shall represent his dead brother's name, and his name shall not be blotted out in Israel.*
> 7 *And if the man does not wish to take his sister-in-law, his sister-in-law shall go out to the elders at the gate and shall say: My brother-in-law will not raise up a name for his brother in Israel. He does not want to act like a brother-in-law to me.*
> 8 *And the elders of his city shall summon him and shall speak to him; but if he stands firm and says: I do not wish to take her,*
> 9 *then his sister-in-law shall go up to him in the sight of the elders, and she shall remove his sandal from his foot and shall spit in his face, and she shall respond, saying: Thus let it be done to the man who will not build his brother's house.*
> 10 *And in Israel its name shall be called: "House-of-the-removed-sandal."*

The legislation concerning levirate marriage is peculiar to the presentation of the law in Deuteronomy; the practice, however, was an old one,[5] and here it is given legal authority in the covenant

---

3. However, the ox is the subject of other legislation; Exod. 21:28-32, 35-36.
4. Thus this passage is used in the NT to illustrate the principle that "the laborer is worthy of his hire"; 1 Tim. 5:18; cf. 1 Cor. 9:9. For a more detailed study of this law in Deut., with particular reference to the history of its interpretation, see G. Lisowsky, "Dtn. 25:4," in F. Maass, ed., *Das ferne und nahe Wort.* BZAW 105 (1967), pp. 144-152.
5. See, e.g., Gen. 38. For similar legislation in the Near East, see Middle Assyrian Laws, A, §§ 30, 31, 33; *ANET*, p. 182. For general discussions of levirate marriage, see S. R. Driver, *Deuteronomy*, pp. 280-85; R. de Vaux, *Ancient Israel*, pp. 37f.; N. H. Snaith, "The Daughters of Zelophehad," *VT* 16 (1966), pp. 124-27. That the practice

community of Israel. The passage falls into two sections: (i) the legislation concerning levirate marriage is stated (vv. 5-6); (ii) the procedure is stated which is to be followed in the event that a man was unwilling to fulfil his responsibilities (vv. 7-10).

(i) The law of levirate marriage was that a man should accept responsibility for his deceased brother's childless widow by marrying her. However, the law applied only under certain conditions. First, the two brothers must have been living together for the law to be applicable; they would thus be part of a large family unit, and both would already be sharing certain responsibilities. Second, the widow was to be childless in a particular sense — she was not to have had a *son;* apparently the law would still be in effect if she had a daughter, but not a son, for the first-born son was the legal and responsible inheritor of his father's estate. Under both these conditions, the woman was not to look for another husband (*a strange man*) outside the immediate family. The brother of the deceased husband, already resident in the home, was to marry her. *Brother-in-law* — the Hebrew term (*yābām*) has a more specific sense than the English equivalent implies,[6] for it refers specifically to that brother-in-law who was liable to levirate marriage under the conditions specified above.[7] The first-born male son, resulting from the levirate marriage, was to *represent his dead brother's name.*[8] That is, in law, he would be equivalent to the son of the deceased and he would provide the deceased man with a posterity in Israel. There may be several reasons underlying the legislation in addition to providing the deceased with posterity. First, of course, there was the matter of the inheritance of the dead man's property.[9] But a further reason may lie in the nature of the covenant, for since the time of Abraham, the covenant promises of God were made "to you and your descendants after you" (Gen. 17:7-9). Though each man participated in the covenant relationship during his lifetime, there was always a future for the family of God; and though he could not participate in that future in person, he could share in it through those he left behind him. Thus the provision of posterity through levirate marriage was an act, once again, in harmony with the covenant between Israel and God.

(ii) The brother-in-law had a legal right to refuse his obligations to his brother's widow, though the exercise of that right would

---

was still in use in NT times seems evident from the question put to Jesus by the Sadducees; Matt. 22:23-33; Mark 12:18-27; Luke 20:27-40.
6. The same restriction applies to the feminine form of the word, translated *sister-in-law* (v. 7).
7. Cf. Ugar. *ybmt* (*UT* 19.1065; p. 408); see the discussion in J. Gray, *The Legacy of Canaan*², p. 271.
8. Heb.: "he shall rise upon the name of his (viz., the real father's) brother."
9. For the laws relating to inheritance, see Num. 27:8-11.

incur the strong disapproval of the community. If the brother-in-law refused to marry the woman, she took her case to the legal authorities (*the elders*) *at the gate*, the place where law was conducted officially; see 21:19 and commentary. First, she laid her charge: *My brother-in-law will not raise up a name* . . . — *name* here has the sense of "posterity,"[10] namely, a child who would perpetuate the father's name. Then the man was summoned and he formally stated that he did not desire to marry the woman. Then, in the presence of the court, the woman symbolically humiliated the man, by removing his sandal and spitting in his face. The action was not simply one of anger, but publicly reflected her feelings and those of the community about the man's refusal. The removal of the shoe or sandal indicated that the brother had abandoned his responsibility,[11] and therefore deserved the shame symbolized by the spitting. The title given to the house (v. 10) further indicated the shame on the brother, who would continue to live in the house, but a house in which there was no living representative of his own deceased brother. The reason why a brother might refuse to marry the widow probably is to be found in a desire for personal gain. If he married the woman and there was a male child, that child, who would legally be the son of the deceased man, would inherit his "father's" property. In the absence of such a child, however, the surviving brother might hope to inherit the property of his deceased brother (Num. 27:9; this would apply only if the widow had no children at all, male or female). If such were the motive, it deserved the reprobation of the community.

(d) Stopping a Fight (vv. 11-12)

> 11 *When men are wrestling together, a man and his brother, and the wife of one of them approaches to rescue her husband from the power of his assailant, and she puts out her hand and grasps his private parts,*
> 12 *then you shall cut off her hand; you shall have no pity.*

Two men are wrestling together, both of whom are Israelites (*a man and his brother*). The wife of the man who has been attacked seeks to break up the fight by grasping the private parts of the assailant; such action, however, is forbidden and the woman's hand is to be cut off.

This is the only occurrence of the law in the Pentateuch,[12] though there is other legislation relating to men wrestling.[13] The law illustrates, in general terms, that the end does not justify the means.

10. Cf. G. A. Cooke, *A Text-book of North-Semitic Inscriptions*, pp. 197f.
11. On the symbolism of removing a shoe, see M. H. Farbridge, *Studies in Biblical and Semitic Symbolism*, p. 274.
12. For a parallel in Middle Assyrian Law, see A, § 8 (*ANET*, p. 181).
13. Exod. 21:22-25.

Though the end (rescuing her husband from an assailant) was honorable, the particular means could not be tolerated. The specific reason for the prohibition, however, is less certain. It may have been a matter of protecting womanly modesty.[14] More probably, it may be implied that the woman's action would cause permanent injury to the male.[15] If this is the case, it may be significant that such injury could result in the inability of the man to father children; in that event, the position of the law is important, for it follows legislation (vv. 5-10) relating to a man who through premature death was unable to father children. To some extent, therefore, both portions of legislation have a common theme.

It should be noted, finally, that the punishment prescribed for this violation of the law is an extension of the *lex talionis* (see 19:21 and commentary); for obvious reasons, given the different sexes of the persons involved in the incident, the *lex talionis* could not be applied literally. It may be that this very particular piece of casuistic law is intended as an example of how *lex talionis* was able to be interpreted when it could not be applied literally.

(e) Weights and Measures (vv. 13-16)

> 13 *You shall not keep two kinds of weights in your bag, a large one and a small one.*
> 14 *You shall not keep two kinds of measures in your house, a large one and a small one.*
> 15 *You shall keep a full and exact weight; you shall keep a full and exact measure, in order that you may prolong your days upon the land which the Lord your God is about to give to you.*
> 16 *For anyone doing these things, anyone acting unjustly, is an abomination of the Lord your God.*

For parallel legislation, see Lev. 19:35-37; similar injunctions are known in Near Eastern texts.[16]

Just as the administration of justice was to conform to the highest moral standards (16:18-20), so too commercial activities were to be conducted in accord with rigid ethical principles; in both cases the result would be long life in the promised land (v. 15b; see also 16:20b).

False weights and measures, by which a merchant could exploit his customers (cf. Amos 8:5), are prohibited.[17] When buying,

---

14. See M. Weinfeld, *Deuteronomy and the Deuteronomic School*, pp. 292f.
15. See A. Phillips, *Ancient Israel's Criminal Law*, p. 94.
16. In Egypt, see the sixteenth chapter of the Instructions of Amenemope *(ANET*, p. 423); cf. A. S. Yahuda, *The Language of the Pentateuch in Its Relation to Egyptian*, p. 76. For Mesopotamia, see H. W. F. Saggs, *The Greatness That Was Babylon*, p. 282.
17. For a detailed study of weights and measures, see R. B. Y. Scott, "Weights and Measures of the Bible," *BA* 22 (1951), pp. 22-40.

a merchant could obtain more than he paid for by using a large *weight* (lit. "stone") or *measure* (Heb. *'êpāh*). When selling, he could cheat the customer with a light weight or measure, by providing less than the customer paid for. Instead of having two sets of false weights or measures, the merchant was to have one set of each, for both buying and selling, which were to be the legally ordained size. On v. 16, see 18:12; 22:5.

(f) "Remember Amalek" (vv. 17-19)

17 *Remember what Amalek did to you on the route of your exodus from Egypt:*
18 *how he attacked you on the road and launched an assault against your rear, against all the stragglers behind you, when you were faint and weary. And he did not fear God.*
19 *And it shall be that when the Lord your God grants you rest from all your enemies who are round about you in the land, which the Lord your God is going to give you as an inheritance to possess, you shall blot out the memory of Amalek from under heaven. You shall not forget.*

Remember what Amalek did to you (v. 17) — see Exod. 17:8-16. The account in Exodus describes a particular encounter between Israel and Amalek[18] at Rephidim. Verses 17-18 in this passage, however, probably have in mind a number of encounters with the Amalekites, of which that referred to in Exod. 17 is the first. It is known that the Amalekites, in conjunction with certain Canaanites, inflicted a defeat on Israel near Hormah (Num. 14:39-45), and there may have been a number of other skirmishes along the way, of which no detailed record has survived. The attacks in the rear, directed against the weary stragglers who had fallen some distance behind the main body of the Israelites (v. 18), suggest that apart from particular battles, the Amalekites were a constant source of distress to the Israelites. The enmity of the Amalekites, together with the underhand nature of their attacks, evoked the severe punishment described in v. 19.

This short passage on the Amalekites, coming near the end of the presentation of law, seems at first sight to be out of place in its present context; in substance, it cannot be related to the earlier material on foreign nations (23:3-8), which is particularly concerned with admission to the assembly of the Lord. However, as with the substance of the presentation of the law, these verses are directly related to what was to be done in the land, once God had given his people possession of the promised land. They relate, in other words, to "unfinished business," and the importance of the subject is made clear in Exod. 17:14. The behavior of the Amalekites had been so

18.   On the Amalekites, see G. M. Landes, *IDB* I, pp. 101f.

grave that their future judgment had been written down in a book; the entry in the book consisted of God's words and was a promise that the memory of the Amalekites would be blotted out from under heaven. Now the significance of vv. 17-19 in the context of the law becomes clearer. The presentation of law in Deuteronomy has as its basis the law of the covenant, which was written in a book (Exod. 24:4, 7). So too, the extermination of the Amalekites was written in a book; it was presented again to the Israelites as a reminder that there was unfinished business to perform once they had settled in the promised land. *You shall not forget* (v. 19) — in Israel's future history, the continuing aggressiveness of the Amalekites gave the Israelites little chance to forget, until at last the Amalekites seem to have ceased to be a nation, about the time of Hezekiah (1 Chr. 4:43).

15. THE CEREMONIAL FULFILMENT OF THE LAW (26:1-15)

1 *And it shall be that when you enter the land which the Lord your God is about to give you as an inheritance, and you take possession of it and you live in it,*

2 *then you shall take part of the first of all the fruit of the ground which you gather in from your land, which the Lord your God is about to give to you, and you shall put it in a basket and you shall go to the place that the Lord your God shall choose to establish his name there.*

3 *And you shall go to the one who shall be priest in those days and you shall say to him: I declare today to the Lord my God that I have entered the land which the Lord promised by oath to our fathers to give to us.*

4 *Then the priest shall take the basket from your hand and he shall put it down before the altar of the Lord your God.*

5 *And you shall respond and say before the Lord your God: An ailing Aramean was my father, and he went down to Egypt and lived as an alien there, few in number; and there he became a great and powerful and populous nation.*

6 *And the Egyptians treated us badly and afflicted us, and they imposed on us hard labor.*

7 *But we cried out to the Lord God of our fathers, and the Lord listened to our voice and he saw our affliction and our toil and our distress,*

8 *and the Lord brought us out from Egypt with a powerful hand and an outstretched arm, and with great awesomeness, and with signs and wonders.*

9 *And he brought us in to this place and he gave us this land, a land flowing with milk and honey.*

10 *And now, behold, I have brought the first of the fruit of the ground which you have given to me, O Lord. Then you shall put it down before the Lord your God and you shall bow down in worship before the Lord your God.*

11 *And you shall rejoice in all the goodness that the Lord your God has granted to you and to your household —you, and the Levite, and the resident alien who is in your midst.*

12 *When you have completed tithing all the tithe of your produce in the third year, the year of the tithe, and you have given it to the Levite, to the resident alien, to the orphan, and to the widow,and they have eaten in your settlements and had their fill,*

13 *then you shall say before the Lord your God: I have completely removed the holy portion from the house, and furthermore I have given it to the Levite, to the resident alien, to the orphan, and to the widow, according to all your commandment which you commanded me. I have not passed over any of your commandments and I have not forgotten.*

14 *I have not eaten any of it trusting in my own strength, and I have not removed any of it in a state of uncleanness, and I have not given any of it to the dead. I have obeyed the voice of the Lord my God. I have done according to all that you commanded me.*

15 *Look down from your holy residence, from heaven, and bless your people, Israel, and the ground which you have given to us, just as you promised by oath to our fathers—a land flowing with milk and honey!*

Whereas the main substance of the specific stipulations (Deut. 12–26) anticipates the continuing future life of Israel in the promised land, the legislation contained in 26:1-15 relates to two particular ceremonies which were to be held as soon as Israel had taken possession of the land and begun its new (agricultural) style of life. In this sense, 26:1-15 follows naturally from 25:17-19, which also refers to particular action to be taken once the land had been possessed; it precedes naturally the legislation of 27:1-26, in which the particular renewal of the covenant in the vicinity of Shechem is commanded, to be undertaken after the crossing of the Jordan and the initial stages of the conquest.

The two particular ceremonies, which would be held at different times and in different places, were: (i) the offering for the first time of the firstfruits of the land (vv. 1-11); (ii) the first celebration of the triennial tithe (vv. 12-15). Although these verses describe two particular ceremonies, the substance of the verses is also valuable for the insight provided into the normative and continuing celebration of the related festivals. The view that 26:1-15 deals with two particular ceremonies, each to be held once only on particular occasions, is implied not only by the wording and the location of the passage at the end of the specific stipulations, but also by the fact that the general legislation relating to the normal celebration of both ceremonies has been mentioned earlier in the discourse on the law.

(i) The first offering of the firstfruits of the ground (vv. 1-11). This ceremony was to take place in the promised land (*when you enter the land*), after the conquest (*you take possession of it*), and when the

Israelites had begun to live in the land and be supported by its produce (*you live in it:* v. 1). The firstfruits of the harvest were offered at the Feast of Weeks (16:9-12; cf. 18:4); on the link between the Feast of Weeks and the offering of the firstfruits, see Num. 28:26. Unlike passover and the covenant ceremony, the offering of firstfruits would be a new religious institution in Israel; before taking possession of the land, they were not an agricultural people and therefore had no harvest festival. Thus this first offering of the firstfruits by the Israelites, once they had taken possession of the land, would mark the inauguration of the new life which had been anticipated for so long on the basis of the covenant promise of God.

The feast would be celebrated at the sanctuary — *the place that the Lord your God shall choose* . . . (v. 2). When they were at the sanctuary, the people would take a part of the firstfruits which they had brought with them and place it in a basket; the part in the basket symbolized the whole which they had brought with them, for the purposes of the ceremony that followed. Then, carrying his basket, each man would go in to the priest officiating at the sanctuary and would make a declaration before the priest (v. 3). The declaration was a personal testimony that the man had entered the promised land, and the basket he carried symbolized that already he was beginning to experience the blessing of the new land and the new life given by God. But the declaration did not only reflect man's experience; it was a testimony also to the faithfulness of God, who had promised the land long ago and now had fulfilled that ancient promise by giving the land to his people.

It is difficult to be certain of the procedure that was to be followed in the remainder of the ceremony, for the account is very concise. The priest took the basket from the man and put it down before the altar of the Lord (v. 4); in v. 10, however, it is stated that the man himself put down his basket *before the Lord* (i.e., the altar), and this has sometimes been taken as a contradiction and as being indicative of editorial revision of diverse material. What is probably intended, however, is that the priest performed an action and spoke some words; then both the action and the words were repeated by the man. Thus the declaration that was to be made by the worshipper (vv. 5b-10a) is introduced by the words: *you shall respond and say* . . . (v. 5a). Although this is a common idiomatic expression for introducing direct speech in Hebrew, here it may have the precise sense of responding to the words (and later to the action) of the priest; see also the commentary on 21:7. On this interpretation, the priest would take the basket from the worshipper and speak certain words, either those of vv. 5b-10a (to be repeated by the worshipper) or other words to which vv. 5b-10a were the response. Then the basket would be returned to the worshipper, who would make his own statement (vv. 5b-10a) prior to setting it down before the altar.

The words that were to be spoken by the worshipper have been the subject of considerable debate in recent OT scholarship. G. von Rad has argued that the verses have all the characteristics and attributes of a *creed* and that this short passage may be the earliest recognizable example of a creed in the history of Israel's religion.[1] Although von Rad's thesis contains many valuable insights into the nature of the verses,[2] the context in which the passage appears weighs against the view that vv. 5b-10a are a creed. According to the context, these words were to be spoken by the worshipper at a particular time celebrating a particular event,[3] the beginning of the full settlement of the promised land; primarily, the words reflect that particular occasion, though no doubt they continued to be used in the subsequent worship of Israel.

An ailing[4] Aramean was my father — the reference is to Jacob, who entered Egypt with his sons. By the time he went down into Egypt, Jacob was already an old man (130 years old: Gen. 47:9) and ready to die (Gen. 45:28; 46:30). Jacob is described as an *Aramean,* perhaps reflecting his marriage to Leah and Rachel, both Aramean women.[5] That Jacob, the head of the family that moved into Egypt, was *ailing* or "perishing" emphasizes all the more the astonishing work of God in making good his covenant promises. *And lived as an alien there* — the words serve to contrast the state of the man who is making the declaration. He now has a land of his own and has brought to God the firstfruits of that land; in contrast, his forefather had no

---

1. See G. von Rad, *The Problem of the Hexateuch and Other Essays* (E.T. 1966), pp. 3-8; the relevant essay was first published in German in 1938. The hypothesis of von Rad has found considerable support in OT scholarship. For a recent study of the creed hypothesis, with conclusions different from those of von Rad, see C. Carmichael, "A New View of the Origin of the Deuteronomic Credo," *VT* 19 (1969), pp. 273-289.
2. The hypothesis, however, has been subjected to a number of critiques; for a useful summary, with some new critical observations, see J. P. Hyatt, "Were There an Ancient Historical Credo in Israel and an Independent Sinai Tradition?" in H. T. Frank and W. L. Reed, eds., *Translating and Understanding the OT.* Festschrift H. G. May, pp. 152-170.
3. Cf. D. Kidner, "The Origins of Israel," *TSF Bulletin* 57 (1970), pp. 3-12 (*p. 9). It is doubtful whether there was anything quite equivalent to a *credo* in early Israelite religion; if there was, then the *Shema'* would have a stronger claim to the title (see Deut. 6:4-9 and commentary) than the passage under discussion.
4. Heb. *'ᵃrammî 'ōbēd.* The verb *'ābad* means primarily "perish, die," though it may also indicate something "lost" (Deut. 22:3). Here, it could mean "lost, wandering," though it will be suggested in the commentary that "perishing, ailing" provides the better sense.
5. Cf. K. A. Kitchen, "Aram, Aramaeans," *NBD,* pp. 55-59. On the "Proto-Aramean" origins of the patriarchs, see J. C. L. Gibson, "Light from Mari on the Patriarchs," *JSS* 7 (1962), pp. 51f.; *idem,* "Observations on Some Important Ethnic Terms in the Pentateuch," *JNES* 20 (1961), pp. 229-234. Note also that *'arm* (Aram) is used in a personal name in the Ugaritic texts; *PRU* 2.46 (=*UT* 1046), line 5, *bn. arm;* lines 7, 9, *bn army.* See further the discussion in F. Gröndahl, *Die Personennamen der Texte aus Ugarit,* pp. 219f.

land he could call his own and lived in a foreign country. *Few in number* — see the list contained in Gen. 46:8-27, where it is noted that there were seventy people in Jacob's family at that time. From that small beginning, the descendants of Jacob became a "nation" in Egypt.

The declaration begins with Jacob, in the land of Canaan, and then describes his move into Egypt; the second part (vv. 6-8) starts with Egypt and then describes the great Exodus from Egypt. The people of God were maltreated in Egypt and cried out for help; God heard their cry and brought them out from that land with a great display of power. On the Exodus from Egypt, see further the commentary on Deut. 6:20-25. After the Exodus comes the third section; God brought his people into his promised land, *a land flowing with milk and honey* (see also 6:3). From this structure, it is clear that the worshipper's declaration is not exactly a creed. The motive expressed in the verses is thanksgiving for the *land,* and hence the progression is as follows: (i) Jacob, the head of a small family, did not have the land; (ii) in Egypt, Israel was a "nation," but had no land and did not have good prospects of acquiring a land; (iii) God, in his graciousness, had overcome every barrier and had given his people a *land.* Hence, the absence of any mention of the making of the covenant at Horeb (Sinai) is quite natural, though it would be a curious omission if the passage were in fact a creed. The passage does not recount *all* the major events in Israel's past history, but selects those which most naturally highlight God's gift of a land to his people.

The climax of the declaration comes in v. 10a. Remembering all those events in which God had been moving to bring his people to the land, the first generation of true residents return to God with an offering of the fruit of the land which had been given to them. It would be a dramatic moment, the culmination of several centuries during which the promise of God had been anticipated, and it was fitting that the moment should be marked with an offering and with thanksgiving. Though a solemn moment, it was to be a time of great rejoicing (v. 11), not only for the land-owning Israelite, but also for the Levite and resident alien, who participated in a less direct manner in the blessing of God.

(ii) If the first offering of firstfruits took place in the first year of full settlement in the land, the ceremony described in vv. 12-15 would take place two years later during the third year of full settlement. The tithe of the third year took place in the Israelite towns or *settlements,* and that which was tithed was to be distributed among various classes of underprivileged persons (v. 12); see the legislation on the topic in 14:28-29. After distributing the tithe, the worshipper made a declaration *before* (or "in the presence of") *the Lord your God;* since the words were probably to be spoken in the *settlements,* not at the central sanctuary, these words may indicate that this worship and declaration in the third year of settlement were performed in the home (see further on v. 15, below). The declaration has three parts: (a) a positive statement (v. 13); (b) a negative statement (v. 14); (c) a prayer in conclusion (v. 15).

(a) In the positive statement, the Israelite declares his fulfilment of the law relating to the tithe of the third year; the statement finishes with two negative clauses emphasizing the complete fulfilment of the law. (b) The negative statement (v. 14) affirms that the task has been carried out properly. The three negative remarks in this part of the declaration, though no longer completely clear in their meaning, seem to point to certain factors which, if present, would have nullified the fulfilment of the tithe law. *Trusting in my own strength*[6]— the one offering the tithe was to remember that what he offered was part of the blessing of God and not something he had produced through his own cleverness or agricultural skill.[7] *I have not given any of it to the dead* — on the prohibition of religious practices associated with the dead, see 14:1 and commentary. It is possible that a Canaanite practice is implied in these words and that the offerer is affirming that no part of his tithe has been offered to Baal, the "Dead One."[8] These three negative affirmations are followed by two positive declarations (v. 14b) that all of God's law has been fulfilled.

(c) The declaration ends with a prayer (v. 15). *Look down from your holy residence* — perhaps because the prayer is uttered in the home or in the settlement, it is to God in *heaven* that the prayer is addressed, with no reference to *the place that the Lord your God shall choose* (v. 2), namely the sanctuary. *Heaven* is a theological manner of referring to the "residence" of the transcendent God; it would probably be wrong to assume that according to Hebrew belief God literally lived "up there," for both heaven and earth were a part of God's order of creation.[9] However, the language of the opening words of the prayer is quite remarkable, for it at once affirms the utter transcendence of God, and yet makes plain that God could hear the words of his people, spoken in their homes and settlements through-

6.   Heb. *be'ōnî*. Cf. G. Fohrer, "Twofold Aspects of Hebrew Words," in P. R. Ackroyd and B. Lindars, eds., *Words and Meanings*, p. 98. A. S. Yahuda (*The Language of the Pentateuch in Its Relation to Egyptian*, pp. 271-73) has suggested "in my lifetime," on the basis of Egyptian *wn*.
7.   There may be a suggestion that the farmer had somehow depended on Canaanite means in producing his substance; if such was the case, then even though he tithed it to God, it would be unacceptable.
8.   Cf. H. Cazelles, *Le Deutéronome*, p. 106; *idem*, "Sur un rituel du Deutéronome" (Deut. 26:14), *RB* 55 (1948), pp. 54-71. See also J. Gray, *The Legacy of Canaan*[2], pp. 65n., 253.
9.   Gen. 1:1. See also P. C. Craigie, "Hebrew Thought about God and Nature and Its Contemporary Significance," *Canadian Journal of Theology* 16 (1970), pp. 3-11.

out the land. The prayer requests God's *continued* blessing — *continued,* because the tithe is a sign that already the Israelites were experiencing the blessing of God. They pray that both *Israel* and the *ground* (not so much the *land* as the ground which brings forth the harvest) might be blessed, and the basis on which the prayer is offered is the promise of God to their forefathers. When a man prays to God that he fulfil a divine promise, that man can rest assured that God is able and willing to answer his prayer. *A land flowing with milk and honey* — see 6:3.

D. CONCLUSION TO THE DECLARATION OF THE LAW (26:16-19)

16 *This day the Lord your God is commanding you to do these statutes and judgments, and you shall be careful to do them with all your heart and with all your soul.*

17 *Today you have proclaimed that the Lord is your God, that you will walk in his ways, and that you will keep his statutes and his commandments and his judgments, and that you will listen to his voice.*

18 *And today the Lord has proclaimed concerning you, that you are to be his highly prized people, just as he said to you, and that you are to keep all his commandments,*

19 *and that he will set you high above all the nations whom he has made, for praise and for a name and for honor, and that you will be a holy people for the Lord your God, just as he said.*

This short passage concludes the address on the law, but more exactly it is a conclusion to the discourse on the specific stipulations. The brief introduction to the specific stipulations in the address itself (12:1) is reflected in v. 16; all this section is still within the address — that is, these are still the words spoken, not a part of the written introduction (see 4:44-49). The specific stipulations have been presented; the people are urged to obey them, *with all your heart and with all your soul* (see also 6:5).

Verses 17-19 relate to a part of the covenant renewal ceremony;[1] although the ceremony itself is not made explicit, the words spoken by Moses give a clue to its nature. After the full declaration of the law, the people, who are gathered on the plains of Moab, make a declaration of their allegiance to God. God in turn declares his faithfulness to his people, the divine declaration being spoken by Moses, the mediator in the covenant renewal ceremony. The spoken words

---

1. For a detailed study of this passage, together with an examination of other studies, see N. Lohfink, "Dt. 26:17-19 und die Bundesformel," *Zeitschrift für katholische Theologie* 91 (1969), pp. 517-553.

would serve as a binding commitment on both parties in the renewal ceremony.[2] The substance of vv. 17-19 assumes that such declarations have just been made, and the words of the address summarize the content of those declarations.

Today (vv. 17, 18) — the time is that in which the address on the law was delivered on the plains of Moab. *You have proclaimed* (vv. 17, 18) — the verb indicates a formal declaration of commitment and may be a technical term in treaty/covenant vocabulary.[3] The Israelites declare that the Lord is their God; their declaration commits them to a life totally dominated by God. Hence, they will *walk in his ways* (see also 8:6), keep all his law, and *listen to* (or "be obedient to")[4] *his voice*. On the proclamation of God concerning his people, see also 7:6; 28:1. *For praise and for a name and for honor* — Israel, remaining faithful to the covenant God, would be renowned among other nations, not because of inherent merit, but because the covenant community would reflect the glory of the covenant God in its national life. This glory was the potential of the community of God's people; but in the two chapters that follow, a solemn warning is issued concerning the natural disasters that would fall upon Israel in the event of unfaithfulness to the covenant God.

2.   In the political treaties, a parallel is to be found in the exchange of oaths between the parties to the treaty; see the treaty between an Assyrian King and his vassal in the Zagros mountains, *ANET(S)*, p. 192.
3.   The verb is the Hiph. form of *'āmar*, which in OT usage occurs only in these two verses. Some commentators understand the verb, in a literal sense, as direct causative of *'āmar;* see G. A. Smith, *The Book of Deuteronomy*, p. 298. The sense of v. 17 would then be: "You have caused the Lord to say . . ."; on this interpretation, v. 17 would be God's covenant declaration, vv. 18-19 that of the people. But this rendering makes the syntax of the subsequent portions of vv. 17-19 extremely awkward. On the meaning "proclaim" for the Hiph. form here, see *TDOT* I, pp. 328f. (Wagner).
4.   See 5:1 and commentary.

IV. THE ADDRESS OF MOSES: BLESSINGS AND CURSES (27:1–28:69 [Eng. 29:1])

A. THE RENEWAL OF THE COVENANT COMMANDED (27:1-26)

1. THE WRITING OF THE LAW AND THE OFFERING OF SACRIFICES (27:1-10)

1 *Moses and the elders of Israel commanded the people, saying: Keep the whole commandment which I am commanding you today.*

2 *And it shall be, on the day that you cross the Jordan to the land which the Lord your God is about to give you, that you shall raise up for yourselves large stones, and you shall whitewash them with lime.*

3 *And you shall write all the words of this law upon them when you have crossed over, in order that you may go into the land which the Lord your God is about to give to you, a land flowing with milk and honey, just as the Lord God of your fathers said to you.*

4 *And it shall be, when you have crossed over the Jordan, that you shall raise up these stones — as I am commanding you today — on Mount Ebal and you shall whitewash them with lime.*

5 *And there you shall build an altar to the Lord your God, an altar of stones; you shall not work on them with an iron tool.*

6 *You shall build an altar of the Lord your God with complete stones, and upon it you shall offer burnt offerings to the Lord your God;*

7 *and you shall sacrifice peace offerings, and you shall eat there and you shall rejoice before the Lord your God.*

8 *And you shall write all the words of this law upon the stones, doing it clearly and well.*

9 *Then Moses and the priests, the Levites, addressed all Israel, saying: Be silent and hear, O Israel: this very day you have become the people of the Lord your God.*

10 *Therefore you shall listen to the voice of the Lord your God and you shall perform his commandments and his statutes, which I am commanding you today.*

The main section of specific stipulations (Deut. 12–26) is sandwiched between two sections in which the future renewal of the covenant is anticipated: 11:26-32 and 27:1-26. The structure at this point is significant for understanding the nature of the covenant relationship and the renewing of that relationship on the plains of Moab. The renewal of the covenant in Moab has two focal points: (1) the remembrance of the past, specifically the forming of the covenant at Horeb (Sinai); (2) the anticipation of the future, when again the covenant would be renewed. This perspective is a part of the Hebrew understanding of history; it is not simply that the Hebrews had a linear concept of time. Rather, they believed that there was a close relationship between the present moment, the events leading up to that moment, and those events still lying in the future, when the essence of God's ancient promise to the patriarchs would be fulfilled. Thus, throughout the renewal of the covenant in Moab, which had its roots in the past, the focal point and indeed the purpose of the renewal lay in the anticipation of the future. The specific details concerning the continuity of leadership in the covenant community are stated in chs. 29–30, but in ch. 27 the general principle is given, namely, that in the future there would have to be a further renewal of obedience and commitment to God's law, which had just been declared and expounded (chs. 12–26).[1]

1 *Moses and the elders of Israel* — the coupling of Moses and the elders is unusual, since in Deuteronomy Moses normally addresses the people by himself. But this joint address probably has particular significance: at the renewal of the covenant which is commanded, Moses would not be present (since he would die before the others entered the promised land). Therefore a particular responsibility would fall on the elders of the people to ensure that the injunction was carried out. It is probable that the joint form of address is designed to impress more urgently on the elders their future responsibilities in the leadership of the people. *Keep the whole commandment which I am commanding you today* — the injunction refers not only to the specific legislation of chs. 12–26, but also to the command to renew the covenant in the promised land (see also vv. 9-10, below, and 11:26-29).

In the verses that follow,[2] instructions are given concerning

---

1. See Josh. 8:30-35 for a description of the renewal that is demanded in Deuteronomy.
2. The repetitive nature of the verses, particularly with reference to the preparation of the stones, has given rise to a number of attempts to clarify the literary structure and sources of the chapter. See M. H. Segal, *The Pentateuch*, pp. 95f.; E. Nielsen, *Shechem. A Traditio-Historical Investigation* (²1959), pp. 50-75. It is possible, however, that the repetitive nature of the verses serves an emphatic function, reinforcing the necessity of obeying the injunctions.

two ceremonies which were to be carried out: (1) the preparation of stones on which the law was to be written; (2) the building of an altar on which sacrifices were to be offered. These two particular activities were both a part of the longer renewal ceremony, which also included the pronouncing of blessings and curses (vv. 11-26). The time and place are specified as being after the crossing of the river Jordan into the promised land (v. 2; see also 11:29, 31).

2-4, 8 The recording of the law on stones. Stones were to be erected and were then to be prepared for writing by whitewashing; when the law was written on the stones, the white background would make it clearly visible and easily read. The method of preparation and of writing described here is typically Egyptian in technique, rather than Palestinian or Mesopotamian.[3] The stones not only served to carry the written text of the law, but they also functioned as silent witnesses to the renewal of the covenant.[4] *The words of this law* (vv. 3 and 8) — in general terms, the phrase describes the legislation contained in chs. 12–26, but whether it should be interpreted literally as referring to a transcription of those chapters is uncertain. The law in Deuteronomy is presented as a part of Moses' address and includes elements such as exhortation and warning; but the address is based on the law of the covenant made at Horeb (Sinai). Therefore, the intention may be that the law of the covenant, on which Moses' exhortation was based, was that which was to be written on the stones.

The stones were to be set up *on Mount Ebal* (v. 4). Mount Ebal and Mount Gerizim[5] were located west of the Jordan, approximately 40 miles north of the city of Jerusalem. An important east-west trade route passed between the two mountains, and toward the eastern end of the pass nestled the ancient town and sanctuary of Shechem. This location is some distance to the north of the point at which the Israelites would cross the Jordan in order to begin their invasion of the promised land. The site for renewal, however, was no doubt deliberately chosen, for it had particular associations for the Hebrews. Abraham had built an altar there and the place had been associated from the time of the patriarchs with the Lord's promise of the gift of the land;[6] hence it was a particularly appropriate place at which to renew the covenant for the first time *within* the promised land.

3. See S. R. Driver, *Deuteronomy*, p. 296. Black ink, prepared from soot and gum (see J. R. Harris, ed., *The Legacy of Egypt*[2], p. 218), would stand out clearly on a white background. See also the article by R. J. Williams, *IDB* IV, pp. 909-921.
4. See Josh. 24:27. Cf. D. J. McCarthy, *Treaty and Covenant*, p. 126.
5. For Mount Gerizim, see v. 12 (below). The Samaritan version reads Gerizim for Ebal in v. 4, but this is more likely to reflect the religious attitudes of the Samaritans (for whom Gerizim had special significance) than an original textual variant.
6. Gen. 12:6-7. Jacob, too, had built an altar in the vicinity of Shechem; see Gen. 33:18-20. The sacred associations of the place are also emphasized by the burial of Joseph's bones there; Josh. 24:32.

5-7 In addition to setting up the stones, the Israelites were to build a rough altar of complete, uncut stones. The construction requirements follow the instructions already given at Sinai: "If you make me an altar of stone, you will not build it of cut stones, for if you wield your tool upon it, you profane it" (Exod. 20:25). The older law clarifies the injunction in v. 5: *you shall not work on them with an iron tool.* However, it is not altogether certain why an iron tool should profane the stones and make them unsuitable for God's altar.[7] An event from Israel's later history may illustrate the significance of the prohibition. The Israelites did not themselves work with iron and in Saul's day they had to go to Philistine smiths, who charged exorbitant prices, in order to have iron implements repaired (1 Sam. 13:19-23). Thus, it is possible that even from an early date, the use and maintenance of iron tools was indicative of dependence on non-Hebrews, a thing discouraged by the exclusive nature of the covenant relationship. On the altar which was constructed in this manner, *burnt offerings* (v. 6) and *peace offerings* (v. 7) were to be offered, and together the people would rejoice in God's presence (see Exod. 20:24). The injunctions concerning this future ceremony reflect the ceremony already undertaken at the initial making of the covenant at Sinai (Exod. 24:5-11).

9-10 Once again (see also v. 1), all Israel are exhorted to hear and obey God's words. *This very day you have become the people of the Lord your God* (v. 9) — see also 26:16-19 and commentary. The meaning is that in the renewal of the covenant, the Israelites renewed their status as God's people. They were already the people of God, of course, but the ceremony on the plains of Moab reminded them of that status and renewed its reality. This consciousness of being God's people is used here to reinforce the Israelites' sense of responsibility in renewing again their covenant with God, once they had passed over into the promised land.

2. BLESSINGS AND CURSES AT THE COVENANT RENEWAL (27:11-26)

11 *And Moses commanded the people on that same day, saying:*
12 *When you have crossed over the Jordan, these shall stand on Mount Gerizim to bless the people — Simeon, and Levi, and Judah, and Issachar, and Joseph, and Benjamin.*

---

7. In general, it may be assumed that the prohibited method has associations with Canaanite religion and therefore was to be forbidden in Israel. Iron objects are known in Egypt from the 14th century B.C., though iron working was not introduced until a later date; J. R. Harris, "Technology and Minerals," in *The Legacy of Egypt*[2], p. 90. The art of smelting and iron working seems to have been developed by the Hittites about the middle of the second millennium B.C.; see F. V. Winnett, "Iron," *IDB* II, pp. 725f. See also the reference to iron in Deut. 8:9.

13 *And these shall stand on Mount Ebal for the curse — Reuben, Gad, and Asher. and Zebulun, Dan, and Naphtali.*

14 *Then the Levites shall respond and say to every man of Israel with a loud voice:*

15 *Cursed be the man who makes an idol or molten image, an abomination of the Lord, the work of a craftsman's hands, and sets it up in secret! Then all the people shall respond and say: Amen.*

16 *Cursed be the one who dishonors his father and his mother! And all the people shall say: Amen.*

17 *Cursed be the one who displaces his neighbor's boundary marker! And all the people shall say: Amen.*

18 *Cursed be the one who leads astray a blind man in the road! And all the people shall say: Amen.*

19 *Cursed be the one who perverts the justice due to the resident alien, the orphan, and the widow! And all the people shall say: Amen.*

20 *Cursed be the one who lies with his father's wife, because he has uncovered his father's skirt! And all the people shall say: Amen.*

21 *Cursed be the one who lies with any kind of animal! And all the people shall say: Amen.*

22 *Cursed be the one who lies with his sister, the daughter of his father or the daughter of his mother! And all the people shall say: Amen.*

23 *Cursed be the one who lies with his mother-in-law! And all the people shall say: Amen.*

24 *Cursed be the one who kills his neighbor in secret! And all the people shall say: Amen.*

25 *Cursed be the one who takes a bribe in order to kill an innocent person! And all the people shall say: Amen.*

26 *Cursed be he who does not elevate the words of this law by doing them! And all the people shall say: Amen.*

11-14 The scene is now set for the ceremony of blessing and cursing which would take place at the renewal of the covenant to be held in the vicinity of Shechem (see also 11:26-32). Six of the tribes would stand on the slopes of Mount Gerizim and six would stand on the slopes of Mount Ebal;[1] they would represent respectively the blessing that followed upon obedience of the law and the cursing that was subsequent to the disobedience of the law. On the basis of the description of the ceremony given in Josh. 8:30-35, the ark, together with the Levitical priests who attended it, would be set in the middle of the valley, with the two groups of tribes on either side of it.

1. The division of the tribes seems to be based on their maternal relationship to the patriarch Jacob. The tribes descended from Leah and Rachel, Jacob's legitimate wives, represented the blessing; those descended from Zilpah and Bilhah, together with the tribes Reuben and Zebulun, represented the curse.

Although the details of the ceremony are no longer certain, the symbolism seems fairly clear. The ark, containing the covenant tablets, was in the middle. The people were either obedient to the law of the covenant or disobedient; there was no half-way house. The cursing and blessing would be a solemn reminder of the responsibility imposed by the covenant law and of the alternatives open to the Israelites. In v. 14, the Levites[2] addressed the Israelites and declared first of all the curses. There is no mention in the chapter of the subsequent declaration of the blessings, and the reason for this omission is uncertain. In the interpretation of the Mishnah,[3] the Levites (by the ark) address the blessings to Mount Gerizim and the six tribes standing there are to respond "Amen"; then the Levites address the curses to those tribes standing on Mount Ebal and they too respond "Amen." This is a possible interpretation,[4] though the text itself does not provide all the details that would be necessary for a complete reconstruction of the ceremony. It is not unlikely, however, that the twelve blessings, which are not mentioned here, would have been the exact reverse of the twelve curses that are stated.[5]

There now follow in vv. 15-26 the twelve curses, the so-called Dodecalog. To each curse *all the people*[6] respond "Amen." This word, which refers back to what has immediately preceded, indicates assent and agreement to what has been proclaimed.[7] Thus, by saying "Amen," the people indicate understanding and agreement and thereby remove any possible excuse for their conduct, if at some subsequent time they were to disobey the law of the covenant. It is difficult to determine a single unifying theme underlying the various acts that are placed under the curse. It is possible, however, that *secrecy* (see *in secret*, vv. 15, 24) might be considered such a theme. That is to say, there were certain crimes committed which by their very nature might not be discovered and therefore would not be brought to trial. If secrecy is the theme, then the curses pronounced here make it clear that crime is not determined merely by its discovery and punishment; whether or not an illegal act was ever discovered, it was nevertheless a crime against God and therefore deserved the curse of God.

2. The Levites here are those Levites whose specific duty it was to attend to the ark. They do not constitute the whole tribe of Levi, who have already taken their place on Mount Gerizim (v. 12) to represent the blessing.
3. *Sota* vii.5.
4. But see the comments and suggestions of I. Lewy, "The Puzzle of Dt. 28," *VT* 12 (1962), pp. 207-211.
5. Compare 28:3-6 and 16-19 for an example of direct opposites in blessing/curse passages.
6. Either all twelve tribes present, or (following the interpretation of the Mishnah) all the six tribes representing the curse say "Amen."
7. Cf. J. C. L. Gibson, *Textbook of Syrian Semitic Inscriptions* I, p. 30.

15 The first curse is called down on the man who makes an *idol* (carved from wood) or *molten image* (cast in metal). The crime envisaged could be a breach either of the first commandment (if it were an idol of a god other than the Lord) or of the second commandment (if it were an attempt to represent God himself in some visual and physical form). An idol or image was particularly reprehensible because it was *the work of a craftsman's hands,* the implication being that a man-made object could in some manner be an object through which worship could be directed. Since the crime was a breach of the Decalog, it would be appropriately punished in normal circumstances; but if the idol or image were kept *in secret,* the authorities in Israel might never learn that a sin was being committed. The curse emphasizes that lack of knowledge of a crime makes it no less an *abomination* of the Lord.

16 The second curse relates to the one who *dishonors*[8] *his father and his mother.* Thus it describes one who, by his actions, would be breaking the fifth commandment ("Honor your father and your mother . . ."). The precise law on this subject (Deut. 21:18-21) required the parents to prosecute their stubborn and rebellious son, but in practice this would have been a very difficult law to carry out because of the various conflicting emotions that would be involved. The stern requirements of the law would conflict with the continuing love for the son or daughter, and in this tension it would be difficult to know at what point the actions of the sibling necessitated recourse to the law, which carried the harsh penalty of death. But the curse covers the eventuality in a less direct fashion, for whether or not the rebellious sibling was brought to the courts of law, the act of dishonoring parents incurred automatically the curse of God.

17 The third curse relates to property rights, namely, to the illegal moving of a boundary marker, with the intention of acquiring territory that by right belonged to another man (see also 19:14 and commentary). It may be that more than just a boundary marker is intended; the reference may be to something like the Mesopotamian *kudurru-*stone.[9] This stone was not simply a marker, but it contained in addition an inscription giving details of property rights and invoking divine sanction and protection. Thus the crime envisaged could be total appropriation of another person's property. The nature of the crime is such that it would not normally be attempted, except in circumstances that might lead the offender to think he could do it with

8. For the meaning of the word in context, see M. A. Klopfenstein, *Scham und Schande nach dem AT* (1972), pp. 190-93. The word is the opposite in meaning from "honor" in the fifth commandment.
9. See A. L. Oppenheim, *Ancient Mesopotamia* (1964), pp. 123, 159; M. G. Kline, *The Structure of Biblical Authority,* pp. 32-34.

impunity. The curse emphasizes once again that the action was condemned within the covenant community, whether or not the offender was brought to the courts of the law.

18 The fourth curse is directed against the man who *leads astray a blind man in the road* (see also Lev. 19:14). The words may be taken literally, or they may have a more metaphorical sense; that is, they may indicate some kind of treatment of a blind man, which would result in personal gain, and yet which could not be brought to law because the blind man would not be able to identify the offender. If, for example, money is stolen from a blind man, he is not in a position to identify the thief. In contrast, the spirit of the covenant law prescribes just and humane treatment for all fellow Israelites; hence the curse is invoked on the one who offends against the spirit of charity and justice implicit in the covenant.

19 In a similar tone, the fifth curse is directed against all those who, by acting unjustly, might seek to take advantage of those members of society who could be easily abused, *the resident alien, the orphan, and the widow* (see also 24:17). Once again, the status in law of those offended against was such that they might fear to bring proceedings against the offender, but the curse nevertheless brings the offender under the judgment of God.

20-23 There now follow four curses directed against sexual offenses of various types;[10] in the nature of these acts they would normally be done in secret or in private, and therefore they would not always be brought to the attention of the courts of law. The sixth curse (v. 20) is directed against the person who has sexual relationships with his father's wife (presumably his step-mother). *He has uncovered his father's skirt* — to "cover (a woman) with the skirt" describes metaphorically the taking of a woman in marriage (cf. Ruth 3:9). Hence, *uncovering* the skirt seems to be a euphemistic manner of describing the invasion of the privacy of the sexual relationship between the father and (step-)mother by the father's son. The seventh curse is directed against the person who commits the crime of bestiality (v. 21), which again is an act normally committed in privacy or in the open countryside.[11] The eighth curse is directed against the man who commits incest with his sister (v. 22); even if the brother and sister had only one parent in common, incest (whether or not discovered) brought down the curse of God. In the ninth curse, sexual cohabitation with a mother-in-law[12] is prohibited.

10. For general parallels in the Code of Hammurabi, see laws 154-58; *ANET*, pp. 172f.
11. For Hittite laws on bestiality, and the differences between Hittite and Hebrew legislation, see H. A. Hoffner, *TB* 20 (1969), pp. 41f.
12. On the meaning of the Heb. word, see T. C. Mitchell, "The Meaning of the noun ḤTN in the OT," *VT* 19 (1969), pp. 93-112 (*p. 112).

24-25 The tenth and eleventh curses have to do with various ways in which murder might be committed, thereby breaking the sixth commandment. First a man might kill his neighbor in secret and therefore he might never be brought to trial for his crime. Second, a man might take a bribe in order to kill an innocent person; a paid assassin of this kind naturally would not commit the crime unless he thought he could avoid the penalty of the law, for otherwise his *bribe* would be of little value to him. Both types of murder come under the curse.

26 The twelfth and final curse has a summary and all-inclusive nature; it describes that man who does not take positive action which obedience to the law demanded. There is a sense in which the previous eleven curses are only examples, the twelfth curse making it quite clear that any action that does not *elevate the words of this law* brings an offender under the curse of God.

This last curse Paul expounds in his letter to the Galatians (3:10-14). The reach of the law is so all-pervasive that man cannot claim justification before God on the basis of "works of the law." This all-embracing nature of the law turns our eyes to Christ, who "redeemed us from the curse of the law, having become a curse for us, for it is written: Cursed be every one who hangs on a tree."[13]

B. THE BLESSINGS AND CURSES PRONOUNCED IN MOAB
(28:1-69 [Eng. 28:1-29:1])

1. THE BLESSINGS (28:1-14)

1 *And it shall be that if you listen carefully to the voice of the Lord your God, in order to keep and to do all his commandments, which I am commanding you today, then the Lord your God will set you high above all the nations of the earth.*
2 *And all these blessings shall come upon you and overtake you, because you listen to the voice of the Lord your God.*
3 *Blessed shall you be in the city and blessed shall you be in the countryside.*
4 *Blessed shall be the fruit of your womb, and the fruit of your ground, and the fruit of your animals — the offspring of your cattle and the young ones of your flock.*
5 *Blessed shall be your basket and your kneading-trough.*
6 *Blessed shall be your coming in and blessed shall be your going out.*
7 *The Lord will grant that your enemies, who rise up against you, shall be struck down before you; they shall come out to you by one road, but they shall take flight before you by seven roads.*

---

13. See also Deut. 21:23; for fuller discussion, see the Introduction, section VIII, "Theology."

8 *The Lord will command the blessing to be with you in your granary and in everything you put your hand to; and he will bless you in the land which the Lord your God is about to give to you.*

9 *The Lord will raise you up to be a holy people for himself, just as he promised you by oath, if you keep the commandments of the Lord your God and walk in his ways.*

10 *Then all the peoples of the earth shall see that the name of the Lord is proclaimed over you, and they shall be afraid of you.*

11 *And the Lord will grant you more than enough prosperity in the fruit of your womb, and in the fruit of your animals, and in the fruit of your ground, which the Lord promised by oath to your fathers to give to you.*

12 *The Lord will open up for you his good storehouse, the heavens, to give rain for your land in its season, and to bless every work of your hand; and you shall lend to many nations, but you shall not borrow.*

13 *And the Lord shall make you the head and not the tail; and you shall be above only, and you shall not be beneath, if you give heed to the commandments of the Lord your God, which I am commanding you today, by taking care and by doing them.*

14 *And you shall not turn aside, to the right hand or to the left, from all the words that I am commanding you today, by going after other gods to serve them.*

The conclusion to the specific stipulations (26:16-19) was followed in the address by instructions relating to the future renewal of the covenant in the vicinity of Shechem, after the initial stages of the conquest. In that future renewal ceremony, blessings and curses would be declared to the people (27:11-26). Now the focus in the address of Moses returns to the present moment, and in ch. 28 the substance of the address is an exhortation based upon the blessings and curses pronounced during the renewal of the covenant on the plains of Moab. The blessings are stated first (28:1-14) and then are followed by a much larger section dealing with the curses (28:15-68). In both parts of ch. 28, the actual blessings and curses which were pronounced formally in the ceremony are stated very succinctly; the blessings are stated in vv. 3-6 and find their direct opposites in the curses contained in vv. 16-19. Whether these were all the blessings and curses pronounced during the ceremony, or only extracts from them, is uncertain; the twelve curses of 27:15-26 indicate that the blessings and curses pronounced in Moab may have been longer. However, in ch. 28 there is not an explicit description of the blessing/cursing ceremony; the chapter contains only the sermon of Moses based upon the blessing/cursing theme, and the substance of vv. 3-6 and 16-19 may only be the "text" that Moses chooses as a basis for his sermon. On this interpretation of the chapter, vv. 7-14 and 20-68 are a part of the sermon of Moses, not a part of the basic ceremony of pronouncing the blessings and curses. The ceremony per se would probably be conducted along the lines indicated by 27:11-14.

1   The passage begins with language directly reflecting the substance of 26:16-19. A conditional statement (v. 1a) is followed by a promise (v. 1b); if Israel obeys the commandments of God, then blessing will follow. This principle, together with its converse (v. 15), provides the basic foundation for interpreting ch. 28. *High above all the nations of the earth* — see also 26:19. The setting, within which the blessing or cursing of God was to be experienced, was an international one; given this large perspective of men and nations, it is easy to forget that Israel at this time was a people without a land. The international theme emerges clearly in the sermon that follows and it is given two emphases. (a) There is an emphasis on the *internal* blessing of God on his people, indicating the health and prosperity of the nation per se. (b) There is also an emphasis on the strength and vitality of Israel vis-à-vis other nations. The converse of both these emphases appears in the following section dealing with curses; Israel not only would experience disaster within her communal life as a result of disobedience, but would be openly humiliated among other nations.

2-6   The blessings are stated. Verse 2 serves to introduce the blessings that form the starting point for this portion of Moses' sermon. "The blessings are represented as actual powers, which follow the footsteps of the nation, and overtake it."[1] The blessing of God would extend to every sphere of Israel's life: to urban life and rural life (v. 3); to fertility, in man, in the ground, and in animals (v. 4); to the provision of household necessities (v. 5);[2] to the daily activities that a man might undertake (v. 6).[3]

Verses 7-14, exhortation based on the blessings pronounced, either elaborate on the meaning of the foregoing blessings, or else deal with related topics evoked by those blessings.

7   First, a prerequisite for the continuing experience of divine blessing is stated. Any enemies of Israel, whose attack would threaten their peaceful and blessed existence, would be defeated; God would grant his people victory. Here the security granted by God against external threats is stated to emphasize the reality of God's blessing within the community. It was a promise in which the Israelites could trust, for already they had experienced the victory God had

---

1.   Keil and Delitzsch, *The Pentateuch,* pp. 435f.
2.   The *kneading-trough* was a kitchen utensil, a wide shallow bowl employed for the preparation of dough with which to make bread. The blessing of v. 5 thus refers to the ample provision of daily food for the family.
3.   *Your coming in . . . your going out* — see also 31:2 for the same idiom. The idiom refers to a man's daily work; the blessing indicates that a man would be blessed abundantly in the fulfilment of his responsibilities each day.

provided against the military might of Egypt. On God's provision of victory, see further 7:17-26.

8 The Lord's blessing would be seen *in your granary.* The noun *'āsām* (RSV "barn") seems to denote specifically a place where grain is stored.[4]

9 See also 7:6 and 26:19. The condition is stated once again for emphasis (see v. 1); the blessing of God would be granted only if the people were obedient to his commandments.

10 The blessing of God would result in the exaltation of Israel among all other peoples; they would *be afraid of* (or "revere") Israel because of the manifest blessing and presence of God. *The name of the Lord is proclaimed over you —* the exaltation of Israel would be a result not of her own merit, but of God's blessing. Thus Israel's glorious estate would be a proclamation of God's *name* (see also 26:19) and a testimony to God's power and grace within the world.

11 See also v. 4. God, in his goodness, would *grant . . . more than enough prosperity. . . .* The Hebrew is literally: "the Lord will cause you to have an excess of prosperity."

12 One of the roles of God in the promised land would be the provision of fertility; fertility depended primarily on the rains. Without the rains, the crops could not grow, and without the crops and the other produce of the field, neither man nor his domestic animals could survive. Thus in v. 12, there is a very rich expression of the blessing of God, for in providing the rains, God was providing what would be the mainspring of life in Israel's land. The language of the verse is poetic and the imagery may serve a particular religious purpose. The heavens are described as God's *storehouse;* whenever he opened that storehouse, the rains would come down to fertilize the land. The imagery at this point is reminiscent of Ps. 104:3, 13, where God is described as watering the mountains from his lofty abode. But both Hebrew passages find a parallel in the Canaanite myth of Baal, as it is known from the Ugaritic texts. According to the myth, when a house was built for Baal, a window or skylight was set in the roof of the house, so that through this opening Baal could release the rains over the earth.[5] The myth points to a primary function of Baal in the religion of the Canaanites; as a provider of rain, he was a fertility god. When the Israelites entered the promised land, they would be faced with the temptations of the fertility cult of Baal, which had served the previous residents in the land. Such temptations were to be resisted,

---

4. The noun is used only twice in the OT: see also Prov. 3:10. On the meaning *granary,* see the Yavneh-Yam letter; J. C. L. Gibson, *Textbook of Syrian Semitic Inscriptions* I, p. 29; D. Diringer and S. P. Brock, "Words and Meanings in Early Hebrew Inscriptions," in P. R. Ackroyd and B. Lindars, eds., *Words and Meanings,* pp. 41f.
5. For the text, see *CTA* 4.7.15-30 (=*UT* 51.7.15-30).

337

for though the Lord was not a fertility God in the restricted sense, yet fertility was within his power, for he was the creator and sustainer of the world. It may be that the language of v. 12 (and also of Ps. 104) deliberately echoes the Canaanite myth in order to emphasize that the Lord, and not Baal, would provide the needed rains. On God's provision of the rain, see further 11:11-17 and commentary. On v. 12b, see 15:6 and commentary.

13 The blessing of God is now given another form of expression, but the blessing is qualified once again by the condition of obedience (see also vv. 1, 9). God would make Israel to be the *head*, not the *tail*, [6] and to be *above only*, and not *beneath*. The context in which the idiom is to be understood is provided by the *peoples of the earth* (v. 10) and the *many nations* (v. 12). Israel would be a prince among nations, rich in produce and harvest, strong against her enemies, glorious in the presence of God in her midst — always provided that the commandments of God were obeyed (v. 13b).

14 The promise of blessing is concluded by a further admonition to obey God, never deviating from the path marked out for the people of God, and steadfastly refusing to be drawn into the web of the cults of foreign gods. On the language used in this verse, see 5:32; 8:19; 13:2-19.

2. THE CURSES (28:15-69 [Eng. 29:1])

(a) The Curses Pronounced During the Ceremony (vv. 15-19)

15 And it shall be that if you will not listen to the voice of the Lord your God, in order to keep and to do all his commandments and his statutes which I am commanding you today, then all these curses shall come upon you and shall overtake you.
16 Cursed shall you be in the city, and cursed shall you be in the countryside.
17 Cursed shall you be in your basket and in your kneading-trough.
18 Cursed shall be the fruit of your womb and the fruit of your ground, the offspring of your cattle and the young ones of your flock.
19 Cursed shall be your coming in and cursed shall be your going out.

This introductory section to the curses provides a parallel to vv. 1-6; every blessing of the earlier portion here finds its converse in a curse. Once again, the curses are introduced by a conditional statement; the curses would fall upon the people only *if* they were disobedient to the law of God (v. 15).[1] For the substance of the curses, see the commentary on vv. 2-6.

6. A similar idiom, though serving a different purpose, is employed in Isa. 9:15-16; cf. E. J. Young, *The Book of Isaiah* I, pp. 351f.

1. The curse sections of certain Near Eastern treaties also begin with a conditional

In the long elaboration on the curses that follows (vv. 20-68), there are a number of general difficulties which must be examined briefly prior to going on to the detailed commentary. First, there is the difficulty of attempting to define the relationship between these verses and the many parallels that occur in curse-texts in ancient Near Eastern literature.[2] M. Weinfeld, among others, has argued that large portions of vv. 20-68 were directly borrowed from Assyrian sources, particularly from the vassal treaties of Esarhaddon, which are dated in the seventh century b.c.[3] That there are close parallels between the substance of Deut. 28 and Esarhaddon's vassal treaties is beyond question; the difficulty lies in interpreting the significance of those parallels. One example of Weinfeld's larger argument will be examined to illustrate the difficulties. There are parallels in substance between 28:26-35 and VTE, lines 419-430;[4] the significance of the parallels, in Weinfeld's argument, lies not only in the substance of the curses, but also in the "almost identical order"[5] in which they are presented. After discussing the evidence in detail,[6] Weinfeld concludes that the evidence "attests that there was a direct borrowing by Deuteronomy from the Assyrian treaty documents."[7] To these remarks, it may be responded: (i) There are many differences in detail between the wordings of the two passages; these differences preclude the possibility of direct *borrowing*, but still leave open the possibility of *adaptation*.[8] (ii) If it be granted that there is an "almost identical order" in the presentation of curses in the two sections under examination, then it must be noted that the similarity in sequence does not extend to *all* the parallels between Deut. 28 and the Vassal Treaties of Esarhaddon.[9] (iii) Several of the curses in 28:26-35 have parallels in other (older) Near Eastern texts, which reduce the significance of the parallels with VTE, 419-430.[10] (iv) There are several aspects of the

---

clause. See, e.g., the Hittite treaty between Muršiliš II and Duppi-Teššub; J. A. Thompson, *The Ancient Near Eastern Treaties and the OT,* p. 17.
2.   For a convenient tabulation of the more important external parallels, see D. J. McCarthy, *Treaty and Covenant,* p. 122.
3.   *Deuteronomy and the Deuteronomic School,* pp. 116-129.
4.   For an English translation of the latter, see *ANET(S),* pp. 98-105.
5.   Weinfeld, p. 118. The exception to the order is 28:26, which must be transposed to follow 28:29 in order to provide an exact parallel.
6.   Detailed points will be taken up in the commentary (below); in this context, only the general thrust of Weinfeld's argument is noted.
7.   Weinfeld, pp. 121f.
8.   On the distinction between *borrowing* and *adapting* in the comparative study of texts, see P. C. Craigie, *TB* 22 (1971), pp. 28-30. For an example, Deut. 28:26 refers to "birds" and "beasts" in a general fashion; *VTE,* 425-27 refers specifically to "eagles" and "vultures."
9.   This can be seen clearly in the table provided by D. J. McCarthy, *Treaty and Covenant.* p. 122.
10.   For example, the sickness noted in Deut. 28:27 has a parallel in *VTE.* Deut. 28:27, however, specifies the sicknesses as ones that cannot be healed; there is no parallel to

curses noted in 28:26-35 that have no parallel whatever in the Esarhaddon texts.[11] (v) Several of the curses in 28:26-35 can be interpreted in relation to earlier portions of Deuteronomy, but must be stretched beyond their natural meaning to provide a parallel to *VTE*, 419-430.[12] (vi) Further specific points will be noted in the commentary; see particularly the commentary on vv. 27-29. To summarize, though the presence of parallel material in the Vassal Treaties of Esarhaddon is beyond doubt, a direct relationship between the two texts is highly unlikely. It is more likely that there was a body of common conceptions in the Near East associated with curses, whether in treaties, law codes, or other types of texts. Both Deut. 28 and the Assyrian texts indicate that they have drawn on these resources, but in both texts they have been adapted to their immediate context.

A second difficulty in this section of curses relates to the length of the curse-section vis-à-vis the blessings; the section containing the curses seems to be excessively long in relation to that containing the blessings.[13] This imbalance has given rise to a number of suggestions concerning the structure of the chapter; portions of the chapter are thought to come from later periods in Israel's history, some from as late as the Exile,[14] so that in its present form, Deut. 28 is a composite narrative. Although it is possible that there have been minor accretions over the course of time, the following points may be noted with regard to the length of the chapter. (i) The imbalance finds several parallels in other Near Eastern texts containing blessings and curses.[15] (ii) The imbalance finds an obvious reason in light of the purpose of the exposition of the curses in the address of Moses. The curses come close to the end of the ceremony of covenant renewal; they provide the speaker with an excellent opportunity for one final warn-

---

this point in *VTE*, but a parallel can be found in the curse of sickness noted in the epilog of the Law Code of Hammurabi, xxviii.50-60; *ANET*, p. 180.

11. For example, the vineyard (v. 30b), the ox, ass, and flock (v. 31), have no parallel in *VTE*.

12. For example, Weinfeld (p. 118) compares v. 30a *(you shall betroth a wife . . .)* with *VTE*, 428-29. It should be noted, however, that all three parts of v. 30 are to be interpreted against the background of the exemptions from military service stated in Deut. 20:5-7, which provide a direct parallel (see the commentary on 28:30, below). In contrast, the Assyrian text describes the wife being taken by an *enemy*, not simply by another man, as is the case in both Hebrew passages.

13. See also ch. 27, where only the curses are given in detail, the blessings simply being referred to in general terms.

14. For example, P. R. Ackroyd suggests that vv. 36-68 probably reflect Judah's experience of siege and exile; *Israel under Babylon and Persia* (1970), p. 146. Cf. M. H. Segal, *The Pentateuch*, p. 96.

15. K. A. Kitchen refers to the Lipit-Ishtar laws, where curses outnumber blessings by approximately 3:1, and the Law Code of Hammurabi, where the proportion of curses to blessings is approximately 20:1; *Ancient Orient and OT* (1966), p. 97 (n. 41).

ing to the people of the dangers of disobeying the law of God. Moses was about to die, the congregation were about to cross the Jordan, and the whole future of Israel depended on faithful obedience to the law of God. Thus the long and solemn sermon on the curse of God provides a final incentive for wholehearted commitment in renewing the covenant.

There is one further matter to be noted before returning to the text. When the substance of Deut. 28:15-68 is read with a knowledge of the subsequent history of Israel as a nation, the curses seem to assume an awful inevitability. And when it is recalled further that the Israelites were not an exceptional people, but reflected in their perversity the nature of sinful man, then the inevitability of the curse weighs equally on the modern reader. It is at this point that the gospel message of the New Testament casts light into the darkness evoked by the curse. The point can be illustrated with a quotation from William Blake's poem, "The Everlasting Gospel."[16]

> Jesus was sitting in Moses' chair.
> They brought the trembling woman there.
> Moses commands she be stoned to death.
> What was the sound of Jesus' breath?
> He laid his hand on Moses' law.
> The ancient heavens in silent awe,
> Writ with curses from pole to pole.
> All away began to roll.

The inevitability of the curse can be removed only by Jesus, and that is possible only because "he redeemed us from the curse of the law, having become a curse for us" (Gal. 3:13). For further discussion, see Introduction, VIII ("Theology"), section 5.

(b) Death, Sickness, and Drought (vv. 20-24)

> 20 *The Lord will send on you cursing, confusion, and fierce anger in every enterprise that you undertake, until you are destroyed and until you perish quickly because of the evil of your deeds in which you have forgotten me.*
> 21 *The Lord will make the pestilence cling to you until he has wiped you out from upon the ground to which you are going in order to take possession of it.*
> 22 *The Lord will afflict you with consumption, and with fever, and with inflammation, and with raging fever, and with drought, and with scorching, and with mildew, and they shall pursue you until you perish.*
> 23 *And your heavens which are above your head shall be bronze, and the earth which is beneath you shall be iron.*

16. See W. B. Yeats, ed., *Poems of William Blake* (n.d.), p. 115. The quotation is taken somewhat out of context, but nevertheless serves to illustrate the point at issue.

24 *The Lord will make the rain of your land to be dust and powder; it shall descend upon you from heaven until you are destroyed.*

20 Disobedience to the law would result in God afflicting his people with a series of calamities, which would result finally in death. *Fierce anger* (RSV "frustration"; RV "rebuke") — the Hebrew (*mig'eret*) denotes the physical expression of God's anger.[17] The root cause of the disaster would be forgetfulness (see also 8:11-20 and commentary); the people would forget God, and in forgetting God they would forget his commandments. Having forgotten the commandments of God, the people would inevitably commit evil deeds and bring upon their own heads disaster. God sends the curse (v. 20a), but man invites it by his deeds (v. 20b).

21 *Pestilence* probably refers to a disease of epidemic proportions, which would cling to the people (i.e., it would be impossible to halt its progress) until they were wiped out from the promised land.

22 Seven afflictions are noted in this verse, four of them human diseases and three relating to plant life; as in the previous verse, the afflictions would result in death for the people. Although the identity of the four diseases cannot be specified with any certainty in modern medical nomenclature, there seems to be a common element to all four diseases which distinguishes them from those mentioned in vv. 27-28 (below).[18] All are related to "heat." If *consumption* is in fact tuberculosis, it may be noted that fever and intense sweating are among the symptoms of that disease. The other three diseases also seem to be associated with heat, either in the form of fever or as a burning sensation resulting from inflammation of the tissues. Plant life would also suffer from the afflictions sent by God. *Drought*[19] — heat and lack of water would cause plants to die. *Scorching* — the reference is probably to the hot wind (sirocco) blowing in from the desert, *scorching* plant life as it blew. *Mildew* — the reference may be to that form of mildew which extracts moisture from plants (causing them to die) and forms a white powdery substance on the leaves.

23 Cf. Lev. 26:19 and *VTE*, 528-531. The verse follows the meaning of v. 22b. The *bronze* heavens would be bright with the sun, but no rain would fall from them to water the ground; the earth underfoot would be as hard as iron, unable to support life. The dryness of the cursed land stands in marked contrast to the blessed

---

17. See A. A. Macintosh, "A Consideration of Hebrew *g'r*," *VT* 19 (1969), pp. 471-79; cf. S. C. Reif, "A Note on *g'r*," *VT* 21 (1971), pp. 241-44.
18. For a thorough treatment of *disease* in the Bible, see R. K. Harrison, *IDB* I, pp. 847-854.
19. The translation assumes the pointing *hōreb* (for *hereb*).

land described in v. 12, which was watered freely by God from his heavenly storehouse.

24 Instead of rain, dust and powder would descend from heaven, making the once blessed land a lifeless desert; the dusty sand would be swept in from the desert by the sirocco wind (see v. 22).

(c) Defeat in Battle and Ignoble Death (vv. 25-26)

> 25 *The Lord will give you up to be smitten before your enemies. You shall go out to him by one road, but you shall flee before him by seven roads, and you shall become an object of terror to all the kingdoms of the earth.*
>
> 26 *And your corpses shall become food for every bird of the sky and for the animals of the earth, and there shall be no one to disturb them.*

The curse described in these two verses is the converse of the blessings contained in vv. 7, 10. Instead of victory, there would be defeat. Instead of the enemy fleeing in terror by seven different roads, Israel would be put to flight. Disobedience to the law of God separated the people from him, and in this state of separation they could not expect to experience the presence of God in the midst of their army; without God in the midst of Israel's army, defeat was inevitable. *You shall become an object of terror*—the meaning is quite different from v. 10, *they shall be afraid of you.* The Israelites would become such devastated specimens of humanity, that other men would find it too terrible to look at them. They would be recognized, however, by birds and beasts of prey, not as human beings, but simply as a source of meat. Man who was created to master the world (Gen. 1:28) would be mastered by it, if he fell under the curse of God.

(d) Diseases and the Consequences of Defeat (vv. 27-35)

> 27 *The Lord will smite you with Egyptian boils, and with hemorrhoids, and with eczema, and with scabies, of which you cannot be healed.*
>
> 28 *The Lord will smite you with madness, and with blindness, and with derangement of the mind;*
>
> 29 *and you shall be groping about at midday, just like the blind man who gropes about in the darkness, and you shall not make your ways prosperous, but you shall only be wronged and robbed continually, and there shall be no one to deliver you.*
>
> 30 *You shall betroth a woman, but another man shall lie with her; you shall build a house, but you shall not live in it; you shall plant a vineyard, but you shall not put it to use.*
>
> 31 *Your ox shall be slaughtered before your eyes, but you shall not eat of it; your ass shall be seized in your presence, but it shall not be returned to you; your flock shall be given over to your enemies, and there shall be no one to deliver you.*

32 *Your sons and your daughters shall be given over to another people and your eyes shall see and fail with longing for them the whole day long, but you shall be powerless to help.*

33 *A people whom you have not known shall eat the fruit of your ground and all the produce of your toil, and you shall only be wronged and crushed continually,*

34 *so that you are driven mad by the sight you see with your eyes.*

35 *The Lord will smite you with terrible boils on the knees and on the legs, of which you cannot be healed, from the sole of your foot to the top of your head.*

27 Further diseases with which God will afflict the people are noted. As was the case at v. 22, the specific identity of each disease is uncertain. *Egyptian boils* — this is presumably the disease with which God afflicted the Egyptians, prior to the Exodus (Exod. 9:19).[20] *Hemorrhoids* — though the exact identification is uncertain, some type of anal disorder seems to be intended.[21] All four diseases, if their identification is even approximately correct, are diseases of the skin, or at least have dermatological symptoms. See also v. 35 (below).

28 The reference to *blindness*, preceded by *madness* and followed by *derangement of the mind*, indicates that this verse may still be referring indirectly to disorders of the skin. The tertiary stage of syphilis includes both blindness and insanity among its symptoms.[22] If this interpretation of the verse is correct,[23] then the significance of the curse becomes all the more apparent. The spread of syphilis would indicate that the laws on sexual behavior had been abandoned, and that people had brought upon themselves the curse of God by their licentious activities.[24]

20. P. Montet finds what seems to be a similar disease mentioned in an Egyptian medical text; *Egypt and the Bible*, p. 98.
21. For a fuller discussion of the identification of the disease, see O. Neustätter, "Where Did the Identification of the Philistine Plague as Bubonic Plague Originate?" *Bulletin of the History of Medicine* 11 (1942), pp. 36-47. Neustätter, though uncertain of "hemorrhoids," thinks nevertheless that it is closer to the meaning than "plague (boils)." The Douay version refers to "the part of thy body, by which the dung is cast out."
22. See, e.g., Sir Stanley Davidson, *The Principles and Practice of Medicine* ([6]1963), pp. 58, 1009.
23. Weinfeld (pp. 121f.) interprets *gārāb* (v. 27) as some kind of leprosy, noting cognate terms in Syriac/Aramaic and Akkadian (p. 117, n. 5). He couples leprosy with what he calls "judicial blindness" (vv. 28-29) and notes a similar coupling of curses in *VTE*, 419-424. Even if the translation "leprosy" is correct, it should be noted that the parallel is not precise. (i) 28:27 lists four incurable diseases; *VTE*, 419-420 mentions only leprosy. (ii) 28:28-29 mentions madness and blindness; *VTE*, 422-24 mentions only blindness.
24. The interpretation of the verse in terms of syphilis is open to doubt. It is possible that blindness and madness are intended in a general sense as typical cures. For the curse of blindness in the Ugaritic texts, see *CTA* 19.IV.167 (=*UT* 1 Aqht I:167); in this text, the curse of blindness is invoked because of murder.

29 The substance of v. 28 is now vividly illustrated. In broad daylight, the cursed blind man gropes around. He cannot see and does not know how to make himself prosperous, but he can be seen by others; his fumbling ineptitude makes him an easy prey for robbers. Having brought about his sad state through disobedience to the law of God, he is now at the mercy of those who live outside the law, and there is no one to offer help. His fellows are equally cursed, and he has gone too far from God to call for his deliverance.

30-34 There now follows a series of curses which would come in the wake of defeat in battle. The three main clauses in v. 30 all relate to the exemptions from military service granted in time of war; see Deut. 20:5-7 and commentary. The exemptions were possible only because God would be present with his people in battle and would grant them victory. Disobedience to the law of God, however, would mean that God would no longer be a force in the army of Israel. In the absence of God's presence, the enemy would be more threatening than ever before; and in order to meet the menace, all exemptions from military service would be cancelled. Those normally exempted from military service would be killed and the consequence of v. 30 would follow. The enemy would take control of their livestock (v. 31) and even their children would be treated like animals. *Given over to another people* (v. 32) — the meaning is that they would be sold into slavery to a foreign nation. A foreign nation would eat the fruit of the ground and the produce of their labor (v. 33); compare this curse with the blessings of vv. 8, 11 (above). In vv. 32, 34, there is a return to the theme of sight and blindness. Earlier, blindness was associated with sickness (vv. 27-28); now the horrors of what the people would see indicate that even blindness could be a blessing. They would see their children being taken away and would be powerless to do anything. Instead of madness being experienced as a disease, the people would be driven to insanity by what they saw.

35 In this verse there is a further reference to diseases of the skin which would afflict the people cursed by God; the disease mentioned here is reminiscent of that from which Job suffered (see Job 2:7).

(e) Exile, Poor Harvests, and Decline in Status (vv. 36-46)

36 *The Lord will bring you and your king, whom you raise up over you, to a nation whom neither you nor your fathers have known, and there you shall serve other gods, wood and stone!*

37 *And you shall become a horror, a proverb, and an object of taunt among all the peoples to whom the Lord leads you.*

38 *You shall take out to the field abundant seed, but you shall gather in little, for the locust shall consume it.*

39 *You shall plant vineyards and till them, but you shall not drink wine and you shall not gather in fruit, for the worm shall eat it.*

40 *You shall have olives in all your territory, but you shall not anoint yourself with oil, for your olives shall drop off.*

41 *You shall bear sons and daughters, but they shall not belong to you, for they shall go off into captivity.*

42 *A swarm of crickets shall take possession of every one of your trees and of the fruit of your ground.*

43 *The resident alien who is in your midst shall rise over you higher and higher, but you shall go down, lower and lower.*

44 *He shall lend to you, but you shall not lend to him; he shall be the head, but you shall be the tail.*

45 *And all these curses shall come upon you, and they shall pursue you and overtake you until you are destroyed, for you did not listen to the voice of the Lord your God, in order to keep his commandments and his statutes which he commanded you.*

46 *And they shall be for a sign and for a wonder upon you and upon your posterity forever.*

36-37 The Israelites who were gathered on the plains of Moab could still remember their servitude in Egypt, and now the threat of a similar experience is held before them again. Disobedience to the law of God could lead to the curse of deportation from the promised land; the covenant with God would be exchanged for vassaldom to an earthly power. Although the memory of Egypt no doubt lies behind this curse,[25] it is not Egypt that would be the instrument of God in the curse, but rather *a nation whom neither you nor your fathers have known.* Having lost the privileges of the covenant, the Israelites would be forced into the service of strange gods, not a living God like their Lord,[26] but lifeless gods of wood and stone. *Your king* — see 17:14-20 for the legislation relating to kings. *You shall become a horror . . .*— see also v. 25.

38-42 The substance of these verses is a more detailed elaboration on the curse of the *fruit of your womb and the fruit of your ground* (v. 18). The Israelites would work hard, seeding their fields (v. 38), planting and tilling[27] their vineyards (v. 39), tending their olive trees (v. 40), and bearing children (v. 41), but all their work and all the initial signs of prosperity would vanish under the curse of God. The locust, the grapeworm, disease in the olive trees, foreign powers, and

25. Deportation of enemies was a common military practice, not only by the Egyptians but by most military powers of the Near East; men might be taken as hostages or in order to be put to work as slaves. Cf. J. M. Sasson, *The Military Establishments at Mari*, pp. 48f.; H. W. F. Saggs, *The Greatness That Was Babylon*, p. 97; G. Steindorff and K. C. Seele, *When Egypt Ruled the East* ([2]1957), p. 56; D. J. McCarthy, *Treaty and Covenant*, p. 124.

26. Cf. Deut. 5:26.

27. On the verb *'āḇaḏ* with the sense "to till," compare the use of the cognate verb in line 7 of the Aramaic Zenjirli inscription, *y'bdw. 'rq. wkrm.* Cf. G. A. Cooke, *A Text-book of North-Semitic Inscriptions*, p. 166.

crickets,[28] are the instruments with which God would afflict his disobedient people.

43-44   The curse of God would affect each area of Israel's life, so that the people would enter upon a path of steady decline, sinking even lower than the underprivileged member of their own community, the *resident alien*. The curses here are the reverse of the blessings contained in vv. 12-13.

45-46   These two verses provide a brief pause in the solemn elaboration of curses and remind the audience once again of the reasons that would give rise to such terrible disaster. Disobedience to the word of God would result inevitably in disaster. With v. 45, compare vv. 15 and 20. *For a sign and for a wonder* — the disasters that would befall the Israelites, if they were disobedient to God, would serve to illustrate the ways of God to other nations, who would be prompted to ask questions when they saw the plight of the Israelites. For a fuller treatment of this theme, see 29:22-29 and commentary.

(f) Siege and the Horrors of the Besieged (vv. 47-57)

> 47 *Because you will not have served the Lord your God with rejoicing and with a good heart on account of the abundance of everything,*
>
> 48 *then you shall serve your enemies, whom the Lord sends out against you, in hunger, and in thirst, and in nakedness, and in need of everything; and he will set a yoke of iron upon your neck until he has destroyed you.*
>
> 49 *The Lord will raise up against you a nation from far away, from the end of the earth, which soars like an eagle soars, a nation whose language you do not understand,*
>
> 50 *a nation of fierce appearance, who pay no respect to an elder and show no favor to a youngster.*
>
> 51 *And they shall eat the fruit of your animals and the fruit of your ground until you are destroyed. They are a nation who will not leave behind for you any grain, new wine, and fresh oil, the offspring of your cattle and the young ones of your flock, until they have caused you to perish.*
>
> 52 *And they shall besiege you in all your settlements, until the high and fortified walls, in which you place your trust, come down, throughout all your land; and they shall besiege you in all your settlements throughout all your land which the Lord your God will have given to you.*
>
> 53 *And you shall eat the fruit of your womb, the flesh of your sons and your daughters, whom the Lord God will have given to you, in the siege and in the distress with which your enemy shall distress you.*
>
> 54 *As for the man among you who is delicate and very dainty, his eye*

---

28. The specific identity is uncertain, but the creature would be some member of the locust species with enormous destructive power.

THE BOOK OF DEUTERONOMY

will be evil against his brother, and against his beloved wife, and against the last of his sons that remains.
55 *so that he will not give to one of them any of the flesh of his sons which he is eating, in case there is nothing left for him in the siege and in the distress with which your enemy shall distress you in all your settlements.*
56 *As for the delicate and dainty woman among you, who would hardly venture to set the sole of her foot upon the earth on account of her daintiness and delicacy, her eye shall be evil against her beloved husband, and against her son, and against her daughter,*
57 *and against her afterbirth which came out from between her feet, and against her sons to whom she has given birth, because she will eat them in secret, in need of everything in the siege and in the distress with which your enemy shall distress you in your settlements.*

The potential horrors that would result from the curse of God are now presented in even more terrible detail. The passage can be divided loosely into three subsections: (i) The covenant with God is exchanged for a "yoke of iron" (vv. 47-48). (ii) The Lord will raise up a foreign power to besiege Israel in her settlements (vv. 49-52). (iii) During the distress of the siege, the Israelites would descend to the depth of depravity in practicing cannibalism (vv. 53-57).

(i) *Because you will not have served . . .* (v. 47). The verb is translated in the future perfect tense. Within the address on the curse, the speaker is so carried away by his theme that it now seems that the curse is inevitable, and the words are almost as if the curse had already been put into effect.[29] Because of God's abundant provision for all his people's needs, they should have learned to serve God *with rejoicing and with a good heart;* but to receive the blessing of God and then to find no joy in it and offer no thanks for it, was to invite the curse of God. *On account of the abundance of everything* — these words, which point to the prosperity of the community of God, provide a point of contrast for those cursed of God, who are *in need of everything* (vv. 48, 57). Because Israel would at some future point reject the service of God, they would be assigned by God to serve their enemies. The curse of God here reverses the history of salvation: God had brought his people out of Egypt, where they served an enemy; but because in the course of time they rejected God's love, they would be assigned once again to serve an enemy, forfeiting all the privileges of the covenant. Whereas they enjoyed abundant provision within the community of God, the Israelites would serve their

29. There is thus a similarity with the legislation relating to the poor, where the fact that there *need* not be any poor in the land is held in tension with the fact that inevitably there *will* be poor in the land. See 15:1-11 and commentary.

enemies, in need and destitution, feeling the iron yoke of God's curse weighing constantly more heavily upon them, until at last they died.

(ii) The sermon on the curse now becomes more specific; God would raise up a nation to act as his own instrument of judgment against his ungrateful people. *Like an eagle soars* — the idiom is used frequently in the OT to describe the speed and strength of an enemy power.[30] *A nation of fierce*[31] *appearance* — the Hebrew involves a play on words for emphasis: "a nation fierce of face who do not lift up faces" (i.e., *pay no respect*).[32] This foreign nation would consume all produce, both meat and crops (v. 51); see also vv. 33-34 (relating to human enemies) and vv. 38-42 (of locusts and other creatures devouring the harvest). The foreign nation would not leave over any *grain, new wine, and fresh oil* for Israel's consumption; this is in marked contrast to 7:13, where these three products are promised as a part of God's blessing to his people. The enemy would besiege Israel in her settlements; the Israelites, trusting not in God but in their *high and fortified walls*, would experience the bitterness of defeat. They should have known from past experience that a fortified city was of no significance — it was the presence of God that made victory certain, just as his absence made defeat inevitable (see also 1:28 and commentary).

(iii) The focus now shifts from the enemy who would be besieging Israel's cities, to the Israelites within these cities, who would be undergoing the stress of siege conditions. The theme of this section is cannibalism, which is introduced in general terms in v. 53, and then vividly and horrifyingly illustrated in the verses that follow. Israel now appears in a stark moral contrast to the fierce enemy of the foregoing verses. The enemy would eat *the fruit of your animals and the fruit of your ground* (v. 51), but the Israelites would eat their own children, *the fruit of your womb* (v. 53), who were in fact God's blessed gift to them (see v. 4, above). The two illustrations that follow (vv. 54-55, 56-57) make the cannibalism seem even more terrible, because it is mentioned almost casually. The delicate and daintily bred man would be too mean to share his "meat" with members of his own family; by emphasizing the man's meanness, and virtually taking the cannibalism for granted, the speaker unfolds the terrible reversal of standards that would take place within the community who deserted God. *His eye will be evil* (v. 54; cf. v. 56) — the sense is that a man would be unfriendly (cf. 15:9) and would grudge sharing what he

30. See Hos. 8:1; Jer. 48:40. For *eagle* in a different simile, see Deut. 32:11.
31. On '*az*, "fierce," similar to Akk. *ezezu*, cf. J. Gray, *The Legacy of Canaan*[2], p. 185.
32. Cf. the use of the same Heb. idiom in 10:17 (where it is rendered by "impartial," referring to God).

had with those closest to him. *His beloved wife* (v. 54; cf. v. 56) — literally "the wife of his bosom" (see also 13:7).

This section of Moses' address takes on a prophetic tone when it is related to the later history of Israel; see, for example, 2 K. 6:24-31; Lam. 2:20; 4:10.[33]

(g) Summary Section on the Curses (vv. 58-68)

58 *If you will not be careful to keep all the words of this law, written in this book, by revering this glorious and fearful name, the Lord your God,*

59 *then the Lord will inflict upon you and upon your posterity extraordinary afflictions, great and permanent afflictions, and severe and permanent sicknesses.*

60 *And he will make every Egyptian disease, of which you were afraid, return to you; and they shall cling to you.*

61 *In addition, the Lord will bring upon you every sickness and every affliction that is not written in the book of this law, until you are destroyed.*

62 *You shall be left in small numbers, for though you were as the stars of heaven in multitude, yet you would not listen to the voice of the Lord your God.*

63 *And it shall be that just as the Lord took delight in you by doing good for you and by increasing your numbers, so too the Lord will take delight in you by causing you to perish and by destroying you, and you shall be wrenched from the ground to which you are about to go, in order to take possession of it.*

64 *And the Lord will scatter you among all the peoples, from one end of the earth and to the other end of the earth, and there you shall serve other gods whom you have not known, nor have your fathers — wood and stone!*

65 *And among those nations, you shall not find rest, and there shall be no resting place for the sole of your foot, and there the Lord will give you a quaking heart, and failing eyes, and a languishing soul.*

66 *And your life shall be suspended in front of you, and you shall be in dread by night and by day and you shall have no confidence in your life.*

67 *In the morning you shall say: If only it were evening! And in the evening you shall say: If only it were morning! — because of the dread of your heart which you dread and because of the things seen by your eyes which you see.*

68 *And the Lord will make you return to Egypt in ships in the way concerning which I said to you: You shall see it no more. And there*

---

33. For parallel references to cannibalism in Near Eastern Texts, see M. Weinfeld, *Deuteronomy and the Deuteronomic School*, pp. 126-29. Cannibalism, in time of stress, was apparently known from ancient times, as is indicated by references to it in the Epic of Atrahasis; see W. G. Lambert and A. R. Millard, *Atra-ḫasīs: The Babylonian Story of the Flood*, pp. 112-15.

you will put yourselves up for sale to your enemies, for male slaves
and for female slaves, but there will be no buyer.

In this section, which summarizes the curse of God, the horrifying details of the preceding verses give way to a broader picture; the effect of this final section, however, is no less terrifying, for little by little the speaker unfolds to his audience the manner in which every basic expression of God's covenant love for his people could be reversed. First, the general principle is expressed; disobedience to the law of God invites the curse of God (vv. 58-59). The potential actions of God described in the verses that follow are not the mindless or capricious acts of an unknown and malevolent deity; they are the just acts of a righteous God whose covenant love would have been spurned by his own people. The curses following, reversing the blessings of God which the Israelites had already begun to experience, constitute a final, awesome warning to the Israelites who are now engaged in the last part of the renewal of the covenant in Moab.

(i) In Egypt, before the Sinai Covenant had been made, God afflicted the Egyptians with severe diseases, in order to bring his blessing upon Israel. In the curse of God, the diseases of Egypt would afflict Israel, not her enemies, and for good measure they would suffer from disease and afflictions that even the Egyptians had not known (vv. 60-61). (ii) In the blessing of God, Israel's forefathers had descended into Egypt in small numbers; they had increased there, left in force, and were constantly growing in number, according to the ancient covenant promise of God. In the curse of God, they would shrink again, their numbers growing smaller and smaller until at last they were destroyed by God (vv. 62-63a). (iii) In the blessing of God, the Israelites constantly anticipated the gift of the promised land; for those gathered in Moab, a few already possessed their land, but for most, the fulfilment of the promise lay in the immediate future. In the curse of God, the people would be forcibly removed from the promised land and scattered abroad among many other peoples (vv. 63b-64a). (iv) The fullness of the covenant blessing lay in serving and loving the Lord alone. The emptiness of living under the curse would be experienced in serving other gods, the lifeless gods of wood and stone (v. 64b). (v) In the blessing of God, foreign nations would fear Israel, while Israel remained confident in God. In the curse of God, the Israelites would themselves be constantly bound by fear (vv. 65-67). (vi) The blessing of the covenant was long life in the promised land. The man under the curse would not know from one minute to the next whether his life would be spared (v. 66). (vii) In the blessing of God, the people had been brought out of Egypt and freed from that old servitude. In the curse of God, they would return to Egypt once again,

351

and there they would experience the depth of humiliation; in offering themselves for sale, they would be deemed by the Egyptians to be substandard, not even worth making into slaves (v. 68). Having rejected the service of their loving God, they would no longer be fit even to act as slaves to their fellow human beings.

Some more detailed notes on the content of the section now follow:

58 *Written in this book* — the reference is probably to the Book of the Covenant, which may have formed the basis of the renewal ceremony.[34]

60 *Egyptian disease* — see also v. 27 and commentary. Within the blessing of God, the people would have been protected against Egyptian disease; see 7:15.

63 *By causing you to perish* — the wording implies a strong contrast with 26:5. Beginning with an *ailing* (or "perishing") *Aramean,* God could make his people grow in number, provided they were obedient. If they were disobedient, he could diminish those numbers again by making his people *perish* (or "ail"); the same root is used in both instances (*'bd*).

64 Although the verse has a prophetic tone, in the light of Israel's subsequent history, it should be noted that banishment from the land is a natural form of punishment to be envisaged, given the strong emphasis on possession of the land within the covenant promise of God.[35]

66 *And your life shall be suspended in front of you* — it "shall be, as it were, suspended in front of thee on a thread, which threatens every moment to break."[36]

68 *Return to Egypt in ships.* The significance of these words is uncertain. They may simply describe a mode of travel to Egypt, though sailing to Egypt from Palestine would not be an altogether natural means for a relatively short journey. Hence several scholars have suggested that the words imply the slave trade between the Phoenician coast and Egypt.[37] Such an interpretation is unlikely, however, since v. 68b indicates that the Israelites, under the curse, would return to Egypt voluntarily and, once there, they would offer themselves for sale into slavery. Hence it is possible that the Heb. *b'nywt* should not be translated "in ships," but should be rendered: "in ease, casually" (on the basis of Ugaritic evidence).[38] Although

34. See further 17:18 and commentary, and Introduction, IV, "Date and Authorship," n. 32.
35. Cf. R. E. Clements, *God's Chosen People,* p. 57.
36. S. R. Driver, *Deuteronomy,* p. 318.
37. *Ibid.,* p. 319; Buis and Leclercq, *Le Deutéronome,* p. 181.
38. The suggestion is based on the evidence J. Gray offers for a similar rendering in Judg. 5:17; see Gray, *Joshua, Judges and Ruth,* pp. 287f. The Heb. has not been pointed, since the vocalization of the word with this meaning is uncertain.

such a rendering is uncertain, it would offer a further contrast between the blessing and the curse. God had brought his people out of Egypt, and together they had fought every inch of the way. Forgetting that great redemption, the people under the curse would be permitted to return casually to Egypt, the land of their bondage.

(h) Conclusion of the Basic Renewal Ceremony (28:69 [Eng. 29:1])

> 69 *These are the words of the covenant which the Lord commanded Moses to make with the Israelites in the land of Moab, besides the covenant that he made with them in Horeb.*

There is some doubt whether this short verse serves as a conclusion to the preceding chapters or as an introduction to the following chapters;[39] the difficulty is reflected in the differences in the numbering of the verse. The most natural sense would seem to emerge from interpreting the verse as a conclusion to the preceding chapters; the verse refers back to 1:1-5 in which the whole section was introduced.

With the proclamation of the blessings and curses, the formal ending of the renewal ceremony[40] is reached. However, there was further business to be conducted in Moab, for in addition to the renewing of the Horeb covenant, there was to be a new leader among the Israelites. Moses' death was close at hand, and in the remaining chapters of Deuteronomy the question of new leadership is taken up. Although not all renewal ceremonies would involve a change of leadership, when such a change was to take place, the covenant ceremony (or an addition to it) would be the proper occasion for the transfer, for a part of the leader's role was to act as mediator in the ceremony, as did Moses (. . . *the covenant which the Lord commanded Moses to make* . . .). This theme of new leadership, together with Moses' last words of exhortation, dominate the remaining chapters of Deuteronomy.

---

39. See N. Lohfink, "Der Bundesschluss im Land Moab. Redaktionsgeschichtliches zu Dtn. 28:69–32:47," *BZ* N.F. 6 (1962), pp. 32-56. Lohfink takes this to be the first verse of a new unit and traces elements of the treaty pattern in the section that follows.
40. With the reference to *two* covenants in this verse, Horeb and Moab, the continuity expressed within the book of Deuteronomy becomes clear. In Moab, the Horeb covenant is renewed, and yet both are new covenants in a sense, for both reflect the continuing living relationship between God and his people.

V. THE ADDRESS OF MOSES:
A CONCLUDING CHARGE
(29:1 [Eng. v. 2]–30:20)

A. AN APPEAL FOR COVENANT FAITHFULNESS
(29:1-28 [Eng. vv. 2-29])

1 *And Moses summoned all Israel and he said to them: You have seen all that which the Lord has done before your own eyes in the land of Egypt, to Pharaoh, and to all his servants, and to all his land —*

2 *the great trials which your eyes saw, the signs, and those great wonders.*

3 *But the Lord has not granted you, up to this day, a mind to understand, and eyes to see, and ears to hear.*

4 *And I directed you for forty years in the wilderness; your garments did not wear out upon you, and your sandals did not wear out upon your feet.*

5 *You did not eat bread and you did not drink wine or strong drink, so that you might know that I am the Lord your God.*

6 *Then you came to this place. And Sihon, king of Heshbon, together with Og, king of Bashan, came out to meet us for battle, but we destroyed them.*

7 *And we took their land and we gave it for an inheritance to the Reubenites, and to the Gadites, and to the half-tribe Manasseh.*

8 *So you shall keep the words of this covenant, and you shall do them, so that you may be successful in all that you do.*

9 *Today, all of you are stationed before the Lord your God — your heads, your tribes, your elders and your officers, every man of Israel;*

10 *your children, your wives, and the resident alien who is in the midst of your camp, from the one who gathers wood to the one who draws your water —*

11 *so that you might enter into the covenant of the Lord your God and into his oath, which today the Lord your God is making with you;*

12 *in order that today he might raise you up as a people for himself, and he shall be God for you, just as he said to you, and just as he swore to your fathers, to Abraham, to Isaac, and to Jacob.*

13 *And it is not with you alone that I am making this covenant and this oath,*

14 *but with the one who is here with us today, standing before the Lord our God, and with the one who is not here with us today.*

15 *But you know how we lived in the land of Egypt, and how we passed through the midst of the nations whom you passed;*

16 *and you saw their detestable things and their idols, the wood and stone, silver and gold, which were with them.*

17 *So beware lest there be among you a man, or a woman, or a family, or a tribe, whose mind is diverted today from the Lord our God to go and serve the gods of those nations, and lest there be among you a stock bearing poisonous fruit or wormwood.*

18 *And it shall be that when a man hears the words of this oath, then blesses himself in his heart, saying: "I shall have peace, even though I walk in the stubbornness of my heart," then the moist along with the parched shall be swept away.*

19 *The Lord will not be willing to pardon him, but rather the Lord's anger and his jealousy shall smoke against that man, and all the oath that is written in this book shall rest on him, and the Lord will obliterate his name from under the heavens.*

20 *And the Lord will single him out from all the tribes of Israel for disaster, according to all the oaths of the covenant that are written in this book of the law.*

21 *Then the later generation, your sons who rise up after you and the foreigner who comes from a distant land, shall say, when they see the plagues of that land and the sicknesses with which the Lord has made it sick —*

22 *brimstone and salt; the whole land burning; nothing is sown and nothing sprouts up; and no grass at all rising up in it; like the overthrow of Sodom and Gomorrah, of Admah and Zeboiim, which the Lord overthrew in his anger and in his wrath —*

23 *then all the nations shall say: For what reason has the Lord acted thus to this land? What is the reason for the burning of this great anger?*

24 *Then men shall say: It is because they abandoned the covenant of the Lord God of their fathers, which he made with them when he brought them out from the land of Egypt;*

25 *and they went and served other gods, and they bowed down in worship to them, gods whom they had not known and whom he had not appointed for them.*

26 *Therefore the anger of the Lord was burning in that land, bringing upon it the whole curse that is written in this book;*

27 *and the Lord plucked them up off the ground in anger, and in wrath, and in great fury, and he threw them to another land, as it is this day.*

28 *The secret things belong to the Lord our God; but the revealed things belong to us and to our children for ever, so that we might do all the words of this law.*

In the concluding charge, Moses returns first of all to dwell briefly on some of the themes already contained in the earlier discourses (vv. 1-8.[1] The substance of the material presented here in summary form is a recollection of God's acts in history, from the Exodus, through the testing period in the wilderness, and up to the arrival of the people on the plains of Moab. To the reader, the repetition may seem somewhat tedious at first sight, but the significance of the repetition appears in v. 3: *the Lord has not granted you,*[2] *up to this day, a mind*[3] *to understand, and eyes to see, and ears to hear.* With the perspective of time, the Israelites could learn to see God's presence in their past experience, but it required insight and perception. God's participation in the course of human events was not always in a dramatic form, such as miracle. When we read today the accounts of Hebrew history, the divine perspective has already been provided, and it is easy to forget that for the Israelite in ancient times, beset by anxieties of various kinds, that perspective was not automatically present, but required from him the vision of faith. Hence there is a continual return to the theme in the address of Moses, in order that the audience might be brought to real *understanding* of the ways of God, real *seeing* of the acts of God, and real *hearing* of the words of God. If the days ahead were to be successful, it was necessary to have this profound understanding which was so closely associated with faith in God.

In v. 8, the purpose of the recollection is emphasized again. On the basis of what they had seen and heard and come to understand, the Israelites should take great care to abide by *the words of this covenant.* Only then, as they began to take possession of the promised land, would they have success in their undertaking.

Following the historical recollection, the focus of the address now centers on the essence and meaning of the Israelites' covenant relationship with God (vv. 9-14). The people were all *stationed*[4] *before the Lord* (v. 9) in order *to enter into the covenant* (v. 11); the sentence is interrupted by an aside (vv. 9b-10) in which all the categories of people standing before Moses are enumerated (see also Josh. 24:1). The leaders and males are mentioned first,[5] then the

1. The following are selected references to earlier mention of similar themes. On vv. 1-2, see 1:30; 5:1; 7:18-19; 11:2-3. On vv. 4-5, see 8:2-4. On vv. 7-8, see 2:32–3:6. On v. 8, see 4:34; 11:3-7.
2. On this phrase, see the comments of G. T. Manley and R. K. Harrison, *NBC(R),* p. 225: "In attributing such incapabilities to God, the Hebrew lawgiver in merely following OT traditions generally in relating everything to Him as the ultimate source or ground of existence." For Paul's exegesis and use of this verse, see Rom. 11:8.
3. The Heb. is lit. "heart"; see the commentary on 4:9 (n. 2).
4. The verb translated *stationed* (Niph. of *nātsaḇ*) implies some kind of formal arrangement (almost a "parade"); the more general verb is *'āmaḏ,* "stand" (see v. 14).
5. See also 1:13-15 and commentary.

women and children, and finally the resident aliens.[6] The wood-gatherers and water-drawers[7] were probably classes of people within the group resident aliens, on whom many of the more menial tasks would have fallen.[8] All these people were assembled *to enter into the covenant* and *into his oath.* The word *oath,* while virtually synony-mous with *covenant* in this context, may serve to emphasize not only the renewal of the *relationship* (signified by the covenant), but also the entering into the *legacy* (that which was promised by oath) of the covenant relationship, which God had initiated with their forefathers.

The emphasis in this passage is upon the present (*today* is used five times), not in the sense that a new covenant was being initiated, but rather in the sense that the renewing of the covenant was a revitalizing of the relationship. The essence of the covenant is de-scribed in v. 12. God would raise up the Israelites to be a *people for himself;* that is, God willingly and freely took upon himself certain obligations toward his chosen people. The people, in response, were bound to him as their God (*he shall be God for you*). Thus both "parties" to the covenant undertook obligations,[9] but the nature of the obligations differed (the relationship was one of "suzerainty," not one of "parity"). God, in sovereignty and grace, initiated the rela-tionship and in so doing committed himself in a promise to the chosen people; the people's obligation to commit themselves in the covenant was based not simply on law or demand, but on a response of love, for the purpose of the covenant relationship elicited such a response.

13-14 The scope of the covenant. As is often the case in Deuteronomy, the future implications of the covenant relationship are drawn out again. The people on the plains of Moab were indeed renewing their covenant with God, but they were not to forget that they were but one part of a larger community, a community not limited by the passage of time. *The one who is not here with us today* — the reference is not to those who could not be present for some reason such as ill health. Rather, the words indicate the generations to be born in the future.[10] The reference to future generations impressed even more firmly the responsibility incumbent on those who were present on the plains of Moab, for not only their own future, but also the future of their posterity would be contingent upon their obedience

6. On the *resident alien*, see 1:16 and commentary.
7. In the Ugaritic Keret Legend, the cognate word is employed in the feminine form: *CTA* 14.III.113. The menial task of drawing water seems to have been the lot of women; for a translation of the text, see G. R. Driver, *Canaanite Myths and Legends,* p. 31.
8. For an illustration from subsequent history, see Josh. 9:21-27.
9. This feature is not new with the Sinai Covenant, as sometimes supposed, but it is already explicit in the covenant with the patriarchs, to whom God bound himself by oath (v. 12b).
10. See also 5:3 for a different expression of the same principle.

to the law of the covenant. The potential failure of any one generation, already potential in the elaboration of curses in ch. 28, reintroduces a solemn note in the subsequent discourse in ch. 29.

15-17 The Israelites already had some knowledge of foreign forms of worship; they had experience of foreign religion in Egypt and during their travels through the desert and to the east of the Dead Sea. They knew already the nature of that worship, its *detestable things* and *idols*, [11] which were made from wood or stone and decorated with silver or gold. Thus, although the Israelites would meet an alien form of worship when they entered the promised land, they had already experienced various forms of alien culture and should be equipped to deal with it. Nevertheless, Moses warns the people once again: *beware . . .* (v. 17). The danger was that an individual (*a man, or a woman*), *a family,* or even a whole *tribe* might turn aside from true faith in the Lord and break the first commandment of the Decalog by serving foreign gods. This danger is one of the commonest themes in the whole book of Deuteronomy, but here it is given a particular emphasis, stated first in v. 17 and then elaborated upon in the subsequent verses. The emphasis is indicated thus: *lest there be among you a stock* [12] *bearing poisonous fruit or wormwood.* [13] The metaphor indicates the permeation of evil throughout Israel because of the action of an individual, family, or tribe. To express it in another way, "no man is an island"; when a man or group sinned by serving other gods, that sin was like a poisonous branch with bitter fruit, which by its nature spoiled the whole tree. The emphasis is thus placed on Israel's nature as a covenant *community*, the whole of which was affected, for good or evil, by the actions of its constituents. As a community, Israel would stand or fall; as a community, it would experience blessing or cursing. However, the anonymity of the individual within the community could lead to a wrong attitude of independence and a feeling of false security within the community, regardless of a man's own righteousness — or lack of it. The theme is developed further in the following verses.

18-20 A man might hear *the words of this oath* and yet persist in pursuing his own willful and sinful path, gaining his confidence

11. On the Heb. terminology employed, see S. R. Driver, *Deuteronomy*, pp. 323f. The terms indicate considerable contempt for the objects of foreign worship.
12. "Stock" is a tentative translation of Heb. *shōresh;* see H. L. Ginsberg, " 'Roots Below and Fruits Above' and Related Matters," in D. W. Thomas and W. D. McHardy, eds., *Hebrew and Semitic Studies* (1963), p. 75. The LXX, however, renders the more traditional meaning "root." The idiom is used both in the NT (see Heb. 12:15) and in the Qumran texts; for discussion, see F. F. Bruce, *Commentary on the Epistle to the Hebrews.* NICNT (1964), pp. 365f.
13. *Wormwood* is used metaphorically to denote distress, bitterness, and trouble; see Jer. 9:15; 23:15; Prov. 5:4; Lam. 3:15,19; Amos 5:7. See also M. H. Farbridge, *Studies in Biblical and Semitic Symbolism,* pp. 48f.

from being part of the larger community. He could say, *"I shall have peace . . .,"* not because he merited peace or blessing, but because the community would continue to receive God's blessing and he was a part of that community. Moses stresses in his address the interrelationship between the parts and the whole within the covenant community of God. It was the community as a whole which was bound to God in the covenant and which would receive God's blessing in the promised land. Yet the emphasis on the community did not mean that the individual was an anonymous nonentity. The health and vitality of the whole community depended on the health and vitality of the religious commitment of each individual within it. Far from being anonymous, each individual carried a heavy burden of responsibility for the whole community. The element of responsibility is emphasized by another metaphor, which may have been an ancient proverb: *the moist along with the parched shall be swept away.*[14] That is, because of the evil acts of one man (the one who thought to himself, *I shall have peace*), the whole community was in immediate danger of God's judgment. The individual, however, would carry the heavy burden of responsibility (vv. 19-20); the curse of God would come upon him in its awesome dimensions.[15]

21-27   These verses are similar in form and content to language used both by the later prophets and in Near Eastern historical texts.[16] The situation envisaged lies in the future, when already the curse of the covenant has fallen upon the land because of the people's disobedience. The land is described as being afflicted by *plagues* and *sicknesses* (v. 21), sent by God as a retribution for its sin; this preliminary description is then expanded further with the horrifying details of v. 22.[17] The language employed in v. 22 uses a previous example of God's judgment as a basis for comparison; it is strongly reminiscent of the description of the destruction of Sodom and Gomorrah (Gen. 19:24-29).[18] The details of the scene that is described (*brimstone and salt; the whole land burning . . .*) are related to the metaphor used for

---

14. Although the particular sense of the saying is no longer clear, the general implication seems clear enough: no one would escape judgment.
15. In vv. 19-20, the individual aspect of God's judgment is emphasized, but in vv. 21-27 the broader implications appear once again.
16. See Jer. 5:18-19; 22:8-10; 1 K. 9:8-9; *ANET*, pp. 299f. For discussion, see B. Albrektson, *History and the Gods*, pp. 105f.; D. E. Skweres, "Das Motif der Strafgrunderfahrung in biblischen und neuassyrischen Texten," *BZ* N.F. 14 (1970), pp. 181-197; B. O. Long, "The Question and Answer Schemata in the Prophets," *JBL* 90 (1971), pp. 129-139.
17. Grammatically, the sentence is very terse and interrupts the main sequence of thought which begins in v. 21 and continues, after the break, in v. 23. The terseness of v. 22 is an effective rhetorical device to accentuate the horror of the devastated land.
18. Admah and Zeboiim were located close to Sodom and Gomorrah, probably near the south end of the Dead Sea.

God's anger; in Hebrew, anger is like a fire, scorching or *burning* (see v. 23) everything before it. Thus the land would be burned up; the ground would be parched so that no plant or grass could grow. When men *(the later generation, the foreigner,* v. 21; *all the nations,* v. 23) saw the devastation of the land, they would ask the question: *For what reason has the Lord acted thus to this land?*

The reason for the devastation would be that the people of Israel had abandoned their covenant with God, made first at Sinai after the Exodus from Egypt (v. 24) and subsequently renewed on the plains of Moab. The tragic condition resulting from the abandoning of the covenant is in stark contrast to the high ideals of the covenant described earlier in the chapter (vv. 9-14). The way in which Israel had abandoned the covenant was by serving other gods, *gods whom they had not known and whom he had not appointed for them* (v. 25; see also 4:19; 13:2, 6, 13), and breaking thereby the very first commandment of the Decalog. The curse of the covenant (v. 26) was the inevitable result of breaking the law of the covenant and betraying the total allegiance demanded by the Lord. The curse not only brought devastation to the land, but the people went into exile — *he threw them to another land* (v. 27; see also the curses contained in ch. 28). *As it is this day* (v. 27) — these words may be a part of the answer (vv. 24-27) given to the question posed in v. 23, implying that at the future point envisaged in these verses, the Hebrews would be exiled from their land. Alternatively, the words may be an editorial gloss, added perhaps during the Exile, when the warning theme of the passage came to be understood in a more prophetic sense.

28 *The secret things belong to the Lord our God* — the immediate sense of this verse is determined by the context supplied in the future reflection contained in the preceding verses. The picture painted so vividly in vv. 21-27 is not a prophecy about something that was going to happen inevitably. On the other hand, *if* the Israelites were persistently disobedient and failed in their obligations, a fate such as the one portrayed would become inevitable; the fate, in other words, was conditioned by the proper or improper maintenance of the covenant relationship. The stark portrayal of the possible future, however, was not designed to cause apathy and despair among the people. If such a future was inevitable, the people might ask, then what was the point of obedience? Rather, the dark picture of the future was intended to have the opposite effect: *the revealed things belong to us and to our children for ever, so that we might do all the words of this law.* That is to say, one thing was certain and *revealed,* namely, *the words of this law.* The law placed upon the people the responsibility of obedience, the result of which would be God's blessing in the land they were going in to possess. This general principle was clearly revealed; obedience would lead to God's continuing blessing, but disobedience would bring about the curse of God. To go beyond that and speculate about the future things (*the secret things*) was not man's prerogative.

The verse has also broader, theological implications. It would be presumptuous of man to assume that in revelation he has been given total knowledge of God. The revelation given is adapted to man, *so that we might do all the words of this law*. The latter clause does not reduce religion to the sphere of law and ethics, as Spinoza would have it, but rather indicates the means by which a living relationship with God might be maintained. It may never be possible to *know* all things, the *secret things*, for man's mind is bound by the limits of his finitude; though the nature of God's revelation is not such as to grant man total knowledge of the universe and its mysteries, however, it does grant to him the possibility of knowing God. And it is possible to know God in a profound and living way, through his grace, without ever having grasped or understood the *secret things*.

B. THE CALL TO DECISION: LIFE AND BLESSING OR DEATH AND CURSING (30:1-20)

1 *And it shall be that when all these things come upon you, the blessing and the curse which I have set before you, then you shall return to your senses among all the nations to which the Lord your God banished you;*

2 *and you shall return to the Lord your God and you shall listen to his voice with all your mind and all your desire, according to all that I am commanding you today, both you and your sons.*

3 *Then the Lord your God will restore your fortunes and he will have compassion on you; and he will gather you once again from all the peoples among whom the Lord your God scattered you.*

4 *Even if your banished ones should be on the horizon of the heavens, from there the Lord your God will gather you and from there he will take you;*

5 *and the Lord your God will bring you into the land which your fathers possessed and you shall take possession of it. Then he will make it go well for you and he will make you more numerous than your fathers.*

6 *And the Lord your God will circumcise your heart and the heart of your offspring, to enable you to love the Lord your God with all your mind and with all your desire, so that you might live.*

7 *Then the Lord your God will put all these curses upon your enemies, and upon those that hate you who pursue you.*

8 *But you shall listen once again to the voice of the Lord and you shall do all his commandments, which I am commanding you today.*

9 *And the Lord your God will grant you abundance of prosperity in all your undertakings, in the fruit of your womb, and in the fruit of*

your animals, and in the fruit of your ground; for the Lord will again rejoice over you for good, just as he rejoiced over your fathers,

10 *if you listen to the voice of the Lord your God, keeping his commandments and his statutes, which are written in this book of the law, if you return to the Lord your God with all your mind and with all your desire.*

11 *For this commandment, which I am commanding you today, is not too difficult for you, nor is it beyond your grasp;*

12 *It is not in the heavens, so that it might be said: Who will ascend to the heavens for us and bring it to us? —then he will make us listen to it and we will do it!*

13 *And it is not beyond the sea, so that it might be said: Who will cross over the sea for us and bring it to us? —then he will make us listen to it and we shall do it!*

14 *But the word is very close to you; it is in your mouth and in your mind, so that you may do it.*

15 *Look, today I have set before you life and good, and death and evil.*

16 *But if you listen to the commandments of the Lord your God, which I am commanding you today, by loving the Lord your God, by walking in his ways, and by keeping his commandments and his statutes and his judgments, then you shall live and you shall grow in number, and the Lord your God shall bless you in the land into which you are entering in order to take possession of it.*

17 *But if your mind turns aside and you do not listen, and you are pulled aside and you bow down to other gods and you serve them,*

18 *I declare to you today that you shall certainly perish. You shall not prolong your days upon the land to which you are about to cross over the Jordan, in order to enter into it and have possession of it.*

19 *Today I call the heavens and the earth as witnesses against you. Life and death have I set before you, the blessing and the cursing. But you shall choose life, in order that you and your offspring may live;*

20 *by loving the Lord your God, by listening to his voice, and by sticking close to him. For that is your life and the length of your days, so that you may dwell upon the land which the Lord promised by oath to your fathers, to Abraham, to Isaac and to Jacob, to give to them.*

1-10 The possibility of restoration. The gloomy picture of the curses of the covenant (28:15-68) is balanced in this part of the address by a more distant prospect. *When all these things come upon you, the blessing and the curse* — the reference point of vv. 1-10 is ch. 28 as a whole, both the blessings and the cursings, but the latter dominate the subsequent verses of this section of Moses' address. The address employs the now familiar style of repetition for sake of emphasis, but the technique is slightly different here. Various themes are repeated emphatically, which have appeared earlier in the book; other themes are stated here in reverse terms (i.e., the negative aspects of many of the curses in Deut. 28 are stated here positively). The following table indicates some of the main parallels, both similar and antithetical, with earlier portions of the book:

Deut. 30:1	4:29	[cf. ch. 28]
30:2	4:30	
30:3	4:31	cf. 28:64
30:4		
30:5	28:62-63	
30:6	10:16	
30:7	28:60	
30:8	28:1	
30:9	28:4	
30:10	28:58	

At some future point, when disobedience brought on the curse of the covenant and the people were dispersed among foreign nations, there would come a turning point. The turning point would be followed by certain steps; the process described here was to influence in many ways the preaching of the prophets in subsequent generations.

(a) *You shall return to your senses* (v. 1) — the people would remember that the circumstances in which they found themselves were not the result of "fate," but an inevitable consequence of disobeying the covenant with the Lord, which resulted in the curse of the Lord.

(b) *Return to the Lord* (v. 2) — once they knew the reason for the curse that had befallen them, the course of action would become clear. In repentance, they must return to the Lord of the Covenant, individually and as families.

(c) *You shall listen to his voice* (v. 2) — the repentance involved not only turning back from the evil past, but a new and wholehearted commitment of obedience to God's voice, which was expressed for them in God's law and was written in a book (see v. 10).

(d) *Then the Lord your God will restore your fortunes* [1] (v. 3) — the nature of exile would be such that repentance alone could not lead to freedom, for the people would be in foreign lands under foreign authorities. Having remembered, repented, and obeyed, then the people could look to God for his aid in restoring them to that previous position; only then could they expect to know once again his *compassion* (v. 3). God, acting in the course of human history (just as he had

---

1. On the idiom employed, see S. R. Driver, *Deuteronomy*, p. 329.

363

done in bringing his people out of Egypt), would regather his people from the places to which he had scattered them in judgment.

(e) *Bring you into the land* (v. 5) — the restoration would be a further renewing of the promises of the ancient covenant with the patriarchs. The people would come back to the promised land, they would be prosperous and numerous again.

In one sense, this material is not *primarily* prophetic. Moses, in his address, employs both the experience of the past and his notion of the potential future to force home upon the Israelites the need for obedience in the present. Before they have even entered the land, he warns of their being driven out again and scattered, and then brought back in. This great vision in Moses, encompassing both past and future, does nevertheless come to be seen as prophetic over the course of time.[2] The prophetic element becomes clearer in vv. 6-10, which anticipate in many ways the teaching of Jeremiah on the "New Covenant" (Jer. 31:31-34) and Ezekiel's teaching on the "new heart" (Ezek. 36:24-32).

And the Lord your God will circumcise your heart . . . (v. 6) — see also 10:16 and commentary. The emphasis is quite different in this context. In 10:16, the "circumcision of the heart" is a part of the exhortation to obedience; it was something required of the people that they could do. In 30:6, it is seen rather to be an act of God and thus indicates the new covenant, when God would in his grace deal with man's basic spiritual problem.[3] When God "operated" on the heart, then indeed the people would be able to *love the Lord* and *live* (v. 6). Being once again within a true relationship to God, the people would see the curses, under which they had suffered, transferred to their enemies by whom they had been persecuted (v. 7). They would experience once again the true blessing of God (vv. 8-9), but still the note of contingency dominates Moses' vision of the future. The future blessing would still be contingent upon obedience: *if you listen to the voice of the Lord your God* . . . (v. 10). The new covenant, involving the direct operation of God in man's heart, would still involve obedience, an obedience springing out of love for God in his continuing mercy and grace.

11-14 The emphasis returns once again to the present, the renewal ceremony being enacted on the plains of Moab. *This commandment* (v. 11) refers to the law of the covenant, to which the people were being urged to commit themselves in obedience. The commandment did not impress on the people conditions that were totally impossible to fulfil: it *is not too difficult for you, nor is it beyond*

---

2. The theme appears not only in the writings of the great prophets (e.g., Jer. 29:14; Ezek. 36:24), but also in the NT (Matt. 24:31; Mark 13:27).
3. Cf. Buis and Leclercq, *Le Deutéronome*, p. 187.

your grasp (v. 11). The following verses illustrate this principle in two ways.[4]

It is not in the heavens (v. 12) — metaphorically the commandment is not inaccessible because of its height or loftiness, so that some especially qualified person would be needed to make it all clear. Somewhat more literally, the implication is that the law was given or revealed to man; it was particularly designed for man's living and not a part of the mystery of God that man could not approach[5] and that was retained "in the heavens." There was therefore no ground for excuse in relation to the law; the question, *Who will ascend to the heavens for us?*[6] would be at best a misunderstanding, and at worst a deliberate evasion of the responsibility imposed upon man by the law of the covenant.

It is not beyond the sea (v. 13) — the verse indicates in another way that the commandment was practical and realistic. The objective of the commandment, and obedience to it, was *life* (cf. vv. 15-20); and the emphasis on the immediacy and the practical nature of the commandment is in striking contrast to Near Eastern literature and religion at this point. The Mesopotamian hero Gilgamesh,[7] following the death of his intimate friend Enkidu, set out on a quest for life, a quest that was in many ways fruitless. In the course of his quest, he had to cross the sea,[8] searching for Utnapishtim, the survivor of the flood, whom Gilgamesh hoped might provide him with an answer to his quest. In contrast to this heroic yet tragic quest, life was to be found by the Hebrews in the law of the covenant which Moses set before them: *it is in your mouth and in your mind* (lit. "heart"), *so that you may do it.* With these words on the very essence or purpose of the law, Moses then concludes with a call for decision.

15-20   The call to choice. The options in the choice set before

---

4.   Paul, in his letter to the Romans, employs the words to illustrate the basic character of the new covenant (Rom. 10:6-8); he adapts the words to suit his new purpose. See Calvin's comment: "Moses mentions *heaven* and the *sea*, as places remote and difficult of access to man. But Paul, as though there was some spiritual mystery concealed under these words, applies them to the death and resurrection of Christ. If anyone thinks that this interpretation is too strained and too refined, let him understand that it was not the object of the Apostle strictly to explain this passage, but to apply it to the explanation of his present subject." J. Calvin, *Commentaries on the Epistle of Paul the Apostle to the Romans* (E.T. 1849), p. 389.
5.   Cf. 29:29; see also Job 28:12-14, where *wisdom* (in contrast to *law*) does indeed have dimensions that are beyond human grasp.
6.   Cf. the enigmatic reference to the shepherd-king Etana, in the ancient Sumerian King List, "who ascended to heaven" (*ANET*, p. 265). It is possible that the Hebrew verse implies criticism of views held sacred in other Near Eastern religions.
7.   For a good English rendering, see N. K. Sandars, *The Epic of Gilgamesh* (1960); *ANET*, pp. 72-99.
8.   See tablet X of the Epic of Gilgamesh (*ANET*, p. 92).

the people are the most important that any man — whether in the plains of Moab or in the modern world — has to face: *life and good* on the one hand, or *death and evil* on the other.[9] The choice had been set down in the clearest terms: the law had been stated and expanded; the history of God's dealing with his people had been called to mind; the basic operating principle of love had been enunciated; the potentialities of the future, with both blessing and cursing, had been declared. But in the last resort, the matter came down to a decision that had to be made. God and his ability were not for one moment in question; the responsibility now rested on the people themselves.

The making of a decision, however, involved more than simple affirmation; it involved a whole way of life based upon that decision. The way of *life and good* is described in v. 16: The verse summarizes the whole of the positive aspects of Moses' address: *if you listen to the commandments . . . loving the Lord your God . . . walking in his ways . . . then you shall live.* This ready and loving obedience would be the "catalyst," releasing the full potentiality of God's ancient promise to the fathers — they would increase in number and prosper in the promised land. Then there follows the way of *death and evil* in vv. 17-18: *if your mind turns aside . . . you do not listen . . . you bow down to other gods . . . you shall certainly perish.* This wrong decision would preclude the possibility of experiencing the fulfilment of the ancient promises.

Moses then urges the people to make the proper choice. He does not ask for a dispassionate choice, for the whole course of his address has been leading up to this moment in the renewal ceremony when the people would declare their allegiance. Hence his words are virtually a command: *you shall choose life, in order that you and your offspring shall live* (v. 19b). The solemnity of the choice is reinforced by summoning "witnesses" — *I call the heavens and the earth as witnesses against you.* The heavens and the earth, permanent and unchanging features of God's creation, would bear silent witness in the future to the faithfulness of the people in living out the implications of their choice. (See further on this topic 4:26; 32:1 and commentary.) Only in making and abiding by the right decision would the Israelite find God's true purpose — *for that is your life and the length of your days* (v. 20).

9. Both the contrast between life and death, and the choice between *two ways,* are familiar in other biblical and Near Eastern literature. On life and death, see Gilgamesh, X. vi (*ANET,* p. 93); the "Hymn to Aten" (*ANET,* p. 371). For the idea of *two ways,* see Jer. 21:8; Ps. 1; Prov. 1:1-7; Matt. 7:13-14.

VI. THE CONTINUITY OF THE COVENANT FROM MOSES TO JOSHUA (31:1–34:12)

A. DEPOSITION OF THE LAW AND THE APPOINTMENT OF JOSHUA (31:1-29)

1 *Then Moses went on and addressed these words to all Israel,*
2 *and he said to them: Today, I am one hundred and twenty years old. I am not able to go out and to come in any more. And the Lord has said to me, "You shall not cross over this Jordan."*
3 *The Lord your God, he is about to cross over before you. He will destroy these nations before you, and you shall dispossess them. And Joshua, he is about to cross over before you, just as the Lord said.*
4 *And the Lord will do to them just as he did to Sihon and Og, kings of the Amorites, the ones whom he destroyed, and to their lands!*
5 *And the Lord will set them before you, and you shall do to them according to all the commandment that I commanded you.*
6 *Be strong and be courageous! Do not fear and do not tremble because of them, because the Lord your God, he is the one marching with you. He will not forsake you.*
7 *And Moses called Joshua and said to him in the sight of all Israel: Be strong and be courageous, for you shall bring this people into the land which the Lord promised by oath to their fathers to give to them, and you shall make them inherit it.*
8 *And the Lord, he is the one marching before you. He will be with you. He will not fail you and he will not forsake you. You shall not fear and you shall not be dismayed.*
9 *And Moses wrote this law and he gave it to the priests, sons of Levi, the ones carrying the ark of the covenant of the Lord, and to all the elders of Israel.*
10 *Then Moses commanded them, saying: At the end of seven years, at the time of the year of release, in the Feast of Booths,*
11 *when all Israel comes to appear in the presence of the Lord your God in the place that he chooses, you shall recite this law before all Israel in their hearing.*
12 *Make the people come together, the men, the women, and the children, and your resident alien who is in your settlements, in*

367

order that they may hear and in order that they may learn, and they shall fear the Lord your God and they shall be careful to do all the words of this law.

13 *And their sons, who have not known, shall hear and shall learn to fear the Lord your God, for all the days during which you live on the ground to which you are about to cross over the Jordan in order to take possession of it.*

14 *And the Lord said to Moses: Behold, the time of your death is approaching. Call Joshua and take your place in the tent of meeting, and I will give him orders. And Moses went, and Joshua, and they took their places in the tent of meeting.*

15 *And the Lord appeared in the tent in a pillar of cloud, and the pillar of cloud stood by the entrance of the tent.*

16 *And the Lord said to Moses: Behold, you are about to lie with your fathers. Then this people will rise up and consort with gods foreign to the land, to which they are going to be among them, and they will forsake me and break the covenant that I made with them.*

17 *Then my anger will be hot against them on that day and I will forsake them and I will hide my face from them, and they shall be devoured. And many evils and distresses shall happen to them, and they shall say on that day: Is it not because our God is not in our midst that these evils have happened to us?*

18 *And I will certainly hide my face on that day, on account of all the evil that they will have done, because they will have turned to other gods.*

19 *And now write down this song for yourselves and teach it to the sons of Israel. Put it in their mouths, in order that this song might serve as a witness for me against the sons of Israel,*

20 *when I have brought them to the ground flowing with milk and honey, which I promised by oath to their fathers, and they eat and are full and grow fat, but turn to other gods and serve them and scorn me and break my covenant.*

21 *And it shall be that when many evils and distresses happen to them, then this song shall confront them as a witness, for it shall not be forgotten by their posterity; for I know their intention which they are forming today, even before I have brought them into the land which I promised by oath.*

22 *And Moses wrote this song on that day and he taught it to the sons of Israel.*

23 *And he gave orders to Joshua, son of Nun, and he said: Be strong and be courageous, for you are about to bring the sons of Israel into the land which I promised them by oath, and I will be with you.*

24 *And when Moses had finished writing the words of this law in a book, to their completion,*

25 *then Moses commanded the Levites, those carrying the ark of the covenant of the Lord, saying:*

26 *Take this book of the law and set it beside the ark of the covenant of the Lord your God, and it shall be there as a witness against you.*

27 *For I know your rebellion and your stubbornness. Behold today,
when I am still with you alive, you were rebelling against the Lord,
and how much more after my death!*
28 *Gather together to me all the elders of your tribes and your
officers, and let me speak these words in their hearing and let me
summon the heaven and the earth as witness against them.*
29 *For I know that after my death you shall certainly act corruptly
and turn aside from the way that I commanded you, and evil will
befall you in the coming days, for you will do the thing that is evil
in the eyes of the Lord, provoking him with the work of your hands.*

The approaching decease of Moses, which has already been anticipated (see 1:37-38 and 3:23-29), now becomes the central focus for the
remaining chapters of the book.[1] Moses is aware of his approaching
death, and in the light of that fact he once again encourages the people
in their faith and takes care of some final practical matters relating to
the covenant community. First he encourages the people as a whole
(vv. 1-6), and then, in the presence of the people, he encourages
Joshua in particular, who would soon be assuming the role of leadership (vv. 7-8).

1-2 *Then Moses went on and addressed . . .* — if this translation is correct, it links the material following to the previous section of
the address, particularly chs. 29–30. It is possible, however, to render
the verse as follows: "And Moses finished[2] addressing these words to
all Israel." In this case, v. 1 serves as a conclusion to the foregoing
section of the address and v. 2 introduces the substance of the remaining chapters. *I am not able to go out and to come in any more* (see also
28:6 and commentary) — Moses would no longer be able to fulfil his
normal daily responsibilities, not only because of his great age, but
also because he would not be permitted to cross the Jordan with the
people.

3-6 In his exhortation to the people, Moses returns once
again to familiar themes from earlier portions of his address. Soon the
people were to cross the Jordan and to begin the most critical phase of
their conquest of the promised land. The people would not enter the
battle alone: they would be preceded by the Lord (cf. 9:3) and their
new leader, Joshua. The Israelites had already experienced God's
victory against Sihon and Og (cf. 2:26-37; 3:1-11) and thus they could

---

1. On Deut. 31, see N. H. Ridderbos, "Die Theophanie in Ps. 50:1-6," in *The Priestly
Code and Seven Other Studies* (1969), pp. 213-16; Ridderbos discusses the relationship
between Deut. 31 and Ps. 50, suggesting that the psalm might have been used at a later
date in the context of the reading of the law. For a study of the relationship between
Deut. 31 and the Song of Moses in Deut. 32, see S. C. Alday, "Contexto redaccional del
Cántico de Moisés," *Estudios Bíblicos* 26 (1967), pp. 383-393.
2. The consonantal text of the MT is *wylk;* the alternative translation is based on the
Qumran text, *wykl* (*DJD* I, p. 60), which has some support from the rendering of the
LXX.

advance in the certain knowledge, based on experience, of further victories through God's strength. They are urged to *be strong and be courageous* (v. 6); the strength and courage would come not from confidence in their own abilities, but from confidence in God, *the one marching with you.* The strength and courage of the warriors of God would lie in the disposition of their minds during the battle. Though they would be engaged physically in the fighting, their minds would not be focused on the enemy, whose threatening presence could easily undermine confidence, but rather their minds would be fixed on God, who would not *fail* or *forsake* them (v. 6b). With full confidence in the presence of God in their midst, the army of the Lord could not fail to be victorious in the conquest, and soon the land which had been promised so long ago would become their possession in reality.

7-8 Moses formally repeats the substance of his exhortation, this time addressing it specifically to Joshua in the presence of the people. The formal and public words spoken to Joshua serve not only to encourage Joshua, but also to remind the people that the leadership was properly being assumed by him, with the full approval of God and of Moses, who was the incumbent of the office up to that time. *You shall bring*³ *this people into the land* — Joshua would assume not only responsibility, but also an enormous privilege. He would be instrumental in the realization of God's ancient promise that he would give his people a land. But as in all cases of leadership, the greater the privilege, the greater the responsibility; and Joshua, more than his fellow Israelites, would need the strength, courage, and freedom from fear that found their roots in God's ability and trustworthiness.

9-13⁴ Provision for future covenant ceremonies. Just as the Hittite political treaties made stipulations for their public reading from time to time,⁵ so too the written document of the covenant between God and his people was to be publicly read out on certain occasions. *This law* (v. 9) — the reference may be to the whole book of Deuteronomy (or at least chs. 1–30), or it may refer simply to the substance of the law upon which the address of Moses was based. The written law was entrusted to the joint care of the Levitical priests and elders. The priests shared in the responsibility, for already they were

---

3. MT renders the verb in the Qal form (see the translation in RSV). The translation above assumes an original Hiph. form of the verb (cf. v. 23 below), for which there is some evidence from the versions (Peshitta, Sam.). Cf. A. R. Hulst, *OT Translation Problems,* p. 17; B. Grossfeld, "Targum Neofiti I to Deut. 31:7," *JBL* 91 (1972), pp. 533f.

4. For a literary-critical analysis of the following verses and their relation to the Song of Moses (Deut. 32) and the foregoing law (Deut. 1–30), see O. Eissfeldt, *Kleine Schriften* III, pp. 322-334.

5. See, e.g., the treaty between Suppiluliumas and Mattiwaza, *ANET,* p. 205. Cf. M. G. Kline, *The Structure of Biblical Authority,* pp. 121-23; M. Weinfeld, *Deuteronomy and the Deuteronomic School,* pp. 64f.; K. A. Kitchen, *Ancient Orient and OT,* p. 97.

charged with the care of the *ark of the covenant,* within which the tablets basic to the covenant relationship were contained. The elders shared in the responsibility, for it was their role to ensure that the people under their care lived in accord with the covenant stipulations.

The periodical public recitation of the covenant document was to take place in the future, at seven-year intervals. In the sabbatical year, during the Feast of Booths (or Tabernacles), the law was to be recited in the hearing of all Israel; on the Feast of Booths, see the more detailed legislation in 16:13-15. *In the place that he chooses* (v. 11; cf. 16:15)—the ceremony would be held at the sanctuary, where both the covenant tablets and the written law (see v. 9, above) would be kept.

The ceremony in which the law would be recited, as it is described in these verses, is not in the strict sense a *renewal* of the covenant. The covenant renewal was reserved for particular occasions — the renewal described in the book of Deuteronomy as a whole immediately preceded the major stage of the conquest, for example. The ceremony prescribed in these verses has more the character of a regular commemoration of the covenant. The function of the ceremony would be educational; the people would be summoned together *in order that they may hear and in order that they may learn* (v. 12). For the older people in the covenant community, the educational value of the ceremony would lie in remembering the covenant with God and in renewed dedication to the God of the covenant. The renewed dedication would find its expression in the fear of God and in obedience to his law (v. 12b). The younger generation, however, would learn for the first time the full meaning of the covenant (v. 13). Although they would know about it beforehand, its significance would dawn on them fully only as they left their homes and villages and heard the public reading of the law in the presence of *all Israel* (cf. v. 11). There, in the presence of the larger family of God's people, they would begin to perceive the greater community of which they were a part, and they too would learn to fear God. As each generation learned to fear God and to obey him, so would the continuing community of Israel ensure their lasting possession of the promised land.

14-15   The public words of exhortation are followed by a private ceremony in the tent; only Moses and Joshua are present for this intimate meeting with God, which is called because of the imminent death of Moses (v. 14a). Moses is instructed to enter *the tent of meeting* along with Joshua, and there Joshua would be commissioned for his new role of leadership (. . . *I will give him orders*). The presence of God would be experienced in the pillar of cloud standing at the door of the tent; for further details, see Exod. 33:7-11. In the private ceremony, the Lord first of all addresses Moses (vv. 16-21) and then commissions Joshua as the new leader of Israel (v. 23).

16-21 The words that the Lord addresses to Moses on the eve of his death must have caused great sadness in the aging leader. The substance of his long address to the Israelites had been faithfulness to God and a warning against the dangers of resorting to foreign gods and their cults. But now, about to die, Moses is told that *this people will rise up and consort with gods foreign to the land.* The words of God are not primarily prophetic; they portray rather divine insight into the basic character of the people and their constant tendency to unfaithfulness. In spite of all that God had done, the people would forsake him and *break the covenant.* [6] Having forsaken God, the people would then be forsaken by God, with the inevitable result that disaster would fall upon them at every turn. The awful realization would dawn that the disaster was a result of God's absence from their midst, but then the people would call upon God in vain, for he would have hidden his face from them (v. 18). When his people turned to foreign gods, God turned from his people.

This somber note in the words of God to Moses serves as an introduction to the song Moses was to write and teach to the people (v. 19). *For yourselves* (v. 19) — the plural form probably refers to both Moses and Joshua. The song would serve a solemn function; as the people learned the song and took its words upon their own lips, they would be bearing witness against themselves, not only of their commitment to God, but also of their knowledge of the inevitable consequences of unfaithfulness. Verse 20 recalls the substance of vv. 18-20, but employs different words to emphasize the point. The very prosperity that God would give his people, the prosperity of the land and the abundance of food, could contribute to a sense of ease in which the source of that prosperity was forgotten. [7] The song was to be remembered from one generation to the next and was never to be forgotten. It would serve as a warning of the dangers that would constantly beset Israel, perhaps preventing the people from going astray. But if they went astray, its words would resound in condemnation against them. *I know their intention which they are forming today* (v. 21) — God perceived the intentions latent in the hearts of his people, even before they were themselves fully aware of them. But the goodness of God is perceived in the gift of the song, for a part of its function would be to warn the people of their emerging intentions and turn them back to God before it was too late. The role of the Song of Moses in the life of ancient Israel portrays clearly at least one of the roles the Bible plays in our Christian life in the modern world. On v. 22, see the commentary on v. 30.

6. The expression *hēpēr bᵉrît,* which occurs 20 times in the OT with the Hiph. form of the verb, has been studied in detail in its various contexts by W. Thiel, "Zum Bundbrechen im AT," *VT* 20 (1970), pp. 214-229. Cf. 31:20 (below).
7. With v. 20, compare the more detailed elaboration of a similar theme in Ezek. 16.

23 After addressing Moses in the tent, the Lord then speaks to Joshua, who was soon to assume the office held for so long by Moses. *Be strong and be courageous* — see also vv. 6, 7 (above). The words that would be the source of continuing strength to Joshua come at the end of the verse: *I will be with you*. Of the forms of loneliness that a man can experience, there are few so bleak as the loneliness of leadership. But Joshua assumed his lonely role with an assurance of companionship and strength. God's presence with him would be sufficient to enable him to meet boldly every obstacle that the future could bring. See also Josh. 1:5 and 3:7.

24-29 *The words of this law* (cf. vv. 9, 12) — it is possible that *law (tôrāh)* here may be the song of instruction referred to already in v. 19.[8] In its written form, the song would be appended to the written covenant document which was entrusted to the care of the Levites who carried the ark of the covenant. The words of Moses to the people in vv. 27-29 reflect Moses' response to the words God addressed to him (vv. 16-18). Knowing the natural tendency toward rebellion among his people, he is all the more anxious to be sure they know the words of the song. The song was to be taught to all the people, but in order to achieve this end, the elders and officers are summoned first. The song was to be recited in their hearing (v. 28) and then, no doubt, they would assist in the instruction of all the people when Moses recited the song in the presence of the full congregation (v. 30).

B. THE SONG OF MOSES (31:30–32:44)

30 Then Moses spoke the words of this song to their completion in the hearing of the whole assembly of Israel.

These words serve as the prose introduction to the Song of Moses, which follows in its entirety in 32:1-43, Normally, ancient Hebrew poetry is introduced as having been sung (see Exod. 15:1; Judg. 5:1); here, the song is said to have been spoken. It may be that the song was recited initially and that in this manner it was taught to the people (cf. 31:19), with a view to being sung by them subsequently. The recital (or subsequent singing) of the song would be a part of the covenant renewal ceremony, and it should not be considered simply as an appendix to the book of Deuteronomy. The song functions as a part of the witness to the renewal of the covenant; when the Israelites sang it, they would bear witness to their understanding and agreement to the full terms and implications of the covenant.[1] This part of the renewal

---

8.   Cf. M. Fishbane, "Varia Deuteronomica," *ZAW* 84 (1972), pp. 350f.

1.   See particularly M. G. Kline, *The Structure of Biblical Authority*, p. 141.

ceremony, however, is related in particular to the approaching demise of Moses and Joshua's assumption of leadership. In this context, the song was not only a song of witness for the present, but one that would continue to be sung in the future, thus bearing a continuing witness of the covenant commitment and reminding the people of the implications of a breach of the covenant.

Because of its poetic form, in contrast to the prose form of the foregoing chapters of Deuteronomy, the Song of Moses has been the subject of a large number of detailed and particular studies (see the select bibliography below). Several of these studies have emphasized the antiquity of the song,[2] its many points of similarity with the prophetic literature[3] and with the wisdom literature.[4] However, the song does not refer to particular events;[5] it is generally prophetic in expressing Moses' vision of the future, in both its gloomy and its brighter aspects, in a manner not unsimilar to the elaboration on the blessings and curses in chs. 27-28. It is similar to the wisdom literature in that it includes very practical advice (cf. vv. 7, 28-29); its function is to remind and to educate the people in the way they should take (cf. 31:19) — it is not simply a song of praise. Thus the similarities with literary forms that became common at a later date may indicate a source for those literary forms, but they do not necessarily indicate that the song is to be classified as "prophecy" or "wisdom" in form.

The text of the song is difficult to translate in some places. This difficulty may lie in the fact that poetry in general, and early poetry in particular, draws on rich resources of vocabulary that are not always familiar from the more straightforward prose sources. There are at least fourteen *hapax legomena* in the song[6] and a number of verses are exceptionally difficult to translate with any certainty (see particularly the notes on vv. 5, 8). The style of the song is somewhat different from that of other early Hebrew poetry. In other early songs, the style is largely characterized by the dramatic staccato-type short line; the

2. See the studies of Eissfeldt and Albright noted in the select bibliography (below); see also D. A. Robertson, *Linguistic Evidence in Dating Early Hebrew Poetry* (diss., Yale University, 1966), pp. 230f. On the subject of early Hebrew poetry, see further the Introduction, section IX.5.
3. See the article by G. E. Wright in the select bibliography (below); Wright deals with the divine lawsuit or *rib* pattern in the song, which has also been analyzed in form-critical studies of prophetic literature and is present in some of the psalms. See also the article by E. Baumann (below).
4. See the article in the select bibliography by J. R. Boston.
5. Thus the various attempts to date the song by identifying the "enemy" of vv. 19-29 have been somewhat fruitless; Arameans, Assyrians, Babylonians, and Philistines have been suggested, and all these suggestions may have some validity in the later interpretation of the song during its history in Israel's worship. But as composed and taught, the song does not refer to any specific enemy.
6. This is the number given by S. R. Driver, *Deuteronomy*, p. 348. There may be more if certain difficult verses are taken into account where the meaning is still unclear.

short line (often only two words) is a feature of the function of those songs, most of which are victory songs celebrating a dramatic and joyous event.[7] The Song of Moses in Deut. 32 is characterized by longer lines and more polished forms of poetic parallelism, which are suited in function to the solemn subject matter of the song.

The nature of the structure of the song is a matter of continuing debate;[8] in the presentation of the song here, it has simply been divided into what seem to be natural units of thought, and comment has been added section by section. Problems relating to the translation and meaning of particular lines or words are discussed in the footnotes to the translation, rather than in the main body of the commentary. The select bibliography that follows will provide alternative avenues of approaching the study of the song.

Select Bibliography on the Song of Moses

Only the more recent articles and studies are included here. The notes and bibliographies in the material listed below will provide information on earlier studies.

O. Eissfeldt, *Das Lied Moses, Deuteronomium 32:1-43 und das Lehrgedicht Asaphs samt einer Analyse der Umgebung des Mose-Liedes* (1958).

W. F. Albright, "Some Remarks on the Song of Moses," *VT* 9 (1959), pp. 339-346.

G. E. Wright, "The Lawsuit of God: A Form-critical Study of Deuteronomy 32," in B. W. Anderson and W. Harrelson, eds., *Israel's Prophetic Heritage* (1962), pp. 26-67.

P. W. Skehan, "The Structure of the Song of Moses in Deuteronomy," *CBQ* 13 (1951), pp. 153-163.

J. R. Boston, "The Wisdom Influences upon the Song of Moses," *JBL* 87 (1968), pp. 166-178.

S. Carillo Alday, "El Cántico de Moisés," *Estudios Bíblicos* 26 (1967), pp. 227-248.

E. Baumann, "Das Lied Moses auf seine gedankliche Geschlossenheit untersucht," *VT* 6 (1956), pp. 414-424.

E. Sellin, "Wann wurde das Moselied Deut. 32 gedichtet?" *ZAW* 43 (1928), pp. 161-173.

On the text and versions of the song, see P. W. Skehan, *BASOR* 136 (1954), pp. 12-15 (re the Qumran text, 4QDeut. 32).

7. See particularly Exod. 15:1-18; Judg. 5. Cf. P. C. Craigie, *JBL* 88 (1969), pp. 263f.
8. See the article by Skehan in *CBQ* 13 (1951), pp. 153-163. Skehan divides the song into three principal parts of (approximately) equivalent length: (I) vv. 1-14; (II) vv. 15-29; (III) vv. 30-43. Skehan divides the song as a whole into 69 verses (note that the present verse divisions are late additions to the text) and suggests that this was the author's way of writing a 70-line song, a number with considerable implications. Skehan's suggestive analysis may be fruitful, but it is difficult to determine the extent to which he is reading the implications of later Jewish sources back into the ancient song.

A. Vööbus, *Peschitta und Targumim des Pentateuchs.* Papers of the Estonian Theological Society in Exile 9 (1958), with reference to the Syriac text of Deut. 32 and Exod. 15.

1. INTRODUCTION TO THE SONG (32:1-3)

1 *Give ear, O heavens, and let me speak,*
And hear,⁹ O earth, the words of my mouth!
2 *My teaching shall drop like rain;*
My speech shall distil like dew;
Like raindrops¹⁰ upon fresh grass
And like heavy rain upon vegetation,
3 *For I shall proclaim¹¹ the name of the Lord.*
Ascribe greatness to our God!

The first verse opens the song by calling upon the *heavens* and *earth* to hear the words that are to be spoken; the poetic form is that of synonymous parallelism, but the point of reference for this verse is the earlier mention of heaven and earth as the silent witnesses to the renewal of the covenant (see 4:26; 30:19; 31:28 and commentary). In those verses, Moses called on heaven and earth to act as witnesses. It must be remembered, however, that the song was being taught to the people in order that they might sing it (31:19); thus, the people now vocally commit themselves to the covenant, invoking the unchanging elements of the physical and created world to be witness to their commitment. It should be noted that the song is not *addressed* to the heaven and the earth — it is addressed to the Lord (v. 3), but they are called upon to hear it. In the event of the people's unfaithfulness in the future, the created world would itself stand in silent condemnation of the Israelites.

The *teaching/speech* (v. 2) refers directly to the content of the song which follows.¹² Employing four similes, the poet describes the potential of the song's teaching for the lives of the covenant people. If all the teaching of the song were to penetrate and saturate the hearts and minds of the Israelites, then it could only make them grow in the

9. Heb. "and the earth shall hear"; however, the context indicates the imperative form of the verb.
10. Heb. *sᵉˁîrîm (hapax legomenon)*; though the meaning of the word is uncertain, the context has always suggested the meaning. The Ugaritic texts now provide more direct evidence; there, the words *ṭl* (dew), *rbb* (rain), and *šrˁ* occur in triple parallelism. It seems likely that Heb. *sᵉˁîr* = Ugar. *šrˁ*, and that metathesis has taken place. See U. Cassuto, *The Goddess Anath*, p. 122; *idem, Orientalia* 8 (1939), p. 239; J. Gray, *The Legacy of Canaan²*, p. 44 (n.).
11. For a similar introduction in Ugaritic poetry, see *CTA* 23 (=*UT* 52), line 1: *'eqr'a.'elm. n['mm..]*, "I proclaim the gods gracious. . . ."
12. Indirectly, it refers to the content of Deut. as a whole, which finds concise expression in the song. The word *teaching (leqaḥ)* is one of several words in the song reminiscent of wisdom literature (cf. Prov. 1:5).

fear and strength of the Lord. But the reason why the words of the song can be likened to the beneficial rain is to be found in its subject matter, indicated in v. 3a: *I shall proclaim the name of the Lord.* The *name,* which has various implications in Deuteronomy (cf. 5:11; 12:5; etc.), here gathers together the various attributes of God indicated by his name,[13] which will be set forth in the verses of the song which follow. Then the singer makes a broader appeal for all to *ascribe greatness*[14] *to our God* (v. 3b), a theme that is elaborated in the verses immediately following.

2. A FAITHFUL GOD AND A FAITHLESS PEOPLE (vv. 4-9)

> 4 *The Rock! His work is perfect,*
> *For all his ways are justice.*
> *A God of faithfulness, without injustice,*
> *He is righteous and upright.*
> 5 *They have dealt corruptly with him;*
> *They are no longer his children because of their blemish:*[15]
> *A perverted and tortuous generation!*
> 6 *Is this what you render to the Lord?*
> *You foolish people, with no wisdom!*
> *Is he not your father? He created you,*
> *He made you and he established you.*
> 7 *Remember the days of old!*
> *Consider the years, generation by generation.*[16]
> *Ask your father and he will declare it to you,*
> *Your elders, and they will tell you.*
> 8 *When the Most High gave the nations an inheritance,*
> *When he separated the sons of mankind,*[17]

13. See Exod. 33:19 and G. A. Smith, *The Book of Deuteronomy,* pp. 344f.
14. The word *greatness (gōḏel)* is common in Deut., though rare in other biblical books; cf. Keil and Delitzsch, *The Pentateuch,* p. 467; M. Weinfeld, *Deuteronomy and the Deuteronomic School,* p. 329; *TDOT* II, p. 400 (Mosis).
15. The translation of the first two lines of v. 5 follows RSV. The Heb. is difficult; tentatively, the following reconstruction of the line is suggested: *šḥtw lw l'bn' mrmh* — "They destroyed him! Treacherous stones!" (a) *šḥtw* is read as a plural form, following the hint of the LXX. (b) *l'bn' mrmh* involves a new division of the radicals of the consonantal text, plus emendation of *mwmm* to *mrmh.* (c) The */l/* in *l'bn'* is taken to have an asseverative function. The significance of the rendering (which is hypothetical) is seen in contrast to v. 4. There the Lord is described as a *Rock;* his ways are *perfect (mishpāṭ)* and without *injustice ('āwel).* In contrast, his people are *treacherous stones;* that is, they are like false weights. For the expression *'bn' mrmh,* see Mic. 6:11. *mrmh* ("treacherous, deceitful") occurs as the opposite of *mishpāṭ* (see Prov. 12:5) and as similar in meaning to *'āwel* (see Ps. 55:24). The rendering should not be pressed, but it would provide a striking contrast to v. 4 — a faithful God, the *Rock,* and an unfaithful people, *treacherous stones!*
16. The synonyms employed in the parallelism of this verse (*'lm//dr wdr*) are also employed in Ugaritic poetry; see U. Cassuto, *The Goddess Anath,* p. 26.
17. The translation of the first two lines seems fairly certain; for an alternative suggestion, see G. R. Driver, "Three Notes," *VT* 2 (1952), pp. 356f.

He fixed the boundaries of peoples
According to the number of the sons of God.[18]
9 But[19] *the Lord's portion is his people;*
Jacob is his allotted inheritance.

In this section, a sharp contrast is drawn first of all between the perfection of God (v. 4) and the imperfection of his people (v. 5); then the imperfection of the people is made all the more stark as it is declared against the background of a loving God and his purpose for his people (vv. 6-9). The tone of the passage (as of much of the song) is prophetic, but it may also reflect past failures of the people, such as those already described in the historical portions of Deut. 1–4.

The Lord is described as *the Rock;* the word is placed at the very beginning of the verse for emphasis and it is followed by a series of lines in poetic parallelism which systematically elaborate the attributes of God as the Rock of Israel. The epithet or name, *Rock,* emphasizes the stability and permanence of the God of Israel.[20] It is one of the principal themes in the song (see also vv. 15, 18, 30, 31 and compare v. 37),[21] stressing the unchanging nature of the God of the covenant and contrasting with the fickle nature of the covenant people.

Although the translation of v. 5 is difficult (see n. 15), the sense seems clear enough; Israel, unlike its Rock, is *perverted and tortuous.*[22] The perversity of the Israelites was all the worse in that it was

18. MT reads "sons of Israel," though the evidence of the LXX suggests an original Heb. text meaning "sons of God," or "sons of gods" (LXX "angels of God"). A Qumran manuscript indicates that the LXX may reflect the original text in this instance. For fuller discussion, see P. W. Skehan, *BASOR* 136 (1954), pp. 12-15; R. Meyer, "Die Bedeutung von Deuteronomium 32.8f. 43 (4Q) für die Auslesung des Moseliedes," in *Verbannung und Heimkehr.* Festschrift W. Rudolph (1961); J. Hempel, "Zu 4Q Deut. 32:8," *ZAW* 74 (1962), p. 70; P. Winter, "Nochmals zu Deuteronomium 32:8," *ZAW* 75 (1963), pp. 218-233 (cf. *idem, ZAW* 67 [1955], p. 292).
19. Alternatively, the line can be rendered: "Indeed, the Lord's portion is his people!" by taking the initial word to be emphatic *kî;* cf. J. Gray, *The Legacy of Canaan*[2], p. 278.
20. J. G. Herder has suggested that the imagery reflects Sinai and the rocks of Arabia; on Mount Sinai the covenant was formed, "and on the part of God it was as enduring as the everlasting rocks." See *The Spirit of Hebrew Poetry* (E.T. 1833), I, p. 280. In the "Testament of Jacob," a similar epithet is employed; God is described as the "Stone of Israel" (Gen. 49:24). During and after the Mosaic period, however, "Rock" becomes the more common term to be applied to God (cf. Keil and Delitzsch, *The Pentateuch,* pp. 467f.).
21. See also Ps. 95:1, "the rock of our salvation" (cf. Deut. 32:15). In Isa. 44:8, the word *Rock* is employed to contrast the permanence of God with the impermanence of false deities (see also Ps. 18:31). The word *Rock* may indicate also the personal aspect of devotion to the Lord, whose very permanence makes him the source of absolute trust: Ps. 19:14, "O Lord, my Rock and my Redeemer."
22. The phrase is used by Jesus (Matt. 17:17) of a faithless generation, and it is used in Phil. 2:15 to describe the dark world within which the Christian is to shine as a bright light.

totally out of harmony with the Lord's dealings with them: *Is this what you render to the Lord?* (v. 6). In their foolishness, they failed to recognize him as their father and failed to recognize that all his dealings with them were not onerous impositions, but a reflection of God's covenant love. *He created you, He made you and he established you.* The verb translated by "create" is *qānāh,* not the more familiar *bārā'* which is employed in Gen. 1:1. The same verb (*qānāh*) is used in Exod. 15:16 in the song celebrating the Exodus from Egypt. Thus the phrase *he created you,* in its context, alludes to both the Exodus and Sinai as the events connected with the "creation" of the people of the Lord. That "creation" was initiated in the grace and covenant love of the Lord, and for Israel to forget that grace and to act perversely was tantamount to forgetting its very *raison d'être.* The call to *remember the days of old* (v. 7) is thus a call to reflect on past history and to inquire about its meaning: *ask your father . . . your elders . . .* (v. 7b). For Israel, the historical events of the past were like a map, on which the movements of God in the plane of human events could be traced. But the significance of history lay not in antiquarian interest, but in the conviction that the God who had acted in the past would continue to act in the lives and affairs of his people, and that his acts in the past were of continuing significance for the present and future.

In vv. 8-9, the sovereignty of God over all men and nations is expressed, but it is stated in such a way as to emphasize his particular concern for his chosen people. God is given the title *'Elyon* ("Most High"),[23] which is used only here in Deuteronomy.[24] The title emphasizes God's sovereignty and authority over all nations, whereas in relation to his own people he is called Yahweh or Lord (v. 9). All nations received their *inheritance* and had their boundaries fixed by this sovereign God (v. 8),[25] whose role was in no way restricted to the sphere of Israelite life and history (see also Ps. 74:17). The boundaries were fixed *according to the number of the sons of God* (v. 8b; see n. 18). The exact sense of the phrase is difficult to determine, but the reference seems to be to the divine council of the Lord.[26] His council consisted of "holy ones" (see 33:2 and commentary), who are called "angels" in the LXX; the poetry indicates that the number of nations is related to the number of these Sons of God. Among all these

23. On the use of this title in Canaanite religion, see H. Gese *et al., Die Religionen Altsyriens, Altarabiens und der Mandäer,* pp. 116f.
24. See G. T. Manley, *The Book of the Law,* p. 45; Manley notes that two earlier uses of the title both have Gentile associations, as in the present context: Gen. 14:18 (Melchizedek) and Num. 24:16 (Balaam).
25. See T. H. Gaster, *Thespis,* p. 450; Gaster compares this passage with *Enuma Elish* VI, 56-57.
26. For similar language, see the following selected passages: Ps. 29:1 (see RSV footnote); 82:1, 6; Job 1:6; 2:1; 38:7. Cf. F. M. Cross, "The Council of Yahweh in Second Isaiah," *JNES* 12 (1953), pp. 274-77.

nations, Israel[27] was God's particular *portion* and *allotted inheritance* (v. 9). With such a high calling and noble position, the perversity of the people (v. 5) was all the more wretched.

3. THE GOODNESS OF GOD (vv. 10-14)

10 *He found him in a desert land*
And in a wasteland, a howling wilderness.
He encircled him; he took care of him;
He watched over him like the apple of his eye.[28]

11 *As an eagle stirs up its nest,*
It hovers over its young ones,
It spreads out its wings; it takes one,
It lifts him on its pinions;

12 *The Lord alone guided him,*
And with him there was no strange god.

13 *He made him ride upon the high places of the earth*
And he made him eat the produce of the field,
And he made him suck honey from the crag
And oil from the flinty rock.

14 *Curd of the herd and milk of the flock,*
With the fat of lambs,
And rams of Bashan-breed and he-goats,
Along with the choicest of the grains of wheat;
And of the blood of grapes, you drank wine.

The goodness of God is described in a series of poetic images and similes; the language alludes to God's care for his people in Egypt, his bringing them out of that land, and the guidance and provision that he grants them during their travels. God is seen as a Father-figure,[29] caring for his people in every dimension of their lives.

10 The point of reference in this verse is probably Egypt, not specifically the wilderness. The first two lines of the verse do not describe Egypt in a precise sense, but contrast it, by implication, with the richness of the promised land. But in another way, Egypt was a "desert" in the experience of the people of God. It was not a place they could live in, but a place through which they must pass. It was not the land God was going to give them, but a land of testing and preparation for the travels lying ahead of the Israelites. In this foreign land, however, in which God's people had no continuing city, the Lord protected his people and watched over them with fatherly care.

27. Israel is here called *Jacob*, a regular poetic synonym for Israel; Num. 23:7, 10, 21, 23; 24:5, 17, 18-19.
28. The Heb. idiom is literally: "like the little man (*'îshôn* is a diminutive form of *'ish*) of his eye."
29. On the contrast between this conception and that current in the ancient Near Eastern religions, see H. Frankfort *et al., Before Philosophy* (1964), pp. 245f.

11 The simile of the *eagle*[30] may have been prompted by the language of the wilderness in the previous verse; the picture in this verse is that of the eagle's nest, perhaps located in some remote place in the wilderness. *As an eagle stirs up* (or perhaps "guards") *its nest*[31] — see also v. 10b for the protective character of God's love. Apparently the eagle taught its young to fly by throwing one out of the nest, and then swooping down and allowing the young bird to alight on its mother's wings.[32] The poetry illustrates vividly God's dealings with his people, casting them from security to the fierce wilderness, but remaining beneath them to give them strength for the fearful experience, and gradually teaching them to "fly" on their own. It is implied that Israel is still in its youth, brought out of Egypt as a child and still learning to stand and walk during the years in the wilderness.

12 During the wilderness travels, the Lord alone guided his people, with no help from a *strange god;* compare the goodness of God at this point with the perversity of his people in 31:16, where the Israelites are described as prone to resorting to "gods foreign to the land."

13-14 The focus now shifts to the future, when the people would possess the promised land and experience the goodness of God in the rich produce of the land. *He made him ride upon the high places of the earth* (v. 13a) — the metaphor seems to refer to the conquest and the invincibility of the people of God in their possession of the land. *Honey from the crag* — infertile places would be rich in produce in God's land; it is possible that the specific reference may be to · honeycombs located in the fissures of the cliff-faces.[33] Likewise, the *oil from the flinty rock* may refer to olive trees growing in places otherwise bereft of fruit-growing trees.[34] The people would have in abundance *curd* (or "butter") and *milk,*[35] meat, cereals, and wine. *The blood of grapes* (v. 14) — the idiom means *wine* and it is known in both Hebrew and Ugaritic poetry.[36]

---

30. Although Heb. *nesher* has the specific sense of "griffon-vulture," the word may also be employed as a generic term covering all birds of prey. With the imagery in this verse, compare lines 38-46 of the Epic of Lugalbanda; C. Wilcke, *Das Lugalbandaepos* (1969), pp. 94f.
31. See J. Gray, *The Legacy of Canaan*[2], p. 268.
32. See M. H. Farbridge, *Studies in Biblical and Semitic Symbolism,* pp. 82-84; G. R. Driver, *PEQ* 19 (1958), pp. 56f.; S. E. Loewenstamm, *BASOR* 194 (1969), pp. 52-54.
33. See S. R. Driver, *Deuteronomy,* p. 359. Cf. U. Cassuto, *The Goddess Anath,* pp. 108f.
34. The olive tree can grow in rocky soil and requires very little water.
35. The terms *curd* and *milk* are used together in poetic parallelism in both Hebrew and Ugaritic poetry; see *RSP* I, p. 182.
36. The full idiom varies, though the *blood* (meaning "juice") element remains constant. See Gordon, *UT,* p. 95, n. 4; H. P. Rüger, "Zu RS 24.258," *UF* 1 (1969), p. 206. In v. 14b, *you drank wine* could perhaps be rendered: "you drank *by the bowl*

4. ISRAEL'S PROSPERITY AND APOSTASY (vv. 15-18)

15 But Jeshurun grew fat and kicked.
 You grew fat, you grew thick, you became gross!
 Then he abandoned God, who made him,
 And scorned the Rock of his salvation.
16 They made him jealous with strangers;
 With abominations they offended him.
17 They sacrificed to demons, not God,
 Gods whom they knew not,
 New ones that came in of late;
 Your fathers did not know about them.
18 You were mindless of the Rock that begot you
 And forgot the God that delivered you in pain.

The goodness of God is now contrasted sharply with a description of the fickleness of the people of God. Having grown fat on the graciousness of God's provision, the Israelites relax in their newly found prosperity and forget the Source of their benefit. Forgetting their own God, they turn ungratefully to the attractive, but shallow, temptations of foreign gods.

15 *Jeshurun* is a hypocoristicon for Israel. The name is employed in a positive context in 33:5, but in the song, the use of Israel's "pet-name" serves only to emphasize all the more sharply Israel's ingratitude to God. The people *grew fat* on the bountiful provision of God, but *kicked,* resisting his love and control. The general statement of the first line of v. 15 is then made intensely personal by the shift in number to the second person singular — you *grew fat . . . !*[37] The condemnation falls not only on the impersonal "Jeshurun" or "Israel," but on each individual within that larger community. The meaning of the verbs *abandoned* and *scorned* (v. 15b) is accentuated by the objects of the verbs; Israel abandoned the source of its creation and scorned the basis of its salvation, acts of incredible folly — but the incredible becomes the credible when God's people forget the source of their blessing.

16-17 The parallel terms *strangers* and *abominations* allude to foreign gods and their cults. By abandoning God to go after strange gods, the Israelites break the first commandment of their covenant with God, upon which their whole life depends. On *abominations,* see also 7:25; 18:9, 12. Having forsaken God, they make their sacrifices to *demons,*[38] not to the true God. Neither the Israelites nor their fathers *knew* (v. 17) the demons, the foreign gods, in the way that they knew from experience their Living Lord.

(ḥāmer)"; see M. Dahood, "Hebrew-Ugaritic Lexicography, II," Biblica 45 (1964), p. 408.
37. The three verbs are in the 2nd person *singular.*
38. Cf. 1 Cor. 10:20: "I do not want you to be partners with demons."

18   Parental imagery is used of God once again; he is described as a mother who *begot* and *delivered in pain*[39] the Israelites. In their apostasy, the Israelites *were mindless*[40] even of a love as intimate as that which a mother bears for her own child; such mindlessness invited God's reaction, as the following verses make clear.

5. THE RESULT OF ISRAEL'S APOSTASY (vv. 19-22)

19 *And the Lord saw and condemned,*
    Because of the vexation of his sons and daughters.
20 *And he said:*
    I will hide my face from them.
    I see what their latter end is to be,
    For they are a perverse generation,
    Sons in whom there is no faithfulness.
21 *They made me jealous with a "no-god";*
    They vexed me with their idols.
    But I will make them jealous with a "no-people";
    With a foolish nation I will vex them.
22 *For a fire will be kindled in my nostrils*[41]
    And it will burn to Sheol down below.
    And it will devour the land and its produce,
    And it will scorch the foundations of the mountains.

And the Lord saw (v. 19) — he saw the apostasy of Israel described in the foregoing verses (vv. 15-18). The behavior of the Israelites vexed God; he had a fatherly concern for them as *his sons and daughters,* so that to see them rejecting his love caused him not only anger, but also pain. *I will hide my face from them* (v. 20) — again the words indicate not only anger (cf. 31:18), but also sorrow, for a loving Father finds it hard to look on while his children invite disaster by their sinful behavior. Although God was faithful (see v. 4), the unfaithfulness of his sons separated him from them. They substituted a *"no-god"* for their Living God (5:26) and made a travesty of true religion by serving lifeless *idols* (v. 21). The result was inevitable; if they wanted to trust in a *"no-god,"* then they would experience the judgment of God at the hands of a *"no-people."*[42] If Israel trusted in their Living God, a *"no-people"* would present no threat; but having deserted their Lord, they would cry in vain to their *"no-god"* for

39. For other uses of these parallel terms in Ugaritic and Hebrew poetry, see *RSP* I, p. 186.
40. MT *teshî* is difficult; the form should probably be vocalized *tishsheh,* from the verb *nāshāh.* Cf. G. Rinaldi, *Bibbia e Oriente* 13 (1971), p. 26.
41. On the translation *nostrils ('appî),* see M. Dahood, *Biblica* 45 (1964), p. 283.
42. The contention of W. F. Albright (*VT* 9 [1959], p. 344) and others, that the expression *no-people* refers to Israel, is unlikely, given the context. The poet probably has no specific nation in mind and is simply enunciating the manner in which God's judgment is executed.

deliverance from a threatening *"no-people."* The political powers of
the world were real, however insignificant, and only the Lord could
grant victory to his people, who had no strength apart from God's
strength. In v. 22, the anger takes precedence over pity; and the
divine fire of anger, once kindled, knows no limits in its destructive
force, reaching to *Sheol* (the underworld), devastating the produce of
the land, scorching the foundations of the mountains. The anger of
God is like the love of God, knowing no limits in the places to which it
extends (see Rom. 8:38); but the anger of God is an awesome and
terrible thing exactly because it follows from a rejection of the equally
pervasive love of God.

6. THE EXECUTION OF GOD'S JUDGMENT (vv. 23-27)

23 *I will make evils sweep over them.*
I will expend my arrows against them.
24 *Gnawing hunger of famine,*
And ravages of pestilence,
And bitter stinging;
The teeth of beasts will I send upon them,
Along with venom of snakes of the dust.
25 *Outside, the sword makes childless,*
And inside there is terror –
Even for the young man, even for the maiden,
For the suckling child along with the grey-haired man.
26 *I would have said: "I will cut them in pieces,*[43]
I will make the memory of them cease among men,"
27 *Had I not feared the vexation of the enemy;*
Lest their adversaries had misconstrued,
Lest they say: "Our hand is high,
And it is not the Lord who has done all this."

23 The judgment of God is described first in general terms;
God would afflict his people with *evils* (these are elaborated in v. 24)
and *arrows,* namely, enemies who would defeat Israel in war (the
substance of vv. 25-27 expands on this theme).

24 The judgment of God would be experienced in *famine.* If
the people were obedient to God, they would receive his ample
provision; but when that blessing was withdrawn, famine would
follow. They would also be afflicted by *pestilence,*[44] apparently some

43. On the meaning of the root *p'h,* see KB, p. 749, and on the cognate Ugar. word,
see G. R. Driver, *Canaanite Myths and Legends,* p. 162. The Heb. verb appears to be a
hapax legomenon.
44. The Heb. *reshep* here does not mean "fire-bolt" (cf. S. R. Driver, *Deuteronomy,*
p. 367) but *pestilence;* in the Ugaritic texts, the deity Reshef was a god of pestilence.
See J. Gray, *The Legacy of Canaan²,* p. 276.

form of disease.[45] Even the animal world, *beasts* and *snakes,*[46] would pose a threat to Israel under the condemnation of God.

25 God would further afflict his people in war; the war would affect not only the warriors (those *outside*) but also the noncombatants (those *inside*). *The sword makes childless* — the death caused by the sword of the enemies would result in childless widows at home. *Inside* (lit. "in the chambers")[47] *there is terror* — even those who did not participate in the fighting (children, young people, old men) would experience the horrors of war, for Israel's defeat would mean that the enemy in their wrath could penetrate even the security of private homes in Israel.

26-27 The only thing that would prevent the Lord from permitting the complete destruction of his people would be concern that the *adversaries* employed in the divine judgment might claim for themselves the honor of victory over Israel. The poetic irony thus shows a brief hope, but not for any merit that could be found in Israel. *Our hand is high* (v. 27) — the metaphor indicates military arrogance.[48]

7. ISRAEL'S LACK OF DISCERNMENT (vv. 28-33)

28 *For they are a nation deaf to advice,*
   And there is no discernment among them.
29 *If they were wise, they would comprehend this;*
   They would discern their latter end.
30 *How could one pursue a thousand*
   Or two make a multitude flee,
   If it were not that their Rock had sold them,
   And the Lord had handed them over?
31 *For their rock is not like our Rock.*
   And even our enemies may be judges!
32 *For their vine is from the vine of Sodom*
   And from the terraces[49] *of Gomorrah.*
   Their grapes are the grapes of venom.
   They have bitter clusters of grapes.
33 *Their wine is the poison of serpents*
   and the cruel venom of snakes.

45. Compare the use of the same word in Hab. 3:5.
46. The translation *snakes* is uncertain; the term may simply refer to poisonous insects.
47. In literary terms, the "chambers" are the traditional resort for safety from an enemy; cf. U. Cassuto, *The Goddess Anath,* p. 147.
48. See A. S. Yahuda, *The Language of the Pentateuch,* p. 68, who notes that the Egyptian god Min is described as "He with the uplifted arm." Cf. P. Montet, *Eternal Egypt,* p. 223.
49. Heb. *shaḏmoṯ* (see KB, p. 950). The meaning may be less specific, in which case it would be translated "vineyard"; see G. R. Driver, *Canaanite Myths and Legends,* p. 148, on the cognate Ugar. term (cf. *RSP* I, p. 161).

The reason why God's judgment would be executed on his people (vv. 20-25) was to be found in Israel's lack of discernment; they would see the signs that indicated all was not well with their relationship to God, but they would fail to understand fully, in such a way that would lead to their turning aside from evil. *If they were wise* (v. 29), they would be able to interpret the events that God permitted to happen to them; they would then *discern their latter end* and see the disaster toward which their life style was leading them inevitably. The beginning of God's judgment is not a hidden thing; the signs are there to be read, but the pathos of the people of God lay in their lack of discernment.

And example is provided in v. 30 by way of a rhetorical question. The language employed in the rhetorical question may have a proverbial character, for it is used in similar form elsewhere in the OT. In 1 Sam. 18:7,[50] Saul and David are met on their return from battle by women who are chanting a song:

> *"Saul has slain his thousands,*
> *And David his ten thousands."*

When God was with his people, there would be great victory. But in the rhetorical question of v. 30, the situation is imagined in reverse. Israel's armies would be pursued by *one* and put to flight by *two*. The rhetorical question implies that the only way such a situation could happen would be if God (*their Rock*) had delivered his people into the enemies' power. Since neither the enemy nor the enemy gods (*their rock,* v. 31) were in themselves sufficiently powerful to defeat the God of Israel, the defeat of God's people had to be interpreted as having happened with the permission of God. *Even our enemies may be our judges* (v. 31) — the principle, which recurs in the later prophets, is made clear that the enemies of the people of God could be instrumental in the execution of God's judgment.

The substance of vv. 32-33 refers to the enemies of God's people, who would be instrumental in the execution of divine judgment. Employing the metaphor of a vineyard, its grapes, and the product of wine, the poet declares that the enemies are basically corrupt, having their roots in *Sodom* and *Gomorrah,* places associated with evil since ancient times (see also 29:23). Given the corruption of Israel's enemies, God's use of them could in no way reflect some merit inherent in the enemies, but it did indicate the ignominy Israel brought upon itself by its sinful behavior.

8. THE POSSIBILITY OF COMPASSION (vv. 34-38)

34 *Is that not stored up with me,*
   Sealed up in my treasure houses?
35 *To me belong vengeance and recompense*

50. For similar imagery, see also Isa. 30:17.

For the time when their foot shall slip;
Because close is the day of their calamity
And impending doom hastens upon them.
36 For the Lord will vindicate his people
And will have compassion upon his servants,
When he sees that their strength is exhausted
And become nothing, for bound and free alike.
37 Then he will say:
Where are their gods,
The rock in whom they sought refuge?
38 Who ate the fat of their sacrifices
And drank the wine of their drink offering?
Let them rise up and help you;
Let them be[51] protection for you.

The poet now turns his attention to the *impending doom* which would come upon those enemies of Israel whom God would employ as his instruments of judgment (vv. 34-35). *That* (v. 34) — the antecedent is the judgment of God implicit in the description of Israel's enemies contained in the metaphor of the vine (vv. 32-33). God could use foreign nations to execute judgment on his own people; within the divine providence, however, they would remain responsible for their acts. In the course of time *vengeance* and *recompense, stored* and *sealed* for the appropriate time, would afflict those enemies of the people of God.

Eventually, God would *vindicate* his people and *have compassion* on them (vv. 36-38). There was a prerequisite to the vindication of God, however. Before the people could experience once again the compassion of God, they had to be totally drained of self-assurance and totally freed from their alliance with foreign gods. *Their strength is exhausted and become nothing* (v. 36) — since Israel's defection was largely a result of the arrogance of believing in their own strength, that arrogance and belief in human strength had to be totally demolished before the people were in a position to realize their need of God's strength. The rhetorical question posed in vv. 37-38 is designed to create awareness that other possible sources of strength were also useless. *Where are their gods . . . ?* — the events God had permitted to happen to his people would make it very clear that foreign gods, in whom Israel so lightly could place its trust, were unable to offer help in crisis, and that they were in fact responsible for the crisis in the first place. Only when the Israelites reached rock-bottom would they be able to turn away from the lifeless *rock in whom they sought refuge* (v. 37), and turn again to their God, the living *Rock* (cf. v. 4).

51.   The translation assumes a plural form of the verb, following the evidence of the majority of the versions.

9. THE VINDICATION AND VENGEANCE OF GOD (vv. 39-44)

39 *See now that I, even I, am he,*
And there is no god beside me.
I indeed cause death and I cause life.
I wound and indeed I heal,
And none can deliver from my hand.
40 *For I raise my hand to heaven*
And say: As I live for ever,
41 *If I sharpen my flashing sword,*
And my hand takes hold of judgment,
I will return vengeance to my adversaries
And I will recompense those that hate me.
42 *I will make my arrows drunk with blood,*
And my sword shall consume flesh —
With blood of the slain and the captive
From the head of the enemy's willing volunteers.[52]
43 *Praise his people, O nations,*
For he will avenge the blood of his servants.
And he will return vengeance to his adversaries
And make atonement for the land of his people.[53]
44 *And Moses came and recited all the words of this*
song in the hearing of the people, he and Joshua,[54]
son of Nun.

The noble declaration of the nature of God (v. 39) is presented in contrast to the powerlessness of foreign gods (vv. 37-38). *I . . . am he* — the God of Israel is *he,* the living God, the only one who can offer help and protection (cf. v. 38). *There is no god beside me* — on the monotheistic nature of Israel's faith, see 4:35 and commentary. In the hands of God lay the power of life and death, the power of sickness and health, the power of victory in war. The significance of this affirmation is to be seen vis-à-vis the events that would befall Israel. Everything that happened to the people of God happened only under his power. Life, health, and victory were a result of God's blessing.

52. Heb. *par'ôt;* cf. Judg. 5:2. On the translation above, see P. C. Craigie, *VT* 18 (1968), pp. 397-99.
53. Heb. "his land, his people"; the translation above follows the LXX. In the LXX, v. 43 is twice as long as it is in the MT, and in Heb. 1:6 there appears to be a quotation from the LXX version of v. 43. A Hebrew manuscript from Qumran appears to give evidence of the longer text available to the Greek translators; cf. P. W. Skehan, "A Fragment of the Song of Moses from Qumran," *BASOR* 136 (1954), pp. 12-15. For full discussion of the problems relating to this verse, see J. de Waard, *A Comparative Study of the OT Text in the Dead Sea Scrolls and in the NT,* pp. 13-16, 81; F. M. Cross, *The Ancient Library of Qumran,* pp. 182f. Cross offers a hypothetical reconstruction of the original text (p. 182, n. 30).
54. Heb. "Hoshea'," though it seems clear that *Joshua* is intended, and the Hebrew form is presumably an alternate spelling (cf. Num. 13:8).

But death, disease, and defeat were equally a part of God's dealings with his people; they did not indicate any diminution of God's power, but showed only that the actions of the Israelites deserved divine judgment. An important principle emerges from this passage: when the blessing of God appears to be withdrawn, man should not question the ability of God, but should examine the state of his relationship to God.

I raise my hand to heaven (v. 40) — the action symbolized the making of an oath, which is introduced by the formula that follows, *As I live forever. . . .*[55] In the oath, the Lord declares that he will take *vengeance* (v. 41; cf. v. 35) on his adversaries; although they had been instrumental in the execution of God's judgment on Israel, they themselves would eventually experience the wrath of God for their evil acts. As a result of the execution of God's vengeance, all nations would be called upon to praise Israel, (v. 43), who would have a new beginning in their land, for which God would make atonement. Through the darkness of the judgment expressed so vividly in the Song of Moses, there lay beyond a more distant hope of atonement, and a restoration of the relationship between God, his people, and their promised land.

Verse 44 serves as a prose conclusion to the song, referring back to the similar prose introduction in 31:30.

C. THE IMPENDING DEATH OF MOSES (32:45-52)

45 *And Moses finished reciting all these words to all Israel.*
46 *And he said to them: Set your heart on all the words which I am repeating to you today, and which you must command to your children, that they may be careful to do all the words of this law.*
47 *For it is not merely a vain word for you, but it is your life, and by this word you shall prolong your days upon the land, toward which you are about to cross the Jordan in order to possess it.*
48 *And the Lord addressed Moses on this very same day, saying:*
49 *Ascend this mountain of the Abarim, Mount Nebo, which is the land of Moab, which is opposite Jericho, and see the land of Canaan which I am about to deliver to the sons of Israel to be seized.*
50 *And die in the mountain which you are about to ascend and be gathered to your people, just as your brother Aaron died in Mount Hor and was gathered to his people;*
51 *because you acted unfaithfully with me in the midst of the sons of Israel by the waters of Meribath-kadesh, in the wilderness of Zin; because you did not uphold my holiness in the midst of the sons of Israel.*

55. On the grammatical structure of the oath formula here, see M. R. Lehmann, "Biblical Oaths," *ZAW* 81 (1969), pp. 74-92.

52 *For you shall see the land before you, but you shall not go in there, to the land which I am about to give to the sons of Israel.*

45-47 When Moses had finished reciting the song to the assembled Israelites (v. 45), he urged them one last time to commit themselves wholeheartedly to the covenant. *Set your heart on all the words* (v. 46) — the heart, the seat of the mind in the Hebrew conception, was to be solidly established upon the words of God which were spoken through Moses. The *words* (v. 46a) may either be the words of the song, or they may be *the words of this law* (v. 46b). If the former is the case, then the function of the song can be seen once again; it serves not only as a public witness to covenant commitment, but as a warning against the dangers of leaving the covenant faith. Knowing the dangers of falling from the true faith, the Israelites should be diligent in instructing the younger generation in the true faith; the education of the new generation is an important theme running throughout Deuteronomy (cf. 4:9; 6:7; 11:19; 31:13). *It is not merely a vain word* (v. 47) — that is, *the words of this law* (v. 46) were not merely human words, Moses' words, or even written words, but they were words spoken by God with the specific intention of imparting *life*. The law did not bind men in a straitjacket of legalism, but pointed toward that life which God purposed for them. In the law lay the secret of Israel's longevity and prosperity in the promised land which they were soon to possess.

48-52 When Moses had finished his last address to Israel, once again the Lord addressed words personally to Moses. With this passage, compare Num. 27:12-14. The Lord instructed Moses to climb Mount Nebo, a peak in the Abarim range of mountains to the east of the north end of the Dead Sea; from there he would be able to see the promised land which he was not permitted to enter (see also 3:25-27). On the prohibition of Moses' entering the promised land, see 1:37 and commentary; in this context (v. 51), however, there is a more explicit allusion to the incident described in Num. 20:10-13. Having seen the promised land, Moses would die; on the death of Moses, see the fuller account in 34:1-8.

D. THE BLESSING OF MOSES (33:1-29)

1 *And this is the blessing with which Moses, the man of God, blessed the sons of Israel before his death.*

Moses, who is now at the end of his life of service, pronounces a blessing before he dies; the structure and content of the passage that follows are reminiscent of the Testament of Jacob, which was uttered shortly before Jacob's death (see Gen. 49:1-27). The "blessings" to be uttered by the ancient leader would carry with them the authority of God, for Moses, despite being prohibited from entering the promised land, was dying as a *man of God*. He had served God long and faithfully, and now the time had come to bless the people who had been committed to his charge before he finally took leave of them.

The Blessing of Moses, like the Song of Moses (ch. 32), is set in poetic form. It may well have been recited or sung at some special ceremony bringing to a close the renewal of the covenant in Moab; the tribes, gathered together for the solemn renewal of the covenant, each in turn received their blessing. The blessings, however, and also the introductory and concluding sections of the blessing as a whole (vv. 2-5, 26-29), serve to turn the attention to the immediate future. There is a strong militaristic thread running throughout this chapter, which serves to remind the reader that this blessing is not only the last act of a dying man, but also a word of encouragement and an anticipation of the victories that would soon be won as the Israelites began their conquest of the promised land. The death of Moses marked the end of an era, but it also introduced a new era in which the people of God would receive the gift of God's land, which had been anticipated since the promise made to Abraham.

Select Bibliography on the Blessing of Moses

The Blessing of Moses has been the subject of a number of special studies, as has the Song of Moses in Deut. 32. In addition to the studies of the blessing as a whole noted below, the reader is referred to the many studies of particular passages which are noted in the footnotes to the text and translation.

U. Cassuto, "Il Cap. 33 del Deut.," *Revista degli Studi Orientali* II (1928), pp. 233-253.

F. M. Cross and D. N. Freedman, "The Blessing of Moses," *JBL* 67 (1948), pp. 191-201.

T. H. Gaster, "An Ancient Eulogy on Israel," *JBL* 66 (1947), pp. 53-62.

I. L. Seeligmann, "A Psalm from Pre-regal Times," *VT* 14 (1964), pp. 75-92.

With particular reference to the tribal blessings, see A. H. J. Gunneweg, "Über den Sitz im Leben der sog. Stammessprüche," *ZAW* 76 (1964), pp. 245-255.

H.-J. Zobel, *Stammesspruch und Geschichte.* BZAW 95 (1965).

On matters relating to date and historical significance, see also P. C. Craigie, "The Conquest and Early Hebrew Poetry," *TB* 20 (1969), pp. 76-94.

1. THE EXORDIUM (vv. 2-5)

2 *And he said:*[1]

The Lord came from Sinai
And he shone forth from Seir for us.[2]
He beamed forth from Mount Paran,
And with him were myriads of holy ones;
At his right hand were warriors of God,
3 *Yea, the pure ones of the peoples.*[3]

All his holy ones are at your hand,
They hurry on at your heels,
They set off walking behind you.[4]
4 *Moses commanded for us a law,*
A possession for the assembly of Jacob!
5 *So let there be*[5] *a King in Jeshurun,*
When the chiefs of the people are gathered together,
When together are the tribes of Israel!

The difficulty in translating these four verses means inevitably that it is difficult to interpret them with any certainty. The following comments seek to elaborate the structure of the verses in general terms. First, there are words containing a recollection of the theophany at Mount Sinai; other early Hebrew poems contain a similar recollection of Sinai.[6] The words are set in the mouth of Moses to serve as an introduction to the blessings. Second, however, there is a section (vv. 3b-5) which may be the response made by the assembled people to Moses' initial words. Although this second suggestion is uncertain, it provides a viable means of dealing with the explicit reference to Moses in v. 4.

1. The Heb. text of vv. 2-3 is particularly difficult to translate. A list of special studies follows, but it should be noted that my translation follows largely the work of P. D. Miller and J. T. Milik. A. F. L. Beeston, "Angels in Deut. 33:2," *Journal of Theological Studies* N.S. 2 (1951), pp. 30f.; G. R. Driver, "Hebrew Homonyms," in *Hebräische Wortforschung.* Festschrift W. Baumgartner. SVT 16 (1967), pp. 50-64; O. Komlós, "Tukku Leraklaeka," *VT* 6 (1956), pp. 435f.; B. Margulis, "Gen. 49:10/Deut. 33:2-3," *VT* 19 (1969), pp. 202-210; J. T. Milik, "Deux documents inédits du désert de Judah," *Biblica* 38 (1957), pp. 245-254; P. D. Miller, "A Critical Note on Deut. 33:2b-3a," *Harvard Theological Review* 57 (1964), pp. 241-43. See also M. Dahood, *Ugaritic-Hebrew Philology* (1965), p. 52; J. Barr, *Comparative Philology and the Text of the OT* (1968), pp. 59, 230, 322.
2. Heb. "for them"; the 1st plur. suffix is read following the evidence of the versions (LXX, Syriac, and Vulgate). Or it is possible to read "for his people" (*le'amô*); see Margulis, *loc. cit.,* p. 207.
3. The translation of the last two lines of v. 2 and the first line of v. 3 follows Miller's reconstruction of the text.
4. For the translation of the last two lines of v. 3, see Milik, *loc. cit.,* pp. 252-54.
5. The translation here assumes a simple *waw* plus verb (as is normal in poetry), rather than a *waw* consecutive.
6. See Judg. 5:4-5; Ps. 68:7-8. Cf. Hab. 3:3-4.

First, then, the theophany at Mount Sinai is recalled; this is the only occasion in Deuteronomy where the word *Sinai* is used rather than Horeb, and its use here may have been determined by poetic considerations.[7] The theophany at Sinai is described as having been a time of brilliant light with the brightness emanating from the presence of God on the mountain. With God were the members of his divine council, *holy ones* and *warriors of God* (cf. 32:8). In the NT interpretation of the law of Moses, it is probably this verse (v. 2; cf. LXX) that stands behind the view that the law of Moses was mediated through angels (see Acts 7:53; Gal. 3:19; Heb. 2:2).

It should be noted that in blessing the tribes of Israel, Moses was assuming the role of a father. In Gen. 49, the parallel passage to Deut. 33, Jacob/Israel blesses his sons. Moses acts in a similar fashion, for though the tribes were not literally his sons, he had acted as a father to them. It is probably for this reason that Sinai is mentioned at the beginning of the blessings, for it was the position of Moses within the covenant family of God, which was established at Sinai (see 5:23-33), that enabled him to bless his "children" before he died. And it may also be significant that on the eve of his death, Moses maintained the two foci of the faith; he remembered Sinai and the covenant with God which had made the present moment possible, but in the blessings, it was the future that dominated his thinking. The meaning of that great moment in the past, the covenant at Sinai, always found its significance in the present and the future of God's people.

It has been suggested tentatively that vv. 3b-5 are a response which the people make to the opening words of Moses, before he announces the particular blessings. In v. 3b, the people affirm the role of the members of the divine council in assisting Moses in his task: *his* (i.e., God's[8]) *holy ones are at your* (i.e., Moses') *hand. . . .* The reference is to the assistance given to Moses by members of the divine council when Moses mediated the law of God to the people at Mount Sinai. In v. 4, the people respond further, relating the theme of the words of Moses in v. 2 to their own situation: *Moses commanded for us a law.* The law received at Sinai was to be the constitution of the new state of Israel, which was to come into existence in the near future; the lawgiver would be the head of the new state. Hence the people acclaim their leader, namely, God (the lawgiver): *Let there be*

---

7. Cf. G. T. Manley, *The Book of the Law*, p. 51. If it is correct that Horeb refers to the general vicinity, and *Sinai* to the particular mountain, then the latter term is particularly appropriate in the context recalling the manifestation of the power and glory of God on the mountain. The references to *Seir* and *Paran* are used in poetic parallelism to *Sinai;* from a literary point of view, however, it is clear that one specific place is intended in the verse, namely, Sinai.

8. MT has a 3rd masc. sing. pronominal suffix. O. Komlós (*loc. cit.*), however, suggests reading "your holy ones"; in this case, lines 2-4 of v. 3 would all refer to God, not Moses, and would continue the thought of v. 2.

a King in Jeshurun.[9] The kingship of God in early Israel rests on three basic premises: (i) the liberation of his people in the Exodus (see Exod. 15:18); (ii) the giving of the law at Sinai; (iii) the victory (still lying in the future) by which God would grant to his people the promised land. The affirmation of God's kingship at the beginning of the blessings, in the context of a gathering of the tribes with their chiefs, points up that although Moses would utter the blessings, their fulfilment would lie in the hands of God, provided that the people continued to acknowledge and serve him as their King. And Moses, about to die, could leave his people with the knowledge that they recognized God as their King, so that his death did not mean that the Israelites were bereft of a leader; his departure might even make them depend more heavily on God.

2. THE BLESSING OF REUBEN (v. 6)

> 6 *Let Reuben live and not die,*
> *But let him be few in number.*[10]

The tribe of Reuben (Jacob's firstborn son by Leah) find their blessing in the promise of continuity, even though they would never be strong numerically. In Jacob's blessing (Gen. 49:4), the instability of the tribe had already been hinted, and in a later military affair the Reubenites were criticized for their lack of participation (Judg. 5:15-16). After an incident toward the end of the eleventh century B.C. (see 1 Chr. 5:18-22), very little is heard of the Reubenites, though they continued to exist and are mentioned as late as the time of Ezekiel (48:7). In light of these facts, the blessing of Reuben appears to have a prophetic character to it.

3. THE BLESSING OF JUDAH (v. 7)

> 7 *And this he said to Judah:*
> *Hear, O Lord, the voice of Judah,*
> *And bring him to his people.*
> *With his hands, he contended for himself,*[11]
> *But may you be a help against his enemies.*

The meaning of this blessing is not entirely certain, though it seems clear from the last line that it has reference to military matters. The Targum (Onqelos), which paraphrases the first two lines, is nevertheless suggestive as to the meaning: "Hear, Lord, the prayer of Judah when he goes into battle, and bring him back in peace." If this information is added to Num. 2:9, a sense may be found for the

9. On the name *Jeshurun,* see 32:15 and commentary. See also 33:26.
10. Cf. KB, p. 581.
11. The meaning of this line is uncertain.

blessing. According to the passage in Numbers, Judah was to march at the head of the army as the vanguard.[12] In this position, Judah would hold a very dangerous place in battle. Thus the blessing may be interpreted hypothetically as follows: (i) a prayer that God may hear Judah's call for help in battle (line 1); (ii) a prayer that the tribe might be brought back in safety from the danger of their position in the vanguard (line 2); (iii) although the tribe would fight with their own hands, God is urged to bless them with the *help* of his presence (lines 3-4).

4. THE BLESSING OF LEVI (vv. 8-11)

8 *And to Levi he said:*[13]
  Your Thummim and your Urim are for your pious man,
  Whom you tested at Massah,
  With whom you contended at the waters of Meribah;
9 *The one who says to his father and his mother:*
  "I have not seen them,"
  And he does not recognize his brothers
  And he does not know his sons.
  For they kept your word
  And they guarded your covenant.
10 *They shall instruct*[14] *Jacob in your judgments*
  And Israel in your law.
  They set incense in front of you[15]
  And a whole-offering upon your altar.
11 *Bless, O Lord, his might*
  And accept the work of his hands.
  Crush the loins of his opponents
  And those that hate him — whoever[16] *opposes.*

For the legislation relating to the role of the Levites in Israelite society, see 18:1-8. The Blessing of Levi, which is difficult to interpret at many points,[17] indicates the priestly role of the tribe, in contrast to the more secular tone of the comments directed to Levi in the last words of Jacob (Gen. 49:5-7).

12. See also Gen. 49:8-12, where the blessing of Judah has strong military overtones.
13. On the Qumran text of vv. 8-11 (4QTestimonia), see J. M. Allegro, *JBL* 75 (1956), pp. 174-187; F. M. Cross, *The Ancient Library of Qumran*, p. 225.
14. On the later interpretation of this passage, as reflected in the Qumran text, see T. H. Gaster, "A Qumran Reading of Deut. 33:10," *VT* 8 (1958), pp. 217-19.
15. Heb. *bᵉʾappᵉkā*: on the translation, cf. Gordon, *UT*, p. 362 (19.264).
16. On the translation of *min-* as an indefinite interrogative, similar to Ugaritic, see W. F. Albright, *CBQ* 7 (1945), p. 23 (n. 64).
17. For detailed critical studies of this blessing, see A. H. J. Gunneweg, *Leviten und Priester* (1965), pp. 37-44; A. Cody, *A History of OT Priesthood* (1969), pp. 114-120; L. Ruppert, "Das Motiv der Versuchung durch Gott in vordeuteronomischer Tradition," *VT* 22 (1972), pp. 56-59.

In vv. 8-9, the tribe is characterized representatively, in the person of Moses and (perhaps) Aaron (v. 8), and collectively (v. 9). The characterization refers to a number of different events which are blended together in the structure of the poetry; the testings of the representatives of the tribe at both *Rephidim* (Exod. 17:1-7) and *Kadesh* (Num. 20:1-13) are noted first (v. 8). Then the collective action of the tribe, which resulted in its being set aside for divine service (see Exod. 32:26-29), is recalled (v. 9). After Israel's apostasy in the incident of the "Golden Calf," the Levites had executed God's judgment even on their own brethren, their neighbors and their companions (Exod. 32:27), and it is this incident that is expressed in different language in v. 9.

The blessing then indicates the three principal duties that were to be assigned to the tribe of Levi on the basis of their past actions and dedication to divine service. (i) They were to be responsible for the *Thummim* and *Urim* (v. 8), by which the Lord's will would be made known to the people in matters where decision was difficult to make.[18] (ii) They were to have an educational role[19] in teaching the Israelites the law of God (v. 10a). (iii) They were to be responsible for Israel's formal system of worship (v. 10b). The blessing of the tribe of Levi consists in the strength they would be given for these tasks and the protection from their enemies which God would grant to them (v. 11).

5. THE BLESSING OF BENJAMIN (v. 12)

12 *To Benjamin he said:*
The beloved of the Lord dwells in safety;
'Eli[20] surrounds him all the day long,
And between his weapons[21] he dwells.

In Gen. 49:27 (the last words of Jacob), Benjamin is given a very warlike and fierce character. Likewise, in the Song of Deborah (Judg.

18. Cf. 1 Sam. 23:9-12. For discussion and bibliography, see R. Press, *BHH* III, cols. 2066f.
19. It is possible, however, to interpret v. 10a in relation to the earlier reference to the Thummim and Urim; the instruction of the Levites would then consist in interpreting God's law in relation to difficult matters on the basis of the Urim and Thummim. Cf. A. Haldar, *Associations of Cult Prophets among the Ancient Semites,* pp. 99f.
20. On the reading *'Elî*, an ancient name or epithet of God, see M. Dahood, "The Divine Name 'Eli in the Psalms," *Theological Studies* 14 (1953), pp. 452-57; Gordon, *UT,* p. 456. The meaning would be "Most High"; cf. Ps. 7:9 and M. Dahood, *Psalms, I,* p. 45.
21. The Heb. *kātêp,* normally "shoulders, shoulder blades," may here have the sense "weapons, blades," similar to Ugar. *ktp* (in parallel with *ṣmd;* see *CTA* 6.V.2 = *UT* 49.V.2). The meaning, in context, is suggested in the commentary. Cf. R. T. O'Callaghan, "The word *ktp* in Ugaritic and Egypto-Semitic Mythology," *Orientalia* 21 (1952), pp. 37-46.

5:14), Benjamin seems to have played a prominent part in the war against the Canaanite armies under the command of Sisera.[22] In the present context, there may also be an emphasis on Benjamin's military prowess, but it is given dramatic form in the first two lines by the mention of the security in which the tribe of Benjamin would dwell.

The reference to the tribe as the *beloved of the Lord* may reflect the memory of how Benjamin, in earlier times, had been especially loved by his father (Gen. 44:20). Benjamin's safety and security (lines 1-2) were not to be a result of the tribe's refusal to enter the arena of battle. The security of the tribe would be found in the encompassing presence of God, which would be experienced most vividly in the midst of battle. Thus, the allusion of the third line of the blessing (*between his weapons he dwells*) points to the fact that it would be in battle that Benjamin would be blessed, made safe between the *weapons* of the Lord, who was a "Man of War" (Exod. 15:3).

6. THE BLESSING OF JOSEPH (vv. 13-17)

13 *And to Joseph he said:*
   May his land be blessed by the Lord,
   With the best of the heavens above[23]
   And of the deep lying beneath;
14 *And with the best of the produce of the sun,*
   And with the best of the yield of the months;[24]
15 *And with the best*[25] *of the ancient mountains;*
   And with the best of the everlasting hills;
16 *And with the best of the earth and its fullness;*
   And with the favor of the one who dwells in the bush.[26]
   May it come upon the head of Joseph
   And upon the forehead of the foremost of his brethren.
17 *His first-born bull has majesty,*
   And his horns are the horns of a wild bull.
   With them he shall gore the peoples,[27]
   Together, to the ends of the earth.
   And such are the ten thousands of Ephraim,
   And such are the thousands of Manasseh.

22.   See further, on this passage, P. C. Craigie, *JBL* 88 (1969), p. 257.
23.   Reading *mē'āl* for *miṭṭāl;* cf. Gen. 49:25.
24.   Heb. *yᵉrāḥîm;* there may be a deliberate play on words, for this word may also be translated "moons" (cf. "sun" in the preceding line).
25.   Reading *mimmeged,* as in the preceding and following lines.
26.   Heb. *sᵉneh.* Cf. M. A. Beek, "Der Dornbusch als Wohnsitz Gottes," *Kaf-He: 1940-65 Jubilee Volume. OTS* 14 (1965), pp. 153-161. Alternatively, the text could be translated as *Sinai,* assuming an old consonantal text *sn* (before the *mater lectionis* was added).
27.   The metaphorical language employed in this verse is reminiscent of other early Hebrew poetry (see Num. 23:22 and 24:8) and of Ugaritic poetry (see *CTA* 6.VI.16-18 = *UT* 49.VI.16-18).

The blessing of Joseph is longer than most of the blessings in the chapter (with the exception of that of Levi); the length of the blessing is in keeping with the prominence of the tribe in the early period of Israel's history. The blessing has a number of similarities with the older blessing of Joseph spoken by Jacob (Gen. 49:22-26). In the older passage, there is no reference to Ephraim and Manasseh, who are mentioned, however, in the last verse of the passage under discussion. Already, the tribe of Joseph was beginning to split into its two separate parts (cf. 3:13-14). At a somewhat later date, during the time of the judges, the two half-tribes are mentioned, but there is no reference to Joseph (see Judg. 5:14).

The blessing of Joseph relates to two spheres in the life of the tribe: (i) their material prosperity from the produce of the land (vv. 13-16); (ii) their military might vis-à-vis foreign nations (v. 17). The material prosperity that would come upon the tribe is described in a series of beautiful poetic images which reach their climax in v. 16. *The best* (Heb. *meged*) — literally "choice fruits, excellent things." *The best of the heavens above* were the rains, and subsequent dew, which gave growth to the crops. *The deep lying beneath* is a poetic description of the subterranean waters which were believed to be the source of springs and rivers, which in turn watered the land and contributed to its fertility. The *produce of the sun* and *yield of the months* (v. 14) refer to the crops that would be nurtured by the sun and would come to fruition at different seasons of the year. The wealth of the *ancient mountains* and the *everlasting hills* would lie in the forests growing so densely on mountains such as Carmel.[28] The climax of the prosperity provided by nature is reached in the first line of v. 16 — *the earth and its fullness* — but immediately the poet points to the source of the wealth of the natural world: *the one who dwells in the bush.* The words allude to the encounter of Moses with God (Exod. 3:2-4), an encounter that led to the Exodus and the covenant at Sinai; it was because of those great moments in the past that the tribe of Joseph would experience in the future the blessing of God in the land of promise.

In v. 17, there is a reference to the two tribes, Ephraim and Manasseh, into which the tribe of Joseph was beginning to divide. Ephraim is the one given preeminence in this final section of the blessing. The *first-born* son, in the strict sense, was Manasseh, but because of Jacob's reversal in blessing the two sons of Joseph (see Gen. 48:8-20), Ephraim took precedence. This reversal is given dramatic poetic form in the last two lines of v. 17. The normal poetic usage in parallelism would be *thousands//ten thousands,*[29] but here

28. Cf. D. Baly, *Geographical Companion to the Bible*, p. 49.
29. Cf. 32:30; 1 Sam. 18:7; 21:12; 29:5.

the order of the terms is reversed, just as the natural order of the sons was reversed. The blessing of military strength is described dramatically in the imagery of a powerful bull, goring its enemies before it (see also n. 27).

7. THE BLESSING OF ZEBULUN AND ISSACHAR (vv. 18-19)

18 *And to Zebulun he said:*[30]
Rejoice, O Zebulun, in your going forth,
And Issachar, in your tents.
19 *Peoples are summoned to the mountain.*[31]
There they shall sacrifice sacrifices of righteousness.
For they suck out the abundance of the seas
And the hidden treasures of the sand.

The two tribes are called upon to rejoice: Zebulun, *in your going forth,* and Issachar, *in your tents.* It has been suggested that this language is a poetic variation of the frequent Hebrew idiom, "going out/coming in" (see 28:6; 31:2),[32] so that the meaning is that the tribes were to rejoice in every aspect of their daily lives.

The meaning of the first two lines of v. 19 is uncertain.[33] In general terms, the sense seems to be that the prosperity of the tribes would be so great, that from time to time they would hold sacrificial festivals; there they would thank God for their prosperity and summon their fellow Israelites (viz., *peoples*) to participate with them in God's beneficence. The source of their prosperity would be found in the *seas* (in fishing, maritime commerce, etc.) and at the seashores (in shellfish; dye, made from shellfish; glass, made from sand). In the last words of Jacob (Gen. 49:13-15), only Zebulun is associated with the sea, and the emphasis on the sea in the present context (v. 19b) may be the reason why only Zebulun is mentioned in the opening line (v. 18a).

---

30.   Although the introductory words refer only to Zebulun, the blessing applies to both Zebulun and Issachar. The two tribes are also grouped together in the last words of Jacob (see Gen. 49:13-15) and in the Song of Deborah (Judg. 5:14-15).
31.   The syntax of the line makes the translation uncertain. The rendering above follows essentially the Syriac version (cf. Sam.). The verb is pointed as a Niphal form. The problem with this rendering (and that of the RSV) is the absence of a preposition before *mountain.* J. G. Herder attempts to avoid this difficulty by translating: "The tribes shall proclaim your mountain . . . " (*The Spirit of Hebrew Poetry* II, p. 160). He argues that the *tribes* (Heb. "peoples") are Israelites, not foreign people.
32.   S. R. Driver, *Deuteronomy,* p. 408.
33.   Various attempts have been made to identify the *mountain* (Tabor, Carmel, etc.), and although these identifications may have some significance in the later history of the use and interpretation of the blessing, the initial expression of the blessing indicates that no particular place is intended.

THE BOOK OF DEUTERONOMY

8. THE BLESSING OF GAD (vv. 20-21)

20 *And to Gad he said:*
Blessed be the broad lands[34] of Gad.
Like a lion, he lies in wait;[35]
Then he tears an arm — a head too!
21 *And he provides himself[36] with the lion's share,[37]*
For there,[38] a commander's portion is reserved for him.
And he comes to the heads of the people.
He performs the victory of the Lord
And his judgment, along with Israel.[39]

The broad lands of Gad — the tribe of Gad had already been allocated its territory prior to the renewal of the covenant in Moab. Their land lay to the east of the river Jordan (see 3:12-16 and commentary). Although the tribe of Gad already possessed its territory, it still had responsibilities in the coming military conquest, and the remainder of the blessing (vv. 20b-21) relates to Gad's coming role in the victorious war of the Lord. The tribe fulfilled its responsibilities, as is made clear in a later report (Josh. 22:1-6). The blessing indicates that Gad was to play an important part in the battle, and that as a result the tribe would deserve a *lion's share* of the fruit of victory. *And he comes to the heads of the people* (v. 21) — the sense of the Hebrew is uncertain (cf. LXX), though the words seem to stress the military role of Gad. "Heads" here may mean "chiefs" (cf. 33:5), and "people" (*'am*) may have the meaning "army." Thus the words may indicate the ready response Gad would give to the call to war. *The victory of the Lord* — see also the similar language in Judg. 5:11.[40] *Along with Israel* — the meaning seems to be that although Gad already possessed its promised land, nevertheless the tribe would cooperate faithfully along with the rest of Israel in the completion of the conquest.

9. THE BLESSING OF DAN (v. 22)

22 *And to Dan he said:*
Dan, a lion's whelp,

---

34. Reading *mrḥby;* see Cross and Freedman, *JBL* 67 (1948), pp. 191-201.
35. Lit. "he dwells."
36. On this rendering of the Hebrew idiom, see S. R. Driver, *Deuteronomy*, p. 411.
37. Heb. "the first, the choicest." The English metaphor is chosen in keeping with the metaphor of the two preceding lines.
38. Cross and Freedman (*loc. cit.*) suggest reading *ky yšm:* "for he pants. . . ." The present MT, on this reading, would be conflated.
39. The verbs in this verse are perfect in form, or (in the Massoretic pointing) *waw* consecutive imperfect. The apparently *waw* consecutive form (he comes) is rendered as simple imperfect (see also n. 5). The perfect form (*he performs, 'āśāh*) indicates aspect, not time, so that it is the certainty of victory that is emphasized in the blessing.
40. Cf. J. Gray, *Joshua, Judges and Ruth*, p. 283.

400

Shies away from the viper.[41]

The tribe of Dan is described as a *lion's whelp,* an expression used of Judah in the last words of Jacob (Gen. 49:9). The metaphor implies the timidity of youthfulness, but indicates that there would be great strength in the future, when the tribe had grown to its full strength. *Shies away from the viper* — the words may be a play on the saying addressed to Dan by Jacob (Gen. 49:17), where the metaphor describes Dan as a serpent or viper. Dan now has the potential for greater strength, but is still a little nervous in the presence of a viper.

10. THE BLESSING OF NAPHTALI (v. 23)

23 *And to Naphtali he said:*
  Naphtali is satisfied with favor
  And full of the blessing of the Lord.
  The west and the south he will inherit.[42]

This blessing, like the previous one, is of a general nature,[43] pointing to the blessing of God which Naphtali would experience in the land God would grant to them. There is no apparent relationship between this blessing and the last words of Jacob to Naphtali (Gen. 49:21).

11. THE BLESSING OF ASHER (vv. 24-25)

24 *And to Asher he said:*
  Most blessed of sons is Asher.
  Let him be the favorite of his brethren
  And dip his foot in oil.
25 *Iron and bronze are your bolts,*
  And as your days, so shall your strength[44] *be.*

The blessing of Asher takes the form of an exposition of the name of the tribe,[45] which means "happy, blessed." The tribe of Asher would be the most blessed, the most happy among the tribes of Israel. *Dip his foot in oil* (v. 24b) — although there may be a reference here to the territory Asher would possess, which was rich in olive trees, the words are more likely a general allusion to the fertility of the land that

---

41. Heb. *bāshān* (cf. Ugar. *bṯn*); on this rendering, see Cross and Freedman, *loc. cit.*
42. Reading *yîrash,* after the LXX, Syriac, and Vulgate.
43. See Buis and Leclercq, *Le Deutéronome,* p. 211. The word *yām* is translated "west," in keeping with the following word *dārôm,* "south." Although *yām* may be translated "sea," and then related to Naphtali's settlement in the vicinity of Chinnereth (Galilee), the general nature of the blessing makes such an interpretation unlikely. Cf. S. R. Driver, *Deuteronomy,* p. 413.
44. The meaning *strength* seems clear from the cognate Ugar. term, *db'at.* See Gordon, *UT,* p. 383; J. Gray, *The Legacy of Canaan*², p. 259.
45. See Keil and Delitzsch, *The Pentateuch,* p. 511.

would belong to Asher (cf. Job 29:6). *Bolts* — the line points, in a poetic manner, to the strong fortifications (metal door-bolts) that would protect the tribe from its enemies. Secure from their enemies, the tribe would be blessed with the strength to live life to its fullest throughout the lifespan God granted it.

12. CONCLUDING HYMN OF PRAISE (vv. 26-29)

> 26 *There is none like the God of*[46] *Jeshurun,*
> *Who rides the heavens*[47] *to your aid*
> *And the skies in his majesty.*[48]
> 27 *A dwelling place is the eternal God,*
> *And underneath*[49] *are the everlasting arms.*
> *And he thrusts out the enemy before you*
> *And says: "Destroy!"*
> 28 *So Israel shall dwell in safety;*
> *Alone, Jacob dwells*[50]
> *Upon*[51] *a land of grain and new wine —*
> *Even his heavens drop down with dew!*
> 29 *How blessed you are, Israel!*
> *Who is like you?*
> *A victorious army*[52] *in the Lord!*
> *A shield is your aid!*
> *A*[53] *sword is your majesty!*
> *And your enemies shall come cringing to you,*
> *But you shall trample upon their backs!*[54]

46. The reading follows LXX, Syriac, Targums, and Vulgate, and affects only the Massoretic pointing.
47. Similar language is used of the god Baal: *rkb . 'rpt.* For a valuable discussion of the texts and of the secondary literature, see P. J. van Zijl, *Baal. A Study of Texts in Connexion with Baal in the Ugaritic Epics.* AOAT 10 (1972), pp. 329-331. See also H. Gese *et al., Die Religionen Altsyriens, Altarabiens und der Mandäer,* pp. 122f.
48. Lines 2-3 of v. 26 are translated differently by F. M. Cross and D. N. Freedman, "A Note on Deuteronomy 33:26," *BASOR* 108 (1947), pp. 6f.; their translation is based on a partially reconstructed text. However, the text gives reasonable sense in its present form; and two key words (*'ezer* and *ga'ᵃwāh*), the first of which is removed in the proposed reconstruction, reappear together in v. 29b, suggesting a link between the imagery of vv. 26 and 29.
49. Cf. R. Gordis, "The text and meaning of Deut. 33:27," *JBL* 67 (1948), pp. 69-73. Gordis proposes the following translation: "The out-stretching of the everlasting arms . . . ," arguing that the first word in the line is from the root *mth,* "spread out, stretch out."
50. Heb. "well/eye of Jacob" (*'ên*). The translation is based on a reading *'ān,* "he dwells"; see also *mᵉ'onāh,* "dwelling place" in v. 27.
51. Heb. *'el-;* the translation assumes *'al-* (cf. Sam.).
52. For this translation, see Gaster, *JBL* 66 (1947), pp. 53-62, and Seeligmann, *VT* 14 (1964), pp. 75-92.
53. The word *'ᵃsher* is omitted in the translation; it may be a dittography (see *'ashrēḵā* at the beginning of v. 29).
54. Heb. *bāmôt;* the translation "backs," which is preferable in this context to "high

The reference to *Jeshurun* (v. 26) links these concluding verses of praise to the introductory portion of the blessing, where Jeshurun is also mentioned (see v. 5). The words *let there be a king in Jeshurun* (v. 5) now find their complement in the conclusion: *there is none like the God of Jeshurun.* God, who is Israel's king, has none with whom he may be compared, and his kingship is celebrated in these concluding verses by the reference to his own power, and the power he gives to his people, which would win great victories in the coming conflict. After a victory in the past, the Israelites had sung: "Who is like you among the gods, O Lord?" (Exod. 15:11). Now, before battle, the old rhetorical question is turned into an affirmative note of praise: *there is none like the God of Jeshurun!*

Who rides the heavens . . . the skies (v. 26) — the poetic imagery indicates the great power of God, not in an abstract sense, but in relation to the people of God. His majestic passage through the heavens takes him to the aid of his people. The warlike theme continues in v. 27, where it is presented in terms of a contrast similar to that contained in the blessing of Benjamin (v. 12, above). The people of God would find their dwelling place and their security in the presence of God, enveloped by the *everlasting arms.* But the same arms that protected the people of God would be active in the struggle against Israel's enemies (v. 27, line 3). *And says: "Destroy!"* — God would fight in the coming conquest on behalf of his people (cf. 3:22), but the people also had a part to play in the execution of God's judgment. The substance of vv. 26-28 expresses once again the apparent paradox of Israel's existence. The path lying ahead was not one of peaceful existence and quiet solitude, but it was one beset on every side with danger. Yet it was within this danger and war that Israel would find its *safety* (v. 28), because the path of danger was the path in which the presence and help of God would be found. The only criterion for Israel's security and eventual victory was the presence of God, and alternative routes, safer by human standards, would lead only to disaster in the absence of God's presence. In v. 28b, the possession of the promised land, which would follow the victorious conquest, is anticipated in glowing terms (cf. 7:13).

The Blessing of Moses concludes with a meditation on the blessed estate of Israel: *How blessed you are . . . ! Who is like you?* — the answer could only be, "None." But Israel's preeminence lay not in its own merit, but because *there is none like the God of Jeshurun* (v. 26). The power and incomparability of Israel's God imparted to Israel power and incomparability. Israel would be a *victorious army,* not through military genius, but because God, a Man in Battle (Exod.

places," is based on the Ugar. cognate *bmt* (see Gordon, *UT,* p. 373). See further J. Gray, *The Legacy of Canaan²,* p. 259; E. Jacob, *Ras Shamra et l'AT,* p. 63.

15:3), would be fighting on behalf of Israel (3:22). Israel would be protected in battle by the *shield,* which was God (see also Exod. 15:2).[55] Israel would be granted victory by the *sword* of God's presence. Enemies, *cringing* in terror, would be trampled underfoot by the victorious people of God.

E. THE DEATH OF MOSES AND LEADERSHIP OF JOSHUA (34:1-9)

1 *And Moses went up from the plains of Moab to Mount Nebo, the summit of Pisgah, which is opposite Jericho, and the Lord showed him the whole land: Gilead, as far as Dan;*
2 *and all Naphtali, and the land of Ephraim and Manasseh, and the whole land of Judah as far as the western sea;*
3 *and the Negeb, and the Plain, namely, the valley of Jericho, the city of palms, as far as Zoar.*
4 *And the Lord said to him: This is the land which I promised by oath to Abraham, to Isaac, and to Jacob, saying: "I will give it to your posterity." I have let you see it with your eyes, but you shall not cross over there.*
5 *And Moses, servant of the Lord, died there in the land of Moab, as the Lord decreed.*
6 *And he buried him in the valley in the land of Moab, opposite Beth-peor, and to this very day, no man knows his grave.*
7 *And Moses was a hundred and twenty years old when he died. His eyesight had not failed and his vitality had not departed.*
8 *And the Israelites wept for Moses for thirty days on the plains of Moab; then the days of weeping for Moses were ended.*
9 *And Joshua, son of Nun, was full of the spirit of wisdom, for Moses had laid his hands upon him, and the Israelites obeyed him, and they did what the Lord had commanded Moses.*

1-3 After giving his blessing, Moses leaves the plains of Moab, where the covenant renewal ceremony had been conducted, and ascends Mount Nebo, as he had been instructed (see 3:27 and 32:49). *The summit of Pisgah* — see the commentary on 3:17. The context here suggests more strongly that the word *Pisgah* (used in Hebrew always with the definite article) means "ridge, serrated ridge"; thus the verse could be rendered: "Mount Nebo, the summit of the ridge, which is opposite Jericho. . . ." From the top of the mountain, Moses saw the vast panorama of the land God was about to give to his people; whether he could see all the places, or simply saw on every horizon the different directions in which the promised land would extend, is uncertain. The places are listed as they would appear

---

55. On the translation of Exod. 15:2, with its implications of God's protective role, see P. C. Craigie, *VT* 22 (1972), pp. 145f.

to an observer facing north, following the horizon round to the west, and then down to the south; then the eye travels, as it were, back to the starting point by encompassing the great rift valley, containing the Dead Sea. Gilead was to the north of Mount Nebo, lying to the east of the Jordan. Naphtali's territory was northwest, beyond Chinnereth. The lands of Ephraim and Manasseh were west-northwest, situated in the hill country west of the Jordan. Judah's territory was west-southwest, situated in the hills beyond the Jordan and the Dead Sea. The Negeb lay south of Judah. The *Plain* refers to the region immediately north of the Dead Sea, but given the reference to Zoar (apparently at the southern tip of the Dead Sea), the term may apply to the areas at both ends of the Dead Sea.

4   See also Exod. 33:1. Moses is permitted to see the land, but not to enter it (see 3:27; 4:21-22; 32:52).

5-6   *The servant of the Lord* — again, it is emphasized that in his death, Moses was faithful, and that the prohibition against entering the land had not separated him from God's presence (see also the expression *man of God,* 33:1). *He buried him* — the specific subject of the clause (*he*) is uncertain. The context would indicate *the Lord* (v. 5), which would suggest that the death and burial of Moses was a private matter between God and Moses. Although it is possible to take *he* either as Joshua or as a collective term referring to the people, nevertheless the latter part of the verse (*no man knows his grave*) indicates that there was something special about the burial of Moses, and that man did not have a part in it.[1]

7   On the age of Moses, see also 31:2; although his vision and vigor[2] were not impaired, he was no longer able to fulfil all the onerous responsibilities of leadership.

8-9   The mourning for Moses lasted thirty days, apparently a conventional period of mourning, as the same time was given to mourning for Aaron (Num. 20:29). *Moses had laid his hands on him* (Joshua) — see Num. 27:22-23. With Moses dead, Joshua now assumed the leadership, having been duly commissioned by Moses and by God (see 31:23).

1.   In Martin Noth's treatment of the history of Israel, one of the few exceptions to his generally skeptical view of the "historical Moses" is the "concrete fact" concerning the tradition of the tomb of Moses: Noth, *The History of Israel* (E.T. 1965), p. 136 (n. 2). A slightly more positive attempt to trace the tradition of Moses' tomb, though presented within the framework of a similar understanding of early Israel, is offered by S. Schwertner, "Erwägungen zu Moses Tod und Grab in Dtn. 34:5-6," *ZAW* 84 (1972), pp. 24f. For the historical perspective within which the present commentary is written, see n. 2 in the Introduction, together with the comments in Appendix I.
2.   Heb. *lēḥōh,* "vitality, vigor" may refer to a man's sexual force, either literally or as a means of describing full health. On this sense, and the relation of the word to the Ugar. root *lḥḥ,* see W. F. Albright, "The 'Natural Force' of Moses in the Light of Ugaritic," *BASOR* 94 (1944), pp. 32-35.

F. CONCLUSION (34:10-12)

10 *And a prophet like Moses did not rise again in Israel, one whom the Lord knew face to face —*
11 *none like him for all the signs and the wonders which the Lord sent him to do in the land of Egypt, against pharaoh, and against all his servants, and against all his land;*
12 *and none like him for all his mighty power and all the great awesome deeds which Moses did in the sight of all Israel.*

The last three verses of the book constitute, as it were, the literary epitaph of Moses; they form a fitting conclusion to the Pentateuch, of which the last four books contain an account of the life and work of Moses in Israel. Moses was a prophet, but in his epitaph it is not his knowledge of God that is stressed, but rather the Lord's knowledge of him. God had sought him out and appointed him to a particular task; over the years, the relationship had become intimate, so that to those Israelites who knew Moses, it was evident that his highest communion was with God. And so in his epitaph, written in a book because the grave was not known, God's intimate knowledge of Moses was the most striking memory of the man now departed.

In v. 10, the exceptional nature of Moses' prophetic office is stressed; *a prophet like Moses did not rise again in Israel.* The significance of these words does not lie simply in the character of Moses, but rather it is to be found in the nature of his achievement, in God's strength. The content of the comparison (*a prophet like Moses*) is made clear in vv. 11-12. In v. 11, the role of Moses in the Exodus from Egypt is referred to; in v. 12, it is the great events following the Exodus that are implied. Thus the unique aspect of Moses' prophetic ministry is to be found in the role he played in a unique and vitally important event in Israel's history. That unique event, emerging from the Exodus and the forming of the covenant at Sinai, was the formation of the kingdom of God in the nascent, theocratic state of Israel, in which the Lord was King (Exod. 15:18; Deut. 33:5). The event began with the great liberation from Egypt and it was sealed by the new commitment at Sinai. Consequently, however distinguished a subsequent prophet in Israel might be, his ministry would be *within* the community of God's people; the work of the prophet Moses, however, was instrumental, under God, in the formation of that community.

Hence, for the Christian reader, Deuteronomy ends with a pointer toward the future. The earthly kingdom of God, in the founding of which Moses played so important a part, came to an end as an independent state early in the sixth century B.C. The prophets who followed Moses at a later date began to point forward to a New

Covenant (see 18:15-22 and commentary). It was in the formation of the New Covenant that at last a prophet like Moses appeared again, but he was more than a prophet. Whereas Moses was a *servant* in the household of God, the coming prophet was a *son,* Jesus Christ (Heb. 3:1-6), who brought with him the liberation of a new exodus and established the relationship of the New Covenant.

I. INDEX OF CHIEF SUBJECTS

II. INDEX OF AUTHORS

Wagner, S., 325
Wallace, R. S., 151
Watt, W. M., 282
Watts, J. D. W., 71, 156
Weinfeld, M., 25, 26, 45, 50, 51, 71, 72, 73, 81, 170, 179, 186, 204, 217, 236, 267, 270, 300, 316, 339, 340, 344, 350, 370, 377
Weippert, M., 271
Weiss, M., 22
Welch, A. C., 71, 297
Wellhausen, J., 60f.
Wenham, G. J., 49, 50, 52f., 72, 215, 217, 300
Whitaker, R. E., 239
Wijngaards, J. N. M., 45, 71
Wilcke, C., 381

Wild, J., 76
Williams, D., 72
Williams, R. J., 103, 328
Wilson, J. A., 80
Winnett, F. V., 187, 329
Winter, P., 378
Wiseman, D. J., 188, 239
Wood, J. L. R., 238
Wright, G. E., 19, 71, 258, 374, 375

Yahuda, A. S., 143, 156, 182, 243, 316, 323, 385
Yeats, W. B., 341
Young, E. J., 106, 338

Zijl, J. P. van, 402
Zobel, H. J., 391

III. INDEX OF PERSONS AND PLACES

415

417

IV. INDEX OF SCRIPTURE REFERENCES

V. INDEX OF UGARITIC TEXTS

424

55542

Ɫ.Ɫ.Ɫ.1507
C8869
c.2

LINCOLN CHRISTIAN COLLEGE

3 4711 00164 9534